An Introduction to Japanese Linguistics

Blackwell Textbooks in Linguistics

The books included in this series provide comprehensive accounts of some of the most central and most rapidly developing areas of research in linguistics. Intended primarily for introductory and post-introductory students, they include exercises, discussion points and suggestions for further reading.

An Introduction to
Japanese Linguistics
SECOND EDITION

Natsuko Tsujimura

Blackwell
Publishing

BLACKWELL PUBLISHING
350 Main Street, Malden, MA 02148-5020, USA
9600 Garsington Road, Oxford OX4 2DQ, UK
550 Swanston Street, Carlton, Victoria 3053, Australia

First published 1996 by Blackwell Publishers Ltd
Second edition published 2007 by Blackwell Publishing Ltd

1   2007

Library of Congress Cataloging-in-Publication Data

Tsujimura, Natsuko.
  An introduction to Japanese linguistics / Natsuko Tsujimura. — 2nd ed.
    p. cm. — (Blackwell Textbooks in Linguistics)
  "First published 1996 by Blackwell Publishers Ltd."—ECIP data sheet.
  Includes bibliographical references and index.
  ISBN-13: 978-1-4051-1066-2 (hardcover : alk. paper)
  ISBN-10: 1-4051-1066-X (hardcover : alk. paper)
  ISBN-13: 978-1-4051-1065-5 (pbk. : alk. paper)
  ISBN-10: 1-4051-1065-1 (pbk. : alk. paper)   1. Japanese language.   I. Title.
II. Series.

PL523.T74 2007
495.6—dc22
                                                              2006017116

A catalogue record for this title is available from the British Library.

Set in 10/12pt Sabon
by Graphicraft Limited, Hong Kong
Printed and bound in Singapore
by COS Printers Pte Ltd

For further information on
Blackwell Publishing, visit our website:
www.blackwellpublishing.com

To Stuart

Contents

List of Figures, Tables, and Maps

Preface to the Second Edition

In revising this book for the second edition, I tried to keep the same goals in mind as in the original version. Its primary goal is to examine spoken Japanese, presenting linguistic description and analyses of a wide range of phenomena. It is hoped that the book serves as a descriptive source and a theoretical foundation for an audience that includes students and scholars in linguistics as well as those who are interested in the Japanese language more generally. This book is also intended to be used as a pedagogical tool to provide basic notions and terminology in linguistics, and to introduce students to linguistic argumentation. Admittedly, the book may not always seem to be consistent in balancing the descriptive and theoretical illustrations of phenomena, or diverse theoretical treatments for them. Depending on the chapter and on the reader's background, the user may feel that the extent of details and the levels of complexity are either too advanced or not adequate. In a classroom setting, supplementary materials should be considered; or this book could be used as a supplement to the instructor's primary material. The student's orientation and interest should be taken into consideration in deciding the amount of time to be allocated to each chapter and the topics in it. My undergraduate students in humanities, for example, take more interest in general descriptions of phenomena and sociolinguistic issues rather than technical discussions of syntax. For this group, I minimized the theoretical argumentation and spent more time on discussion of social topics such as dialectal variation and gender differences reflected in the language. Used as a textbook in a college-level class, this book should not be seen as a self guide to a general introduction to Japanese linguistics; rather, it should be used in conjunction with the instructor's own orientation and focus in order to accommodate the students' level and needs.

Extensive revisions have been made in chapters 4 (morphology) and 6 (semantics), and a new chapter on first language acquisition (chapter 8) has been added. Chapter 7 (language variation), although still needing a more extensive discussion, has been moderately revised particularly to reflect more updated research in sociolinguistics. The chapters on phonetics (chapter 2), phonology (chapter 3), and syntax (chapter 5) are kept virtually the same. The fields of phonology and syntax in the generative tradition have renewed their outlook by focusing on Optimality Theory and the Minimalist program, respectively, but these changes are not mirrored in this edition. I came to this decision with the primary goal in mind: the book is intended to present descriptions of a wide range of linguistic phenomena in Japanese and introduce a very basic level of theoretical foundation needed in linguistic analysis. Instructors' discretion is called for to fill whatever gap is found. The chapters serve as a launch-point for more detailed theoretical discussion, should the instructor and students decide to pursue it.

Completing this second edition turned out to be even a greater challenge than the original version, and certain decisions that I faced have often been more difficult than the first time. Without constructive comments and warm encouragement from colleagues and friends, I would still have had a number of blank pages with no visible light at the end of the tunnel. Over the past several years, Stuart Davis, Masanori Deguchi, Bill McClure, Donna Jo Napoli, Peter Sells, Andrew Spencer, and Ichiro Yuhara all made enormous contributions to the current version by providing me with professional advice on how I could improve each chapter. I did not always agree with their criticisms, but they helped me tremendously to see the relevant issues much more clearly than I had ever done before. My students in the Department of East Asian Languages and Cultures and those in the Department of Linguistics inspired me during the courses of J421 (Introduction to Japanese Linguistics) and L490/L590 (Structure of Japanese) respectively. Their deep interests in the Japanese language, linguistic or otherwise, have motivated me to stick with this project. These students led me to the modest hope that their understanding and appreciation of the language will grow in their lifetime and the book will somehow serve as a seed for that growth. I consider myself immensely lucky to have been able to work with the staff at Blackwell: Ada Brunstein, Sarah Coleman, and Tami Kaplan have been simply a pleasure to be in the same team with. Their persistence, professionalism, and warmth made it so much easier to tackle this challenging task. Tami took a new job a year before the completion of this book, but without her initial word of encouragement to publish a second edition, this book would not have existed. My sincere gratitude for Steve Smith still remains with me for the opportunity to publish the original form in the first place. It has given me delight and relief to have had another opportunity to work with Fiona Sewell as my copy-editor. Once again, her meticulous editing and insightful suggestions have made for a better product. I received generous support from the Department of East Asian Languages and Cultures through the funding for the project. Andrea Tews did a wonderful job in indexing and cleaning the monumental mess of references into an orderly bibliography.

Although it has been almost a routine for me to acknowledge Stuart Davis in my linguistic publications, he deserves very special thanks here for zillions of reasons: he probably read parts of both editions more often than anybody I know; everywhere he went, he served as my book agent, advertising the first edition to whomever he met and talked to (without any commission); he made sure that the second edition would be completed on time (well, almost on time); and he continues to demonstrate how precious a great sense of humor is in life. The list goes on, but most importantly, Stuart never failed to assure me that this project and other linguistic work of mine means something to the field, although I am still not all that sure he is right on this. I dedicate this book to him.

Acknowledgments

The author and publisher gratefully acknowledge the following for permission to reproduce the copyright material in this book:

Figures 2.2 and 2.4, vocal tract, from A. Akmajian, R. A. Demers, A. K. Farmer, and R. M. Harnish, *Linguistics: An Introduction to Language and Communication*, second edition, p. 109, figure 4.5. Cambridge, MA: MIT Press, 2001. © 2001 by The MIT Press. Reprinted by permission of The MIT Press.

Figure 4.1, distribution of phonological constraints, adapted from Junko Itô and R. Armin Mester, "Phonological Constraints," in John A. Goldsmith (ed.), *The Handbook of Phonological Theory*, p. 823, figure 8. Oxford: Blackwell, 1995. © 1995 by Blackwell Publishing Ltd. Reprinted by permission of the authors and Blackwell Publishing.

Map 7.1, map of Japan, from Masayoshi Shibatani, *The Languages of Japan*, map 3, p. 188. Cambridge: Cambridge University Press, 1990. © 1990 by Cambridge University Press. Reprinted by permission of Cambridge University Press.

Every effort has been made to trace copyright holders and to obtain their permission for the use of copyright material. The publisher apologizes for any errors or omissions in the above list and would be grateful if notified of any corrections that should be incorporated in future reprints or editions of this book.

1 Introduction

We use language every day to communicate with each other. Even young children use language. Children naturally acquire the language (or languages) spoken in the community around them: it could be English, Japanese, Russian, Tagalog, Zulu, or, in the case of the hearing impaired, American Sign Language (ASL), for example. While language consists of sounds (or signs as in ASL), words, and sentences, it is not simply a random sequence of sounds, words, or signs. For instance, a native speaker of English knows that a sequence of sounds like "abpmeshnsch" or the string of words "the walked yellow a yesterday pet three where quickly" do not represent utterances of English. Rather, language is a more systematic, rule-governed mechanism. Sounds pattern in certain regular ways in forming words, and words combine to form sentences in a consistent manner as well.

The field of study where language is investigated in a systematic way is called linguistics. A primary goal of much linguistic research then is to discover the patterns that underlie languages. When linguists find such patterns in a particular language, they posit that there are rules or constraints in the language that produce these patterns. Linguists hypothesize that when children acquire their native language during early childhood, they subconsciously learn the rules and constraints of their language which enable them to speak and understand the language in a fluent manner without hesitation. Thus, linguists are particularly interested in uncovering rules or constraints that speakers must subconsciously know when they speak a language, rules that speakers themselves are completely unaware of.

Some people have thought that children learn their first language by imitating what their parents say. That is, children were thought to learn their first language gradually, by listening to what their parents say to them and by imitating it. However, this assumption has been questioned for various reasons. For example, children have the ability to create sentences they have never heard before. If they learned their first language simply by imitating their parents, it would be impossible for them to create sentences that are completely novel to them. The fact that children are capable of constantly creating new sentences immediately casts doubt on the assumption that children learn their first language by imitation.

Another piece of evidence against the assumption that children learn their first language by imitating their parents comes from the nature of the mistakes they make. In learning their native language, children make mistakes, but the mistakes often reflect their ability to make rather sophisticated generalizations concerning their first language on the basis of their observations. There are plenty of examples of this sort. One instance can be seen in English-speaking children's mistakes in the irregular past tense verb forms. In English, regular past tense verbs are formed simply by adding *-ed* to the present tense verb. So, we get *laughed* from *laugh* and *smiled* from *smile*. English has a large class of irregular verbs including *go–went*, *bring–brought*, and *break–broke*. For the irregular verbs, many children go through a stage where they use *goed* instead of *went* and *bringed* instead of *brought*. Adult speakers of English know irregular past tense verb forms, and hence they would not utter *goed*, *bringed*, and *breaked*; instead, they would say the correct forms, *went*, *brought*, and *broke*. If children learn their first language simply by imitating what their parents say, they should never produce incorrect past tense verb forms such as *goed*, *bringed*, and *breaked* because their parents do not say them. Rather than imitating their parents' speech, children subconsciously make an observation concerning the formation of past tense verb forms on the basis of regular forms such as *laughed* and *smiled*, and then make a generalization that past tense verbs are formed by adding *-ed* to present tense verbs. The incorrect outputs like *goed*, *bringed*, and *breaked* result from an overgeneralization of such a "rule" to irregular verbs. Hence, children do have the ability to generalize on the basis of their observations.

Children also make mistakes in their use of verbs. Some English verbs have causative counterparts. Consider the pairs in (1)–(2), which are taken from Pinker (1989).

(1) a. The horse walked/galloped/trotted/raced/ran/jumped past the barn.
     b. I walked/galloped/trotted/raced/ran/jumped the horse past the barn.
                                                              (Pinker 1989: 131)

(2) a. The log slid/skidded/floated/rolled/bounced.
     b. Brian slid/skidded/floated/rolled/bounced the log.
                                                              (Pinker 1989: 130)

The verbs of the (b) sentences in (1)–(2) display causative use. For example, in (1a) the horse voluntarily performed the action of walking, galloping, trotting, etc. In (1b), on the other hand, I instigated some action that leads to the horse's walking, galloping, trotting, etc. That is, I caused the horse to walk, gallop, trot, etc. Similarly, in (2b), Brian caused the log to slide, skid, float, etc., while such a causative interpretation is not available in the (a) sentence. So, the same verb can be used to induce the causative interpretation. Children observe this phenomenon, but their output is not necessarily grammatical; (3)–(6), taken from Pinker (1989: 305–306), are actual utterances by children (cf. Bowerman 1982; Pinker 1989).

(3) You can drink me the milk.

(4) Will you have me a lesson? [Request to adult friend in swimming pool]

(5)   Andrea, I want to watch you this book.

(6)   Remember me what I came in for.

The verb *drink* in (3) is used with a causative interpretation, although such a reading is not allowed with this verb in adult English. So, the child used the verb to mean "to feed" or "to help to drink". Similarly, *have* in (4) is used as "give", the causative counterpart of *have* ("let me have"); in (5) *watch you* is used to mean "have you watch"; and in (6) *remember* is meant to be "remind" ("let me remember"). Another example that is often observed in children's speech is sentences like "He learned me real good", in which *learn* is intended to be "make me learn". In these errors which actually occur in children's speech, we can see that they are analyzing *drink/have/watch/remember/learn* as causative verbs just like *walk*, *run*, and *roll* in (1)–(2), for instance. Notice that children would not make these sorts of mistakes if they spoke the language just by imitating their parents, because adult speakers would not make such mistakes. Instead, children are making a generalization and applying it to new words and sentences based on what they hear. What is important here is that children are actively making generalizations, trying to figure out the language, although this task is largely subconscious.

Noam Chomsky, the most influential American linguist in the second half of the twentieth century, is a strong proponent of the hypothesis that there must be something innate in the human cognitive system which enables children to create sentences they have never heard before, and enables them to figure out and learn their language. Under this view, one of the main tasks of a linguist is to figure out the exact nature of the innateness. In undertaking this sort of task, linguists first observe some language-related phenomenon and describe it. Second, they try to figure out whether the phenomenon is of an arbitrary nature, or whether there is some systematic pattern associated with it. When the latter is found to be the case, they formulate a hypothesis on the basis of this pattern. Often the hypothesis makes further predictions about patterns in the language. Third, the hypothesis is tested against a new set of data. If the new data are inconsistent with the predictions, the hypothesis is falsified, and hence needs to be discarded or modified in order to account for the patterns found in the language.

We shall see that this notion and strategy of hypothesis testing will play an important role in the presentation of the language data in many of the chapters in this book. To this end we will primarily examine the Japanese language, but on occasion we will also compare Japanese with English.

Suggested Readings

A general introduction to the field of linguistics can be found in Akmajian et al. (1984), Fromkin and Rodman (1993), Finegan (1994), Parker and Riley (1994), Napoli (1996, 2003), and Pinker (1999), among many other textbooks and introductory books. Parker and Riley (1994) is particularly accessible to those who have no prior knowledge of linguistics. Chomsky's program of linguistic research can be found in Chomsky (1986b), Cook (1988), and Pinker (1994). Chapter 3 of Cook (1988) explains concisely the motivation of Chomsky's innateness theory. Pinker (1994) achieves the same goal but in a more technical fashion.

2 Phonetics

When we try to list all the sounds in a language, it is important not to confuse orthography, i.e. the writing system, with the actual sounds. For example, the sound [k] in English can be exemplified by various spellings, as in _kiss_, _sick_, _choir_, _quit_, _cow_, _Iraq_, and _unique_. (Note: The brackets "[ ]" are used when representing the pronunciation of each sound. This symbol will be further explained in chapter 3.) Even though we are looking at seven different ways of spelling here, we are nonetheless referring to the single sound [k].

Confusing spelling and actual sounds is a particular problem in Japanese because, as figure 2.1 (p. 6) shows, the majority of the Hiragana syllabary – one of the writing systems used for Japanese – consists of the combination of a consonant and a vowel, i.e. two separate sounds.

Take さ and て for instance.

(1)

The さ stands for the consonant [s] and the vowel [a]; and て stands for the consonant [t] and the vowel [e]. Thus, the Hiragana syllabary fails to isolate the individual sounds of Japanese, and so does not reflect the phonetic inventory (i.e. the list of sounds) of the language.

Another option would be to consider utilizing the specific Romanization system that has been developed for Japanese in order to isolate the individual sounds. However, even this system does not necessarily reflect the actual sounds. Consider the series in (2), which is part of a commonly used Romanization system for Japanese (i.e. the "Kunrei"-style Romanization).

(2) a. ta
     b. ti
     c. tu
     d. te
     e. to

あ	い	う	え	お
a	i	u	e	o

か	き	く	け	こ
ka	ki	ku	ke	ko

さ	し	す	せ	そ
sa	si	su	se	so

た	ち	つ	て	と
ta	ti	tu	te	to

な	に	ぬ	ね	の
na	ni	nu	ne	no

は	ひ	ふ	へ	ほ
ha	hi	hu	he	ho

ま	み	む	め	も
ma	mi	mu	me	mo

や		ゆ		よ
ya		yu		yo

ら	り	る	れ	ろ
ra	ri	ru	re	ro

わ
wa

を
o

ん
n

Figure 2.1   Hiragana syllabary

Under this Romanization system, the same consonant is shared by the five in (2a–e), and the only difference is supposed to be the vowel that accompanies it. However, the consonant that is represented by t in (2a–e) is not pronounced the same. The consonant t in (2a, d, e) is a sound similar to the t sound in the English words *tease* and *cat*; the consonant in (2b) is similar to the sound represented by ch as in the English word *cheese*; and the consonant in (2c) is pronounced very much like the sequence ts as in the English word *cats*.

This illustration of the Hiragana syllabary and the Romanization system clearly shows that writing systems do not correlate with the phonetic inventory of the language, and hence we need a system which enables us to describe a sound as it is pronounced. This is why we focus on *spoken* language rather than *written* language when we investigate the phonetic system of a language. To avoid the confusion that we have demonstrated above, we use phonetic symbols to transcribe the sounds that exist in a language.

1   Phonetic Inventory

In describing the sounds of a language, a major distinction can be made between consonants and vowels. Consonants are sounds made with an obstruction in the mouth while no such obstruction occurs with vowels. We first describe the consonants of both English and Japanese, and then turn to the vowel sounds.

1.1   *Place/Manner of Articulation and Voicing*

In describing the consonant sounds of a language, there are three notions that help us distinguish one sound from another. They are **place of articulation, manner of articulation**, and **voicing**. With reference to the anatomical structure of the mouth, place of articulation indicates the place in the mouth where the sound is made. The lips and the various regions along the roof of the mouth, which can be seen in figure 2.2, are all places of articulation. Different sounds, then, are made at different places of articulation by placing articulators such as the tongue at these different locations.

Manner of articulation refers to how the articulators, such as the lips and the tongue, achieve contact with the places of articulation. For instance, the sound produced when an articulator has complete contact with a place of articulation and the sound produced with partial contact are different.

Voicing refers to the vibration of the vocal cords. The English sounds [s] and [z], for example, are pronounced at the same place, the alveolar ridge (immediately behind the upper teeth). In other words, these sounds share the same place of

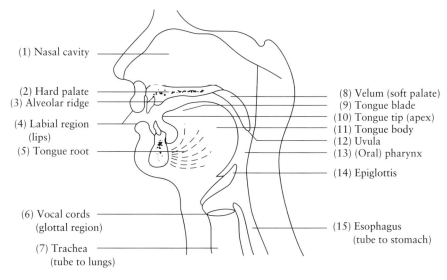

(1) Nasal cavity

(2) Hard palate
(3) Alveolar ridge

(4) Labial region
(lips)
(5) Tongue root

(6) Vocal cords
(glottal region)

(7) Trachea
(tube to lungs)

(8) Velum (soft palate)
(9) Tongue blade
(10) Tongue tip (apex)
(11) Tongue body
(12) Uvula
(13) (Oral) pharynx

(14) Epiglottis

(15) Esophagus
(tube to stomach)

Figure 2.2   Vocal tract

articulation, i.e. alveolar. Furthermore, the manner in which these sounds are made is identical. The airflow coming from the lungs is forced through a narrow opening at the alveolar ridge. The difference between [s] and [z] results from the presence or absence of vocal cord vibration. When [s] is pronounced, the vocal cords do not vibrate, whereas when [z] is articulated, the vocal cords do vibrate. This voicing difference can be felt by placing a finger on one's throat while pronouncing [s] and [z]: you should feel the vibration of the vocal cords while pronouncing [z] out loud whereas nothing will be felt in pronouncing [s].

In addition to these three notions, it is also important to keep in mind whether the airflow from the lungs passes through the oral cavity (the mouth) or through the nasal cavity. When the velum is raised, the passage through the nasal cavity is completely blocked, and the air from the lungs goes out through the oral cavity. Sounds made in this way are called **oral** sounds. When the velum is lowered, on the other hand, the airflow from the lungs travels through the nasal cavity as well as into the oral cavity. The sounds created in this manner are referred to as **nasal** sounds.

Thus, consonants in a language are described by place of articulation, manner of articulation, voicing, and whether they are oral or nasal. Each sound can then be given a unique phonetic symbol.

1.2   *Phonetic Inventory of English – Consonants*

Let us now look at the different examples of place of articulation, manner of articulation, and voicing together with the oral vs. nasal distinction by examining the English phonetic system. Our goal here is not to present a detailed account of English phonetics, but rather to introduce a terminology and transcription system of English examples that we will later make use of in our discussion of Japanese phonetics.

1.2.1   *Stops*

The first group of sounds that we will consider is one that is characterized by its manner of articulation, namely, **stops**. Stops are divided into two types, oral and nasal. Oral stop sounds (often referred to simply as stop sounds) are produced when the airflow originating from the lungs and coming through the oral cavity, or mouth, is completely blocked. What separates oral stops from nasal stops is that the former occur when the velum is raised, preventing airflow escaping through the nasal cavity. Nasal stops are articulated when a complete obstruction takes place in the oral cavity and the air goes through the nasal cavity because of the lowered velum. Nasal stops will be discussed in section 1.2.5 below.

The location of complete air blockage in the oral cavity reflects the place of articulation. When the blockage is made at the lips by placing the upper lip and lower lip together, a bilabial stop is produced. Furthermore, when the **bilabial** stop is accompanied by vocal cord vibration, a **voiced** bilabial stop is produced, and we transcribe it as [b]. The voiced bilabial stop in English is exemplified by words such as *carbon* and *label*. On the other hand, when the vocal cords do not vibrate, a **voiceless** bilabial stop is articulated. We represent this sound as [p]. Examples of words with the voiceless bilabial stop [p] are *pen* and *pop*.

A stop sound made at the alveolar ridge, where the airflow would be completely blocked by the tip of the tongue at the alveolar ridge, is referred to as an **alveolar** stop. There are two types of alveolar stop, depending on whether it is accompanied by vocal cord vibration or not. The voiced alveolar stop is represented as [d] and its voiceless counterpart as [t]. They are exemplified by *sad/adapt* and *tiny/pet*, respectively.

When the air obstruction takes place by raising the tongue body to the velum or soft palate, **velar** stops are produced, and sounds such as the first consonant of words like *cat* and *agree* are articulated. The first example contains a voiceless velar stop, [k], and the second a voiced velar stop, [g].

1.2.2 *Fricatives*

Fricatives are sounds produced when the airflow in the oral cavity is forced through a narrow opening in the vocal tract, so that air turbulence is generated, resulting in a friction noise. The friction noise sounds different depending on where the narrow opening occurs. The first consonants of words like *fin* and *vase* are fricative sounds. These sounds are produced when the upper teeth and the lower lip achieve contact, so the place of articulation for them is called **labio-dental**. The air passes between the upper teeth and lower lip creating friction noise. The voiceless labio-dental fricative is [f] and its voiced counterpart is [v].

A partial blockage of the airflow can also occur when the tip of the tongue is between the upper and lower teeth. Since the sound is made between the teeth, these fricative sounds are called **interdental**. The voiceless and voiced interdental fricatives are [θ] and [ð], respectively, and they are exemplified by *three/truth* and *they/those*.

Recall that the alveolar stops, [t] and [d], are made by a complete blockage of airflow at the alveolar ridge. When we try to create a narrow opening keeping the same place of articulation with the tip of the tongue at the alveolar ridge, we obtain **alveolar** fricatives, as exemplified by the first consonants of the words *sun* and *zoo*. The voiceless alveolar fricative as in *sun* is represented as [s] while the voiced counterpart as in *zoo* is transcribed as [z]. Thus, the voiceless alveolar stop [t] and the voiceless alveolar fricative [s] share the same place of articulation, alveolar, and voicing feature, voiceless, but differ in manner of articulation. Similarly, [d] and [z] share the same place of articulation and voicing, but the former is a stop and the latter is a fricative. Therefore, they have different manners of articulation.

When a fricative sound is made with the blade of the tongue just behind the alveolar ridge, the sound is characterized as a **palato-alveolar** or **alveo-palatal** fricative. The voiceless alveo-palatal fricative is represented as [š], and is exemplified by the first sound in words like *shoe* and *shine*. The voiced alveo-palatal fricative is [ž]: there are not many words that have this sound in English, but it can be exemplified by the middle consonant of *vision* and the second consonant of *measure*. For many English speakers, the alveo-palatal fricatives in English are accompanied by rounding of the lips.

Finally, when the air is partially blocked at the narrow opening between the vocal cords (also called the **glottis**), it creates friction and a glottal fricative sound is produced. The **glottal** fricative is represented as [h]. There is no vibration of the vocal cords in this case, and hence the glottal fricative is voiceless.[1] English words that include the glottal fricative are *heart* and *hotel*.

1.2.3 Affricates

When we pronounce English words such as *church* and *judge*, we notice that the first and the last consonants of each word are produced by the combination of a brief stop followed by a fricative. That is, at first, the air is blocked at a designated place of articulation but then is released with a partial blockage. A sequence of a stop immediately followed by a fricative is called an **affricate**. English has two affricate sounds, [č] and [ǰ], both of which are alveo-palatal. The former is voiceless and is exemplified by the consonants in *church*; and the latter is voiced and is exemplified by the consonants in *judge*. Associated with the pronunciation of these affricate sounds is a slight rounding of the lips.

1.2.4 Approximants

The initial consonants of *land*, *run*, *wish*, and *yield* are produced with constriction in the vocal tract, but the air flows freely from the mouth without any blockage of air or friction. These sounds are called **approximants**. The first two, indicated by [l] and [r], are called **liquids**. Both [l] and [r] are alveolar, but the difference is that with [l] the air channel is on the side of the tongue while with [r] it is in the middle of the mouth. English [l] is normally pronounced with the tongue tip touching the alveolar ridge, but with the sides of the tongue lowered. The air flows freely over one or both sides of the tongue. Consequently, [l] is referred to as a lateral sound. The American English [r] sound is often made with the tongue tip curled back. Both [l] and [r] are accompanied by vibration of the vocal cords, and are hence voiced. The other two approximants, represented as [w] and [y], are referred to as **glides**, the former being a **labio-velar** glide and the latter a **palatal** glide. Glides are made without any contact in the mouth. In the articulation of [w], the body of the tongue approaches the velum and the lips are rounded; and, in the articulation of [y], the front part of the tongue approaches the hard palate. These two glide sounds are also accompanied by vocal cord vibration, and are therefore voiced.

1.2.5 Nasals

In producing a nasal stop, the velum is lowered and a complete obstruction occurs in the oral cavity. The airflow, however, passes freely through the nasal cavity. The sounds produced in this way are **nasal stops** or simply **nasals**. The nasals are like the oral voiced stops [b, d, g] in that they are voiced and are produced with a complete blockage in the oral cavity. There are three nasal sounds in English:

[m], [n], and [ŋ]. The first one, [m], is a bilabial nasal sound, and occurs as the first sound in the word *mother*. The second nasal sound, [n], is alveolar, and is exemplified by the first and last consonants in the word *nun*. Finally, the velar nasal, [ŋ], does not occur in word-initial or syllable-initial position in English. The final consonant in the pronunciation of the word *sing* is an example of this nasal sound.

A summary of the consonant system in English is shown in table 2.1 (p. 12).

1.3 Phonetic Inventory of Japanese – Consonants

In this section we will look at the phonetic inventory of consonants in Japanese. As we will see, some of the sounds are very similar to those in English while there are others that do not occur in English.

1.3.1 Stops

Japanese has a similar set of oral stops to those of English, i.e. [p, b, t, d, k, g]. Each sound is exemplified by the underlined sound of the following Japanese words: *pan* "bread", *binboo* "poor", *tensai* "genius", *doko* "where", *koko* "here", and *gaikoku* "foreign country". Although these stop sounds are roughly the same as those in English, a difference can be observed with the voiceless stops [p, t, k]. When these voiceless stops occur at the beginning of a word or syllable in English, they are accompanied by **aspiration**, i.e. a puff of air. This can be felt by placing a piece of paper in front of your mouth, and then trying to pronounce the English word *pin*. The initial consonant should be accompanied by a puff of air, and hence is aspirated, as is indicated by the movement of the paper. When a native speaker of Japanese pronounces the word *pan* "bread", by contrast, we notice that the paper does not move, or if it does, not as much as in English. This is because the voiceless stops in Japanese are not aspirated. One other difference is that [t] and [d] in Japanese are made by the front part of the tongue blade contacting the alveolar ridge while the relevant articulator in English is the tongue tip. Consequently, [t] and [d] in Japanese are pronounced slightly further forward than those in English with the tongue tip almost touching the back of the upper teeth (cf. Vance 1987). Throughout this book, we will treat them as alveolar stops.

1.3.2 Fricatives

There are no labio-dental and interdental fricatives in Japanese, but there are both voiced and voiceless alveolar fricatives, [z] and [s], which are exemplified by the Japanese words *kaze* "wind" and *san* "three", respectively. The voiceless alveo-palatal fricative, [š], also occurs, for example in *sinbun* "newspaper" and *sika* "deer". This consonant is produced when the airflow is partially obstructed between the blade of the tongue and the back of the alveolar ridge. The pronunciation of [š] in Japanese does not involve the rounding of the lips, unlike pronunciation in English. The voiced counterpart of [š], i.e. [ž], is not usually

Table 2.1 Summary of English consonants.

		bilabial	labio-dental	interdental	alveolar	alveo-palatal	palatal	velar	labio-velar	glottal
Stops:	[+V]	b			d			g		
	[−V]	p			t			k		
Fricatives:	[+V]		v	ð	z	ž				
	[−V]		f	θ	s	š				h
Affricates:	[+V]					ǰ				
	[−V]					č				
Approximants:										
liquid	[+V]				r, l					
glide	[+V]						y		w	
Nasals:	[+V]	m			n			ŋ		

[+V] = voiced
[−V] = voiceless

found in Japanese.[2] The voiceless glottal fricative, [h], can be found in the word *hanbun* "half".[3] Fricative sounds that Japanese has but English does not are the voiceless bilabial fricative, [Φ], and the voiceless palatal fricative, [ç], although their voiced counterparts do not exist in the language. The voiceless bilabial fricative [Φ] is similar to the sound that is made when one blows out a candle but without much lip protrusion. The voiceless palatal fricative [ç] is similar to the sound in the German word *ich* "I" or to the first sound in the English word *huge* as pronounced by many native speakers of American English. The bilabial fricative [Φ] occurs as the first sound in the Japanese words *hurui* "old" and *hukai* "deep", while the palatal fricative [ç] occurs as the initial sound in the words *hiroi* "spacious" and *hitotu* "one". As we will discuss in chapter 3, the occurrences of the voiceless bilabial fricative [Φ] and the voiceless palatal fricative [ç] are largely predictable in that they appear when specific vowels follow them. Notice that although these sounds are written in Romanization as h, as in *hurui* "old" and *hiroi* "spacious", the actual pronunciation is not to be confused with the glottal fricative [h].

1.3.3 Affricates

The affricates in Japanese are the alveo-palatal [č] (voiceless) and [ǰ] (voiced) and the alveolar [tˢ] (voiceless) and [dᶻ] (voiced). The alveo-palatal affricates, [č] and [ǰ], are exemplified by the first sounds in the words *tikaku* "near" and *zikan* "time", respectively. They are less rounded than their English counterparts. The voiceless alveolar affricates are made with a short alveolar stop that is released into an alveolar fricative. The voiceless alveolar affricate [tˢ] is exemplified in Japanese by the first sounds in the words *tumi* "sin" and *turi* "fishing". The voiced alveolar affricate, [dᶻ], does not seem to display a clear contrast with the alveolar fricative, [z], in the pronunciation of most Japanese people (cf. Vance 1987; Shibatani 1990). For example, the pronunciation of the second consonant of *mazusii* "poor" and that of the third consonant of *mikazuki* "crescent moon" varies between [dᶻ] and [z], with perhaps a slight preference for the voiced alveolar affricate. In pronouncing the word *tizu* "map", on the other hand, the second consonant for many speakers is invariably the alveolar fricative [z]. Thus, while [dᶻ] and [z] in Japanese do not contrast in many cases, we can observe a consistent occurrence of one sound or the other depending on individual words.

1.3.4 Approximants

There are three approximants in Japanese, [r], [w], and [y]. The alveolar liquid, [r], in the words *sora* "sky" and *roku* "six", is quite different from either the English sound [l] or [r]. The alveolar liquid in Japanese sounds very similar to the "d" sound in American English words like *tidy* and *steady* in that with both sounds the tongue achieves very quick contact at the alveolar ridge. Technically this sound is called a "flap", and the phonetic symbol [ɾ] is used for a more accurate transcription. This similarity between English and Japanese explains why native speakers of English learning Japanese are often unable to make a distinction between [r] and [d] in Japanese words. For the sake of simplicity, we will use the transcription symbol [r] for the Japanese alveolar liquid sound throughout this book.[4]

The unrounded velar glide [w] and the palatal glide [y] are found in words like *wakaru* "understand" and *yasui* "cheap", respectively. The Japanese velar glide [w] differs from English [w] in that the former is frequently not accompanied by vigorous movement of the lips. It should be noted, however, that lip movement has been observed in the pronunciation of [w], and it may be subject to dialectal and individual variation as well as to casual vs. careful speech difference (cf. Vance 1987).

1.3.5 Nasals

The same set of nasal sounds found in English occurs in Japanese. The bilabial nasal [m] appears in words like *mikan* "orange" and *mame* "beans", and the alveolar nasal [n] is found in *neko* "cat" and *naka* "inside". The occurrence of the velar nasal within a word depends on the speaker. For example, some speakers pronounce the "g" in the word *kagaku* as [ŋ] while others pronounce it as the velar stop [g]. Even when a speaker consistently uses the velar nasal sound in her or his speech, however, it never appears in word-initial position. Thus, the initial consonant of the word *gakkoo* "school" can only be pronounced as [g].

Some works describe the nasal sound, before a pause, in words like *yon* "four" and *ken* "ticket" as being pronounced with the tongue body touching the uvula (cf. Vance 1987). The uvular nasal is represented as [N]: the words mentioned above are thus transcribed as [yoN] and [keN] before a pause.[5]

Nasal sounds in Japanese present an illustration of a phonetic phenomenon called **coarticulation**. Coarticulation occurs when place of articulation extends to a neighboring sound and as a result the pronunciation of adjacent sounds overlaps. Consider the following examples.

(3) a. ken   made   [kem made]
         ticket even
     b. ken   desu   [ken desu]
         ticket is
     c. ken   ga   [keŋ ga]
         ticket Nom

Careful attention should be paid to the pronunciation of the nasal sound at the end of the word *ken* "ticket". Its pronunciation depends on the nature of the consonant that immediately follows it: when the immediately following sound is the bilabial nasal [m] as in (3a), the bilabial nasal is pronounced at the end of the word *ken* "ticket"; when the immediately following sound is the voiced alveolar stop [d] as in (3b), the alveolar nasal occurs at the end of *ken*; and when the following sound is the voiced velar stop as in (3c), the velar nasal surfaces. In these examples, the place of articulation of the immediately following consonant, i.e. [m, d, g], extends to the preceding nasal consonant, so that the nasal sound is pronounced with the same place of articulation. Hence,

Table 2.2 Summary of Japanese consonants.

		bilabial	alveolar	alveo-palatal	palatal	velar	uvular	glottal
Stops:	[+V]	b	d			g		
	[–V]	p	t			k		
Fricatives:	[+V]		z	(ž)*				
	[–V]	ɸ	s	š	ç			h
Affricates:	[+V]		dᶻ	ǰ				
	[–V]		tˢ	č				
Approximants:								
liquid	[+V]		r					
glide	[+V]				y	w		
Nasals:	[+V]	m	n	(ň)**	(ɲ)**	ŋ	N	

[+V] = voiced   *See note 2 at the end of this chapter.
[–V] = voiceless   **See note 6 at the end of this chapter.

coarticulation accounts for the variety of the nasal sounds observed in the last consonant of *ken* "ticket" in (3).[6]

Japanese has a series of **palatalized** consonants (cf. Bloch 1950; Vance 1987). Such sounds are produced by raising the tongue body toward the hard palate when certain consonants are pronounced. We will transcribe a palatalized consonant with a superscript [ʸ]. Examples of palatalized consonants in Japanese include *sanbyaku* [sambʸaku] "three hundred", *ryokan* [rʸokan] "inn", *myaku* [mʸaku] "pulse", and *kyaku* [kʸaku] "guest". The palatalization phenomenon will be taken up in the discussion of mimetics in chapter 3.

Table 2.2 shows the Japanese consonantal system.

Finally, there are instances in which lengthened consonants appear in Japanese. These are called **long consonants**, or more technically, **geminates**. Long consonants contrast with single consonants, as is illustrated in (4).

(4)   a.   sakka "author"   vs.   saka "hill"
      b.   katta "won"   vs.   kata "shoulder"
      c.   assari "simply"   vs.   asari "clam"

Long consonants are transcribed as [C:], where [C] stands for some arbitrary consonant. So, for example, the first word of (4a) is transcribed as [sak:a]. It should be noted that a long consonant is phonetically a single segment. Long consonants are observed in English as well. Examples include *white tape* and *black kite* as pronounced in rapid speech, where the [t] in *white tape* and the [k] in *black kite* are each pronounced as one elongated stop consonant.

1.4   *Phonetic Inventory of English – Vowels*

Vowels are different from consonants in that there is no obstruction in the vocal tract so that the airflow from the lungs is not blocked and thus freely passes through the mouth.[7] Different vowels are produced by changing the location of the tongue. For instance, if you pronounce the vowel in the English word *hat* and gradually try to move the tongue to the back of the mouth, you will find the resulting vowel is like the vowel in the word *hot*. If you pronounce the vowel in the word *meat*, and then gradually try to lower your tongue as far down as possible, there are several vowels that you produce as you lower the tongue: first is a vowel that sounds like the one in the word *mit* and then as you continue to lower the tongue, you should notice a transition from the vowel in the word *mit* to *mate* to *met* to *mat*. So, various positions of the tongue produce different vowels. For the purpose of describing the vowels and presenting their transcription, we divide the mouth by the parameters of height and frontness/backness. On the basis of tongue height we get three vowel qualities, **high, mid,** and **low,** while the frontness/backness dimension of the tongue identifies another three qualities, **front, central,** and **back**.[8] Given the division based on the height of the tongue, for example, the vowels in *meat* and *mit* are considered high vowels; those in *mate* and *met* are mid vowels; and the vowel in *mat* is a low vowel. With respect to frontness/backness, on the other hand, the vowel in *hat* is regarded as front while the vowel in *hot* is back. An example that comes between these two vowels, i.e. a central vowel, is *hut* (although the vowel in *hut* is higher than those in *hat* and *hot*).

The English vowel system is illustrated in figure 2.3, and examples of each vowel, with their corresponding transcription symbol, are listed in (5), below.[9]

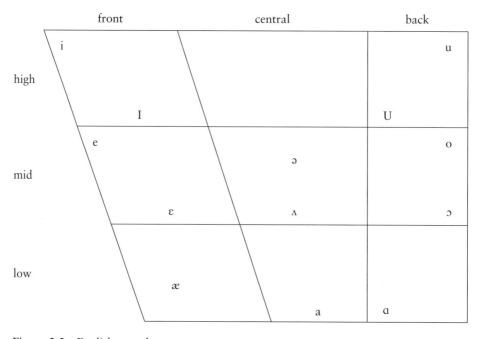

Figure 2.3   English vowel system

(5)   Examples of English Vowels (taken from Finegan 1994: 40)

	front		*central*		*back*	
high	i	Pete, beat			u	pool, boot
	I	pit, bit			U	put, foot
mid	e	late, bait	ə	about, sofa	o	poke, boat
	ɛ	pet, bet	ʌ	putt, but	ɔ	port, brought
low	æ	pat, bat	a	park (Boston dialect)	ɑ	pot, father

1.5   *Phonetic Inventory of Japanese – Vowels*

Japanese exhibits five vowels: high front, high back, mid front, mid back, and low central. The high front vowel is similar to the vowel observed in the English word *beat*, but the lips are not spread. The mid front vowel in Japanese is pronounced slightly higher than the vowel in the English word *pet*. The mid back vowel resembles the vowel in the English word *brought*, although the Japanese mid back vowel is somewhat higher and slightly more front than the English [ɔ]. The low central vowel is pronounced at about the same height as the vowel in *father*; however, the Japanese low central vowel is more forward. In this book, the Japanese high front, mid front, mid back, and low central vowels are represented by [i], [e], [o], and [a], respectively.

The English high back vowel is accompanied by lip rounding. So, for example, when we pronounce the English word *pool*, we notice that our lips are rounded. Such lip rounding is not associated with the Japanese high back vowel. The symbol [ɯ] is used to indicate the **unrounded** high back vowel. The lack of lip rounding is more prominent in the Tokyo dialect; in the Western dialects of Japanese it has been reported that the high back vowel is more rounded (cf. Shibatani 1990). On the other hand, Vance (1987) reports that the Tokyo speakers he observed showed some movement of the lips (technically called "lip compression" as opposed to "lip rounding") in very careful speech.[10] This vowel appears in the Japanese words u̲sagi "rabbit" and mu̲ra "village". For the rest of this book, however, we will use the symbol [u] in place of [ɯ] for the sake of simplicity, unless specification of [ɯ] is necessary.

The summary of the Japanese vowel system along with examples is illustrated in (6).

(6)   Japanese Vowels

	front		*central*		*back*	
high	i	ika "squid"			u	usiro "behind"
		iti "one"				usagi "rabbit"
mid	e	e "painting"			o	oto "sound"
		eki "station"				oka "hill"
low			a	asa "morning"		
				asi "leg"		

There are a number of words in Japanese that contain a long vowel. Such words contrast with words containing a vowel that is not lengthened, as is shown in (7).

(7) a. too   "ten"   vs. to   "door"
     b. suu   "inhale"   vs. su   "vinegar"
     c. satoo   "sugar"   vs. sato "hometown"
     d. biiru   "beer"   vs. biru "building"
     e. meesi   "business card" vs. mesi "meal"

In the words with long vowels in (7), each vowel is elongated. As can be seen, the contrast between a long vowel and a short vowel leads to completely separate words. Long vowels are transcribed as [V:], where "V" stands for an arbitrary vowel. So, for instance, the two words in (7a) are given the following transcription: [to:] vs. [to].

When vowels are produced, they are normally accompanied by vibration of the vocal cords: that is, they are voiced. In Japanese, however, certain vowels in certain positions of a word are often pronounced without vocal cord vibration. These vowels are called **voiceless vowels**, and we refer to this phenomenon as **vowel devoicing**. When vowels are voiceless, we indicate it by a diacritic: [V̥]. In this book we will use this diacritic only when the devoicing is crucial to our discussion. The examples of voiceless vowels include *sika* "deer" [ši̥ka] and *kusai* "smelly" [ku̥sai]. As we will see in chapter 3, vowel devoicing is most frequently observed with high vowels in Japanese, and the vowels become devoiced when a particular set of conditions is met. There is also dialectal variation with voiceless high vowels: in the Tokyo dialect, voiceless vowels are frequently observed, while the devoicing of high vowels is less obvious in western dialects, such as the Osaka and Kyoto dialects.

Notes

---

1   It should be noted that between vowels, the glottal fricative is often accompanied by vocal cord vibration, and hence it is not fully voiceless, as is exemplified by a*h*ead.
2   Some native speakers seem to have [ž] in rapid speech. See Bloch (1950) and Vance (1987) for some discussion of this sound in Japanese.
3   As is the case with the glottal fricative in English, [h] in Japanese is often accompanied by vocal cord vibration when it is between vowels, such as in *tehon* "model".
4   Note that the pronunciation of Japanese [r] is known to vary considerably depending on word position, speaker, and even regional dialect.
5   Sometimes a nasal before a pause may make no contact with the root of the mouth. Such a nasal could be described as a nasalized glide.
6   The coarticulation involving the nasal consonants can also be observed before alveo-palatal and palatal consonants. In these situations, the nasal is realized as alveo-palatal nasal [ň] and palatal nasal [ɲ], respectively. Examples include *ken zya (nai)* [keň ja (nai)] "it is not a ticket" and *ken ya (kane)* [keɲ ya (kane)] "things like ticket and (money)".

7 Note that this definition of vowels appears similar to that of approximants. However, the difference between the two is that with approximants there is constriction in the vocal tract but it does not block the airflow, while with vowels there is no obstruction in the vocal tract whatsoever; although for both, the airflow freely passes through the vocal tract.

8 Vowel classification based on the articulatory position of the tongue is mostly conventional and only approximate. It is useful for labelling vowels, but identification and transcription of vowels should rely more on the acoustic or other perceived qualities than on how they are produced (i.e. where the tongue is).

9 There is considerable dialectal variation with [ɔ] and [ɑ].

10 Vance (1987: 11) explains the difference between "lip rounding" and "lip compression" as follows: "In rounding, the corners of the mouth are brought forward and the lips are protruded. In compression, the jaws are closed, bringing the lips together vertically so that the side portions are in contact."

Suggested Readings

General terminology in phonetics: Ladefoged (1982), Finegan (1994). Ladefoged (1982) is an excellent introductory book for those who are interested in articulatory and acoustic phonetics. Further discussion of the consonant and vowel systems of English is found in both these books.

General issues in Japanese phonetics: Bloch (1950), J. McCawley (1968), Vance (1987), Shibatani (1990). Vance (1987) provides a very detailed literature survey on various phonetic treatments of Japanese sounds.

One of the topics that the present chapter does not include is intonation, and a discussion on it can be found in J. McCawley (1968), Higurashi (1983), Poser (1984), Beckman (1986), Vance (1987), Pierehumbert and Beckman (1988), N. Williams (1990), and Kubozono (1993).

EXERCISES

1   The points marked in the vocal tract (figure 2.4) are places involved in
    the articulation of Japanese consonants. List all the phonetic symbols of
    Japanese consonants that can be articulated at each indicated location.

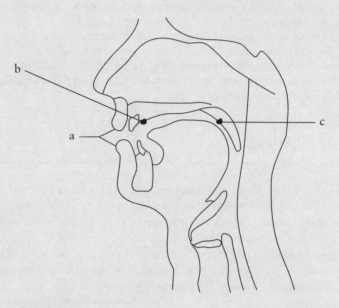

Figure 2.4   Vocal tract

2   Following the style of the examples given below, provide a phonetic
    description of the sounds below them. For consonants, include voicing,
    and place and manner of articulation; for vowels, include height and
    a frontness/backness dimension.

    Examples: [s] = voiceless alveolar fricative
                    [e] = mid front vowel

    Consonants: [n] [r] [š] [tˢ] [b] [č]

    Vowels: [o] [a] [u]

3   Give the Japanese speech sound symbol that corresponds to the follow-
    ing articulatory description. In addition, if you know Japanese, give
    Japanese words that contain these sounds.

    a.   voiced velar stop
    b.   high front vowel
    c.   voiceless bilabial stop

   d. bilabial nasal

   e. voiceless palatal fricative

4 In each of the following pairs of sounds, one or more features are shared. Provide a single relevant feature that is shared by the following pairs. Two examples are given:

Examples: [p]:[g] stop
            [i]:[e] front

   a. [b]:[ǰ]
   b. [k]:[ŋ]
   c. [e]:[o]
   d. [tˢ]:[d]
   e. [u]:[i]

5 Have a native speaker of Japanese pronounce the following words that are written in Romanization ("Kunrei"-style) and provide transcriptions of these words.

   a. isi "stone"
   b. hon "book"
   c. tetudau "help"
   d. itta "went"
   e. matimasyoo "let's wait"
   f. zibun "self"
   g. san kamosirenai "it might be three"
   h. syasin mo nakusita "(I) lost pictures, too"

6 [Exercise for those who know the Hiragana syllabary.] Write out the following transcription using Hiragana syllabary.

   a. [ašita]
   b. [sap:ari]
   c. [asat:e iko: to omot:e irundesu]
   d. [kočira de oyoŋimašita]
   e. [tanakasan wa ǰo:zu ni setˢume:šitekudasaimašita]
   f. [mot:o yoku kaŋ:aetekara oteŋami o sašiaŋetaindesu]

3 Phonology

Given the phonetic inventory introduced in chapter 2, we shall investigate how the sounds are put together in Japanese. We will in particular observe that a number of sound-related phenomena occur in Japanese, and that these phenomena are quite systematic. The area of **phonology** deals with the systematic patterning of speech sounds.

In comparing the phonetic inventories of English and Japanese in chapter 2, we noted that the voiceless stops in English are aspirated, i.e. associated with a puff of air, while those in Japanese are not. When we look at the distribution of such aspirated voiceless stops in English, however, we notice that not all occurrences of the voiceless stops in the language are aspirated. As we will see below, the occurrence of aspirated voiceless stops in English is restricted to certain positions in a word, and in that sense is predictable.

Let us transcribe these sounds in more detail by indicating the aspirated voiceless stops as $[p^h, t^h, k^h]$ and non-aspirated ones as $[p, t, k]$. Let us now try to pronounce the following words: *pin*, *spin*, *stop*, and *propose*. As was described in chapter 2, the aspiration can be detected by placing a piece of paper in front of the mouth and observing whether there is any movement in pronouncing those voiceless stops. The distribution of the aspirated and non-aspirated bilabial stop, "p", is reflected in (1). (The period "." in (1d) marks the syllable boundary.)

(1) a. pin → $[p^h \text{ɪn}]$
     b. spin → [spɪn]
     c. stop → [stɑp]
     d. propose → $[p^h \text{rə.}p^h \text{oz}]$

Compare (a) with (b) and (c). The voiceless bilabial stop is aspirated at the beginning of the word, but when it follows [s], it is not aspirated. The place where the bilabial stop is aspirated is not limited to word-initial position, however. Notice that in (d), "p" is aspirated at the beginning of the second syllable as well. We can generalize that voiceless stops are aspirated when they are in syllable-initial position; and they are unaspirated elsewhere. So, we can see that even though the characterization of "p" is voiceless bilabial stop, its actual phonetic realization can vary, that is, either aspirated "p" ($[p^h]$) or unaspirated "p" ([p]). We can, then, regard the aspirated "p" and the unaspirated "p" as variants of a more general (or more abstract) "p". This general "p" is referred to as a **phoneme**, and the variants of a phoneme are called **allophones**. So, in the present case, the aspirated "p" and the unaspirated "p" are said to be the allophones of the phoneme "p". We indicate a general transcription of a phoneme by using the notation "/ /", and call it a **phonemic transcription**. The transcription of allophones involves a more detailed description, including the presence or absence of aspiration, for instance. The detailed transcription of allophones is called a **phonetic transcription**, and we indicate the phonetic transcription with the notation "[ ]". Using this type of notation, then, we can say that the phoneme /p/ is realized either as the aspirated [pʰ] or as unaspirated [p], and the environments in which the allophones of /p/, i.e. [pʰ] and [p], occur are predictable. That is, the allophone [pʰ] appears in the syllable-initial position while the allophone [p] occurs elsewhere. Given that there are two kinds of transcription types, the phonemic transcription of the word *pin* is given as /pɪn/, and the phonetic transcription as [pʰɪn]. Similarly, the phonemic transcription of the word *spin* is /spɪn/ and its phonetic transcription is [spɪn].

We have observed above that a difference between phonemes and allophones resides in the fact that where allophones occur can be predictable while this is not the case with phonemes. It should be pointed out, in addition, that allophones are not contrastive in different words while phonemes can be. For example, the two allophones of /p/ in English, i.e. [pʰ] and [p], are never contrastive in different words. That is, in English there does not exist a pair of words, such as [spʰɪl] and [spɪl], containing the aspirated [pʰ] and the unaspirated [p], respectively, that have different meanings. It is a phoneme, instead, that serves as a contrastive unit. For instance, /p/ and /b/ are separate phonemes in English, and hence, we find a contrastive pair of words such as *pill* /pɪl/ and *Bill* /bɪl/.

The field of phonology deals to a great extent with the regularity with which sounds are distributed, with one of its goals being to determine the condition under which such regularities are defined. In this chapter we will discuss various phenomena in the Japanese sound system.

1   Phonological Rules in Japanese

1.1   *Devoicing of High Vowels*

Just as the English phoneme /p/ has allophonic variants, phonemes in Japanese display allophonic variants as well. As we have briefly mentioned in chapter 2, certain vowels in Japanese exhibit the devoicing phenomenon in a particular environment (cf. Vance 1987). The vowels that most frequently undergo devoicing are the high vowels, i.e. /i/ and /u/.[1] Not all the dialects of Japanese exhibit high vowel devoicing, however. For example, the phenomenon is quite wide-spread in the Tokyo dialect, while in the Kansai area, including Osaka and Kyoto, the devoicing phenomenon is not common, if it occurs at all. In this section we will examine the condition under which the high vowels are devoiced in Tokyo Japanese.

First, consider the following data, where the circle under a vowel indicates that it is devoiced.[2]

(2) a.   [ika]   "squid"
     b.   [šikaru]   "scold"
     c.   [kidesu̥ka]   "Is it a tree?"
     d.   [ki̥ta]   "north"
     e.   [tˢuda]   (person's name)
     f.   [čikai]   "near"
     g.   [ku̥sai]   "smelly"
     h.   [kigeN]   "mood"
     i.   [šizuka]   "quiet"
     j.   [ki̥seN]   "steamship"
     k.   [kagitai]   "(I) want to sniff."
     l.   [točida]   "It's land."
     m.   [su̥kida]   "(I) like (it)."
     n.   [miǰikai]   "short"
     o.   [taku̥saN]   "a lot"
     p.   [kokugo]   "Japanese language"
     q.   [udoN]   "noodle"
     r.   [izumo]   (place name)
     s.   [çi̥tˢuyo:]   "necessary"
     t.   [katˢu̥çi̥to]   "person to win"
     u.   [uširo]   "back"
     v.   [pi̥kaso]   "Picasso"
     w.   [ki̥čigai]   "crazy person"
     x.   [Φu̥šiN]   "suspicion"

When we concentrate on where the voiceless high vowels appear, we notice that the devoicing phenomenon is observed in a restricted situation. What, then, is the condition under which the high vowel devoicing is induced? In determining the environments in which the high vowel devoicing takes place, it is important to pay attention to the nature of consonants that precede and follow the high vowels. In doing so, it is often helpful to list all the sounds that can possibly occur before and after the sound in question. The list in (3) below illustrates the range of possible sounds that precede and follow the voiceless high vowels on the basis of the data given in (2).

(3)   š | i̥/u̥ | k
      s | | t
      k | | s
      p | | č
      tˢ | | ç
      ç | | tˢ
      č | | š
      Φ | |

Is there any regular environment in which the high vowels are voiceless? More specifically, is there any property that is common among these sounds surrounding the voiceless high vowels? The place of articulation and the manner of articulation both have a wide range of distribution. What is shared by the preceding and following sounds in (3), however, is their voicing feature: that is, all of them are voiceless consonants. So, when the high vowels are preceded and followed by voiceless consonants, devoicing takes place.

Notice that in order to become devoiced, the high vowels require two voiceless consonants, one preceding AND one after, rather than just one, either preceding or following. This strict condition is confirmed by examples like (2e, h, i, k, l, n, p, u, w). In these examples the high vowel is either preceded or followed by a voiceless consonant, but remains voiced. In (2e), for instance, the high vowel /u/ is preceded by a voiceless consonant, namely [tˢ], but is followed by a voiced consonant, [d]. In this situation, the high vowel does not undergo devoicing. Similarly, in (2k), the first occurrence of the high vowel /i/ is followed by the voiceless consonant [t] but preceded by the voiced consonant [g], and as a consequence, the high vowel is pronounced as voiced. Therefore, the high vowels need to be preceded AND followed by voiceless consonants in order for the devoicing to occur. The environment in which high vowel devoicing takes place can be stated in (4).

(4)　The high vowels, /i/ and /u/, are voiceless between voiceless consonants. Otherwise, they are voiced.

The generalization in (4) specifies the situation in which the high vowels are realized as voiceless. It also states that when the environment is not met, high vowels are realized as voiced. Another way of stating the generalization in (4) is by rules like those in (5), where the phonological change is described on the left of the notation "/" and the environment in which the change occurs is stated on the right of the notation.

(5)　a.　i → i̥ / voiceless consonant _____ voiceless consonant
　　　b.　u → u̥ / voiceless consonant _____ voiceless consonant

The underlined position in (5) is where the phonological change of the high vowels occurs. Notice that the two rules in (5) are very similar in that the environment of the phonological change (i.e. on the right of the symbol "/") is identical. To avoid this type of overlapping, we can further generalize the two rules in (5) by referring to /i/ and /u/ as high vowels. This is shown in (6).

(6)　high vowel → voiceless / voiceless　　　　　voiceless
　　　　　　　　　　　　　　consonant _____ consonant

The rule stated in (6) can further be formalized by using notations that are convenient in stating phonological rules. This is accomplished in (7), where "V" and "C" stand for vowel and consonant, respectively.

(7)   V   → V̥ / C   ___   C
        [+high]   [−voice]   [−voice]

In the rule formula of (7), the vowel height is expressed by [+high], and the voicing feature of the surrounding consonants is indicated by the notation [−voice].
The rules in (6) and (7) do not include a statement indicating where the voiced
counterparts of the high vowels appear. We have seen above that the situation
where voiceless high vowels occur is more restricted than the situation where
their voiced counterparts appear. So, although the rules in (6) and (7) are stated
on the basis of a more restricted environment, i.e. the environment for voiceless
high vowels, a less restricted environment is implied as a default case. That is,
the rules should further be interpreted such that when the conditions stated in
the rules are not met, voiced high vowels appear.
   The condition of high vowel devoicing becomes more complicated when we
consider the following additional set of data.

(8)   a.   [muki̥]   "direction"
      b.   [kamisori]   "razor"
      c.   [kazu]   "number"
      d.   [deguči]   "exit"
      e.   [gasu̥]   "gas"
      f.   [kagi]   "key"
      g.   [kaki̥]   "oyster"
      h.   [kagu]   "sniff"
      i.   [haši̥]   "chopsticks"
      j.   [kači̥]   "value"
      k.   [kaǰi]   "fire"
      l.   [seki̥]   "seat"
      m.   [katˢu̥]   "win"

Pay close attention to the high vowel at the end of each word. Some of the
word-final high vowels get devoiced while others do not. This is not what we
expect given our rule in (4). The rule in (4) requires two voiceless consonants, one
preceding and the other following the high vowels. What separates the examples
in (8) from those in (2), over which the rule in (4) has its effect, is the fact that
the high vowels in (8) are in word-final position. So, focusing on the data given
in (8), let us concentrate on what sort of conditions may be placed on the consonant that precedes the high vowels. The range of consonants which cause the
high vowel to become devoiced is in (9a) while the consonants in (9b) do not
seem to induce devoicing.

(9)   a.   /k, č, s, š, tˢ/
      b.   /r, z, g, ǰ/

It is quite obvious that when the high vowels at the end of the word are
preceded by a voiceless consonant, they undergo devoicing; while when a voiced
consonant precedes them, they do not become devoiced. This observation can
be expressed in the following rule.

(10) a. The high vowels, /i/ and /u/, are voiceless when they are at the end
of the word and are preceded by a voiceless consonant.

  b. $\begin{array}{ccc} V & \rightarrow \underset{\circ}{V} / & C \\ [+\text{high}] & & [-\text{voice}] \end{array}$ _____ #

The notation "#" indicates the end of a word.[3]

Let us now compare the rules stated in (4) and (10). We can immediately
notice the similarity: that is, the condition on what precedes the high vowels
is the same in both statements. The only difference is what follows the vowels.
It is customary to collapse two or more rule environments if the other aspects
of the rules are the same. This indicates that the two rules can be viewed as
a single process. Hence, the rules in (4) and in (10) can be reduced into one by
using the notation in (11).

(11) $\begin{array}{ccc} V & \rightarrow \underset{\circ}{V} / & C \\ [+\text{high}] & & [-\text{voice}] \end{array}$ _____ $\left\{ \begin{array}{c} C \\ [-\text{voice}] \\ \# \end{array} \right\}$

The curly brackets in (11) indicate the alternatives: a voiceless consonant can
immediately follow the high vowel, or the word can end with the high vowel
itself. When either condition is met, high vowel devoicing occurs as long as the
consonant before the high vowel is voiceless.

In this section we have observed that the high vowels in Japanese are phonetically realized sometimes as voiceless and sometimes as voiced. Since the situation
under which the voiced and voiceless variants appear is completely predictable,
these two variants are each allophones of the phonemes /i/ and /u/. That is, [i̥]
and [i] are allophones of /i/, and [u̥] and [u] are allophones of /u/.

1.2 Nasal Assimilation

In chapter 2 we have illustrated that the pronunciation of nasal sounds often
involves coarticulation. When the nasal sound /n/ is followed by a bilabial sound,
the nasal is phonetically realized as [m]; and when /n/ is followed by a velar sound,
its phonetic realization is the velar nasal [ŋ]. Thus, depending on the place of
articulation of the following consonant, the phonetic realization of /n/ varies.
For example, the nasal consonant of the word *san* "three" exhibits different
phonetic realizations depending on the nature of the consonant that follows it.
This is illustrated in (12).[4]

(12) a. /sanban/   → [sambaN]   "number 3"
         /sanpun/   → [sampuN]   "3 minutes"
     b. /sannen/   → [san:eN]   "3 years"
         /santen/   → [santeN]   "3 points"
         /sansatu/   → [sansatˢu]   "3 books"
         /sandan/   → [sandaN]   "3 steps"
     c. /sanko/   → [saŋko]   "3 (objects)"
         /sangoositu/ → [saŋgo:šitˢu] "Room 3"

The phenomenon of coarticulation as exemplified in (12) is called **assimilation:**
that is, the phenomenon entails adjacent sounds becoming phonetically similar,
sharing some features such as place of articulation. In our example above, the
place of articulation of a consonant, namely, the labial consonants (/b/ and
/p/) in (12a), the alveolar consonants (/n/, /t/, /s/, and /d/) in (12b), and the velar
consonants (/k/ and /g/) in (12c), is extended to the immediately preceding
nasal sound. The assimilation phenomenon illustrated in (12) is systematic in
that the nature of the nasal sound can be predictable given the place of articulation of the following consonant. This regularity can be stated in terms of
the rules in (13).

(13) a. /n/ is realized as the bilabial nasal [m] when it is immediately followed
          by a bilabial consonant.
      b. /n/ is realized as the alveolar nasal [n] when it is immediately followed
          by an alveolar consonant.
      c. /n/ is realized as the velar nasal [ŋ] when it is immediately followed
          by a velar consonant.

These generalizations can also be stated by the rules in (14).

(14) a. n → m / ___   C
                          bilabial
      b. n → n / ___   C
                          alveolar
      c. n → ŋ / ___   C
                           velar

Notice that although both these sets of rules in (13) and (14) account for the
range of data given in (12), they fail to capture the important generalization pertinent to the assimilation phenomenon. What is crucial in the nasal assimilation
case we are discussing here is the fact that the place of articulation is identical
between the nasal segment and the consonant immediately following it. So, it
is not necessary to refer to the individual place of articulation as long as the rule
indicates that the two adjacent segments in question share the same place of
articulation. The generalization stated in (15) achieves this effect.

(15) /n/ is realized as the nasal sound that shares the same place of articulation
      as the immediately following consonant.

The generalization in (15) can also be formulated in terms of the rule in (16).

(16) n →   nasal / ____   C
          [α place]   [α place]

The notation "[α place]" under the nasal sound and the consonant immediately following it indicates that the place of articulation of these two sounds is
identical. For example, when the place of articulation of the following consonant

is bilabial, the nasal sound is also bilabial, i.e. [m]. Note that the rules in (15) and (16) are preferable to the individual rules stated in (13) and (14), because the former can capture the regularity of the nasal assimilation as a more general phenomenon.[5]

Notice that the phonological changes described in (15) occur when the nasal sound is at the end of a syllable and is followed by another consonant.[6] Given the generalization of (15), we might want to analyze [m], [n], and [ŋ] as always being allophones of /n/ since their occurrences are predictable. However, the three nasal sounds under discussion can also appear freely before vowels. Before vowels, furthermore, their occurrences are not predictable. Consider the examples in (17).

(17) a.   [matˢu]   "pine"
            [sumo:]   "Sumo wrestling"
            [amai]   "sweet"
            [me]   "eye"
            [imi]   "meaning"
     b.   [natˢu]   "summer"
            [kino:]   "yesterday"
            [neko]   "cat"
            [niku]   "meat"
            [nuru]   "paint"
     c.   [kaŋaku] or [kagaku] "science"
            [kaiŋo:] or [kaigo:]   "meeting"
            [kuŋi] or [kugi]   "nail"
            [do:ŋu] or [do:gu]   "instrument"
            [kaŋe] or [kage]   "shadow"

The examples in (17a) and (17b) show that the distribution of [m] and [n] is not predictable. For this reason, the nasals should be treated as independent phonemes, /m/ and /n/ (especially note the minimally different pair involving the words [matˢu] "pine" and [natˢu] "summer"). In order to account for the assimilation data in (12a) as well as the set of data given in (17a), it is necessary to analyze certain instances of [m] in Japanese as being an allophone of the phoneme /n/, shown in (12a), while other instances of [m] reflect the phoneme /m/ as in (17a).

As for [ŋ], there does not seem to be any clear evidence for a separate phoneme /ŋ/. First, as seen in (12c), [ŋ] is an allophone of (a syllable-final) /n/ when it occurs before a velar sound. Second, while one can find minimally different pairs like [matˢu] vs. [natˢu] shown in (17a–b), which supports /m/ and /n/ as separate phonemes, the sound [ŋ] can never appear at the beginning of a word, and so a sequence like [ŋatˢu] with an initial [ŋ] does not occur. Third, while [ŋ] can occur in the middle of a word between vowels as shown by examples like [kuŋi] "nail" and [kaŋe] "shadow" in (17c), these words can always be pronounced with a [g] instead, yielding [kugi] and [kage]. Notice, though, that when [g] occurs at the beginning of the word, as in *gakkoo* [gak:o:] "school", it can only be pronounced as a [g]. This suggests that the instances of [ŋ] that

occur in words like [kuɲi] and [kaɲe] are indeed allophones of the phoneme
/g/. Technically speaking, we can say that [ŋ] and [g] are in **free variation**
between vowels. That is, in between vowels, /g/ can be pronounced as either
[g] or [ŋ]. Thus, some instances of [ŋ] are allophones of the phoneme /g/ as in
(17c) while other instances are allophones of /n/ as in (12c). There is no separate
phoneme /ŋ/ in Japanese.

1.3   Alveolar Alternations

Another instance of allophonic alternation can be observed with alveolar sounds
in Japanese. Let us begin with the allophonic variants that are exhibited with
the Japanese voiceless alveolar stop, /t/. Consider the data in (18).

(18)   /atami/   →   [atami]   (place name)
       /tukau/   →   [tˢukau]   "use"
       /tokei/   →   [toke:]   "clock"
       /uta/   →   [uta]   "song"
       /tatu/   →   [tatˢu]   "stand"
       /heta/   →   [heta]   "unskillful"
       /tetudau/   →   [tetˢudau]   "help"
       /koto/   →   [koto]   "thing"
       /katu/   →   [katˢu]   "win"
       /utusu/   →   [utˢusu]   "reflect"
       /tateru/   →   [tateru]   "build"
       /setomono/   →   [setomono]   "pottery"
       /itu/   →   [itˢu]   "when"
       /utu/   →   [utˢu]   "hit"
       /kita/   →   [kita]   "came"
       /oto/   →   [oto]   "sound"

Focus on the difference between the phonemic transcriptions on the left of the
arrows and the phonetic transcriptions on the right. First, notice that in (18)
the phoneme /t/ can actually be realized in two different ways: either [t] or [tˢ].
Second, we should ask ourselves the question as to whether the two different
realizations of /t/ are completely arbitrary, or whether their distribution is regular
in that we can determine a specific environment in which only one of them can
occur. Let us assume that their distribution is regular and try to find an appropriate environment.

Recall that when we attempt to figure out what the environment is in which
a specific allophone occurs, it is important to pay close attention to its surrounding sounds. In the present case, we are interested in where [t] and [tˢ] each occur:
(19) illustrates the possible sounds that can precede and follow these two variants
of /t/ based on the data in (18). We note that [t] and [tˢ] can be surrounded by
vowels on both sides or can occur before a vowel at the beginning of a word.
(The symbol "#" preceding [t] or [tˢ] means that the consonant occurs at the
beginning of the word.)

(19)

a	t	a		a	tˢ	u
e		e		e		
i		o		i		
o				o		
u				u		
#				#		

Is there any generalization that can be captured in contrasting these two? Let us first compare the range of vowels that can precede [t] and [tˢ]. The illustration in (19) shows that there does not seem to be any special condition holding for the nature of the vowels that precede [t] and [tˢ]: rather, they each can be preceded by any vowel; also, they can each appear at the beginning of the word not preceded by any vowel at all. What about the range of vowels that can follow [t] and [tˢ]? It is quite clear from (19) that only the high back vowel /u/ can follow [tˢ], and other vowels follow [t].[7] On the basis of these observations, then, we can state the generalization in (20).

(20) /t/ is realized as [tˢ] when it is followed by the high back vowel. Otherwise, /t/ is realized as [t].

The statement in (20) can further be formalized as a rule like (21).

(21) t → tˢ / ____ u

The rule in (21) says that /t/ becomes [tˢ] when it is followed by [u], which is equivalent to what (20) states. The rule of the form in (21) can be stated in terms of place and manner of articulation along with the specification of a voicing feature. This is accomplished by (22).

(22) voiceless   → voiceless   / ____ high back vowel
      alveolar stop   alveolar affricate

The rules stated in (21) and (22) do not mention anything about the condition under which [t] appears. As we have dealt with in our discussion of high vowel devoicing, by stating a condition defined by a more specific and restricted situation, we are also implying a condition for the other. That is, when the more specific environment for [tˢ] is not met, [t] is realized instead. Consequently, [t] appears in more varied environments. Hence, even though the rules in (21) and (22) do not mention anything about where [t] occurs, it should be interpreted as "if the condition is not met, [t] appears".

We have seen the distribution of [t] and [tˢ], and discussed the condition under which they occur. Since both sounds are variant pronunciations of /t/, they are considered allophones of /t/.

Another instance of an allophonic change is displayed in (23).

(23)　/tikaku/　→　[čikaku]　"near"
　　　/otiru/　→　[očiru]　"fall"
　　　/tatari/　→　[tatari]　"spell"
　　　/ita/　→　[ita]　"board"
　　　/keti/　→　[keči]　"stingy"
　　　/satori/　→　[satori]　"realization"
　　　/uti/　→　[uči]　"house"
　　　/otoko/　→　[otoko]　"man"
　　　/tabete/　→　[tabete]　"eating"
　　　/akiti/　→　[akiči]　"empty land"
　　　/moti/　→　[moči]　"rice cake"
　　　/kati/　→　[kači]　"value"

Again, pay close attention to the phonetic realization of /t/ in (23). You will notice that /t/ can be realized either as [t] or as [č]. Is this alternation totally arbitrary? Or is the environment in which one of the allophones appears conditioned by a certain rule? Recall that what we need to do is concentrate on the surrounding sounds, in particular, the type of vowels in this case, in order to determine the condition pertinent to the occurrence of each sound. The range of possible vowels that precede and follow [t] and [č] is displayed in (24).

(24)
a	t	a		a	č	i
e		e		e		
i		o		i		
o				o		
u				u		
#				#		

The distribution of the surrounding vowels demonstrated in (24), as well as the distribution we have examined in (19) above, lead us to the conclusion that [č] appears only when it is followed by the high front vowel, /i/, while [t] occurs when it is followed by vowels other than /i/ (and /u/). Furthermore, the nature of the preceding vowel does not seem to be crucial in this set of data. So, we can come up with the generalization stated in (25).

(25)　/t/ is realized as [č] when it is followed by the high front vowel /i/. Otherwise, /t/ is realized as [t].

Or we can state the generalization in terms of a rule like (26).

(26)　t → č / ＿＿ i

Since /t/ can be realized as [t] or [č] and their appearances are conditioned by a rule such as (25) or (26), we can regard [t] and [č] as allophones of /t/. Together with the preceding discussion concerning the data in (18), then, we can conclude that [t], [tˢ], and [č] all constitute allophones of /t/.

Now, consider the following sets of data.

(27) /sakura/   →   [sakura]   "cherry blossom"
      /kesa/   →   [kesa]   "this morning"
      /asita/   →   [ašita]   "tomorrow"
      /osoi/   →   [osoi]   "late, slow"
      /simasu/   →   [šimasu]   "(I will) do (it)"
      /musi/   →   [muši]   "insect"
      /kusaru/   →   [kusaru]   "spoil"
      /kesiki/   →   [kešiki]   "scenery"
      /ase/   →   [ase]   "sweat"
      /isi/   →   [iši]   "stone"
      /miso/   →   [miso]   "soy bean paste"
      /tosi/   →   [toši]   "year"

(28) /zenbu/   →   [zembu]   "all"
      /ozisan/   →   [oǰisaN]   "uncle"
      /izen/   →   [izeN]   "before"
      /kazi/   →   [kaǰi]   "fire"
      /kuzira/   →   [kuǰira]   "whale"
      /kazoku/   →   [kazoku]   "family"
      /zannen/   →   [zan:eN]   "regrettable"
      /kuzu/   →   [kuzu]   "trash"
      /izi/   →   [iǰi]   "maintenance"
      /tozan/   →   [tozaN]   "mountain climbing"
      /kezuru/   →   [kezuru]   "sharpen, scrape"
      /meziro/   →   [meǰiro]   (place name)

Let us begin with the data in (27), focusing on the variants of /s/. Notice that the voiceless alveolar fricative has two variants, [s] and [š]. Observe further that [š] is realized only when it is followed by the high front vowel, /i/. The preceding vowel does not seem to contribute to this phonological change at all. The other variant, [s], on the other hand, does not seem to be as restricted as the occurrence of [š]: except when /s/ is followed by /i/, [s] always surfaces irrespective of the type of vowel that precedes it. On the basis of these observations, we can capture the generalization in terms of a statement, as in (29a), or in terms of rule notation, as in (29b).

(29)   a.   /s/ is realized as [š] when it is followed by the high front vowel /i/.
            Otherwise, it is realized as [s].
       b.   s → š / ____ i

Hence, we can conclude that [s] and [š] are allophones of /s/, and the phonological change is conditioned by the rules stated in (29).

Let us turn to (28). This set of data is intended to illustrate the phonological change associated with the voiced alveolar fricative, /z/. This fricative sound has two phonetic realizations: [z] and [ǰ], the latter of which is the voiced alveopalatal affricate. In examining their distribution, it can be seen that the preceding vowel does not make any contribution to the phonological change: any vowel can precede [z] or [ǰ] including none. What about the following vowel? As we have seen with the three phonological changes of alveolar sounds above, the following vowel is indeed the crucial key to determine the environment. After examining the vowels that can follow [ǰ] and those that cannot, we can reach the conclusion that the high front vowel is the determining factor for the appearance of [ǰ]. This generalization is stated in (30).

(30) a. /z/ is realized as [ǰ] when it is followed by the high front vowel /i/. Otherwise, it is realized as [z].

   b. z → ǰ / ____ i

The sounds [z] and [ǰ] are two variants of /z/, and since the environments in which they occur are predictable, they are considered allophones of the phoneme /z/.

1.4 [h]/[Φ]/[ç] Alternations

In the previous section, we have examined cases where a single phoneme has two possible allophones, such as /s/, which has the allophones [s] and [š], and we have also examined the case of /t/, which has three allophones, [t], [tˢ], and [č]. There are other cases in Japanese where a phoneme can have more than two allophones. The phonological changes observed with the phoneme /h/ are another case. Let us consider the distributions of /h/ and its phonetic realizations in (31).

(31)

/yohoo/	→	[yoho:]	"forecast"
/toohu/	→	[to:Φu]	"Tofu"
/hosi/	→	[hoši]	"star"
/oahu/	→	[oaΦu]	"Oahu"
/suhada/	→	[suhada]	"bare skin"
/ehime/	→	[eçime]	(place name)
/haha/	→	[haha]	"mother"
/huku/	→	[Φuku]	"clothes"
/tehon/	→	[tehoN]	"model"
/saihu/	→	[saiΦu]	"wallet"
/hahen/	→	[haheN]	"broken piece"
/koohii/	→	[ko:çi:]	"coffee"
/hako/	→	[hako]	"box"
/hito/	→	[çito]	"person"
/hukai/	→	[Φukai]	"deep"
/sihon/	→	[šihoN]	"capital"
/kuuhuku/	→	[ku:Φuku]	"hunger"
/hen/	→	[heN]	"strange"
/kuuhi/	→	[ku:çi]	"waste"
/kihin/	→	[kiçiN]	"grace"
/sihai/	→	[šihai]	"control"
/ehu/	→	[eΦu]	"F"

Compare the phonemic transcription and the phonetic transcription. We should find three different realizations of /h/: [h], [Φ], and [ç]. When we try to list all the vowels preceding and following /h/ in an attempt to determine the environments for the three allophones, we notice that the environments for [Φ] and [ç] are more restricted than that for [h]. As was the case in some of the previous phonological rules discussed above, the nature of the vowel that follows is the crucial factor. First, the bilabial fricative, [Φ], occurs only when /h/ is followed by the high back vowel /u/. Second, the palatal fricative, [ç], appears only when /h/ is followed by the high front vowel /i/. And, finally, the glottal fricative, [h], surfaces when other vowels, /a/, /e/, and /o/, follow it. This three-way realization of the phoneme /h/ can be summarized as in (32), which can be formalized as in (33).

(32) a. /h/ is realized as [Φ] when it is followed by the high back vowel /u/.
      b. /h/ is realized as [ç] when it is followed by the high front vowel /i/.
      c. Otherwise, /h/ is realized as [h].

(33) a. h → Φ / ＿＿ u
      b. h → ç / ＿＿ i

Again, the phonological rules pertinent to the phoneme /h/ are conditioned by the type of vowels that follow it. Since the occurrences of the variants of /h/, i.e. [Φ], [ç], and [h], are predictable, they are regarded as allophones of /h/.

1.5 Digression on the Phoneme Status of [tˢ, č, š, ǰ, Φ, ç]

We have thus far discussed the fact that the allophones of certain phonemes in Japanese are predictable, and the regularity of the occurrence of specific allophones has been stated in terms of phonological rules. At this point, let us examine the phonological rules that we have formulated in sections 1.3 and 1.4 above. The relevant rules are repeated in (34).

(34) a. t → tˢ / ＿＿ u
      b. t › č / ＿＿ i
      c. s → š / ＿＿ i
      d. z → ǰ / ＿＿ i
      e. h → Φ / ＿＿ u
      f. h → ç / ＿＿ i

What the rule in (34c) states, for example, is that the phoneme /s/ is realized as [š] when it is followed by the high front vowel /i/, and that when it is followed by vowels other than /i/, /s/ is realized as [s]. This means that as long as [s] is analyzed only as an allophone of /s/, it is expected that the occurrence of [š] is restricted to the environment in which /s/ is followed by /i/ and would not occur before vowels such as /a, e, u, o/, for instance. Similar predictions are also made for the rest of the rules in (34). Upon closer examination, however, these predictions are not borne out, as is shown by the following sets of data.[8]

(35)   [kantˢo:ne]   "canzone"
       [otottˢaN]   "father"
       [gottˢo:]   "feast"

(36)   [česu]   "chess"
       [ča]   "tea"
       [čokore:to]   "chocolate"
       [ču:i]   "attention"

(37)   [šačo:]   "company president"
       [šo:bai]   "business"
       [senšu:]   "last week"
       [šeru]   "Shell"

(38)   [ǰanru]   "genre"
       [ǰose:]   "woman"
       [ǰu:su]   "juice"
       [ǰesuča:]   "gesture"

(39)   [Φaito]   "fight"
       [Φeminisuto]   "feminist"
       [Φirumu]   "film"
       [Φo:ku]   "fork"

(40)   [çaku]   "hundred"
       [çu:çu:]   "sound of wind blowing"

If we analyze [tˢ, č, š, ǰ, Φ, ç] as always being allophones of /t, t, s, z, h, h/, respectively, none of the examples in (35)–(40) should occur, given the phonological rules in (34). We might wonder if [tˢ, č, š, ǰ, Φ, ç] are not allophones of the respective phonemes /t, t, s, z, h, h/ at all and hence disregard the phonological rules in (34), and instead treat them as separate phonemes. However, there are reasons to maintain the analysis that [tˢ, č, š, ǰ, Φ, ç] are indeed allophones of /t, t, s, z, h, h/, respectively. Recall our sound inventory of Japanese examined in chapter 2. We have observed that Japanese exhibits the voiceless alveolar stop, /t/. We have also seen that the (unrounded) high back vowel, /u/, constitutes one of the vowels in Japanese. Given that these two sounds are unquestionably phonemes of Japanese, it is reasonable to expect that the sequence of /t/ and /u/ should occur since it is typically the case in language after language that any consonant phoneme can be followed by any vowel phoneme. At the phonetic level, then, we might expect the realization of [tu], just as we expect the combination of /t/ with other vowels in the language. While the phonetic sequences of [t] with [a] and [e], for example, are attested as [ta] and [te], [tu] never appears in Japanese. A similar observation can be made for the other sounds under discussion: [ti], [si], [zi], [hu], and [hi] simply do not exist in Japanese. Given these observations together with the fact that any consonant phoneme should appear before any vowel phoneme, we would contend that phonetic sequences such as [tˢu] [či], [ši], [ǰu], [Φu], and [çi] and be analyzed phonemically as /tu/, /ti/, /si/, /zu/, /hu/, and /hi/, respectively. In this way, consonant phonemes like /t/, /s/, and /h/ can occur before any vowel at least at the phonemic level. Hence, the phonological rules in (34) should be maintained.

Further evidence for the rules in (34) will come in our discussion of various endings associated with verbs to be given in section 1.6. For example, if one considers a verb base like /mat/ "wait", the /t/ of the verb base is phonetically realized sometimes as [t] as in /mat + anai/ [matanai] "do/will not wait", sometimes as [tˢ] as in /mat + u/ [matˢu] "(will) wait", and sometimes as [č] as in /mat + itai/ [mačitai] "want to wait" (where the symbol "+" is used to separate the verb base from endings). Thus, the realization of the last consonant of this verb base is [tˢ] only before /u/, and [č] only before /i/. It is realized as [t] in all other contexts. This strongly supports the reality of the rules in (34), and that sounds like [tˢ] and [č] as well as [š], [ǰ], [Φ], and [ç] can be allophones of /t/, /s/, /z/, and /h/.

Nonetheless, the data in (35)–(40) show that [tˢ, č, š, ǰ, Φ, ç] can also be separate phonemes. This means that while certain instances of the sounds like [tˢ], [č], [š], [ǰ], [Φ], and [ç] are allophones of phonemes like /t/, /s/, /z/, /h/, as is most clearly demonstrated by the brief discussion of the verb base /mat/ "wait" given above, other instances of the sounds [tˢ], [č], [š], [ǰ], [Φ], and [ç] reflect the status of these as the phonemes /tˢ/, /č/, /š/, /ǰ/, /Φ/, and /ç/, as best evidenced by the words in (35)–(40). It should be noted that the status of /tˢ/ as a phoneme is quite marginal, occurring infrequently and mainly in loan words.

We have observed instances of phonological rules in Japanese. Recall that in chapter 2 we listed the allophones we have discussed in this section as sounds that occur in Japanese. It does not mean, however, that all the sounds appear arbitrarily. The discussion in this section leads to the conclusion that some sounds in Japanese, as is the case in every language in the world, are restricted to certain environments. So far as we can figure out what the environments are, we can predict where a particular sound in a language occurs.

1.6 *Verbal Conjugation Rules*

Many verbs in English produce their past tense by adding *-ed* to the present form. For instance, the verb *laugh* has its past tense form *laughed*. Similarly, the present participle form can be obtained by the addition of *-ing* to the present tense form as in *laughing*. This sort of paradigm is called a **conjugation**.

The Japanese verbal system exhibits intricate conjugation patterns, and it is particularly of interest in this section since it displays several intriguing phonological changes. As will be shown below, phonological changes exhibited in the verbal conjugation system in Japanese are somewhat different from the type of changes we have observed earlier in this chapter, such as nasal assimilation and alveolar alternations, in that the phonological changes observed in verbal conjugation are triggered by the addition of particular endings. (Technically, these changes are called **morphophonological** changes: cf. Tsujimura and Davis 1989;

Davis and Tsujimura 1991.) Let us first consider the paradigms in (41), given in Romanization, where non-past tense, negative, past tense, conditional, and provisional forms are illustrated.

(41)   "eat"   "stand"
    non-past   taberu   tatu
    negative   tabenai   tatanai
    past   tabeta   tatta
    conditional tabetara   tattara
    provisional tabereba   tateba

Let us attempt to identify the base form of the verbs and the endings that derive the non-past, negative, past, conditional, and provisional forms. Notice that within each paradigm, a substantial portion is shared by all the forms. For instance, all the forms of the word for "eat" share *tabe*. Similarly, the portion *tat* is shared by all the forms of the verb for "stand". Recall that in section 1.3 above, we discussed the fact that [t] and [tˢ] are allophones of /t/ in Japanese, and we stated that the environment in which /t/ is realized as [tˢ] is when it is followed by the high back vowel. The phonetic transcription of the non-past tense form of the verb for "stand" is [tatˢu]. Notice that the verbal form contains [tˢ] immediately before the high back vowel, and it suggests that this sound is underlyingly /t/. This means that all the conjugated forms of the verb for "stand" contain /tat/. The identical portion that is shared by all the conjugated forms amounts to the base form to which the different verbal endings are attached. This base form is called the verbal **root**. That is, a verbal root is the most basic meaningful form to which various endings are added. In the examples in (41), for instance, /tabe/ and /tat/ are verbal roots.

   Given that the roots of the verbs in (41) are /tabe/ and /tat/, we can now identify the endings for non-past, negative, past, conditional, and provisional. When we look at the paradigm for /tabe/, the endings in (42A) are extracted; while when we examine the paradigm for /tat/, those in (42B) are extracted.

(42)   *A*   *B*
    non-past   -ru   -u
    negative   -nai   -anai
    past   -ta   -ta
    conditional -tara   -tara
    provisional -reba   -eba

A question that immediately arises is whether the paradigm endings in *A* and the paradigm endings in *B* are completely different sets that arbitrarily apply to verbs. That is, is it arbitrary or not that the non-past tense endings /ru/ and /u/ go with the roots /tabe/ and /tat/ respectively? Or is the question of which paradigm ending should apply to a given verb determined by predictable factors? In order to answer these questions, we need to look at more data. The verbal roots in (43a) take the pattern of endings seen in (42A) while those in (43b) take the pattern of endings seen in (42B).

(43) a. yame   "quit":   *non-past*   yameru
                             negative   yamenai
                             past   yameta
                             conditional   yametara
                             provisional   yamereba

       same   "cool"
       kare   "wither"
       kari   "borrow"
       koware   "break"
       kotae   "answer"
       todoke   "deliver"
       tasuke   "help"

      b. mat   "wait":   *non-past*   matu
                             negative   matanai
                             past   matta
                             conditional   mattara
                             provisional   mateba

       kak   "write"
       kat   "win"
       sir   "know"
       nom   "drink"
       sas   "stick"
       tomar   "stop"
       tikazuk   "approach"

A significant difference can be found with respect to how these roots end. Observe that the verbal roots in (43a) all end in a vowel, while those in (43b) all end in a consonant. So, taking the non-past tense ending as an example, we can state the generalization as follows.

(44) a. If the root ends in a vowel, the non-past tense ending is *-ru*.
      b. If the root ends in a consonant, the non-past tense ending is *-u*.

The distributions of forms such as the negative and the provisional can be generalized similarly to the rules in (44). That is, given the two contrastive forms for the verbal conjugation in Japanese, as exemplified in (42), what is crucial in determining which paradigm ending a verbal root should take depends on the phonological form of the individual root: in our case here, whether a verbal root ends in a consonant or in a vowel is the determining factor.

     Once the conjugation patterns are selected, various verbal forms are produced, as is seen in (41). Interestingly enough, when the way in which each ending is attached to a root is further examined, we can see that several phonological changes take place. An example can be illustrated by the phonological changes that are involved in the formation of the past tense. Compare (45) through (48), where all the verbal roots are consonant-ending. The symbol "+" is used to mark the boundary between a verbal root and the past tense ending /ta/. (Recall that a colon ":" after a sound in transcription means that the sound is long or geminate.)

(45) a. /kat + ta/   → [kat:a]   "won"
      b. /mat + ta/   → [mat:a]   "waited"
      c. /ut + ta/   → [ut:a]   "hit (past)"
      d. /tat + ta/   → [tat:a]   "stood"

(46) a. /kaer + ta/ → [kaet:a]   "returned"
      b. /hair + ta/ → [hait:a]   "entered"
      c. /magar + ta/ → [magat:a]   "made a turn"
      d. /sir + ta/   → [šit:a]   "got to know"

(47) a. /yob + ta/   → [yonda]   "called"
      b. /tob + ta/   → [tonda]   "flew"
      c. /sakeb + ta/ → [sakenda]   "screamed"
      d. /korob + ta/ → [koronda]   "tripped, fell"
      e. /asob + ta/ → [asonda]   "played"

(48) a. /nom + ta/   → [nonda]   "drank"
      b. /yom + ta/   → [yonda]   "read (past)"
      c. /tanom + ta/ → [tanonda]   "asked"
      d. /sum + ta/   → [sunda]   "lived"
      e. /kam + ta/   → [kanda]   "bit"

Contrast the phonemic representation of a word and the past tense ending on the left of the arrow with the phonetic realization of the sequence on the right of it. No change is observed in (45): everything in the phonemic representation is in the phonetic transcription without any loss or addition. As is described in (45), the root ending /t/ and the initial consonant of /ta/ are phonetically realized as a single long consonant.

In (46)–(48), however, we see several phonological changes. Let us start with (46). What is unique about this set is that the verbal roots in this group end with /r/, and when the past tense ending /ta/ is added to them, the final consonant of the root changes to [t]. As a consequence, the root ending /t/ and the initial consonant of the past tense /ta/ are phonetically realized as a long consonant, as is illustrated in (46). This change is stated in (49).

(49) /r/ at the end of the verbal root becomes [t] before the past tense -*ta*.

Alternatively, we can state (49) in terms of a rule schema. This is accomplished in (50).

(50) r → t / ____ + ta

Next, consider (47). The verbal roots in this group share the characteristic that the consonant at the end of the root is /b/. In contrasting the underlying phonemic representation on the left and the phonetic transcription on the right, we notice two phonological changes: (i) the root-final /b/ becomes [n]; and (ii) the initial consonant of the past tense ending /ta/ changes to its voiced counterpart, i.e. [d]. Let us state this generalization as in (51) or (52).

(51) /b/ at the end of the verbal root becomes [n] before the past tense ending -*ta*, and the initial consonant of /ta/ becomes [d] when it is preceded by a root that ends in [n].

(52) a. b → n / ____ + ta
     b. t → d / n + ____

Finally, the forms in (48) also undergo two changes. The verbal roots in this set all end in /m/, which changes to [n] before the past tense ending -*ta*. Subsequently, the initial consonant of the past tense ending becomes voiced. These changes are stated in (53) and (54).

(53) /m/ at the end of the verbal root becomes [n] before the past tense ending -*ta*, and the initial consonant of /ta/ becomes [d] when it is preceded by a root that ends in [n].

(54) a. m → n / ____ + ta
     b. t → d / n + ____

Notice that (52b) and (54b) are the same rule. (52a) and (54a), on the other hand, are not the same, and yet they are substantially similar: both /b/ and /m/ are characterized as bilabial stops. And in both rules the output is the same, i.e. deriving the alveolar nasal. Since we are dealing with phonological changes that are involved with the addition of the past tense ending -*ta* in all the cases under discussion, we can consider the (a) rules virtually the same, and can try to collapse them into one. The way to accomplish this is to use the common phonetic feature shared by both /b/ and /m/, i.e. bilabial stop. The collapsed rule is in (55).

(55)
$$\left\{ \begin{array}{c} b \\ m \end{array} \right\} \rightarrow \quad n \quad / \text{____} + ta$$

voiced   alveolar
bilabial   nasal
stop

The advantage of collapsing two (or more) rules into one is that the collapsed rule can capture the generality of the rule process in question. That is, if we have what seem to be different rules applying to more than one phoneme that share some phonetically significant properties and if the phonological change brought about is the same, then it can be posited that there is a single more general rule. It is a traditional goal in phonology to find regularity in the sound patterning and come up with the significant generalizations given the data. In this sense, the rule in (55) is stated broadly in that it applies to voiced bilabial stops.

Now, consider the additional forms in (56) and (57).[9]

(56) a. /kak + ta/   →   [kaita]   "wrote"
      b. /sak + ta/   →   [saita]   "blossomed"
      c. /wak + ta/   →   [waita]   "boiled"
      d. /manek + ta/   →   [maneita]   "invited"
      e. /somuk + ta/   →   [somuita]   "disobeyed"

(57) a. /tug + ta/   →   [tˢuida]   "poured"
      b. /kag + ta/   →   [kaida]   "sniffed"
      c. /tog + ta/   →   [toida]   "sharpened"
      d. /katug + ta/   →   [katˢuida]   "lifted (it) on the shoulder"
      e. /oyog + ta/   →   [oyoida]   "swam"

All the roots in (56) end in /k/ while the roots in (57) have /g/ as the root-final consonant. Let us first examine (56). In this derivation, the root-final consonant /k/ seems to change to the vowel [i] before the past tense -*ta*. On the basis of this observation, then, we might state the phonological change as in (58).

(58) a. /k/ at the end of the verbal root becomes [i] before the past tense ending -*ta*.
      b. k → i / ____ + ta

Although (58) appears to describe the phonological change involved in (56) correctly, there is reason not to pursue this possibility. First, notice that all the phonological changes we have examined so far display cases in which a vowel changes to another vowel (or a variant of the vowel) or a consonant changes to another consonant. The phonological change stated in (58), in contrast, involves a change from a consonant to a vowel. It turns out that phonological derivations that change consonants to vowels or vice versa are very rare.

Second, verbal forms such as *kakita* "wrote", *sakita* "blossomed", *wakita* "boiled", etc., in which both /k/ and /i/ appear in a past tense form of a verb, have been historically attested. This historical evidence strongly suggests that /k/ and /i/ are separate segments, rather than that one is derived from the other. For these reasons, the phonological change from /k/ to /i/ in (56) should better be described by the combination of two changes: that is, the insertion of /i/ and the deletion of /k/. Thus, we can restate the phonological change in (56) as in (59).

(59) a. When the verbal root ends in /k/ and the past tense ending -*ta* follows it, the high front vowel /i/ is inserted at the end of the verbal root, and subsequently /k/ is deleted.
      b. Ø → i / k ____ + ta
      c. k → Ø / ____ i + ta

In (b) and (c), "Ø" stands for no segment. The change from no segment to /i/ in (b) amounts to the insertion of /i/, while the change from /k/ to no segment entails the deletion of /k/. Given these two separate rules, the underlying form of (56a), /kak + ta/, for example, first becomes /kaki+ta/, and then /k/ before the inserted /i/ is deleted, yielding /kai+ta/.

Let us now turn to (57). We immediately detect there is a similar phonological change in this derivation. That is, the consonant /g/ at the end of the verbal root changes to the vowel /i/. In this case, however, an additional change is associated with it, namely, the voicing of the initial consonant of the past tense ending *-ta*. As we have discussed concerning the forms of (56), the first change should be considered as the combination of the insertion of /i/ and the subsequent deletion of /g/. The first change, then, can be stated as in (60), which is parallel to (59).

(60)   a.   Ø → i / g ____ + ta
       c.   g → Ø / ____ i + ta

A question that immediately arises, then, is why the voicing of the first consonant of the past tense ending *-ta* takes place in (57) but not in (56). Notice that the only difference between the two sets of data is the nature of the consonant that is at the end of the verbal root: when the root-final consonant is /k/, the voicing does not occur, while when the root-final consonant is /g/, the voicing takes place. So, it seems reasonable to hypothesize that the voicing of /t/ can be attributed to the difference between /k/ in (56) and /g/ in (57). What this observation suggests is that in stating the voicing rule, the presence of the voiced consonant /g/ is necessary as a pertinent environment. The relevant rule should look like (61).

(61)   t → d / g + ____

It should be remembered, at this point, that a similar voicing of the first consonant /t/ of the past tense ending *-ta* has already been observed in the paradigms of (47) and (48) above. We have come up with the same rule of voicing, which was conditioned by the presence of the preceding /n/ segment at the end of a verbal root. The voicing rule is repeated below as (62).

(62)   t → d / n + ____

The voicing change stated in (61) and (62) is identical although the environment in which the voicing takes place is not. When we focus on the phonetic characteristics inherent to /g/ and /n/, however, we find a property that is shared by both sounds: that is, /g/ and /n/ are both voiced. The similarity between (61) and (62), then, shows our hypothesis that voicing is triggered by the root-final /g/ in (57) while not being triggered by the voiceless root-final consonant /k/ in (56). This is indeed on the right track. Let us summarize the rules that are relevant to the derivation of the verbal conjugation observed in (57).

(63)   a.   t → d / g + ____
       b.   Ø → i / g ____ + ta
       c.   g → Ø / ____ i + ta

It is interesting to note that the voicing rules of (61) and (62) are reminiscent of the nasal assimilation phenomenon we have discussed in section 1.2. Recall that assimilation is a phenomenon in which a phonetic feature extends to a neighboring sound. The voicing of /t/ observed with the past tense ending /ta/, then, can be characterized as a case of assimilation, i.e. voicing assimilation. That is, in both rules, the feature of voicing inherent to /g/ and /n/ spreads to the segment /t/, which immediately follows them. Hence, the phonological rules stated in (61) and (62) can be considered assimilation rules.

We should now examine whether the set of rules in (63) indeed derives the well-formed past tense verbal forms in (57). Let us consider the verbal form in (57a), i.e. /tug + ta/, as our example. First, (63a) applies to the underlying form, /tug + ta/, since the environment of this rule is met: the root-ending consonant is /g/. The application of this rule is described in (64).

(64) underlying: tug + ta
    (63a):   tug + da

Second, the rule (63b) is expected to apply to the output of (64), i.e. [tug + da], but this rule cannot apply to [tug + da]. Is the condition for the rule in (63b) met in [tug + da]? No. It is because this rule requires that the environment contain the past tense ending of the form /ta/ rather than /da/, even though the latter is derived from the former. It means that we need to modify the rule in (b) so that the insertion rule can apply to the output of (64). We can achieve this by changing /ta/ in (63b) to /da/, as is described in (65).

(65) Ø → i / g ____ + da

Let us apply the modified insertion rule in (65) to the result of (64), which meets the environment that the insertion rule requires. This is shown in (66).

(66)   tug + da
    (65): tugi + da

Finally, the deletion rule of (63c) needs to be applied to the result of the derivation in (66) above, but we immediately notice that this rule cannot apply. As was the case with (63b), the deletion rule also specifies the presence of /ta/, rather than /da/, as the environment in which the rule should apply. As (66) shows, in order for the deletion rule of (63c) to apply to the output of (66), the /ta/ in the rule needs to be modified to /da/. The modified rule is in (67).

(67) g → Ø +/ ____ i + da

Since the condition that is required by the rule in (67) is met in the output of (66), the deletion rule can now be applied, as is depicted in (68).

(68)   tugi + da
    (67): tui + da

What we obtain as a result of applying the three rules is [tˢuida], which is an acceptable past tense form. The three rules, two of which underwent some modifications, are summarized in (69).

(69) a. t → d / g + _____
      b. Ø → i / g _____ + da
      c. g → Ø / _____ i + da

Thus, the sequence of the rules of (69) sufficiently accounts for the derivation of the set of verbs given in (57).

When we look at the set of rules in (69), we readily notice a strong similarity between (69) and (59). The relevant portions of the two sets of rules are repeated below.

(59) b. Ø → i / k _____ + ta
      c. k → Ø / _____ i + ta

(69) b. Ø → i / g _____ + da
      c. g → Ø / _____ i + da

There are two differences between the two sets of rules contrasted above. The first difference is the type of consonant that conditions the insertion rules as well as the type that undergoes the deletion rules: in (59) the consonant is /k/, and in (69) it is /g/. The second difference is the past tense ending form that partially conditions the rules: in (59) the past tense ending has the form of /ta/ while in (69) it is /da/.

We have earlier explained the relevance of stating rules as generally as possible. In order to generalize rules, it is important to look for common properties that are shared by the sounds under investigation. When we focus on the two sets of insertion and deletion rules we have come up with above, we notice /k/ and /g/ do share the place and manner of articulation, namely, velar stop. As for the second difference, what is crucial to the rules is the segments /t/ and /d/. That is, we do not necessarily refer to the past tense ending as a whole for the purpose of the rule application as long as the segments /t/ and /d/ are present in the rule formula. We can, then, find a common feature inherent to /t/ and /d/ as well: they are both alveolar stops. Thus, the insertion and deletion rules stated in (59) as well as in (69) above can be generalized by using terms such as velar stop and alveolar stop. This is demonstrated below.

(70) a. Ø → i / velar consonant _____ + alveolar stop
      b. velar consonant → Ø / _____ i + alveolar stop

It should be pointed out that we can reduce the number of rules from four separate ones to two by generalizing the insertion and deletion rules, as illustrated in (70).

1.7   Rule Ordering

In the previous section we have discussed several generalizations involved in
phonological changes. We have observed that some changes consist of more than
one rule. When a phenomenon involves two or more rules, it should be kept in
mind that the rules sometimes need to be ordered in certain ways. The set of
rules that we have discussed in (52) presents an example. The rules in question
are repeated below.

(52)   a.   b → n / ____ + ta
       b.   t → d / n + ____

Since we have these two rules to account for the derivations of the verbs in (47),
there are two things we need to find out: (i) should they be ordered?; and (ii) if
they should be ordered, in what order? To find out the answers to these questions,
we need to consider all potential orders that are logically possible. It means that
if there are two rules involved, there should be two logical possibilities; and
if there are three rules, there should be six logical possibilities. Given logically
possible rule orderings, if certain orderings result in a permissible form while
others do not, then it means that the rules must be ordered, and furthermore
that they must be sequenced in the order that produces well-formed results. If,
on the other hand, any ordering results in the correct form, then it suggests that
the ordering among the rules is not relevant.

Let us investigate the ordering of the rules in (52). Since there are two rules, the
possibilities are either (a) before (b), as in (71a), or (b) before (a), as in (71b). We
can examine these two possibilities by using (47a) as our sample. ("*" indicates
an ill-formed result, and "DNA" means that the rule does not apply.)

(71)   a.   yob + ta   b.   yob + ta
           (52a)   yon + ta   (52b)   DNA
           (52b)   yon + da   (52a)   yon + ta
                   _____   _____
           output: yonda   output: *yonta

In the derivation illustrated in (71a), rule (52a) applies to the underlying form
since the condition is met, changing the root final /b/ to /n/. Rule (52b) subsequently applies to the output of the application of rule (52a), yielding [yonda],
the acceptable form.

The derivation of (71b), on the other hand, ends in an unacceptable verbal
form. In this derivation, rule (52b) is intended to apply first. However, the
rule does not apply ("DNA") because the initial consonant of the past tense
ending /ta/ must find the segment /n/ preceding it in order to meet the environment for the rule application. So, this rule fails to apply to the underlying
form. Rule (52a) then applies to the unchanged underlying form. This time,
the condition for the rule application is met: the segment /b/ precedes the past
tense forming /ta/. (52a) thus changes /b/ to /n/, but the output *[yonta] is an
unacceptable form.

These results of the two different rule orderings suggest that first, these two rules must be ordered and second, they must be ordered in such a way that (52a) applies before (52b).

Another instance where rule ordering is crucial in a derivation can be drawn from the past tense forms of the verb roots that we have observed in (57) above. The relevant data are repeated as (72).

(72) a. /tug + ta/   → [tˢuida]   "poured"
      b. /kag + ta/   → [kaida]   "sniffed"
      c. /tog + ta/   → [toida]   "sharpened"
      d. /katug + ta/ → [katˢuida] "lifted (it) on the shoulder"
      e. /oyog + ta/   → [oyoida]   "swam"

We have come up with three rules to account for the derivation of the past tense forms in (72). They are repeated in (73).

(73) a. t → d / g + _____ (voicing)
      b. Ø → i / velar consonant _____ + alveolar stop (insertion)
      c. velar consonant → Ø / _____ i + alveolar stop (deletion)

As was mentioned above, when three rules are involved, there are six logically possible orderings. The six possibilities are listed in (74), each of which describes an order of the rule application.

(74) a. voicing–insertion–deletion
      b. voicing–deletion–insertion
      c. insertion–voicing–deletion
      d. insertion–deletion–voicing
      e. deletion–voicing–insertion
      f. deletion–insertion–voicing

In order to determine whether they need to be ordered and if so how, we must first examine each ordering to see if it results in an acceptable form. Let us take up the investigation using (72a) as an example. Each derivation according to the orderings of (74) is demonstrated in (75) through (80).

(75)   tug + ta
      voicing: tug + da
      insertion: tugi + da
      deletion: tui + da
      _____

                    [tˢuida]

(76)   tug + ta
      voicing: tug + da
      deletion: DNA
      insertion: tugi + da
      _____

                    *[tˢugida]

(77)   tug + ta
            insertion: tugi + ta
            voicing: DNA
            deletion: tui + ta
            _____

                            *[tˢuita]

(78)   tug + ta
            insertion: tugi + ta
            deletion: tui + ta
            voicing: DNA
            _____

                            *[tˢuita]

(79)   tug + ta
            deletion: DNA
            voicing: tug + da
            insertion: tugi + da
            _____

                            *[tˢugida]

(80)   tug + ta
            deletion: DNA
            insertion: tugi + ta
            voicing: DNA
            _____

                            *[tˢugita]

The ordering of (74a), as is illustrated in (75), is the only one that results in an acceptable form. In this derivation, the voicing rule first applies and changes the consonant of the past tense ending /t/ to /d/. The insertion rule then applies and the vowel /i/ is inserted at the end of the verb root. Finally, the deletion rule deletes the /g/, deriving an acceptable past tense form. The rest of the orderings, on the other hand, all end up with ungrammatical forms. In (74c), which is depicted in (77), for example, the insertion rule applies first and /i/ is inserted at the end of the verb root. The next rule, i.e. the voicing rule, does not apply because the environment is not met: that is, in order for this rule to apply, there should be a /g/ immediately before the past tense ending. But the form to which the voicing rule would apply here has the vowel /i/ at the end of the verb root, and hence, the rule cannot apply. Finally, the application of the deletion rule leads to the deletion of /g/. The resulting form is the ungrammatical *[tˢuita]. As can be seen by the derivations illustrated in (76)–(80), the rest of the orderings also yield unacceptable verbal forms. The examination in (75)–(80) suggests that the three rules in (73) must be ordered, and the only permissible ordering is voicing–insertion–deletion.

Finally, let us examine one case in which rules need not be crucially ordered. We have just discussed that the three rules in (73) must have the ordering of

(74a). As was pointed out in note 9, the example we have seen above (i.e.
/tug + ta/) technically involves one more rule, namely, the phonological rule of
t → tˢ. So, we need to examine whether this allophonic rule should be ordered
in relation to the voicing, insertion, and deletion rules that we have discussed.
The allophonic rule is repeated below as (81), and the orderings among the four
rules are illustrated in (82)–(85). (We will assume that the ordering of (74a) is
already determined.)

(81)   t → tˢ / ____ u

(82)
	tug + ta
(81)	tˢug + ta
voicing	tˢug + da
insertion	tˢugi + da
deletion	tˢui + da

[tˢuida]

(83)
	tug + ta
voicing	tug + da
(81)	tˢug + da
insertion	tˢugi + da
deletion	tˢui + da

[tˢuida]

(84)
	tug + ta
voicing	tug + da
insertion	tugi + da
(81)	tˢugi + da
deletion	tˢui + da

[tˢuida]

(85)
	tug + ta
voicing	tug + da
insertion	tugi + da
deletion	tui + da
(81)	tˢui + da

[tˢuida]

Unlike the two cases we have seen earlier, all the orders depicted above derive
the well-formed past tense verb [tˢuida]. It suggests that the ordering of (81) in
relation to the voicing, insertion, and deletion rules is not crucial.

We have shown how rule ordering is sometimes important and sometimes
unimportant by examining three cases. In order to determine the correct ordering,

we need to examine each logical possibility. The one that generates an acceptable form indicates the correct ordering, although there are cases where the ordering is not crucial.[10]

2 Sequential Voicing – "Rendaku"

Most people know what *susi* is. Even those who do not know what it is exactly probably have heard the name of the Japanese cuisine. As some people already know, there are several kinds of *susi*: to name a few, we have *makizusi*, *inarizusi*, *tirasizusi*, and so on. We can figure out that these words share the portion -*zusi*, and realize that this part is somehow related to the word *susi*. What is curious is why they are not called *makisusi*, *inarisusi*, and *tirasisusi*, rather than *makizusi*, *inarizusi*, and *tirasizusi*, respectively. This phenomenon is quite common in Japanese, especially when two or more words are combined in the process called **compounding**. (We will discuss the compounding process in more detail in chapter 4.) The phenomenon shown as the difference between *susi* and *zusi* can be roughly described as the word-initial consonant of the second word of the compound becoming voiced. If the second word of a compound begins with a vowel followed by a consonant, this phenomenon is not observed. The voicing process is termed **sequential voicing** or **Rendaku** (cf. J. McCawley 1968; Kindaichi 1976a; Otsu 1980; Ito and Mester 1986; Vance 1987).

Examples of Rendaku are shown in (86)–(95), given in phonetic transcription.

(86) [take] + [sao] → [takezao]
     bamboo pole bampoo pole

(87) [çito] + [tˢuma] → [çitozuma] or [çitodᶻuma]
     person wife someone's wife

(88) [hana] + [či] → [hanaǰi]
     nose blood nose bleeding

(89) [buta] + [širu] → [butaǰiru]
     pig soup pork soup

(90) [hoN] + [tana] → [hondana]
     book shelf book shelf

(91) [ko] + [taiko] → [kodaiko]
     small drum small drum

(92) [yo:] + [karaši] → [yo:garaši]
     western mustard western mustard

(93)   [tabi]   + [çito]   →   [tabi<u>b</u>ito]
       travel   person   traveler

(94)   [asa]   + [Φuro]   →   [asa<u>b</u>uro]
       morning   bath   morning bath

(95)   [nihoN] + [haši]   →   [nihom<u>b</u>aši]
       Japan   bridge   (place name)

The Rendaku phenomenon observed above can be summarized as in (96).

(96)   a.   s   →   z
       b. t^s →   z/d^z
       c.   č   →   ǰ
       d.   š   →   ǰ
       e.   t   →   d
       f.   k   →   g
       g.   ç   →   b
       h.   Φ   →   b
       i.   h   →   b

In (86) while there is no phonological change in the first word, the initial voice-less consonant of the second word becomes voiced, i.e. [s] to [z], when the two words are compounded. In (87) we notice a change occurs from [t^s] to [z] or [d^z]. Recall our discussion of the Japanese phonetic inventory: in most cases, [z] and [d^z] are in free variation for many speakers. Consequently, the voiced counterpart of [t^s] is either [z] or [d^z] in the Rendaku examples. In (88) the initial consonant of the second word, [č], changes to its voiced counterpart, [ǰ]. In (89) we observe the change from [š] to [ǰ]. Notice that the latter (voiced alveo-palatal affricate) is not a voiced version of the former (voiceless alveo-palatal fricative). It should be remembered that the alveo-palatal fricative [ž] is not detectable in most speakers. So, [š] is changed to [ǰ], which is close to [š] in that they share the same place of articulation. They can also be considered near counterparts since the affricate involves the fricative quality. So, the applica-tion of Rendaku in this example results in [ǰ]. In both (90) and (91) the initial consonant of the second word is [t], which becomes its voiced counterpart, namely, [d]. Similarly, in (92), the voiceless velar stop undergoes voicing, and the initial consonant surfaces as [g].

   What about (93)–(95)? In these examples the initial consonants are all allo-phones of /h/, and the application of Rendaku to them results in the voiced bilabial stop, [b]. This is not what we would expect given the examples in (86)–(92). Recall that there is no voiced version in Japanese of the allophones of /h/. Why, then, does Rendaku change [h], [ç], and [Φ] to the voiced bilabial stop [b]? There is a historical reason for this seemingly unexpected result (cf. Vance 1987). It has been claimed that the present glottal fricative /h/ can be traced

back to the voiceless bilabial stop, /p/, which underwent a historical change,
leading to the present /h/. Given that the origin of /h/ is historically /p/, then,
it is not surprising that in contemporary Japanese, Rendaku changes the voiceless
allophones of /h/ to [b], i.e. the voiced counterpart of [p].

   Although Rendaku is observed quite extensively with compounds, researchers
have noted that it applies only under certain circumstances. Otsu (1980) summarizes the relevant conditions for Rendaku as follows. First, the second member
of a compound should be a native Japanese word for Rendaku to apply. This
immediately excludes second members that are Sino-Japanese words, i.e. words
that are of Chinese origin, or other loan words. This situation is illustrated by
(97)–(99). Contrast each pair, taken from Otsu (1980: 208–209). Examples
hereafter are given in Romanization.

(97)   a.   ato   +   harai   →   atobarai
            afterward   payment   deferred payment
       b.   ato   +   kin   →   atokin
                         money   balance, money left

(98)   a.   binboo +   kami   →   binboogami
            poverty   god   god of poverty
       b.   binboo +   syoo   →   binboosyoo
                         disposition   disposition to living stingily

(99)   a.   yasu   +   heya   →   yasubeya
            cheap   room   cheap room
       b.   yasu   +   hoteru   →   yasuhoteru
                         hotel   cheap hotel

The second members of the compounds in the (a) examples are all native words,
and hence voicing occurs: [h] → [b] in (97a) and (99a), and [k] → [g] in (98a).
The (b) examples, on the other hand, do not undergo voicing, but rather, the
voiceless consonants stay voiceless. The second members of these compounds
are either of Sino-Japanese origin, as in (97b) and (98b), or of English origin, as
in (99b).

   The condition that the second member of a compound should be a native word
is not entirely without exception, however. We find cases in which Sino-Japanese
words and other loan words are sometimes treated as if they were native words.
In such cases, then, the second member of a compound undergoes Rendaku.
Examples of such "exceptional" cases are discussed in Otsu (1980: 209) and
illustrated by (100)–(101).

(100)   booeki + kaisya   →   booekigaisya
        trade   company   trading company

(101)   uta   + karuta   →   utagaruta
        song   cards   playing cards with *waka* on

The words *kaisya* "company" in (100) is a Sino-Japanese compound, and *karuta* "cards" in (101) a loan word from Portuguese, and hence the condition under discussion is expected to disallow the effect of Rendaku, contrary to fact. An explanation given for these "exceptional" cases is that the second members of the compounds in examples like (100)–(101) occur frequently enough to be considered as native words. If this explanation is correct, however, a word like *hoteru* "hotel" in (99), for example, should also be regarded as a native word because it occurs quite frequently, at least as frequently as *kaisya* "company" and *karuta* "cards". But *hoteru* does not show the effect of Rendaku.

Second, Rendaku does not occur when the second member of a compound has a voiced stop, voiced fricative, or voiced affricate. Technically, stops, fricatives, and affricates are grouped together and are called **obstruents**, and so we can say that voiced obstruents have the effect of preventing or blocking Rendaku. This constraint is called **Lyman's Law**, and is illustrated by the pairs in (102) and (103) (taken from Otsu 1980: 210).

(102) a. oo   + kata   →   oogata
           big   size   big size
       b. oo   + kaze   →   ookaze
                   wind   big wind

(103) a. zyuzu + tama   →   zyuzudama
           rosary beads   (prayer) beads
       b. zyuzu + tunagi →   zyuzutunagi
                   sequence   roping together

The pair in (102) shows that when the second member of a compound contains a voiced obstruent, specifically the voiced fricative /z/ in (102b), Rendaku does not apply: when there is no voiced consonant in the second member, the word-initial voiceless consonant undergoes voicing, as in (102a). The pair in (103) indicates the same phenomenon. The (a) example of (103), furthermore, shows that it does not matter whether the first member of a compound contains a voiced obstruent or not: the first member of the compound in (103a) includes a voiced affricate, [ǰ], as well as a voiced fricative, [z], and yet Rendaku applies to the initial consonant of the second member, /t/, to yield [d].

Third, as is extensively discussed in Otsu (1980) and Ito and Mester (1986), when a compound consists of three or more members, the internal structure of the compound comes into play to determine whether Rendaku can apply or not. We first need to discuss what the internal structure of a compound is. When, for example, three words are put together to form a compound, as in (104), there are two possible meanings associated with it, depending on which two words are first compounded.

(104) nuri   + hasi   + hako
       lacquered   chopsticks   box

The two potential interpretations are as follows:

(105)   a.   chopstick box which is lacquered
        b.   box for lacquered chopsticks

Under the interpretation of (105a) the object that is lacquered is the box, not the chopsticks. The meaning of (105b), in contrast, implies that the chopsticks are lacquered rather than the box. So, in order to induce the reading of (105a), the word for "chopsticks" and the word for "box" are first compounded, and then the resulting compound is further put together with the word for "lacquered". This can be schematically illustrated in (106).

(106)

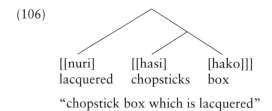

```
[[nuri]      [[hasi]      [hako]]]
lacquered    chopsticks   box
```

      "chopstick box which is lacquered"

Under the interpretation of (105b), on the other hand, the word for "lacquered" and the word for "chopsticks" must be compounded first, the result of which is subsequently compounded with the word for "box". This compounding process is shown in (107).

(107)

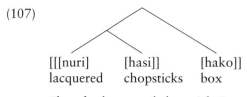

```
[[[nuri]     [hasi]]     [hako]]
lacquered    chopsticks   box
```

      "box for lacquered chopsticks"

   Let us now turn to Rendaku and discuss why the internal structure of compounds is crucial in determining whether voicing should occur or not. The internal structure of compounds is important to consider because Rendaku refers to a specific position of the compound structure. For example, Rendaku derives different outputs for (106) and (107) since their internal structure is not alike. Compare the difference in the Rendaku outputs in (108) and (109).

(108)   "chopstick box which is lacquered"

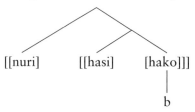

```
[[nuri]      [[hasi]      [hako]]]
                              |
                              b
```

(109) "box for lacquered chopsticks"

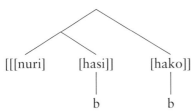

In (108), in which *hasi* and *hako* are the members of the first compound, the initial consonant of the second member of this compound, *hako* "box", undergoes voicing and no other voicing occurs. That is, in forming the next compound, in which *nuri* and *hasibako* are the members, the initial consonant of the second member, i.e. *hasibako*, does not undergo voicing. Why? Lyman's Law contributes to the failure of the Rendaku phenomenon here. Once the first compound was formed (i.e. hasi + hako → hasibako), the second member undergoes voicing, and this compound now contains a voiced stop, i.e. /b/. When the word *nuri* "lacquered" is further added forming a three-word compound, Lyman's Law blocks the voicing of /h/ in *hasi* "chopsticks" because /b/ in *hasibako* is a voiced obstruent. As a result, only one instance of Rendaku is observed in this example.

In contrast, (109) undergoes voicing twice. When *nuri* and *hasi* are first compounded, the initial consonant of the second member, i.e. *hasi*, becomes voiced, yielding *nuribasi*. Then, when *nuribasi* and *hako* are compounded next, the initial consonant of the second member, i.e. *hako*, undergoes voicing. There is no voiced obstruent in *hako*, and so Lyman's Law is not effective in this example. Hence, the entire compound in (109) surfaces as *nuribasibako* while that in (108) surfaces as *nurihasibako*.

Given the internal constituent structure of a compound along with Lyman's Law, we can predict where Rendaku should occur. The additional examples of (110) confirm our conclusion thus far.

(110) a.

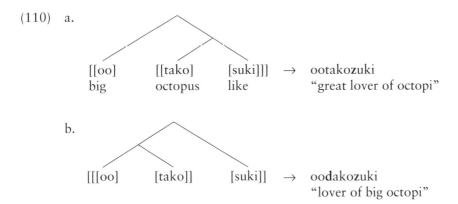

In (110a) the meaning of the compound is "great lover of octopi", so we can determine that *tako* and *suki* are compounded first, which is further modified by *oo.* The opposite situation is obtained in (110b): *oo* and *tako* are first grouped together, and subsequently *suki* is compounded with the result of the first compounding process. It is expected that only one application of Rendaku takes place in (110a) to yield *takozuki*, since when *oo* is added, the /z/ of *takozuki* serves to block the next potential application of voicing to the word-initial consonant /t/ due to Lyman's Law. Hence, the result is *ootakozuki*. (110b), on the other hand, is predicted to undergo Rendaku twice. The first application to the compound *oo* + *tako* should yield *oodako*. When *oodako* and *suki* are compounded, Lyman's Law does not apply since there is no voiced obstruent in the second member, *suki*. Hence, Rendaku applies to the initial consonant of this word, and the derived form is *oodakozuki*.

Given the demonstration of the two sets of three-word compounds, it seems that Lyman's Law along with the appropriate internal structure of the compounds can predict when the Rendaku phenomenon occurs. The following example, however, shows that the above-mentioned conditions are not sufficient. Consider (111).

(111) a. nuri   + kasa   + ire
           lacquered   umbrella   case

       b. nurigasaire   "case for lacquered umbrellas"

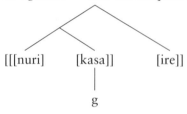

       c. nuri<u>k</u>asaire   "lacquered umbrella case"

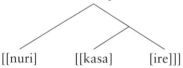

The three words in (111a), i.e. *nuri*, *kasa*, and *ire*, display two possible compounding structures, as is illustrated in (111b) and (111c). Given the internal structure of (111b), one occurrence of the Rendaku phenomenon is expected: in the first compound, the initial consonant of the second member, *kasa*, undergoes voicing, while in the second compound, the second member, *ire*, does not begin with a voiceless consonant. As a result, Rendaku is observed only once.

A problem arises in (111c), however. In the first compound, where *kasa* and *ire* are its members, Rendaku does not take place since the second member does not start with a voiceless consonant. In the next step, *nuri* and *kasaire* are compounded, and the second member should undergo voicing: *kasaire* begins with a voiceless consonant, and there is no voiced obstruent that would block the voicing. Contrary to this expectation, Rendaku does not take place, and the result is *nurikasaire*. This derived form satisfies the conditions we have discussed thus far: Lyman's Law does not apply because the second member of the compound (in each compounding) does not contain a voiced obstruent; and the compounding processes properly took place exactly the way the internal structure shows.

What we need in order to solve this problem is to add a further condition to include cases like (111c). Recall that Rendaku does not take place a second time in examples (108) and (110a) above, and that we explained this as a result of Lyman's Law blocking the second application of Rendaku. On the other hand, as long as we rely on Lyman's Law, the lack of Rendaku application in (111c) is left unexplained. Instead of the explanation on the basis of Lyman's Law, however, Otsu (1980: 219) proposes the following condition in order to account for the problematic case we have seen above.

(112)   Rendaku applies only when a potential Rendaku segment is in a right branch constituent. (Right Branch Condition, RBC)

The Right Branch Condition by Otsu refers to a specific point in the internal structure of a compound. The term "branch" is used to view the internal structure of a compound as a tree: whenever a point in a structure has two dividing paths under it, we refer to this situation as "branching". So, "right branching constituent" refers to an item that is on the right of such a branching situation. In (113), for instance, "x" indicates a right branching constituent.

(113)   a.   b.

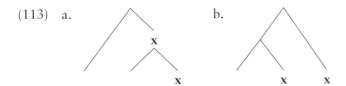

According to Otsu, furthermore, the right branching constituent stated in (112) refers to such a constituent at the lowest level of the internal structure of a compound. Given the Right Branch Condition above, let us examine (108), for example, which can be schematized as in (114).

(114)

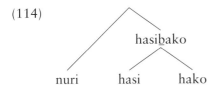

When *hasi* and *hako* are first compounded, *hako* is the right branch constituent at the lowest level, and hence the initial voiceless consonant undergoes Rendaku, deriving *hasibako*. Notice, however, that when *nuri* and *hasibako* are put together as the second compounding process, the second member can be considered a right branching constituent, but it is no longer at the lowest level in this internal structure. Hence, the voicing does not take place.

The internal structures of (110a) and (111c) look like (115) and (116), respectively.

(115)

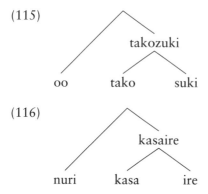

(116)

The first Rendaku application turns the voiceless consonant of (115), /s/, to /z/ while no change is made in (116) since there is no potential segment for Rendaku. When Rendaku applies for the second time, the second members, i.e. *takozuki* and *kasaire*, are not at the lowest level. Thus, by attributing the absence of Rendaku to the second members in these cases to the Right Branch Condition, rather than attributing it to Lyman's Law, we can account for problematic cases like (116) as well as instances like (114) and (115).

The two situations in (115) and (116) should be contrasted with (110b), where no problem is created. The second application of Rendaku in (110b) applies to the lowest level, and hence *suki* undergoes voicing to derive *zuki*. It should be pointed out that while we accounted for (115)–(116) on the basis of the Right Branch Condition rather than Lyman's Law, Lyman's Law indeed accounts for the Rendaku phenomenon observed especially in the two-word compounds earlier. Hence, we conclude that Lyman's Law is still a crucial factor to be taken into consideration for the Rendaku phenomenon.[11]

Let us summarize the conditions pertinent to the Rendaku phenomenon we have discussed above.[12]

(117) a. Lyman's Law: If the second member of the compound contains a voiced obstruent (i.e. a stop, a fricative, or an affricate), then the initial consonant of the second member cannot undergo Rendaku.
       b. Right Branch Condition: Rendaku applies only when a potential Rendaku segment is in a right branch constituent at the lowest level.

3   Mora vs. Syllable

If we ask a native speaker of English how many parts there are in the word *London*, she or he would be most likely to answer "two". If we ask a native speaker of Japanese the same question, however, she or he would probably say "four". This difference resides in how English and Japanese speakers divide words into smaller units. Specifically, English speakers divide words into **syllables** while

Japanese speakers divide them into **morae**. Because of this difference, a native speaker of English divides *London* into two syllables whereas a native speaker of Japanese considers the word to consist of four morae.

Let us first consider the syllable. A syllable is traditionally said to have an internal structure that can be divided into three sub-units. They are **onset**, **nucleus**, and **coda**, and are illustrated in (118).

(118)

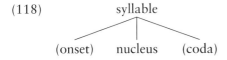

The parentheses in (118) indicate that onset and coda can be optional while nucleus is an obligatory member of the syllable. Onset refers to the syllable-initial consonant(s); nucleus corresponds to a vowel; and coda coincides with the syllable-final consonant(s). So, for instance, one-syllable words in English like *strand* and *print* have the syllable-internal structures of (119) and (120), respectively.

(119)   strand [strænd]

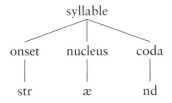

(120)   print [prɪnt]

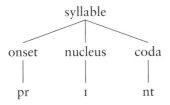

The syllable in English is essential in order to account for various phonological phenomena such as aspiration. Recall from chapter 2 that /p/ (as well as the other voiceless stops) is aspirated when it is in the initial position of the syllable. In Japanese, in contrast, the notion of mora is predominantly used to account for various phonological phenomena. The mora has one of three realizations shown in (121).[13]

(121)   a.   (C)V
        b.   the first part of a long consonant (or the first part of a geminate)
        c.   syllable-final, or "moraic", nasal /n/

(121a) refers to a vowel optionally preceded by a consonant. So, according to this definition, the word /aki/ "autumn" has two morae: /a/ being one and /ki/

being the other. The former is not preceded by any consonant while the latter is. Nonetheless, each is counted as one mora. (121b) suggests that in a case where a long consonant or a geminate occurs, such as /gakki/ "musical instrument", the first part of the long consonant, i.e. the first occurrence of /k/, is considered one mora. Hence, /gakki/ consists of three morae, as is illustrated in (122).

(122)   /ga.k.ki/

The "moraic" /n/ in (121c) refers to an occurrence of /n/ that is not followed by an accompanying vowel. In such a case the /n/ stands by itself as a single unit and is considered a mora. Examples of this case include /mikan/ "orange" and /nenkin/ "pension". The final /n/ of /mikan/ and the second and the third occurrences of /n/ in /nenkin/ represent a moraic /n/. Hence, these two words are divided on the basis of the mora as in (123).

(123)   a.   /mi.ka.n/
        b.   /ne.n.ki.n/

Similarly, the word for *London* in Japanese, transcribed as /rondon/, displays two instances of moraic /n/. The word contains four morae altogether and has the division shown in (124).

(124)   /ro.n.do.n/

There is a traditional assumption that mora is a timing unit, and that each mora is supposed to bear the same length of time. Some experimental works including Beckman (1982) and Port et al. (1987) discuss the validity of this assumption. Although there have been certain disagreements among the researchers, it can be concluded that mora is considered a timing unit especially within the larger context of words. That is, if two sets of three-mora words are compared with respect to their length, the general durations of the two words come out more or less the same. To this extent, then, the mora can be regarded as a temporal unit (cf. Port et al. 1987).

Given the exemplification of mora in (121), words like *mikan* "orange", *gakkoo* "school", and *rondon* "London" are divided differently depending on which notion, syllable or mora, is the basis for the division. This is illustrated in (125).

(125)   *mora-based*   *syllable-based*
        a.   mi.ka.n   mi.kan
        b.   ga.k.ko.o   gak.koo
        c.   ro.n.do.n   ron.don

Although, as was briefly mentioned above, a number of phonological phenomena can be explained in terms of mora, there are some instances in which syllable is also relevant to Japanese (cf. Kubozono 1993/1994). A good example is observed in accentuation patterns in various dialects, which will be discussed in section 4.3 of this chapter. Moreover, there are certain distributional requirements in Japanese that refer to syllable structure. For example, unlike in English, no words in Japanese can begin with two or more consonants. This reflects the fact that a syllable can begin with at most a single consonant. Furthermore, as reflected in (125b, c), a syllable-final consonant is very restricted in Japanese. Such consonants can only be a nasal (125c) or the first part of a geminate (125b). In the remainder of this sub-section, however, psycholinguistic evidence from speech errors and language games will be presented to show that the mora is indeed a crucial notion in the phonology of the Japanese language.[14]

3.1 Speech Errors

Speech errors (also known as slips of the tongue) provide evidence that Japanese is a mora-based language while the English language is syllable-based. Let us first observe the speech error phenomenon in English.

3.1.1 English

There are many types of speech errors, as discussed by Fromkin (1971, 1973). (126) lists some of these errors and provides examples. (126) is taken from Kubozono (1985: 222); his original source is Fromkin (1973: 243–269).

(126) a. Substitution
           (i)   Anticipation: a <u>r</u>eading <u>l</u>ist → a <u>l</u>eading list
           (ii) Perseveration: <u>she</u> can <u>see</u> it → she can <u>she</u> it
      b. Transposition (Reversal; "Spoonerism")
           <u>H</u>ockett or <u>L</u>amb → <u>l</u>ocket or <u>h</u>am
      c. Omission
           <u>s</u>peech error → peach error
      d. Addition
           optimal number → <u>m</u>optimal number
      e. Movement
           <u>d</u>inner at eight → inner at <u>d</u>ate
      f. Blend
           Ross/<u>Ch</u>omsky → <u>R</u>omsky

Additional data are given in (127), taken from Kubozono (1985: 223) (also see Fromkin 1973: 227); hyphenation indicates syllable boundary.

(127) a. ma-ga-<u>z</u>ine → ma-<u>z</u>a-gine
      b. cor-<u>t</u>i-cal → cor-<u>k</u>i-cal
      c. <u>R</u>o-man <u>J</u>a-kob-son → <u>Y</u>o-man <u>R</u>a-kob-son
      d. <u>t</u>o-nal pho-no-lo-gy → <u>f</u>o-nal pho-no-lo-gy
      e. <u>a</u>d hoc → odd h<u>a</u>ck
      f. g<u>rou</u>p thr<u>ee</u> → g<u>ree</u>p three
      g. go<u>ne</u> to see<u>d</u> → god to see<u>n</u>

All the examples in (126) and (127) are attested speech errors by native speakers of English. Recall our discussion of the internal structure of the syllable. The internal structure depicted in (118) is repeated as (128).

(128)   syllable

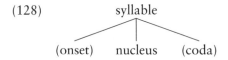

         (onset)   nucleus   (coda)

When we investigate the examples in (127), paying particular attention to where in the syllable these errors occur, we notice certain regularities. Consider (127a) and (127c), which are examples of transposition errors. Notice that in each example only the onsets are exchanged. Furthermore, in (127e) and (127g), which are also examples of transposition errors, two nuclei and two coda positions, respectively, are switched. Errors in which an onset exchanges with an onset, a nucleus with a nucleus, and a coda with a coda are quite common. On the other hand, we do not find errors, for example, that would exchange a nucleus with either an onset or a coda. Moreover, errors that involve the exchange of an onset with a coda are very rare. Thus, the observed pattern of exchange errors provides evidence for the internal structure of a syllable as depicted in (128). That is, without such internal structure, it would be difficult to describe and account for the range of speech error phenomena that is observed here (cf. Davis 1988).

   An extensive range of research on speech errors in English has revealed interesting characteristics pertinent to the language. Kubozono (1985), for instance, summarizes the following two generalizations. First, vowels are never replaced by consonants. For instance, although we have attested errors of the type seen in (127a), no errors are attested that are represented in (129).

(129)   m<u>a</u>-ga-zine → *<u>am</u>-ga-zine

In this example, the first consonant and the following vowel interchange position. Second, a long vowel or a sequence of a vowel followed by a glide (called a **diphthong**) never splits into two segments. Thus, although (130a) is a possible speech error in English, we would not expect to have the type of errors shown in (130b).[15]

(130)   a pipe smoker [p<u>ay</u>p sm<u>o(w)</u>kər]
        a.   a pope smiker [p<u>o(w)</u>p sm<u>ay</u>kər]
        b.   *a pop smoyker *[p<u>a</u>p sm<u>oy</u>kər]

In (130a) two nuclei are exchanged, keeping the diphthong [ay] (i.e. the sequence of a vowel and a glide) intact. In (130b), on the other hand, the diphthong is split and the [y] of the diphthong is combined with another vowel. It is this sort of error, where a long vowel or diphthong is split, that English does not display. Two characteristics of English speech errors are summarized in (131).

(131)   a.   Vowels are never replaced by consonants.
        b.   Long vowels and diphthongs never split into two elements.

3.1.2 *Japanese*

Let us observe the speech error phenomenon in Japanese (cf. Tabusa 1982). The following examples, taken from Kubozono (1985: 228), are errors that have been attested; hyphenations indicate the division into morae. The intended utterance is on the left of the arrow and the actual utterance with the speech error is on the right of the arrow.

(132) Substitution
      a. ka-<u>a</u>-ta-a da-<u>i</u>-to-o-ryo-o → ka-<u>i</u>-ta-a da-i-to-o-ryo-o
          "President Carter"
      b. mo-<u>o</u>-ta-a-ba-<u>i</u>-ku → mo-<u>i</u>-ta-a-ba-i-ku
          "motor bike"
      c. be-<u>i</u>-tyu-u ka-<u>n</u>-ke-i → be-i-tyu-u ka-<u>i</u>-ke-i
          "China–US relation"

(133) Transposition
      a. da-<u>n</u>-ga-i sa-<u>i</u>-ba-n-syo → da-<u>i</u>-ga-<u>n</u> sa-i-ba-n-syo
          "Court of Impeachment"
      b. ka-<u>n</u>-ke-<u>i</u> ka-i-ze-n → ka-<u>i</u>-ke-<u>n</u> ka-i-ze-n
          "improvement in relationship"

(134) Blend
      a. mu-u-do hu-n-i-ki → mu-n-i-ki
          "mood-atmosphere"
      b. to-ma-re su-to-p-pu → to-ma-p-pu
          "stop (imperative)"

Keeping in mind the characteristics of the speech error phenomenon observed in English and summarized in (131) above, let us now see the following character-istics of Japanese speech errors that have been observed by Kubozono (1985). First, consider (132a, b). In these examples, long vowels are split, with the second part of the long vowel being substituted for by another vowel. Recall that this is what we do not expect in English. (135), taken from Kubozono (1985: 228), adds another example of this sort.

(135) ko-o-zu-<u>i</u> tyu-<u>u</u>-i-ho-o → ko-o-zu-<u>u</u> tyu-u-i-ho-o
      "flood warning"

Second, it is possible for long consonants to split into two segments. This is illustrated by (136) (from Kubozono 1985: 228).

(136) zi-n-ke-n mo-n-da-i de ko-ma-<u>t</u>-te i-ru
      "We are troubled with the problem of human rights."
      → zi-n-ke-n mo-n-da-i de ko-ma-<u>n</u>-te i-ru

Notice that the first member of the long consonant is replaced by a moraic /n/.

Third, examine (132c) as well as (133a, b). In these examples, it is clear that a moraic /n/ is replaced by a vowel or vice versa. That is, consonants and vowels can replace each other. Again, this is not observed in English speech errors. More data of this kind are shown in (137) (from Kubozono 1985: 228).

(137) a. bo-<u>n</u> sa-<u>i</u>-ba-n-tyo-o → bo-n sa-<u>n</u>-ba-n-tyo-o
           "Chief Justice Bon"
       b. ku-<u>u</u>-<u>bo</u> mi-d-do-we-e → ku-<u>b</u>-bo mi-d-do-we-e
           "Aircraft Carrier Midway"

(137b), in particular, shows that a consonant that replaces a vowel is not limited to a moraic /n/. As this example illustrates, a vowel can be replaced by a consonant that comprises the first part of a long consonant.

The characteristics of speech errors in Japanese that are observed by Kubozono are summarized in (138).

(138) a. Long vowels can split into two components.
       b. Long consonants can split into two parts.
       c. Vowels can be replaced by consonants, and vice versa.

In comparing (138) with (131), it is important to point out that these differences arise because Japanese is a mora-based language while English is a syllable-based language. Long vowels and long consonants referred to in (138a) and (138b) each count as two morae, and hence there is no problem splitting these segments into two in Japanese. A long vowel (or diphthong) in English, in contrast, forms an inseparable unit, i.e. nucleus. Moreover, in Japanese the type of consonants that can replace, and be replaced by, a vowel includes a moraic /n/ and the first part of a long consonant, each of which consists of a single mora. Therefore, replacement of the type we have observed in Japanese above does not interrupt any unbreakable unit. Instead, all the instances of speech errors in Japanese seen here refer to the mora unit, keeping the basic phonological notion constant. There are no attested speech errors in Japanese in which a syllable-initial consonant exchanges with an immediately following vowel since these would not constitute two independent moraic units. The Japanese speech errors exemplified here all involve a moraic unit being exchanged with or replaced by another moraic unit. In English, on the other hand, the basic notion is syllable, and hence errors can refer to the internal constituents of a syllable, but separating within a nucleus constituent, such as separating the parts of a long vowel or diphthong, results in impossible and unattested speech errors. Hence, speech error facts show that the mora, rather than the syllable, is an important unit in Japanese.[16]

3.2 Language Games: "Babibu" Language

Many languages have their unique language games. Most native speakers of English have probably heard of Pig Latin, which is a language game in English.

One of the language games in Japanese, known as the "babibu" language, will be introduced in this section to demonstrate that this language game provides another piece of evidence suggesting that the mora is a crucial unit in Japanese phonology (cf. Haraguchi 1991). How the "babibu" language is played is illustrated in (139).

(139) a. tegami → tebegabamibi   "letter"
        b. susi → subusibi   "sushi"
        c. hosi → hobosibi   "star"
        d. sensoo → sebenbusoboobo   "war"
        e. imooto → ibimoboobotobo   "younger sister"
        f. sinbun → sibinbububunbu   "newspaper"

This language game is described as follows. Take the first mora (C)V. To this mora, add another mora that consists of a /b/ immediately followed by the vowel identical to that of the first mora. Using an index, the result can be depicted as $(C)V_1$-bV_1. Next, take the second mora of the base word, and repeat the same process that we took to form the $(C)V_1$-bV_1 sequence. The output of the second process is $(C)V_1$-bV_1-$(C)V_2$-bV_2. This process is repeated until we reach the last mora of the word. In the case of a long vowel, the vowel is split up into two parts with each vowel part considered as one mora. Furthermore, this language game also treats a moraic /n/, which is not accompanied by a vowel, as a single mora. Consequently, the insertion of /b/ occurs after it in the language game. When /b/ is inserted after such an /n/, /u/ is inserted after /b/ as is exemplified by (139d) and (139f).

A question arises as to the "babibu" forms of words with long consonants. Haraguchi (1991) mentions that their "babibu" forms are made based on their kana transcriptions (see figure 2.1 in chapter 2 above for examples of the Hiragana syllabary). In the kana writing system, the first member of a long consonant is transcribed by a small form of the kana syllabary corresponding to /tu/. So, the first member of a long consonant is always transformed into /tu-bu/ in this language game regardless of what the actual consonant is. This situation is illustrated in (140).

(140) a. gakkoo → gaba**tubu**koboobo   "school"
        b. nippon → nibi**tubu**pobonbu   "Japan"
        c. kitto → kibi**tubu**tobo   "surely"
        d. kissaten → kibi**tubu**sabatebenbu   "coffee house"

The pronunciation of the long consonant varies depending on the word in (140): /k, p, t, s/. Despite this variation, the first parts of these long consonants are uniquely represented as /tubu/ in the language game.

From the observation above, it is clear that the "babibu" language game refers to each mora of a word: a long vowel is treated as consisting of two morae, and /n/ not accompanied by a vowel, namely, moraic /n/, counts as one mora. In no instance does the language game make crucial reference to syllable structure. This point may be more explicitly demonstrated by comparing the "babibu" language with a language game in English, "abi-dabi" language. The "abi-dabi" language is instantiated by (141).

(141) a. give   [gɪv]   → [gabɪv]
       b. tree   [tri]   → [trabi]
       c. window [wɪndo]   → [wabɪndabo]
       d. frozen   [frozən] → [frabozabən]
       e. eat   [it]   → [abit]
       f. intend   [ɪntɛnd] → [abɪntabɛnd]
       g. eye   [ay]   → [abay]
       h. coin   [koyn]   → [kaboyn]

We can describe this language game as follows. Insert /ab/ immediately before the nucleus of a syllable. If we analyzed English based on mora structure and if this language game were sensitive to mora, (141g), for example, would result in (142).

(142) *[abaaby]

Therefore, in playing the "abi-dabi" language, it is critical to refer to a syllable, and moreover, to be able to identify the internal structure of a syllable.

4   Accentuation in Japanese

4.1   Stress vs. Pitch

The world's languages are typically divided into three types with respect to how stress and pitch are realized on words. There are **stress(-accent)** languages, **tone** languages, and **pitch-accent** languages. In stress languages like English, a certain syllable in a word is perceived by speakers as being the most prominent, and this syllable is said to carry the primary stress. In these languages the prominence of the stressed syllable is realized by the combination of pitch, vowel duration (length), and greater intensity (i.e. loudness). One factor alone, such as high pitch, is not sufficient to indicate stress. For example, in the sentence "Is that a rabbit?" the last syllable of *rabbit* receives a high pitch due to the rising intonation associated with a question. However, stress is placed on the first syllable since the vowel of the first syllable of the word is longer and greater in intensity than the vowel of the last syllable. Also, in stress languages it is usually the case that the location of primary stress in the word is predictable. For example, in Hungarian, primary stress always occurs on the first syllable of the word. However, in some stress languages, like English, the pattern of word stress is quite complicated, though predictable (cf. Halle and Vergnaud 1987).

In tone languages, each syllable of the word is associated with a separate tone such as high tone or low tone. The occurrence of the specific tones on the syllables in a word cannot be predicated and must therefore be individually learned.

Moreover, in tone languages, it is common for words to be differentiated solely by the tone, as in (143). Example tone languages include Chinese and Igbo (an African language). To illustrate the tonal pattern of these languages, consider the Chinese words in (143), taken from Hyman (1975: 214), where the tone with which these words are pronounced is indicated in the parentheses.

(143)   Chinese
        a.   [mā] "mother"   (high)
        b.   [má] "hemp"   (high–rising)
        c.   [mǎ] "horse"   (dipping/falling–rising)
        d.   [mà] "scold"   (high–falling)

Chinese has the four words shown in (143), all of which are pronounced with the same sound sequence [ma]. They differ, however, in the distribution of tones. Each tone is a property associated with the word (or syllable) itself as part of its pronunciation, just as the meaning is a property associated with the word. The word in (143a) is pronounced with a high tone, the word in (143b) with a high rising tone, and so on. So, when the meaning of the word [mā] in (143a) is learned as "mother", the high tone must also be learned as part of the pronunciation of that word. The same point can be shown by the examples from Igbo in (144), taken from Hyman (1975: 213), where each word has two syllables with a tone on each.

(144)   Igbo
        a.   [ákwá] "crying"   (high–high)
        b.   [ákwà] "cloth"   (high–low)
        c.   [àkwá] "egg"   (low–high)
        d.   [àkwà] "bed"   (low–low)

In (144a) there is high tone on both the first and second syllable; in (144b) there is high tone on the first syllable and low tone on the second; in (144c) low tone is on the first syllable while high tone is on the second; and in (144d) there is low tone on both the first and second syllable. The phonetic representations of the four words in (144) are identical except for their tonal patterns. In this case, too, the tonal pattern accompanies the word along with the word's meaning and its pronunciation. That is, the tonal pattern must be learned along with the sounds and the associated meaning. There is no way of predicting the tonal pattern.

4.2   Accentuation in Japanese

The third type of language is pitch-accent languages, of which Japanese is an example, and that we now consider. Pitch-accent languages are similar to tone languages in that each mora in a word is associated with a specific tone or pitch (such as high pitch, low pitch, falling pitch, etc.), just as in Chinese and Igbo. However, in pitch-accent languages, the pitch or tonal pattern of the entire word is predictable given the location of the accent of a word. For example, consider the Japanese words (Tokyo dialect) in (145), where the location of the accent of the word is indicated by the diacritic "*".

(145)

a.   s*o*ra   "sky"   (high–low)

b.   ka*w*a   "river"   (low–high)

c.   ko*k*oro "heart"   (low–high–low)

d.   oto*k*o   "man"   (low–high–high)
e.   katati   "shape"   (low–high–high)

The location of the accent is not predictable. The information regarding it comes with the word as part of its pronunciation along with the meaning of the word. In linguistic terminology, we would say that the accent is lexically indicated. That is, the location of the accent must be learned separately for each word. However, given the location of the accent, the pitch pattern of the word is predictable, unlike the case with tone languages such as Chinese and Igbo.

First, the accent, as is indicated by "*", marks the location in the word where the pitch falls: that is, the accent diacritic tells us that the accented mora as well as the morae preceding it all receive a high pitch or tone and that the morae after the accented mora are realized with low pitch. Second, in Tokyo Japanese, there is a rule called **Initial Lowering Rule** by Haraguchi (1977), which says that the pitch of the first mora of the word is low unless the accent is placed on that mora. Given these two generalizations, the pitch pattern of the entire word should be predictable in Tokyo Japanese.

Let us take the word in (145b) as an example. We know that the second mora has the accent marker, which means that this vowel receives high pitch and that the initial mora should also be pronounced with high pitch, because all morae preceding the accent diacritic receive high pitch. The Initial Lowering Rule, however, changes the high pitch of the first vowel to low, and the resulting pitch pattern is low–high. The accent of (145c) is placed on the second mora, so we know that the first and second morae have a high pitch. On the other hand, the last mora receives a low pitch since the accent marks the location of the pitch fall. (That is, the mora after the one with the accent diacritic receives low pitch.) The Initial Lowering Rule lowers the pitch of the first mora, and hence the pitch pattern of the word is low–high–low. Similarly, in (145d), the accent marker is on the last mora, which means that all the morae should be realized with high pitch. However, the Initial Lowering Rule applies and the high pitch on the first mora is lowered. Hence, the word is realized as the low–high–high pattern. (145e) presents an interesting case. There is no accent marker in this word. This means that every mora receives a high pitch because there is no accent marker that indicates the pitch fall. The Initial Lowering Rule applies to the first mora, and the word is pronounced as low–high–high. Note that even though the word in (145d) and that in (145e) are specified differently with respect to the placement of the accent marker, they surface identically as a result of the interaction of the accent placement and the Initial Lowering Rule.

The difference between tone languages like Chinese and pitch-accent languages like Japanese is that in the latter, given the location of the accent, which must be individually learned for each word, the realization of the pitch pattern for the word is predictable. In Tokyo Japanese the accented mora and those preceding it receive high pitch while those after it receive low pitch. Coupled with the Initial Lowering Rule, we know which pitch is realized with each mora. In Chinese or in Igbo, on the other hand, such a prediction does not hold, and for each syllable of the word, the speaker must learn whether it is associated with high pitch, low pitch, etc.

A pitch-accent language is similar to a tone language in that if a word is pronounced with the wrong tone, the word could mean an entirely different thing. That is, pitch is a crucial factor in identifying words. To illustrate this point, consider (146), where each pair differs only in the pitch pattern of the word. (The pitch patterns of the words in (146) are based on the Tokyo dialect.)

(146) a. hasi (high–low) vs. hasi (low–high)
    "chopsticks"   "bridge"

   b. ame (high–low) vs. ame (low–high) [no accent]
    "rain"   "candy"

   c. aki (high–low) vs. aki (low–high) [no accent]
    "autumn"   "vacancy"

   d. hai (high–low) vs. hai (low–high) [no accent]
    "yes"   "ashes"

   e. kan (high–low) vs. kan (low–high) [no accent]
    "can"   "sense"

These pairs illustrate a minimal contrast in that in each case the two words are exactly identical except for their pitch pattern. So, if a speaker pronounces *hasi* with the low–high pitch pattern, the word will not be interpreted by a Tokyo Japanese speaker to mean "chopsticks" without a context. Stress in stress languages like English, on the other hand, usually does not contrast words in this manner. Even when a speaker mispronounces the word *mountain* with the stress on the second syllable, the listener is able to understand the word to mean "mountain" with or without an appropriate context. Nevertheless, it is also true that pitch does not necessarily contrast words. That is, as Kubozono (1995) points out, we often observe two (or more) words that have the same pronunciation and pitch pattern, and yet they can have totally different meanings. Consider the following examples from Kubozono (1995: 22).

(147)   *
    a. o-syokuzi-ken   "meal ticket"
       honorific-meal-ticket
                  *
    b. osyoku-ziken   "bribery incident"
       bribery-incident

(148)   *
    a. kooki "second semester"
           *
    b. kooki "noble"
           *
    c. kooki "chance"

In spite of the fact that the words in each example have identical pronunciation and pitch pattern, they have different meanings. Hence, while the examples in (146) suggest that pitch can contrast words, the examples in (147)–(148) illustrate that pitch does not always play this role.

It is worth pointing out that there are still several differences between pitch-accent languages like Japanese and stress languages like English. The following two examples are differences that Kubozono (1995) discusses. First, as we have observed in (146) above, there are words that do not bear accent, and Japanese indeed exhibits a large number of such words without accent. In contrast, stress languages do not have content words lacking stress: all such words in English, therefore, have at least one stress (i.e. primary stress) to indicate the prominence of the word. Second, words in stress languages like English can have a secondary stress. For example, the word *education* has its primary stress on the third syllable and its secondary stress on the first syllable. A parallel situation is absent in Japanese: that is, an equivalent of secondary stress, i.e. "secondary accent", does not exist.

As we have observed above, since Japanese is a pitch-accent language, the pitch pattern of the word is predictable. Consider the pitch pattern of some words in Tokyo Japanese, where "H" and "L" refer to high pitch and low pitch, respectively.

(149) a. inoti   "life"
         HLL
     b. kokoro "heart"
          LHL
     c. atama   "head"
         LH H
     d. miyako "capital"
          LHH

In (149a) a high pitch is found in the first mora of the word. In (149b) a high pitch is found on the second mora. The words in (149c) and (149d) display an identical pitch pattern. However, this similarity in pitch pattern between (149c) and (149d) is only apparent; they can be differentiated by adding the Case particle *-ga* immediately after them. Compare the two nouns in (150).

(150) a. atama-ga   b. miyako-ga
           LH H L   LH H H

Although the pitch pattern within the noun is identical, once the particle is added, the pitch pattern of the sequence of the noun and the particle is different: *-ga* receives low pitch in the first example while it is associated with high pitch in the second.

  In considering the two words in (150), recall that the location of the pitch fall is where the accent occurs. This means that the two words in (150) would have the representation in (151a) and (151b), respectively, where the location of accent is represented by the accent diacritic "*".

(151) a.   *
           a ta ma (-ga)
       b. mi ya ko (-ga)

Since the form in (151a) has the accent diacritic on the final mora when the Case particle is added, the particle is realized with a low pitch as shown in (150a). However, the form in (151b) is **accentless** or **unaccented**, and there is no pitch drop when the Case particle is added, so it surfaces with a high pitch as shown in (150b). Thus, while the two forms in (151) have an identical pitch pattern in isolation as in (149c, d), they are differentiated when Case particles are added.

4.3 Mora vs. Syllable

In section 3 above we have discussed the fact that the mora is an important notion in Japanese, and we have seen that speech errors and language games provide some evidence for it. Accentuation patterns also show that the mora plays an important role in some dialects. On the other hand, we shall observe that the syllable also plays a significant role in accounting for the distribution of accents in other dialects.

  It should be remembered that a single mora consists of one of the following.

(152) a. (C)V
       b. the first part of a long consonant
       c. "moraic" /n/

Recall also our observation that native speakers of Japanese divide words into smaller parts on the basis of mora. As Shibatani (1990) reports (and see the reference cited there), however, this is not always the case when various dialects of Japanese are taken into consideration. For example, a speaker of the Takajocho dialect (Miyagi prefecture in northern Japan) would not divide the word *mikan* "orange" into three parts: rather, she or he would divide the word into two, *mi-kan*. Similarly, speakers of this dialect would regard *gakkoo* "school" as consisting of two parts. What it means is that the syllable, rather than the mora, plays an important role in dividing a word in this dialect.

Shibatani also points out that a similar observation is made in accounting for the accentuation pattern of the Takajocho dialect. In this dialect, the accent is placed on the last syllable of a word. So, Shibatani (1990: 160) notes that the words in (153) are pronounced with the indicated pitch pattern.

(153)   a.   koko.ron (low–high)   "of heart"
        b.   hei.tai (low–high)   "soldier"

Therefore, we expect that there is no pitch pattern of the sort illustrated in (154), in which the last syllable is split into two morae.

(154)   a.   *ko ko ro n
                 L L L H
        b.   *he i ta i
                 LL LH

This is because in the Takajocho dialect, the accentuation pattern is determined on the basis of the syllable instead of the mora.

Shibatani, on the other hand, demonstrates that in the Osaka dialect, the determination of the pitch patterns invokes the notion of mora rather than syllable. Consider the examples of the dialect in (155) (from Shibatani 1990: 160).

(155)   a.   so tu ro n   "graduation thesis"
                 L L L H
        b.   he n ta i   "pervert"
                 LL LH

If it is syllable structure that contributes to the accentuation pattern, it would be impossible to break up the last syllable of each of these words, *ron* in (155a) and *tai* in (155b), so that various parts of a syllable receive different pitches. If we consider the pitch pattern to be explained in terms of mora, what we see in (155) is totally what we expect: /n/ without a vowel following it counts as a mora, and two consecutive vowels count as two morae. That is, different pitches are assigned to different morae.

Recall that we have observed above that the pitch pattern of the Tokyo dialect is also sensitive to mora, just as is the Osaka dialect. In the Tokyo dialect, thus, it is natural to see a syllable consisting of two vowels receiving two distinct pitches. Similarly common is a syllable consisting of a vowel and a moraic /n/ receiving two distinct pitches. These two cases are exemplified by the pitch pattern of (156) and (157), where both words have the accent on the initial mora.

(156) ta i si   "ambassador"
     HL L

(157) ka n ri "management"
     HL L

These examples clearly show that the notion of mora pertains to the pitch patterns of a word in the Tokyo dialect.[17]

In summary, by examining pitch patterns, we have observed that the dialectal variation between the Takajocho dialect, on the one hand, and the Osaka dialect and the Tokyo dialect, on the other, suggests that the notion of syllable structure is not entirely missing in Japanese. Rather, it seems necessary to invoke syllables in accounting for some variation in the accentuation patterns existing in diverse dialects.[18]

4.4 Accentuation of Long Nominal Compounds

Although in section 4.3 above we have seen some relevance of the syllable in accentuation patterns of dialects, there is enough evidence to show that Japanese is primarily a mora-based language. We have indeed observed this in two pieces of evidence earlier, i.e. speech errors and language games. In this section, we will discuss further support for this claim. The support comes from the accentuation pattern of long nominal compounds in the Tokyo dialect. This phenomenon has been extensively discussed by J. McCawley (1977), Higurashi (1983), and Tsujimura and Davis (1987), and we will compare these three approaches. At the end of section 8, however, we will examine a new analysis of accentuation of compounds put forth by Kubozono and Mester (1995).

Compounds are **long** when the second member consists of three morae or more (cf. J. McCawley 1968, 1977). Short compounds are, in comparison, those that are formed with a second member being a one- or two-mora word. The accentuation of long compound nouns is very interesting in that the original accent of the second word, before compounding, sometimes stays after compounding, but it often shifts to a different location. Examples illustrating this variation are given in (158)–(162).

(158)   *   *   *
       huyu   + kesiki   →   huyugesiki
       winter   scenery   winter scenery

(159)   *   *   *
       yama   + hototogisu → yamahototogisu
       mountain   quail   mountain quail

(160)   *   *   *
       hanauri   + musume   → hanaurimusume
       flower selling   girl   girl who sells flowers

(161)   *   *

        ni   + kuruma   →   niguruma

        load   car   cart

(162)   *   *   *

        noogyoo + kumiai   →   noogyookumiai

        agriculture   association   agricultural association

Consider (158) and (159), first. The original accent of the second member stays on the same mora before and after the compounding, and this accent becomes the accent of the newly formed compound word as a whole. It means that the original accent on the first member is eliminated. In fact, this last point holds for all the cases in (158)–(162), and we will be assuming that it is the accent of the second member that plays a significant role in determining the accent of the compound.

Let us move to (160)–(162). In these examples, the accent of the second member shifts after compounding: in (160) the accent on the last mora of the original word moves to the initial mora of the compound word; in (161) the second member is accentless and after compounding it receives an accent on the first mora; and in (162) the accent on the third mora of the second member shifts to the first mora of the word. On the basis of these observations, J. McCawley (1977) proposed the rule of accent placement stated in (163).

(163)   a.   The accent of the second element predominates.

        b.   If, however, the second element has its accent on the final syllable or is unaccented, put the accent on the first syllable of the second element.

(163a) says that the accent of the first member does not count in considering the accentuation of the whole compound, and hence it is deleted. It is important to notice that (163b) is stated in terms of syllable rather than mora. So, let us look for the cases in which the second member is accented on the last syllable or is not accented. (160)–(162) are subsumed under such a category: the second member of (160) has its accent on the last syllable *me*; in (161) the second member has no accent; and in (162) the last syllable corresponds to *ai*, which has the accent on it. According to (163b), then, a new accent should be placed on the first syllable of the second member in these cases. The results of the application of these rules properly coincide with the accentuation patterns illustrated in (158)–(162).

Recall that we have repeatedly discussed the relevance of mora in accentuation patterns in Japanese, but if McCawley's analysis is correct, it somewhat undermines such an observation. This is because McCawley's rule in (163) is stated in terms of the syllable, rather than the mora. Although McCawley's syllable-based analysis is one of the first attempts to account for the accentuation of nominal compounds, capturing the basic intuition of the phenomenon, it is not totally without problems in that there are some counter-examples to his rule. Examine the compounds in (164) and (165).

(164)
                           *   *

     sato   + kokoro   →   satogokoro

     country   heart   homesickness

(165)   *   *   *

     denki   + kamisori → denkikamisori

     electric   razor   electric shaver

Let us apply the rule of (163) to these two instances. (163a) says that the accentuation of the first member does not play a role. According to (163b), since *kokoro* in (164) does not have its accent on the final syllable, nor is it unaccented, the original accent should stay at the same location. Consequently, we should expect the result to be as in (166).

(166)   *

     satogokoro

Contrary to this prediction, the accent of the compound is on the first mora of the second member, as is indicated in (164).

    Similarly, *kamisori* in (165) does have an accent and the accent is on the third mora, i.e. not on the final syllable. So, the rule in (163b) does not apply to this case, and hence the original accent should stay where it is before the compounding. The predicted location of the accent of the compound is as in (167).

(167)   *

     denkikamisori

Again, the prediction is not borne out, and the resulting accent is not in the correct location, as (165) shows. Therefore, although McCawley's syllable-based approach seems intuitively on the right track, it predicts an incorrect placement of accent.[19]

    Higurashi (1983), in comparison, has proposed a mora-based analysis of the accentuation of long nominal compounds. She argues that the generalization in (168) holds for the accentuation patterns of long nominal compounds in Japanese.

(168)   If the second member of a compound is a native word (excluding any loan words), the accent always falls on the first mora of the second member of the compound.

What is essential in this generalization is the origin of the second member: that is, whether it is native or loan. Regardless of where the original accent is placed, the accent should be found on the first mora as long as the second member of a compound is a native word. It is implied that if the second member is a loan word, then the accent of the word should stay and become the accent of the whole compound.

    Let us examine how the generalization in (168) is captured. Consider the compounds in (169), whose second members are all native words (indicated as

[+native]), and those in (170), whose second members are all loan words (indicated as [−native]).

(169)   Second member = [+native]

                             *   *

    a.   sato   + kokoro   →   satogokoro
         country   heart   homesickness

           *   *   *

    b.   isi   + atama   →   isiatama
         stone   head   hard head

           *   *

    c.   ni   + kuruma   →   niguruma
         load   car   cart

(170)   Second member = [−native]

                *   *   *

    a.   sukin   + kuriimu   →   sukinkuriimu
         skin   cream   skin cream

           *   *   *

    b.   hangaa + sutoraiki   →   hangaasutoraiki
         hunger   strike   hunger strike

           *   *   *

    c.   bizin   + konkuuru   →   bizinkonkuuru
         beautiful contest   beauty contest
         person

The second member words in (169) are all of native origin. According to (168), then, the accent of the derived compounds should be consistently placed on the first mora of the second-member words irrespective of where the original accent was. This is indeed what we see in (169). The second-member words in (170), on the other hand, are loan words, borrowed from English. Hence, these words are beyond the scope of the application of (168). As a result, the accent of the original words remain on the same mora, and it serves as the accent for the whole compound.

   Although the prediction seems to be borne out as far as the examples in (169) and (170) are concerned, there are several problems with Higurashi's mora-based analaysis. First, it predicts that as long as the second member is [+native], regardless of the length of the second member or the location of the accent of the second member, the accent of the compound should fall on the first mora of the second element. However, when the second member is longer than three morae, her analysis often predicts wrong results. Consider (171)–(172), in which the second-member words are of native origin. The predicted accentuation on the basis of her generalization is in (a) while the actual accentuation is in (b).

(171)   a.   Prediction
                                        *   *
                         yunyuu + kudamono   →   yunyuukudamono
                         import   fruit   imported fruit
    b. Actual accentuation   *
                    yunyuukudamono

(172) a. Prediction   *   *   *

                              yama   + hototogisu   →   yamahototogisu

                              mountain   quail   mountain quail

    b. Actual accentuation   *

                              yamahototogisu

Observe the discrepancy between the predicted and actual location of accent. Since the second elements in both cases are native words, the accentuation of these compounds should follow (168), deriving the pattern in (a). Contrary to this prediction, the accent on the second-member words stays, as (b) depicts.

Second, Higurashi says that in words like (170) the accent stays on the same mora of the second member because they are loan words. On the other hand, she claims that the second elements of the compounds below are [+native], and therefore the accent shifts, following (168).

(173) a.   *   *   *

        insutanto + koohii → insutantokoohii

        instant   coffee   instant coffee

    b.   *

        tikin   + karee → tikinkaree

        chicken   curry   chicken curry

The second-member words in (173), *koohii* "coffee" and *karee* "curry", are undoubtedly loan words, no less so than *kuriimu* "cream", *sutoraiki* "strike", and *konkuuru* "contest" in (170) are. If *kuriimu*, *sutoraiki*, and *konkuuru* are treated as [−native], then so should *koohii* and *karee* be. But, then, a problem arises. If *koohii* and *karee* are considered [−native], they should not follow (168), and the accent should not shift, giving rise to the incorrect results in (174).

(174) a.   *

        *insutantokoohii

    b. *tikinkaree (unaccented)

In summary, Higurashi's analysis often makes a wrong prediction when the second member is longer than three morae. Furthermore, her criteria to decide whether a word is native or not are not clear, given the different treatment in (170) and (173). It should be pointed out, however, that the feature of [+/−native], in itself, is a legitimate criterion, and is often invoked to account for various phenomena in a variety of languages. However, an analysis of some phenomenon in which both loan words and native words are treated the same in a unified manner would be preferred over one where they are not (cf. Vance 1986).

Tsujimura and Davis (1987) propose yet another mora-based analysis. This basically takes McCawley's insight, but attempts to collapse compounds with loan words and compounds with native words and to state a rule in terms of mora, so that it avoids both McCawley's and Higurashi's shortcomings. An important generalization to be captured is that when the second member is three morae or longer, and the accent of the second member is placed on the last or second-to-last mora or the second member is unaccented, then the accent of the compound is always on the initial mora: otherwise, the accent stays. A mora that is second to the last is called a **penultimate** mora. This generalization is stated in (175).

(175) a. If the accent of the second member is placed on the final mora or the penultimate mora, then shift it to the first mora.
　　　　b. If the second member is unaccented, place an accent on the first mora.

Notice that (175) is stated in terms of mora. Furthermore, it does not matter what the origin of the second word is: all the word types are treated equally. Some examples of the application of (175) are illustrated in (176)–(178).

(176)   *   *   *
　　　　huyu   + kesiki   → huyugesiki   [(175) does not apply.]
　　　　winter   scenery   winter scenery

(177)   *   *   *
　　　　hanauri + musume   → hanaurimusume [(175a) applies.]
　　　　flower-   girl   a girl who sells
　　　　selling   flowers

(178)   *   *
　　　　ni   + kuruma   → niguruma   [(175b) applies.]
　　　　load   car   cart

The second member in (176) has its accent on the first mora, and thus neither rule in (175) applies. Consequently, the original accent becomes the accent of the compound. Since the second member of (177) is accented on the final mora, (175a) comes into play, and shifts the accent to the initial mora. The second member of (178), on the other hand, is unaccented, and so (175b) applies, and an accent is placed on the first mora of the second member.

　　Now, let us consider the examples that are problematic with McCawley's and Higurashi's analyses to examine whether (175) can handle those cases. Consider (179)–(183).

(179)   *   *
　　　　yunyuu + kudamono → yunyuukudamono
　　　　import   fruits   imported fruits

(180)   *   *   *
　　　　sukin   + kuriimu   → sukinkuriimu
　　　　skin   cream   skin cream

(181)
                          *   *

    sato   + kokoro   →   satogokoro

    country   heart   homesickness

(182)
          *   *   *

    insutanto + koohii   →   insutantokoohii

    instant   coffee   instant coffee

(183)
   *

    tikin   + karee   →   tikinkaree

    chicken   curry   chicken curry

The first two examples, (179) and (180), are the cases to which neither (175a) nor (175b) applies because they are accented with their accents neither on the final mora nor on the penultimate mora. Hence, the original accentuation patterns remain intact. Notice that while the second member of (179) is a native word, that of (180) is a loan word. Such a difference, however, is not relevant to this analysis: both cases are treated identically. Let us turn to (181) and (182), where the second members have their accent on the penultimate mora. (175a) is relevant and accounts for these cases: the original accents are moved to the initial mora. In these two examples, again, native words and loan words make no difference with respect to the application of the rule. Finally, (183) is explained by (175b): the second element is unaccented in this case, and the rule of (175b) places an accent on the first mora of this word.

    The examination of (175) in its application to various compounds reveals that it captures the right generalization concerning the accentuation of long nominal compounds. This analysis suggests that mora is a crucial notion to explain the accentuation pattern of long nominal compounds. This is especially seen in comparing (180) with (181). In terms of syllables, the second word in each compound has an accent on the penultimate syllable, but the accent stays in (180) while it shifts to the initial mora in (181). The difference between the two, however, is captured in terms of morae. The accent is on the mora which is third from the last in (180), but it is on the penultimate in (181), so only (181) surfaces with an accent on the initial mora. Furthermore, as we will see in the next section, long compounds demonstrate different behavior from short compounds in their accentuation patterns. Recall that we have adopted the definition of long and short compounds in terms of mora. The fact that the distinction by mora length results in different accentuation patterns provides further evidence that the mora is a critical unit in Japanese phonology.

4.5 Accentuation of Short Nominal Compounds

We have seen in the preceding section that the accentuation of long nominal compounds is given a systematic treatment based on mora structure. The accentuation of **short** nominal compounds, on the other hand, appears to be rather random in that no particular set of rules seems to account for their accentuation patterns.

Higurashi (1983), however, attempts to make some generalizations according to the accentual behavior of individual second-member nouns.

The first group Higurashi describes subsumes short nouns (i.e. comprising one or two morae) whose initial accent survives. According to her, *miso* "bean paste" and *sora* "sky" are included in this group. (184)–(185) illustrate the accentuation pattern of short compounds containing these nouns as their second members.

(184) a.
```
                        *                        *
       inaka        + miso       →    inakamiso
       country        bean paste      country-style bean paste
```
       b.
```
       *              *                        *
       sinsyuu      + miso       →    sinsyuumiso
       Shinshu                        bean paste from Shinshu
```
       c.
```
                        *                        *
       takeya       + miso       →    takeyamiso
       Takeya-brand                   Takeya bean paste
```

(185) a.
```
                        *                        *
       akane        + sora       →    akanezora
       red            sky             red sky
```
       b.
```
                        *                        *
       yuuyake      + sora       →    yuuyakezora
       sunset         sky             sunset sky
```

Both *miso* "bean paste" and *sora* "sky" have their accents on the first mora. Higurashi says that compounds with these words as the second member maintain their accents on the first mora. As she notes, however, there are a few exceptions to this generalization. When the first member is a word that indicates the color of *miso*, then the compound as a whole becomes accentless. This situation is illustrated by the compounds in (186).

(186) a.
```
       *            *
       siro   + miso   →    siromiso [unaccented]
       white
```
       b.
```
       *            *
       aka    + miso   →    akamiso [unaccented]
       red
```

Although her observation may be correct to the extent of what the examples in (186) show, the first member is not necessarily limited to color terms. Consider (187).

(187)
```
                    *
       goma   + miso   →    gomamiso [unaccented]
       sesame               bean paste with sesame seeds
```

Notice that even though *goma* "sesame" does not indicate the color of miso, the compound is accentless. Furthermore, the example in (188) suggests that the accentuation pattern with *miso* as the second member of a compound may depend on the accent and length of the first member.

(188)   *   *   *
        midori + miso   →   midorimiso
        green

Although *midorimiso* "green miso" does not exist as an actual Japanese word, it is a possible word and, therefore, a native speaker would not consider it an incorrect form. So, let us suppose that *midorimiso* exists. As (188) shows, the compound is not unaccented, as is predicted by Higurashi's explanation. Instead, the compound retains the accent of the second member. It may be the case, then, that the length and accent of the first element may need to be examined in order to capture a more adequate generalization.

    The second class Higurashi deals with is cases where the accent of the second member is lost. They include compounds comprising *huro* "bath", *ki* "tree", and *su* "vinegar" as their second members. The examples Higurashi provides are in (189).

(189)   a.   *   *
          asa   + huro   →   asaburo
          morning   bath   morning bath
       b.   *   *
          huyu   + ki   →   huyuki
          winter   tree   winter tree
       c.   *
          goma   + su   →   gomasu
          sesame   vinegar   dressing with sesame seeds

    Finally, there are compounds where an accent is placed on the last mora of the first member regardless of whether the second member is accented or where the accent is. This is illustrated in (190) and (191).

(190)   a.   *   *   *
          asa   + iti   →   asaiti
          morning   market   morning market
       b.   *   *   *
          uma   + iti   →   umaiti
          horse   horse market
       c.   *   *
          setomono + iti   →   setomonoiti
          ceramics   ceramics market

(191)   *   *
         asa   + kaze   →   asakaze
         morning   wind   morning wind

It seems apparent that capturing a generalization pertinent to the accentuation of short nominal compounds is more complicated than Higurashi describes, but it appears to be quite plausible that unlike the cases with long nominal compounds, the first member word plays a significant role in determining the accentuation involved with short nominal compounds.[20]

4.6   *Accentual Variation among Endings*

When we carefully look at various endings in English such as *-ic*, *-al*, *-ity*, and *-ness*, as in *electric*, *commercial*, *maturity*, and *sadness*, we notice that they are not homogeneous with respect to their phonological effects on the entire word. For example, among the endings just mentioned, *-ic*, *-al*, and *-ity* affect the stress pattern of the word to which they are attached, while *-ness* does not. Consider the examples in (192)–(194) illustrating such a contrast.

(192)   a.   sýmbol
        b.   symból-ic

(193)   a.   párent
        b.   parént-al

(194)   a.   grammátical
        b.   grammaticál-ity
        c.   grammátical-ness

As the contrast between (192a) and (192b) demonstrates, the ending *-ic* changes the stress pattern: the stress shifts from the first syllable to the second syllable when *-ic* is added. The endings *-al* in (193b) and *-ity* in (194b) share the property of altering the stress pattern of the word to which they are attached. Thus, *-al* changes the stress of *parent* from the first syllable to the second. Similarly, *-ity* shifts the (main) stress on the second syllable of *grammatical* to the fourth syllable of *grammaticality*. Compare the behavior of *-ity* in (194b) with that of *-ness* in (194c): the stress in *grammatical* does not alter when *-ness* is added to this word. That is, while *-ity* changes the stress of *grammatical*, *-ness* does not.

A similar phenomenon is observed in Japanese with respect to the relation between various endings and accentuation, as is discussed in Higurashi (1983). Some endings have influence on the accentuation patterns in several different ways while others do not. Here, we will introduce four types of endings to observe these properties. Recall first that an accent can be placed in a variety of positions within a word, as our earlier examples have indicated. This is shown in (195).

(195) a.   *

        inoti "life"

     b.   *

        kokoro "heart"

     c.   *

        atama "head"

     d. miyako "capital"

It should be remembered that the realization of pitch is identical between the final-accented word in (195c) and the unaccented word in (195d): both of them surface as low–high–high. Recall also that their difference, however, can be identified by adding the Case particle -*ga* immediately after them: the Case particle receives a low pitch in (195c) while it gets a high pitch in (195d). Let us attach this particle to all the words in (195), as demonstrated in (196).

(196) a.   *

        inoti-ga

     b.   *

        kokoro-ga

     c.   *

        atama-ga

     d. miyako-ga

What (196) indicates is that -*ga* does not alter the location of the accent of the original word. Endings like -*ga* that do not influence the accent of the original word in any way are called **unaccented**.

   Second, when -*made* "even" is added to the words in (195), a slight change occurs. This is displayed in (197).

(197) a.   *   *

        inoti   vs. inoti-made

     b.   *   *

        kokoro vs. kokoro-made

     c.   *   *

        atama vs. atama-made

     d.   *

        miyako vs. miyako-made

As (197a–c) show, if the noun bears its own accent originally, this accent survives, and therefore -*made* has no influence on the accentuation pattern of the whole sequence. When -*made* accompanies an unaccented word, as in (197d), however, an accent is placed on -*made*. This is an **accented** ending. What is characteristic about this kind is that its accentual effect is observed only with unaccented words.

   The third type of ending is termed **pre-accenting**. An example of this type is -*sika* "only". Pre-accenting endings are similar to accented ones in that they do not show any change with words with accents on them, but a difference appears when the word is unaccented. Examine (198).

(198) a.   *   *
           inoti   vs. inoti-sika
       b.   *   *
           kokoro vs. kokoro-sika
       c.   *   *
           atama   vs. atama-sika
       d.   *
           miyako vs. miyako-sika

Notice that when -*sika* is added to the unaccented word in (198d), an accent
ends up on the last mora of the noun to which it is attached. This property of
placing an accent elsewhere other than on the ending itself separates -*sika* from
-*made*. Since the addition of -*sika* results in accenting the final mora of the noun
stem, it is called pre-accenting.

   Finally, some endings bear their own accents that have precedence over the
accent of a word to which they are attached. They are called **accent-deleting**
because they have the effect of deleting the accent of the word to which they
attach so that their own accents win out. This property is shown in (199) by
the behavior of -*gurai* "about".

(199) a.   *   *
           inoti   vs. inoti-gurai
       b.   *   *
           kokoro vs. kokoro-gurai
       c.   *   *
           atama   vs. atama-gurai
       d.   *
           miyako vs.   miyako-gurai

Observe that no matter where the original accents of the nouns are located, the
accent of -*gurai*, which is on the first mora, predominates. The summary of the
four kinds of endings and their characteristics is given in (200).

(200) | *type* | *characteristic* | *example* |
       |---|---|---|
       | unaccented | There is no influence on the accent of the preceding word. | -*ga* |
       | accented | When it follows an unaccented word, an accent is placed on it. | -*made* |
       | pre-accenting | When it follows an unaccented word, an accent is placed on the preceding word. | -*sika* |
       | accent-deleting | It deletes the accent of the preceding word, and its own accent becomes the accent of the entire word. | -*gurai* |

It is interesting to see that the accentuation pattern can be altered not only
by the compounding process that we have observed in sections 4.4 and 4.5 but
also by the attachment of diverse types of endings which display heterogeneous

properties. Each ending in Japanese, then, will fall into one of the four types discussed here.

5 Mimetics

Many languages have sound-symbolic words. There are at least two types of these. One type is **onomatopoeia**; words that sound like what they mean, for example, words depicting animal sounds. The other is a more abstract type and is referred to as an **ideophone**. Ideophones and onomatopoeia together are subsumed under the rubric of **mimetics**. Examples of mimetics in English can be illustrated by onomatopoeic words such as *bow-wow* and *cock-a-doodle-doo* and ideophonic words like *helter-skelter* and *teeter-totter*.

Japanese displays a quite extensive list of mimetics, much larger than in English. Some examples are given in (201).

(201)   a.   pika-pika   "glaring"
        b.   gata-gata   "rattling"
        c.   sowa-sowa   "restlessness"
        d.   beto-beto   "sticky"
        e.   zara-zara   "coarse"
        f.   kati-kati   "tough"
        g.   pota-pota   "dripping"
        h.   zawa-zawa   "noisy"

As the examples in (201) show, mimetic forms in Japanese often involve repetition of the first portion.

What is phonologically very interesting about mimetics in Japanese is the phenomenon called **palatalization**. As briefly mentioned in chapter 2, palatalization occurs when the tongue body approaches the palatal region of the mouth as some consonants are articulated. For instance, the voiceless bilabial stop /p/ is palatalized when the tongue body is raised to the hard palate, producing [pʸ]. Similarly, the voiced velar stop is palatalized by raising the tongue body to the hard palate. The resulting sound is the palatalized voiced velar stop, [gʸ]. There are a number of instances in which mimetic forms contain palatalized consonants, as is exemplified in (202).

(202)   a.   pitya-pitya   [pičapiča]   "splashing"
        b.   bisyo-bisyo   [bišobišo]   "soaking wet"
        c.   hyoro-hyoro   [çoroçoro]   "slender and tall"
        d.   pyon-pyon   [pʸompʸoN]   "hopping"
        e.   hunya-hunya   [ɸuɲaɸuɲa]   "soft"
        f.   zyuu-zyuu   [ǰuːǰuː]   "sizzling"

As the phonetic transcriptions show, the palatalized counterparts of /t/, /s/, /h/, /n/, and /z/ are phonetically realized as [č], [š], [ç], [ɲ] and [ǰ], respectively.

It is often observed that when a non-palatalized consonant in a mimetic form is palatalized, it induces a slightly different meaning. Hamano's investigation (1986) deals extensively with such cases. Consider the pairs in (203)–(208), taken from Mester and Ito (1989: 268), in which a non-palatalized mimetic form is compared with its palatalized counterpart.[21]

(203) a. poko-poko   "up and down movement"
       b. pyoko-pyoko   "jumping around imprudently"

(204) a. kata-kata   "homogeneous hitting sound"
       b. katya-katya   "non-homogeneous clattering sound"

(205) a. kasa-kasa   "rustling sound, dryness"
       b. kasya-kasya   "noisy rustling sound of dry objects"

(206) a. pota-pota   "dripping, trickling, drop by drop"
       b. potya-potya   "dripping in large quantities"

(207) a. zabu-zabu   "splashing"
       b. zyabu-zyabu   "splashing indiscriminately"

(208) a. noro-noro   "slow movement"
       b. nyoro-nyoro   "(snake's) slow wriggly movement"

There are several interesting observations that have been made by Hamano (1986) and Mester and Ito (1989). The meaning is different between the palatalized mimetics and their non-palatalized counterparts. Hamano explains that the mimetic palatalization adds a semantic notion of **uncontrolledness** to the base form that does not include a palatalized consonant. The notion of "uncontrolledness", according to Hamano, includes childishness, immaturity, instability, unreliability, uncoordinated movement, diversity, excessive energy, noisiness, lack of elegance, and cheapness, depending on the meaning of the base form. Incidentally, this semantic characterization of palatalized mimetics as states of uncontrolledness is, in fact, comparable to the sound-symbolic systems found in other languages, such as northwest American Indian languages.

Mester and Ito (1989) further draw several generalizations concerning the phonological properties of palatalization involved in mimetics. Let us go over their generalizations (the examples below are also from Mester and Ito 1989: 270). First, when we pay attention to the length of each mimetic form, we notice the output of palatalization always consists of four morae. As is clear from the non-palatalized forms, however, the generalization that mimetics are four morae long extends to non-palatalized mimetics as well. Although there are some exceptions to this generalization (*pyokon-pyokon*, *dosun-dosun*, and *pisyari-pisyari*), four-mora mimetics are the forms we observe most frequently.

Second, there is a restriction as to how many consonants can be palatalized in a base form. Compare the pairs in (209) and (210).

(209) a. pyokopyoko   "flip-flop"
       b. *pyokyopyokyo

(210) a. potyapotya   "splashing"
       b. *pyotyapyotya

The ill-formed mimetics such as (209b) and (210b) indicate that only one palatalized consonant is allowed per base.

The third generalization has to do with the question of which consonant can undergo palatalization. We have just discussed that only one palatalization is permitted per base. As (209a) and (210a) demonstrate, a palatalized consonant can appear either at the beginning of the first mora or at the beginning of the second mora, assuming that a base form always consists of two morae. On the other hand, the distribution of palatalized consonants does not seem to be arbitrary. Consider the examples in (211) and (212).

(211) a. metyametya vs. *myetamyeta "destroyed"
       b. kasyakasya vs. *kyasakyasa "rustling"
       c. hunyahunya vs. *hyunahyuna "limp"

(212) a. tyokotyoko vs. *tokyotokyo "childish small steps"
       b. zyabuzyabu vs. *zabyuzabyu "dabble in liquid"
       c. nyokinyoki vs. *nokyinokyi "sticking out"

The mimetics in (211) have a palatalized consonant in the second mora of the base form. If a palatalized consonant appears in the first mora of the base form, the mimetic word is not well-formed. The mimetics in (212), in contrast, display the opposite situation: so far as the first consonant is palatalized, the derived mimetic word is well-formed. What the contrast between the two sets of examples indicates is that palatalization is not restricted to any particular position of the base. Rather, the nature of the consonant that is intended to undergo palatalization plays an essential role. To see this point, compare the acceptable and unacceptable mimetics in (211) and (212) again. The palatalized consonants include /t, s, n, z/ while the consonants whose palatalizations lead to unacceptable mimetics are /m, k, h, b/. Notice that what the phonemes in the first group have in common is the same place of articulation, i.e. alveolar. Thus, we can conclude that if a base contains an alveolar sound and a non-alveolar sound, then the alveolar sound has precedence over the non-alveolar sound in palatalization. This should account for the range of data in (211) and (212).

Next, consider the additional data in (213), in which both consonants of the base forms are alveolar sounds.

(213) a. dosyadosya vs. *dyosadyosa "in large amount"
       b. nosyonosyo vs. *nyosonyoso "slowly"
       c. netyanetya vs. *nyotanyota "sticky"

This set of data, then, demonstrates that if there is more than one alveolar consonant in a base, it is always the rightmost alveolar sound that undergoes palatalization.

The fourth generalization is somewhat related to the previous one. We have just discussed the relevance of alveolar sounds to palatalization in mimetics. What will happen if a base does not have any alveolar sound? Examples of this sort are shown in (214).

(214) a. pyokopyoko   vs. *pokyopokyo   "jumping up and down"
       b. hyokohyoko   vs. *hokyohokyo   "lightly, nimbly"
       c. gyobogyobo   vs. *gobyogobyo   "gurgling"

None of the consonants included in these examples is alveolar: /p, k, h, g, b/. Nevertheless, palatalization takes place. In this case, however, it appears that the position of the palatalized consonant is significant. That is, in all grammatical mimetics, palatalization occurs in the first mora of the base form. If the consonant in the second mora undergoes palatalization, on the other hand, the output is always unacceptable. Hence, we can state the generalization that if the base does not contain an alveolar consonant, palatalization takes place in the base-initial position.

Finally, the set of examples in (215)–(219) demonstrates that there is something special about the liquid /r/.

(215) a. noronoro   "slow, lazy"
       b. nyoronyoro
       c. *noryonoryo

(216) a. torotoro   "slow, dumb"
       b. tyorotyoro
       c. *toryotoryo

(217) a. zarazara   "course texture"
       b. zyarazyara
       c. *zaryazarya

(218) a. gorogoro   "goggle-eyed"
       b. gyorogyoro
       c. *goryogoryo

(219) a. horohoro   "weak"
       b. hyorohyoro
       c. *horyohoryo

Let us first look at (215)–(217). All the consonants of the mimetics in these examples are alveolar sounds. According to one of the generalizations that we have discussed above, if there is more than one alveolar sound in the base, the rightmost alveolar sound should undergo palatalization. Since /r, n, t, z/ in these examples are all alveolar and the liquid /r/ is the rightmost alveolar, /r/ is expected to be palatalized. As the (c) forms indicate, the resulting mimetics are ill-formed. On the other hand, if the leftmost alveolar undergoes palatalization, the output is acceptable, as the (b) forms show.

The peculiarity of /r/ with respect to palatalized mimetics is also detected by (218) and (219), where the consonants other than /r/ are not alveolar. Since /g/ and /h/ are not alveolar, /r/, being an alveolar sound, should undergo palatalization. Again, the palatalized /r/ results in ill-formed mimetics. In these cases, instead, the non-alveolar consonants are palatalized, deriving acceptable mimetic forms.

What these observations suggest is that under no circumstances does /r/ undergo palatalization. So, if the other consonant happens to be an alveolar sound, as is the case in (215)–(217), it undergoes palatalization. Moreover, if no alveolar sound is found, the other consonant, which is non-alveolar, becomes palatalized.

The generalizations and restrictions regarding palatalized mimetics discussed in this section are summarized in (220).

(220) a. Mimetic palatalization can be characterized as adding an element of "uncontrolledness" to the base.
       b. The resulting palatalized mimetics are four morae long.
       c. Only one palatalized consonant is allowed per base.
       d. The rightmost alveolar consonant predominantly undergoes palatalization.
       e. If there is no alveolar sound in the base, palatalization occurs in the base-initial position.
       f. The liquid sound /r/ never undergoes palatalization.[22]

6 Loan Words

When a word is borrowed into another language, the pronunciation of the word is inevitably altered. This is because the sounds making up the word may not all exist in the language that borrows it. An example can be seen in Japanese words borrowed into English. We often hear the type of Japanese mattress pronounced as [futən] in English, but the Japanese pronunciation of the word is [ΦutoN]. The substitution of [f] for [Φ] is simply due to the fact that English does not have this bilabial fricative sound. Since both [f] and [Φ] are fricatives, with similar places of articulation, labio-dental vs. bilabial, they are close enough to allow substitution.

This sort of sound alternation is widely observed when English words (as well as loan words from other languages) are borrowed into Japanese (cf. Lovins 1975). As expected, the English sounds that do not belong to the Japanese sound system are substituted for by the sounds that exist in Japanese. Typical sound substitutions take place with respect to the English words that contain [f, v, θ, ð, r] simply because these sounds are missing in Japanese.

The sounds /f/, /v/, /θ/, and /ð/ in English are substituted by [Φ], [b], [s], and [z], respectively, in Japanese. Some examples are in (221)–(224).

			English	*Japanese*
(221)	a.	five	[fayv]	[Φaibu]
	b.	fork	[fork]	[Φo:ku]
	c.	knife	[nayf]	[naiΦu]
(222)	a.	vacation	[vəkešən]	[bake:šoN]
	b.	vanilla	[vənɪlə]	[banira]
	c.	volcano	[vəlkeno]	[borukano]
(223)	a.	three	[θri]	[suri:]
	b.	theater	[θɪətər]	[šiata:]
	c.	thunder	[θʌndər]	[sanda:]
(224)	a.	brother	[brʌðər]	[buraza:]
	b.	feather	[fɛðər]	[Φeza:]
	c.	leather	[lɛðər]	[reza:]

It is interesting to point out that given that [v], [θ], and [ð] are substituted for by [b], [s], and [z], respectively, native speakers do not make a distinction between these pairs. That is, if native speakers are given minimal pairs like (225), the expected pronunciations of these would be identical, without any distinction.[23]

			English	*Japanese*
(225)				
	a.	vase	[ves]	[be:su]
		base	[bes]	[be:su]
	b.	thigh	[θay]	[sai]
		sigh	[say]	[sai]
	c.	tenth	[tɛnθ]	[tensu]
		tense	[tɛns]	[tensu]
	d.	breathe	[brið]	[buri:zu]
		breeze	[briz]	[buri:zu]

Therefore, many native speakers of Japanese, particularly those who do not have exposure to English sounds, would perceive these pairs almost identically. That is, the distinctions between [v] and [b], [θ] and [s], and [ð] and [z] that appear in English are completely lost in Japanese.

Besides [f, v, θ, ð], the English liquid sound [r] finds an interesting distribution once words containing it are borrowed into Japanese. Compare the English and Japanese pronunciations of the words in (226).

(226)   *English*   *Japanese*

a. cream   [krim]   [kuri:mu]
b. color   [kʌlər]   [kara:]
c. parlor   [pɑrlər]   [pa:ra:]
d. rice   [rays]   [raisu]
e. pork   [pɔrk]   [po:ku]
f. fry   [fray]   [Φurai]
g. Colorado [kɑlərɑdo]   [kororado]

Some instances of [r] in English are realized as the Japanese flap (transcribed here as [r]) while others surface as a lengthening of the preceding vowel. For example, the occurrences of the English liquid in (226a, d, f, g) all correspond to the Japanese liquid (flap) while those in (226b, c, e) are substituted for by the lengthened vowel. When we examine these cases more carefully, we notice that the pattern of this distribution is not arbitrary. In the cases where the English [r] corresponds to the Japanese pronunciation of the flap, the former belongs to the onset of the syllable. In the cases where the English [r] is substituted by a lengthened vowel, on the other hand, the English [r] is part of the coda. In this situation, furthermore, the vowel that corresponds to the nucleus of the original word gets lengthened. Hence, the actual realization of [r] in Japanese depends on where in the syllable the [r] occurs in the original English word. For the most part, if [r] belongs to the onset, it appears as the flap sound in Japanese. If, on the other hand, [r] is part of the coda, the preceding vowel is lengthened and [r] does not survive.[24]

Finally, the insertion of a vowel is frequently observed in loan-word phonology (cf. Lovins 1975). Consider the examples in (227).

(227)   *English*   *Japanese*

a. lamp   [læmp]   [rampu]
b. bus   [bʌs]   [basu]
c. hot   [hɑt]   [hot:o]
d. bed   [bɛd]   [bed:o]
e. catch   [kæč]   [kʲač:i]
f. dodge ball [dɑǰbɑl]   [doǰ:ibo:ru]

As these examples show, the range of vowels inserted after consonants varies. Kubozono (1995) makes the following generalizations regarding the type of vowel insertion: (i) /o/ after /t/ and /d/; (ii) /i/ after /č/ and /ǰ/; and (iii) /u/ elsewhere. Recall that in Japanese a consonant can be free-standing without a following vowel only in the case of a moraic nasal or a geminate consonant. The insertion of a vowel in words like those in (227) can be considered an attempt to avoid such an unattested free-standing consonant in the language.[25]

7 Casual Speech and Fast Speech

When we speak casually and/or fast in a very informal situation, it is often the case that words are shortened in various ways. For example, in English *want to* is pronounced as *wanna* and *going to* as *gonna*. Furthermore, a whole sentence sometimes becomes very abbreviated. A good example of this is when we say "*Did you eat yet?*" very fast, pronouncing it as [ʤɪtʸɛt].

Both N. Hasegawa (1979) and Shibatani (1990) demonstrate various cases of casual speech and fast speech phenomena. Although Hasegawa argues that casual speech and fast speech phenomena are different, this section presents a brief phonological description of these two speech phenomena in Japanese without making precise distinctions.

First, certain functional words containing /n/ in Japanese often lose their accompanying vowel, and as a result they stand as a moraic nasal by itself. This phenomenon is called **nasal syllabification**, and is exemplified by (228)–(229); (228a, b) and (229) are from N. Hasegawa (1979: 128) with a slight modification of the gloss.

(228) a. kuru   no   nara   →   kuru **n** nara
           come   nominalizer   if   "if it is that you come"
       b. Taroo no   da   →   Taroo **n** da
           Taro   gen.   nominalizer   "it's Taro's"
       c. kimi   no   uti   →   kimi **n** ti
           you   gen.   house   "your house"

(229) a. gakusya ni naru   →   gakusya **n** naru
           scholar to become   "become a scholar"
       b. genki   ni naru   →   genki **n** naru
           fine   to become   "become fine"

In (228) *no* loses its accompanying vowel and becomes a moraic /n/. As (228c) demonstrates, in addition to the vowel loss, the word-initial vowel of the immediately following word is also deleted. Similarly, the postposition *ni* "to" in (229) undergoes the same nasal syllabification process, and is realized as the moraic nasal /n/.[26] As Shibatani (1990) observes, the nasal syllabification also applies to non-past negative forms of verbs whose root ends in /r/. (230) provides examples illustrating this.

(230) a. sir-a-nai   →   si-**n**-nai   "don't know"
       b. kaer-a-nai   →   kae-**n**-nai   "don't return"
       c. okur-a-nai   →   oku-**n**-nai   "don't send"

As we have seen above, nasal syllabification is widely observed, and yet it is not without exception. For example, consider (231) (N. Hasegawa 1979: 128).

(231) kimi no   namae → *kimi n namae
      you poss. name   "your name"

The possessive marker *no* in (231) is the same as that in (228b, c), and yet the application of nasal syllabification to this example results in an unacceptable phrase.

Second, sequences of vowels such as *ae*, *oi*, and *ai* are realized systematically as *ee* [e:]. The phenomenon is characteristically observed in male speech, and signals toughness or masculinity. This phonological process is termed **vowel fusion**. Examples are shown in (232) (N. Hasegawa 1979: 129).

(232) a. atarimae → atarimee "of course"
       b. kaeru   → keeru   "return"
       c. sugoi   → sugee   "great"
       d. nai   → nee   "not, no"

There are quite a few exceptions to this phenomenon, as is observed word-internally as well as across words. Consider the cases in (233)–(234) in which vowel fusion is not exhibited (N. Hasegawa 1979: 129).[27]

(233) a. koitu   → *keetu   "this man"
       b. saigo   → *seego   "the last"
       c. kiiroi → *kiiree   "yellow"
       d. kimae   → *kimee   "generosity"

(234) a. ore ga   iku → *ore geeku "I go"
           I   Nom go
       b. ore mo iku → *ore meeku "I also go"
           I   also go

Although the same range of vowel sequences is observed in (233) and (234) as in (232), the outputs of vowel fusion are all ill-formed in (233) and (234). The failure of the application of vowel fusion may be explained in (234) by the fact that the fusion takes place across the word boundary. Nevertheless, the same explanation does not apply to the words in (233), and there does not seem to be a straightforward account for the well-formedness of (232) on the one hand and for the ill-formedness of (233) on the other.

Third, there are phenomena similar to the English examples given earlier, such as *wanna* from *want to* and *gonna* from *going to*. This phenomenon is called **contraction**. Contraction phenomena in Japanese are limited to only a certain selection of words. Compare (235) and (236), which are taken from N. Hasegawa (1979: 130).

(235) a. mite   simau → mityau   "have seen"
           see   finish
       b. yonde simau → yonzyau   "have read"
           read   finish

(236) a. kore de simaimasu   →   *kore zyaimasu "finish at this moment"
           this at finish
       b. mite siru   →   *mityu "know by seeing"
           see know
       c. yonde siru   →   *yonzyu "know by reading"
           read know

The type of contraction observed in (235) applies to the gerund form of a verb
followed by the auxiliary verb *simau* "finish". When these two elements are
present, as in (235), contraction takes place. A few restrictions apply, however.
The source of *-te/de* that induces the contraction must be part of the gerund
form of a verb. (236a) contains *de* "at", but since this word is a postposition
rather than part of the gerund of a verb, the contraction cannot apply. Moreover, the second word must be the auxilary word *simau* "finish", as can be seen
by the unacceptable forms in (236b, c). Notice that in these examples, the first
element is indeed a gerund of a verb. However, the required auxiliary verb is
missing here, and hence, the contraction fails to apply.

Another type of contraction that occurs is illustrated in (237), taken from
N. Hasegawa (1979: 130).[28]

(237) a. miru koto wa (nai) →   mikko (nai)   "it is not that he sees"
           see   that Top neg
       b. yomu koto wa (nai) →   yomikko (nai) "it is not that he reads"
           read

The contraction in (237) consists of the non-past tense form of a verb plus *koto
wa nai* "it is not that", deriving a verbal form followed by *-kko nai*. The
restriction with this type of contraction is the verb form: that is, it must be the
non-past tense form of a verb. If the verb is in the past tense, as in (238) below,
the contracted form is ungrammatical.

(238) mita koto wa (nai)   →   *mitakko (nai) "it is not that he saw"
       saw

Therefore, the two instances of contractions observed here are rather sensitive
to a particular kind of construction.

8   Length Requirements

Many languages display constraints on how long a word should be. For instance,
English superlative formation exhibits such a case. When we form a superlative
in English, we normally add the ending *-est* to an adjective. This is demonstrated
in (239).

(239) a. simple   →   simplest
      b. cheap   →   cheapest
      c. happy   →   happiest
      d. smart   →   smartest

However, there are some adjectives that do not form a superlative by adding this ending. For instance, consider (240).

(240) a. intellectual   →   *intellectualest
      b. expensive   →   *expensivest
      c. complicated   →   *complicatedest
      d. ecstatic   →   *ecstaticest

For these words, we have to use the word *most* as in *most intellectual* and *most expensive*, and so on.

What, then, disallows the use of the ending *-est* for the words in (240)? Is it completely irregular, or is there any rule that the native speaker subconsciously knows? The crucial generalization is that the ending *-est* does not attach to long words. More specifically, it does not attach to words which consist of more than two syllables.

What we see here is a constraint that refers to the length of a word. The remainder of this section will be spent discussing such constraints on word length in Japanese. We will see that these constraints are stated in terms of morae, thus providing additional support for and, therefore, adding significance to the notion of the mora in Japanese.

Poser (1990) discusses extensively a number of cases where conditions on word length play a crucial role in Japanese. One example deals with hypocoristic formation (or nickname formation). In forming a nickname in Japanese, the ending *-tyan* [čan] is normally added to a given name, as is illustrated in (241).

(241) a. satiko   →   satiko-tyan
      b. masao   →   masao-tyan
      c. hirosi   →   hirosi-tyan
      d. akiko   →   akiko-tyan
      e. ryuusuke   →   ryuusuke-tyan

However, it is more common to shorten the given name and add *-tyan*. So, consider (242).

(242) a. ayako   →   aya-tyan
      b. hanako   →   hana-tyan
      c. yukiko   →   yuki-tyan
      d. osamu   →   osa-tyan
      e. syuusuke   →   syuu-tyan
      f. keiko   →   kei-tyan
      g. zyunko   →   zyun-tyan

What is important to our discussion is the length of the portion that is taken out of the entire given name. In the examples above, the first two morae are taken and -*tyan* is added to them. This generalization is confirmed by the possible and impossible hypocoristic forms displayed in (243), taken from Poser (1990: 83).

(243) a. kazuhiko → kazu-tyan, *kazuhi-tyan, *ka-tyan
       b. masahisa → masa-tyan, *masahi-tyan, *ma-tyan
       c. takatugu → taka-tyan, *takatu-tyan, *ta-tyan

The range of data in (242) and (243) clearly shows that the shortened name to which -*tyan* is added cannot be three morae or one mora. It has to be exactly two morae long.

What is more interesting is that the two morae need not be extracted from the given name from left to right. That is, as long as the base element can maintain a two-mora length, the two morae can be taken by extracting the first and the third morae, skipping the second mora. Or it is also possible to extract the first mora and lengthen it to two morae. These situations are illustrated in (244)–(245), taken from Poser (1990: 85–86).

(244) a. akiko   → ako-tyan
       b. motoko → moko-tyan
       c. yosiko → oko-tyan

(245) a. hiroko → hii-tyan
       b. izumi   → ii-tyan
       c. masae   → maa-tyan
       d. tiemi   → tii-tyan

The first and the third morae are extracted from the base names in (244a, b). In (244c) the first and the third morae are taken, but the first mora does not include the accompanying consonant /y/. The derived hypocoristic forms are well-formed since they meet the requirement that the base consist of two morae. This requirement is satisfied in (245) as well: in all the examples, only the first mora is selected, but the vowel is lengthened, so that the length of the output is exactly two morae.

Recall, for this matter, that the first consonant of a long consonant is considered one mora. The hypocoristic forms in (246), taken from Poser (1990: 85), are consistent with this notion of mora as well as the length requirement under discussion.

(246) a. etuko   → et-tyan
       b. mitiko → mit-tyan
       c. yasuko → yat-tyan
       d. natuko → nat-tyan

The first member of the long consonant observed in (246) counts as one mora, and hence the base form for the hypocoristic formation maintains the two-mora length in these examples. Consequently, hypocoristic formation in Japanese requires that the base be two morae.

The second instance of a length requirement that Poser discusses is demonstrated by the formation of Geisha/bargirl client names, although this client name formation seems to be slightly more restrictive than the hypocoristic formation. The client name can be formed by the following two steps: (i) take the first mora and lengthen the vowel; and (ii) add *o-* and *-san* before and after the base, respectively. Consider the data in (247), taken from Poser (1990: 92), which include possible and impossible client names.

(247) a. honda → o-hoo-san, *o-hon-san, *o-hos-san
       b. kondoo → o-koo-san, *o-kon-san, *o-kos-san
       c. tanaka → o-taa-san, *o-tana-san, *o-tas-san

Notice that satisfying the two-mora requirement is not simply enough: only the first mora can be extracted, and the vowel is subsequently lengthened to form two morae. Hence, the client name formation demonstrates a minimal-word condition that is stricter than the hypocoristic formation. Nevertheless, the requirement that the base form must consist of two morae plays an important role.

The third example given by Poser is what is known as Renyookei Reduplication. Renyookei is one of the verbal conjugation forms. It involves a reduplicated or repeated form of a verb base and is often used to modify another verb. The verb base for the reduplication corresponds to the verb root when the root ends with a vowel. When the root ends with a consonant, on the other hand, /i/ is inserted immediately after the root, and the base consisting of the root and /i/ is reduplicated. The restriction on the word length in this formation is that the output must contain an even number of morae. Examine (248)–(249), taken from Poser (1990: 94).

(248) a. nak   "cry"   → nakinaki
       b. tabe   "eat"   → tabetabe
       c. yorokob   "rejoice"   → yorokobiyorokobi

(249) a. s "do"   → siisii, *sisi
       b. mi "see" → miimii, *mimi

Since the base is repeated, the output is naturally an even number. What is interesting, however, is the cases in (249). The verb base consists of one mora, and as the unacceptable form suggests, simply reduplicating the mora is not sufficient. Instead, the vowel of the verb base must be lengthened and then the two-mora verb base is reduplicated. The resulting words comprise four morae. So, the constraint pertinent to the Renyookei Reduplication can be stated such that the verb base to be reduplicated must be at least two morae. Or, alternatively, we can say that the output must be at least four morae.

Fourth, Poser discusses a language game played among musicians. The constraint relevant here is that the resulting word be four morae. Examine how this language game is played by observing the data in (250), taken from Poser (1990: 96).

(250) a. koohii   →   hiikoo   "coffee"
       b. maneezyaa   →   zyaamane   "manager"
       c. nioi   →   oinii   "smell"
       d. mesi   →   siimee   "meal"
       e. pan   →   nnpaa   "bread"
       f. ki   →   iikii   "tree"
       g. he   →   eehee   "fart"

The first two forms show that the last two morae are taken and then moved to the beginning of the word. The requirement that the output must be four morae can more clearly be seen in (b) since the original word contains five morae. The examples in (250c–g) exhibit the case where the base word is shorter than four morae, and hence vowel lengthening is called for in order to satisfy the requirement that the resulting form be four morae long. With a three-mora base word like (250c), the last two morae are selected first and moved to the beginning, and the vowel of the original first mora is lengthened, thereby producing the four-mora output. Two-mora base words like (250d, e) reverse the order of the mora and both vowels are lengthened. In (250e) the moraic nasal /n/ is lengthened, and since the long consonant is followed by the bilabial stop, the output is pronounced as [m:pa:]. With one-mora base words such as in (250f, g), the vowel of the mora is lengthened and duplicated so that the output is four morae. All the processes result in four-mora outputs. Hence, this constitutes another instance of a word length requirement ensuring that the resulting forms of the language game be four morae long.[29]

Fifth, clipping (or shortening) of loan-word compounds as described by Ito (1990) illustrates a similar phenomenon. Japanese has numerous loan-word compounds, and they tend to become shortened in the spoken language. When they are shortened, however, the clipping process must follow a constraint in such a way that the shortened compound consists of four morae. (251) presents some examples.

(251) a. purofessyonaru resuringu → puro resu "professional wrestling"
       b. waado purosessaa → waa puro "word processor"
       c. rimooto kontorooru → rimo kon "remote control"
       d. ziinzu pantu → zii pan "jeans"
       e. sekusyaru harasumento → seku hara "sexual harassment"
       f. paasonaru konpyuutaa → paso kon "personal computer"

The clipping occurs by taking two morae from each word (normally the first two morae). The resulting compound contains four morae.

Finally, the phenomenon that occurs in what might be called Nominal Clauses as discussed in Tsujimura (1992) also demonstrates the importance of a condition on word length. Relevant to our discussion are Nominal Clauses that consist of nouns that are derived from their corresponding verbs. Examples of Nominal Clauses are given in (252)–(254).[30]

(252) Taroo-ga Ziroo-to **arasoi**-tyuu . . .
Taro-Nom Ziro-with fighting-while
"while Taro is fighting with Ziro . . ."

(253) tenin-ga sinamono-o **atukai**-tyuu . . .
clerk-Nom merchandise-Acc handling-while
"while a clerk is handling the merchandise . . ."

(254) Hanako-ga huku-no dezain-o **kangae**-tyuu . . .
Hanako-Nom clothes-Gen design-Acc thinking-while
"while Hanako is thinking about the design of her clothes . . ."

The nouns, *arasoi* "fighting" in (252), *atukai* "handling" in (253), and *kangae* "thinking" in (254), are all derived from their corresponding verbs, *arasou* "fight", *atukau* "handle", and *kangaeru* "think", respectively, and hence they are called "deverbal nouns". The deverbal nouns in Nominal Clauses are always accompanied by endings that are related to time. Those endings include *-tyuu* "while", as in the examples above, as well as *-go* "after" and *-izen* "before". Nominal Clauses appear within a complete sentence, and normally function as temporal modifiers (cf. Iida 1987; Shibatani and Kageyama 1988).

As is discussed in Tsujimura (1992) in detail, Nominal Clauses are phonologically interesting in that they impose a length requirement on deverbal nouns that appear in their construction. That is, the deverbal nouns in Nominal Clauses must be at least four morae long. The examples in (252)–(254) satisfy this requirement since the deverbal nouns *arasoi*, *atukai*, and *kangae* are all four morae long. They should be contrasted with Nominal Clauses that contain deverbal nouns whose length is shorter than four morae. As the examples in (255)–(258) illustrate, Nominal Clauses with deverbal nouns that consist of two morae or three morae are not well-formed.

(255) *Taroo-ga kawa-de **turi**-tyuu . . .
Taro-Nom river-at fishing-while
"while Taro is fishing at the river . . ."

(256) *Ziroo-ga taikin-o **tame**-tyuu . . .
Ziro-Nom lots of money-Acc saving-while
"while Ziro is saving lots of money . . ."

(257) *?Hanako-ga daigaku-ni **kayoi**-tyuu . . .
Hanako-Nom college-to commuting-while
"while Hanako is commuting to the college . . ."

(258) *?Mariko-ga uti-de **inori**-tyuu . . .
Mariko-Nom home-at praying-while
"while Mariko is praying at home . . ."

The deverbal nouns in (255) and (256), i.e. *turi* "fishing" and *tame* "saving", are two-mora words while those in (257) and (258), i.e. *kayoi* "commuting" and *inori* "praying", are three-mora words. As the judgments show, they cannot form acceptable Nominal Clauses because the length of the deverbal nouns does not satisfy the length requirement: they are all shorter than four morae. Thus, the length requirement imposed on deverbal nouns that appear in Nominal Clauses illustrates that a length requirement is operative here, and also that the length requirement is stated in terms of morae.

We have observed several instances of conditions on word length. They refer to either two morae or four morae. Poser claims that two morae constitute a unit that is pertinent to the various phenomena observed above. Borrowing the terminology that was originally proposed in the phonological literature for stress languages, Poser calls this two-mora unit a **foot**. Since this unit consists of two morae, he further calls it a **bimoraic foot**. Now, we can say that hypocoristic formation, Geisha/bargirl client name formation, and Renyookei Reduplication all refer to a bimoraic foot. As for the musician's language game, clipping of loan words, and deverbal nouns in Nominal Clauses, the relevant conditions refer to four morae, namely, two bimoraic feet. The unit consisting of four morae is further referred to as a **colon**. It should be remembered that the notion of the mora has been shown to be significant in Japanese phonology. What the discussion above has demonstrated is that the bimoraic foot plays an important role in accounting for various phonological phenomena, and it provides further support to the relevance of the mora in Japanese.

Related to the significance of the bimoraic foot, the notion of the colon introduced just above has a further implication concerning the accentuation of compounds, already discussed in sections 4.4 and 4.5 above. The remainder of this section will be spent examining an analysis of accentuation of compounds advanced by Kubozono and Mester (1995). Recall that the previous analyses of compound accentuation considered earlier all assume that compounds should be divided into two categories on the basis of the length of the second member: if the second member of a compound is three morae or longer, the compound is considered a "long" compound, while if the second member consists of fewer than three morae, i.e. one or two morae, the compound is categorized as a "short" compound. Kubozono and Mester (1995), however, convincingly demonstrate that the standard classification of "long" vs. "short" compounds misses the important generalization that both "long" and "short" compounds exhibit the same accentuation pattern as long as the second member has FEWER THAN FIVE MORAE, i.e. four morae or less. In contrast, the accentuation of a compound whose second member consists of five morae or more clearly patterns differently. Thus, the question as to whether the second member is longer than a colon, namely, two bimoraic feet, leads to a proper generalization of compound accentuation.

On the basis of their new compound classification, Kubozono and Mester reach the following generalization: when the second member consists of four morae or fewer, the accent falls on the penultimate foot. To see the relevance of this generalization, consider (259), in which the second member is three or four morae, and (260)–(262), where the second member consists of one or two morae. Examples are taken from Kubozono and Mester (1995: 2–3) with a slightly modified gloss and notation.

(259)

               *   *

a. me + kusuri → megusuri "eye drop"

        *   *   *

b. isi + atama → isiatama "hard head"

        *   *   *

c. denki + kamisori → denkikamisori "electric razor"

        *   *   *

d. yamato + nadesiko → yamatonadesiko "Japanese woman"

(260)

               *   *

a. itokiri + ha → itokiriba "thread-cutting tooth"

        *   *   *

b. sikago + si → sikagosi "Chicago City"

        *   *   *

c. temuzu + kawa → temuzugawa "the Thames"

                    *

d. abura + musi → aburamusi "cockroach"

           *   *

e. sakura + kai → sakuragai "cherry tree shellfish"

        *   *   *

f. nekutai + pin → nekutaipin "necktie pin"

(261)

           *

a. ratai + ga → rataiga "nude picture"

            *

b. garasu + tama → garasudama "glass bead"

        *   *

c. syakai + too → syakaitoo "Socialist Party"

(262)

              *   *

a. momen + ito → momenito "cotton thread"

           *   *

b. faasuto + kisɯ → faasutokisu "first kiss"

Recall the standard distinction between "long" and "short" compounds: when the second member of a compound is three morae or longer, the compound is "long"; otherwise, a compound is "short". On the basis of this standard distinction, the compounds in (259) are all long while those in (260)–(262) are short. However, Kubozono and Mester show that the accentuation of all the compounds in (259)–(262) exhibits the same pattern.

First, consider (259). Kubozono and Mester claim that, regardless of the location of the original accent of the second member, the accent of the compound always falls on the penultimate foot. It is crucial to point out that a foot is constructed from the end of each word, i.e. from right to left, and that this foot construction operates on each member of a compound. After dividing each member into bimoraic feet, the compounds in (259) can be represented in (263).

(263)   *
    a.   me) (gu) (suri)
              *
    b.   isi) (a) (tama)
                 *
    c.   denki) (kami) (sori)
                 *
    d.   yamato) (nade) (siko)

The three-mora second member *kusuri* (realized as *gusuri* as a result of Rendaku) in (a) consists of two feet: the first two morae from the end of the word, *suri*, are considered to be a foot, and the rest of the word, i.e. *gu*, forms another. When we pay close attention to the location of the accent in (263), we notice that it is always on the penultimate foot that the accent of the compound falls. Hence, the generalization that an accent of a compound is on the penultimate foot correctly predicts the accentuation pattern of the words in (259).

Second, let us turn to the compounds in (260), which are traditionally treated as "short". We apply the same mechanism of foot construction to the second members, and the compounds are now represented as in (264).

(264)   *
    a.   itokiri) (ba)
              *
    b.   sikago) (si)
                *
    c.   temuzu) (gawa)
               *
    d.   abura) (musi)
               *
    e.   sakura) (gai)
               *
    f.   nekutai) (pin)

It should be remembered that a foot is constructed for each member of a compound. So, in the case of (264a) and (264b) above, where the second member consists of a single mora, the word itself forms a single foot. Notice that the accent of each compound falls on the penultimate foot. Hence, while the standard division of "long" and "short" compounds fails to provide a coherent account for the accentuation pattern of "short" compounds, the new approach under discussion generalizes the two classes into one: that is, in both cases, the accent of a compound falls on the penultimate foot.

On the other hand, the patterns illustrated in (261) and (262) appear to be problematic for such a unified account. Consider the same range of data with the constructed foot structure in (265)–(266).

(265) a.   ratai) (ga)   [accentless]
       b.   garasu) (dama) [accentless]
       c.   syakai) (too)   [accentless]

(266)

                              *

    a.   momen) (ito)

                    *

    b.   faasuto) (kisu)

The second member of each compound above consists of one or two morae. As is indicated, the compounds in (265) are all accentless; and the accent falls on the final foot in (266). These two cases, thus, cannot be explained by the generalization that the compound accent falls on the penultimate foot.

Kubozono and Mester, however, claim that when the three accentuation patterns for "short" compounds are statistically compared, the pattern exemplified in (260) is more general than those provided in (261) and (262), and that the vast majority of "short" compound cases still have their accents on the penultimate foot. Thus, they conclude that the compounds that have traditionally been analyzed as "short" and "long" exhibit the same accentuation pattern. Their analysis, then, provides not only an account for "short" compounds, for which no coherent analysis seems to have existed previously, but also a unified generalization for the accent pattern of both "long" and "short" compounds.

The generalization that the compound accent falls on the penultimate foot, however, does not hold for the sets of data in (267) and (268), as Kubozono and Mester further discuss. Examples are taken from Kubozono and Mester (1995: 6) with an additional foot notation.

(267)   *   *

       metiru + arukooru → metiru) (a) (ruko) (oru) "methyl alcohol"

(268)   a.   nyuu + karedonia → nyuu) (ka) (redo) (nia) "New Caledonia"
         b.   minami + kariforunia → minami) (kari) (foru) (nia) "southern California"

The second members of these compounds are all longer than four morae. Notice that the accent of each compound is not on the penultimate foot: it is on the third foot from the end in (267), and there is no accent in (268). According to Kubozono and Mester, when the second member is longer than four morae, i.e. five morae or more, the pattern exemplified in (268) is far more general than that in (267): that is, the accent of the second member predominates. It should be pointed out that while the pattern exemplified by (267) is also predicted by Tsujimura and Davis's (1987) analysis, the pattern in (268) is a crucial case that cannot be explained by their analysis.

Kubozono and Mester's analysis is summarized in (269).

(269)   a.   When the second member of a compound consists of two bimoraic feet or less, the accent of the compound falls on the penultimate foot.
         b.   When the second member of a compound is longer than two bimoraic feet, the accent of the second member predominates.

Previous approaches to the accent of compounds all assumed the division between "short" and "long" compounds, and left the accentuation pattern of "short" compounds unsolved. In contrast, Kubozono and Mester's analysis eliminates such a division and provides a unified explanation for the accent pattern.[31] The analysis summarized in (269) has an important consequence, regarding the notion of the colon introduced earlier. The crucial division that the analysis of (269) intends to capture is whether the second member is longer than two bimoraic feet, namely, a colon. We can now conclude that it is a colon that distinguishes between the two essential accentuation patterns in compounds: if the second member is longer than a colon, its original accent predominates; otherwise, the accent falls on the penultimate foot.

Notes

1   As Vance (1987), for example, notes, devoicing can occur with vowels other than the high vowels. Examples of such cases can be found in the first /o/ of /kokoro/ "heart", the first /o/ of /soko/ "there", and the first /a/ of /katana/ "sword". For further discussion, see Vance (1987) and the references cited there.

2   As was noted in chapter 2, the phonetic transcription [u] will be used, throughout this book, to represent the high back vowel in Japanese, although it should be understood as being unrounded. The phonetic transcription [t] as well as [k] and [p] in Japanese should be understood as being unaspirated.

3   More specifically, it is a high vowel without an accent on it that devoices, as seen by comparing *hasi* "bridge" and *hasi* "chopsticks": the high vowel on the former is accented, and thus does not devoice. See section 4 for a detailed discussion of accent in Japanese. Also, for the discussion of the relation between vowel devoicing and accent, see J. McCawley (1977), Haraguchi (1977), and Vance (1987).

4   We assume that each word, in the examples in (12), is followed by a pause. The phonetic transcription of the word-final /n/ as uvular nasal [N] reflects this assumption.

5   Given our rules in (15) and (16), one may wonder what the phonetic realization of the nasal sound may be when it is immediately followed by an alveo-palatal sound like [š] and [ǰ] and by a palatal sound like [y] and [ç], for instance. As the rules predict, the nasal sound is realized as alveo-palatal nasal, the phonetic symbol for which is [ň], and as palatal nasal, [ɲ], in these situations respectively. These sounds and the examples of assimilation have been briefly introduced in note 6 of chapter 2. Examples of assimilation that involve alveo-palatal nasal and palatal include *kansya* [kaňša] "gratitude" and *sanzyu* [saňǰuː] "thirty" for the former and *honya* [hoɲya] "bookstore" and *hinhin* [çiɲçiN] "neigh neigh" for the latter. Although in the present section we do not discuss these cases, the rules in (15) and (16) correctly account for these nasal sounds as well.

6   The nasal at the end of a syllable has a special status in Japanese phonology, and will be referred to as "moraic" /n/ later in section 3.

7   We will discuss the cases where /t/ is followed by the high front vowel /i/ later.

8   The word for *film* under (39) has another pronunciation, [ɸuirumu]. The occurrence of [ɸ] before [u] is predicted by (34e).

9   The phonetic realization of /tu/ as [tˢu] in (57a) and (57d) shows that the allophonic rule of (21), discussed in section 1.3 above, independently applies to these cases.

10 The necessity of rule ordering may also depend on how the rules are formulated. So, for example, if the rules in (73) are formulated differently by stating the environment differently, the rule ordering that we have come up with in our discussion above may not be the one that would derive an acceptable form.

11 Kubozono (1995) takes up the range of data similar to our (110)–(111) and discusses the relation between the internal structure of compounds and Rendaku in terms of branching.

12 Although the conditions in (117) account for the range of data we have dealt with in this section, there exist a number of examples that still resist Rendaku even when the conditions are met. For this reason, there has been a claim that Rendaku is not predictable (cf. Martin 1952). For a further discussion of examples of this sort, see Vance (1980).

13 Kubozono (1995) reports that the type illustrated in (121a) constitutes the majority (over 90 percent) of Japanese mora.

14 In his comparative investigation of Japanese and English, Kubozono (1995) discusses the relevance of mora to the formation of words that consist of parts of one or more words (technically called **blends**).

15 The phonemic diphthongs in English are /ay/ as in *pipe*, /ɔy/ as in *boy*, and /aw/ as in *cow*. It is possible to view diphthongs as being a sequence of two consecutive vowels that are within the same syllable. Thus, one may phonetically transcribe the English diphthongs as [aɪ], [ɔɪ], and [au]. In Japanese, as noted by Vance (1987: 16), any possible vowel sequence may be a diphthong.

16 It should be emphasized that according to the detailed study of Kubozono (1989), speech errors where an initial consonant of a syllable interchanges with an initial consonant of another syllable are rare in Japanese, though quite common in English as in (127a, c).

17 If the accentuation pattern of the Tokyo dialect were based solely on the mora, we would expect to find words of the pattern (C)VNCV (C = consonant, N = moraic nasal, V = vowel) with a low–high–low pitch pattern where the high pitch is on the moraic nasal. However, there are no such words occurring in the Tokyo dialect. This may suggest that the syllable does play a certain role in accounting for the pitch pattern of the dialect.

18 A study by Kubozono proposes the analysis that the notion of the syllable is more significant to various phonological phenomena in Japanese than it has been thought before. For a detailed discussion, see Kubozono (1993/1994).

19 The words *kokoro* "heart" in (164) and *kamisori* "razor" in (165) have alternative forms; the accent is placed on the last mora of both words. With such alternative accentuation patterns of the second member of the compounds in (164)–(165), the rules in (163) correctly predict the accentuation of these compounds. Nonetheless, this analysis still cannot account for the cases in (164)–(165).

20 See Kubozono and Mester (1995) for an analysis of the accentuation of short compounds. A brief discussion of their analysis will be introduced at the end of section 8 of this chapter.

21 All the examples of mimetics in the remainder of this section are given in Romanization. It should be kept in mind that the palatalized consonants are being interpreted as single consonants (despite the fact that palatalization is indicated as a sequence of two consonants in Romanization) since Japanese does not allow syllable-initial consonant clusters, as mentioned in section 3 of this chapter.

22 It is characteristic of the mimetic vocabulary that /r/ is not palatalized. There are examples of palatalized /r/ in non-mimetic words like *ryuukyuu* "Ryukyu", etc.

23 It should be noted that not all the examples in (225) are commonly used as loan words.

24 There are some exceptions to this generalization, as is exemplified by *beer* pronounced as [bi:ru].
25 For a more detailed analysis of loan-word phonology, see Lovins (1975).
26 Postpositions will be discussed in chapter 4.
27 The label "Nom" is the abbreviation of Nominative Case particle. Particles and their treatment as Case will be discussed in chapter 4, section 1.6.
28 The label "Top" is the abbreviation of Topic marker.
29 For a slightly different version of this language game, see Ito et al. (1996).
30 The label "Acc" is the abbreviation of Accusative Case particle.
31 Crucially, though, in so-called short compound data like those in (260), Kubozono and Mester only consider such forms when the first member is more than two morae. They do not consider data like those in (186) and (189) where the first member is one or two morae. According to Kubozono (personal communication), such forms do not behave phonologically like compounds, and have unpredictable accentuation like single lexical items.

Suggested Readings

General issues in Japanese phonology: J. McCawley (1968), Vance (1987), Shibatani (1990). A number of initial observations on which later analyses have been based are included in J. McCawley (1968). Vance (1987) discusses essential issues in Japanese phonology, and also serves as a source for references.

Verbal conjugation: J. McCawley (1968), Vance (1987), Tsujimura and Davis (1989), Davis and Tsujimura (1991). The last two works present a detailed analysis of the alternations that occur when the past tense marker -*ta* is added to the verb stem. Their analysis is given within the framework of Autosegmental Phonology. Also, see the references cited there for previous analyses.

Rendaku: J. McCawley (1968), Kindaichi (1976a), Otsu (1980), Vance (1980, 1982, 1987), Ito and Mester (1986, 2003), Kuroda (2002). Ito and Mester (1986) provide a theoretical analysis of Rendaku within the theory of Underspecification. Ito and Mester (2003) is a more recent and extended treatment of the phenomenon in Optimality Theory.

Speech errors: Fromkin (1971, 1973) (speech errors in English), Tabusa (1982), Kubozono (1985, 1989). Tabusa (1982) contains a large corpus of speech errors in Japanese. Kubozono (1985, 1989) discusses the theoretical implications of Japanese speech errors on issues related to mora and syllable.

Language games: Tateishi (1989), Poser (1990), Haraguchi (1991), Ito et al. (1996). Tateishi (1989), Poser (1990), and Ito et al. (1996) deal with musicians' language while Haraguchi (1991) discusses the "babibu" language. All these four works consider the theoretical implications of the language games they discuss.

Mora vs. syllable: Beckman (1982), Port et al. (1987), Kubozono (1993/1994, 1995, 1999, 2003), Davis and Ueda (2003). A controversy concerning the status of the mora as a timing unit is observed in the first three works. They discuss experimental phonetic evidence. Kubozono (1993/1994, 2003) examine the role of the syllable in Japanese phonology. Kubozono (1999) gives an overview of the topic. Davis and Ueda (2003) examines the relevance of mora demonstrated in a dialect.

Accent: J. McCawley (1968, 1977), Haraguchi (1977), Hyman (1977), Higurashi (1983), Poser (1984), Beckman (1986), Tenny (1986), Tsujimura and Davis (1987), Vance (1987), Pierrehumbert and Beckman (1988), Tsujimura (1989), Shibatani (1990), Kubozono (1994), Kubozono and Mester (1995), among many others. Haraguchi (1977) and Shibatani (1990) both provide a detailed illustration of dialectal variation of accentuation patterns, and in addition Haraguchi (1977) develops a theoretical account of accentuation patterns of various dialects within the Autosegmental Theory. Issues concerning the accentuation patterns observed with compounds are included in J. McCawley (1977), Higurashi (1983), Tsujimura and Davis (1987), and Kubozono and Mester (1995). Accentual variation among different endings is discussed in Higurashi (1983), Tenny (1986), and Tsujimura (1989). The last two works consider implications for the theory of Lexical Phonology. Poser (1984), Beckman (1986), Pierrehumbert and Beckman (1988), and Kubozono (1994) investigate issues related to accent in Japanese from an experimental phonetics viewpoint.

Mimetics: Hamano (1986, 1998), Mester and Ito (1989). Hamano (1986, 1998) contain a very detailed description of Japanese mimetics. Mester and Ito (1989) provides a theoretical analysis of the palatalization phenomenon observed in mimetics.

Loan words: Lovins (1975), Katayama (1998), Shinohara (2000). Katayama (1998) presents an Optimality Theoretic analysis of loan words.

Casual speech and fast speech: N. Hasegawa (1979), Shibatani (1990).

Length requirement: Tateishi (1989), Ito (1990), Poser (1990), Tsujimura (1992), Kubozono and Mester (1995), Suzuki (1995), Kurisu (2005). Poser (1990) provides a thorough investigation of length requirements as well as their theoretical implications. Kurisu (2005) examines the effects of minimality on a number of different reduplicative structures in Japanese.

EXERCISES

1 The items under list A are linguistic terms that have been introduced in this chapter, and those under list B are the examples and definitions of those terms. Choose an appropriate example(s) that matches each linguistic term.

List A	*List B*
allophones	the second consonant of a long consonant
onset	*nuri-basi* "lacquered chopsticks"
mora	*potapota* "dripping"
Rendaku	the syllable-final consonant
phonetic transcription	/aki/

obstruents   moraic /n/
contraction   the syllable-initial consonant
palatalization   fricatives and liquid
long compounds   [tˢ], [č], and [t]
"babibu" language   [aki]
                              netyanetya "sticky"
                              /z/
                              kobokoborobo
                              stops and affricates
                              yunyuu-kudamono "imported fruits"
                              mite simau → mityau "have seen"

2 Provide phonetic transcriptions for the following nonsense words in
   Japanese, and for each word, state the consonant changes (or formalize
   the rules) with a clear description of their environments.

   a. /misutuka/
   b. /yasosin/
   c. /setuhita/
   d. /tiisahu/
   e. /aenbusi/
   f. /ozikaze/
   g. /satigahi/
   h. /humonkezi/
   i. /metinrengetu/

3 How many morae are there in the following words?

   a. kankei
   b. ikebana
   c. sekken
   d. aizyoo
   e. sikenkan
   f. saiban

4 Recall our discussion of the "babibu" language game in Japanese.
   How would a speaker of the "babibu" language form the following
   words? Provide the appropriate forms in the "babibu" language.

   a. kamisori
   b. azisai
   c. kuukoo
   d. kekkan
   e. oisii

5   In section 1.6 of this chapter, we have discussed several (morpho)-
    phonological rules involved in verbal conjugation. Consider the follow-
    ing two rules that have been observed.

    a.   t → d / n + ____ (= (52b))
    b.   t → d / g + ____ (= (61))

    These two rules are very similar in that they both change /t/ to [d].
    Show how these two rules can be put together into one. Also, discuss
    why this change in voicing might occur.

6   The following set of data illustrates one type of verbal conjugation
    pattern not discussed in the text. (The symbol under the high front
    vowel indicates that it is voiceless.)

    a.   /sas + ta/   →   [sašita]   "pointed"
    b.   /kas + ta/   →   [kašita]   "lent"
    c.   /sagas + ta/ →   [sagašita]   "looked for"
    d.   /utus + ta/   →   [utsušita]   "reflected"
    e.   /kaes + ta/   →   [kaešita]   "returned"
    f.   /kos + ta/   →   [košita]   "changed one's living place"

    A.   Describe all the phonological changes involved in the formation
         of the past tense form of the verbs listed above.
    B.   Discuss the ordering of the rules you have come up with in
         deriving the set of data above.

7   In section 6 we have examined some of the phonological changes
    involved when a word is borrowed into Japanese. Find 10 words in
    Japanese that have been borrowed from English (you may ask a native
    speaker of Japanese). In phonetic transcription, transcribe the original
    English words and similarly the words after being borrowed into
    Japanese; compare the two sets of transcription. Keeping in mind
    the sorts of phonological changes discussed in section 6, describe the
    differences between the English pronunciation and the Japanese pro-
    nunciation of the words that you collected. Do you think the changes
    that have occurred are unpredictable or is there a certain pattern to
    some of them? Briefly discuss.

8   Explain how the following nonsense words are realized with respect
    to their pitch pattern in the Tokyo dialect. Indicate the pitch patterns
    by using "H" and "L", and justify your answers.

    *

a. kaimi LHLL

      *

b. sisatare LHHLL

    *

c. toraaho HLLL

d. hamesu (unaccented) LHHH

     *

e. katabako LHLL

9 Assuming that the initial consonant of the second member of each compound is a potential Rendaku site, how would these words phonetically be realized? Give the phonetic transcriptions of the resulting compounds.

  a. siro + kuti
  b. misi + hikori
  c. yoko + tazu
  d. wasa + sine
  e. ora + tigo
  f. name + huzuna
  g. mesa + tukasa
  h. tene + hazesi

10 Draw an analysis tree and predict the output of Rendaku for each of the following compounds.

  a. ori + kami → "paper for folding"
    folding paper
  b. ori + kami + tana → "shelf for paper for folding"
    folding paper shelf
  c. ori + kami + tana +tukuri → "making a shelf for paper
    folding paper shelf making for folding"

11 There are two honorific markers for nouns, i.e. *o-* and *go-*. The addition of these markers to nouns demonstrates changes in accentuation. Focusing on the locations of the accent before and after the addition of these honorific markers, come up with two generalizations. You should base your analysis solely on the following data.

  *   *

hasi → ohasi "chopsticks"

 *   *

hon → gohon "book"

```
 *
kome → okome "rice"
kane → okane "money"
mizu → omizu "water"
 *        *
rikai → gorikai "understanding"
 *        *
genki → ogenki "good health"
 *        *
syuzin → gosyuzin "husband"
 *
kokoro → okokoro "heart"
 *
atama → oatama "head"
 *
zasiki → ozasiki "room with tatami mats"
ryokoo → goryokoo "travel"
kigen → gokigen "feeling"
sakana → osakana "fish"
maturi → omaturi "festival"
 *        *
aisatu → goaisatu "greetings"
 *
aisoo → oaisoo "friendliness"
kyooryoku → gokyooryoku "cooperation"
benkyoo → (g)obenkyoo "studying"
```

12 We have discussed how the accent of a word can shift in com-
    pounds, and also how various endings have effects on accentuation
    shifts. Given the verbal stem on the left of the arrow, the output of
    the additional verbal tentative -(y)oo and that of the present tense
    -(r)u on the right of the arrow result in a different accentuation
    pattern. (The accentuation of the verbal stem is judged on the basis
    of the accent on its gerundive form; you can ignore how it was
    determined.)

List A
```
        *                 *
a.  tabe + yoo → tabeyoo "let's eat"
                          *
b.  yorokob + (y)oo → yorokoboo "let's get pleased"
           *                 *
c.  araware + yoo → arawareyoo "let's appear"
                      *
d.  ire + yoo → ireyoo "let's put in"
```

List B

a.   tabe + ru → taberu "eat"

b.   yorokob + (r)u → yorokobu "get pleased"

c.   araware + ru → arawareru "appear"

d.   tanom + (r)u → tanomu "ask"

e.   kangae + ru → kangaeru "think"
f.   ire + (r)u → ireru "put in"
g.   sawar + (r)u → sawaru "touch"

Answer the following questions on the basis of the above data.

A.   Where does the accent fall on the derived verbal tentative words featured in list A?
B.   What is the condition of the accent shift involved in the addition of the verbal tentative ending -(y)oo?
C.   Where does the accent fall on the derived verbal present tense words featured in list B?
D.   What is the condition of the accent shift involved in the addition of the present tense ending -(r)u?

13   It has been observed that the accentuation pattern of loan words in Tokyo Japanese is largely predictable. Answer the following questions.

A.   On the basis of the following data, describe the location of the accent.

a.   masuku   "mask"

b.   kurasu   "class"

c.   razio   "radio"

d.   aisu   "ice"

e.   hausu   "house"

f.   raito   "light"

g.   sutoobu   "heater"

h.   sutoraiku "strike (baseball)"

B. Now, consider the following set of the data. Observe the location of the accent. Can the description given in A above fit the data below? If it does not, provide a generalization that describes the accent location of the words listed below. (You do not need to consider the set of data under A above.)

   a.　ere̊beetaa　　"elevator"

   b.　wåsinton　　"Washington"

   c.　kare̊ndaa　　"calendar"

   e.　mane̊ezyaa　"manager"

   f.　ko̊ronbusu　"Columbus"

   g.　saidåa　　　"cider"

   h.　esukareetaa　"escalator"

C. On the basis of the two generalizations you have given above, try to unify them so that a single generalization would account for both sets of data.

D. Discuss what sort of bearing your generalization might have on the notion of syllable and/or mora.

14　Given the discussion of the conditions pertinent to the mimetic palatalization, consider the following nonsense mimetic words. Which are well-formed mimetics? Which ones are ill-formed? State the reason for your answer.

   a.　gutyagutya
   b.　pyasupyasu
   c.　guzyaguzya
   d.　zumyozumyo
   e.　ryaburyabu
   f.　syakusyaku

4 Morphology

How do we identify words? In spoken language words are pronounced continuously. There are no pauses between words. This is true in both English and Japanese. In English writing, however, words are spelled individually and space is given between words, at least to some degree providing us with a means to identify words. In Japanese writing, on the other hand, there is no space between words, so we cannot rely on such a visual device.

The question of how to identify words perhaps boils down to a more fundamental question, "What is a word?" This is indeed a very difficult question. For example, ask yourself whether *waterbed*, *fortune-teller*, *salad dressing*, *book return*, *teapot*, and *round-trip* each constitute a single word. Also, ask yourself whether *don't*, *wouldn't*, *wanna*, *gonna*, *I'm*, and *you're* are each one word or two words. You will immediately realize it is not always straightforward to identify words. A more extreme example is seen in an American Indian language, Potawatomi. A string of sound *kwapmuknanuk* means "They see us" (cf. Fromkin and Rodman 1993). Is it a word, a sentence, or something else?

Despite the lack of clues with which to identify words in written Japanese, as well as for spoken language in general, native speakers know the words of the language. Knowing a word means knowing the sound and meaning of the word; this, in turn, relies on various sorts of information. Such information primarily comes from four different areas: phonology, morphology, syntax, and semantics. The speaker knows how the word is pronounced (phonological information) and can figure out what it means (semantic information). She or he is also aware of whether a word consists of more than one meaningful element (morphological information), and knows how a word is used in a larger context such as in a phrase or in a sentence (syntactic information). Granting that any attempt to define the word leaves at least some questions unanswered, we characterize it as a free-standing sound–meaning unit.

This chapter focuses on the **morphology** of Japanese, the area that deals with how words are formed and the internal structure of words. Moreover, we will take a brief look at how morphological processes interact with phonology, semantics, and syntax.

1 Parts of Speech Categories

Words have syntactic labels which are essential in forming phrases and sentences in syntax. These labels are called **parts of speech categories** or simply **categories**. As we will see below, it is often the case that a single property cannot define a category. For this reason, it is important to keep in mind that a cluster of characteristics eventually leads to the identification of each category.

1.1 Nouns

The first category we take up is **nouns**. Nouns can co-occur with demonstratives such as *kono* "this" and *sono* "that", as in *kono hana* "this flower" and *sono hon* "that book".

Nouns can take noun modifiers which precede them, and these noun modifiers take the particle *no* (the Genitive Case particle). For example, consider the phrases in (1).[1]

(1) a. Taroo-no hon
         Taro-Gen book
         "Taro's book"
     b. kinoo-no   sinbun
         yesterday-Gen newspaper
         "yesterday's paper"
     c. Tookyoo-no tizu
         Tokyo-Gen map
         "a map of Tokyo"
     d. sensoo-no hanasi
         war-Gen   story
         "a story about the war"

Hon "book", *sinbun* "newspaper", *tizu* "map", and *hanasi* "story" in these examples are nouns that are modified by a preceding noun. In (1a), for instance, the noun *hon* "book" is modified by the preceding noun, i.e. *Taroo*. In order to mediate the possessive relation between these two nouns, the Genitive Case particle *-no* intervenes between the two. The type of prenominal modification mediated by the Genitive Case particle *-no* is not limited to the possessive relation. As the rest of the examples in (1) shows, it ranges over a variety of relations between the two nouns.

A noun can also be a member of a conjunct linked by *to* "and", as in *otoko to onna* "man and woman" and *susi to sasimi* "sushi and sashimi". Unlike in English, the conjunctive word *to* can combine only nouns, disallowing conjoined adjectives like **ookii to ii* "big and good" and conjoined verbs such as **iku to kau* "go and buy", and hence *to* "and" serves as a helpful clue to the identity of nouns.

While English can identify nouns by the distribution of articles such as *a/an* and *the*, as in *an apple* and *the cat*, Japanese lacks articles entirely, and thus they cannot be used to identify nouns. Furthermore, the equivalent of the singular and plural distinction in English is generally not available in Japanese: that is, there is no plural marking such as the English ending *-(e)s*. Although the plural marker *-tati*, as in *kodomo-tati* "children" and *gakusei-tati* "students", is available, its use is extremely limited in that it can apply only to humans, and hence plurality cannot be a good gauge for the status of nouns.[2]

What further separates Japanese nouns from English nouns is that Japanese nouns are associated with a conjugational paradigm, illustrated in (2) with the noun *hon* "book".[3]

(2) a. *non-past*   hon-da   "it is a book"
     b. *non-past neg.* hon-zya na-i   "it's not a book"
     c. *past*   hon-dat-ta   "it was a book"
     d. *past neg.*   hon-zya na-kat-ta   "it wasn't a book"
     e. *tentative*   hon-daroo   "it is probably a book"

When a noun appears with the noun conjugation paradigm, as is shown above, it is used as a predicate of a clause. Recall that I have stated earlier that the conjunctive word *to* can combine only nouns. However, when nouns are used predicatively, appearing with the conjugation pattern depicted in (2), they cannot be conjoined by *to*. This is shown in (3).

(3) a. Taroo-wa nihonzin-da.
         Taro-Top Japanese-is
         "Taro is a Japanese person."
     b. Taroo-wa doitugo-no   sensei-da.
         Taro-Top German-Gen teacher-is
         "Taro is a German teacher."
     c. *Taroo-wa nihonzin-to   doitugo-no   sensei-da.
         Taro-Top   Japanese-and German-Gen teacher-is
         "Taro is a Japanese person and German teacher."

1.2 Verbs

Verbs in Japanese are most readily identified by the various conjugational endings that can be placed on them. For example, the non-past tense ending *-(r)u* is attached exclusively to verbal roots, where the term "root" refers to a meaningful unit which cannot be given further morphological analysis. Consider the examples in (4).

(4) a. tabe-ru "eat"
     b. yom-u   "read"
     c. mi-ru   "see"
     d. nom-u   "drink"
     e. kaer-u   "return"

When the ending *-(r)u* is added to a verbal root, the resulting form is a non-past tense form of the verb.

The past tense ending *-ta/da* as well as the gerund-forming ending *-te/de* can also be added to a verbal root without being interrupted by anything between them. The examples in (5) are the past tense forms and the gerundive forms of the verbs listed in (4) above.

(5) | | *past tense* | *gerund* | *gloss* |
|---|---|---|---|
| a. | tabe-ta | tabe-te | "eat" |
| b. | yon-da | yon-de | "read" |
| c. | mi-ta | mi-te | "see" |
| d. | non-da | non-de | "drink" |
| e. | kaet-ta | kaet-te | "return" |

Notice that the past tense forming *-ta/da* and the gerund forming *-te/de* are added immediately to the right of the verbal root. Some phonological changes take place as a consequence of these additions, as was discussed concerning the past tense ending in chapter 3.

Verbal roots can be accompanied by the ending *-(i)ta-* "want to" in the desiderative form of a verb, as in *tabe-ta-* "want to eat", *nom-ita-* "want to drink". The desiderative ending is realized as *-ita-* when the verbal root ends in a consonant and as *-ta-* when it ends in a vowel. Again, the desiderative ending *-ta-* is attached only to verbs.

Verbs can be divided into two types, transitive verbs and intransitive verbs. The former take a direct object while the latter do not. (6) and (7) present examples of transitive verbs and intransitive verbs, respectively.

(6) a. Taroo-ga ringo-o tabe-ta.
    Taro-Nom apple-Acc eat-past
    "Taro ate an apple."
  b. Hanako-ga doresu-o kat-ta.
    Hanako-Nom dress-Acc buy-past
    "Hanako bought a dress."

(7) a. Kodomo-ga warat-ta.
    child-Nom laugh-past
    "A child laughed."
  b. Ziroo-ga oyoi-da.
    Ziro-Nom swim-past
    "Ziro swam."

The words *tabe-ta* "ate" and *kat-ta* "bought" in (6) are verbs since they are accompanied by the past tense ending *-ta* and nothing intervenes between the roots and *-ta*. Furthermore, they are both transitive verbs because they occur with direct objects, i.e. *ringo* "apple" in (6a) and *doresu* "dress" in (6b). The verbs in (7), also so identified by the past tense ending, are intransitive. Being intransitive, these verbs do not appear with direct objects.

The transitive vs. intransitive dichotomy has some relevance to morphology, and it is reflected in the presence of morphologically related transitive and intransitive verb pairs (cf. Shibatani 1973a; Jacobsen 1981; Tsujimura 1989). Some transitive verbs and intransitive verbs resemble each other, and form morphologically related verb pairs. These pairs are generated by adding a set of transitive/intransitive-forming endings to verbal roots. This is illustrated in (8)–(11).

		intransitive	*transitive*	*gloss*
(8)	a.	tao-**re**	tao-**s**	"fall"
	b.	tubu-**re**	tubu-**s**	"press"
	c.	naga-**re**	naga-**s**	"float"
(9)	a.	nao-**r**	nao-**s**	"mend"
	b.	noko-**r**	noko-**s**	"leave behind"
	c.	too-**r**	too-**s**	"pass"
(10)	a.	tasuk-**ar**	tasuk-**e**	"help, rescue"
	b.	sag-**ar**	sag-**e**	"lower"
	c.	kim-**ar**	kim-**e**	"decide"
(11)	a.	ok-**i**	ok-**os**	"get up"
	b.	ot-**i**	ot-**os**	"fall"
	c.	horob-**i**	horob-**os**	"destroy"

In each pair of transitive and intransitive verbs, a root portion is shared by the two: *tao*, *tubu*, and *naga* in (8), for instance. The endings -*re*/-*s*, -*r*/-*s*, -*ar*/-*e*, and -*i*/-*os* are added to the roots to form the intransitive–transitive verb pairs. The intransitive/transitive-forming endings are not limited to those illustrated above, as is demonstrated in detail by Jacobsen (1981), and it is not clear why a certain ending is selected by a particular verbal root. However, there are a restricted number of transitive/intransitive-forming endings available in Japanese, and by recognizing these endings, we can determine which member is transitive and which member is intransitive for most cases. Thus, by recognizing the shared verbal root as well as a limited set of endings that are placed adjacent to it, we can morphologically relate transitive and intransitive verb pairs like those in (8)–(11). We will examine morphologically related transitive and intransitive verb pairs again, more closely, in section 5.

As a sub-class of the category verb, some of the verbs in Japanese can also be used as **auxiliary verbs**. When used as such, they are added to certain forms of regular verbs. The auxiliary verbs often lose their basic meanings, and sometimes add a meaning that is only somewhat related to the basic meanings that they have as independent verbs. For instance, the verb *ku-ru* (come-non-past) counts as a full-fledged verb that means "come", but it can also follow a gerund form of another verb, serving as an auxiliary verb. When it is used as an auxiliary verb, it induces the meaning of "begin V-ing". Compare the two sentences in (12) and (13).

(12) Taroo-ga asita ku-ru.
Taro-Nom tomorrow come-non-past
"Taro will come tomorrow."

(13) Ame-ga hut-te-<u>ku</u>-ru.
rain-Nom fall-gerund-come-non-past
"It begins to rain."

In (12) *ku-ru* is a full-fledged verb and means "come". In (13), by contrast, *ku-ru* immediately follows the gerund form of the verb *hur* "fall", serving as an auxiliary verb.[4] Notice that the original meaning "come" is not apparent in (13). Instead, together with the verb to which it is added, it induces a construction-specific meaning, i.e. "begin V-ing". It should also be pointed out that auxiliary verbs carry the verbal conjugation paradigm. Other examples of verbs that can be used as auxiliary verbs include *simau* "put X away" and *miru* "see": when they are added to the gerund of a verb, they respectively mean "finish V-ing" and "try X-ing", as is illustrated in (14)–(15).

(14) Taroo-ga susi-o zenbu tabe-te-<u>simat</u>-ta.
Taro-Nom sushi-Acc all   eat-gerund-put away-past
"Taro finished eating all the sushi."

(15) Hanako-ga akai doresu-o ki-te-<u>mi</u>-ta.
Hanako-Nom red dress-Acc put on-gerund-see-past
"Hanako tried the red dress on."

1.3 Adjectives

As was the case with verbs, **adjectives** are identified by a variety of conjugational endings, such as the non-past tense ending *-i*, the non-past negative ending *-ku-na-i*, and the past tense ending *-kat-ta*, as is illustrated in (16).

(16)

	non-past	*non-past negative*	*past*
a.	ooki-i	ooki-ku-na-i	ooki-kat-ta
	"it is big"	"it's not big"	"it was big"
b.	aka-i	aka-ku-na-i	aka-kat-ta
	"it is red"	"it's not red"	"it was red"
c.	taka-i	taka-ku-na-i	taka-kat-ta
	"it is high"	"it's not high"	"it was high"
d.	too-i	too-ku-na-i	too-kat-ta
	"it is far"	"it's not far"	"it was far"
e.	samu-i	samu-ku-na-i	samu-kat-ta
	"it is cold"	"it's not cold"	"it was cold"

All the adjectives in their non-past tense forms contain the ending *-i*; those in their non-past negative forms exhibit *-ku-na-i*, where *-i* is the non-past tense ending; and those in their past tense forms end with *-kat-ta*. Notice that the past tense ending *-kat-ta* in (16) resembles the past tense ending *-ta* for verbs, as we have observed in (5). This similarity can be explained by isolating *-ta* as signaling past tense for both verbs and adjectives. The only difference between the two, then, is that in the case of adjectives, the past tense ending cannot be immediately adjacent to the adjectival root; rather, it must be preceded by *-kat-*.

Adjectives are placed before nouns to modify them. For example, the adjective *ooki-i* "big" modifies *kuruma* "car" in *ooki-i kuruma* "big car". A similar modification relation is observed between the adjective *taka-i* "high, expensive" and the noun *uti* "house" in *taka-i uti* "expensive house".

1.4 Adverbs

Just as adverbs in English are often formed by adding *-ly* to adjectives, so are many Japanese **adverbs** formed from adjectives by adding *-ku* to the adjectival root. Compare the adjectives in the non-past tense forms (i.e. the citation forms) and the adverbs derived from them in (17).

(17)　　*adjective*　*adverb*　*gloss*
　　a.　ooki-i　　ooki-ku　　"big"
　　b.　aka-i　　　aka-ku　　　"red"
　　c.　taka-i　　　taka-ku　　"high, expensive"
　　d.　too-i　　　too-ku　　　"far"
　　e.　samu-i　　samu-ku　　"cold"

Given the list in (17), we immediately notice the similarity between these adverbs and the non-past negative adjectives in (16) above. That is, the non-past negative forms of adjectives and adverbs share the adjectival root plus *-ku* sequence, and yet the two belong to different categories, i.e. the one belonging to the adjective category and the other to the adverb. The difference is that the adjective roots can take *-ku*, but at the same time they further need to add more endings immediately to their right. The negative ending of *-na-i* is one such example. On the other hand, an adverb consists of an adjectival root and *-ku*, and nothing more. So, such words end with *-ku* and cannot be further added to. Hence, the category of the word should be adverb, rather than adjective.

Although many adverbs are derived from adjectival roots, there are also independent adverbs which do not find their corresponding adjectives. They include *totemo* "very", *zutto* "by far", *motto* "more", *zenzen* "(not) at all", *zettai* "never", *ainiku* "unfortunately", *kanarazu* "always, for sure", and *tabun* "probably", among many more.

In sentences, adverbs modify adjectives, verbs, other adverbs, and even whole sentences, as is illustrated in (18).

(18)　a.　Ano eiga-wa　　**totemo** kanasi-i.
　　　　　that movie-Top　very　　sad-non-past
　　　　　"That movie is very sad."

b. Niku-wa **zettai** tabe-na-i.
meat-Top never eat-not-non-past
"(I) never eat meat."

c. Taroo-wa Hanako-yori **zutto** haya-ku ki-ta.
Taro-Top Hanako-than by far early come-past
"Taro came a lot earlier than Hanako."

d. **Ainiku** ame-ga huri-dasi-ta.
unfortunately rain-Nom fall-start-past
"Unfortunately it started to rain."

The adverb in (18a), *totemo* "very", modifies the adjective *kanasi-i* "sad". The adverb *zettai* "never" in (18b) modifies the negative form of the verb *tabe* "eat". In (18c) *zutto* "by far" modifies another adverb *haya-ku* "early", which is based on the adjective *haya(-i)* "early". Finally, *ainiku* "unfortunately" in (18d) modifies the entire sentence.

1.5 Postpositions

The four categories described thus far, i.e. nouns, verbs, adjectives, and adverbs, are available in both Japanese and English. There are several categories that are present in Japanese but not in English, however. Postpositions constitute an example. **Postpositions** are the Japanese counterpart of **prepositions** in English, and as the term indicates, postpositions are placed AFTER nouns while prepositions occur BEFORE nouns. This positional difference can be observed by comparing the examples in (19) with the accompanying English translation.

(19) a. uti-de
house-at
"at home"

b. gakkoo-e
school-to
"to school"

c. tomodati-to
friend-with
"with a friend"

d. gozi-made
5 o'clock-until
"until 5 o'clock"

e. yama-kara
mountain-from
"from the mountain"

Postpositions in Japanese include *de* "at", *e* "to", *to* "with", *made* "until", and *kara* "from" in (19). As these examples show, the postposition is placed after the noun. The English translation of each phrase indicates that the corresponding prepositions appear before the noun.

Postpositions cannot stand independently. That is, if a postposition is stranded by itself in a phrase or in a sentence, there is no way we can interpret it. Thus, postpositions always occur with accompanying nouns in order to form a meaningful unit. The illustration in (19) also shows that postpositions in Japanese tend to be phonetically short, either monomoraic (i.e. consisting of a single mora) or comprising two morae. Recall that at the beginning of this chapter, we characterized a word as a free-standing sound–meaning unit. Under this characterization, then, their dependent nature places Japanese postpositions outside the word class.

It is worth noting that the conjugation paradigm of nouns observed in (2) above is sometimes found with the noun–postposition sequence. This is illustrated in (20).

(20) a. Gozi-made **da.**   "It is until 5 o'clock."
      b. Gozi-made **zya nai.**   "It is not until 5 o'clock."
      c. Gozi-made **dat-ta.**   "It was until 5 o'clock."
      d. Gozi-made **zya na-kat-ta.**   "It was not until 5 o'clock."
      e. Gozi-made **daroo.**   "It is probably until 5 o'clock."

As Jorden with Noda (1987) notes, however, the noun–postposition sequence with the conjugation pattern as depicted in (20) does not appear without a prior context. Instead, Jorden explains that *da, zya nai, dat-ta*, etc. in (20) are in fact "used as a replacement for the specific predicate of the previous utterance" (p. 209).

1.6 Case Particles

Case particles constitute an interesting element among Japanese categories. Case particles include Nominative (Nom) -*ga*, Accusative (Acc) -*o*, Dative (Dat) -*ni*, and Genitive (Gen) -*no*, and to these we add the Topic (Top) marker -*wa*. Examples are shown in (21).

(21) a. Taroo-ga   hasit-ta.
          Taro-Nom run-past
          "Taro ran."
      b. Kodomo-ga hon-o   yon-da.
          child-Nom   book-Acc read-past
          "The child read the book."
      c. Ziroo-ga Yosio-ni   ringo-o   age-ta.
          Ziro-Nom Yoshio-Dat apple-Acc give-past
          "Ziro gave an apple to Yoshio."
      d. Hanako-no   musuko-ga warat-ta.
          Hanako-Gen son-Nom   laugh-past
          "Hanako's son laughed."
      e. Ano uti-wa   ooki-i.
          that house-Top big-non-past
          "As for that house, it is big."

The Nominative Case *-ga*, exemplified in (21a–d), normally indicates that the accompanying noun is the subject of the sentence. The Accusative Case *-o*, as in (21b, c), marks the noun that immediately precedes it as the direct object. The Dative Case *-ni* in (21c) is primarily associated with verbs of giving, and together with a noun, it implies the recipient. The Genitive Case *-no* is used to establish a modification relation to the following noun, as in (21d). The nature of this modification includes the possessor–possessed relation, and in such a case, the Genitive Case particle is similar to English *'s* as in *Tony's car*. And, finally, the Topic marker *-wa* singles out an accompanying noun as the topic of the sentence. So, the Case particles in Japanese, for the most part, resemble the Case system in languages like Latin. Consider the Latin sentence in (22), taken from Napoli (1993: 51).

(22) Galli   gentem   expugnaverant.
      gaul-II-P-Nom people-III-S-Acc take by storm-3P-Pluperfect
      "The Gauls had taken the people by storm."
      (P = plural; S = singular; 3 = third person; II = second declension; III = third declension. A DECLENSION is a noun class, and membership in a declension determines the Case endings for singular and plural.)

In this Latin sentence, the Nominative Case and Accusative Case are used to mark the accompanying nouns, respectively, as the subject and as the object of the sentence.

Despite the apparent functional similarity to Case systems employed in various languages such as Latin, Russian, and Old English, Japanese Case particles exhibit unique properties that give them a distinct status. For example, in many Case systems, individual Case endings are considered a part of nouns, as the Classical Latin examples in (23) on the basis of the noun *lupus* "wolf" show, and it is not conceivable to represent a noun without a Case; in Japanese, on the other hand, Nominative and Accusative Case particles may sometimes be dropped, especially in casual speech, as is illustrated in (24).

(23)

Case	*noun stem*		*Case ending*		
nominative	lup	+	us	lupus	The wolf runs.
genitive	lup	+	i	lupi	A sheep in *wolf's* clothing.
dative	lup	+	ō	lupō	Give food *to the wolf*.
accusative	lup	+	um	lupum	I love *the wolf*.
ablative	lup	+	ō	lupō	Run *from the wolf*.
vocative	lup	+	e	lupe	*Wolf*, come here!

(Fromkin and Rodman 1993: 328)

(24) a. Tomodati(-ga) kita?
          friend(-Nom) came
          "Has my friend come?"
      b. Atarasii eiga(-o)   mita?
          new   movie(-Acc) saw
          "Have you seen the new movie?"

Furthermore, Nominative and Accusative Case particles in Japanese can be replaced by some morphemes including *mo* "also" and *sae* "even", which constitutes another property that is not observed in other Case systems. The examples in (25)–(26) demonstrate Case particle substitution.

(25) a. Hanako-ga   otya-o nonda.
        Hanako-Nom tea-Acc drank
        "Hanako drank tea."
     b. Taroo-mo otya-o nonda.
        Taro-also tea-Acc drank
        "Taro also drank tea."

(26) a. Taroo-wa zitensya-o   motteinai.
        Taro-Top bicycle-Acc not have
        "Taro does not have a bicycle."
     b. Taroo-wa zitensya-sae motteinai.
        Taro-Top bicycle-even not have
        "Taro doesn't even have a bicycle (e.g., let alone a car)."

Hence, Japanese Case particles resemble the Case systems in other languages in that they mark the grammatical functions of accompanying nouns in a sentence, but they also exhibit a unique set of properties that are not commonly observed in other Case systems.

It should be pointed out that Case particles in (21) resemble the postpositions in (19): they cannot stand by themselves and always seem to attach to a noun, and furthermore, they are all monomoraic. In this sense, Case particles are also outside the word class. However, the difference between these two categories is significant. Postpositions, in general, bear an inherent meaning. For example, *de* "at" implies location, and *to* "with" has comitative meaning. Case particles, in contrast, do not bear specific semantic content. Rather, their roles are more functionally determined within a sentence in that they indicate that in a sentence the accompanying noun functions as subject, object, and so forth. Furthermore, while Case particles can often be absent in a sentence, particularly in a casual speech situation, postpositions must be present in order to retain their meanings. This contrast is described in (27)–(28).[5]

(27) a. A, ame(-ga)   hut-te-ir-u.
        oh rain(-Nom) fall-gerund-be-non-past
        "Oh, it's raining."
     b. Kono ringo(-o)   tabe-ta?
        this apple(-Acc) eat-past
        "Did you eat this apple?"

(28) a. Taroo-ga   tosyokan-*(de) hon-o   yon-de-ir-u.
        Taro-Nom library-(at)   book-Acc read-gerund-be-non-past
        "Taro is reading a book at the library."
     b. Hanako-ga   tomodati-*(to) koohii-o   non-da.
        Hanako-Nom friend-(with)   coffee-Acc drink-past
        "Hanako had coffee with her friend."

Notice that Case particles can be omitted in casual speech, as in (27), whereas the omission of postpositions results in unacceptable sentences, as (28) suggests. So, even though Case particles and postpositions look alike, the roles that they play in sentences are distinct.[6]

We might add that while it is true that Case particles accompany nouns, and there are many examples of this type of combination, nouns are not the only category that can immediately precede them, as is exemplified by (29).

(29)   Koko-made-ga omosiro-i.
       here-until-Nom interesting-non-past
       "Up to this point is interesting."

In this sentence, *made* "until, as far as" is a postposition and the Nominative Case particle immediately follows it. Therefore, Case particles can follow postpositions although particles following nouns comprise a far more general pattern.

1.7 *Adjectival Nouns*

Let us turn to a category called **adjectival nouns**.[7] The name of this category seems contradictory, but it describes the nature of this class of words: they have characteristics both of adjectives and of nouns. They are similar to adjectives in that they modify the nouns that follow them. Furthermore, as adjectives, generally, they can be modified by an adverb like *totemo* "very". This is demonstrated by the examples in (30), where the first word in each example is an adjectival noun, and *-na* is added to it when it modifies the following noun.

(30)   a.   kirei-na kami   totemo kirei-na kami
            pretty   paper   very   pretty   paper
            "pretty paper"   "very pretty paper"
       b.   benri-na   kaban   totemo benri-na   kaban
            convenient bag   very   convenient bag
            "convenient bag"   "very convenient bag"
       c.   genki-na hito   totemo genki-na hito
            energetic person   very   energetic person
            "energetic person"   "very energetic person"

The adjectival noun in (30a), *kirei* "pretty", for instance, modifies the noun *kami* "paper". At the same time, *kirei* can be modified by the adverb *totemo* "very". So, adjectival nouns are like adjectives in that they play a role in modifying nouns and also because they can be modified by the adverb *totemo*.

Adjectival nouns, on the other hand, are similar to nouns especially in their conjugation pattern. Nouns are accompanied by varieties of endings, including those for the non-past tense, past tense, negative, and so on. Adjectival nouns take the set of conjugational endings that is identical to that taken by nouns. Such a similarity in the conjugation pattern is observed in (31), where *hon* "book" and *kirei* "pretty" serve as examples of nouns and adjectival nouns, respectively.

(31)   *nouns*   *adjectival nouns*

		nouns	*adjectival nouns*
a.	*non-past*	hon-da	kirei-da
b.	*non-past neg.*	hon-zya na-i	kirei-zya na-i
c.	*past*	hon-dat-ta	kirei-dat-ta
d.	*past neg.*	hon-zya na-kat-ta	kirei-zya na-kat-ta
e.	*tentative*	hon-daroo	kirei-daroo

The paradigm depicted above should be contrasted with that of adjectives. The conjugation pattern that the adjective *ooki-* "big" demonstrates, for instance, is given in (32).

(32)			
	a.	*non-past*	ooki-i
	b.	*non-past neg.*	ooki-ku na-i
	c.	*past*	ooki-kat-ta
	d.	*past neg.*	ooki-ku na-kat-ta
	e.	*tentative*	ooki-i daroo

The comparison between (31) and (32) clearly indicates that adjectival nouns take the conjugation paradigm of nouns rather than that of adjectives. In this sense, they are called "nouns".

However, adjectival nouns do not display some of the other properties that full-fledged nouns have. First, as is already observed in (30) above, when an adjectival noun modifies a noun, *-na* is added to establish the modification relation, while such a modification relation is mediated by the Genitive Case particle *-no* when a noun modifies another noun, as in *Taroo-no hon* (Taro-Gen book) "Taro's book". Second, adjectival nouns cannot be accompanied by Case particles while full-fledged nouns can. So, occurrences of adjectival nouns with Case particles, such as **kirei-ga* "pretty-Nom" and **kirei-o* "pretty-Acc", are not possible. Third, while full-fledged nouns can be modified by demonstratives, such as *kono* "this" and *sono* "that", as well as by other nouns, adjectival nouns cannot. This is illustrated in (33).[8]

(33) a.   kono hon   vs. *kono kirei
           this   book   this   pretty
           "this book"   "*this pretty"
     b.   Taroo-no hon   vs. *kami-no kirei
           Taro-Gen book   paper-Gen pretty
           "Taro's book"   "*beauty of paper"

Incidentally, when loan words modify nouns, they tend to belong to the category of adjectival nouns (cf. Shibatani 1990). For instance, the English loan *tough* and the French loan *chic* are used in Japanese as *tahu-na hito* "tough person" and *sikku-na doresu* "chic dress", respectively. As mentioned, the *-na* ending indicates that the word preceding it is an adjectival noun.

1.8 Verbal Nouns

The last category in Japanese to be considered is the class of words called **verbal nouns** (cf. Martin 1975; Kageyama 1976–1977; Iida 1987; Miyagawa 1987a; Shibatani and Kageyama 1988; among others).[9] Again, the contradictory term suggests their dual status, i.e. both as verbs and as nouns. Many verbal nouns in Japanese come from Sino-Japanese compounds, but they also include loan words as well as deverbal nouns (i.e. nouns derived from their corresponding verbs) of Japanese origin. Examples of verbal nouns are displayed in (34).

(34) a. *Sino-Japanese* benkyoo (ben-kyoo) "studying"
                            ryokoo   (ryo-koo)   "traveling"
                            kenkyuu (ken-kyuu) "research"
                            dokusyo (doku-syo) "reading"
                            kookoku (koo-koku) "advertising"
      b. *English loans* kisu   "kiss"
                            deeto   "date"
                            doraibu "drive"
                            zyogingu "jogging"
      c. *Japanese*   torihiki   (tori-hiki)   "trading"
          (deverbal)   toriatukai (tori-atukai) "handling"
                            torisimari (tori-simari) "picking up"
                            ukekotae   (uke-kotae)   "answer"

These verbal nouns are clearly nouns in that they can co-occur with demonstratives such as *kono* "this" and *sono* "that", and also can be marked with Case particles. This is shown in (35).

(35) a. Ano **kenkyuu**-ga   Tanaka-sensei-o   yuumei-ni si-ta.
          that research-Nom Tanaka-teacher-Acc famous-to do-past
          "That research made Professor Tanaka famous."
      b. Taroo-to-no   **deeto**-wa totemo tanosi-i.
          Taro-with-Gen date-Top very   fun-non-past
          "The date with Taro is a lot of fun."
      c. Nihon-wa tyuugoku-to **torihiki**-o   hazime-ta.
          Japan-Top China-with trading-Acc start-past
          "Japan started trading with China."

(35a) illustrates that the verbal noun *kenkyuu* "research" can be modified by the demonstrative *ano* "that". Furthermore, the three verbal nouns in these examples are accompanied by Case particles, *-ga*, *-wa*, and *-o*. This suggests that the verbal nouns demonstrated in (35) are nouns.

Verbal nouns often occur with the verb *su-ru* (do-non-past) "do", and when this situation occurs, the verbal noun with *su-ru* is regarded as a verb. Consider the examples in (36) illustrating this point.

(36) a. Taroo-ga   suugaku-o ni-zikan   **benkyoo**-si-ta.
          Taro-Nom math-Acc two-hour studying-do-past
          "Taro studied math for two hours."
      b. Hanako-ga   Masao-to   kamakura-e   **doraibu**-si-ta.
          Hanako-Nom Masao-with Kamakura-to driving-do-past
          "Hanako took a drive to Kamakura with Masao."
      c. Gakusei-ga   **ukekotae**-si-te-ir-u.
          student-Nom answering-do-gerund-be-non-past
          "Students are answering."

The verb *su-ru* by itself is a full-fledged verb, meaning "do", but when it is
combined with a verbal noun, its own meaning is hardly retained. Rather, the
meaning of the complex verb consisting of a verbal noun and *su-ru* is attributed
mostly to the meaning of the verbal noun. The primary role of *su-ru* is, then,
to carry the verbal conjugation, such as non-past, past, progressive, and so on.
    As Iida (1987) and Shibatani and Kageyama (1988) discuss, verbal nouns can
appear with endings that bear some temporal meanings such as *-tyuu* "while",
-go "after", *-gatera* "at the same time", and *-izen* "before". What is interesting
about this situation is the distribution of Case particles. Consider the data in
(37)–(39), taken (with minor changes) from Iida (1987: 104).

(37) John-wa gakui-o   **syutoku-go**, nihon-e ki-ta.
      John-Top degree-Acc getting-after Japan-to come-past
      "John came to Japan after getting a degree."

(38) Keisatu-wa supiido-ihan-o   **torisimari-gatera**   kootuuryoo-o
      police-Top speed-violation-Acc checking-same time traffic-Acc
      tyoosa-si-ta.
      investigate-do-past
      "The police investigated the traffic situation while stopping cars for
      speeding."

(39) Rooma-gun-ga **sinnyuu-izen**,   soko-wa sizukana mura dat-ta.
      Romans-Nom invasion-before there-Top tranquil village be-past
      "Before the Roman invasion, that was a tranquil village."

The endings that indicate temporal meanings are attached to the verbal nouns.
Notice that a complex of a verbal noun and a temporal ending should be considered a noun according to our criteria, for example, the possible co-occurrence
with Case particles, as is demonstrated in (40).

(40) Nihon-e iku-nara gakui-o   **syutoku-go-ga**   i-i.
      Japan-to go-if d egree-Acc getting-after-Nom good-non-past
      "If you (plan to) go to Japan, it's better to go after getting a degree."

If the complex of a verbal noun and a temporal ending should count as a noun,
we should expect the Genitive Case particle to appear for prenominal modifiers.
And this prediction is indeed borne out, as in (41)–(42).

(41) Gakui-**no** syutoku-go, John-wa nihon-e ki-ta.
degree-Gen getting-after John-Top Japan-to come-past
"John came to Japan after getting a degree."

(42) Supiido-ihan-**no** **torisimari-gatera,** keisatu-ga kootuuryoo-o
speed-violation-Gen checking-same time police-Nom traffic-Acc
tyoosa-si-ta.
investigate-do-past
"The police investigated the traffic situation while stopping cars for speeding."

(43) Rooma-gun-**no sinnyuu-izen,** soko-wa sizukana mura dat-ta.
Romans-Gen invasion-before there-Top tranquil village be-past
"Before the Roman invasion, that was a tranquil village."

What is interesting is the fact that in addition to taking the Genitive marking on prenominal modifiers, a characteristic of nouns, a verbal noun with a temporal ending demonstrates an array of other Case particles that are normally observed with verbal and adjectival predicates. We have already seen that this is indeed the case in (37)–(39). That is, such a characteristic is normally attributed to the property of predicates in general, rather than to the property of nouns.[10]

2 Morpheme Types

A native speaker of English knows that *grammar* is a word. She or he also knows that *grammatical* is a word, and that this word is somehow related to the word *grammar*. Similarly, *ungrammatical* is a word whose meaning is the opposite of *grammatical*, and it can further be expanded into *ungrammaticality*. The native speaker is aware that these words are composed of *grammar* and *-ic, -al, un-,* and so on, and each one of them contributes to the meaning difference. These meaningful units that comprise the word are called **morphemes**. So, *grammar, -ic, -al, -un,* and *-ity* exemplify morphemes in English.

We have already observed many examples of morphemes in Japanese. For instance, what we have referred to as the non-past tense "ending" *-(r)u* and the past tense "ending" *-ta/da,* as well as independent words such as *hon* "book" and *hana* "flower", are all examples of morphemes.

There are several types of morphemes. Morphemes are divided into two classes depending on whether they can stand by themselves or whether they must be attached to another morpheme. If morphemes can appear by themselves, they are called **free morphemes**. They are exemplified by *book, elephant,* and *go* in English, and *tomodati* "friend", *genki* "energetic", and *hontoo* "true" in Japanese. All words, as they are characterized at the beginning of this chapter, hence are also free morphemes. If, on the other hand, morphemes cannot stand by themselves and instead count as parts of words, they are considered **bound morphemes**. Japanese verbal conjugation endings, such as the non-past tense morpheme -(r)u, the past tense morpheme -ta/da, and Case particles such as -ga and -o, are members of this type. They cannot stand by themselves, and thus need to be attached to another word or morpheme without exception.

Bound morphemes can further be divided into **derivational morphemes** and **inflectional morphemes**. Derivational morphemes are bound morphemes that may change the meaning and/or the category of the word to which they are attached. For example, the morpheme *su-* "bare" can be added to a noun and can change its meaning, as in (44).[11]

(44) a. asi   "leg"   → su-asi   "bare leg"
      b. hada   "skin" → su-hada   "bare skin"
      c. te   "arm"   → su-de   "bare arm"
      d. kao   "face" → su-gao   "bare face"

In this case, the morpheme *su-* does not change the category of the word to which it is attached: the words on the left of the arrow as well as those on the right of it are nouns. However, the meaning of the resulting word is clearly different from that of the word without it. That is, the morpheme *su-* supplies the base noun with the meaning of bareness.

Other examples are observed with the morphemes -(i)ta- and -sa. Unlike the morpheme *su-*, these two morphemes change the category of the word to which they are attached. Consider the examples in (45)–(46).[12]

(45)   *verb root*   *adjective*
      a. ik   "go"   → ik-i-ta-i   "want to go"
      b. tabe   "eat"   → tabe-ta-i   "want to eat"
      c. kak   "write" → kak-i-ta-i   "want to write"
      d. oyog   "swim"   → oyog-i-ta-i "want to swim"

(46)   *adjective root*   *noun*
      a. hiro   "wide"   → hiro-sa   "width"
      b. omo   "heavy" → omo-sa   "weight"
      c. huka   "deep"   → huka-sa   "depth"
      d. taka   "high"   → taka-sa   "height"

The words on the left of the arrow in (45) are verbal roots. The addition of the morpheme -(i)-ta-i turns the verbs into adjectives, as the non-past tense morpheme -i suggests. Furthermore, -(i)ta- adds the desiderative meaning, "want to", to the original meaning of the verb. Similarly, the morpheme -sa in (46) is added to the adjectival roots, and changes the adjectives to nouns. Thus, *su-*, -(i)ta-, and -sa change the meaning and/or the category of the word to which they are attached, and hence they are considered derivational morphemes.

Inflectional morphemes do not generate different words, unlike the derivational morphemes discussed above. Instead, inflected forms are variants of the same word, and for this reason inflectional morphemes do not change the category of the word. Many of the morphemes that are involved in verbal and adjectival conjugations can be considered examples of inflectional morphemes. For instance, the non-past tense morpheme *-(r)u* and the past tense morpheme *-ta/da* for Japanese verbs are inflectional morphemes. The non-past tense and past tense morphemes for adjectives, *-i* and *(-kat)-ta*, are also inflectional morphemes. Consider (47).

(47) a. *non-past tense (verb): -(r)u*

tabe	"eat"	→	tabe-ru	"eat, will eat"
nom	"drink"	→	nom-u	"drink, will drink"
kak	"write"	→	kak-u	"write, will write"
mi	"see"	→	mi-ru	"see, will see"

 b. *past tense (verb): -ta/da*

tabe	"eat"	→	tabe-ta	"ate"
nom	"drink"	→	non-da	"drank"
kak	"write"	→	kai-ta	"wrote"
mi	"see"	→	mi-ta	"saw"

 c. *non-past tense (adjective): -i*

ooki	"big"	→	ooki-i	"is big"
oisi	"delicious"	→	oisi-i	"is delicious"
aka	"red"	→	aka-i	"is red"
omo	"heavy"	→	omo-i	"is heavy"

 d. *past tense (adjective): -kat-ta*

ooki	"big"	→	ooki-kat-ta	"was big"
oisi	"delicious"	→	oisi-kat-ta	"was delicious"
aka	"red"	→	aka-kat-ta	"was red"
omo	"heavy"	→	omo-kat-ta	"was heavy"

The forms on the left of the arrow and those on the right are the same word, but different variants. Furthermore, the addition of these inflectional morphemes does not change the categories of the base words, i.e. all the words in (47a, b) are verbs and those in (47c, d) are adjectives.

The distinction between derivational and inflectional morphemes is one way of categorizing bound morphemes. The basic criteria for this division focus on whether a given morpheme has the effect of changing the meaning and/or the category of the word to which it is attached, and also whether it is a separate word or a variant of the word. Independent of this distinction, bound morphemes can also be divided into diverse classes according to where in a word they appear. This kind of categorization divides bound morphemes into prefixes, suffixes, and infixes, which are generally referred to as **affixes**.

An affix which occurs before a base form is called a **prefix**, while one that appears after it is called a **suffix**. We have already observed an instance of a prefix in (44) above, which is repeated below.

(44)
a.	asi	"leg"	→	su-asi	"bare leg"
b.	hada	"skin"	→	su-hada	"bare skin"
c.	te	"arm"	→	su-de	"bare arm"
d.	kao	"face"	→	su-gao	"bare face"

The derivational morpheme *su-* "bare" in (44) is prefixed to a noun and the resulting word is also a noun. Thus, the morpheme *su-* in these examples is a derivational morpheme because the new word is treated as an independent word with a different meaning, and at the same time it is a prefix because of the position in which it occurs, namely, before the base noun.

Prefixes in Japanese can be either of native origin or loans. The prefix *su-* is an example of a native prefix. Although there are not so many native prefixes, those in (48) are quite commonly used.

(48)   a.   *oo-* "big"
            e.g. oo-daiko "big drum", oo-ame "heavy rain", oo-yuki "heavy snow"
       b.   *ko-* "small"
            e.g. ko-gaisya "branch company", ko-tori "small bird"
       c.   *huru-* "old"
            e.g. huru-hon "old book", huru-mono "old things", huru-ike "old pond", huru-ido "old well"
       d.   *o-* (honorific, beautificatory)
            e.g. o-denwa "telephone", o-hasi "chopsticks", o-hana "flowers", o-tegami "letter"

In contrast with prefixes of native origin, there are many Sino-Japanese prefixes, i.e. those of Chinese origin. Some of the Sino-Japanese prefixes often change nouns to adjectival nouns. Consider the examples in (49)–(51).

(49)   a.   tyuui "attention" → **hu**-tyuui "careless"
       b.   tyuui-**no**   kotoba
            attention-Gen word
            "words for attention"
       c.   **hu**-tyuui-**na** hito
            careless   person
            "a careless person"

(50)   a.   zyoosiki "common sense" → **hi**-zyoosiki "senseless"
       b.   zyoosiki-**no**   koto
            common sense-Gen thing
            "things that are common sense"
       c.   **hi**-zyoosiki-**na** hito
            senseless   person
            "a senseless person"

(51)   a.   sinkei "nerve" → **mu**-sinkei "insensitive"
       b.   sinkei-**no**   byooki
            nerve-Gen illness
            "illness from nerve"
       c.   **mu**-sinkei-**na** hito
            insensitive   person
            "an insensitive person"

The prefixes *hu-*, *hi-*, and *mu-* are all of Chinese origin, and they add a negative meaning to the base form. It should be remembered that *-na* is used with adjectival nouns to establish a modification relation with the following noun. In contrast, when a prenominal modifier is a noun, a modification relation is mediated by the Genitive Case particle *-no*, as is observed with the phrases in the (b) examples above. The fact that the prefixed nouns take *-na*, rather than *-no*, to mediate a modification relation with the following nouns in the (c) examples suggests that these prefixed words, *hu-tyuui* "careless" in (49), *hi-zyoosiki* "senseless" in (50), and *mu-sinkei* "insensitive" in (51), are adjectival nouns.

On the other hand, we also observe prefixes that are attached to nouns and yet do not change the category. Examples of this type are shown in (52)–(53).

(52) a. kaihatu "development" → **mi**-kaihatu "under-developed"
     b. kaihatu-**no**   keikaku
        development-Gen plan
        "a plan for development"
     c. **mi**-kaihatu-**no**   kuni
        under-developed-Gen country
        "developing country"

(53) a. seihin "product" → **sin**-seihin "new product"
     b. seihin-**no**   happyoo
        product-Gen announcement
        "announcement of a product"
     c. **sin**-seihin-**no**   happyoo
        new-product-Gen announcement
        "announcement of a new product"

As these examples show, prefixes such as *mi-* and *sin-* do not change the category of the words to which they are prefixed although they change the meaning of the original nouns.

Loan prefixes, particularly from English, are increasingly common in Japanese. The prefixes in (54) are all loans from English (cited in Shibatani 1990: 220) and do not change the category of the word.

(54) a. new   → nyuu-seihin   "new product"
     b. post → posuto-nakasone "post Nakasone"
     c. all   → ooru-nippon   "all Japan"
     d. mini → mini-kan   "mini-can (of beer)"
                 mini-keisanki   "mini-calculator"

The non-past tense and past tense morphemes for verbal inflection are examples of suffixes. We have also observed the inflectional paradigms of nouns, adjectives, and adjectival nouns. These paradigms are repeated below.

(31)   *nouns*   *adjectival nouns*
   a.   *non-past*   hon-da   kirei-da
   b.   *non-past neg.*   hon-zya na-i   kirei-zya na-i
   c.   *past*   hon-dat-ta   kirei-dat-ta
   d.   *past neg.*   hon-zya na-kat-ta   kirei-zya na-kat-ta
   e.   tentative   hon-daroo   kirei-daroo

(32)   *adjectives*
   a.   *non-past*   ooki-i
   b.   *non-past neg.*   ooki-ku na-i
   c.   *past*   ooki-kat-ta
   d.   *past neg.*   ooki-ku na-kat-ta
   e.   *tentative*   ooki-i daroo

The morphemes attached to the right of the noun, adjectival noun, and adjectival root are all instances of suffixes. There are many more. For instance, the causative-forming morpheme *-(s)ase* appears after the verbal root and so does the passive-forming morpheme *-(r)are*. These suffixes are illustrated in (55)–(56).

(55)   Hanako-ga   kodomo-ni kaimono-e   ik-ase-ta.
      Hanako-Nom child-Dat   shopping-to go-causative-past
      "Hanako made her child go shopping."

(56)   Musuko-ga sensei-ni   home-rare-ta.
      son-Nom   teacher-by praise-passive-past
      "My son was praised by the teacher."

Both the causative morpheme *-ase* in (55) and the passive morpheme *-rare* in (56) appear to the right of the verbal root, and hence they are suffixes. Notice, furthermore, to the right of the causative and passive suffixes is the past tense morpheme *-ta*, and thus as we have mentioned above, the past tense morpheme is an example of a suffix.

Infixes are bound morphemes that are inserted in the middle of a word rather than being placed before or after it. Japanese does not have any example of infixes. Infixes are not widely exhibited in English, either, but they can be exemplified by the use of *bloody* in words like *fantastic*, deriving *fan-bloody-tastic* (British English). In this example *bloody* is regarded as an instance of an infix. Another example is drawn from Tagalog, the major language spoken in the Philippines. As is discussed in Spencer (1991: 12), the infix *-um-* is inserted in a single word *sulat* "writing", as in *s-um-ulat* "to write" (subject focus).

It should be pointed out, in passing, that given the varieties of morphemes existing in Japanese, it is important to keep in mind that the relative order among the morphemes plays a crucial role in forming words in case more than one suffix is sequenced. For example, the passive suffix *-(r)are* and the desiderative suffix *-(i)ta-* take a verbal form on their left, but when they are both suffixed to a verb, the passive suffix must precede the desiderative suffix. This is illustrated in (57).

(57)   a.   home-rare-ta(-i)   "want to be praised"
            praise-passive-desiderative
       b.   *home-ta-rare(-ru)

In (57a) the passive morpheme is suffixed to the verbal root, and then the desiderative morpheme is suffixed to the resulting form of the first suffixation operation. The output is well-formed, and means "want to be praised". In (57b) the order of the two suffixes is reversed, and the resulting form is not acceptable or interpretable. Hence, the relative order among bound morphemes is not arbitrary.

   We have thus far examined various types of morphemes attested in Japanese. Morphemes can also be classified depending on their phonological properties (cf. J. McCawley 1968; Ito and Mester 1993, 1995, 1999). According to such a classification, morphemes can be divided into the following four categories: **Native**, **Sino-Japanese**, **Mimetic**, and **Foreign**. Native refers to words and morphemes that are of Japanese origin. Sino-Japanese are those that are borrowed from Chinese and of which we have already observed a number of examples. Mimetics are not a category based on origin, but they have their own properties that make them separate from other types of morphemes, as we will mention below (and as was discussed in chapter 3). Foreign words and morphemes include those loans from languages other than Chinese. Given these four categories, the same object or notion can be expressed differently depending on the classification. The list in (58), slightly modified from Ito and Mester (1993: 2), exemplifies this.

(58)   *native*   *Sino-Japanese*   *mimetic*   *foreign*
      "shine"   kagayaku   -koo-   kira-kira   syain
      "dog"   inu   -ken-   wan-wan   doggu

As Ito and Mester (1993) (and also J. McCawley 1968 for the original observations) demonstrate, this type of classification is motivated by phonological behavior: that is, these classes of words and morphemes do not exhibit the same phonological behavior. First, when native and Sino-Japanese words and morphemes contain an instance of the phoneme /p/, it always appears as a part of a long consonant, i.e. /pp/ ([p:]), or immediately after a moraic /n/, i.e. /np/ ([mp]). For example, we have *kappa* [kap:a] "river imp" and *nippon* [nip:oN] "Japan" as well as *kanpai* [kampai] "cheers" and *sinpai* [šimpai] "worry", but a single occurrence of /p/, as in **kapa* [kapa] and **nipon* [nipoN], is not tolerated by these classes. On the other hand, there is no such restriction imposed on mimetics and foreign words and morphemes, as can be seen with the mimetic words *pota-pota* [potapota] "dripping" and *pika-pika* [pikapika] "shining" and the English loans *pen* [peN] "pen" and *peepaa* [pe:pa:] "paper".

   Second, according to Ito and Mester, with native and mimetic words, a consonant following a nasal sound must be voiced. This constraint thus disallows native and mimetic words from containing the sequences **[nt], **[mp], and **[ŋk]. This can be illustrated by observing native words such as *tonbo* [tambo] "dragonfly", *kande* [kande] "chewing", and mimetic words like *syombori*

[šombori] "lonely" and *unzari* [unzari] "disgusted", where the consonant following the nasal sound is voiced. This constraint, however, does not apply to Sino-
Japanese and foreign words, as is seen with the Sino-Japanese words *sanpo*
[sampo] "walk" and *hantai* [hantai] "opposition" as well as the English loan
santa [santa] "Santa".[13]

Third, all the classes except foreign words and morphemes disallow long
consonants consisting of voiced stops, fricatives, and affricates. This disallows
sequences such as */bb/ [b:], */dd/ [d:], */gg/ [g:], and */zz/ [z:]. So, instances of
long consonants observed in native, mimetic, and Sino-Japanese must be voiceless. This is shown by the native word *asatte* [asat:e] "the day after tomorrow",
the mimetic *nikkori* [nik:ori] "smiling", and the Sino-Japanese word *sippai* [šip:ai]
"failure". Foreign words and morphemes are exempt from this constraint, as
words such as *doggu* [dog:u] "dog", *beddo* [bed:o] "bed", and *baggu* [bag:u]
"bag" illustrate.

The distribution of the phonological constraints to which each morpheme class
is subject is graphically illustrated in figure 4.1 (slightly modified from Ito and
Mester 1995). The four-way classification of words and morphemes discussed
above can be crucial in accounting for the diversity of phonological constraints
that restrict various combinatorial possibilities.

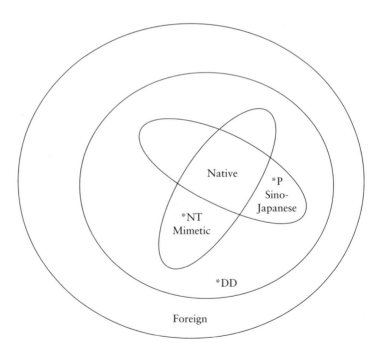

*P: no single occurrence of [p]
*NT: no voiceless consonant after nasal
*DD: no long consonants of voiced obstruents (stops, fricatives, and affricates)

Figure 4.1   Distribution of phonological constraints

3 Word Formation

Given the different kinds of morphemes described above, there are several ways to put them together so that a new word is formed. Although the types of word formation have already been introduced in informal terms earlier, let us discuss them in more detail here.

3.1 *Affixation*

A very common process of word formation is **affixation**, which subsumes **prefixation** and **suffixation**. These are processes that prefix or suffix a morpheme to a base form.

The suffixation of the noun-forming derivational morpheme -*te* (agentive) exemplifies how morphological operations can interact with other aspects of the grammar (cf. Sugioka 1986). The agentive suffix -*te* is affixed to a verbal root and forms a noun. In the case of a verbal root that ends in a consonant, -*i*- is inserted between the root and -*te*. Since it changes the category, it is a derivational morpheme. Examine (59).

(59) a. kak-i-te   "writer"
         write
      b. odor-i-te   "dancer"
         dance
      c. hanas-i-te "speaker"
         speak
      d. ur-i-te   "seller"
         sell

The suffix -*te* is affixed to a verbal root, and changes the category of verb to that of noun. Semantically, the derived noun implies the agent who does the action named by the verb. Furthermore, it is interesting to observe that this suffixation displays the phonological property of accentuation shift illustrated in (60).[14]

(60) a.   *   *
         kak   →   kak-i-te
      b.   *   *
         yom   →   yom-i-te
      c.   *
         hanas   →   hanas-i-te   [unaccented]
      d. odor   →   odor-i-te   [unaccented]
      e. ur   →   ur-i-te   [unaccented]

When the accent of the verbal root is on the first mora, the accent shifts to -*te*, as in (60a, b). If the accent is elsewhere other than the first mora, or there is no accent, then the resulting noun is unaccented, as the rest of the examples demonstrate. Thus, the *-te* suffixation influences the accentuation pattern.

We have thus far seen that *-te* suffixation interacts with syntax, semantics, and phonology. When we consider various word formation processes, there is an additional matter that should be kept in mind, i.e. the productivity of the word formation process under discussion. Morphological productivity refers to how regularly a rule or process applies to form a new word. How productive is *-te* suffixation? Does this process apply to any verbal root? To answer these questions, we must compare the set of examples in (61) with (59).

(61)   a.   *ir-i-te   "a person who needs something"
            need
       b.   *ni-te   "a person who resembles someone"
            resemble
       c.   *deki-te   "a person who can do something"
            be capable of
       d.   *wakar-i-te   "a person who understands something"
            understand

The *-te* suffixation to verbal roots like *ir* "need", *ni* "resemble", *deki* "be capable of", and *wakar* "understand" produces unacceptable words. We have mentioned earlier that the semantic property of this suffix is as agent of the action denoted by the verb. Notice that what verbs like "need", "resemble", "be capable of", and "understand" denote cannot be achieved by an individual doing some action. That is, an individual has no control over what the verbs denote. These verbs belong to the class called **stative verbs**. So, whenever the verb is a stative verb, the result of this suffixation is ungrammatical. This suggests that the *-te* suffixation is productive only when the output nouns refer to an agent of some action and the verbs are not of the stative class.

3.2   Compounding

A second type of word formation process we will discuss is **compounding** (cf. Kageyama 1982; Sugioka 1986; Shibatani 1990; Kubozono 1995). Since Japanese employs a great number of compounds and they raise interesting issues, we will return to this topic again in section 7. This section gives a brief sketch of them.

Compounds are formed by combining two or more words. We have examined the instances of compounds in discussing the accentuation of long nominal compounds as well as the Rendaku phenomenon in chapter 3. In many cases compounds are composed of two or more independent words. For example, English compounds such as *bathroom* and *towel-rack* consist of two words. On the other hand, some compounds are formed by combining bound morphemes. English examples of this sort might include *photograph*, *telegraph*, *erythrocyte*, and *hemocyte*, where each composite is not an independent word (cf. Spencer 1991). Compounds in Japanese can be formed in a variety of ways. For instance, composites of compounds can be solely native words, Sino-Japanese, or a combination of words of different origin. These are demonstrated in (62)–(64), taken from Shibatani (1990: 237–238).

(62) Native Compounds
    a. *noun–noun*   aki-zora   "autumn sky"
    b. *adjective–noun* tika-miti   "short cut"
    c. *verb–noun*   nomi-mizu "drinking water"
    d. *noun–verb*   yuki-doke   "snow-melting"
    e. *verb–verb*   tati-yomi   "reading while standing"
    f. *noun–adjective* hara-ita   "stomachache"

(63) Sino-Japanese Compounds[15]
    a. ki-soku   "rule"
    b. koo-ri   "high interest"
    c. satu-zin   "manslaughter"
    d. kei-koku   "warning"
    e. ken-kyuu "research"

(64) Hybrid Compounds
    a. *Sino-Japanese + native* dai-dokoro   "kitchen"
    b. *Sino-Japanese + foreign* sekiyu-sutoobu "oil stove"
    c. *foreign + Sino-Japanese* taoru-zi   "towel cloth"
    d. *native + foreign*   ita-tyoko   "chocolate bar"
    e. *foreign + native*   garasu-mado   "glass window"
    f. *foreign + foreign*   teeburu-manaa "table manner"

Native compounds consist of two native words or morphemes; each composite word can come from a variety of different categories, as is demonstrated in (62). For example, *aki-zora* "autumn sky" in (62a) is formed by putting together the individual nouns *aki* "autumn" and *sora* "sky". The voicing of the initial consonant of the second member is a result of Rendaku. Many of the Sino-Japanese compounds are formed in Chinese, and have been borrowed as complete compounds even though each composite does not necessarily correspond to any individual word in Japanese. (64) presents a variety of combinations in terms of the origin of composite words in forming compounds.

There is another type of compound in Japanese that displays a cluster of properties that make them distinct from the compounds of the type observed in (62)–(64) above. All the compounds that we have seen thus far exhibit the property that one member (normally the first) modifies or specifies the other. For example, in the compound of (62c), the first member *nomi* "drinking" modifies the second member *mizu* "water", specifying the type of the water. The set of compounds depicted below, on the other hand, do not demonstrate such a modification relation between the two members of the compound; (65a–c) are taken from Kageyama (1982: 236) and (65d–f) are from Sugioka (1986: 106).

(65) a. oya-ko   "parent and child"
      b. ten-ti   "sky and earth"
      c. nori-ori   "getting in and out (of a vehicle)"
      d. eda-ha   "branches and leaves"
      e. iki-kaeri   "coming and going"
      f. yomi-kaki   "read and write"

These compounds are called **dvandva** compounds. The relation that each member of the compound has to the other is that of coordination. That is, unlike the compounds in (62)–(64), dvandva compounds do not refer to a single individual or object as a whole, but rather make reference to two individuals or objects that each member of that compound names. In (65a), for example, *oya-ko* "parent and child" reflects the meaning of both members of the compound, i.e. *oya* "parent" and *ko* "child". Hence the modification relation between the members of a compound is not a characteristic that dvandva compounds exhibit.

It is also worth pointing out that dvandva compounds often do not undergo the Rendaku phenomenon (cf. Otsu 1980). Observe all the examples except (c) in (65). In these dvandva compounds, the initial consonant of the second member is voiceless. Furthermore, these second-member words do not contain voiced obstruents that would block the voicing (i.e. Lyman's Law). So, the environment for these initial consonants to undergo Rendaku is there, but they remain voiceless. The absence of the Rendaku phenomenon is, hence, another property that isolates dvandva compounds from other compounds.

3.3 Reduplication

A third type of word formation process is **reduplication**. Reduplication is a process in which a part of a word or a whole word is repeated to create a new word. Two instances of reduplication in Japanese have been discussed in chapter 3, i.e. mimetics and Renyookei reduplication. Examples are shown in (66)–(67).

(66) a. pota-pota   "dripping"
      b. hena-hena   "weak"
      c. bisyo-bisyo   "soaking wet"
      d. pitya-pitya   "splashing"
      e. zawa-zawa   "crowded, noisy"

(67) a. Hanasi-o sii-sii tabe-ta.
          talk-Acc do-do eat-past
          "We ate and talked at the same time."
      b. Sono ko-wa   naki-naki kaet-ta.
          that child-Top cry-cry   return-past
          "The child went home crying."

As the examples in (66) show, the mimetic forms involve reduplication, usually of a two-mora base. The Renyookei reduplication forms in (67) are produced by repeating a verbal base and serve to modify the following verb. It should be remembered that in cases like (67a) where the verbal base consists of only one mora, *si*, the vowel is lengthened so that the base is at least two morae long. As we discussed in chapter 3, this is due to the length requirement imposed on Renyookei Reduplication, according to which the verbal base to be reduplicated must be at least two morae long.

3.4   Clipping

Another type of word formation is **clipping**, which is a process that shortens words, as seen in the examples in (68); (68c–f) are taken from Shibatani (1990: 255).

(68)   a.   keisatu   "police"   →   satu
       b.   denki takuzyooki   "electric calculator"   →   dentaku
       c.   seiyoo-siki   "western-style"   →   yoo-siki
       d.   suupaa maaketto   "supermarket"   →   suupaa
       e.   purattohoomu   "platform"   →   hoomu
       f.   gakusei-waribiki   "student discount"   →   gakuwari

The words in (68a, c, d, e) undergo clipping by leaving some parts of the words out. In the case of compounds like (68b, f), the first two morae of each composite are taken. This is reminiscent of the clipping pattern that we have observed with the shortening of loan words discussed in chapter 3. The relevant examples are repeated in (69).

(69)   a.   purofessyonaru resuringu   →   puro resu   "professional wrestling"
       b.   waado purosessaa   →   waa puro   "word processor"
       c.   rimooto kontorooru   →   rimo kon   "remote control"
       d.   ziinzu pantu   →   zii pan   "jeans"
       e.   sekusyaru harasumento   →   seku hara   "sexual harassment"

In all the examples in (69), two morae are taken from each element. Thus, the clipping process follows certain restrictions imposed by the length requirement that has been discussed in chapter 3.

3.5   Borrowing

As a final process, we can mention **borrowing**.[16] All the loan words, including Sino-Japanese compounds, belong to this group. As we have discussed in chapter 3, when words are borrowed from another language, some phonological changes are observed so that the pronunciation of borrowed words is consistent with the phonological system of Japanese. For instance, consider the phonological differences involved in the words in (70) borrowed from English.

(70) a. three [θri] → [suri:]
  b. magazine [mægəzin] → [magaǰin]
  c. singer [sɪŋər] → [šiŋga:]
  d. voice [voys] → [boisu]

Japanese lacks the voiceless interdental fricative [θ], and so it is substituted for by [s], as in (70a). In (70b) the sequence of the alveolar fricative [z] and the high front vowel [i] is not attested in Japanese, and hence the consonant is replaced by the alveo-palatal affricate [ǰ]. The voiceless alveolar fricative [s] in (70c) exists in Japanese, and as we discussed in chapter 3, when it is followed by the high front vowel [i], it undergoes the allophonic change that turns /s/ to [š]. Finally, the voiced labio-dental fricative [v] does not exist in Japanese, and thus, the voiced bilabial stop [b] acts as its substitute (cf. Lovins 1975).

Modifications associated with borrowings are not limited to phonological change. When foreign words are borrowed into Japanese, categories need to be adjusted so that the borrowed words are consistent with the inflectional patterns that a particular category displays. Consider (71).

(71) a. paniku-ru "panic (V)" (← panic)
  b. nau-i   "modern" (← now)
  c. sikku-na "chic" (← chic)

The word *paniku-ru* "panic" in (71a) comes from the English word *panic*. Once it is regarded as a verb in Japanese, it must pattern with other Japanese verbs, following the verbal inflectional paradigm, and this is why the non-past tense suffix *-ru* is added to it. This new verb, of course, has other conjugated forms including negative, past tense, and so on. The word *nau-i* in (71b) originates from the English word *now*, and the word is given adjectival status. As an adjective, the non-past tense suffix *-i* is added. As is the case for *paniku-ru*, *nau-i* takes other inflected forms such as negative and past tense, patterning with native adjectives. The French word *chic*, on the other hand, is given adjectival noun status, as is indicated by the *-na* ending used to modify a noun that follows it.

It is interesting to note that when borrowing takes place, some change in semantic content of the original words seems to be inevitable. J. McCawley (1993) observes, for instance, that the loan word *raisu* "rice" does not mean rice in general, but specifically refers to "rice served on a plate or a western-style bowl rather than a rice-bowl and is to be eaten with a fork or a spoon rather than with chopsticks" (p. 473).

It also seems that the different origins of loan words contribute to a certain orientation that the words have. For instance, J. McCawley (1993) makes the interesting observation that Sino-Japanese loan words tend to appear in science and technology fields while foreign loans are frequently observed in the areas of cooking, fashion, and entertainment. Hence we can detect some regularity in the way loan words of different origin are adopted.

4 Head

We have examined morpheme types above and have noted that derivational morphemes can change categories of words. Change in categories is also observed in other word formation processes like compounding. For example, the noun *awa* "foam" can be compounded with the verb *tateru* "stand" to form the word *awa-dateru* "make foam". The new compound word is a verb. To this verb, we can further add the noun suffix *-kata* "the way of", deriving *awa-date-kata* "the way of making foam". The category of this compound is a noun. Notice that the category can alter every time we add a new morpheme. The pattern of category change, however, is not random. That is, it is always the right member of the word resulting from a word formation process that determines the category. The element that determines the category of the newly created word is called the **head**. Thus, in the above-mentioned examples, *tateru* in *awa-dateru* is the head, while in the word *awa-date-kata*, *kata* is the head. Notice, furthermore, it is always the case that the head that determines the category of the word is the rightmost morpheme of the word. This generalization that the head is always on the rightmost morpheme is called the **Righthand Head Rule** by E. Williams (1981). Observe that the Righthand Head Rule is maintained in the examples in (72).

(72) a. denki (N) + sutoobu (N) → denki-sutoobu (N)
      electricity   heater   electric heater
   b. ama-zuppai (A) + sa (N) → ama-zuppa-sa (N)
      sweet and sour   degree   the degree of sweet and sour
   c. aka (N/A) + kuroi (A) → aka-guroi (A)
      red   black   reddish black
   d. koke (N) + musu (V) → koke-musu (V)
      moss   grow   moss grows

In all the examples in (72), the head is the rightmost element, whether it is a free morpheme or a bound morpheme, and this rightmost element determines the category of a new word as a result of word formation.

5 Issues in Japanese Morphology (1): Transitive and Intransitive Verb Pairs

In section 1.2 we have briefly mentioned morphologically related transitive and intransitive verb pairs. In this section we will examine the transitive dichotomy a bit more closely, as researchers have considered it a crucial aspect of Japanese grammar (Jacobsen 1992; Kageyama 1993, 1996; Suga and Hayatsu 1995). Let us begin by repeating in (73)–(76) the examples given earlier.

		intransitive	*transitive*	*gloss*
(73)	a.	tao-**re**	tao-**s**	"fall"
	b.	tubu-**re**	tubu-**s**	"press"
	c.	naga-**re**	naga-**s**	"float"
(74)	a.	nao-**r**	nao-**s**	"mend"
	b.	noko-**r**	noko-**s**	"leave behind"
	c.	too-**r**	too-**s**	"pass"
(75)	a.	tasuk-**ar**	tasuk-**e**	"help, rescue"
	b.	sag-**ar**	sag-**e**	"lower"
	c.	kim-**ar**	kim-**e**	"decide"
(76)	a.	ok-**i**	ok-**os**	"get up"
	b.	ot-**i**	ot-**os**	"fall"
	c.	horob-**i**	horob-**os**	"destroy"

As these examples indicate, an identical verbal root is further suffixed by intransitive- and transitive-forming suffixes of various kinds. The closest analogy in English is observed in pairs such as *raise* and *rise*, *lay* and *lie*, and *fell* and *fall*, but it is more common to find transitive and intransitive verb paradigms in identical verbal forms like *break*, *melt*, and *sink* in English.

Transitive and intransitive verb pairs in Japanese are related to each other not only on morphological grounds but also on syntactic and semantic grounds. Consider the examples in (77)–(80).

(77) a. *transitive*   Taroo-ga ki-o   tao-si-ta.
                        Taro-Nom tree-Acc fell-past
                        "Taro felled a tree."
     b. *intransitive* Ki-ga   tao-re-ta.
                        tree-Nom fall-past
                        "A tree fell."

(78) a. *transitive*   Hanako-ga   kodomo-o tasuk-e-ta.
                        Hanako-Nom child-Acc rescue-past
                        "Hanako rescued a child."
     b. *intransitive* Kodomo-ga tasuk-at-ta
                        child-Nom is rescued-past
                        "A child was rescued."

(79) a. *transitive*   John broke a toy.
     b. *intransitive* A toy broke.

(80) a. *transitive*   Mary melted ice.
     b. *intransitive* Ice melted.

As both the Japanese and English examples show, the direct object of the transitive verb (marked with the Accusative Case in the Japanese sentences) in the

(a) sentences is consistently the subject of the intransitive verb in the (b) sentences. In (77a), for instance, *ki* "tree" is the direct object of the transitive verb *taosita* (the past tense form of *taosu*), but in (77b), it appears as the subject of the morphologically related intransitive counterpart, i.e. *taoreta* (the past tense form of *taoreru*). This systematic relationship has its semantic correlation. Intransitive sentences such as (77b) and (78b) describe an event in which some change takes place in an individual expressed by the subject, and their transitive counterparts mean that there is some individual that causes the change. For example, (77b) describes the change in a tree, from standing straight to falling down to the ground; and (77a) expresses that Taro did something to cause the change in the tree. Because of this semantic relationship, morphologically related transitive and intransitive verbs are often referred to as (lexical) **causative and inchoative verbs**, respectively.

Jacobsen (1981, 1992) extensively investigated morphologically related transitive and intransitive verb pairs, and classified them according to the morphological make-up of suffixes that distinguish between transitive and intransitive verbs. (81) lists the suffix pairs along with a few examples for each pair (taken from Jacobsen 1992: 258–268).

(81)

suffix pair	*intransitive*		*transitive*	
-e-/-Ø-	oreru	"break"	oru	"break"
	yakeru	"burn"	yaku	"burn"
-Ø-/-e-	aku	"open"	akeru	"open"
	itamu	"hurt"	itameru	"injure"
-ar-/-e-	agaru	"rise"	ageru	"raise"
	hazimaru	"begin"	hazimeru	"begin"
-ar-/-Ø-	togaru	"become sharp"	togu	"sharpen"
	tunagaru	"become connected"	tuagu	"connect"
-r-/-s-	kaeru	"return"	kaesu	"return"
	kieru	"go out"	kesu	"extinguish"
-re-/-s-	koboreru	"spill"	kobosu	"spill"
	kowareru	"break"	kowasu	"break"
-ri-/-s-	kariru	"borrow"	kasu	"lend"
	tariru	"suffice"	tasu	"add, supplement"
-Ø-/-as-	heru	"decrease"	herasu	"decrease"
	naru	"ring"	narasu	"ring"
-e-/-as-	deru	"come out"	dasu	"take out"
	tokeru	"melt"	tokasu	"melt"
-i-/-as-	mitiru	"become full"	mitasu	"fill"
	nobiru	"become extended"	nobasu	"extend"
-i-/-os-	okiru	"get up"	okosu	"get up"
	otiru	"fall"	otosu	"drop"
-Ø-/-se-	niru	"resemble"	niseru	"model after"
	noru	"get on"	noseru	"put on"

suffix pair	*intransitive*		*transitive*	
-e-/-akas-	amaeru	"act dependent on"	amayakasu	"spoil"
	obieru	"become frightened at"	obiyakasu	"frighten"
-or-/-e-	komoru	"be fully present"	komeru	"fill with"
	nukumoru	"become warm"	nukumeru	"warm up"
-are-/-e-	sutareru	"fall into disuse"	suteru	"throw away"
	wakareru	"become divided"	wakeru	"divide"

Jacobsen's detailed survey indicates that the nature of the relationship between morpheme pairs and verb roots is arbitrary. That is, there is no obvious generalization as to which verbal root selects which morpheme pair. The random nature may further be confirmed by observing that an identical morpheme such as -e- and no marking (indicated as "-Ø-") appears both as an intransitive-forming suffix and as a transitive-forming suffix for different verbal roots.

While suffix pairs in (81) appear random in their morphological shapes, upon closer examination, we may notice that -ar- and -e- are shared by many of the intransitive-forming suffixes while -as- and -e- are observed frequently in the transitive-forming suffixes. Shibatani (1990) explains that these corresponding patterns have strong connections to the passive morpheme -rare- and -re- and the causative morpheme -sase- and -se-. Recall that we have noted above that sentences with transitive verbs are the causative versions of those with their morphologically related intransitive counterparts. So, it comes as no surprise that many of the transitive-forming suffixes in (81) can be traced back to the present-day causative morphemes. As for the connection between intransitive-forming suffixes and the passive morphemes, it has often been pointed out that sentences with inchoative verbs are similar in meaning to passive sentences, which are formed by suffixing the passive morpheme to a transitive verb. For example, (82) and (83) are passive sentences based on the transitive sentences in (77a) and (78a), respectively. Compare them with (77b) and (78b).

(82) Ki-ga   (Taroo-ni) tao-s-are-ta.
      tree-Nom (Taro-by) felled-pass-past
      "A tree was felled (by Taro)."

(77b) Ki-ga   tao-re-ta.
      tree-Nom fall-past
      "A tree fell."

(83) Kodomo-ga (Hanako-ni) tasuk-e-rare-ta.
      child-Nom   (Hanako-by) rescue-pass-past
      "A child was rescued (by Hanako)."

(78b)   Kodomo-ga tasuk-at-ta.
        child-Nom   is rescued-past
        "A child was rescued."

The passive sentences and inchoative sentences are similar in meaning in that both describe the change of state that the individual named by the subject undergoes. Furthermore, they are syntactically similar in that the subject of the passive sentence and that of the inchoative sentence both correspond to the direct object of the transitive verb, to which the passive morpheme *-(r)are* is suffixed. It is generally understood, however, that while passive sentences assume the presence of an individual that brings about the change, inchoative sentences do not.

   One of the reasons that morphologically related transitive and intransitive verb pairs are very intriguing comes from the extent to which Japanese allows causative and inchoative verb pairing, a characteristic that is not uncommon in languages that employ morphological marking of transitivity. As mentioned above, a great majority of English causative and inchoative verb "pairs" take morpho-logically identical forms, but compared to Japanese, the number of such "pairs" is relatively small. Put differently, in most, if not all, cases where English finds causative and inchoative verb uses, there are corresponding Japanese verb pairs that are morphologically related; however, the reverse situation does not hold. (84) lists some of the transitive and intransitive verb pairs of Japanese which do not find English counterparts. For example, in English, one cannot say *The child rescued* to mean that the child is rescued.

(84)   *transitive*   *intransitive*   *gloss (of transitive verb)*
       tasukeru   tasukaru   "help, rescue"
       mitukeru   mitsukaru   "find"
       todokeru   todoku   "deliver"
       kiru   kireru   "cut"
       kimeru   kimaru   "decide"
       miru   mieru   "see"
       kiku   kikoeru   "hear"
       umeru   umaru   "bury"
       ueru   uwaru   "plant"
       someru   somaru   "dye"
       horu   horeru   "dig"
       osieru   osowaru   "teach"
       wakeru   wakareru   "divide"
       ireru   hairu   "put in"
       dasu   deru   "take out"
       umu   umareru   "give birth"
       koeru   kosu   "go over"
       nigasu   nigeru   "let escape"
       tukamaeru   tukamaru   "catch"
       nuku   nukeru   "pull out"
       nugu   nugeru   "take off"
       toru   toreru   "take"
       turu   tureru   "fish"
       arawasu   arawareru   "show"

Thus, the extensive nature of morphologically related transitive and intransitive verb pairs is well attested by the list in (84) and many more.

It is interesting to note that there are some, although not many, sets of morphologically related transitive and intransitive verb pairs in which intransitive counterparts unexpectedly take direct objects (Okutsu 1995; Suga 1995). As was shown in the contrast in (77)–(78) above, transitive verbs normally take Nominatively marked subject and Accusatively marked object; while with intransitive verbs, the Accusatively marked object of transitive verbs appears as subject, marked with the Nominative Case. In contrast, some transitive–intransitive verb pairs, as is illustrated in (85)–(88), take the identical Case pattern: that is, both a transitive verb and its intransitive counterpart have Nominative-marked (often substituted by *wa*) subject and Accusative-marked object. In this case, furthermore, intransitive sentences with direct objects, as in the (b) sentences below, are interpreted on a par with transitive sentences. The examples in (85)–(88), taken from Suga (1995: 123–124; the gloss is added), illustrate this situation.

(85) a. Ichiroo-wa katteni zaseki-o <u>kaeru</u>-node,   sensei-ni yoku
        Ichiroo-Top freely   seat-Acc change-because teacher-by often
        shikarareru. (kaeru – tr.)
        is scolded
     b. Ichiroo-wa katteni zaseki-o <u>kawaru</u>-node sensei-ni yoku shikarareru.
        (kawaru – intr.)
        "Ichiro is often scolded by his teacher because he changes his seats as
        he pleases."

(86) a. Hanako-wa tabitabi zyuusyo-o <u>utusu</u>-node   yuumeida.
        Hanako-Top frequently address-Acc change-because famous
        (utusu – tr.)
     b. Hanako-wa tabitabi zyuusyo-o <u>uturu</u>-node yuumeida. (uturu – intr.)
        "Hanako is famous because she often changes her address."

(87) a. Inu-ga   sippo-o <u>tarasite</u>   aruiteiru. (tarasu – tr.)
        dog-Nom tail-Acc make hang is walking
     b. Inu-ga sippo-o <u>tarete</u> aruiteiru. (tareru – intr.)
        "A dog is walking with its tail hanging down."

(88) a. Yamadakun-wa sigoto-o <u>oete</u> uti-ni   kaetta. (oeru – tr.)
        Yamada-Top   work-Acc finish home-to returned
     b. Yamadakun-wa sigoto-o <u>owatte</u> uti-ni kaetta. (owaru – intr.)
        "Yamada went home after finishing his work."

In each pair, the underlined verbs form root-shared transitive and intransitive verb variants. In spite of the morphologically intransitive status, the verbs in the (b) sentences all have the distribution of subject and object identical with their transitive counterparts in the (a) sentences; and as far as the examples in (85)–(88) are concerned, there is virtually no difference in meaning between the (a) sentences and (b) sentences. (See Suga 1995 for further discussion.)

We have observed earlier that transitive and intransitive verb pairs in English, in the majority of cases, take morphologically identical verb forms. There are similar cases in Japanese as well: a few of them are native verbs, but more examples are found with a Sino-Japanese verbal noun accompanied by *-suru*. (89)–(90) are examples of native verbs (adapted from Okutsu 1995: 71–72); (91) is an instance with a Sino-Japanese verbal noun (adapted from Jacobsen 1992); and (92) lists more Sino-Japanese verbal nouns plus *-suru* that can be used both transitively and intransitively.

(89) a. Mado-ga   hiraku. (intr.)
           window-Nom open
           "The window opens."
      b. Taroo-ga mado-o   hiraku. (tr.)
           Taro-Nom window-Acc open
           "Taro opens the window."

(90) a. Sokudo-ga masu. (intr.)
           speed-Nom increase
           "The speed increases."
      b. Kuruma-ga sokudo-o masu. (tr.)
           car-Nom   speed-Acc increase
           "The car increases its speed."

(91) a. Okane-ga   hunsitu-suru. (intr.)
           money-Nom become lost
           "The money gets lost."
      b. Taroo-ga okane-o   hunsitu-suru. (tr.)
           Taro-Nom money-Acc lose
           "Taro loses money."

(92) hason-suru "break", henka-suru "change", idoo-suru "move", kaihuku-suru "recover", kaisi-suru "begin", kakudai-suru "expand", syukusyoo-suru "decrease", syuuryoo-suru "end", tyuusi-suru "stop", zooka-suru "increase", nensyoo-suru "burn", rakka-suru "fall", . . .

One of the most controversial issues that concern transitive and intransitive verb pairs particularly from the morphological point of view is the directionality of the derivation. The central question is this: is a transitive verb the basic form from which its intransitive counterpart is derived by a morphological operation, or vice versa? This question is especially contentious in Japanese because of the complexity of morphology that shapes the verb pairs under discussion. Before examining Japanese, however, let us look at the typological inventory of derivational direction involved in various languages. Haspelmath (1993) surveyed a number of the world's languages and discussed in detail the question we have just raised. First, in languages like Russian, Lezgian (a Nakho-Daghestanian language spoken in southern Daghestan and northern Azerbaijan in the eastern Caucasus), and Hindi-Urdu (an Indo-European language spoken in India), a transitive verb is indeed the base, and an additional morpheme is added in order to form its intransitive counterpart. Consider the examples in (93).

(93) a. *Russian*   katat'-sja   "roll" (intr.)
                         katat'   "roll" (tr.)
      b. *Lezgian*   xkaž x̂un   "rise"
                         xkažun   "raise"
      c. *Hindi-Urdu*   khul-naa   "open" (intr.)
                         khol-naa   "open" (tr.)

(Haspelmath 1993: 91)

The derivation of intransitive verbs in Russian, Lezgian, and Hindi-Urdu is achieved by a suffix, an auxiliary, and stem modification, respectively. Since inchoative verbs are derived on the basis of causative verbs, Haspelmath calls the direction of the process "anticausative alternation".

The reverse of anticausative alternation, namely, "causative alternation", is also attested in various languages. In these, an intransitive (or inchoative) verb is the base from which its transitive (causative) counterpart is formed. Georgian (a Kartvelian language spoken in the republic of Georgia), French, and Arabic represent some of the languages with causative alternation, as (94) illustrates.

(94) a. *Georgian*   duɣ-s   "cook (intr.)"
                        a-duɣ-ebs   "cook (tr.)"
      b. *French*   fonder   "melt (intr.)"
                        faire fonder   "melt (tr.)"
      c. *Arabic*   darasa   "learn"
                        darrasa   "teach"

(Haspelmath 1993: 91)

The formation of transitive verbs in (94) is parallel to that of intransitive verbs in (93): in Georgian, French, and Arabic, transitive verbs are derived from intransitive bases by way of an affix, an auxiliary, and stem modification, respectively.

English represents yet another type. As we have already observed, the majority of inchoative and causative verb pairs in English take morphologically identical forms. To add to a few examples given above, there are verbs like *open*, *close*, *change*, *roll*, *turn*, *dry*, *freeze*, and many more. The reverse is the situation where transitive and intransitive verb pairs demonstrate no morphological relation. For example, the Russian transitive verb for "burn" and its intransitive counterpart are *goret'* and *žeč'*, respectively (Haspelmath 1993: 92).

Given the typological alternation patterns between transitive and intransitive verbs, how are Japanese transitive and intransitive verb pairs classified? As we have already observed, transitive (causative) and intransitive (inchoative) verbs share a verb root, and to it a variety of transitive-forming and intransitive-forming suffixes is added. In this respect there is no particular directionality of derivation in the sense that the anticausative alternation in (93) and the causative alternation in (94) suggest. Haspelmath calls this pattern "equipollent alternation", and gives Japanese, Hindi-Urdu, and Lithuanian as examples of languages that demonstrate such a pattern. His Hindi-Urdu and Lithuanian examples are given in (95).

(95)   a.   *Hindi-Urdu*   šuruu honaa   "begin (intr.)"
                           šuruu karnaa   "begin (tr.)"
       b.   *Lithuanian*   lūžti   "break (intr.)"
                           laužti   "break (tr.)"

                                                    (Haspelmath 1993: 92)

Let us focus on the three alternation types, anticausative, causative, and equipollent alternations, and represent them schematically, as they will be most relevant to the remainder of our discussion in this section. The symbol "M" in (96)–(98) stands for various kinds of morphological operations, ranging from affixation to addition of auxiliary items, that have been shown to be involved in transitivity alternation patterns thus far.

(96)   *anticausative alternation* $[[\text{verb}]_{tr} + M]_{intr}$

(97)   *causative alternation* $[[\text{verb}]_{intr} + M]_{tr}$

(98)   *equipollent alternation* $[[\text{verb}]_{root} + M1]_{tr}, [[\text{verb}]_{root} + M2]_{intr}$

While Haspelmath uses Japanese as an example of languages that adopt equipollent alternation as a major pattern, one may conjecture on the basis of the list in (81) that some of the morpheme pairs suggest anticausative alternation and others causative alternation. When we focus particularly on the morpheme pairs where one counterpart has no overt morpheme, indicated as -Ø-, it is in principle possible to analyze the verb with no morpheme as the base from which the other is derived by suffixation of an overt morpheme. The morpheme pairs that contain no overt marking in (81) include the following: -e-/-Ø-, -Ø-/-e-, -ar-/-Ø-, -Ø-/-as-, and -Ø-/-se-. The first pair, -e-/-Ø-, for instance, is instantiated by the verb pair *or-e-ru* (intr.) "break" and *or-u* (tr.) "break", and since the transitive verb can be considered the base from which the intransitive verb is derived by the suffixation of -e-, this could be an example of anticausative alternation pattern. The converse situation is illustrated by the second pair, -Ø-/-e-, exemplified by *ak-u* (intr.) "open" and *ak-e-ru* (tr.) "open": in this case, the intransitive verb is the morphological base, and its transitive counterpart is derived by adding the suffix -e- to the intransitive verb base. Thus, this may count as an instance of causative alternation. Given this type of analysis, the rest of the morpheme pairs, i.e. those that do not contain -Ø- either as an intransitive-forming affix or as a transitive-forming affix, are considered instances of equipollent alternation: in the third morpheme pair in (81), -ar-/-e-, which derives *agaru* (intr.) "rise" and *ageru* (tr.) "raise", the verbal root is *ag-* and to it the intransitivizer -ar- and the transitivizer -e- are suffixed to derive the intransitive and transitive verb forms, respectively.

Viewed in this fashion, Japanese may be regarded as a language in which all three alternation patterns in (96)–(98) are operative in the formation of morphologically related intransitive and transitive verb pairs. In fact, this is the position that has traditionally been taken by a number of scholars who have dealt with transitivity alternation patterns, although actual morphological and derivational analyses vary according to individual scholars, leading to different classifications of verb pairs. Following this tradition, Okutsu (1995), for one, classifies derivation types into three: they are intransitivization, transitivization, and polarization, and correspond to (96)–(98), respectively. Examples of each type (adapted from Okutsu's 1995 lists) are given in (99)–(101).[17] (Each English gloss corresponds to the transitive verb.)

(99) *intransitivization* hasam-u   →   hasam-ar-u   "insert"
                            husag-u   →   husag-ar-u   "close"
                            sas-u   →   sas-ar-u   "stick"
                            tunag-u   →   tunag-ar-u   "connect"

(100) *transitivization*   kawak-u   →   kawak-as-u   "dry"
                            ugok-u   →   ugok-as-u   "move"
                            her-u   →   her-as-u   "decrease"
                            oyob-u   →   yob-os-u   "extend"

(101) *polarization*   nao-s-u   ↔   nao-r-u   "repair"
                            no-se-ru   ↔   no-r-u   "take in"
                            mawa-s-u   ↔   mawa-r-u   "turn"
                            kobo-s-u   ↔   kobo-re-ru "spill"

As Okutsu himself cautions (and see also Kageyama 1996), however, morphological composition of these transitive and intransitive verb pairs alone is not sufficient to provide a comprehensive analysis of directionality of derivation and more generally the nature of the relationship between the two variants. This is so especially because transitivity alternations involve a number of issues including historical change and sometimes matters beyond morphology. In order to capture an accurate picture of the nature of the relationship between morphologically related transitive and intransitive pairs, we have to consider various factors ranging from morphological shape and morphophonological properties, meaning the relationship between the two, and historical developments to the syntactic relations of nouns that a verb requires. To illustrate the complexity of transitivity alternations, compare the examples in (102)–(103) (adapted from Okutsu 1995: 64).

(102) a. Konogoro atama-ga   bokete-kita. (bokeru – intr.)
           these days head-Nom became senile-came
           "I've been getting senile these days."
       b. *Konogoro atama-o   bokasite-kita. (bokasu – tr.)
           these days head-Acc make senile-came
           "I have been making myself senile these days."

(103) a. Kabe-no iro-ga   boketa. (bokeru – intr.)
           wall-Gen color-Nom faded
           "The color of the wall has faded."
       b. Kare-wa kabe-no iro-o   bokasita. (bokasu – tr.)
           he-Top   wall-Gen color-Acc shaded off
           "He shaded off the color of the wall."

It should be noticed that although the identical set of verb pairs is used in (102) and (103), the transitive variant is natural only in (103): (102b) is odd because becoming senile is not in the control of human beings, and hence the causation of such a situation cannot be expressed by the transitive (and causative) verb *bokasu*. The color of the wall is something that human beings can change, and thus (103b) is straightforwardly interpreted. If we focus only on the morphological composition of the verb pairs in (102) and (103), the two cases are treated on a par: that is, the verbs in the (a) sentences are intransitive verbs and those in the (b) sentences are their transitive verbs; and the former are inchoative verbs while the latter are their causative counterparts. Once they are put in sentences, the difference emerges, and the kind of semantic relationship between (103a) and (103b) cannot equally be obtained between (102a) and (102b), casting doubt on the "relatedness" between the two verbs that their morphological composition appears to suggest. Similar observations have been more extensively made in Kageyama (1996). Thus, the true nature of the relationship between transitive and intransitive variants of transitive alternations that we have discussed in this section is certainly founded on their morphological composition, which shares at least a verbal root, but this relationship calls for examination over a wide range of linguistic behavior.

6   Issues in Japanese Morphology (2): Nominalization

We have seen that one of the hallmarks of derivational morphemes is that they may change the categorial status of the word to which they are affixed. For example, the change in category from verb to noun is observed in English by the derivation of *driver* from *drive*, *creation* from *create*, and *laughter* from *laugh*. In each of these cases, a suffix is clearly identified that is responsible for the categorial change. What about words like *read*, *buy*, and *make* in (104)–(106)?

(104)   Chomsky's *Syntactic Structure* is not an easy <u>read</u>.

(105)   Kittle's is advertising a great <u>buy</u> for their Labor Day sale.

(106)   What is the <u>make</u> of your car?

While we are more accustomed to see words like *read*, *buy*, and *make* as verbs, it is evident in these sentences that they are used as nouns. That is, there are no derivational morphemes attached to them, but they function perfectly as nouns. Such a categorial shift serves as a morphological operation even though no overt change in form is observed, and it is considered a kind of **nominalization**. Nominalization includes any operation that changes the categorial status of a word that is not a noun to a noun, whether it involves affixation or not. The underlined words in (104)–(106) are derived by nominalization, and are often called deverbal nouns. Japanese demonstrates a number of instances of nominalization, both those derived by affixation of overt morphemes and those without them.

Deverbal nouns that parallel those in (104)–(106) are formed in the following two ways in Japanese. When a verb root ends in a vowel, the root itself serves as a noun; on the other hand, when a verb root ends in a consonant, its noun form is derived by suffixing -*i* to the root. These forms correspond to those that have been referred to as Renyookei in traditional grammar terms. Examples of the two cases are given in (107)–(108).

(107)   *vowel-ending root*   *deverbal noun form*
        kangae   "think"   kangae
        kari   "borrow"   kari
        tasuke   "help"   tasuke
        mooke   "profit"   mooke
        araware   "appear"   araware
        kokoromi   "try"   kokoromi
        sasae   "support"   sasae
        oboe   "remember"   oboe
        akirame   "give up"   akirame

(108)   *consonant-ending root*   *deverbal noun form*
        tanom   "request"   tanom-i
        tomar   "stop"   tomar-i
        kat   "win"   kat-i
        kaseg   "earn"   kaseg-i
        ugok   "move"   ugok-i
        sakeb   "scream"   sakeb-i
        tayor   "rely on"   tayor-i
        kurusim   "suffer"   kurusim-i
        kimar   "decide"   kimar-i

Nominalized verbs, namely, deverbal nouns like those in (107)–(108), refer either to the process of the events denoted by the base verbs or to entities that are somehow related to the events named by the base verbs, such as agents of the events, resulting products, and place and time of the events, among others (Martin 1987; Kageyama 2002). The list in (109)–(116) (selected from Martin 1987: 886–887), for instance, illustrates the range of process and entities to which deverbal nouns can refer. These derived nouns are all originated from single verbs, whose present tense forms are given in parentheses.

(109) *process*   oyogi (<oyogu) "swimming", sirabe (<siraberu) "investigation"

(110) *content of process*   kangae (<kangaeru) "thought", osie (<osieru) "instruction", nozomi (<nozomu) "hope", negai (<negau) "request", nayami (<nayamu) "worry", inori (<inoru) "prayer"

(111) *product or result*   tutumi (<tutumu) "bundle", hori (<horu) "ditch", amari (<amaru) "excess", katamari (<katamaru) "clod", atumari (<atumaru) "gathering", kubomi (<kubomu) "dent"

(112) *agent*   suri (<suru) "thief", domori (<domoru) "stammerer"

(113) *object*   tumami (<tumamu) "knob", yatoi (<yatou) "employee"

(114) *means*   hakari (<hakaru) "scales", hataki (<hataku) "duster"

(115) *place*   toori (<tooru) "street", hate (<hateru) "the ends"

(116) *time*   kure (<kureru) "sundown", owari (<owaru) "end"

There are a great many deverbal nouns whose base verbs are compounds, consisting of two verbs. Some examples are given in (117).

(117)   uketori (<uke-toru) "receipt", kasidasi (<kasi-dasu) "lending out", tukisoi (<tuki-sou) "attendant", ukeire (<uke-ireru) "acceptance", moosikomi (<moosi-komu) "application", kumitate (<kumi-tateru) "structure"

We will take up those cases in the next section, where compound verbs will be discussed in detail.

That these deverbal nouns are indeed categorially nouns is shown by observing (i) that they can be modified by demonstrative words like *kono* "this" and *sono* "that", (ii) that they can take noun modifiers with the Genitive Case *-no*, and (iii) that they take the noun conjugation paradigm. These are shown in (118)–(120).

(118)   Demonstratives
        a. kono kangae   "this thought/idea"
            this thought
        b. sono ugoki   "that movement"
            that movement
        c. ano uketori   "that receipt"
            that receipt

(119)   Noun Modification with *-no*
    a.   Taroo-no   kangae   "Taro's thought/idea"
        Taro-Gen   thought
    b.   sensei-no   ugoki   "the teacher's movement"
        teacher-Gen   movement
    c.   sinamono-no uketori   "the receipt of the goods"
        goods-Gen   receipt

(120)   Noun Conjugation Paradigm
    a.   *non-past*   kangae/ugoki/uketori-da
    b.   *non-past neg.* kangae/ugoki/uketori-zha nai
    c.   *past*   kangae/ugoki/uketori-dat-ta
    d.   *past neg.*   kangae/ugoki/uketori-zya na-kat-ta
    e.   *tentative*   kangae/ugoki/uketori-daroo

Nominalization is also attained by the affixation of a variety of morphemes. The suffixation of *-te* to a verbal root that we have discussed in section 3.1 is an instance where a noun is derived from a verb to name an agent of the action denoted by the verb. The examples are repeated in (121).

(121)   a.   kak-i-te   "writer"
        write
    b.   odor-i-te   "dancer"
        dance
    c.   hanas-i-te "speaker"
        speak
    d.   ur-i-te   "seller"
        sell

Other suffixes similar to *-te* include *-kata*, *-kai/gai*, and *-sama*: they are suffixed to verb roots to mean "method", "value", and "manner", respectively, as in (122).

(122)   a.   kak-i-kata   "method of writing"
        tabe-kata   "method of eating"
        yom-i-kata   "method of reading"
    b.   iki-gai   "value of living"
        si-gai   "value of doing"
        tukuri-gai   "value of making"
    c.   iki-zama   "manner of living"
        sini-zama   "manner of dying"
        tukuri-zama "manner of making"

Nominalization is not limited to verbs in its application. Suffixes like *-sa* and *-mi* are suffixed to adjectives to derive nouns, as the examples in (123)–(124) demonstrate. The suffixation of *-sa* derives a noun that refers to an abstract property named by the base adjective, while the *-mi* suffixation picks out a concrete entity with the property (Sugioka 1986).

(123)   atu-sa   "thickness"
        naga-sa   "length"
        yasu-sa   "cheapness"
        atarasi-sa   "freshness"
        akaru-sa   "brightness"

(124)   maru-mi   "a roundness"
        huka-mi   "a deep place"
        taka-mi   "a high place"
        yowa-mi   "a weakness"

In all the instances of nominalization process we have seen thus far, a single lexical form undergoes the nominalization process, whether it involves an overt meaningful morpheme, such as in (121)–(124), or not, as in (107)–(117). That is, in all the cases above, a single non-noun lexical item is converted to a single noun. The source of nominalization, however, is not restricted to a single lexical item; rather, a phrase can also be nominalized (Sugioka 1986; Martin 1987). Consider the examples of the *-te* nominalization in (125)–(129), in comparison with those in (121). ((125)–(126) are adapted from Sugioka 1986: 98, and (127)–(129) from Martin 1987: 224.)

(125)   Kare-wa yome-ni nari-te-o   sagasite-iru.
        he-Top   bride-to become-TE-Acc looking for
        "He is looking for a bride-to-be."

(126)   Inaka-de-wa   isya-ni   nari-te-ga   sukunai.
        country-in-Top doctor-to become-TE-Nom few
        "Few become a doctor in a rural town."

(127)   Zensokui-ni-wa   nari-te-ga   sukunai.
        asthma specialist-to-Top become-TE-Nom few
        "Those becoming asthma specialists are few in number."

(128)   Aite-ni site kure-te-ga   nakatta.
        deal with   favor TE-Nom there was none
        "There was no one who dealt with me."

(129)   Moratte kure-te-ga   arimasen.
        receive   favor-TE-Nom there is none
        "There's none who will marry me."

In (125)–(127) *nari-te* is a deverbal noun whose base verb is *naru* "become", and in this sense, they do not appear to be any different from those in (121). Since the deverbal noun *nari-te* is categorially a full-fledged noun, any noun that is intended to modify it is expected to be marked with the Genitive Case *-no*. Contrary to this prediction, the phrasal expression . . . *ni naru* "become . . ." stays intact just as in cases where *naru* "become" functions as a verb, as in *yome-ni* *naru* "become a bride", *isya-ni naru* "become a doctor", and *zensokui-ni naru* "become an asthma specialist". Furthermore, when we consider the meaning of the *-te* nominalization, the scope of the agent meaning is not just over the verb *naru* "become" alone but over *yome-ni naru* "become a bride" in (125), *isya-ni naru* "become a doctor" in (126), and *zensokui-ni naru* "become an asthma specialist" in (127). Thus, the agent-forming morpheme *-te* should be considered to be suffixed to a phrase, as is schematized in (130a), not to a single word, as in (130b).

(130) a.   [yome-ni   nari]-te
            [isha-ni   nari]-te
            [zensokui-ni nari]-te
       b.   [yome-ni]   [nari-te]
            [isha-ni]   [nari-te]
            [zensokui-ni] [nari-te]

(128)–(129) present a similar case of phrasal nominalization. While *kureru* "give" stands by itself as a verb, as is demonstrated in (131a), it serves as an auxiliary verb in the expression V-*te kureru* to mean "do someone a favor of V-ing", as in (131b).

(131) a.   Taroo-ga   watasi-ni hana-o   kureta.
            Taro-Nom I-Dat   flower-Acc gave
            "Taro gave me flowers."
       b.   Taroo-ga   zitensya-o naosite-kureta.
            Taro-Nom bicycle-Acc repair-gave
            "Taro repaired my bicycle (for me)."
            (lit. Taro did me a favor of repairing my bicycle.)

As these examples illustrate, *kureru* as a free-standing verb has the meaning of possession change of some item, but *kureru* as an auxiliary verb in the sequence V-*te kureru* loses the literal meaning of the concrete action of giving. Instead, the auxiliary verb indicates that the event denoted by the verb (e.g., *naosu* "repair" in (131b)) is a favor from one individual to another. In light of the *-te* nominalization in (128)–(129), then, the agent-forming morpheme should be regarded as nominalizing the entire phrase, *aite-ni site kureru* "do a favor of dealing with" and *moratte kureru* "do a favor of receiving", rather than nominalizing the verb *kureru* alone, since the meanings implied in these nominalization cases retain the meaning of *kureru* as an auxiliary verb. To schematize this situation, the nominalization in (128)–(129) should be analyzed as (132a), rather than (132b).

(132) a.   [aite-ni site   kure]-te
            [moratte   kure]-te
       b.   [aite-ni site] [kure]-te
            [moratte]   [kure]-te

Similar examples of phrase-level suffixation are also found with nominalization of adjectives, such as the *-sa* suffixation in (123). While the morpheme
-sa is added to an adjectival base to derive a noun in (123), the examples in
(133)–(134) (slightly modified from Sugioka 1986: 138) illustrate that the scope
of suffixation extends beyond a single word.

(133)   Taroo-wa [kane-o   hosi]-sa-ni   nusumi-o sita.
        Taro-Top [money-Acc want]-SA-cause theft-Acc did
        "Taro committed a robbery out of desire for money."

(134)   Taroo-wa [tesuto-de ii   ten-o   tori-ta]-sa-no   amari
        Taro-Top [test-in   good mark-Acc get-want]-SA-Gen as a result
        kanningu-o   sita.
        cunning-Acc did
        "Taro cheated in the exam out of the desire to get good marks."

The phrase indicated by square brackets is the portion to which *-sa* is suffixed.
If *-sa* nominalizes just the adjective *hosii* "want" in (133), deriving *hosi-sa*,
the modifying noun, *kane* "money", should be marked with the Genitive Case
-no. In fact, such a possibility is available: *kane-no hosi-sa-ni* . . . is perfectly
acceptable in (133). A point significant to our discussion is that *kane* "money"
can also be marked with the Accusative Case *-o*, just as is expected when
hosii is a predicative adjective: *kane-o hosii* "I want money." That is, the fact
that *kane* "money" is marked with the Accusative Case and at the same time
can appear with the nominalized adjective, *hosi-sa*, suggests that the suffix *-sa*
nominalizes the whole phrase, *kane-o hosii*, rather than a single word. That is,
-sa is suffixed to the phrase *kane-o hosii*, rather than just *hosii*. (134) presents
an even more interesting case. The desiderative suffix *-tai* "want to" suffixes to
a verbal stem, making the whole complex pattern with adjectives in its conjugational paradigm. On the surface, the nominalizing morpheme *-sa* appears
to be suffixed to the adjectival base, *tori-tai* "want to get", but as the square
brackets indicate, it is suffixed to the whole phrase. Notice that *ii ten* "good
mark" is the direct object of the verb *toru* "get", and the locative phrase *tesuto-
de* "in test" modifies the phrase *ii ten-o toru* "get good mark", as is illustrated
in (135).

(135)   Taroo-ga   tesuto-de ii   ten-o   toru/totta/tori-tai.
        Taro-Nom test-in   good mark-Acc get/got/want to get
        "Taro gets/got/wants to get good marks in the test."

Thus, the phrases *tesuto-de* and *ii ten-o* in (134) are exactly the way they appear
as accompaniments of a predicate as shown in (135). This suggests, then, that
what *-sa* nominalizes is the entire phrase surrounded by the brackets. The discussion above makes it clear that the nominalization process operates not only
on individual words but also on phrases. Put differently and in more general terms,
there are both lexical and phrasal sources available to suffixation.

7 Issues in Japanese Morphology (3): Compounding

7.1 Background

Compounding is a very common word formation type in Japanese, and its examples are ubiquitous. When a compound is formed, it displays a set of properties of its own. First, we have already observed examples of phonological phenomena involved in compounding, namely the Rendaku (sequential voicing) phenomenon and accent shift. For instance, in the compound *satogokoro* "homesickness", which results from putting *sato* "country" and *kokoro* "heart" together, the initial consonant /k/ of *kokoro* undergoes voicing; and the original accent on the second mora of *kokoro* moves to the initial mora of that word.

Second, the meaning of a compound is not always a composition of the meanings of the words that constitute the compound, and is often idiosyncratic. For example, *tabe-aruku* "make an eating tour" and *nomi-aruku* "bar hop" are formed by putting together consumption verbs, *taberu* "eat" and *nomu* "drink", and the manner of motion verb *aruku* "walk", but neither compound preserves the meaning of walking. Furthermore, in the case of *nomi-aruku* "bar hop", the drinking action expressed in this compound refers specifically to alcohol consumption. Another semantic property of compounds is that the nouns that comprise them are not referential (Spencer 1991; Kageyama 1993). In Noun–Verb compounds like *kusa-musiri* (weeds-picking) "weeding", *hon-dana* (book-shelf) "bookshelf", and *yama-nobori* (mountain-climbing) "mountain climbing", each noun, *kusa* "weeds", *hon* "book", and *yama* "mountain", does not refer to specific weeds, books, or mountains. The non-referential nature is evidenced by the fact that the noun portions cannot be replaced by demonstrative words, as in *sore-musiri (that-picking), *sore-dana (that-shelf), and *soko-nobori (there-climbing) (Kageyama 1993).

Finally, internal structure is an important property of compounds since it relates directly to their phonological and semantic properties. Recall from our discussion of Rendaku in chapter 3 that different internal structures of a three-word compound change the voicing possibilities of potential Rendaku sites. Furthermore, we have also observed that variation in internal structure changes how resulting compounds are interpreted. Thus, the phonological and semantic properties are indeed consequences of a particular internal structure that a compound has as its essential property.

In putting two (or more) words together to form a compound, the relation between them may be characterized in different ways. Major relations that are often cited include **head–modifier**, **apposition**, and **predicate–argument** (Spencer 1991; Kageyama 1993). Compounds like *hon-dana* "bookshelf", *denki-sutoobu* "electric heater", and *hasi-bako* "chopstick box" are examples of the head–modifier relation. The second member of each of these compounds serves as head (Righthand Head Rule), and the first word describes the head: *hon-dana* refers to a kind of shelf, and the purpose of the shelf is for placing or organizing books. Another compound, *syokki-dana* "dish shelf", which has the same head as *hon-dana*, refers to a type of shelf, and it is further specified as being used for dishes. Similarly, *sutoobu* "heater" in *denki-sutoobu* and *hako* "box" in *hasi-bako* mentioned above are the heads, and the modifiers *denki* "electric" and *hasi* "chopsticks" modify the heads to further specify what sort of heater and box they are.

Examples of the apposition relation are found in dvandva compounds, such as *oya-ko* "parent and child" and *iki-kaeri* "coming and going". As the term suggests, neither of the two members of a dvandva compound has a primary status, such as that of head, or bears any particular dependency relation with the other. Rather, they are simply conjoined in parallel.

In order to explain the predicate–argument relation pertinent to compounds, we need to digress a little and discuss some semantic property of verbs. A native speaker of English knows that active sentences and passive sentences like those in (136) are semantically related.

(136)   a.   John kicked the dog.
        b.   The dog was kicked by John.

Although *John* in (136a) is the subject while *John* in (136b) is the object of the preposition *by*, we know that semantically *John* plays the same role in the action of kicking the dog, namely, the person who initiated the action. Similarly, the dog in the two sentences may have syntactically different functions, but nonetheless it is semantically interpreted in a parallel fashion in both sentences. That is, the dog is the one that received the kick. Thus, even though John as "the kicker" and the dog as "the kicked" may have different syntactic realizations, their semantic roles in active and passive sentences are identical. These semantic roles, in fact, imply participants of the action or the state that is denoted by a verb. In order to make reference to those semantic participants, we need to introduce **thematic roles** or **semantic roles** (cf. Gruber 1965; Fillmore 1968; Jackendoff 1972).

The primary thematic roles that we shall refer to are **agent, theme, goal, source**, and **experiencer**. Agent refers to the instigator of an action. The subjects in (137)–(138) are examples of agent.

(137)   Taroo-ga   ringo-o   tabeta.
        Taro-Nom apple-Acc ate
        "Taro ate an apple."

(138)   Ziroo-ga   hon-o   kaita.
        Ziro-Nom book-Acc wrote
        "Ziro wrote a book."

Taroo in (137) and *Ziroo* in (138) both perform the action denoted by the verbs, *tabeta* "ate" and *kaita* "wrote", respectively, and hence, they are referred to as agents. Theme is characterized as the entity that undergoes a change of state or a transfer. In the above examples, *ringo* "apple" and *hon* "book" are regarded as themes since they undergo a change of state, from not being eaten/ written to being eaten/written. An example of theme as an entity undergoing a transfer is given in (139).

(139)   Taroo-ga   Hanako-ni   hon-o   ageta.
        Taro-Nom Hanako-Dat book-Acc gave
        "Taro gave a book to Hanako."

The noun *hon* "book" undergoes a transfer from Taro's possession to Hanako's possession, and hence it should be considered a theme.

What about the thematic role of *Hanako* in (139)? It is an example of a goal, namely, the ending point of a transfer. The final location of the book in this sentence is Hanako, and hence *Hanako* bears the goal role. Associated with the goal is the source, which refers to the starting point of a transfer. Consider the sentence in (140).

(140)   Ziroo-ga   hon-o   Tookyoo-kara Oosaka-made okutta.
        Ziro-Nom book-Acc Tokyo-from   Osaka-to   sent
        "Ziro sent books from Tokyo to Osaka."

In this example the starting point of the transfer of books is Tokyo and the ending point is Osaka, and hence Tokyo is the source and Osaka is the goal. Needless to say, *Ziroo* and *hon* "book" participate in the transfer as agent and theme, respectively. Notice that *Taroo* in (139) has been identified as the agent, but can also be considered the source since the book was in Taro's possession before it was transferred to Hanako. Therefore, in this sentence, Taro can be regarded as either agent or source.

Finally, the experiencer is normally associated with verbs that denote psychological states, such as *sonkei-suru* "respect", *kirau* "dislike", and *osoreru* "fear". An entity that experiences a psychological state is referred to as an experiencer while an entity that causes a psychological state is called either a theme or a stimulus. In (141) *Taroo* is the experiencer and *Tanaka-sensei* is the theme (or stimulus).

(141)   Taroo-ga   Tanaka-sensei-o   sonkei-site-iru.
        Taro-Nom Prof. Tanaka-Acc respect
        "Taro respects Prof. Tanaka."

Thematic roles are necessary to describe an event denoted by a verb as its key role players, and represent essential elements of verbs. The thematic roles that a verb requires are called **arguments**, and the number and type of a verb's arguments are listed in a verb's **argument structure**. For instance, the argument structures of *taberu* "eat" and *ageru* "give" are given in (142).

(142)   a.   taberu: (agent, theme)
        b.   ageru: (agent, theme, goal)

What is significant about argument structure is that its content, namely, the number and type of roles, is usually consistent within a class of verbs that are semantically coherent. For instance, verbs of motion such as *aruku* "walk", *odoru* "dance", and *hasiru* "run" always take one role and that role is of agent. Verbs of emotion or psychological state like *kirau* "dislike", *nikumu* "hate", and *osoreru* "fear" invariably appear with the experiencer and theme. Thus, as long as we know the semantic class of a verb, we can generally determine the nature of the argument structure with which the verb is associated (cf. Levin 1985).

There are a number of expressions besides arguments that appear in a sentence that further describe an event denoted by a verb. When we depict an event in which Hanako eats pizza, we can give details such as what she eats it with, and when, where, and with whom she eats it. The example in (143) illustrates such a depiction.

(143)   Hanako-ga   kinoo   pizza-o   kooen-de Taroo-to
        Hanako-Nom yesterday pizza-Acc park-at   Taro-with
        hasi-de   tabeta.
        chopsticks-with ate
        "Hanako ate pizza with chopsticks with Taro at a park yesterday."

Given the argument structure of *taberu* in (142a) above, we know that the expressions corresponding to agent, Hanako, and theme, pizza, are arguments that are always associated with the verb. On the other hand, phrases like *kinoo* "yesterday", *kooen-de* "at the park", *Taroo-to* "with Taro", and *hasi-de* "with chopsticks" are not required by the verb, and yet may serve to provide further elaboration of the event denoted by the verb. These expressions are **adjuncts**, as opposed to arguments, and are not members of the argument structure.

Returning to the last type of relations compounds may have, namely the predicate–argument relation, examples of this type are seen in compounds in which one member is a predicate such as a verb and the other serves as its argument. The compounds in (144) consist of a noun on the left and a verb, or its nominalization, on the right. The verbs all take the argument structure of (agent, theme), and the noun corresponds to the theme role of the verb.

(144)   a.   mi-gamaeru   "stand ready"
             body-get set
        b.   tema-doru   "take time"
             time-take
        c.   nezi-mawasi   "screwdriver"
             screw-turning
        d.   kan-kiri   "can opener"
             can-cutting
        e.   kusa-tori   "weeding"
             weed-taking

These dependency relations relevant to compounds do more than serve as a convenient descriptive tool to group compounds together. They often contribute to making important linguistic generalizations. We have already noted that the Rendaku phenomenon, a recurring topic, does not apply to drandva compounds. Sugioka (1986) further observes that compounds of the predicate–argument relation and those that consist of a verb and its adjunct react differently to Rendaku. According to Sugioka, in compounds whose second member is a deverbal noun, the second member generally resists Rendaku when the first member is an argument of the original verb; if, on the other hand, the first member is an adjunct, the second member readily undergoes the voicing phenomenon. The contrast is demonstrated in (145)–(147) (adapted from Sugioka 1986: 107).

(145) a. e-kaki   (< e-o kaku)   [e = argument]
           picture-paint   (< picture-Acc paint)
           "painter"
       b. te-gaki   (< te-de kaku)   [te = adjunct (instrument)]
           hand-paint   (< hand-with paint)
           "hand painted"

(146) a. mono-hosi   (< mono-o hosu)   [mono = argument]
           thing-dry   (< thing-Acc dry)
           "place for dying laundry"
       b. kage-bosi   (< kage-de hosu)   [kage = adjunct (location)]
           shade-dry   (< shade-at dry)
           "drying in the shade"

(147) a. sakana-turi   (< sakana-o turu)   [sakana = argument]
           fish-catch   (< fish-Acc catch)
           "fishing"
       b. iso-zuri   (< iso-de turu)   [iso = adjunct (location)]
           beach-fishing   (< beach-at catch)
           "fishing on the beach"

The compounds in the (a) sentences exhibit the predicate–argument relation between the two members: the first is an argument of the second. These compounds do not undergo Rendaku. In the (b) sentences, the first members are adjuncts of various sorts to the second members. Rendaku is observed in this kind of compound. Hence, Rendaku is conditioned by the nature of relations that members of a compound have to each other.[18]

With the background relevant to compounds given above, in the remainder of this section we shall examine N–V compounds and V–V compounds as well as nominalized compounds more closely, restricting our attention to those consisting of native nouns and verbs.

7.2 N–V Compounds

What will be referred to as N–V compounds here include those consisting of a noun as the first member and a verb as the second member, whether the verb categorially remains as a verb or turns into a deverbal noun. Both instances observe the Righthand Head Rule: in the former, where the head preserves the categorial status of verb, the compound is considered a verb, while in the latter, the head is a deverbal noun, and hence the compound is treated as a noun. The generalizations in (148) by and large hold for N–V compounds in Japanese (Sugioka 1986; Shibatani 1990; Kageyama 1993, 2001a).

(148) a. The noun in N–V compounds may be an argument or an adjunct of the accompanying verb. When the noun is an argument of the verb, it generally resists the agent role.
       b. N–V compounds that are nouns (i.e. those whose verb member is nominalized) exhibit a wide range in their reference, from event, state, agent, result/product, location, and time to instrument.
       c. N–V compounds that are nouns are more common than those that are verbs. In N–V compounds that are verbs, furthermore, having adjuncts for the noun member is extremely rare.
       d. A large number of N–V compounds that are nouns, if not all, do not find their corresponding verbal forms as independently existing words. Some of them co-occur with -*suru* "do" to achieve a function parallel to verbs.

(149)–(150) list some examples of N–V compounds that are verbs and those that are nouns: compounds in the (a) examples have noun members that correspond to the verbs' arguments, and the noun members in the (b) examples correspond to the verbs' adjuncts. (Those in parentheses are archaic.)

(149) N–V Compounds that are Verbs
       a. mi-gamaeru "take a stance", awa-dateru "beat up a froth", tema-doru "take time", na-zukeru "name somebody", iro-datu "get excited/angry", huti-doru "hem", iro-aseru "fade", abura-jimiru "become dirty with oil", nami-utu "dash", myaku-utu "pulsate"
       b. muti-utu "whip", (ama-tobu "fly in the sky")

(150) N–V Compounds that are Nouns
       a. neji-mawasi "screwdriver", kan-kiri "can opener", mono-oki "lumber room", abura-kosi "oil filter", yasai-itame "stir-fried vegetables", syooyu-sasi "soy-sauce pitcher", sake-nomi "heavy drinker", sara-arai "dish washing (person)", yuki-doke "snow melting"
       b. hutuka-yoi "hangover", huna-yoi "sea-sickness", hi-yake "suntan", te-ami "hand-weaving/woven", abura-itame "stir-fry", mizu-arai "washing without soap", mizu-taki "unthickened stew cooked on the table", abura-age "deep-fried tofu", (taki-nomi "like drinking waterfall")

Let us discuss the generalizations in (148), making reference to actual examples in (149)–(150). The noun members of the compounds in (149a) and (150a) are arguments of the co-occurring verb members. As (148a) states, none of the noun members in (149a) and (150a) corresponds to the agent argument of its verb member. If the noun member is the agent of the verb member, a resulting compound is not well-formed, as is illustrated in (151)–(154).

(151) mi-gamaeru   vs.   *teki-gamaeru (intended: "an enemy's getting set")
      body-get set   enemy-get set

(152) awa-dateru   vs.   *kokku-dateru (intended: "a cook's beating up
      froth-beat up   froth")
                             cook-beat up

(153) neji-mawasi   vs.   *daiku-mawasi (intended: "a carpenter's tightening
      screw-revolving   a screw")
                             carpenter-revolving

(154) yasai-itame   vs.   *kokku-itame (intended: "a cook's stir-frying")
      vegetable-stir frying   cook-stir-frying

The restriction on the semantic role in N–V compounds has also been pointed out in English. For example, *truck driver* is an acceptable (and existing) compound, where *truck* is the theme of *drive*, but *child-driver* is not acceptable to refer to a child who drives, since *child* is the agent of the verb. Thus, the recognition of argument structure and its members is relevant to a generalization holding for N–V compounds beyond Japanese.

   N–V compounds in (150) are categorially nouns: the rightmost member is the head and determines category; and in this case, furthermore, the head is a deverbal noun. As nouns, N–V compounds as a whole may refer, and the referential range is very wide, from act and state to object, and from something concrete to something abstract (Sugioka 1986; Kageyama 1993). Of the examples in (150), *sara-arai* "dish washing", *yuki-doke* "snow melting", and *mizu-arai* "washing without soap" refer to acts; *hutuka-yoi* "hangover", *huna-yoi* "seasickness", and *hi-yake* "suntan" all refer to states describing an individual or skin; *sake-nomi* "heavy drinker" and again *sara-arai* "dish washing person" name a person who undertakes the act of alcohol drinking or dish washing; *neji-mawasi* "screwdriver", *kan-kiri* "can opener", *abura-kosi* "oil filter", and *syooyu-sasi* "soy-sauce pitcher" refer to instruments to be used for various purposes; *yasai-itame* "stir-fried vegetables", *te-ami* "hand-woven", *abura-itame* "stir-fry", *mizu-taki* "unthickened stew cooked on the table", and *abura-age* "deep-fried tofu" refer to products; and finally *mono-oki* "lumber room" refers to a location. It may be noted that the thematic role that the noun member bears in relation to the verb member has no implication for the type of interpretation that a compound ends up with. In *sara-arai* (dish-wash), for instance, the noun member serves as theme of the verb *arau* "wash", and yet the compound can mean either an agent of dish washing or the act of dish washing; likewise in *abura-age* (oil-fry), the noun member, *abura* "oil", refers to the instrument with which the frying event takes place, but the compound as a whole names not just any product as a result of frying in oil, but a specific tofu product, i.e. deep-fried tofu.

   Turning to (148c–d), let us pay attention to the contrast between N–V compounds that are verbs and those that are nouns. In our discussion of nominalizations, we have observed that a deverbal noun is generated by taking the Renyookei form of the base verb: this form corresponds to a verb root if it ends in a vowel, or to a verb root plus /i/ if it ends with a consonant. The fact that the number of N–V compounds that are nouns far exceeds that of N–V compounds that are verbs, however, suggests that the former may not always be "derived" from the latter by nominalization. We can make two observations in this connection. First, in many cases the verb member of the compounds in (149) does not find its nominalized form, as an individual word or as a compound. Consider (155).[19]

(155)		N–V compound (V)	N–V compound (N)	nominalization of the verb member
	a.	mi-gamaeru	mi-gamae	kamae
	b.	awa-dateru	*awa-date	?tate
	c.	tema-doru	tema-dori	*tori
	d.	na-zukeru	na-zuke	tuke
	e.	iro-datu	?iro-dati	*tati
	f.	huti-doru	huti-dori	*tori
	g.	iro-aseru	?iro-ase	*ase
	h.	abura-jimiru	*abura-jimi	simi
	i.	nami-utu	*nami-uti	*uti
	j.	myaku-utu	*myaku-uti	*uti
	k.	muti-utu	muti-uti	*uti

Second, in a similar vein, a large number of nominal N–V compounds in (150) do not find their corresponding verbal forms. Furthermore, the nominalized verb member in (150) often cannot stand by itself as an independent deverbal noun. This is shown in (156).

(156)		N–V compound (N)	N–V compound (V)	nominalization of the verb member
	a.	neji-mawasi	*neji-mawasu	mawasi
	b.	kan-kiri	*kan-kiru	?kiri
	c.	mono-oki	*mono-oku	*oki
	d.	abura-kosi	*abura-kosu	*kosi
	e.	yasai-itame	*yasai-itameru	*itame
	f.	syooyu-sasi	*syooyu-sasu	?sasi
	g.	sake-nomi	*sake-nomu	?nomi
	h.	sara-arai	*sara-arau	arai
	i.	yuki-doke	*yuki-dokeru	*toke
	j.	hutuka-yoi	*hutuka-you	yoi
	k.	huna-yoi	*huna-you	yoi
	l.	hi-yake	*hi-yakeru	yake
	m.	te-ami	*te-amu	*ami
	n.	abura-itame	*abura-itameru	*itame
	o.	mizu-arai	*mizu-arau	arai
	p.	mizu-taki	*mizu-taku	*taki
	q.	abura-age	*abura-ageru	age

The situation in (155) and (156) indicates that there is very little connection between verbal and nominal N–V compounds in terms of their "derivational" relationship. Nominal N–V compounds, in particular, are clearly not based on verbal N–V compounds. Moreover, we cannot assume that nominal N–V compounds are formed by putting existing nouns and deverbal nouns together: the nouns in these compounds do exist as free-standing nouns while deverbal nouns are not necessarily found in the existing Japanese vocabulary.

Recall that N–V compounds in (150) are nouns and can exhibit a wide referential spectrum. When they refer to act or state, the verb -*suru* "do" may follow them, turning the entire compounds into predicates. Of the examples given in (150), *sara-arai* "dish washing", *te-ami* "hand-weaving", *abura-itame* "stir-fry", and *mizu-arai* "washing without soap" can appear with -*suru* and function as predicates; and *hutuka-yoi* "hangover", *huna-yoi* "sea-sickness", and *hi-yake* "suntan" generate the inchoative meaning of getting into a certain state. For instance, *sara-arai-suru* and *hutuka-yoi-suru* mean "wash dishes" and "get a hangover", respectively. Needless to say, when a nominal N–V compound refers to a concrete object, such as *neji-mawasi* "screwdriver", -*suru* cannot appear with it, as in **neji-mawasi-suru*. Recall, furthermore, some deverbal nouns that are derived from single base verbs can refer to process, as in (109), but they do not function as verbs by adding -*suru* to them. This is presumably because corresponding predicates can readily be found by tracing back to the original verbs from which they are derived. Thus, rather than **oyogi-suru*, it is much more straightforward to use the verb *oyogu* "swim". Below are given additional nominal N–V compounds that can appear with -*suru* (taken from Sugioka 1986: 80; Kageyama 2001b: 246).

(157) a. kane-mooke-suru   "make profit"
           money-profit
       b. tera-mairi-suru   "go to temple"
           temple-visit
       c. ie-de-suru   "run away from home"
           house-leave
       d. suna-asobi-suru   "play with sand"
           sand-play
       e. yo-asobi-suru   "go out and have fun at night"
           night-play
       f. waka-zini-suru   "die young"
           young-die
       g. ne-age-suru   "raise price"
           price-raise
       h. nori-zuke-suru   "starch"
           starch-put

It is interesting to note that the verb -*suru* makes it possible for nominal N–V compounds to function as verbs, compensating for the absence of corresponding verbal forms, such as **kane-mookeru* for (a) or **tera-mairu* for (b), for example.

7.3 V–V Compounds

Compound words that consist of two verbs are particularly common in Japanese. As we have already seen in some examples of V–V compounds, the first verb appears in the Renyookei form. In comparing Japanese with English, we notice that expressions for which phrases are used in English often find corresponding V–V compounds in Japanese. For example, the inception, termination, or continuation of an action is described by main verbs like *start, stop/finish*, or *continue* with the gerundive or infinitival form of the verb that denotes a particular action, as is illustrated by *start eating, stop/finish writing a book*, and *continue to investigate the case*. These phrases correspond to Japanese V–V compounds like *tabe-hazimeru* (eat-start), *kaki-owaru* (write-finish), and *sirabe-tuzukeru* (investigate-continue). Similarly, a verb–particle combination in English like *run up the hill* is expressed by a V–V compound such as *kake-agaru* (run-go up). Furthermore, English is rich in resultative expressions such as *shake someone awake* and *cut a tree down*: *awake* describes the state of someone as a result of shaking her or him, and *down* describes the state of a tree as a result of cutting it. In contrast, Japanese is rich in compound verbs like *yuri-okosu* (shake-wake) and *kiri-taosu* (cut-fell).

Besides their sheer number, V–V compounds present several interesting properties. Each verb represents a set of linguistically significant characteristics, ranging from phonological, morphological, and semantic to structural. When two verbs are put together, however, it is not the case that the resulting compound is a composition of the characteristics that each verb has. How these characteristics interact and which set of characteristics survives in a V–V compound become important questions to investigate. In what follows, we will examine various issues revolving around these questions.

7.3.1 Lexical vs. Syntactic V–V Compounds

As a major classification, V–V compounds are divided into two types, **lexical V–V compounds** and **syntactic V–V compounds**, based on the nature of the second verb and the relationship between the two verb members of a compound (Kageyama 1989, 1993; Masuoka and Takubo 1992; Yo Matsumoto 1996). It is generally agreed that many syntactic V–V compounds are made up of verbs that have **aspectual** meaning as the second verb. By **aspectual** is meant that the beginning, ending, and continuation of an event are described. Included in verbs that have aspectual meaning are *hazimeru* "begin", *dasu* "begin", *owaru* "finish", *oeru* "finish", *ageru* "finish", *agaru* "finish", *tuzukeru* "continue", and *kakeru* "be about to". Of these verbs, *dasu, ageru, agaru*, and *kakeru* exhibit aspectual meaning, but such a meaning emerges only when they serve as the second member of a V–V compound. Some researchers, furthermore, include second verbs not showing aspectual meaning in the class of syntactic V–V compound (Masuoka and Takubo 1992; Kageyama 1993). The following, for example, may be analyzed as syntactic V–V compounds: *au* "do something to each other", *nareru* "get accustomed to", *naosu* "do something over", *wasureru* "forget", *sugiru* "overdo", and *sokonau* "fail to do", among others. The English gloss that accompanies these verbs corresponds to the meaning that these verbs contribute as the second member of a V–V compound, as the verbs may have different meanings as independent verbs.

Examples of syntactic and lexical V–V compounds are given in (158)–(159).

(158)   Syntactic V–V Compounds
      a.   kaki-hazimeru   "begin to write"
          yomi-hazimeru   "begin to read"
          kangae-hazimeru   "begin to think"
      b.   kaki-owaru   "finish writing"
          yomi-owaru   "finish reading"
          tabe-owaru   "finish eating"
      c.   kaki-ageru   "complete writing"
          tukuri-ageru   "complete making"
          sirabe-ageru   "investigate thoroughly"
      d.   kaki-tuzukeru   "continue to write"
          yomi-tuzukeru   "continue to read"
          kangae-tuzukeru   "continue to think"
      e.   kaki-kakeru   "about to write"
          oki-kakeru   "about to put"
          korosi-kakeru   "about to kill"
      f.   kaki-nareru   "get used to writing"
          yomi-nareru   "get used to reading"
          tabe-nareru   "get used to eating"
      g.   kaki-naosu   "re-write"
          yomi-naosu   "re-read"
          kangae-naosu   "re-think"
      h.   kaki-wasureru   "forget to write"
          kiki-wasureru   "forget to ask"
          kai-wasureru   "forget to buy"
      i.   tabe-sugiru   "overeat"
          nomi-sugiru   "drink too much"
          kangae-sugiru   "think too much"
      j.   kaki-sokonau   "misspell"
          sini-sokonau   "fail to kill oneself"
          ii-sokonau   "make a mistake in one's use of words"

(159)   Lexical V–V Compounds
      uti-korosu (shoot-kill)   "shoot to death"
      kiri-taosu (cut-fell)   "cut down"
      tataki-kowasu (hit-break)   "break by hitting"
      tobi-mawaru (fly-circle)   "fly about"
      hikari-kagayaku (shine-sparkle)   "shine"
      tabe-aruku (eat-walk)   "make an eating tour"
      uke-toru (receive-take)   "accept"
      tori-atukau (take-treat)   "handle"

omoi-agaru (think-rise)   "be arrogant'"
mi-okuru (see-send)   "see off"
arai-nagasu (wash-pour)   "wash away"
tori-kesu (take-erase)   "cancel"
harai-modosu (pay-return)   "pay back"
maki-komu (roll-congested)   "involve"
kami-tuku (bite-attach)   "bite at"

Martin (1987) explains that syntactic V–V compounds depart from lexical V–V compounds in the three respects listed in (160).

(160) a. They [= syntactic V–V compounds] carry with them the grammar of the verbal from which the infinitives comes (e.g., the selection and marking of adjuncts);
       b. The meanings are wholly predictable from the components; and
       c. The formations are productive – some widely, some narrowly, but more productive than patterns found in compound lexical verbs [= lexical V–V compounds].

(Martin 1987: 438)

By (160a) is meant that the argument structure and syntactic distribution of arguments and adjuncts of the first verb are preserved at the compound level. For example, the argument structure and the argument/adjunct distribution of *kaki-hazimeru* "begin to write" in (158a) are the same as *kaku* "write". The verb *kaku* takes agent and theme, and they are realized as subject and object, respectively; and *kaki-hazimeru* shows the identical property. The second compound in (158e) consists of the first verb *oku* "put", which requires three arguments, agent, theme, and location, and they are syntactically realized as subject, object, and a locational phrase. The compound *oki-kakeru* "about to put" patterns exactly the same way. (161)–(162) illustrate these two cases.

(161) a. Taroo-ga   tegami-o kaita.
           Taro-Nom   letter-Acc wrote
           <agent>   <theme>
           "Taro wrote a letter."
       b. Taroo-ga   tegami-o kaki-hazimeta.
           Taro-Nom   letter-Acc began to write
           <agent>   <theme>
           "Taro began to write a letter."

(162) a. Hanako-ga   kabin-o   teeburu-no ue-ni   oita.
           Hanako-Nom   vase-Acc table-Gen top-on put
           <agent>   <theme> <location>
           "Hanako put a vase on the table."
       b. Hanako-ga   kabin-o   teeburu-no ue-ni   oki-kaketa.
           Hanako-Nom   vase-Acc table-Gen top-on was about to put
           <agent>   <theme> <location>
           "Hanako was about to put a vase on the table."

Lexical V–V compounds, on the other hand, do not always preserve the grammatical properties of the first member. The best example comes from the last item
in (159), i.e. *kami-tuku* "bite at". Consider the examples in (163).

(163) a. Inu-ga   ude-o   kanda.
           dog-Nom arm-Acc bit
           "The dog bit my arm."
       b. Inu-ga   ude-ni/*o   kami-tuita.
           dog-Nom arm-onto/*Acc bit
           "The dog bit my arm."
       c. Kahun-ga   ude-ni   tuita.
           pollen-Nom arm-onto attached
           "Pollen got onto my arm."

These examples show that the argument/adjunct property of the first verb *kamu*
"bite" is not all reflected as the property of the compound; rather, the unexpected
marking of the postposition *-ni* on *ude* "arm" comes from the property of the
second verb, *tuku* "attach". As we will examine later, lexical V–V compounds
are much less systematic and predictable in argument distribution than syntactic
V–V compounds.

The predictability of meanings in syntactic V–V compounds and lack thereof
in lexical V–V compounds as stated in (160b) is evident from the glosses given
in (158)–(159). Lexical compounds like *tabe-aruku* "make an eating tour",
mi-okuru "see off", *tori-kesu* "cancel", and *maki-komu* "involve" are particularly
unpredictable given the meaning of each member. The meanings of syntactic V–
V compounds, in contrast, are much more regularly compositional than lexical
compounds.

The property in (160c) is somewhat related to that in (160b). Since the
meanings of syntactic compounds are compositional and hence predictable, this
type of compound is more productive. For instance, if we select the verb *hazimeru*
"begin" as the second member of a compound, it is predicted that the meaning
will be "begin to do something", so garden-variety verbs can serve as the first
member as long as the meaning of the resulting compound fits the pattern of
"begin to do something". In this sense there is not much selectional restriction
between the two members of syntactic V–V compounds. Lexical V–V compounds,
in contrast, have meanings that cannot always be predictable, and in this sense,
a combination of two verbs in this class of compounds is not something that
we can freely create; rather, combinatory possibilities are predetermined with
fixed meanings.

In addition to the differences Martin spells out in (160), syntactic and lexical
V–V compounds are distinct from each other in various constructions. Kageyama
(1989, 1993), for one, demonstrates that phenomena such as the *soo-suru* substitution, Subject Honorification, and passive, among others, elucidate the contrastive
properties between the two types of V–V compounds. First, *soo-suru* "do so"
can substitute for the first member of a syntactic V–V compound whereas such
substitution is not possible in a lexical V–V compound. The contrast is shown
in (164)–(165).

(164) Syntactic V–V Compounds

a.	kaki-hazimeru	→ soo-si-hazimeru
	begin to write	so-do-begin
b.	yomi-owaru	→ soo-si-owaru
	finish to read	so-do-finish
c.	kangae-tuzukeru	→ soo-si-tuzukeru
	continue to think	so-do-continue
d.	kangae-naosu	→ soo-si-naosu
	rethink	so-do-do again
e.	oki-wasureru	→ soo-si-wasureru
	forget to put	so-do-forget
f.	tabe-sugiru	→ soo-si-sugiru
	overeat	so-do-exceed
g.	sini-sokonau	→ soo-si-sokonau
	fail to die	so-do-fail

(165) Lexical V–V Compounds

a.	uti-korosu	→ *soo-si-korosu
	shoot to death	so-do-kill
b.	kiri-taosu	→ *soo-si-taosu
	cut down	so-do-fell
c.	tataki-kowasu	→ *soo-si-kowasu
	break by hitting	so-do-break
d.	tobi-mawaru	→ *soo-si-mawaru
	fly about	so-do-circle
e.	hikari-kagayaku	→ *soo-si-kagayaku
	shine	so-do-shine
f.	tabe-aruku	→ *soo-si-aruku
	make an eating tour	so-do-walk
g.	uke-toru	→ *soo-si-toru
	accept	so-do-take
h.	tori-atukau	→ *soo-si-atukau
	handle	so-do-treat

While a part of a compound can be substituted for by *soo-suru* only in syntactic V–V compounds, both types can undergo the substitution of an entire compound, deriving an identical form, as is shown in (166). In both examples, *soo-suru* refers to the whole compound words, i.e. *kaki-hazimeru* "begin to write" (syntactic V–V compound) and *uti-korosu* "shoot to death" (lexical V–V compound), rather than parts of the compounds.

(166) a. Syntactic V–V Compound
Taroo-ga tegami-o <u>kaki-hazimeta</u>-node Hanako-mo soo-sita.
Taro-Nom letter-Acc began to write-because Hanako-also did so
"Since Taro began to write a letter, Hanako did so (= began to write a letter), too."

b. Lexical V–V Compound
Taroo-ga   tori-o   <u>uti-korosita</u>-node   Hanako-mo soo-sita.
Taro-Nom bird-Acc shot to death-because Hanako-also did so
"Since Taro shot a bird to death, Hanako did so (= shot a bird to death), too."

Second, Subject Honorification, which will be discussed again in chapter 5, refers to a construction that takes a form of o-Verb-*ni naru*, and is used to express respect for an individual named by the subject. In (167), for instance, the verb is *kaku* "write" and the individual for whom the honorific expression is used is Professor Tanaka.

(167)   Tanaka-sensei-ga   gengogaku-no hon-o   o-kaki-ni natta.
Tanaka-Prof.-Nom linguistics-Gen book-Acc o-write-*ni naru* (past)
"Professor Tanaka wrote a book on linguistics."

The Subject Honorifications in the form of o-Verb-*ni naru* may apply to the first member of a syntactic V–V compound but not to that of a lexical V–V compound. On the other hand, it can apply to an entire compound regardless of the compound type. (168)–(169) show the point.

(168)   Syntactic V–V Compounds
a.   kaki-hazimeru   →   o-kaki-ni nari-hazimeru
begin to write   o-kaki-hazime-ni naru
b.   yomi-owaru   →   o-yomi-ni nari-owaru
finish reading   o-yomi-owari-ni naru
c.   kangae-tuzukeru   →   o-kangae-ni nari-tuzukeru
continue to think   o-kangae-tuzuke-ni naru
d.   kangae-naosu   →   o-kangae-ni nari-naosu
rethink   o-kangae-naosi-ni naru
e.   tabe-sugiru   →   o-tabe-ni nari-sugiru (mesiagari-sugiru)
overeat   o-tabe-sugi-ni naru
f.   oki-wasureru   →   o-oki-ni nari-wasureru
forget to put   o-oki-wasure-ni naru

(169)   Lexical V–V Compounds
a.   uti-korosu   →   *o-uti-ni nari-korosu
shoot to death   o-uti-korosi-ni naru
b.   kiri-taosu   →   *o-kiri-ni nari-taosu
cut down   o-kiri-taosi-ni naru
c.   tataki-kowasu   →   *o-tataki-ni nari-kowasu
break by hitting   o-tataki-kowasi-ni naru
d.   tobi-mawaru   →   *o-tobi-ni nari-mawaru
fly around   o-tobi-mawari-ni naru
e.   tabe-aruku   →   *o-tabe-ni nari-aruku (*mesiagari-aruku)
make an eating tour   o-tabe-aruki-ni naru
f.   uke-toru   →   *o-uke-ni nari-toru
accept   o-uke-tori-ni naru
g.   tori-atukau   →   *o-tori-ni nari-atukau
handle   o-tori-atukai-ni naru

Third, the passive morpheme, *-(r)are-*, can appear in the first verb of a syntactic V–V compound, but not in the first verb of a lexical V–V compound. As is the case with the previous situations, however, both types of compounds allow the passive morpheme to be suffixed to an entire compound verb.

(170)   Syntactic V–V Compounds
    a.   kaki-hazimeru   →   [kak-are]-hazimeru
        begin to write   [kaki-hazime]-rareru
    b.   kangae-tuzukeru   →   [kangae-rare]-tuzukeru
        continue to think   [kangae-tuzuke]-rareru
    c.   kaki-sokonau   →   [kak-are]-sokonau
        fail to write   [kaki-sokone]-rareru
    d.   korosi-kakeru   →   [koros-are]-kakeru
        about to kill   [korosi-kake]-rareru

(171)   lexical V–V compounds
    a.   uti-korosu   →   *[ut-are]-korosu
        shoot to death   [uti-koros]-areru
    b.   kiri-taosu   →   *[kir-are]-taosu
        cut down   [kiri-taos]-areru
    c.   tataki-kowasu   →   *[tatak-are]-kowasu
        break by hitting   [tataki-kowas]-areru
    d.   uke-toru   →   *[uke-rare]-toru
        accept   [uke-tor]-areru
    e.   tori-atukau   →   *[tor-are]-atukau
        handle   [tori-atukaw]-areru
    f.   kami-tuku   →   *[kam-are]-tuku
        bite at   [kami-tuk]-areru

The behavior that the two types of V–V compounds exhibit in the three phenomena above can roughly be generalized in terms of how tight the relation between two verbs is. Syntactic V–V compounds consistently allow certain elements to intervene between two composite verbs while lexical V–V compounds resist breaking up two members. That is, the relation between two verbs is tighter in lexical V–V compounds than in syntactic V–V compounds. Put another way, lexical V–V compounds are treated strictly on a par with a single verb while two verbs in syntactic V–V compounds are less tightly put together. This, however, is not to say that syntactic V–V compounds can freely allow intervention of any element. As Kageyama (1993: 76) shows, for example, particles such as *mo* "too" and *sae* "even" can appear in phrasal expressions like *ginza-e iku* "go to Ginza", as in *ginza-e-mo iku* "go to Ginza too" and *ginza-e-sae iku* "go even to Ginza". However, both types of V–V compounds resist the intervention of these particles: **kaki-sae-hazimeru* "begin even to write" and **uti-sae-korosu* "even shoot to death".

Due to the various differences, it has often been claimed that, as the label suggests, syntactic V–V compounds are derived in the syntax rather than the lexicon (Kageyama 1993; Yo Matsumoto 1996). Given that word formation in the lexicon takes place at an earlier stage than word formation in the syntax, a consequence of the lexical vs. syntactic compound dichotomy is that verbs that serve as the second member of syntactic V–V compounds, many of which are aspectual, can be further compounded to lexical V–V compounds, but the reverse situation does not hold true (Kageyama 1989, 1993). These two contrastive situations are shown in (172).

(172) a.   Lexical Compound + Syntactic V2
             uti-korosu + hazimeru → [uti-korosi]-hazimeru "begin to shoot to
             shoot to death + begin   death"
             kiri-taosu + tuzukeru → [kiri-taosi]-tuzukeru "continue to cut down"
             cut down + continue
       b.   Syntactic Compound + Lexical V2
             kaki-hazimeru + korosu → *[kaki-hazime]-korosu
             begin to write + kill
             kangae-tuzukeru + kowasu → *[kangae-tuzuke]-kowasu
             continue to think + break

The two compounds in (172a), *uti-korosu* "shoot to death" and *kiri-taosu* "cut down", are lexical compounds. Additional verbs, *hazimeru* "begin" and *tuzukeru* "continue", bear aspectual meanings and are very common V2 members of syntactic V–V compounds, as we have observed earlier. Thus, adding these aspectual verbs to the lexical compounds raises no problem, and is a productive process. (172b) presents the opposite situation, i.e. the addition of a non-aspectual verb to a syntactic V–V compound in the attempt to form a lexical V–V compound. As the ungrammaticality indicates, such a process is not allowed.

   Although the two-way classification of compound types seems straightforward, it should be noted that some verbs can appear as the second verb of both compound types. Consider the pairs in (173)–(175).

(173) a.   kodomo-ga hasiri-<u>nuku</u> [syntactic]
             child-Nom run-do thoroughly
             "A child runs through."
       b.   kugi-o   hiki-<u>nuku</u> [lexical]
             nail-Acc pull-pull
             "pull a nail out"

                                                      (Himeno 1999: 185)

(174) a.   ko-ga   aruki-<u>toosu</u> [syntactic]
             child-Nom walk-do completely
             "A child walks (some distance) completely."
       b.   hari-o   tuki-<u>toosu</u> [lexical]
             needle-Acc push-go through
             "push a needle through"

                                                      (Himeno 1999: 190)

(175) a. inu-ga   sini-<u>kaketa</u> [syntactic]
           dog-Nom die-was about to
           "A dog almost died."
       b. kabe-ni motare-<u>kaketa</u> [lexical]
           wall-to lean-hang
           "leaned on the wall"

In each of these pairs, the V2 member is identical. When appearing in syntactic
compounds, as the (a) examples show, *nuku* and *toosu* mean "do completely,
thoroughly, persistently", and *kakeru* means "almost, be about to". As parts of
lexical compounds, as in the (b) examples, they no longer bear the same range
of aspectual readings. The distinction is supported by the diagnostics that we have
discussed above. For instance, the *soo-suru* substitution is allowed only in syntactic
compounds, as is shown in (176)–(178).

(176) a. kodomo-ga soo-si-nuku (= (173a))
       b. *kugi-o soo-si-nuku (= (173b))

(177) a. ko-ga soo-si-toosu (= (174a))
       b. *hari-o soo-si-toosu (= (174b))

(178) a. inu-ga soo-si-kaketa (= (175a))
       b. *kabe-ni soo-si-kaketa (= (175b))

Some compounds, furthermore, can be interpreted in the two different ways, i.e.
one as a syntactic compound and the other as a lexical one. Examples illustrating
such a situation include *tukuri-dasu* and *mi-naosu*.

(179) a. Sanzi-ni   keeki-o <u>tukuri-dasita</u>-ga mada dekinai. [syntactic]
           3 o'clock-at cake-Acc make-started-but yet   not completed
           "I started to make a cake at 3:00, but it hasn't been made."

           cf. soo-si-dasita

       b. Geizyutuka-ga utukusii tyawan-o   <u>tukuri-dasita</u> [lexical]
           artist-Nom   beautiful teacup-Acc produced
           "An artist produced a beautiful teacup."

           cf. *soo-si-dasita

(180) a. Kotae-o   moo itido <u>mi-naosita</u>. [syntactic]
           answer-Acc more once look-redid
           "(I) checked my answer one more time."

           cf. soo-si-naosita

       b. Subarasii kooen-no   ato, kare-o <u>mi-naosita</u>. [lexical]
           great   lecture-Gen after he-Acc changed my opinion
           "After his great lecture, I changed my opinion of him."

           cf. *soo-si-naosita

These demonstrate minimum pairs in that identical compounds serve as both syntactic and lexical. The contrast, however, is clear on the basis of their meanings as well as the availability of the *soo-suru* substitution.

Finally, syntactic V–V compounds are not homogeneous, and at least some of them can further be divided into two types. We have seen above that syntactic V–V compounds are partially characterized by the aspectual meaning. In particular, compounds that contain verbs such as *hazimeru* "begin", *tuzukeru* "continue", and *owaru* "finish" as the second member have been argued to exhibit two senses (Shibatani 1973c; Kuno 1983; Yo Matsumoto 1996). To use Yo Matsumoto's (1996: 173) terms, they are compounds with the "non-intentional beginning reading" and those with the "intentional initiation reading". Consider the examples in (181)–(182).

(181)   The Non-Intentional Beginning Reading
        a.   Hanako-wa   hutori-hazimeta.
             Hanako-Top   become fat-began
             "Hanako began to become fat."

                                                         (Shibatani 1973c: 88)

        b.   Taroo-wa eraku nari-hazimeta.
             Taro-Top great become-began
             "Taro began to become a great man."

                                                                      (ibid.)

        c.   Ame-ga   huri-hazimeta.
             rain-Nom fall-began
             "It began to rain."

                                                         (Yo Matsumoto 1996: 171)

(182)   The Intentional Initiation Reading
        a.   Taroo-ga   susi-o   tabe-hazimeta.
             Taro-Nom sushi-Acc eat-began
             "Taro began to eat sushi."
        b.   Hanako-ga   tegami-o kaki-hazimeta.
             Hanako-Nom letter-Acc write-began
             "Hanako began to write a letter."

As Shibatani (1973c) explains, the subjects of the sentences in (181) cannot intentionally bring about the events, as is evidenced by the fact that they cannot form imperative sentences based on them, e.g., *Hutori-hazime-ro!* "Begin to become fat!" or *Eraku nari-hazimero!* "Begin to become a great man!" Those events in (182), on the other hand, can be initiated intentionally by individuals. So, their imperative counterparts are straightforwardly acceptable, e.g., *Susi-o tabe-hazimero!* "Begin to eat sushi!" or *Tegami-o kaki-hazimero!* "Begin to write a letter!" While the distinction between (181) and (182) may be thought to result from the semantic nature of V1 or the compound itself, Yo Matsumoto (1996) points out that focus on members of compounds or compounds themselves does not always provide a clue to a particular interpretation. The examples in (183)–(184) show his point (adapted from Yo Matsumoto 1996: 172–173).

(183) John-wa sono koro-kara   ii   ronbun-o kaki-hazimeta.
　　　 John-Top that period-since good paper-Acc write-began
　　　 "John's writing of good papers began around that time."

(184) John-wa kinoo   ronbun-o kaki-hazimeta.
　　　 John-Top yesterday paper-Acc write-began
　　　 "John (intentionally) began to write the paper yesterday."

Despite the identical V–V compound form, *kaki-hazimeta*, (183) has the non-intentional beginning reading while (184) has the intentional initiation reading.

7.3.2 Lexical V–V Compounds: Semantic Relations

We have observed the meanings of lexical V–V compounds are often not predictable. It would be trouble-free if the meaning of a compound verb were obtained by summing up the meaning of each compound member: e.g., the meaning of compound [V1–V2] were "doing/becoming/being V1 and doing/becoming/being V2". In fact, there are some compound verbs that fit such a description. Many other compounds, however, exhibit several interesting semantic relations, including one event causing another and one event describing another. In some compounds, the meaning of one member has lost the original meaning as an independent verb, giving a more primary semantic status to the other member. More extreme cases reveal that neither compound member has maintained the original definition: in these cases, the meaning of a compound is idiomatic. Below we will roughly categorize the semantic relations between V1 and V2 of a lexical compound into four types (cf. Tagashira and Hoff 1986; Kageyama 1993; Yo Matsumoto 1996; Himeno 1999 – most examples below are taken from these works).

　　First, the least controversial among researchers seem to be compounds in which V1 and V2 hold a semantically parallel relation, without giving either member primary status. Although relatively low in number, the compounds in (185) fall into this class.

(185) hikari-kagayaku (shine-glitter)　　　　　　　"shine"
　　　 ukare-sawagu (be happy-be noisy)　　　　　　"have a spree"
　　　 naki-sakebu (cry-shout)　　　　　　　　　　"cry"
　　　 tobi-haneru (jump-leap)　　　　　　　　　　"jump up and down"
　　　 awate-hutameku (be confused-be agitated)　　"make a great fuss"
　　　 tae-sinobu (endure-bear)　　　　　　　　　　"endure"
　　　 koi-sitau (miss-long for)　　　　　　　　　　"long for"
　　　 yorokobi-isamu (be pleased-be encouraged) "rejoice and get excited"

In each compound in (185), the two composite verbs have similar meanings and both meanings contribute equally to the meaning of the compound as a whole. This parallel situation is reminiscent of dvandva compounds such as *oya-ko* "parent-child" and *eda-ha* "branches and leaves" in that compound members are conjoined. Although V1 and V2 semantically hold an equal status, it should be noted that the order cannot be reversed. Thus, *kagayaki-hikaru* and *sawagi-ukareru*, for instance, are not existing compounds. This may reflect the unpredictable, unproductive nature of lexical compounds.

A second relation is one where the meaning of a compound reflects both of the meanings of its members and one member describing the other in various ways. Examples are given below: in each group, an identical V2 is shared by all in (186) while an identical V1 is shared in (187).

(186) a. uti-korosu (shoot-kill)   "shoot to death"
          naguri-korosu (hit-kill)   "hit to death"
          kiri-korosu (slash-kill)   "slash"
          sasi-korosu (stab-kill)   "stab to death"
          sime-korosu (strangle-kill)   "strangle to death"
      b. daki-okosu (hold-get someone up)   "raise somebody in one's arm"
          hiki-okosu (pull-get someone up)   "help someone get up"
      c. tobi-saru (fly-leave)   "fly away"
          moti-saru (hold-leave)   "take away"
          nugui-saru (wipe-leave)   "wipe off"
      d. kaki-atumeru (rake-gather)   "gather by raking"
          kiki-atumeru (hear-gather)   "gather by asking people around"
          yobi-atumeru (call-gather)   "call together"
      e. hari-tukeru (paste-attach)   "paste"
          nui-tukeru (paint-attach)   "sew on"
          uti-tukeru (hit-attach)   "drive (a nail into a wall)"
      f. sui-ageru (suck-raise)   "suck up"
          uti-ageru (hit-raise)   "shoot up"
          kumi-ageru (pump-raise)   "pump up"
          osi-ageru (push-raise)   "push up"
      g. nagare-deru (flow-come out)   "flow out"
          nizimi-deru (run-come out)   "ooze out"
          ahure-deru (overflow-come out)   "overflow"

(187) a. tobi-koeru (fly/jump-pass)   "jump over"
          tobi-agaru (fly/jump-ascend)   "jump up"
          tobi-mawaru (fly/jump-go around)   "fly/jump around"
          tobi-noru (fly/jump-get on)   "jump onto"
          tobi-okiru (fly/jump-get up)   "jump out of bed"
      b. osi-dasu (push-take out)   "push out"
          osi-tateru (push-raise)   "hoist"
          osi-tumeru (push-stuff)   "pack"
          osi-nokeru (push-remove)   "push aside"
      c. hiki-ageru (pull-raise)   "pull up"
          hiki-ireru (pull-put in)   "draw in"
          hiki-simeru (pull-tighten)   "tighten"
          hiki-dasu (pull-take out)   "pull out"
          hiki-hanasu (pull-separate)   "pull apart, separate"

In all the examples above, V1 describes the event named by V2. In (186a), for example, V2 is *korosu* "kill" and V1 provides various manners or means of killing: killing can be achieved by shooting (by a gun), hitting, slashing or stabbing (by a knife), or strangling (by a hand/rope). Similarly in (187a), V2s denote events of passing, ascending, going around, getting on (a step/train, etc.), and getting up, and the manner in which each event is described is expressed by V1, i.e. *tobi-* "flying/jumping". V2 in these examples serves to shape a core meaning of a compound with V1 adding further information. In light of the position of head, then, the compounds in (186)–(187) are consistent with the Righthand Head Rule.

In many lexical compounds one member loses its original meaning, although to varying degrees (Tagashira and Hoff 1986; Kageyama 1993; Yo Matsumoto 1996; Himeno 1999). Instead of making no semantic contribution to a compound, however, such member can add functional senses to the meaning of the other member, serving as being emphatic or adverbial. This situation constitutes a third type of semantic relation between compound members. For example, the verb *tukeru*, as an independent verb, means attaching something somewhere, denoting a change of location of some object: we have seen that this meaning is reflected in a compound like *hari-tukeru* "paste", *nui-tukeru* "sew on", and *uti-tukeru* "drive a nail into wall" in (186e) above. On the other hand, when the same verb appears in compounds like *donari-tukeru* (shout-attach) and *nirami-tukeru* (stare-attach), it no longer implies change of location but instead adds a sense of harshness. Thus, *donarii-tukeru* and *nirami-tukeru* mean "thunder at somebody" and "give a fierce look", respectively. The list in (188), taken from Yo Matsumoto (1996: 218), illustrates a range of V2s that have lost their original meanings.

(188) a. tukeru (lit. "attach")   →   "hard, harshly"
           sikari-tukeru (scold-)   "scold harshly"
           nage-tukeru (throw-)   "throw hard"
           humi-tukeru (stamp-)   "stamp on hard"
           nirami-tukeru (stare-)   "glare at"
       b. tuku (lit. "be attached")   →   "after some effort"
           omoi-tuku (think-)   "think of, hit upon"
           kaŋgae-tuku (think-)   "think of, hit upon"
       c. kaesu (lit. "return")   →   "back to the original state"
           hiki-kaesu (draw back-)   "retreat"
           tori-kaesu (take-)   "regain"
       d. tateru (lit. "stand")   →   "actively"
           donari-tateru (yell-)   "yell violently"
           seme-tateru (attack-)   "attack violently"
       e. hateru (lit. "come to an end")   →   "completely"
           tukare-hateru (get tired-)   "get exhausted"
           nayami-hateru (agonize-)   "agonize to death"
       f. komu (lit. "go in")   →   "to a great extent, enough"
           damari-komu (be silent-)   "become utterly silent"
           huke-komu (get old-)   "become very old"

g.　ageru (lit. "lift")　　　　　→　"loudly and clearly"
　　yomi-ageru (read-)　　　　　　"read out"
　　utai-ageru (sing-)　　　　　　"sing beautifully"
h.　wataru (lit. "cross")　　　　→　"with a far-reaching effect"
　　hare-wataru (clear up-)　　　　"clear up all over the sky"
　　hibiki-wataru (resound-)　　　"reverberate"

As for instances of V1 losing its original meaning, Yo Matsumoto (1996) gives *sasu* "thrust" as an example, as in *sasi-semaru* (-come close) "become near at hand, become urgent", *sasi-osaeru* (-hold) "seize", *sasi-tomeru* (-stop) "suspend", to give the sense of "urgency or forcefulness" (p. 219). Kageyama (1993) includes *kaku* "scratch" and *toru* "take" as examples of V1 serving as emphasizing or intensifying what is denoted by V2: compounds like *kaki-atumeru* (-collect) "rake/scrape up together", *kaki-midasu* (-disturb) "be confused", and *kaki-tateru* (-stand) "arouse (interest in)" are examples of the former; and those including *tori-sumasu* (-be unruffled) "be unruffled", *tori-hakarau* (-manage) "manage", and *tori-sikiru* (-settle) "manage" are examples of the latter. In addition, we may consider *osu* "push" as in *osi-toosu* (-carry through) "persist to the end" and *osi-yoseru* (-come near) "rush for", where *osi-* adds a sense of forcefulness to the events denoted by the V2s. Although it is not clear how to characterize the sense it adds, *tatu* "stand" may play a similar role in *tati-mukau* (-face) "confront", *tati-komeru* (-include) "hang over, envelope", *tati-okureru* (-be late) "make a slow start".

Finally, both members of a compound sometimes lose their original meanings as independent verbs, and when this happens, the meaning of the compound is more or less idiomatic. In the examples in (189), compare the composites' original meanings (given in the parentheses) and the compound meanings.

(189)　oti-tuku (fall-arrive)　　　　　"settle down, keep calm"
　　　　omoi-agaru (think-rise)　　　　"get conceited"
　　　　tate-kaeru (stand-change)　　　"pay temporarily for someone"
　　　　kiri-nukeru (cut-pass)　　　　　"struggle through"
　　　　dasi-nuku (take out-pull)　　　"outwit"
　　　　tuki-au (attach-meet)　　　　　"go steady with, get along (well)"
　　　　itami-iru (hurt-enter)　　　　　"feel extremely obliged"
　　　　kagi-tukeru (smell-attach)　　　"detect"
　　　　ii-yoru (say-come close)　　　　"make advances"
　　　　kai-kaburu (buy-put on)　　　　"overestimate"
　　　　tori-nasu (take-achieve)　　　　"mediate"
　　　　yuki-todoku (go-reach)　　　　　"be careful, be attentive to details"
　　　　yari-au (do-meet)　　　　　　　"compete"
　　　　sime-kukuru (shut-bind)　　　　"finish off"

Given the individual meanings of V1 and V2, it is unlikely that one would be able to determine the meaning of these compounds, and in this sense, their meanings are idiomatic. Interestingly, some compounds have more than one meaning, one that reflects the meaning of one or both members and the other that is idiomatic. The examples in (190)–(193) describe the situation.

(190)   moti-agaru (hold-rise): (i) be lifted; (ii) happen
    a.   zimen-ga   moti-agatta
         ground-Nom be lifted
         "the ground is lifted"
    b.   ziken-ga   motiagatta
         incident-Nom happened
         "an incident happened"

(191)   mi-awaseru (see-put together): (i) look at each other; (ii) postpone
    a.   kao-o   mi-awaseru
         face-Acc look at each other
         "look at each other's faces"
    b.   ryokoo-o mi-awaseru
         trip-Acc postpone
         "postpone a trip"

(192)   hiki-tukeru (pull-attach): (i) draw; (ii) charm
    a.   kodomo-o tikaku-ni hiki-tukeru
         child-Acc near-to   draw
         "draw a child toward me"
    b.   hito-no   kokoro-o hiki-tukeru
         person-Gen heart-Acc charm
         "attract/charm people"

(193)   hari-kiru (stretch-cut): (i) stretch completely; (ii) be in high spirits
    a.   himo-o   hari-kiru
         string-Acc stretch completely
         "stretch a string completely"
    b.   kodomo-ga hari-kitte-iru
         child-Nom be in high spirits
         "a child is being in high spirits"

In (190), for example, the compound has at least two meanings, one that reflects the meanings of V1 and V2, i.e. "be lifted", and the other that is not predictable from the composites' meanings and is hence idiomatic, i.e. "happen, take place". The context, however, can normally disambiguate the multiple meanings. In some cases, furthermore, the argument structures and the nature of arguments, such as animacy, are different depending on the meaning. For example, *hari-kiru*, under the more literal meaning of "stretch completely" in (193i), takes agent and theme, which are realized as subject and object, respectively. The same compound under the idiomatic meaning of "be in high spirits" in (193ii) is an intransitive verb and the sole argument is normally human. Given these differences, the presence of the Accusatively marked object, *himo-o*, in (193a) and the human subject, *kodomo-ga*, in (193b) clearly lead to appropriate interpretations of the compound.

As Tagashira and Hoff (1986) observe, many compounds have come to be treated almost as single-member verbs, with their original compound status hardly recognized. These include *mi-tukeru* (see-attach) "find", *si-tateru* (do-erect) "tailor", *ni-au* (resemble-meet) "be becoming", *hik-kosu* (pull-go over) "move to a new residence", and *hiki-zuru* (pull-rub) "drag along".

7.3.3   *Lexical V–V Compounds: Transitivity and Argument Structure*

Just as the meaning of a compound can undergo various degrees of changes from its members' original meanings, the range of arguments that a compound verb ends up taking may differ from the argument structure properties that each of V1 and V2 has. Since two verbs, each of which is associated with an independent argument structure, are involved to form a compound verb, and the compound verb is accompanied by a single argument structure, various questions arise. For example, which argument structure, i.e. V1's or V2's, becomes the argument structure of the compound? Is a totally new argument structure created for a compound, independent of V1 or V2? Or does the argument structure of a compound verb somehow consist of parts of V1's and V2's argument structures? In order to find answers to these questions, we will now turn our focus to the distribution of a compound verb's arguments in terms of transitivity and to the distribution of arguments and adjuncts. In so doing, we shall primarily discuss compound verbs whose composites' meanings are more or less preserved, for reasons that will be made clear later in this section (Yamamoto 1984; Tagashira and Hoff 1986; Kageyama 1993; Yo Matsumoto 1996; Himeno 1999).

To begin with, when the members of a compound verb are identical in their transitivity, i.e. both intransitive verbs or both transitive verbs, the output is normally of the same kind. Examples in (194) consist of intransitive composite verbs, while those in (195) are formed from two transitive verbs. The compounds are intransitive in (194) and transitive in (195).

(194)   Vi+Vi → Vi
        tobi-haneru (jump-jump)   "jump up and down"
        naki-sakebu (cry-scream)   "cry"
        kake-agaru (run-ascend)   "run up"
        nagare-deru (flow-exit)   "flow out"
        tobi-aruku (jump-walk)   "run about"

(195)   Vt+Vt → Vt
        kiri-taosu (cut-fell)   "fell"
        moti-ageru (hold-raise)   "lift"
        humi-tubusu (step on-crush)   "trample down"
        hori-dasu (dig-get out)   "dig out"
        kai-modosu (buy-return)   "buy back"
        damasi-toru (deceive-take)   "trick and take away"

The transitivity of V1, V2, and the compound are all identical, and the semantic roles of the arguments are also matching. For example, *tobi-haneru* "jump up and down" takes a single argument, agent, and so do *tobu* "jump" and *haneru* "jump": *Kodomo-ga tobu/haneru/tobi-haneru* "A child jumps/jumps/jumps." Another compound in (194), *nagare-deru*, consists of *nagareru* "flow" and *deru* "exit", both of which take a sole argument, theme; and the compound also takes a single argument, theme: *Mizu-ga nagareru/deru/nagare-deru* "Water flows/comes out/flows out." In (195) all the composite verbs of the compounds are associated with agent and theme, which are realized as subject and object, respectively, and that is how the arguments of the compounds appear in sentences: *Taroo-ga ki-o kiru/taosu/kiri-taosu* "Taro cuts/fells/fells down a tree." Thus, (194)–(195) present the most straightforward situations concerning transitivity and argument structure relation between compound members and the compounds themselves. This is also consistent with the Righthand Head Rule.

There are many compounds, however, that do not match in transitivity and/or argument structure between the two composite verbs. Consider the two sets of examples in (196)–(197), where one member is intransitive and the other is transitive.

(196) Vi+Vt
      de-mukaeru (exit-greet)   "go out to meet"
      hane-kaesu (jump-return)   "hit back"
      naki-otosu (cry-drop)   "get one's way by crying"
      nori-kaeru (get on-change)   "transfer (to another car)"
      tare-nagasu (hang-pour)   "discharge"

(197) Vt+Vi
    a. tumi-kasanaru (pile-be piled up)   "be piled up, accumulate"
        tuki-sasaru (poke-be stuck)   "stick in"
        tuki-deru (poke-exit)   "stick out"
        maki-tuku (wrap-attach)   "wrap around"
        kesi-tobu (erase-fly)   "vanish"
    b. uri-aruku (sell-walk)   "peddle"
        nomi-aruku (drink-walk)   "barhop"
        moti-kaeru (hold-go back)   "take out"
        moti-yoru (hold-come near)   "bring together"
        ture-saru (take-leave)   "take away"

In (196) the compounds consist of intransitive verbs as V1 and transitive verbs as V2; and the compounds as a whole are transitive. All the compounds in (197) have transitive verbs as V1 and intransitive verbs as V2. The compounds in (197a) are intransitive while those in (197b) are transitive. Taking an example from the first compound in (196), *de-mukaeru* "go out to meet", the intransitive status of the V1 and the transitive status of the V2 are illustrated in (198).

(198) a. Taroo-ga heya-kara <u>deta</u>. [intransitive]
        Taro-Nom room-from exited
        "Taro came out from the room."
    b. Taroo-ga tomodati-o kokoro-kara <u>mukaeta</u>. [transitive]
        Taro-Nom friend-Acc heart-from welcomed
        "Taro sincerely welcomed his friend."
    c. Taroo-ga tomodati-o <u>de-mukaeta</u>. [transitive]
        Taro-Nom friend-Acc went out to meet
        "Taro went out to meet his friend."

Turning to (197), first, besides the transitivity property, the compounds in this group take the argument structure pattern of V2. Consider *tumi-kasanaru* "be piled up, accumulate" and *tuki-sasaru* "stick in", and their composite verbs concerning their argument and adjunct distribution.

(199) a. Taroo-ga   isi-o   <u>tunda</u>. [transitive]
           Taro-Nom stone-Acc piled
           "Taro piled stones."
       b. Isi-ga   <u>kasanatta</u>. [intransitive]
           Stone-Nom got piled
           "Stones got piled."
       c. Isi-ga   <u>tumi-kasanatta</u>. [intransitive]
           stone-Nom got piled up
           "Stones got piled up."

(200) a. Taroo-ga hari-de   yubi-o   <u>tuita</u>. [transitive]
           Taro-Nom needle-with finger-Acc pricked
           "Taro pricked his finger with a needle."
       b. Hari-ga   yubi-ni   <u>sasatta.</u> [intransitive]
           needle-Nom finger-into was stuck
           "A needle was stuck in a finger."
       c. Hari-ga   yubi-ni   <u>tuki-sasatta</u>. [intransitive]
           needle-Nom finger-into was stuck in
           "A needle was stuck in a finger."

Second, the situation becomes much more complicated in (197b). As is the case with (197a), the compounds in this group consist of a transitive V1 and an intransitive V2, but end up with compound verbs that are transitive, unlike those in (197a). Speaking in terms of argument structure, these compounds basically carry over the argument structure pattern of V1, but at the same time allow adjuncts associated with V2 to appear. This is shown in (201)–(203).

(201) a. Taroo-ga oosaka-kara tookyoo-made kottoohin-o uri-aruita.
           Taro-Nom Osaka-from Tokyo-to   antique-Acc peddled
           "Taro peddled antique pieces from Osaka to Tokyo."
       b. Taroo-ga   kottoohin-o utta.
           Taro-Nom antique-Acc sold
           "Taro sold antique pieces."
       c. Taroo-ga oosaka-kara tookyoo-made aruita.
           Taro-Nom Osaka-from Tokyo-to   walked
           "Taro walked from Osaka to Tokyo."
       d. *Taroo-ga (kottoohin-o) oosaka-kara tookyoo-made utta.
           Taro-Nom (antique-Acc) Osaka-from Tokyo-to   sold
           "Taro sold (antique pieces) from Osaka to Tokyo."

(202) a. Hanako-ga   tabenokosi-o uti-ni   moti-kaetta.
           Hanako-Nom leftovers-Acc home-to took out
           "Hanako took the leftovers home."

    b.   Hanako-ga   tabenokosi-o motte-iru.
        Hanako-Nom leftovers-Acc hold
        "Hanako has/holds/carries the leftovers."
    c.   Hanako-ga   uti-ni   kaetta.
        Hanako-Nom home-to returned
        "Hanako went home."
    d.   *Hanako-ga (tabenokosi-o) uti-ni   motta.
        Hanako-Nom (leftovers-Acc) home-to held/carried
        "Hanako carried (the leftovers) home."

(203) a.   Otoko-ga kodomo-o kooen-kara ture-satta.
        man-Nom child-Acc park-from   took away
        "A man took a child away from the park."
    b.   Otoko-ga kodomo-o turete-iru.
        man-Nom child-Acc take
        "A man has taken (i.e. is with) a child."
    c.   Otoko-ga kooen-o/kara   satta.
        man-Nom park-Acc/from left
        "A man left the park."
    d.   *Otoko-ga (kodomo-o) kooen-o/kara   tureta.
        man-Nom (child-Acc) park-Acc/from took
        "A man took (a child) from the park."

As the examples illustrate, the theme object of the compound is associated with V1 while the locative adjunct is specified by V2. Crucially, these locative adjuncts cannot independently appear with the first verbs of the compounds. Thus, these compounds demonstrate the cases in which both compound members contribute to the argument and adjunct distribution pattern of the compounds. In fact, this sort of mixed case is not restricted to compounds that consist of a transitive verb as V1 and an intransitive verb as V2. Kageyama (1996: 108) discusses the compounds *katari-akasu* "talk the night away", *nageki-akasu* "spend the night in grief", and *nomi-akasu* "drink all night long", where all the compound members are transitive verbs, to demonstrate a situation similar to (201)–(203) above. Consider the example in (204).

(204) a.   Natu-no   itiya-o   gakuseizidai-no   omoide-o
        summer-Gen one night-Acc student days-Gen memory-Acc
        katari-akasita.
        talked the night away
        "(We) talked a summer night away reminiscing (about) our student days."
    b.   omoide-o   kataru
        memory-Acc talk
    c.   itiya-o   akasu
        one night-Acc spend
    d.   *(omoide-o) itiya-o   kataru
        (memory-Acc) one night-Acc talk
    e.   *(itiya-o)   omoide-o   akasu
        (one night-Acc) memory-Acc spend

As (204b–d) indicate, *omoide* "memory" is selected by the verb *kataru* "talk", not by the verb *akasu*; similarly, the time expression *itiya* "one night" is associated only with *akasu* "spend". The fact that both *omoide* and *itiya* can appear with *katari-akasu* in (204a) in Accusative Case suggests that the argument distribution pattern of the compound may come from the properties of both compound members.

Related to the compounds in (197), another intriguing compound type with respect to the contrast between the argument distribution pattern of compounds and that of their composite verbs is discussed by Kageyama (1996). Consider the argument distribution of the two compounds in (205)–(206), *arai-otosu* (wash-take away) "wash off" and *huri-mazeru* (shake-mix) "shake together" (adapted from Kageyama 1996: 104–105), where all the compound members are transitive verbs.

(205)   a.   Taroo-ga   huku-no   yogore-o arai-otosita.
             Taro-Nom cloth-Gen dirt-Acc   washed away
             "Taro washed away the dirt of the cloth."
        b.   huku-o   arau; yogore-o otosu
             cloth-Acc wash dirt-Acc   remove
        c.   *yogore-o arau; *huku-o   otosu
             dirt-Acc   wash cloth-Acc remove

(206)   a.   Hanako-ga   bin-no nakami-o   huri-mazeta.
             Hanako-Nom jar-Gen contents-Acc shook   together
             "Hanako shook together the contents of the jar."
        b.   bin-o   huru; nakami-o   mazeru
             jar-Acc shake contents-Acc mix
        c.   *nakami-o   huru; *bin-o mazeru
             contents-Acc shake jar-Acc mix

Both compounds in (205)–(206) have the same argument distribution pattern: (i) the theme object of the compound includes a Genitive modifier that holds a possessor–possessed relation, i.e. the cloth has the dirt and the jar has the content, as is shown in the (a) sentences; and (ii) V1 is associated with the possessor but not with the possessed, while V2 is specified for the possessed but not the possessor, as the (b–c) sentences illustrate. In these examples, the compound verbs express mutually exclusive arguments of the composites in the form of a possessive phrase. Thus, there is more than one way for composite verbs to contribute to the argument and adjunct distribution properties of compound verbs.

7.3.4   *Transitive and Intransitive Compound Verb Pairs*

In section 4 above we have discussed morphologically related transitive and intransitive verb pairs. Verb pairs like *agaru/ageru* "rise/raise", *deru/dasu* "come out/take out", *tuku/tukeru* "attach/put on", and *naoru/naosu* "be fixed/fix" frequently appear as the second member of V–V compounds as well (Jacobsen 1992; Kageyama 1996; Himeno 1999). Recall that the transitive verb generally takes two arguments that are distributed in a sentence as subject, marked with the Nominative Case particle -*ga*, and object, marked with the Accusative Case particle -*o*, while the intransitive counterpart takes one argument that appears as subject, marked with the Nominative Case particle -*ga*; and semantically the intransitive verb denotes an inchoative event, and its transitive counterpart describes causation of the corresponding inchoative event. Interestingly, these consistent syntactic and semantic patterns between morphologically related verb pairs often break down once they appear as the second member of V–V compounds. Below we will examine two verb pairs, *agaru/ageru* and *deru/dasu*, to illustrate how their properties as independent verbs get altered once they serve as compound members. In particular, we will focus on combinatory possibilities based on transitivity, i.e. the question of whether *agaru* "rise" and *deru* "come out", for instance, as intransitive V2 members can be compounded with both transitive and intransitive verbs as V1 members, and on the nature of the meanings.

Let us begin with *agaru* (Vi) and *ageru* (Vt). These verbs do not behave the same with respect to the transitivity of V1. For example, *ageru* (Vt) tends to reject intransitive verbs as its V1 members. That is, instances of Vi-*ageru* are scarce. Semantically, compounds with *agaru/ageru* as the second member could have one of the following three meanings: (i) upward movement, (ii) completion of an event or creation, or (iii) addition of an emphatic tone to an event. The combinatory possibilities based on the transitivity of V1 and V2 are illustrated in (207)–(209) according to the meanings of the resulting compounds.

(207)   Upward Movement

    A. Vi-agaru(Vi)/*ageru(Vt)
          kake-agaru/*ageru (run-)   "run up"
          hai-agaru/*ageru (crawl-)   "crawl up"
          mai-agaru/*ageru (fly-)   "fly up"
          uki-agaru/*ageru (float-)   "surface"
          tobi-agaru/*ageru (fly-)   "fly/jump up"

        a. Taro-ga   nikai-ni   kake-agatta.
            Taro-Nom upstairs-to ran up
            "Taro ran up to the upstairs (floor)."

    B. Vt-agaru(Vi)/ageru(Vt)
          moti-agaru/ageru (carry-)   "be lifted"/"lift"
          turusi-agaru/ageru (hang-)   "be lifted"/"lift up"
          tuki-agaru/ageru (push-)   "be pushed up"/"push up"
          maki-agaru/ageru (roll-)   "roll up"/"roll up"
          uti-agaru/ageru (shoot-)   "be shot up"/"shoot up"
          osi-agaru/ageru (push-)   "be pushed up"/"push up"

        a. Zisin-de   zimen-ga   moti-agatta.
            earthquake-because ground-Nom be lifted up
            "The ground got lifted up because of the earthquake."

    b. Taroo-ga   nimotu-o   moti-ageta.
        Taro-Nom luggage-Acc lifted up
        "Taro lifted up the luggage."

C. Vt-*agaru(Vi)/ageru(Vt)
    hakobi-*agaru/ageru (carry-)   "carry up"
    kakae-*agaru/ageru (hold-)   "hold up"
    tasuke-*agaru/ageru (rescue-) "rescue, pick up"
    tori-*agaru/ageru (take-)   "pick up"

    a. Taroo-ga   nimotu-o   nikai-ni   hakobi-ageta.
        Taro-Nom luggage-Acc upstairs-to carried up
        "Taro carried up the luggage to the upstairs (floor)."

(208) Completion (Creation)

A. Vi-agaru(Vi)/*ageru(Vt)
    deki-agaru/*ageru (be completed-) "be completed"
    nie-agaru/*ageru (boiled-)   "be boiled"
    hare-agaru/*ageru (clear up-)   "(sky) clear up"

    a. Subarasii sakuhin-ga deki-agatta.
        great   work-Nom was completed
        "A great work was completed."

B. Vt-agaru(Vi)/ageru(Vt)
    yaki-agaru/ageru (bake/burn-)   "be baked"/"finish baking"
    taki-agaru/ageru (cook-)   "be cooked"/"finish cooking"
    ori-agaru/ageru (weave-)   "be woven"/"finish weaving"
    yude-agaru/ageru (boil-)   "be boiled"/"finish boiling"
    hori-agaru/ageru (carve-)   "be carved"/"finish carving"
    kaki-agaru/ageru (write-)   "be written"/"finish writing"
    si-agaru/ageru (do-)   "be finished"/"finish"

    a. Oisii   keeki-ga   yaki-agatta.
        delicious cake-Nom was baked
        "A delicious cake has been baked."
    b. Taroo-ga oisii   keeki-o   yaki-ageta.
        Taro-Nom delicious cake-Acc finish baking
        "Taro finished baking a delicious cake."

C. Vt-*agaru(Vi)/ageru(Vt)
    kazoe-*agaru/ageru (count-)   "enumerate"
    narabe-*agaru/ageru (line up-)   "finish lining up"
    enzi-*agaru/ageru (perform-)   "perform beautifully"
    tutome-*agaru/ageru (work-)   "complete working"
    utai-*agaru/ageru (sing-)   "sing beautifully"

a. Taroo-ga   Hanako-no   tyoosyo-o   kazoe-ageta.
Taro-Nom Hanako-Gen strong points-Acc enumerated
"Taro enumerated Hanako's strong points."

(209)   Emphasis

A.   Vi-agaru(Vi)/*ageru(Vt)
hurue-agaru/*ageru (tremble-)   "be terrified"
obie-agaru/*ageru (be frightened-)   "be frightened"
sukumi-agaru/*ageru (crouch-)   "be scared"
mukure-agaru/*ageru (get angry-)   "get furious"
nobose-agaru/*ageru (be crazy-)   "be conceited"

a.   Taroo-ga   osorosisa-ni hurue-agatta.
Taro-Nom horror-at   was terrified
"Taro was terrified of horror."

B.   Vt-*agaru(Vi)/ageru(Vt)
sibari-*agaru/ageru (bind-)   "bind securely"
donari-*agaru/ageru (shout-)   "shout"
odosi-*agaru/ageru (threaten-) "threaten"
sime-*agaru/ageru (tighten-)   "strangle"
home-*agaru/ageru (praise-)   "praise"

a.   Gootoo-ga   kodomo-o sibari-ageta.
robber-Nom child-Acc   bound securely
"A robber bound the child securely."

In (207) *agaru* and *ageru* imply upward movement and V1 members further specify the manner of the movement. As the schematic descriptions under (207A–C) indicate, not all logical possibilities, namely, Vi-*agaru*, Vi-*ageru*, Vt-*agaru*, and Vt-*ageru*, are attested. The completion and emphasis senses in (208) and (209) are more functional meanings that are generally given rise to when *agaru* and *ageru* serve as the V2 members of compounds. All the compounds under (208) denote completion of an event described by their V1 members. The V1 transitives in (208B) tend to be creation verbs, that is, verbs that denote creation of artifacts, such as baking a cake, knitting a sweater, carving a statue, and writing a book, among others. As for the combinatory possibilities, the same range of combinations as in (207) is available to the compounds under the completion sense. Compounds with *agaru* and *ageru* as V2 members are more restricted in (209) in that only Vi-*agaru* and Vt-*ageru* are available combinations. As mentioned above, *agaru* and *ageru* in this class add an emphatic tone to, or intensify, the event denoted by the V1 members. As the example sentences show, all the acceptable compounds described in (207)–(209) follow the transitivity pattern of the V2, i.e. either *agaru* (Vi) or *ageru* (Vt), regardless of the transitivity of V1: that is, if V2 is *agaru*, the compound is intransitive, and if V2 is *ageru*, it is transitive. This suggests that the transitivity of these compounds follows the Righthand Head Rule.

Recall that we have noted earlier that intransitive verbs rarely serve as a V1 member when *ageru* appears as V2. There are only a handful of exceptional compounds that are counter to this generalization. These compounds mostly describe involuntary bodily movements (Himeno 1999), as is demonstrated in (210), along with a few others such as *nori-ageru* (get on-) "run around" and *nanori-ageru* (give one's name-) "give one's name".

(210)   syakuri-ageru (scoop-)   "sob"
        musebi-ageru (be choked-)   "be choked up [in the physical sense]"
        seki-ageru (cough-)   "cough frequently"

   a.   Kodomo-ga sibaraku   syakuri-ageta.
        child-Nom for a while sobbed
        "A child sobbed for a while."

Besides the fact that these verbs are counter-examples to the generalization on combinatorial possibilities, they are also counter to the Righthand Head Rule: as (210a) indicates, the compound verbs in (210) are intransitive despite the transitive status of the second member, *ageru*.[20]

The behavior of morphologically related transitive and intransitive verb pairs, when they serve as the second member of V–V compounds, varies depending on which pair is being examined. As shown below, for instance, the pair *deru/dasu* "come out/take out" exhibits a set of properties different from *agaru/ageru*. The verbs *deru* (Vi) and *dasu* (Vt), as V2 members of V–V compounds, induce three meanings: (i) movement to outside or surface, (ii) making something appear, creation, or discovery, and (iii) beginning an event, although the second and third meanings are associated only with the transitive verb, *dasu*.

First, under the first meaning, i.e. movement to outside or surface, the intransitive verb *deru* may combine with both intransitive and transitive verbs as a V1 member, while the transitive verb *dasu* combines with transitive verbs. These combinations are illustrated in (211).

(211)   A.   Vi-deru(Vi)
             hai-deru (crawl-)   "crawl out"
             tobi-deru (fly/jump-)   "fly out"
             hasiri-deru (run-)   "run out"
             huki-deru (blow out-)   "blow out"
             nagare-deru (flow-)   "flow out"
             susumi-deru (advance-)   "come forward"

             Taroo-ga   tiisai ana-kara   hai-deta.
             Taro-Nom small hole-from crawled out
             "Taro crawled out of a small hole."

        B.   Vt-deru(Vi)
             todoke-deru (report-)   "report"
             negai-deru (request-)   "file an application"
             moosi-deru (say-)   "propose"

Taroo-ga siyakusyo-ni tenkyo-o todoke-deta.
Taro-Nom city hall-to   move-Acc reported
"Taro reported a change of address to the city hall."

C. Vt-dasu(Vt)
    hakobi-dasu (carry-)   "carry out"
    okuri-dasu (send-)   "send out"
    tuki-dasu (push-)   "push out"
    hiki-dasu (pull-)   "pull out"
    ture-dasu (take-)   "take out"
    osi-dasu (push-)   "push out"
    tori-dasu (take-)   "take out"
    nagasi-dasu (pour-)   "pour out"
    sasoi-dasu (invite-)   "invite out"
    tasuke-dasu (rescue-) "help somebody out of"
    moti-dasu (hold-)   "take out"

Taroo-ga isu-o   uti-kara   hakobi-dasita.
Taro-Nom chair-Acc house-from carried out
"Taro carried a chair out of the house."

The compounds in (211A) are intransitive while those in (211B) and (211C) are transitive. That is, the compounds in (211B) are counter to the Righthand Head Rule. The pattern of argument/adjunct distribution of the compounds in (211B) comes from V1. As for those in (211C), since both the transitive verbs that serve as V1 and *dasu* seem to have a similar argument/adjunct pattern, allowing for a theme object and locative expressions, it may appear to be difficult to determine which pattern the compounds follow. At least one example, *moti-dasu* "take out", however, suggests that they actually pattern with *dasu*. Consider the contrast in (212).

(212) a. Taroo-ga kyoositu-kara hon-o   moti-dasita.
           Taro-Nom classroom-from book-Acc took out
           "Taro took out a book from the classroom."
       b. *Taroo-ga kyoositu-kara hon-o   motta.
           Taro-Nom classroom-from book-Acc held
           "Taro held a book from the classroom."
       c. Taroo-ga kyoositu-kara hon-o   dasita.
           Taro-Nom classroom-from book-Acc took out
           "Taro took out a book from the classroom."

As the contrast between (212b) and (212c) suggests, *dasu*, but not *motu*, can be accompanied by a locative expression, *kyoositu-kara*. The fact that the compound verb *moti-dasu* can occur with the locative expression as in (212a) indicates that the argument/adjunct distribution pattern is a contribution that the V2 member, *dasu*, makes. On the other hand, it is not the case that the contribution that V1 makes is moot or absent. It is clear that V1 defines the nature of the action denoted by *dasu*, i.e. taking something or someone out. Related to it, V1 further semantically restricts the type of direct object a compound takes. Compare (213) and (214).

(213) a. Taroo-ga   musuko/*zitensya-o kooen-ni ture-dasita.
           Taro-Nom son/*bicycle-Acc   park-to   took out
           "Taro took his son/bicycle out to the park."
       b. musuko/*zitensya-o turete iku
           son/bicycle-Acc   take   go
           "take (his) son/bicycle (to somewhere)"

(214) a. Taroo-ga   zitensya/*musuko-o kooen-ni moti-dasita.
           Taro-Nom bicycle/*son-Acc   park-to   took out
           "Taro took his bicycle/son out to the park."
       b. zitensya/*musuko-o motte iku
           bicycle/son-Acc   hold   go
           "take (his) bicycle/son (to somewhere)"

As (213b) and (214b) show, these V1 verbs, *tureru* "take" and *motu* "hold", put an animacy restriction on the direct objects they take: *tureru* appears with an animate object and *motu* with an inanimate object. As the (a) examples indicate, this semantic restriction is carried over to V–V compounds that contain them as the V1 member.

Under the interpretation of movement to outside or surface, V–V compounds with *deru/dasu* as the V2 member further exhibit an intriguing property. Some of the first members that appear in the pattern illustrated in (211A) can co-occur with both *deru* and *dasu* without any difference in meaning, and in both cases the compounds function as intransitive verbs. Examples are given in (215).

(215) tobi-deru/dasu (fly/jump-)   "jump out"
       huki-deru/dasu (blow-)   "blow out"
       uki-deru/dasu (float-)   "surface"
       simi-deru/dasu (soak-)   "ooze"
       nuke-deru/dasu (escape-)   "get/sneak out"
       hai-deru/dasu (crawl-)   "crawl out"
       nagare-deru/dasu (pour-)   "pour out"

       a. Booru-ga ana-kara   tobi-deta/dasita.
           ball-Nom hole-from jumped out
           "A ball jumped out of a hole."
       b. Tumaranai kaigi-na-node   sotto   nuke-deta/dasita.
           boring   meeting-be-because quietly snuck out
           "Since it was a boring meeting, (I) quietly snuck out."

Compounds with *deru* and those with *dasu* are interchangeably used without difference in meaning or transitivity: both are intransitive verbs.

The second meaning, i.e. making something appear, creation, or discovery, is induced only by compounds with the transitive verb *dasu* as V2. (216) shows some examples.

(216) migaki-dasu (polish-) "reveal by polishing"
kezuri-dasu (scrape-) "reveal by scraping"
terasi-dasu (shine-) "illuminate"
kaki-dasu (write-) "write out"
hari-dasu (spread-) "post"
aburi-dasu (broil-) "make appear over a fire"
tukuri-dasu (make-) "produce"
kangae-dasu (think-) "think out'"
ori-dasu (weave-) "create by weaving"
egaki-dasu (draw-) "describe by drawing"
sagasi-dasu (search-) "find out"
sirabe-dasu (investigate-) "find out by investigating"
kiki-dasu (ask-) "obtain information by asking"
kagi-dasu (smell-) "smell out"
mituke-dasu (find-) "find out"

As these examples show, verbs that serve as V1 are restricted to transitive verbs, and many of these compound verbs are verbs of creation, i.e. verbs that denote an event in which something is created.

Finally, V–V compounds that imply the beginning of an event are restricted to those with the transitive verb *dasu* as V2. V1 can be either an intransitive or transitive verb, as is shown in (217).

(217) A. Vi-dasu(Vt)
naki-dasu (cry-) "begin to cry"
warai-dasu (laugh-) "begin to laugh"
aruki-dasu (walk-) "begin to walk"
huri-dasu (fall-) "begin to rain/snow"
hasiri-dasu (run-) "begin to run"
ugoki-dasu (move-) "begin to move"

Akanboo-ga naki-dasita.
baby-Nom began to cry
"A baby began to cry."

B. Vt-dasu(Vt)
tukai-dasu (use-) "begin to use"
tukuri-dasu (make-) "begin to make"
utai-dasu (sing-) "begin to sing"
uti-dasu (hit-) "begin to hit"
kaki-dasu (write-) "begin to write"

Atarasii konpyuutaa-o sensyuu-kara   tukai-dasita.
new   computer-Acc last week-from began to use
"I began to use a new computer last week."

The transitivity of the compounds matches that of the V1 member: in (217A) the V1 members are intransitive, and so are the compounds; similarly, in (217B) both V1 members and the compounds are transitive. This class of compounds departs from those under the first two meanings discussed above in that the compounds in (217A) and (217B) are syntactic compounds. In addition to the fact that the V2 member, *dasu*, contributes the aspectual meaning to mark the beginning of event, these compounds pattern like other syntactic compounds with respect to the diagnostic tests that we have observed before. Consider (218)–(220).

(218)   Taroo-ga   aruiki-dasu-to,   musuko-mo soo-si-dasita.
        Taro-Nom walk-start-when son-also   do so-started
        "When Taro walked, his son started to do the same."

(219)   Sensei-ga   o-aruki-ni nari-dasita.
        teacher-Nom o-walk-*ni naru*-started
        "The teacher started to walk."

(220)   IBM-no   konpyuutaa-ga tukaw-are-dasita.
        IBM-Gen computer-Nom use-passive-started
        "IBM computers started to be used."

The fact that the *soo-suru* substitution, the Subject Honorification, and passive can all apply to V1 in (218)–(220) along with the aspectual meaning of marking the beginning of an event points to the identification of the compounds in (217A) and (217B) as syntactic.

As we have observed above, morphologically related transitive and intransitive verb pairs often appear as the V2 member of V–V compounds, but the relationship between a transitive verb and its intransitive counterpart as independent verbs does not always transfer to the derived compounds. That is, transitive verbs and their intransitive counterparts often vary in combinatorial possibilities as well as the meanings of the resulting compounds, and in some cases, furthermore, only a transitive verb and not its intransitive counterpart, or vice versa, is allowed as a V2 member of a compound.

7.3.5   *Compound Verbs and Nominalization*

In section 5 we have examined nominalization of individual verbs, i.e. deverbal nouns. As was briefly mentioned there, nominalization of V–V compounds is also frequently observed. On the other hand, not all V–V compounds find their nominalized forms; and conversely, we find "deverbal nouns" whose corresponding verbal forms do not exist (Tagashira and Hoff 1986). Examples of each situation are given in (221)–(223).

(221)   *nominalization*   *V–V compounds (verbal forms)*
         tabe-aruki   tabe-aruku (eat-walk) "make an eating tour"
         kasi-dasi   kasi-dasu (lend-take out) "lend out"
         harai-komi   harai-komu (pay-put in) "pay"
         kari-tori   kari-toru (cut-take) "mow"
         uti-age   uti-ageru (shoot-raise) "shoot up"
         ire-kae   ire-kaeru (put in-change) "replace"
         tabe-sugi   tabe-sugiru (eat-exceed) "overeat"

(222)   *nominalization*   *V–V compounds (verbal forms)*
         *osi-hiraki   osi-hiraku (push-open) "push open"
         *maki-tuki   maki-tuku (wrap-attach) "twine around"
         *mai-agari   mai-agaru (fly-rise) "get into the air"
         *ture-sari   ture-saru (take-leave) "take somebody away"
         *tabe-aki   tabe-akiru (eat-fed up) "tired of eating"
         *sagasi-dasi   sagasi-dasu (search-take out) "find out"
         *donari-tuke   donari-tukeru (yell-attach) "shout"

(223)   *nominalization*   *V–V compounds*
                                                                       (verbal forms)

      a.   tori-hiki   "dealings"   *tori-hiku (take-pull)
           momi-arai   "washing by rubbing"   *momi-arau (rub-wash)
           mi-gorosi   "leaving one to his fate"   *mi-gorosu (see-kill)
           ue-zini   "starving to death"   *ue-zinu (starve-die)
           tati-gui   "eating while standing"   *tati-guu (stand-eat)
           osi-uri   "high-pressure selling"   *osi-uru (push-sell)
           ki-daore   "extravagance in dress"   *ki-daoreru (wear-fall)
           tuke-yaki   "broiling with soy sauce"   *tuke-yaku (put-broil)
           tukai-sute   "disposable (things)"   *tukai-suteru
                                                            (use-discard)

      b.   iki-ki   "coming and going"   *iki-kuru (go-come)
           kasi-kari   "borrowing and lending"   *kasi-kariru
                                                            (lend-borrow)
           nomi-kui   "eating and drinking"   *nomi-kuu (drink-eat)
           iki-kaeri   "going and returning"   *iki-kaeru (go-return)
           okuri-mukae   "taking someone to and   *okuri-mukaeru
                           from somewhere"   (send-greet)
           uri-kai   "buying and selling"   *uri-kau (sell-buy)
           dasi-ire   "taking in and out"   *dasi-ireru (take
                                                            out-put in)
           kati-make   "winning and losing"   *kati-makeru (win-lose)
           yomi-kaki   "reading and writing"   *yomi-kaku (read-write)

The V–V compounds in (221) display corresponding nominalized forms. Those
in (222), in contrast, do not nominalize. The "nominalized" compounds in
(223) exist without corresponding verbal forms: those in (223b) illustrate a case
where the relation between the first and second member is that of dvandva.

Although there are no verbal forms for the compound nouns in (223), they can be "verbalized" by adding *suru* "do": most of them are directly followed by *suru*, as in *tori-hiki-suru* "trade", *momi-arai-suru* "wash by rubbing", *iki-ki-suru* "go and come", and *nomi-kui-suru* "eat and drink", but a few in (223a) take *-ni suru*, like *mi-gorosi-ni-suru* "leave someone to his fate", *tuke-yaki-ni-suru* "broil with soy sauce", and *tukai-sute-ni-suru* "use something once and throw it away".

Notes

---

1   The label "Gen" in the examples in (1) is the abbreviation of Genitive Case particle.
2   In fact, it is somewhat misleading to call *-tati* a plural marker because N(oun)-*tati* does not always mean more than one N. For example, *Yamada-sensei-tati* (Yamada-teacher-*tati*) refers to a group of individuals of which Professor Yamada is a member, and does not mean more than one Professor Yamada. For this reason, Martin (1975) regards *-tati* as a "collectivizer".
3   The abbreviation "neg." is for negative.
4   The underlying form of the verb root *hut* "fall" in (13) is *hur*. As is the case with the past tense ending *-ta* that we have discussed in chapter 3, a (morpho)phonological change takes place in the root-final consonant when the gerund-forming ending *-te* is added. The derived form *hut* in the example is a result of such a (morpho)phonological change.
5   The symbol "*( )" indicates that the sentence is unacceptable in the absence of the item within the parentheses.
6   In addition to the differences discussed above, Case particles and postpositions in Japanese are given distinct syntactic treatments. That is, a noun accompanied by a Case particle is analyzed as a noun phrase while a noun followed by a postposition is considered a postpositional phrase. A consequence of this syntactic difference at the phrasal level can be observed in the behavior of numeral quantifiers, as is extensively discussed by Miyagawa (1989a).
7   This category has also been referred to as "nominal adjective".
8   There are some words that can be classified both as a noun and as an adjectival noun. For example, *ziyuu* "free, freedom" is an adjectival noun, because when it modifies a following noun, *-na* rather than *-no* intervenes between them, as in *ziyuu-na zikan* "free time", although there is at least one instance in which *-no* is used, e.g. *ziyuu-no megami* "the Statue of Liberty". On the other hand, *ziyuu* can be accompanied by Case particles, as in *ziyuu-ga hosi-i* ("freedom-Nom want-non-past") "I want freedom", and also can be modified by another noun, as in *genron-no ziyuu* ("speech-Gen freedom") "freedom of speech". A similar situation can be found in English: adjectives like *rich* and *poor* can be used as nouns with the definite article *the*, as in *the rich* and *the poor*. Also, the word *hontoo* "true" is used to modify a noun, mediated by the Genitive Case *-no*, as in *hontoo-no hanasi* "true story", but it cannot be accompanied by a Case particle, as is exemplified by **hontoo-ga/o*. These cases suggest that categorial distinctions are not always clear-cut.
9   This section treats verbal nouns as an independent category primarily because of the property observed with Case particles discussed at the end of this section. However, it is quite possible to analyze them as a sub-class of nouns.
10 Uehara (1998) examines in detail various criteria that have been proposed to identify nouns, nominal adjectives (the same as adjectival nouns in this chapter), adjectives,

verbal nouns, and verbs. He points out problems with past criteria and proposes a new set of categorial criteria based on the prototype theory. For the basic idea leading to the prototype theory, see Rosch (1978).

11   (44c) and (44d) undergo Rendaku, which means that Rendaku is observed not only when two independent words are combined but also when a certain bound morpheme is added to a word.

12   It should be recalled that when the desiderative morpheme *-ta-(i)* is added to a verbal root that ends in a consonant, *-i-* appears between the root and *-ta-(i)*, as is observed in *ik-i-ta-i* "want to go" in (45a). The adjectives on the right of the arrow in (45) are given in their citation forms (i.e. the non-past tense forms).

13   One may claim that the native word *sirankao* [širaŋkao] "pretending not to notice" and the mimetic word *pyonpyon* [pʸompʸoN] "hopping" are counter-examples to the constraint discussed above: that is, in these examples, a nasal sound is immediately followed by a voiceless consonant. Although Ito and Mester do not discuss these examples, it may be argued that *sirankao* is analyzed underlyingly as /siranu-kao/ ("not know-face"), from which /sirankao/ is derived by the application of nasal syllabification (discussed in chapter 3), and hence it is not subject to the constraint. As for the second example, *pyonpyon*, it seems that in the case of reduplicated mimetics, the constraint should be interpreted as applying only to the non-reduplicated base, i.e. *pyon* in the present case. In fact, cross-linguistically, it is not uncommon for phonological constraints to fail to apply to reduplicated forms if it helps to maintain phonological identity between the reduplicated part and the base (cf. Wilbur 1993).

14   The accentuation of the verbal roots is determined on the basis of the accentuation of the gerunds of these verbs.

15   The hyphenation indicates the morpheme boundary, but it does not necessarily mean that each morpheme corresponds to an independent word in Japanese.

16   Although borrowing is often discussed in historical linguistics, we will take up the topic in this section, focusing on its role as a way of introducing new words into Japanese.

17   Okutsu's (1995) classification is based on more than the morphological make-up of verb pairs, and often takes traditional conjugation patterns and historical change, among other factors, into consideration. See his discussion for details.

18   The argument vs. adjunct opposition claimed to be operative in the Rendaku application, however, is not without counter-examples. Iida (1999: 21) observes that contrary to Sugioka's generalization, there are compounds of the predicate–argument relation that undergo Rendaku, as in (i), while there are also compounds that consist of the nominalization of a verb and its adjunct that do not exhibit the voicing phenomenon, as in (ii).

(i)   N(argument)-V
        ama-dare (< ame "rain" + tareru "drip")   "raindrop"
        hito-dasuke (< hito "people" + tasukeru "rescue")   "helping hand"
        hito-gorosi (< hito "people" + korosu "kill")   "murder"
        asi-bumi (< asi "feet" + humu "step")   "stamping"
        ie-zukuri (< ie "house" + tukuru "make")   "house building"

(ii) N(adjunct)-V
        mae-kake (< mae "front" + kakeru "hang")   "apron"
        kata-kake (< kata "shoulder" + kakeru "hang")   "shawl"
        mizu-taki (< mizu "water" + taku "cook")   "unthickened stew"
        te-suri (< te "hand" + suku "make")   "handmade"

19 The symbol "*" before an example indicates ungrammaticality while "?" suggests
    that a form may be odd or doubtful.
20 In addition to the three semantic classes discussed in this section, i.e. upward
    movement, completion, and emphasis, we may include one more small class of
    compound verbs with *ageru* as V2: directional behavior (Himeno 1999). This class
    can further be divided into two groups: verbs that denote behavior directed toward
    one's superior with an honorification effect, and those that describe events that have
    adverse or disadvantageous effects on someone with less power and bring benefit
    to an individual corresponding to the subject. Examples of the two groups are
    shown in (i).

(i) a. moosi-ageru (say-)   "tell"
         negai-ageru (request-)   "request respectfully"
     b. tori-ageru (take-)   "take away"
         kai-ageru (buy-)   "buy"
         kari-ageru (borrow-)   "borrow"
         maki-ageru (roll-)   "take away"
     c. Keisatu-ga hannin-kara zyuu-o tori-ageta.
         police-Nom criminal-from gun-Acc took away
         "The police took a gun away from the criminal."

The V2 in (ib), *ageru*, cannot be substituted for by its intransitive counterpart,
agaru, while in (ia) at least *moosi-ageru* allows for *moosi-agaru*.

Suggested Readings

General terminology in morphology: Aronoff (1976), Matthews (1976), Bauer
(1983), Di Sciullo and Williams (1987), Spencer (1991), Spencer and Zwicky
(1998), Haspelmath (2002), Aronoff and Fudeman (2005).

Parts of speech categories: Kageyama (1982), Miyagawa (1987a), Shibatani
(1990), Ohkado (1991), Uehara (1998). Kageyama (1982), Miyagawa (1987a),
and Ohkado (1991) examine some of the Japanese parts of speech whose categorial statuses are ambiguous. Uehara (1998) takes up the issue from a different
theoretical perspective.

Word formation: Miyagawa (1980), Kageyama (1982, 1989, 1999), Shibatani
and Kageyama (1988), Shibatani (1990), Yo Matsumoto (1992, 1996), Kubozono
(1995, 2002).

Transitivity: Jacobsen (1992), Kageyama (1993, 1996), Suga and Hayatsu
(1995). Jacobsen (1992) presents a detailed investigation of morphologically
related transitive and intransitive verb pairs, and is accompanied by an extensive
list of such verb pairs. Suga and Hayatsu (1995) is a collection of articles devoted
to the topic of transitivity. The discussion and analysis in Kageyama (1993, 1996)
touch on a wide range of phenomena revolving around transitivity that also exhibit
interesting interactions with semantics.

Nominalization: Sugioka (1986), Saiki (1987), Hagiwara et al. (1999), Iida
(2002).

Compounding: Makino (1976), Sugioka (1986), Tagashira and Hoff (1986), Kageyama (1993), Yo Matsumoto (1996), Nishiyama (1998), Himeno (1999), Fukushima (2005), Yumoto (2005). Tagashira and Hoff (1986) serves as an excellent source book of compound verbs. Kageyama (1993) and Himeno (1999) also contain a rich set of examples of compounds. Kageyama (1993) and Yo Matsumoto (1996) extensively discuss the matters that relate to argument structure in compounds. Nishiyama (1998) approaches V–V compounds from the perspective of Distributed Morphology, while Fukushima (2005) examines them from a lexicalist point of view.

EXERCISES

1   The terms under list A are those introduced in this chapter. The items under list B are examples of those terms. Match the examples in list B to the linguistic terms in list A.

List A	*List B*
inflectional morpheme	-*ta* in *tabe-ta* "ate"
derivational morpheme	*eda-ha* "branches and leaves"
prefix	*oyogi* (< *oyogu* "swim")
infix	-*te* in *utai-te* "singer"
dvandva	*kooen-de* ("park-in") in *kooen-de ringo-o*
borrowing	*taberu* (park-in apple-Acc eat)
clipping	*tahu-na* "tough"
compounding	*ringo-o* ("apple-Acc") in *kooen-de ringo-o*
nominalization	*taberu* (park-in apple-Acc eat)
argument	*mi-* in *mi-kaihatu* "underdeveloped"
adjunct	*satu* "police"

2   Identify the word-formation type that is involved in the following Japanese words.

a.   kirakira   "sparkling"
b.   tabe-mono   "food"
      eat-thing
c.   kangae (< kangaeru "think")   "idea"
d.   sohuto-da   "it's soft"
e.   paso kon   "personal computer"
f.   tabe-ta-sa   "degree at which one wants to eat"
g.   kaki-ageru   "finish writing"
      write-finish

3 Identify the thematic (semantic) roles of the underlined NPs.

   a. <u>Taroo</u>-ga <u>hon</u>-o   yonda.
       Taro-Nom book-Acc read
       "Taro read a book."
   b. <u>Hanako</u>-ga   <u>tonari-no ko</u>-o   kiratteiru.
       Hanako-Nom neighbor-Gen child-Acc dislike
       "Hanako dislikes the child next door."
   c. <u>Sensei</u>-ga   <u>gakusei</u>-ni <u>enpitu</u>-o   ageta.
       teacher-Nom student-to pencil-Acc gave
       "The teacher gave his student a pencil."
   d. <u>Taroo</u>-ga <u>titioya</u>-kara <u>zitensya</u>-o   moratta.
       Taro-Nom father-from bicycle-Acc received
       "Taro received a bicycle from his father."

4 Compare (a) and (b).

   a. Taroo-ga   kuruma-o tome-ru.
       Taro-Nom car-Acc   stop
       "Taro stops a car."
   b. Kuruma-ga tomar-u.
       car-Nom   stop
       "A car stops."

   A. Identify the transitivity of the verbs in (a) and (b). Discuss the
       relationship of the two verbs with respect to (i) morphological
       shapes, (ii) distribution of the arguments, and (iii) the meanings.
   B. In each of the following verb pairs, the first verb is intransitive
       and the second is transitive. Given the distribution of arguments
       in (a–c) along with the meaning of the verbs shown below, fill in
       the blanks with appropriate verbs.

       mitukaru/mitukeru   "find"
       simaru/simeru   "close"
       kawaku/kawakasu   "dry"

       a. To-ga   (   ).
           door-Nom
       b. Tomodati-ga saihu-o (   ).
           friend-Nom   wallet-Acc
       c. Sentakumono-ga   (   ).
           laundry-Nom

5   Consider the data below.

adjective	gloss	intransitive verb	transitive verb
katai	solid	katamaru	katameru
akai	red	akamaru	akameru
usui	thin	usumaru	usumeru
takai	high	takamaru	takameru
kiyoi	pure	kiyomaru	kiyomeru
kuroi	black	kuromaru	kuromeru
nukui	warm	nukumaru	nukumeru
hayai	fast	hayamaru	hayameru
hiroi	wide	hiromaru	hiromeru
hukai	deep	hukamaru	hukameru
yowai	weak	yowamaru	yowameru

A.   On the basis of the data above, explain how verbs are morpho-
     logically derived from adjectives.
B.   Find two English suffixes that are involved in the formation of
     verbs based on adjectives. Explain the derivation with examples.

Consider the additional data below.

adjective	gloss	intransitive verb		transitive verb
kanasii	sad	*kanasimaru	kanasimu	kanasimaseru
tanosii	pleasant	*tanosimaru	tanosimu	tanosimaseru
kurusii	difficult	*kurusimaru	kurusimu	kurusimaseru
sitasii	friendly	*sitasimaru	sitasimu	sitasimaseru
itosii	longing	*itosimaru	itosimu	itosimaseru
osii	regrettable	*osimaru	osiimu	osimaseru
natukasii	dear	*natukasimaru	natukasimu	natukasimaseru
kuyasii	vexing	*kuyasimaru	kuyasimu	kuyasimaseru
sitasii	friendly	*sitasimaru	sitasimu	sitasimaseru

C.   Explain how this set is different from the first set of data.
D.   Discuss possible characteristics that might differentiate the two sets
     of data.

6   We discussed three kinds of relations by which compounds can be
    characterized. Which type of the relations can describe the following
    compounds?

a.   denki-kamisori   "electric razor/shaver"
     electric-razor
b.   kasi-kari   "borrowing and lending"
     lending-borrowing

c. kan-kiri   "can opener"
    can-cutting
d. gomi-bako   "garbage can"
    garbage-box
e. yasai-itame   "stir fried vegetables"
    vegetable-fring
f. oya-ko   "parent and child"
    parent-child

7   We have observed that morphologically related transitive and intransi-
    tive verb pairs can serve as V2 of a V–V compound; however, the
    relation that they have to one another and the properties that they
    manifest do not always hold when they serve as V2 of a V–V com-
    pound. Consider the case below with *kakeru* and *kakaru*, and answer
    the questions.

    <u>kakeru/kakaru</u>
    a. Taroo-ga katu-ni   soosu-o   kaketa.
        Taro-Nom cutlet-onto sauce-Acc poured
        "Taro poured sauce onto a cutlet."
    b. Katu-ni   soosu-ga   kakatta.
        cutlet-onto sauce-Nom got poured
        "Sauce was poured onto a cutlet."

    A. Which of the two, *kakeru* and *kakaru*, is transitive and which is
        intransitive? Justify the answer. The morpheme *o* as in *o-tegami*
        in (b) (glossed as "hon.") is an honorific prefix added to some
        nouns.

        <u>kaki-kakeru</u> (kaku + kakeru)
        a. Taroo-ga tegami-o kaki-kaketa.
            Taro-Nom letter-Acc write-about to
            "Taro was about to write a letter."
        b. Sensei-ga   o-tegami-o   o-kaki-ni nari-kaketa.
            teacher-Nom hon.-letter-Acc o-write-ni naru-about to
            "The teacher was about to write a letter."
        c. Taroo-ga tegami-o kaki-kaketa.   Mary-mo
            Taro-Nom letter-Acc wrote-about to Mary-also
            soo-si-kaketa.
            do so-about to
            "Taro was about to write a letter. Mary was about to do so,
            too."
        d. Taroo-ga   tegami-o kaita.
            Taro-Nom letter-Acc wrote
            "Taro wrote a letter."

e. *Tegami-ga kaki-kakatta.
   letter-Nom write-about to
   "A letter was about to be written."
   (cf. Denwa-ga   nari-kakatta.
        telephone-Nom ring-about to
        "The telephone was about to ring.")

<u>huri-kakeru</u> (huru + kakeru)

a. Taroo-ga dooro-ni mizu-o huri-kaketa.
   Taro-Nom street-onto water-Acc shake-poured
   "Taro sprinkled water onto a street."

b. *Sensei-ga   dooro-ni mizu-o   o-huri-ni   nari-kaketa.
   teacher-Nom street-onto water-Acc o-shake-ni naru-poured
   "The teacher sprinkled water onto a street."

c. *Taroo-ga dooro-ni mizu-o huri-kaketa. Mary-mo
   Taro-Nom street-onto water-Acc shake-poured Mary-also
   soo-si-kaketa.
   did so-poured
   "Taro sprinkled water onto a street. Mary did so, too."

d. Taroo-ga boo-o   hutta.
   Taro-Nom stick-Acc shook
   "Taro shook a stick."

e. Dooro-ni mizu-ga   huri-kakatta.
   street-onto water-Nom shake-poured
   "Water got sprinkled onto the street."

B. On the basis of the data above, discuss the difference between the two compounds. Include in your discussion the way they differ in types, meanings, and distribution of arguments and adjuncts.

5 Syntax

Given a finite set of words existing in a language, the native speaker of that language is able to create an infinite number of sentences. In so doing, however, the native speaker does not put words together randomly. A native speaker of Japanese, for example, knows that (1a) is a coherent, grammatical Japanese sentence while (1b) is not.

(1) a. Taroo-ga   kinoo   ookii hanbaagaa-o   itutu tabeta.
       Taro-Nom yesterday big   hamburger-Acc five   ate
       "Taro ate five big hamburgers yesterday."
    b. *Itutu tabeta kinoo   hanbaagaa-o   Taroo-ga   ookii.
       five   ate   yesterday hamburger-Acc Taro-Nom big

There is a regularity in putting words together, and when a sentence fails to conform to this regularity, it leads to the ungrammaticality illustrated by the sentence in (1b). How the words are put together to create grammatical sentences is dealt with in **syntax**. In this chapter we will introduce certain syntactic notions that will be relevant to our discussion and then examine some of the major phenomena that are characteristic of Japanese syntax, such as scrambling, null anaphora, reflexives, passives, causatives, relative clauses, unaccusativity, and the light verb construction.

It should be cautioned, however, that syntax is an area full of controversy, partly because there are a great many competing theories and also because syntactic issues tend to be more abstract than, say, phonological ones. For this reason, the current chapter faces a limitation: its coverage is not exhaustive and the discussion of each topic will not employ the degree of depth that syntacticians might wish to see; nor do many of the analyses taken up here reflect the most current syntactic theory. The primary goal of this chapter, instead, is to observe and discuss a wide range of syntactic phenomena and the theoretical issues related to them. Those who wish to pursue further discussions and investigations are encouraged to make use of the suggested readings and references cited in this chapter.

1 Syntactic Structures

1.1 Syntactic Constituency

In discussing the syntactic regularities in a language, it is essential to figure out which words can combine to form units. In (1a), for instance, the native speaker of Japanese knows that *ookii* "big" and *hanbaagaa* "hamburger" form a meaningful unit, where *ookii* describes the size of the hamburger. Such a grouping is referred to as **syntactic constituency**. In (1a), for example, we say that *ookii* "big" and *hanbaagaa* "hamburger" form a constituent. Syntactic constituency is particularly motivated by structural ambiguity. Consider the grammatical phrase in Japanese in (2).

(2) akai hon-no   hyoosi
     red book-Gen cover

There are two interpretations associated with the phrase in (2): one reading is the cover of a red book, and the other is such that the cover is red and the book itself is not necessarily red. Notice that the ambiguous interpretation observed in (2) does not come from lexical ambiguity. That is, none of the three words in (2), i.e. *akai*, *hon-no*, and *hyoosi*, has an ambiguous meaning that could be the cause of the ambiguous interpretation observed above. Rather, the ambiguity has to do with the way these words are put together to form constituents. Hence, this is a case of structural ambiguity rather than lexical ambiguity. The structural ambiguity in (2) can, then, be explained by two different ways of forming constituency. This is illustrated in (3) and (4).

(3) a. [[akai hon]-no hyoosi]   "the cover of a red book"
     b. [akai [hon-no hyoosi]]   "a red cover of the book"

(4) a.

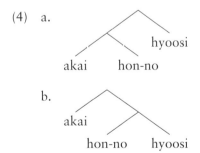

     b.

Although the ordering of the three words is exactly identical in (a) and (b), they are structurally different. As the structures in (3a) and (4a) indicate, when the first two words form a constituent which modifies *hyoosi* "cover", the phrase means "the cover of a red book". The structures in (3b) and (4b), in contrast, indicate that when *hon* "book" and *hyoosi* "cover" form a constituent, modified by *akai* "red", the phrase has the other interpretation, i.e. "a red cover of the book". Hence, different constituencies indicate different interpretations. The order of a sequence of words gives no clue to ambiguity, but the representations of internal structures like (3) and (4) that clearly reflect syntactic constituency do provide an explanation as to why the phrase in (2) can have two different interpretations.

1.2 *Phrase Structures*

A common device to represent syntactic constituency pertinent to phrases and sentences is a **phrase structure tree,** which is similar to the analysis tree of (4) depicted above. Phrase structure trees show what a phrase or a sentence consists of and which words form constituents. The labels that are used in drawing phrase structure trees are those of **lexical categories** and **phrasal categories.** Lexical categories correspond to the major part of speech categories that include noun (N), verb (V), adjective (A), and postpositon (P). Lexical categories can combine with other categories to form a larger unit, i.e. a phrasal category. For example, the N *hon* "book" can optionally combine with the A *akai* "red" and form a constituent. The resulting constituent is called a noun phrase (NP). The A *akai* "red" can further be modified by the adverb (ADV) *totemo* "very", to form another constituent, namely, the phrasal category adjectival phrase (AP). So, the Japanese phrase *totemo akai hon* "very red book" renders itself as an NP that has the constituent structure in (5).

(5)

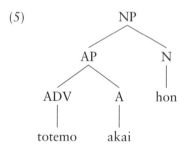

In this tree, the phrasal category NP is built around the lexical category N. Similarly, the phrasal category AP is built around the lexical category A. The specific location in a tree where a category label can appear is called a **node:** "ADV", "A", "N", "AP", and "NP" in (5) are all referred to as nodes. The phrase structure tree of (5) indicates that an N can combine with an AP, forming an NP constituent. In (5) "A" and "N", for instance, correspond to part of speech categories, adjective and noun, respectively, and hence are lexical categories; while the whole phrase "NP" is a phrasal category under which the N *hon* "book" combines with the AP *totemo akai* "very red".

Phrasal categories are not limited to NPs and APs. Postpositions can combine with NPs to form postpositional phrases (PPs). Two examples of PPs are illustrated in (6).

(6)   a.   uti-de   b.   gakkoo-made
           house-at   school-to
           "at home"   "to school"

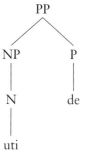   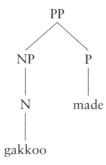

The P *de* "at" combines with an NP, forming a PP in (6a). Similarly, in (6b), the PP is the phrasal node resulting from the combination of the P *made* "to" and the NP *gakkoo* "school".

Verbs can combine with either NPs or PPs. Consider the examples in (7).

(7)   a.   atarasii hon-o   kau   b.   uti-e   kaeru
           new   book-Acc buy   house-to return
           "buy a new book"   "return home"

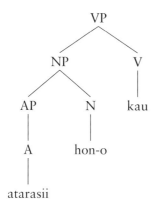   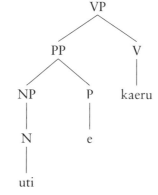

In (7a) the V *kau* "buy" combines with the NP *atarasii hon-o* "a new book", which consists of an AP and an N, to form a VP. (7b) is a case in which the V combines with a PP, i.e. *uti-e* "to the house". In both situations, the whole phrases are labeled as VPs. Furthermore, many verbs can combine with both an NP and a PP. This is shown in (8).

(8) gakkoo-de atarasii hon-o   katta
    school-at new   book-Acc bought
    "bought a new book at school"

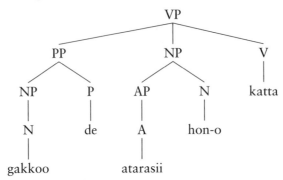

In the phrase structure tree of (8), the V *katta* "bought" combines with the PP, *gakkoo de* "at school", and the NP, *atarasii hon-o* "a new book", forming a VP.

When we add the subject NP to the VP in (8), we now form a sentence, which is abbreviated as "S". Consider the syntactic structure of (9).

(9) Taroo-ga   gakkoo-de atarasii hon-o   katta.
    Taro-Nom school-at new   book-Acc bought
    "Taro bought a new book at school."

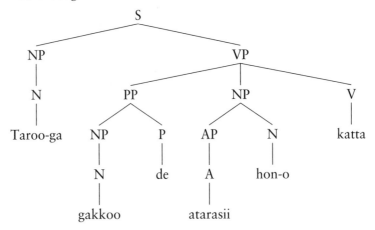

Incidentally, it should be noticed that Case particles are syntactically treated as part of an NP while Ps are considered a lexical category that forms an independent node. For instance, the Accusative Case particle *o* in (7a) and (8) does not have a node separate from the NP that accompanies it: rather, it is treated as part of the NP. Ps such as *de* "at" as in (6a), *made* "to" as in (6b), and *e* "to" as in (7b), on the other hand, are analyzed as distinct from the accompanying NP. This is due to the difference between Case particles and postpositions discussed in chapter 4: postpositions bear specific meanings while Case particles usually indicate the grammatical functions of the accompanying NP in a sentence, such as subject and object. Although there are a few researchers who have analyzed Case particles and postpositions uniformly as constituting independent nodes, in this book we will make a distinction between the two just as we have above. That is, postpositions form a separate node while Case particles such as *ga* (Nominative), *o* (Accusative), *ni* (Dative), and *no* (Genitive) (as well as the Topic marker *wa*) are treated as a part of the NP in which they occur.[1]

Returning to the example of structural ambiguity illustrated in (3)–(4) above, the analysis tree of (4) can be modified as below, using the phrase structure representation that we have discussed thus far.

(10)   a.   b.

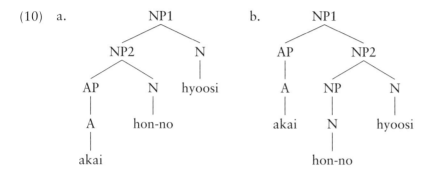

As we have discussed, the phrase *akai hon-no hyoosi* is structurally ambiguous in that it can have either the structure depicted in (10a) or that in (10b), depending on what interpretation is intended. Thus, the ambiguity is explained by the different ways in which certain words are put together in forming a constituent. What is new in these structures is that the NP1 of (10a) and NP2 of (10b) consist of an NP and an N rather than an AP and an N. We shall assume that when a noun has a prenominal modifier, where the modifier is often a noun accompanied by the Genitive Case *no*, as is in the present case, such an expansion is possible.

1.3   Phrase Structure Rules

We have seen that given the limited sets of lexical categories and phrasal categories, we can represent phrases and sentences hierarchically so that syntactic constituency can explicitly be depicted. Given the device of phrase structure trees, we can express an infinite number of sentences clearly illustrating their internal structures. Syntactic structures are not randomly formed, however. As hinted at above and shown in more detail below, there are systematic regularities in forming phrase structures. For example, an S node does not consist of an NP and a PP alone: instead, it regularly has the constituents of an NP and a VP. Nor do we see a PP having the constituents of a VP and a P. So, on the one hand, phrase structures should employ freedom to express an unlimited number of sentences and phrases, but on the other hand, they should also be restrictive enough to be able to specify the regularities of the generation of such syntactic structures. To this end, we will use **phrase structure rules** like those in (11).

(11) a. S → NP VP
      b. NP → (NP) (AP) N
      c. VP → (PP) (NP) (PP) (NP) V
      d. PP → NP P

These phrase structure rules indicate the constituency of each phrasal category as well as the order among the constituents. For instance, (11a) expresses that an S always has an NP and a VP as its immediate constituents, and that the ordering between them is that the NP precedes the VP. The categories in parentheses mean that they are optional. The phrase structure rules in (11) are able to generate the phrases and sentences that we have discussed thus far as well as those in (12). The syntactic structures corresponding to the sentences in (12) are illustrated in (13).

(12) a. Gakusei-ga   kita.
          student-Nom came
          "A student came."
      b. Kodomo-ga kooen-de asonda.
          child-Nom   park-at   played
          "A child played at the park."
      c. Taroo-ga   Hanako-to   Tookyoo-e itta.
          Taro-Nom Hanako-with Tokyo-to   went
          "Taro went to Tokyo with Hanako."
      d. Taroo-ga   sakanaya-de hurui sakana-o katta.
          Taro-Nom fish store-at old   fish-Acc bought
          "Taro bought old fish at a fish store."
      e. Ziroo-ga   Masako-ni   yubiwa-o ageta.
          Ziro-Nom Masako-Dat ring-Acc gave
          "Ziro gave Masako a ring."
      f. Taroo-ga   Hanako-ni   UPS-de hon-o   okutta.
          Taro-Nom Hanako-Dat UPS-by book-Acc sent
          "Taro sent Hanako a book by UPS."

(13) a.   b.

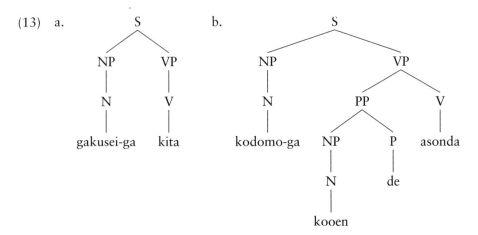

c.

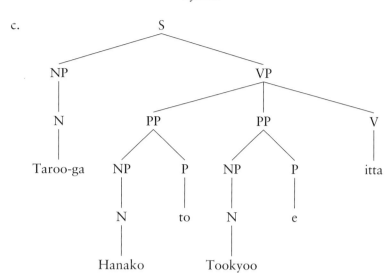

d.

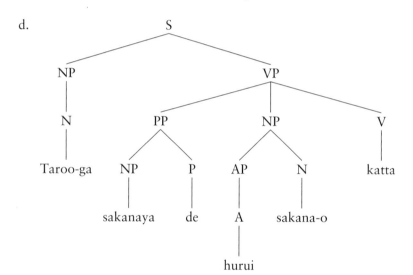

e.

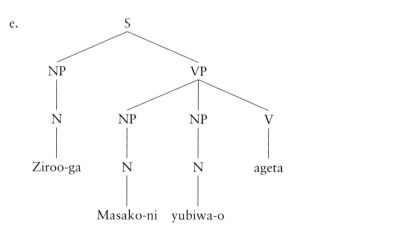

f.

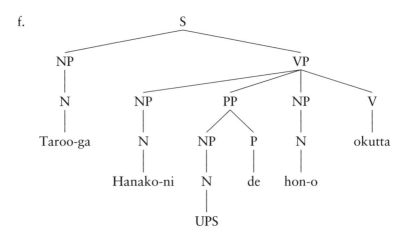

(13d), for example, is generated by the combination of the phrase structure rules in (11). (11a) generates the NP and the VP, which are the immediate constituents of the S. The subject NP, in the absence of an accompanying NP or AP, simply consists of the N, *Taroo*, following (11b). The VP is further expanded to the object NP, *hurui sakana* "old fish", the PP, *sakanaya-de* "at a fish store", and the V, *katta* "bought", which are all generated by (11c). (11b) generates an AP and an N, and this is exemplified by the AP *hurui* "old" and the N *sakana* "fish". Following (11d), the PP consists of the NP *sakanaya* "fish store" and the P *de* "at". This NP is not accompanied by an A or an NP, and is accordingly labeled as N.

   Now, consider the sentences in (14).

(14) a. Hanako-ga   [Taroo-ga   tukutta] susi-o   tabeta.
          Hanako-Nom Taro-Nom   made   sushi-Acc   ate
          "Hanako ate the sushi that Taro made."
      b. [Taroo-ga   tukutta] susi-ga   kusatta.
          Taro-Nom   made   sushi-Nom   spoiled
          "The sushi that Taro made spoiled."
      c. Taroo-ga   [Hanako-ga   oisii   susi-o   tukutta]-to   itta.
          Taro-Nom   Hanako-Nom delicious sushi-Acc   made-COMP   said
          "Taro said that Hanako made delicious sushi."
      d. Taroo-ga   Hanako-ni [sensei-ga   Tookyoo-e itta]-to   itta.
          Taro-Nom Hanako-to teacher-Nom Tokyo-to   went-COMP   said
          "Taro said to Hanako that his teacher went to Tokyo."

The portions surrounded by the square brackets form independent clauses. These independent clauses are instances of sentence modifiers or relative clauses. In (14a) and (14b), for example, *Taroo-ga tukutta* "Taro made" is a clause that modifies *susi*. Notice that the set of phrase structure rules in (11) does not generate sentences with sentence modifiers like (14a) and (14b) simply because an NP cannot have an S as its immediate constituent by the rules in (11). What we need, then, is an additional phrase structure rule that allows for the generation of the syntactic structures as in (15), which respectively correspond to (14a) and (14b). Those examples are repeated below.

(15) a. Hanako-ga   Taroo-ga tukutta susi-o   tabeta.
      Hanako-Nom Taro-Nom made   sushi-Acc ate
      "Hanako ate the sushi that Taro made."

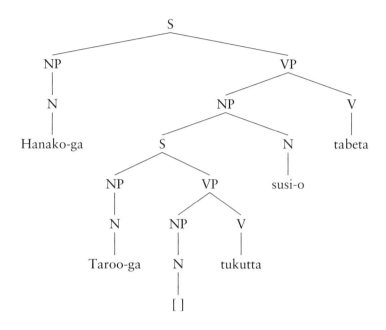

   b. Taroo-ga tukutta susi-ga   kusatta.
      Taro-Nom made   sushi-Nom spoiled
      "The sushi that Taro made spoiled."

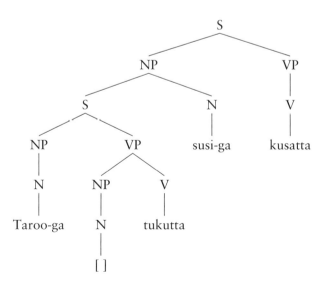

First, in describing the structure of a sentence modifier in Japanese, we note that the sentence modifier and the noun it modifies form an NP. This NP is under the topmost VP in (15a) and under the topmost S in (15b). That is, the noun *susi* can combine with an S to form an NP. In order to generate such an NP, we need to modify the phrase structure rule of (11b) so that an S modifying a noun can be considered as a constituent of another sentence. This can be accomplished by the phrase structure rule in (16).

(16)   NP → (S) (NP) (AP) N

Second, unlike English, there is no word intervening between a sentence modifier and the noun that it modifies. Compare the Japanese sentences in (15) with the English sentences in (17).

(17)   a.   John ate the cake **which** Mary baked.
       b.   The woman **who** donated her furniture to charity is my mother.
       c.   Mary went to the gym **where** Jim usually works out.

Sentence modifiers (or relative clauses) in English often require the presence of words like *which*, *who*, and *where* as in (17); these are called "relative pronouns". Japanese, on the other hand, does not exhibit words corresponding to these relative pronouns which are placed between the sentence modifier and the modified noun. Hence, an NP can have an S and an N as its immediate constituents.

Third, in the phrase structure trees depicted in (15), there is an NP (and consequently an N) node under which no word is expressed. This reflects the intuitive sense that the modified noun "originates" from the position in the associating sentence modifier, indicated by the blank. In other words, one can understand the sentence in (15a) as being like "Hanako ate the sushi that Taro made it" where "it" refers to the modified noun "sushi". In order to keep track of this relationship between the sentence modifier and the modified noun, the two Ns can be co-indexed, as in (18).

(18)   a.   (= (15a))

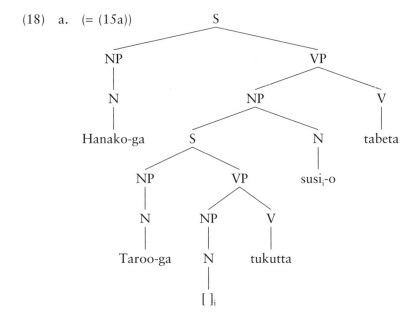

b.   (= (15b))

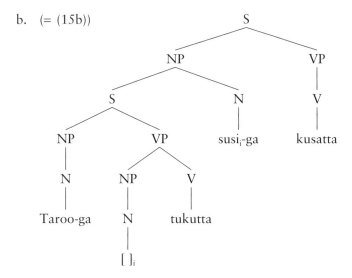

In (18a), for example, the N *susi* "sushi" is interpreted as the direct object of the lower V *tukutta* "made", and such a relationship is established by the use of the index "i". Hence, with a slight modification and the introduction of some diacritics, we can adequately represent the syntactic structure of sentence modifiers.

Let us now turn to (14c) and (14d). As can be observed in the English translation, these are sentences which have indirect quotations in Japanese. Unlike the sentences with sentence modifiers, the quoted sentence functions as a direct object of the verb. Furthermore, the quoted sentence is accompanied by *to* "that". As the gloss indicates, *to* "that" is called a **complementizer (COMP)**. Since complementizers serve to introduce a clause (i.e. a quotation), we use a new category, S' (call it "S-bar"), that consists of a complementizer and an accompanying clause. This can be stated in terms of the phrase structure rule in (19).

(19) S' → S COMP

What we further need is a phrase structure rule that would introduce an S' under a VP. This is shown by (20), as a modified version of the phrase structure rule of (11c).

(20) VP → (PP) (NP) (PP) (NP) (S') V

Given the additional and modified phrase structure rules, we can draw phrase structure trees for (14c) and (14d) as in (21).

(21)   a.   (= (14c))
            Taroo-ga   Hanako-ga   oisii   susi-o   tukutta-to   itta.
            Taro-Nom Hanako-Nom delicious sushi-Acc made-COMP said
            "Taro said that Hanako made delicious sushi."

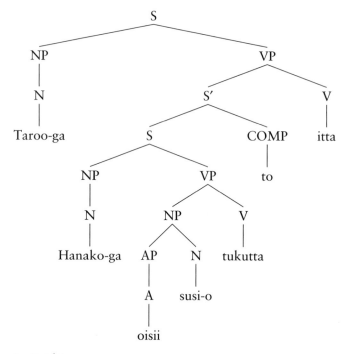

b.   (= (14d))
     Taroo-ga   Hanako-ni sensei-ga   Tookyoo-e itta-to   itta.
     Taro-Nom Hanako-to teacher-Nom Tokyo-to   went-COMP said
     "Taro said to Hanako that his teacher went to Tokyo."

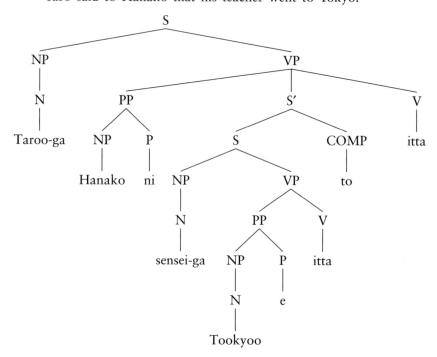

Since an independent sentence is "embedded" under the topmost VP, the lower S is called an **embedded clause**, while the topmost S is referred to as a **matrix** or **main clause**.

1.4 *The Notion of Head*

Consider the phrase structure rules in (22) that we have examined above.

(22) a. S′ → S COMP
      b. S → NP VP
      c. NP → (S) (NP) (AP) N
      d. VP → (PP) (NP) (PP) (NP) (S′) V
      e. PP → NP P

Except for the first two rules in (22), phrasal categories such as NP, VP, and PP require the presence of N, V, and P, respectively. That is, we can observe that these phrasal categories are built around lexical categories of the same type. For instance, a noun phrase is built around a noun, a verb phrase around a verb, and so on. The lexical category around which a phrasal category is formed is called the **head**. So, the N, V, and P in (22c), (22d), and (22e) are all heads of their respective phrasal categories.[2]

There are two characteristics associated with heads. First, they are always present. So, in all the syntactic trees we have examined above, whenever we see an NP, we also observe its head N; whenever we see a VP, we also observe its head V, and so on. Second, the type of meaning associated with the head is always associated with the phrase. For instance, observe the similarity in meaning between (a) and (b) in the pairs in (23)–(24).

(23) a. hon "book"   b. akai hon "red book"

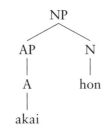

(24) a. kaeru "return"   b. uti-e kaeru "return home"

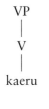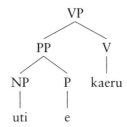

The meaning of the (b) phrases is obviously attributed to the meaning of their heads. The whole NP in (23b) refers to a kind of book, which comes from the meaning of the head, *hon* "book". The accompanying AP simply modifies the head to add further information to the meaning of the head. Similarly in (24b) the primary meaning of the VP comes from the meaning of the head, i.e. the action of returning. This is the meaning that the VP minimally must have. The PP that precedes it then simply supplies more details as to the direction of the returning action. Hence, the meaning of the head is always preserved at the level of its phrasal category.

It is worth noting that the Right Head Rule discussed in chapter 4 is a rule particular to morphology, and hence does not apply to the head used in syntax. This point can readily be shown by comparing the phrase structures in English and Japanese. Consider the instantiations of VP and PP in English in (25).

(25)   a.   ate fish   b.   to school

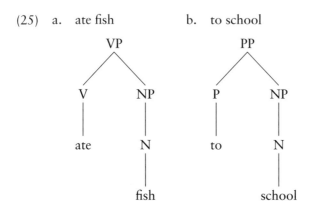

According to the definition of head in phrase structure, the head of the VP in (25a) is the V and that of the PP in (25b) is the P(reposition). Notice that the position of the head is different between Japanese and English: in Japanese we saw that the head is placed on the right while in English it is on the left. This sort of variation is observed across the languages of the world. Hence, on the basis of this illustration, it is clear that the Right Head Rule is not a rule in syntax, and its application is restricted to the domain of morphology.

1.5   Subcategorization

Given the phrase structure rules introduced above, it is interesting to see how the ungrammaticality of the sentences in (26) should be explained.

(26)   a.   *Taroo-ga susi-o   itta.
             Taro-Nom sushi-Acc went
             "*Taro went sushi."

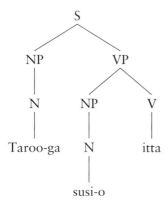

b. *Hanako-ga   Ziroo-ni susi-o   waratta.
    Hanako-Nom Ziro-Dat sushi-Acc laughed
    "*Hanako laughed sushi to Ziro."

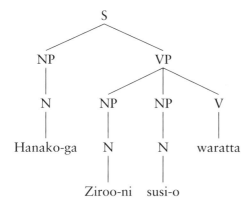

c. *Taroo-ga Hanako-ni   susi-o   tabeta.
    Taro-Nom Hanako-Dat sushi-Acc ate
    "*Taro ate sushi to Hanako."

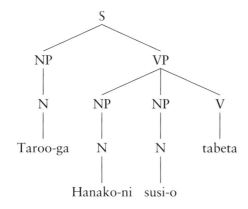

The sentences in (26) are all consistent with the phrase structure rules in (11), as is depicted by the accompanying syntactic structures, and yet they are ungrammatical. The problem with these sentences can be attributed to the fact that there is inconsistency between the nature of the verbs and the number of NPs that are realized in the sentences. For instance, the verb *itta* "went" in (26a) and the verb *waratta* "laughed" in (26b) are examples of **intransitive verbs**, which require only the presence of the subject. Thus, the direct object in (26a), and the direct object and indirect object in (26b) are not what the verbs require. In fact, these intransitive verbs not only do NOT require these NPs but also MUST NOT have them. On the other hand, the verb *tabeta* "ate" in (26c) is a **transitive verb**, requring both a subject and a direct object. Since the transitive verb in this sentence cannot have an indirect object, the sentence is ungrammatical.

What is crucial here is that since phrase structure rules are blind to the nature of the verb in terms of the number of NPs with which it co-occurs, there is no way of avoiding the generation of ungrammatical sentences like those in (26). In order to solve this problem, we use **subcategorization**. This specifies the number and/or type (or category) of constituents (besides subject) with which an individual verb appears. The subcategorization specifications for the verbs in (26), then, should look like (27).

(27) a. *ik* "go": [___]
      b. *waraw* "laugh": [___]
      c. *tabe* "eat": [NP ___]

The underline indicates the location of the verb in question. (27a) and (27b) state that these verbs do not require any object NP while (27c) shows that the verb obligatorily takes an object NP. Certain verbs require a direct and an indirect object, such as *ageru* "give", as is exemplified by (28).

(28) Taroo-ga Hanako-ni hana-o   ageta.
      Taro-Nom Hanako-Dat flower-Acc gave
      "Taro gave Hanako flowers."

The subcategorization frame for *ageru* "give" is given in (29).

(29) *age* "give": [NP NP ___]

There are also verbs that require a PP, as is the case with verbs like *oku* "put". Consider the example in (30)–(31) of such a verb and its subcategorization.

(30) Taroo-ga tana-ni hon-o   oita.
      Taro-Nom shelf-at book-Acc put
      "Taro put a book on the shelf."

(31) *ok* "put": [PP NP ___]

Notice that the constituents, i.e. the NP object and the PP, required by the verb are both specified in the verb's subcategorization frame. In this situation, we say that the verb *ok* "put" subcategorizes for an NP and a PP.

1.6 Structural Relations

Besides the notion of head introduced in section 1.4 of this chapter, there are some technical structural terms that need to be mentioned since they will play a role in our later discussion. Consider the abstract phrase structure tree in (32).

(32)
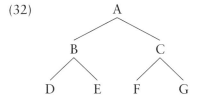

If there is a uniformly downward path from a node at one level to a node at another level, we say the first node **dominates** the other. In (32), for instance, the node A dominates all the node labels below it, i.e. the nodes B, C, D, E, F, and G, because in each case there is a uniformly downward path from A to the node under it. The node B dominates the node D and the node E, but it does not dominate the nodes A, C, F, and G because there is no uniformly downward path from B to those nodes. Similarly, the only nodes that node C dominates are F and G. In (24b), for example, the VP dominates all the nodes that are under it, and the PP dominates the NP and the P, but it does not dominate the V.

Related to the notion of domination is the term **immediate domination**. A node is said to immediately dominate another when the former dominates the latter and they are apart by one hierarchical level. In (32), for example, node A immediately dominates B because A, which is the highest in the hierarchical structure, dominates B and B is at the next highest level lower than A. Similarly, C immediately dominates F. However, A does not immediately dominate D. The relational term "immediately dominate" is quite convenient in defining subject and object. As we will examine in detail later in this chapter, the characterization of subject especially can be rather intricate. Assuming the phrase structure rules given in (22), however, we can always refer to the subject of a sentence as the NP immediately dominated by an S, and to the object of a sentence as the NP immediately dominated by a VP.

Now, consider the nodes B and C in (32). These nodes share the node A that immediately dominates them. In this situation node B and node C are said to be **sisters**. That is, they are in a sister relation. Other nodes in (32) appearing in a sister relation are D and E as well as F and G. However, the nodes E and F are not sisters because they do not share a node that immediately dominates them. For this same reason, C and E are not sisters. In (24b) the PP and V are sisters, and so are the NP and P. The notion of a sister relation will be important to the understanding of the syntactic structure of Japanese.

A final relation, **c-command**, will play an important role in explaining several phenomena in Japanese syntax. To determine whether the node X c-commands the node Y, go upward from X in the tree and stop at the first node that branches (i.e. immediately dominates at least two nodes). If this first branching node also dominates Y and X does not dominate Y, then X c-commands Y. Under this definition, node B in (32) c-commands nodes C, F, and G. However, nodes F and G do not c-command B because the first branching node dominating nodes F and G is node C and node C does not dominate node B. The relevance of this relation will become apparent in our later discussion.

2   Transformational Rules

In this section we will briefly examine some instances of transformational rules. Such rules map one phrase structure tree to another. This has the effect of deriving a new sentence from a related one. In particular, we will focus on yes–no questions (questions that can be answered by *yes* or *no*) and wh-questions (questions introduced by a word that begins with *wh* in English, such as *who*, *what*, and *where*), and we will show that their formation in Japanese is different from English.

2.1   Yes–No Question

Let us first compare declarative and corresponding yes–no interrogative sentences in English, as in (33) and (34).

(33)   a.   John should leave.
       b.   Should John leave?

(34)   a.   Mary can eat fish.
       b.   Can Mary eat fish?

Although we have not discussed phrase structure rules in English, if compared to the set in Japanese we can assume that the (a) sentences can be derived by the English phrase structure rules of (35), where words like *should* and *can* are treated as auxiliary (abbreviated as "AUX").

(35)   a.   S → NP AUX VP
       b.   VP → V (NP)

What about the (b) sentences in (33)–(34)? If we assume that yes–no question sentences are also derived by phrase structure rules, then we need another rule to ensure that the word order will be compatible with the (b) sentences. This can be achieved by the phrase structure rule of (36).

(36)   S → AUX NP VP

Since (35a) and (36) are similar, we might want to determine whether there is a single rule that would generate the same string of words just as (35a) and (36) do. The result might look like (37).

(37)   S → (AUX) NP (AUX) VP

When the second AUX is chosen and the first is not, the effect of (35a) is obtained; and when the first AUX is chosen while the second is not, interrogative sentences are generated just as the phrase structure rule of (36) illustrates. On the other hand, as we have seen above, phrase structure rules by themselves are not sensitive to the type of sentences (i.e. declarative or interrogative), and thus, the rule of (37) would generate ungrammatical sentences like (38).

(38)   a.   *Should John may leave?
       b.   *Can Mary will eat fish?

These sentences are consistent with (37), and yet they are not acceptable.

In order to avoid such an undesirable situation, we can invoke **transformational rules**, which operate on the syntactic structure generated by phrase structure rules to derive a new syntactic structure. That is, transformational rules serve to map a phrase marker (or tree) to another phrase marker. The transformational rule that is relevant to the formation of interrogative sentences in English can be stated in (39).

(39)   Yes–No Question Formation: NP   AUX
                                    1   2   →   2   1

The Yes–No Question Formation in (39) takes declarative sentences like (33a) and (34a), and rearranges the two items stated in the rule, so that the resulting question sentences exhibit the new ordering. The (b) sentences of (33) and (34) are indeed what we obtain after the application of the transformational rule to their respective (a) sentences.

Native speakers of a language know intuitively that declarative sentences and their interrogative counterparts are somehow related. Note that transformational rules generally reflect this intuition: the Yes–No Question Formation transformation preserves the basic meaning that the original declarative sentence has.

The syntactic structure before a transformational rule applies is referred to as **deep structure** or **d-structure** while the syntactic structure after the rule application is called **surface structure** or **s-structure**.

Let us briefly examine yes–no questions in Japanese. Examples are given in (40)–(41).

(40)   a.   Tanaka-san-ga   asita   kimasu.
            Mr Tanaka-Nom tomorrow come
            "Mr Tanaka will come tomorrow."
       b.   Tanaka-san-ga   asita   kimasu ka.
            Mr Tanaka-Nom tomorrow come   Q
            "Will Mr Tanaka come tomorrow?"

(41) a. Hanako-ga   susi-o   tukurimasita.
            Hanako-Nom sushi-Acc made
            "Hanako made sushi."
     b. Hanako-ga   susi-o   tukurimasita ka.
            Hanako-Nom sushi-Acc made   Q
            "Did Hanako make sushi?"

Compare the formation of interrogative sentences in Japanese with those in English. It is clear that Japanese does not exhibit the same type of rearrangement needed among words for the purpose of forming an interrogative sentence based on a declarative sentence, as observed in English. Instead, the question particle *ka* is added at the end of the sentence to form an interrogative sentence. Interrogative sentences in Japanese, then, might arguably be generated by the phrase structure rule of (22b) with the optional specification of the question particle *ka*, as is illustrated in (42).

(42) S → NP VP (ka)

Since a phrase structure rule of the form (42) does not raise a problem of the sort we have observed in English, as especially seen by (37) and the ill-formedness in (38), a transformational operation is not normally called for in the formation of interrogative sentences in Japanese.

2.2 WH-Movement

In the previous section, we noted that interrogative sentences are intuitively related to their declarative sentences. We have seen that given declarative sentences as d-structure, the English Yes-No Question Formation of (39) maps the d-structure onto interrogative sentences (i.e. s-structure), whereby the intuitive sense is reflected. Similarly, we know that the sentence *What will John eat?* is intuitively related to the declarative sentence *John will eat a hamburger*. Thus, the formation of wh-questions can be dealt with by way of a transformational rule. Let us assume that English also has S′ which introduces S and COMP as its immediate constituents, although because of the difference in word order between Japanese and English, we need to analyze COMP as preceding S in English. This is expressed in the phrase structure rule of (43).

(43) S′ → COMP S

Let us now examine a transformational rule that will derive a wh-question sentence. We call this transformational rule WH-Movement, as is stated in (44), where the term "wh-phrase" subsumes interrogative words.

(44) WH-Movement: Move a wh-phrase into the COMP position.

In the sentence *What will John eat?*, we assume that *what* originates from the direct object of the verb, since the verb requires one. That is, we assume that the d-structure configuration of this sentence is *John will eat what*. The derivation of this sentence is depicted in (45). (The position of the AUX in the question sentence is not crucial in our discussion at this point.)

(45)　a.　d-structure:

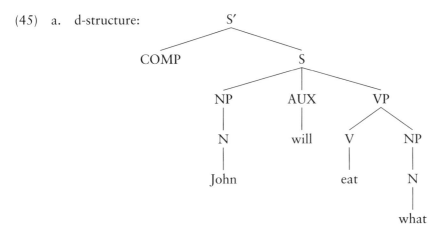

　　b.　s-structure:

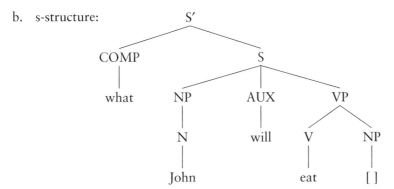

According to the rule stated in (44), *what* in (45a), being a wh-phrase, is moved to the COMP position, deriving the syntactic structure of (45b).

What happens to the NP node after *what* is moved to the COMP position? When a movement transformation moves a constituent to some other position, it leaves a trace (indicated as "t") behind, and in order to keep track of the derivational history of a moved constituent, we co-index the moved element and the trace left behind by the movement operation. This is depicted in (46).

(46)

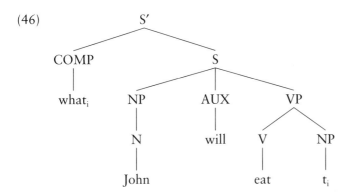

The trace t_i under the direct object NP position is left behind by the movement of *what$_i$* to the COMP position, and the co-indexing suggests this relationship between the two.[3]

The trace as a by-product of a movement rule plays an important role in keeping track of where a movement constituent originally comes from. At this point, however, we should ask ourselves whether a trace left behind by a movement rule is indeed motivated. As it turns out, there is a piece of evidence for the presence of a trace, as has been discussed in many works (cf. Chomsky 1980; Jaeggli 1980; Postal and Pullum 1982; among others). Consider the interrogative sentence in (47).

(47)   Who do you want to succeed?

This sentence is ambiguous in that there are two interpretations associated with it. One is such that there is someone who you want to be successful, and you are asking who that person is. A possible answer would be *I want John to succeed*. Under this interpretation, the word *succeed* is equivalent to *be successful*. In the other reading, the word *succeed* is synonymous with *replace*. In this interpretation, a possible answer would be *I want to succeed John*. Hence, the original position of the wh-phrase *who* is not the same under these two interpretations. This can be shown by using a trace, as the s-structure representations of (48) illustrate.

(48)   a.   [$_{S'}$ [$_{COMP}$ who$_i$] [$_S$ you want t$_i$ to succeed]]
        b.   [$_{S'}$ [$_{COMP}$ who$_i$] [$_S$ you want to succeed t$_i$]]

In colloquial and fast speech, English *want* and *to* are often contracted as *wanna*. So, (47) can be pronounced as (49).

(49)   Who do you wanna succeed?

What is of interest is that many native speakers find that (49) corresponds only to (48b). Differently put, when the verb *succeed* in (47) means "be successful", the contracted form *wanna* cannot be used.

Let us assume, at this point, that for *want* and *to* to be contracted, they have to be immediately next to each other. Now, compare the s-structure representations in (48). In (48b) nothing intervenes between *want* and *to*, and hence the contraction is possible, as is predicted. In (48a), on the other hand, there is a trace left behind by the movement of *who* between *want* and *to*, and since they are not immediately next to each other, the contraction fails and *wanna* is not available in this interpretation.

This suggests that by invoking a trace in the s-structure representation of the ambiguous sentence in (47), it presents a natural account for the unavailability of the contracted form, under the interpretation where *succeed* means *be successful*. Therefore, this contraction phenomenon in English provides a crucial piece of evidence for the validity of a trace as a consequence of a movement transformation. Hence, we will posit a trace whenever a constituent is moved by a movement rule.

Before we leave this subsection, let us take a quick look at wh-questions in Japanese.

(50) a. Hanako-ga   kinoo   tomodati-to susi-o   tukurimasita.
          Hanako-Nom yesterday friend-with sushi-Acc made
          "Hanako made sushi with her friends yesterday."
      b. Dare-ga   kinoo   tomodati-to susi-o   tukurimasita ka.
          who-Nom   yesterday friend-with sushi-Acc made   Q
          "Who made sushi with (his/her) friends yesterday?"
      c. Hanako-ga   itu   tomodati-to susi-o   tukurimasita ka.
          Hanako-Nom when   friend-with sushi-Acc made   Q
          "When did Hanako make sushi with her friends?"
      d. Hanako-ga   kinoo   dare-to   susi-o   tukurimasita ka.
          Hanako-Nom yesterday who-with sushi-Acc made   Q
          "With whom did Hanako make sushi yesterday?"
      e. Hanako-ga   kinoo   tomodati-to nani-o   tukurimasita ka.
          Hanako-Nom yesterday friend-with what-Acc made   Q
          "What did Hanako make with her friends yesterday?"
      f. Dare-ga   itu   dare-to   nani-o   tukurimasita ka.
          who-Nom   when   who-with   what-Acc made   Q
          "Who made what with whom when?"

This range of data is reminiscent of the formation of the yes–no questions in Japanese discussed earlier, in that there is no movement of a constituent associated with the formation of wh-questions: instead, interrogative words replace NPs at the same position, and the question particle *ka* is added at the end of the sentence. Furthermore, multiple wh-questions like (50f) can freely be generated. Hence, we assume that in Japanese there is no obvious movement transformation equivalent to the one in English that we have observed above (cf. Nishigauchi 1990).

3   Word Order and Scrambling

3.1   *Scrambling Phenomenon*

English has a relatively rigid word order among constituents in a sentence. For example, consider the English sentences in (51).

(51) a. John gave Bill Mary.
      b. John gave Mary Bill.
      c. Bill gave John Mary.
      d. Bill gave Mary John.
      e. Mary gave Bill John.
      f. Mary gave John Bill.

We may need to consider John, Mary, and Bill as pets or dolls in order to allow for a more coherent context. In all the sentences, however, the subject is always to the left of the verb, the indirect object is always immediately to the right of the verb, and so on. Consider a set of phrase structure rules like (52) for English: subject is readily defined as the NP immediately dominated by the S, and the object is defined as the NP immediately dominated by the VP.

(52)   a.   S → NP VP
       b.   VP → V NP NP
       c.   PP → P NP

What about languages like Japanese, where the word order among constituents in a sentence employs more freedom than in English? Examine the Japanese sentences in (53), all of which virtually mean the same.

(53)   a.   Kinoo   Taroo-ga   Ginza-de susi-o   tabeta.
            yesterday Taro-Nom Ginza-in sushi-Acc ate
            "Taro ate sushi in Ginza yesterday."
       b.   Taroo-ga   Ginza-de kinoo   susi-o   tabeta.
            Taro-Nom Ginza-in yesterday sushi-Acc ate
       c.   Kinoo   susi-o   Taroo-ga   Ginza-de tabeta.
            yesterday sushi-Acc Taro-Nom Ginza-in ate
       d.   Susi-o   kinoo   Taroo-ga   Ginza-de tabeta.
            sushi-Acc yesterday Taro-Nom Ginza-in ate
       e.   Ginza-de Taroo-ga   kinoo   susi-o   tabeta.
            Ginza-in Taro-Nom yesterday sushi-Acc ate
       f.   Kinoo   Ginza-de susi-o   Taroo-ga   tabeta.
            yesterday Ginza-in sushi-Acc Taro-Nom ate

In general, except for the restriction that the verb must be placed at the end of the sentence, the relative order among other constituents can be random. That is, the order of each constituent is different in the sentences in (53), but they all mean the same. The type of sentences in which some constituents are not in the canonical order of subject–object–verb is called **scrambled** sentences, and the phenomenon is referred to as **scrambling** (cf. Harada 1977; Whitman 1979; Saito 1985).

If the word order among constituents is relatively random, then, how do we know who does what? This is where Case particles come into play. The Case particle *ga* normally indicates that the accompanying NP is the subject, and the Case particle *o* suggests that the NP with which it is associated is the direct object. The Dative Case particle *ni*, which generally occurs with giving verbs such as *ageru* "give" and *yaru* "give", marks an NP as the indirect object. So, Case particles employ a specific function that designates the role of the accompanying NP in a sentence. And, because of this function, NPs do not need to appear in defined positions. English, on the other hand, lacks Case particles, and hence structural positions play an important role in identifying subject and object.

Recall that we have discussed the difference between Case particles and postpositions in Japanese. A more fundamental reason why we give separate treatment to them is that we assume that all languages are like Latin or German, where a rich Case system is observed, regardless of whether individual Cases such as Nominative, Accusative, Dative, and Genitive are overtly manifested. Under this assumption, even if a language does not have an overt manifestation of Cases, they are abstractly present. So, English, for example, has a very impoverished overt Case system while Japanese has the overt manifestation of Cases. Languages with such overt manifestation are more likely to display scrambling than languages like English that lack overt manifestation of Case.

3.2 Configurationality

How, then, do we represent scrambled sentences in syntactic trees? For example, do we need six different syntactic trees for the sentences in (53), each of which is generated by a different phrase structure rule? It should be remembered that the meanings of these sentences are virtually identical. Then, it seems extremely redundant to generate scrambled sentences separately from a different set of phrase structure rules.

Up until the 1980s some researchers assumed that the basic word order of Japanese was subject–object–verb, and that the hierarchical structure of a sentence patterns like English; other researchers assumed that Japanese employed a "flatter" structure, in which there was no constituent corresponding to the VP, and that the subject NP and object NP were both sisters to V. Under the first assumption, the syntactic trees of a sentence in Japanese and English look like (54).

(54)   a.   Japanese   b.   English

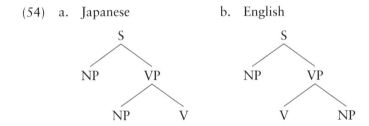

It is important to note that under this assumption the subject NP and the object NP have different hierarchical status in that the subject NP c-commands the object NP, but not vice versa. The first branching node that dominates the subject NP also dominates the object NP; on the other hand, the first branching node dominating the object NP is the VP, and the VP does not dominate the subject NP. That is, subject and object occupy asymmetrical structural positions under this assumption. This point will be of relevance later.

Under the second assumption, in contrast, a Japanese sentence looks like (55).

(55)

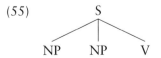

In this structure, there is no VP node that plays a role in hierarchically separating the subject NP from the object NP (cf. Hinds 1973). Consequently, in (55), the subject NP c-commands the object NP while at the same time the object NP c-commands the subject NP.

In the early 1980s, however, a proposal was made by Farmer (1980, 1984) and Hale (1980, 1981) that the world's languages were typologically divided into two groups, languages with the VP node as in (54) and those that exhibited a "flatter" structure similar to (55) above, and that Japanese belonged to the latter type. In this analysis a single phrase structure should generate sentences in which constituents such as subject and object are not hierarchically distinguished. The phrase structure proposed by Farmer and Hale is given in (56).

(56) $X' \rightarrow X'^* \ X$

X is a head and X' ("X-bar") is a level that roughly corresponds to a phrasal level. In (56) X ranges over all the part of speech categories. The diacritic "*" in this rule means that any number of X' including none can be generated. According to this phrase structure, a sentence takes the schematic structure of (57), which is further exemplified by (58).

(57)

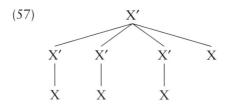

(58)   a.   Hanako-ga   hon-o   katta.
             Hanako-Nom book-Acc bought
             "Hanako bought a book."

        b.

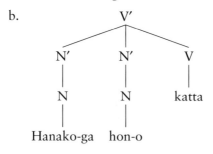

In the case of the multiple occurrence of X', the categories of X need not be unique. So, for example, the structure in (59) can be generated by (56) as well.

(59)   a.   Taroo-ga   kooen-de sanpo-sita.
             Taro-Nom park-in   took a walk
             "Taro took a walk in the park."

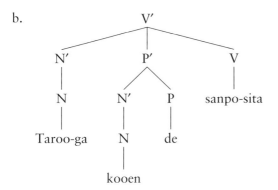

It is important to point out that this approach does not assume that there is a VP node that hierarchically distinguishes subject from object. As the structure of (58) depicts, subject and object are both sisters to V, which is taken to be the head of a sentence.

Under this proposal, scrambling is not an isolated phenomenon, but rather it is a natural consequence of generating a sentence from the phrase structure rule of (56). For example, both sentences in (60) and (61) are generated by the phrase structure rule of (56), as is demonstrated by their accompanying structures.

(60) Taroo-ga susi-o   tabeta.   (61) Susi-o   Taroo-ga tabeta.
      Taro-Nom sushi-Acc ate   sushi-Acc Taro-Nom ate
      "Taro ate sushi."   "Taro ate sushi."

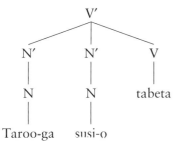
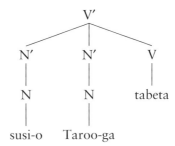

(61) is a scrambled version of (60). This proposal does not treat either structure as basic: instead, both sentences are freely generated by the phrase structure rule in the same fashion. Notice that subject and object are not structurally defined as they are in (54). Crucially, under this analysis, subject and object are of the same status in the hierarchical structure. When Japanese is treated as having a "flatter" structure without a VP node, whereby subject and object are not hierarchically defined, we can say that Japanese is analyzed as a **non-configurational** language. That is, in this treatment, subject and object are not defined in configurational terms. In contrast, the analysis that claims the structure of (54a) for Japanese considers the language as **configurational**.

Almost immediately after the proposal was made that Japanese was a non-configurational language, a group of linguists provided supporting evidence for treating Japanese as a configurational language with a VP node that hierarchically separated subject from object, thereby regarding Japanese and English as parallel in structural terms (cf. Saito and Hoji 1983; Hoji 1985; Saito 1985; to name a few). Saito, for one, demonstrated that basic sentences in Japanese are generated as (54a), in which the subject is immediately dominated by the S while the object is immediately dominated by the VP, and that scrambled sentences where the object precedes the subject are derived by the application of a movement rule.[4]

Let us discuss a basic motivation for this hierarchical (or configurational) analysis in somewhat non-technical terms. It should be pointed out that in almost all world languages, word order in which object precedes subject is more "marked". That is, there are virtually no languages in which the object must precede the subject in a basic transitive sentence. In this sense, the subject–object order is conceived of as more fundamental. This observation holds for Japanese, too. For example, in formal speech or written language, it is rare to see sentences with the object–subject word order, and many Japanese speakers intuitively feel that the subject–object word order is more basic. Given this typological information, if we see a Japanese sentence in which object precedes subject, we want to propose that the object has moved out of the VP and has been fronted over the subject. So, given the basic phrase structure of a Japanese sentence as in (54a), a sentence with the object–subject word order should be represented as in (62).

(62) Susi-o   Taroo-ga   tabeta.
      sushi-Acc Taro-Nom ate
      "Taro ate sushi."

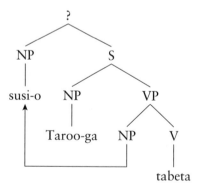

The derivation of the scrambled sentence along the lines sketched in (62) is what Saito basically proposes. Saito, however, further goes on to argue that the fronting of the object NP in (62) should be viewed as an instance of a movement rule that crucially leaves a trace behind, and that the node that dominates the fronted object, identified as "?" in (62), is S. Under this analysis the movement rule that derives a scrambled sentence in Japanese is viewed as parallel to the movement rule that is involved in the wh-movement in English that we observed earlier. The d-structure and s-structure of the sentence in (62) are depicted in (63) and (64).

(63) d-structure:

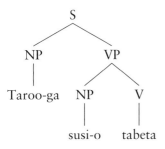

(64) s-structure:

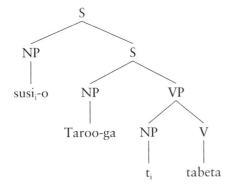

In the s-structure of (64), the trace is left behind by the movement of the object NP, *susi*, and the trace and scrambled NP are co-indexed to indicate the scrambled NP's original position.

In short, this configurational analysis of Japanese departs from the non-configurational treatment in important respects: under the configurational analysis, (i) there is a VP node in Japanese; (ii) as a consequence of (i), subject and object have distinct hierarchical status, i.e. the subject is immediately dominated by the S while the object is immediately dominated by the VP; and (iii) scrambling is an instance of a movement rule that fronts a constituent and leaves a trace behind. We will further examine evidence for the configurational treatment of Japanese below.

3.3 Evidence for the Movement Analysis

Recall the evidence discussed in section 2.2 for traces left by wh-movement in English: the contraction facts have been given a natural account by invoking the presence of a trace as shown in (48). Is there any evidence to support the claim that scrambling results from the application of a movement rule that leaves a trace behind? It is important to find that out because this potential evidence would lead to further support for a hierarchical structure that structurally separates subject from object in Japanese, as is the case with English.

3.3.1 *Numeral Quantifiers*

A piece of evidence for the movement analysis of scrambling comes from the phenomenon known as Quantifier Floating, as is discussed by Kuroda (1980) and Miyagawa (1988, 1989a). Before getting into the detailed discussion of such evidence, however, let us first describe the numeral quantifier system in Japanese (cf. Kamio 1977; Shibatani 1977, 1978; Inoue 1978; Kuno 1978; Haig 1980; Kuroda 1980, 1983; Miyagawa 1988, 1989a; among others). When we count objects, numeral quantifiers are normally associated with them. Numeral quantifiers usually consist of a numeral expression with a classifier that is characteristic of the noun that is counted. Several examples of numeral quantifiers are given in (65).

(65) a. san-nin   "three people"
      b. san-bon   "three long and cylindrical objects"
      c. san-mai   "three thin and flat objects"
      d. san-gen   "three houses"
      e. san-satu   "three bound objects"
      f. san-biki   "three animals (dogs, cats, . . .)"

These numeral quantifiers can be used as modifiers that are placed immediately before the NP that they modify (i.e. as prenominal modifiers), and to indicate the modification relation; the Genitive particle *no* appears after numeral quantifiers. This is illustrated in (66).

(66) a. Sannin-no kodomo-ga uti-e   kita.
          three-Gen child-Nom house-to came
          "Three children came to my house."
      b. Taroo-ga   sanmai-no kami-o   katta.
          Taro-Nom three-Gen paper-Acc bought
          "Taro bought three sheets of paper."
      c. Hanako-ga   sanbiki-no inu-ni   esa-o   yatta.
          Hanako-Nom three-Gen dog-Dat food-Acc gave
          "Hanako gave three dogs food."

As alternative sentences to (66), there are cases in which numeral quantifiers are separated from the nouns that they modify without a significant change in meaning. This phenomenon is referred to as Quantifier Floating. The sentences in (66) look like those in (67) with floated quantifiers.

(67) a. Kodomo-ga sannin uti-e   kita.
          child-Nom   three house-to came
          "Three children came to my house."
      b. Taroo-ga kami-o   sanmai katta.
          Taro-Nom paper-Acc three   bought
          "Taro bought three sheets of paper."
      c. Hanako-ga   inu-ni   sanbiki esa-o   yatta.
          Hanako-Nom dog-Dat three   food-Acc gave
          "Hanako gave three dogs food."

Although quantifiers can be separated from the modified nouns as in (67), they cannot be placed anywhere. As Miyagawa (1989a) argues, there is a structural restriction on Quantifier Floating. (See Shibatani 1977; Haig 1980; Kuroda 1980, 1983; Miyagawa 1988, 1989a; and the references cited there.) Consider the examples in (68)–(69), which are accompanied by the syntactic structures below them. (Numeral quantifiers are indicated as "NQ".)

(68)   a.   Gakusei-ga   sannin [_{VP} sake-o   nonda].
            student-Nom three   Sake-Acc drank
            "Three students drank Sake."

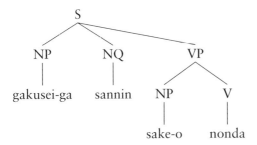

    b.   Taroo-ga   [_{VP} sake-o   sanbon motte-kita].
         Taro-Nom   Sake-Acc three   brought
         "Taro brought three bottles of Sake."

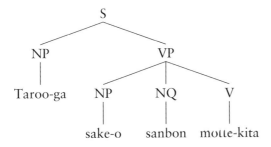

(69)   a.   *Gakusei-ga [_{VP} sake-o   sannin nonda].
            student-Nom   Sake-Acc three   drank
            "Three students drank Sake."

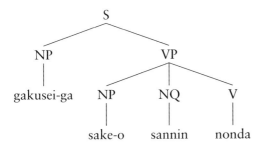

b. *Gakusei-ga [_{VP} hon-o   sannin katta].
    student-Nom   book-Acc three   bought
    "Three students bought books."

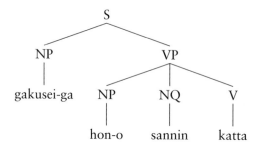

c. *Gakusei-no neko-ga [_{VP} Hanako-to   sannin sanpo-sita].
    student-Gen cat-Nom   Hanako-with three   took a walk
    "Three students' cats took a walk with Hanako."

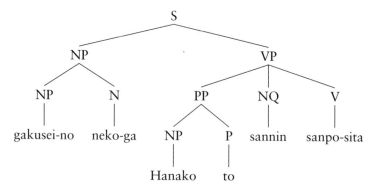

Compare the grammatical sentences with their structures in (68) and the ungrammatical sentences with their structures in (69), concentrating on the structural relation between the NQ and the modified NP. The structural notion of c-command pertains to the difference between the two cases. In (68a) the classifier in *sannin* "three people" is restricted to human beings, and thus, the NQ should modify the subject NP, *gakusei* "student". Notice that the subject NP and its modifying NQ c-command each other: the NP in the subject position, *gakusei* "student", c-commands the NQ, *sannin* "three people" because the first branching node that dominates the subject NP is S, and the S also dominates the NQ; and, the NQ c-commands the subject NP as well. A similar situation is obtained in (68b). The classifier of *sanbon* "three bottles" is used to modify long and cylindrical objects, and thus, we know that the NP is associated with the object NP *sake* "Sake", rather than the subject NP. The direct object NP, sake "Sake", c-commands its NQ, *sanbon* "three long and cylindrical objects": the first branching node that dominates the object NP is the VP, which also dominates the NQ. Furthermore, the NQ also c-commands the object NP. When two nodes c-command each other, this relation is referred to as **mutual c-command**. Miyagawa (1989a) proposes that mutual c-command must hold between the NP and its

NQ. This structural requirement for a NP and its NQ advanced by Miyagawa (1989a) is referred to as the **mutual c-command condition**. In (68) the mutual c-command condition is met, and hence the sentences are acceptable.

Now, we need to examine whether the mutual c-command condition is satisfied in (69). As the associated syntactic structures depict, the condition is violated. In (69a) the NP *gakusei* "student" c-commands the NQ *sannin* "three people": the first branching node dominating the subject NP is the S, and the S dominates the NQ. However, the NQ does not c-command the NP: the first branching node that dominates the NQ is the VP, and the VP does not dominate the NP *gakusei*. The NQ cannot modify the object NP, *sake* "Sake", with which the NQ would maintain the mutual c-command condition, because the classifier *-nin* is used only to modify human beings. Therefore, the condition is not met in this sentence, and as a result the sentence is ungrammatical. A very similar situation is obtained in (69b). The NP *gakusei* "student" c-commands the NQ *sannin* "three people", but the NQ does not c-command the NP: the first branching node dominating the NQ is the VP, and the VP does not dominate the subject NP. Again, the NQ cannot be interpreted to modify the object NP, *hon* "book", which would have a mutual c-command relation with the object NP, because the classifier *-nin* is not compatible with the nature of the noun that represents a bound object, i.e. books. (69c) presents an interesting case. The NQ is intended to modify the NP *gakusei* "student", and the classifier is compatible with the NP. However, neither the NP nor the NQ c-commands the other: the NP *gakusei* "student" cannot c-command the NQ because the first branching node dominating it is the NP immediately dominated by the S, and this NP does not dominate the NQ; nor, does the NQ *sannin* "three people" c-command the NP because the first branching node that dominates the NQ is the VP, and the VP does not dominate the NP *gakusei*. Hence, none of these three structures in (69) satisfies the mutual c-command condition, and therefore these sentences are ungrammatical with the intended modification relation.

Let us now return to our discussion concerning the scrambling phenomenon within the configurational analysis of Japanese. Consider the examples in (70).

(70) a. [$_S$ Sake-o$_i$ [$_S$ Taroo-ga [$_{VP}$ t$_i$ sanbon nonda]]].
           sake-Acc   Taro-Nom   three   drank
          "Taro drank three bottles of Sake."
      b. [$_S$ Hon-o$_i$ [$_S$ gakusei-ga [$_{VP}$ t$_i$ sansatu katta]]].
           book-Acc   student-Nom   three   bought
          "The students bought three books."

In these sentences the direct objects are scrambled over the subjects. Recall that under the configurational analysis that we are assuming now, the object NP is fronted over the subject NP, creating a new S node, and as a consequence of the movement, a trace is left behind in the original object position. The NQs, *sanbon* in (70a) and *sansatu* in (70b) are intended to modify the scrambled object NPs, i.e. *sake* "Sake" and *hon* "book", respectively. We have discussed above the fact that the mutual c-command condition must be satisfied between an NP and its quantifier in order for the sentence to be grammatical, but notice that in (70) this condition is not met. To see this point, consider the structural representations of the examples.

(71)   a.   (= (70a))

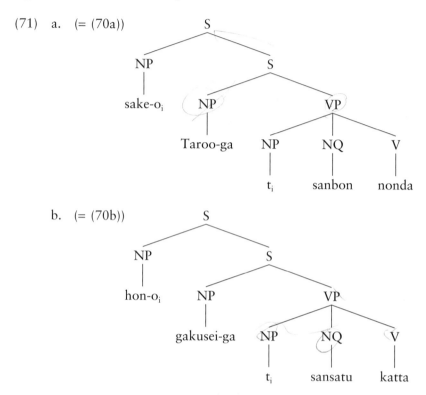

   b.   (= (70b))

In both structures, the scrambled NP c-commands the NQ within the VP, but the NQ does not c-command the NP: the first branching node that dominates the NQ is the VP, and the VP does not dominate the fronted NP. Thus, the mutual c-command condition does not hold in these sentences. It means that these structures are parallel to those in (69) in that neither sentence satisfies the mutual c-command condition. Therefore, we should expect that the sentences in (70) are ungrammatical as those in (69) are. Contrary to this prediction, however, the sentences in (70) are not ungrammatical.

   The unexpected situation we have just observed can readily be explained if we assume that scrambling is an instance of a movement rule that leaves a trace behind. Notice that in the s-structure representations in (71), the mutual c-command condition is not met between the scrambled NP and its NQ, but the condition does hold between the NQ and the trace of the NP that is scrambled. In (71a), for example, the first branching node dominating the trace NP is the VP, which is also the first branching dominating the NQ. It means that the NP-trace and the NQ are sisters, and hence, each c-commands the other. Although the condition is not met between the NQ and the NP itself, it is satisfied between the NQ and the trace left behind by the fronted NP, and hence the sentences are grammatical.

It is clear that it would be rather difficult to explain the difference in grammaticality between (69) and (70), assuming the mutual c-command condition by Miyagawa, if we did not invoke a trace of the scrambled NP. Thus, the NQ facts presented above substantiate the relevance of a trace in structural representations. Furthermore, the presence of a trace amounts to the presence of a movement, and hence the range of data we have just observed provides a crucial piece of evidence, suggesting that scrambling is an instance of a movement rule.

At the same time, the movement analysis of scrambling that has been discussed above supports the configurational analysis of Japanese, namely, the claim that Japanese takes the hierarchical structure of (54a), just as in English, rather than the "flatter" structure of (57). Under the non-configurational analysis, scrambled sentences with the object–subject word order, for instance, are generated by the phrase structure of (56) just like non-scrambled sentences with the basic subject–object order. This analysis does not treat scrambling as an instance of movement, and hence, there is no trace present in the structure of a scrambled sentence. For example, the s-structure representations of (70) would look like (72), assuming that the equivalent of NQ is N′.

(72) a.

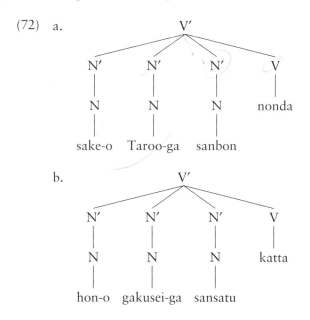

b.

In these non-configurational representations, the scrambled objects *sake* "Sake" in (72a) and *hon* "book" in (72b), and the NQs (each indicated as N′ here), *sanbon* and *sansatu*, respectively, are in a mutual c-command relation. This is because all the constituents under the V′ node maintain the mutual c-command relation with one another. Hence, the grammaticality of (70) is expected. The ungrammaticality of (69), however, is what the non-configurational analysis cannot account for. Under the present assumption, the sentence in (69a) would look like (73).

(73)

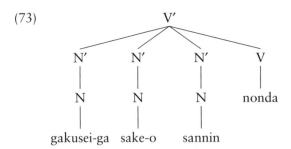

N'   N'   N'   V
| | | |
N   N   N   nonda
| | |
gakusei-ga sake-o   sannin

Since *gakusei* "student" and the quantifier *sannin* "three people" are in a mutual c-command relation, this sentence is predicted to be grammatical. In spite of this prediction, however, we have seen that this sentence is ungrammatical. This is simply because the non-configurational analysis assumes all the constituents are at the same level in a hierarchical structure, which amounts to sisterhood among all the constituents. As long as all the constituents are sisters, it is impossible to differentiate (68) and (69). This type of difficulty does not arise with the configurational analysis, since the VP node plays a role significant for structural notions such as c-command which enables us to account for the range of numeral quantifier phenomena observed above.

3.3.2 *Pronominal Reference*

Another piece of evidence for the hierarchical structure of (54) for Japanese comes from pronouns and their interpretations, as is discussed by Saito (1985). First, consider the examples in English in (74), taken from Saito (1985: 36).

(74) a. John$_i$ loves his$_i$ mother.
      b. *He$_i$ loves John's$_i$ mother.
      c. John's$_i$ mother loves him$_i$.
      d. His$_i$ mother loves John$_i$.

The co-indexing indicates the NP *John* and the pronoun *he/his* refer to the same person. The NP *John* is said to be the **antecedent** of the pronoun *he/his* when such a referential relation is established between a NP and a pronoun. Thus, in (74a), (74c), and (74d) *John* is the antecedent of *he/his* since these pronouns can refer to *John*, whereas in (74b) *John* cannot be the antecedent of *he* since *he* cannot refer to *John* in this sentence; instead, *he* must refer to some male person who is other than *John*. Saito explains that this set of data can be accounted for by the constraint stated in (75).

(75) A pronoun cannot c-command its antecedent.   (Saito 1985: 36)

Let us examine how the constraint in (75) applies to the sentences in (74). Consider (76), where the structures of (74) are given in a somewhat abbreviated manner to show the positions of the pronouns and their antecedents. (A similar set of data is discussed in Saito 1985: 37–38.)

(76)   a.

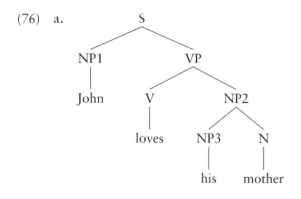

b.   *

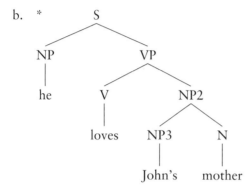

c.

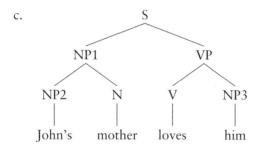

d.

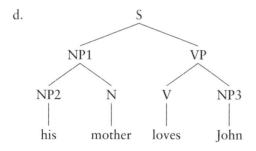

Observe that in (76a), (76c), and (76d) the pronoun does not c-command its antecedent, *John*. In (76a) the first branching node that dominates *his* is NP2, and NP2 does not c-command NP1, *John*. Similarly, in (76c), the first branching node dominating *him* is the VP, which does not dominate the NP2, *John's*. Finally, in (76d), NP1 serves as the first branching node that dominates *his*, and NP1 does not dominate the NP3, *John*. So, the condition of (75) is not violated in these three sentences, and they are grammatical. The pronoun *he* in (76b), on the other hand, does c-command its antecedent: the first branching node that dominates NP1, *he*, is S, and S also dominates the NP3, *John's*. This violates the constraint stated in (75), and as a result, the sentence is ungrammatical.

Let us now examine Japanese pronominal reference (cf. Saito 1985; Whitman 1986). The relevant data are in (77), where the pronoun *kare* "he" is intended to have a referential relation with the NP *Taroo*, and their hierarchical relation is schematically represented in (78).

(77) a. Taroo$_i$-ga [$_{NP}$ Hanako-ga   kare$_i$-ni okutta tegami]-o yonda.
          Taro-Nom   Hanako-Nom he-Dat sent   letter-Acc read
          "Taro$_i$ read the letter that Hanako sent to him$_i$."

      b. *Kare$_i$-ga [$_{NP}$ Hanako-ga   Taroo$_i$-ni okutta tegami]-o yonda.
          he-Nom   Hanako-Nom Taro-Dat sent   letter-Acc read
          "He$_i$ read the letter that Hanako sent to Taro$_i$."

      c. [$_{NP}$ Taroo$_i$-kara okane-o   moratta hito]-ga   kare$_i$-o
          Taro-from   money-Acc received person-Nom he-Acc
          suisensita.
          recommended
          "The person who received money from Taro$_i$ recommended him$_i$."

      d. [$_{NP}$ Kare$_i$-kara okane-o   moratta hito]-ga   Taroo$_i$-o
          he-from   money-Acc received person-Nom Taro-Acc
          suisensita.
          recommended
          "The person who received money from him$_i$ recommended Taro$_i$."

(78) a.

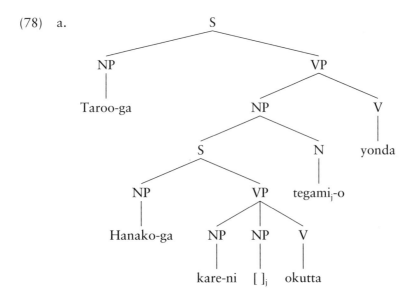

b. *

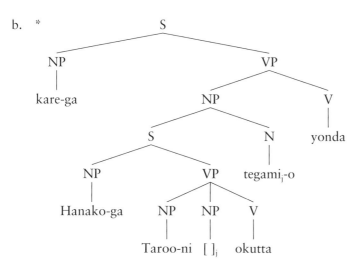

c.

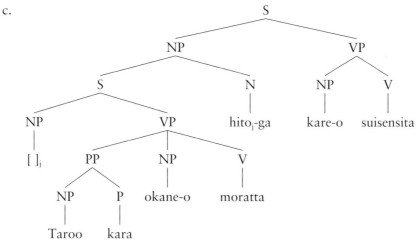

d.

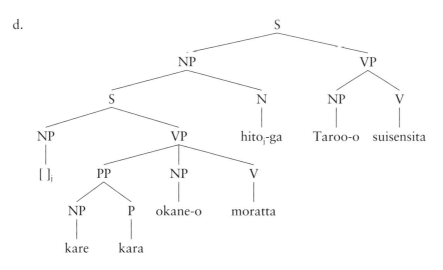

Saito argues that the condition stated in (75) accounts for the range of data given in (77). As the syntactic structures in (78) illustrate, the pronouns in (77a), (77c), and (77d) do not c-command their antecedents. In (77a), whose structure is depicted in (78a), the first branching node that dominates *kare* "he" is the VP under the embedded S, and it is clear that this VP does not dominate the subject NP of the main clause, *Taroo*. In (77c/78c) the first branching node that dominates *kare* is the matrix VP, which does not dominate *Taroo*, which is under the embedded S within the matrix subject NP. Similarly, in (77d/78d), the first branching node dominating *kare* is the PP under the embedded S within the matrix subject NP, and this PP does not dominate its antecedent, *Taroo*. Hence, none of these sentences violates the condition that a pronoun cannot c-command its antecedent. On the other hand, *kare* "he" in (77b), being in the matrix subject position, c-commands its antecedent *Taroo*: the first branching node that dominates *kare* is the topmost S, which also dominates its antecedent *Taroo*. In this sentence, then, the pronoun *kare* does c-command its antecedent, the situation that the constraint in (75) prohibits. Hence, the ungrammaticality of the sentence is straightforwardly explained by the constraint in (75).

Notice that (77c) is crucial in that if we assume a non-configurational structure for Japanese, this sentence should be ungrammatical because it does not satisfy (75). The non-configurational structure representation of the (77c) would look like (79).

(79)

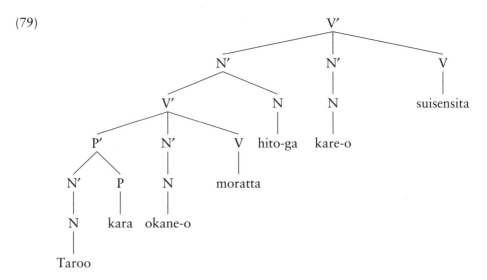

The pronoun *kare* "he" in this structure indeed c-commands its antecedent *Taroo*: the first branching node dominating *kare* is the topmost V', which also dominates the antecedent of *kare*, i.e. *Taroo*. Hence, the sentence is expected to be ungrammatical, contrary to fact. Therefore, if we assume a non-configurational phrase structure representation for Japanese, the range of data concerning pronominal reference cannot be accounted for. Instead, a hierarchical structure containing a VP node under the configurational approach does provide an account for the phenomenon.

Moreover, Saito demonstrates that the pronominal reference examined above also shows that scrambling must be a movement rule because a change in order of constituents necessarily changes the hierarchical relation between a pronoun and its antecedent. To illustrate this point, compare (80) with (81), modified from Saito's (20) (pp. 39–40).

(80) a. *Kare-ga$_i$ [$_{NP}$ Hanako-ga   Taroo-ni$_i$ okutta tegami]-o yonda.
          he-Nom   Hanako-Nom Taro-Dat sent   letter-Acc read
          "He$_i$ read the letter Hanako sent to Taro$_i$."

      b.

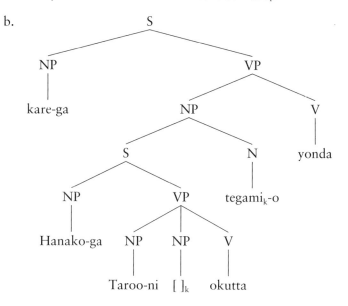

(81) a. [$_{NP}$ Hanako-ga   Taroo-ni$_i$ okutta tegami]-o$_j$ kare-ga$_i$ t$_j$ yonda.
          Hanako-Nom Taro-Dat sent   letter-Acc he-Nom   read
          "He$_i$ read the letter that Hanako sent to Taro$_i$."

      b.

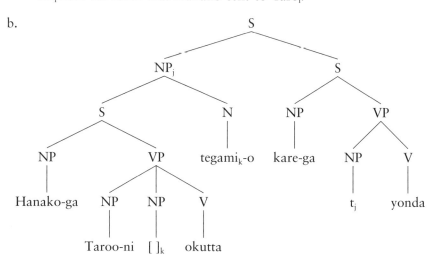

(81) results from fronting the direct object of the matrix clause in (80), i.e.
Hanako-ga Taroo-ni okutta tegami "the letter that Hanako sent to Taro", over
the subject NP, *kare* "he". The ungrammaticality of (80) is explained by the
constraint in (75): the pronoun *kare* c-commands its antecedent, *Taroo*. Once
the direct object, in which the antecedent of the pronoun, *Taroo*, is contained,
is scrambled over the subject *kare* "he", the pronoun *kare* "he" no longer c-
commands its antecedent *Taroo*, as (81b) explicitly shows: in the structure of
(81b), the first branching node dominating *kare* is the original matrix S, and this
S does not dominate its antecedent, *Taroo*. Thus, the sentence is grammatical.
This should be contrasted with the ungrammatical structure of (80b). In this
structure, the first branching node that dominates *kare* is the matrix S, which
also dominates its antecedent, *Taroo*. Hence, the condition that a pronoun cannot
c-command its antecedent is violated here, which results in the ungrammaticality. This suggests, then, that scrambling should be analyzed as an instance of a
movement rule that changes the hierarchical relationship among the constituents,
and that the hierarchical structure depicted in (54a) is justified.

3.4   *Some Restrictions on Scrambling*

Scrambling can rearrange the order among the constituents of a sentence. This
is possible because Case particles such as Nominative *ga*, Accusative *o*, and
Dative *ni* can serve to identify the functions of the accompanying NPs within
the sentence. A question that needs to be asked at this point is whether scrambling
can randomly move any constituent anywhere. Or are there any restrictions on
the way in which scrambling operates?

As is discussed in Harada (1977), scrambling is not totally a free process in
that there are several constraints that should be satisfied. First, compare the sets
of examples in (82)–(83).

(82)   a.   Taroo-ga   honya-de   manga-o   katta.
            Taro-Nom   bookstore-at comic book-Acc   bought
            "Taro bought comic books at a bookstore."
       b.   Taroo-ga   manga-o   honya-de   katta.
            Taro-Nom   comic book-Acc   bookstore-at bought
            "Taro bought comic books at a bookstore."
       c.   Manga-o   honya-de   Taroo-ga   katta.
            comic book-Acc   bookstore-at Taro-Nom   bought
            "Taro bought comic books at a bookstore."

(83)   a.   *Taroo-ga honya-de   katta   manga-o.
            Taro-Nom bookstore-at bought   comic book
       b.   *Taroo-ga katta   manga-o   honya-de.
            Taro-Nom bought   comic book-Acc   bookstore-at
       c.   *Katta manga-o   honya-de   Taroo-ga.
            bought comic book-Acc   bookstore-at Taro-Nom

What is wrong with the sentences in (83) is that the verb is not placed at the end of each sentence. That is, the verb is scrambled in these examples. Although other constituents are rather freely scrambled within a sentence, there is a strong restriction on the position of the verb. That is, the verb must be at the end of a sentence, and hence it cannot be scrambled.

It is worth pointing out that the scrambling of a verb which normally results in ungrammatical sentences like (83) above should be contrasted with a phenomenon called **Right Dislocation**, which involves a movement of some element(s) to the right of the verb. This phenomenon is most notably observed in colloquial speech and is often considered an indication of afterthought. Examples of Right Dislocation are given in (84)–(85): in each example, (b) is the Right Dislocation sentence of (a).

(84) a. Ano uwasa kiita?
          that rumor heard
          "Did you hear the rumor?"
      b. Kiita, ano uwasa?
          heard that rumor
          "Did you hear that rumor?"

(85) a. Kono hon   moo   yonda.
          this   book already read
          "I've already read this book."
      b. Moo   yonda, kono hon.
          already read   this book
          "I've already read this book."

The direct objects of the sentences are moved to the right of the verbs in the (b) sentences. A pause normally occurs after the verb, to indicate that what follows it can be considered an afterthought. As these examples show, a Right Dislocated sentence is not ungrammatical even though the verb is not at the end of the sentence. Thus, if *manga-o* "comic book-Acc" in (83a), for instance, is intended to be a case of Right Dislocation, in which a pause follows the verb, then *manga-o* is interpreted as an afterthought; the sentence is acceptable.[5]

Second, scrambling cannot operate in such a way that it strands Case particles and postpositions. Consider the examples in (86)–(87).

(86) a. Ziroo-ga susi-o   tabeta.
          Ziro-Nom sushi-Acc ate
          "Ziro ate sushi."
      b. Susi-o   Ziroo-ga tabeta.
          sushi-Acc Ziro-Nom ate
      c. *Susi Ziroo-ga   -o   tabeta.
          sushi Ziro-Nom -Acc ate
      d. *-o Ziroo-ga   susi tabeta.
          -Acc Ziro-Nom sushi ate

(87)   a.   Taroo-ga   Hanako-to   suugaku-o benkyoosita.
            Taro-Nom Hanako-with math-Acc   studied
            "Taro studied math with Hanako."
       b.   Hanako-to   Taroo-ga   suugaku-o benkyoosita.
            Hanako-with Taro-Nom   math-Acc   studied
       c.   *Hanako Taroo-ga   -to   suugaku-o benkyoosita.
            Hanako   Taro-Nom -with math-Acc   studied
       d.   *-to   Taroo-ga   Hanako suugaku-o benkyoosita.
            -with Taro-Nom   Hanako math-Acc   studied

Unlike the (b) examples, in the (c) and (d) sentences the Case particle and the postposition are separated from the accompanying NPs and thus are stranded. This situation cannot be allowed as a result of scrambling.

   Third, when two (or more) NPs are conjoined by the connective word *to* "and", a member of the conjoined NP alone cannot be scrambled. This is illustrated in (88).

(88)   a.   Taroo-ga   [susi   to   sasimi]-o   tabeta.
            Taro-Nom   sushi and sashimi-Acc ate
            "Taro ate sushi and sashimi."
       b.   *Susi Taroo-ga   [to   sasimi]-o   tabeta.
            sushi Taro-Nom and sashimi-Acc ate
       c.   *Sasimi-o   Taroo-ga   [susi   to] tabeta.
            sashimi-Acc Taro-Nom   sushi and ate
       d.   [Susi   to   sasimi]-o   Taroo-ga   tabeta.
            sushi and sashimi-Acc Taro-Nom   ate

In (88a) *susi* and *sasimi* are conjoined. This phenomenon is called coordination. As (88b) and (88c) suggest, one part of a coordinated phrase cannot be scrambled. (88d), on the other hand, is grammatical because the coordinated phrase is scrambled as a whole.

   Fourth, consider the pairs in (89)–(90). (A similar set of data is discussed in Harada 1977: 97.)

(89)   a.   Taroo-ga   asita   [$_s$ kyonen   amerika-de atta] hito-to
            Taro-Nom tomorrow   last year America-in met   person-with
            kekkon-suru.
            get married
            "Tomorrow Taro will get married to the person that he met in America last year."
       b.   *Taroo-ga kyonen   asita   [$_s$ amerika-de atta] hito-to
            Taro-Nom last year tomorrow   America-in met   person-with
            kekkonsuru.
            get married

(90) a. Taroo-ga Sibuya-de [s kinoo   Sinzyuku-de atta] gakusei-to
       Taro-Nom Shibuya-in   yesterday Shinjuku-in met student-with
       koohii-o   nonda.
       coffee-Acc drank
       "In Shibuya, Taro had coffee with the student that he met in Shinjuku
       yesterday."
    b. *Taroo-ga Sinzyuku-de Sibuya-de [s kinoo   atta] gakusei-to
       Taro-Nom Shinjuku-in Shibuya-in   yesterday met student-with
       koohii-o   nonda.
       coffee-Acc drank

The (b) sentences are a scrambled version of the (a) sentences, and they are
intended to bear the same meaning. In the scrambled (b) sentences, a constituent that belongs to the embedded clause (marked with "S") is moved out of
that clause. For instance, *kyonen* in (89a) is clearly meant to modify the event
described by the embedded S, but by scrambling it out of the embedded clause,
such a modification relation is lost. In (89b), the only interpretation possible here
is such that *kyonen* "last year" modifies the event described by the main clause.
However, the adverbial *asita* "tomorrow" also modifies the event described by
the matrix clause, giving rise to incompatible temporal interpretation. A proper
construal is not obtained, and hence, the sentence is ungrammatical.
   A similar restriction is observed in sentences like (91).

(91) a. Taroo-ga [s Hanako-ga   gakkoo-de tukutta] susi-o   tabeta.
       Taro-Nom   Hanako-Nom school-at   made   sushi-Acc ate
       "Taro ate the sushi that Hanako made at school."
    b. *Hanako-ga$_i$ Taroo-ga   [s t$_i$ gakkoo-de tukutta] susi-o   tabeta.
       Hanako-Nom Taro-Nom   school-at   made   sushi-Acc ate
    c. *Gakkoo-de$_i$ Taroo-ga [s Hanako-ga   t$_i$ tukutta] susi-o   tabeta
       school-at   Taro-Nom   Hanako-Nom   made   sushi-Acc ate

The sentences above contain a sentence modifier (or relative clause): *Hanako-
ga gakkoo-de tukutta* "Hanako made at school" is the sentence modifier for
the noun *susi*. Notice that in the ungrammatical sentences in (91b) and (91c),
the scrambled constituents, *Hanako* and *gakkoo-de* "at school", both originate
from within the sentence modifier, which constitutes an embedded S. The result
of the scrambling is ill-formed in both cases. Since the scrambling in (91b) and
(91c) involves the movement of a constituent from within the embedded S to
a position outside the S, it is called **long-distance scrambling**. We contrast long-
distance scrambling, as in (89)–(91), with the scrambling that takes place within
a matrix S, as in (82).
   On the basis of the observations concerning the ill-formed long-distance scrambling in (89)–(91), we might conclude that scrambling is restricted to within a
clause (and hence **clause-bound**) and that long-distance scrambling is not allowed.
As Saito (1985) extensively discusses, long-distance scrambling can indeed be
admissible. Consider the examples in (92)–(93).

(92) a. Taroo-ga [s Hanako-ga   atarasii huku-o   katta]-to
          Taro-Nom   Hanako-Nom new   clothes-Acc bought-COMP
          omotta.
          thought
          "Taro thought that Hanako bought new clothes."
      b. Atarasii huku-o$_i$ Taroo-ga [s Hanako-ga   t$_i$ katta]-to
          new   clothes-Acc Taro-Nom   Hanako-Nom   bought-COMP
          omotta.
          thought

(93) a. Taroo-ga [s Hanako-ga   imooto-ni neko-o ageta]-to   itta.
          Taro-Nom   Hanako-Nom sister-Dat cat-Acc gave-COMP said
          "Taro said that Hanako gave her sister a cat."
      b. Neko-o$_i$ Taroo-ga [s Hanako-ga   imooto-ni t$_i$ ageta]-to   itta.
          cat-Acc Taro-Nom   Hanako-Nom sister-Dat   gave-COMP said

Although to some speakers slight awkwardness may be associated with the (b)
sentences, the long-distance scrambling in (92)–(93) is much more readily accepted
than that in (89)–(91). The data above, thus, show that scrambling is not necessarily clause-bound, and that long-distance scrambling takes place.

It is interesting to observe that the presence of long-distance scrambling renders
itself distinct from the Right Dislocation phenomenon discussed earlier. While
long-distance scrambling suggests that scrambling can occur across clause bound-
aries, Right Dislocation takes place strictly internal to a matrix clause. The Right
Dislocated sentence in (94) should be compared with the grammatical scrambled
sentences in (92)–(93) above.

(94)   *Taroo-ga [s Hanako-ga   t$_i$ tukutta]-tte   itta, susi-o$_i$.
        Taro-Nom   Hanako-Nom   made-COMP said sushi-Acc
        "Taro said that Hanako made sushi."

In this sentence, the object of the embedded sentence *susi-o* "sushi-Acc" is Right
Dislocated, as an afterthought, to the right of the matrix verb. Unlike the long-
distance scrambling exemplified by (92)–(93), the sentence is ungrammatical,
suggesting that Right Dislocation is restricted to the matrix clause.

Fifth, scrambling allows only leftward movement of a constituent. Consider
the example of long-distance scrambling observed in (92) above. As is discussed
by Whitman (1979), Tonoike (1980b), and Saito (1985), when the direct object
atarasii huku-o "new cloth-Acc" is scrambled out of the embedded clause to the
right of the complementizer, the sentence is unquestionably ill-formed, as is demonstrated in (95).

(95)   *Taroo-ga [s Hanako-ga   t$_i$ katta]-to   atarasii huku-o$_i$
        Taro-Nom   Hanako-Nom   bought-COMP new   cloth-Acc
        omotta.
        thought
        "Taro thought that Hanako bought new clothes."

Thus, scrambling is restricted to leftward movement.[6]

Another matter related to long-distance scrambling is its restriction on the subject. Although constituents within an embedded clause can be scrambled out of that clause, the subject of the embedded clause cannot undergo long-distance scrambling, as is shown by Saito (1985). The relevant examples are given in (96)–(97), taken from Saito (1985: 210) with minor modifications.

(96) *Sono okasi-ga$_i$ John-ga   [$_S$ t$_i$ oisii]-to   omotte iru (koto)
        that   candy-Nom John-Nom   tasty-COMP think   (fact)
        "John thinks that that candy is tasty."

(97) *Sono giron-ga$_i$ John-ga   [$_S$ t$_i$ omosiroi]-to
        that   argument-Nom John-Nom   interesting-COMP
        omotte iru (koto)
        think   (fact)
        "John thinks that that argument is interesting."

The scrambled subject belongs to the embedded clause. The contrast between these ungrammatical sentences and the acceptable sentences in (92)–(93), in which constituents other than the subject are scrambled, indicates that a subject cannot be scrambled.

Finally, examine the pairs in (98)–(99).

(98) a. Taroo-ga eigo-ga   yoku wakaru.
            Taro-Nom English-Nom well understand
            "Taro understands English well."
      b. *Eigo-ga   Taroo-ga   yoku wakaru.
            English-Nom Taro-Nom well understand
            "Taro understands English well."

(99) a. Hanako-ga   huransugo-ga hanaseru.
            Hanako-Nom French-Nom   can speak
            "Hanako can speak French."
      b. *Huransugo-ga Hanako-ga   hanaseru.
            French-Nom   Hanako-Nom can speak
            "Hanako can speak French."

The verbs in these examples, such as *wakaru* "understand" and *hanaseru* "can speak", are unusual in that both subject and direct object are marked with the Nominative Case particle *ga*. These verbs are called **stative verbs**, which also include *iru* "need" and *aru* "have, be (inanimate)" along with the verbs in (98)–(99). As is discussed by Kuno (1980), the subject of stative verbs precedes the direct object. In the case of the (b) examples above, the objects are scrambled and are placed before the subjects. The subject–object ordering cannot be maintained in these examples, and as a result, they are unacceptable.[7]

The set of data given in both (98) and (99), however, should be contrasted with (100)–(101), in which the Case particle pattern is slightly different.

(100) a. Taroo-ni eigo-ga   yoku wakaru.
           Taro-Dat English-Nom well understand
           "Taro understands English well."
       b. Eigo-ga   Taroo-ni yoku wakaru.
           English-Nom Taro-Dat well understand

(101) a. Hanako-ni   huransugo-ga hanaseru.
           Hanako-Dat French-Nom can speak
           "Hanako can speak French."
       b. Huransugo-ga Hanako-ni   hanaseru.
           French-Nom   Hanako-Dat can speak

In (100) and (101), the verbs are identical to those of (98) and (99), respectively. The verbs *wakaru* "understand" and *hanaseru* "can speak" can take both the Case pattern of *ga*(subject)–*ga*(object), and that of *ni*(subject)–*ga*(object). As we have observed, when the NPs are marked in the *ga*–*ga* pattern, scrambling is not allowed and the word order maintains the order of subject–object. In contrast, when the *ni*–*ga* pattern is taken, i.e. *ni* for subject and *ga* for object, the *ga*-marked object can be scrambled over the *ni*-marked subject NP. Hence the absence of scrambling observed with the stative verbs above is restricted to the sentences where both subject and object are marked with the Nominative Case *ga*.

4 Null Anaphora

In English, constituents such as subject NPs and direct object NPs are required to be present in sentences. So, if these constituents are missing in a sentence, the sentence becomes ungrammatical, as is shown in (102).

(102) a. John bought a book.
       b. *Bought a book.
       c. *John bought.
       d. *Bought.

Instead, English sentences at least require the presence of pronouns, as in (103), to refer to who bought what.

(103) a. John bought a book.
       b. He bought a book.
       c. John bought it.
       d. He bought it.

In comparison, Japanese allows such missing constituents. Consider the examples in (104).[8]

(104) a. Masao-ga   Yosiko-ni   hon-o   ni-satu ageta.
　　　　Masao-Nom Yoshiko-Dat book-Acc two-cl. gave
　　　　"Masao gave two books to Yoshiko."

　　 b. Yosiko-ni   hon-o   ni-satu ageta.
　　　　Yoshiko-Dat book-Acc two-cl. gave
　　　　"(I/You/He/She) gave two books to Yoshiko."

　　 c. Hon-o   ni-satu ageta.
　　　　book-Acc two-cl. gave
　　　　"(I/You/He/She) gave two books to (you/him/her)."

　　 d. Ni-satu ageta.
　　　　two-cl. gave
　　　　"(I/You/He/She) gave two (bound objects) to (you/him/her)."

　　 e. Ageta.
　　　　gave
　　　　"(I/You/He/She) gave (it) to (you/him/her)."

In (104a) all the required constituents which the verb subcategorizes are fully expressed. In the remaining examples of (104), however, one or more constituents are missing: the subject NP in (b); the subject and the indirect object NPs in (c); the subject, the direct object, and the indirect object in (d); and finally all the constituents except the verb in (e). Unlike in English, however, the unexpressed constituents in Japanese are understood in some context, and hence the sentences in (104b–e) are conceived of as complete, and are grammatical. These missing expressions whose interpretations normally rely on contextual information are referred to as **null anaphora** or **zero pronouns** (cf. Kuroda 1965a; Ohso 1976; Kameyama 1985; N. Hasegawa 1986).

4.1   *Syntactic Representation of Null Anaphora*

Although some expressions are missing, all the sentences in (104) are grammatical, as we mentioned above. It means that there is nothing wrong with these sentences, unlike the English sentences in (102b–d). Then how should we represent these sentences syntactically? Notice that in (104b–e) some NPs are not overtly expressed, but the native speakers somehow understand what is missing and what the content of the missing NP might be. As the English translation indicates, null anaphora plays a similar role to pronouns in that it normally refers to what is in the context. The only difference is that null anaphora does not have phonetic content. So, missing NPs, i.e. null anaphora, as long as they are subcategorized for by a verb, should be represented on syntactic trees, in order that they will receive whatever referential content they might have. We will, thus, represent the unexpressed NPs in phrase structure trees, assuming that they are generated by phrase structure rules. Because it has a similar role to that of pronouns, we will represent the node for null anaphora as "pro", whose phonetic content is understood as absent. The abbreviated syntactic trees for the sentences in (104) are illustrated in (105).

(105)   a.

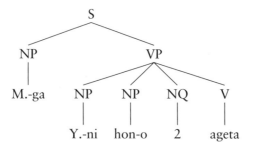

b.

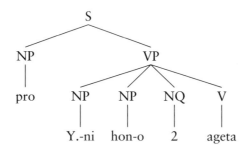

c.

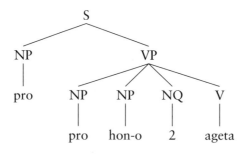

d.

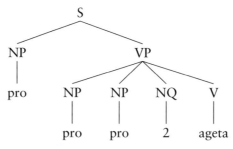

e.

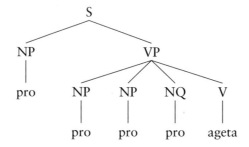

4.2 Interpretation of Null Anaphora

We have mentioned above that null anaphora is represented on syntactic trees as "pro", and that this reflects the native speaker's intuition that she or he somehow understands what is not overtly expressed and what the content of the null anaphora might be. Given the syntactic representation of null anaphora like those in (105), how does null anaphora actually receive interpretation?

The interpretation of null anaphora is normally based on the context in which it occurs. For instance, the null anaphora in (106) is interpreted by the information that is shared by the speaker and the hearer.

(106) a. Taroo-ga [Hanako-ga **pro** nagutta]-to itta.
Taro-Nom Hanako-Nom hit-COMP said
"Taro said that Hanako hit [pro]."

b. Taroo-ga [**pro** Hanako-o nagutta]-to itta.
Taro-Nom Hanako-Acc hit-COMP said
"Taro said that [pro] hit Hanako."

The null anaphora in (106a) is in the direct object of the embedded clause, while that in (106b) is in the embedded subject position. The construal of these instances of null anaphora is completely open in that only context can determine the actual content of the null anaphora. For example, in (106a) the null anaphora in the direct object position of the embedded clause could be Taro or someone else in a given context.[9] Similarly, in (106b) the null anaphora in the embedded subject position could be Taro or someone that has appeared in a previous context. Thus, given sentences like (106), there are many potential ways of interpreting the actual reference of the null anaphora; its identity is not what the rest of the sentence can determine. Null anaphora should be represented in syntactic structures even though there is no phonetic realization of it, but its interpretation is generally not dealt with in syntax. Rather, it relies on the contextual information which the speech participants share given the particular situation.

5 Reflexives

Virtually every language has at least one word or morpheme that expresses a reflexive action or state. Several words that serve this purpose are available in English: *myself, yourself, ourselves, himself, herself, itself,* and *themselves.* These words are called **reflexives** or **reflexive pronouns**, and the NPs to which they refer are termed **antecedents**. The most representative reflexive pronoun in Japanese is *zibun* "self". Although in this section we will primarily deal with the interpretation of reflexives, the issue is significant in syntax because many of the conditions on the interpretation of reflexives invoke several syntactic factors.

5.1   Zibun

It is interesting to observe that English and Japanese reflexives demonstrate a different range of characteristics (cf. Inoue 1976b; Aikawa 1993). Let us first consider the English examples in (107)–(109).

(107)   a. I_i kicked myself$_i$.
        b.   *I_i kicked yourself$_i$.

(108)   a.   John$_i$ hurt himself$_i$.
        b.   *John$_i$ hurt herself$_i$.

(109)   a.   The student$_i$ laughed at himself$_i$.
        b.   *The student$_i$ laughed at themselves$_i$.

The reflexive pronoun and its intended antecedent are co-indexed to indicate the referential relationship. The contrast in each pair shows that the reflexive pronoun and its antecedent must agree in person, gender, and number. In (107b) the reflexive pronoun is in the second person while its antecedent is in the first person, and hence the person agreement fails. The reflexive and its antecedent in (108b) differ with respect to gender, and so the sentence is ungrammatical. Person and gender are in agreement in (109b), but the plural reflexive is inconsistent with the singular antecedent. That is, in English a reflexive word and its antecedent must agree in person, gender, and number.

In Japanese, on the other hand, *zibun* is used for any person and gender. When the antecedent is plural, the suffix *-tati* is optionally added to *zibun*. Examine (110).

(110)   a.   Taroo$_i$-ga   zibun$_i$-o hihan-sita.
             Taro-Nom self-Acc criticized
             "Taro criticized himself."
        b.   Hanako$_i$-ga   zibun$_i$-o semeta.
             Hanako-Nom self-Acc blamed
             "Hanako blamed herself."
        c.   Gakusei$_i$-ga   zibun-tati$_i$-o semeta.
             student-Nom self-pl.-Acc blamed
             "The students blamed themselves."

(110a) and (110b) show that regardless of the person and gender of the antecedent, *zibun* is invariably used. Although the plural morpheme *-tati* is optionally suffixed to *zibun* for its plural antecedent, *zibun* is still used without changing its form, unlike in English.[10]

Second, the antecedent is not limited to animate in English, and hence it can be inanimate, as in (111); while in Japanese the antecedent of *zibun* must be animate (cf. Inoue 1976b). Compare (111) and (114), in particular.

(111)   History$_i$ repeats itself$_i$.

(112) Kodomo-ga zibun-no uti-e   hasitte-itta.
       child-Nom self-Gen home-to run-went
       "The child ran to self's home."

(113) Inu-wa   zibun-no ie-o   sitteiru.
       dog-Top self-Gen home-Acc know
       "Dogs know self's home."   (Inoue 1976b: 119)

(114) *Kuruma$_i$-ga zibun$_i$-no syako-no   hoo-e   hasiridasita.
       car-Nom   self-Gen garage-Gen direction-to began to run
       "The car began to move to self's garage."
                                          (modified from Aikawa 1993: 25)

Hence, the antecedent of *zibun* is restricted to animate, while such a constraint is not observed in English.

Third, *zibun* can appear in the possessive position while reflexive pronouns in English cannot. This contrast is shown in (115)–(116).

(115) John$_i$ studied in his$_i$/*himself$_i$'s room.

(116) Taroo$_i$-ga zibun$_i$-no heya-de benkyoo-sita.
       Taro-Nom self-Gen   room-in studied
       "Taro studied in self's room."

As (115) shows, a pronoun rather than a reflexive must be used in a possessive position in English. In Japanese, on the other hand, *zibun* can freely appear in front of the Genitive Case particle which often marks the possessive relation.

Fourth, the antecedent of *zibun* is restricted to the subject in Japanese while such a subject orientation is not observed in English (cf. Kuroda 1965a; see note 10). Compare the examples in Japanese and English in (117)–(119).

(117) Tanaka-sensei$_i$-ga   Ziroo$_j$-o zibun$_{i/*j}$-no kenkyuusitu-de sikatta.
       Tanaka-prof.-Nom Ziro-Acc self-Gen   office-in   scolded
       "Professor Tanaka scolded Ziro in self's office."

(118) Taroo$_i$-ga Hanako$_j$-ni zibun$_{i/*j}$-no koto-o   hanasita.
       Taro-Nom Hanako-Dat self-Gen   things-Acc told
       "Taro told Hanako (things) about self."

(119) John$_i$ told Bill$_j$ some gossip about himself$_{i/j}$.

In (117) *zibun* can take the subject *Tanaka-sensei* "Prof. Tanaka" as its antecedent, but the direct object *Ziroo* cannot be the antecedent of *zibun*. Similarly, in (118) the subject *Taroo* can be the antecedent of *zibun* but not the indirect object *Hanako*. The Japanese data should be contrasted with the English sentence in (119), where the reflexive pronoun *himself* can refer either to the subject *John* or to the object *Bill*. Hence, *zibun* picks out subject as its antecedent while the antecedents of reflexive pronouns in English are not limited to subject.

Fifth, reflexive pronouns in English must find their antecedents within the same clause, but in Japanese *zibun* and its antecedent need not be within the same clause. Compare the two languages in (120)–(122) in this respect.

(120) John$_i$ told Mary [that Bill$_j$ hurt himself$_{*i/j}$].

(121) Taroo$_i$-ga   Hanako-ni [Ziroo$_j$-ga   zibun$_{i/j}$-o hihan-sita]-to   itta.
       Taro-Nom Hanako-to Ziro-Nom self-Acc criticized-COMP said
       "Taro said to Hanako that Ziro criticized self."

(122) Taroo$_i$-ga [Ziroo$_j$-ga   zibun$_{i/j}$-no kuruma-de Tookyoo-e itta]-to
       Taro-Nom Ziro-Nom self-Gen   car-by   Tokyo-to   went-COMP
       omotteiru.
       think
       "Taro thinks that Ziro went to Tokyo in self's car."

In the English example of (120), as the co-indexing possibilities suggest, the reflexive pronoun *himself* can have the subject of the same clause, *Bill*, as its antecedent, but *John*, not being in the same clause, cannot be considered the antecedent of the reflexive. This restriction is referred to as the **clausemate condition**. In English, thus, the clausemate condition must be satisfied between a reflexive pronoun and its antecedent. The clausemate condition, however, need not be satisfied in Japanese, as (121) and (122) indicate. There are two possibilities for the antecedent of *zibun* in each sentence. In (121) the antecedent can be either *Ziroo*, which is the subject of the embedded clause in which *zibun* is a constituent, or *Taroo*, the subject of the matrix clause. Similarly, the antecedent of *zibun* in (122) can be either the matrix subject *Taroo* or the embedded subject *Ziroo*. The situation in which the antecedent of *zibun* is outside the clause to which *zibun* belongs is referred to as **long-distance reflexivization** or **long-distance *zibun***. The fact that *zibun* can have *Taroo* as its antecedent suggests that the clausemate condition need not be met in Japanese. This means that the interpretation of *zibun* in (121) and (122) is ambiguous: in (121), for example, the individual that Ziro criticized is either Ziro himself or Taro. Notice that even in the case of long-distance reflexivization, the subject orientation maintains. *Taroo* in both (121) and (122), for instance, does not constitute a clausemate with *zibun*, but nonetheless it is the subject of the matrix clause. Therefore, while the clausemate condition need not apply to the Japanese reflexive *zibun*, the subject orientation is observed[11] (cf. Aikawa 1993; Iida and Sells 1988; Katada 1991).

As it turns out, however, the ambiguity observed with a long-distance *zibun*, as in (121), is not always available, as is observed by Howard and Niekawa-Howard (1976). Such an issue particularly arises when a sentence contains more than one occurrence of *zibun*. Consider (123).

(123) [$_S$ Taroo-ga [$_S$ Hanako-ga   zibun-no uti-de   zibun-no koto-o
            Taro-Nom   Hanako-Nom self-Gen house-at self-Gen thing-Acc
       hanasita]-to   itta].
       spoke-COMP said
       "Taro said that Hanako talked (things) about self at self's house."

The embedded clause of this sentence contains two occurrences of *zibun*. The potential antecedents of *zibun* are *Taroo* and *Hanako* since it has been discussed above that *zibun* can serve as a long-distance reflexive. And, indeed, in the case of (123), the antecedent can be either *Taroo* or *Hanako*. What is interesting in this case, however, is that the interpretations of the two *zibuns* in (123) must be unique: that is, if *Taroo* is construed as the antecedent of first *zibun*, then the second *zibun* must also pick up *Taroo* as its antecedent. If the first *zibun* is interpreted to refer to *Hanako*, the second *zibun* is so interpreted as well. Although each *zibun* in this sentence should have two interpretations as logical possibilities, the first *zibun* referring to either *Taroo* or *Hanako* and the second *zibun* also referring to either *Taroo* or *Hanako*, the actual interpretation is limited to two possibilities. That is, among the four logically possible readings of the sentence that are shown in (124), only the first two are indeed attested.

(124) a. Taro said that Hanako talked about him in his house.
      b. Taro said that Hanako talked about her in her house.
      c. *Taro said that Hanako talked about him in her house.
      d. *Taro said that Hanako talked about her in his house.

The number of occurrence of *zibun* is not limited to two. Nevertheless, no matter how many times *zibun* occurs in a sentence, the restriction described above still holds. That is, all the *zibun* instances within a sentence must be interpreted identically.[12]

The restriction on the interpretation of *zibun* in the case of multiple occurrence of the reflexive pronoun demonstrates an interesting interaction with some semantic and/or pragmatic information.[13] To illustrate such cases, consider the examples in (125)–(126) from Howard and Niekawa-Howard (1976: 230).

(125) [s Taroo-wa [s Hanako-ga   zibun-no kawarini zibun-no heya-de
        Taro-Top   Hanako-Nom self-Gen instead   self-Gen room-in
      zibun-no sigoto-o   siteita]-to   itta].
      self-Gen work-Acc was doing-COMP said
      "Taro said that Hanako was doing self's work in self's room in self's
      place."

(126) [s Taroo-wa [s Hanako-ga   zibun hitoride zibun-no heya-de
        Taro-Top   Hanako-Nom self   alone   self-Gen room-in
      zibun-no sigoto-o   siteita]-to   itta].
      self-Gen work-Acc was doing-COMP said
      "Taro said that Hanako was doing self's work by self in self's room."

Notice that each sentence contains three occurrences of *zibun* in its embedded clause. Given our discussion above, the three instances of *zibun* should be interpreted uniformly, and the uniform interpretation is expected to refer to either *Taroo* or *Hanako* as the antecedent of *zibun*, leading to ambiguity. That is, the sentences in (125) and (126) should be ambiguous between (a) and (b) in (127) and (128), respectively.

(127) a. Taro said that Hanako was doing his work in his room in his place.
       b. Taro said that Hanako was doing her work in her room in her place.

(128) a. Taro said that Hanako was doing his work by himself in his room.
       b. Taro said that Hanako was doing her work by herself in her room.

However, the prediction is not borne out and neither sentence is ambiguous: (127a) and (128b) are the only interpretations of (125) and (126), respectively. Why is this so?

As Howard and Niekawa-Howard imply, the lack of ambiguity is in fact attributed to the phrases *kawarini* "in place of someone, instead of someone" in (125) and *hitoride* "by oneself" in (126). Notice that if *zibun* in (125) were interpreted as *Hanako*, the interpretation would correspond to that of (127b), and due to the presence of *kawarini* "in place of someone", the sentence would not be interpretable: that is, Hanako cannot do her work in her place (i.e. instead of herself). Hence, the phrase *kawarini* forces the interpretation of the first occurrence of *zibun* as *Taroo*, and once the specific reading is assigned to this *zibun*, the second and third occurrences of *zibun* must be so interpreted as well. A similar situation is obtained in (126). In this case, the crucial phrase that determines a specific interpretation of *zibun* is *hitoride* "by oneself". With this phrase the only interpretation *zibun* can be assigned is the one in which *zibun* refers to *Hanako*: otherwise, the sentence would be anomalous and not interpretable. Again, the first *zibun* must pick up *Hanako* as its antecedent, and once the first *zibun* receives such an interpretation, then the other two occurrences of *zibun* must have the same antecedent, i.e. *Hanako*. As a result of the interaction between semantics/pragmatics and the properties of *zibun*, (125) and (126), respectively, can only be interpreted as (127a) and (128b).

In relation to the subject orientation of *zibun* and long-distance *zibun*, the examples in (129)–(130) serve to demonstrate their interaction.

(129) Taroo$_i$-ga [zibun$_i$-ga yuumei-da]-to sinziteiru.
       Taro-Nom self-Nom famous-is-COMP believe
       "Taro believes that self is famous."

(130) Hanako$_i$-ga Ziroo$_j$-ni [zibun$_{i/*j}$-ga sono hon-o
       Hanako-Nom Ziro-to self-Nom that
       kaita]-to itta.
       book-Acc wrote-COMP said
       "Hanako said to Ziro that self wrote that book."

In these examples, *zibun* is in the embedded subject position, and hence cannot find its antecedent which would be a clausemate with it (cf. Aikawa 1993). Due to the fact that Japanese allows long-distance reflexivization, *zibun* can pick out *Taroo* and *Hanako* as its antecedent. Notice that in the cases of long-distance *zibun*, the subject orientation of the antecedent is maintained: both *Taroo* and *Hanako* are the matrix subjects. As Aikawa (1993) observes, the fact that reflexive pronouns can appear in the embedded subject position, as in (129) and (130), is a property that is not observed in English. (129) and (130) should be contrasted with the English sentences in (131) and (132).

(131)   *John$_i$ thinks that [himself$_i$ is famous].

(132)   *John$_i$ told Mary that [himself$_i$ wrote the book].

These examples indicate that reflexive pronouns in English cannot appear in the subject position as a consequence of the clausemate condition. Therefore, the embedded subject position being available to *zibun* points toward another characteristic of reflexives that distinguishes Japanese from English.

A sixth way in which English and Japanese reflexives differ is that while English reflexive pronouns, like all pronouns, do not allow any modification, *zibun* can take various prenominal modifiers. For example, it can be modified by an adjective, a numeral quantifier, and a sentence modifier. Examples are shown in (133)–(135); (134) is an example slightly modified from Aikawa (1993: 44).

(133)   Taroo$_i$-ga   kagami-no naka-ni   **atarasii** zibun$_i$-o mituketa.
        Taro-Nom mirror-Gen inside-in new   self-Acc found
        "Taro found a new self in the mirror."

(134)   Hanako$_i$-ga   kagami-no naka-ni   **gonin-no** zibun$_i$-o mita.
        Hanako-Nom mirror-Gen inside-in five-Gen   self-Acc saw
        "Hanako saw five of self in the mirror."

(135)   Ziroo$_i$-ga   **omoidoorini   huruma-e-nakatta**   zibun$_i$-ni
        Ziro-Nom as one wishes behave-potential-didn't self-at
        gakkarisita.
        disappointed
        "Ziro was disappointed at the self that could not behave as he wished."

These examples are frequently observed in fiction, and are not the type of sentences we hear in everyday conversation, but nevertheless they are acceptable. The adjective *atarasii* "new" in (133), the numeral quantifier *gonin* "five people" in (134), and the sentence modifier *omoidoorini hurumaenakatta* "couldn't behave the way he wished" in (135) all modify *zibun*. As the translation shows, a modification of this sort is not possible in English.

Seventh, *zibun* does not always have to find its antecedent within the same sentence. Instead, *zibun* can pick out as its antecedent some individual that has been mentioned or assumed in a discourse context. Consider the discourse context in (136), in which *zibun* refers to an individual that is mentioned in the previous sentence, i.e. John; modified from Aikawa (1993: 27), who cites Koster (1982) and Ueda (1986a).

(136) A: Dareka-ga   **John**-no   kawarini   sono paatii-ni
           someone-Nom John-Gen in place of that party-to
           itta-ndesu-ka.
           went-it is that-Q
           "Is it that someone went to that party in place of John?"
      B: Iie, **zibun**-ga kita-ndesu.
           no self-Nom came-it is that
           "No, it is that self came."

In B's response, since *zibun* appears in the matrix subject position, we know that it cannot find its antecedent within the same sentence. *Zibun* in this case picks out John in A's question as its antecedent. It is interesting to note that the antecedent of *zibun* that is found across sentences in a discourse need not be the subject. Note, too, that English does not exhibit this type of discourse-oriented *zibun* antecedent.

Finally, in some dialects of Japanese, *zibun* can be used to refer to the speaker without any overt expression that corresponds to its antecedent in the same sentence. This use is demonstrated in (137). Of course, such a use of reflexives is not available in English.[14]

(137)   Zibun-ga ikimasu.
        self-Nom go
        "I will go."

(138)   *Myself/Yourself/Himself/Herself/Itself/Themselves will go.

Apparently, this use of *zibun* is more extensively observed in dialects around the Kansai area of Japan.

Despite the various differences we have observed in the behavior of reflexive words in English and Japanese, there is at least one similarity between the two languages. That is, reflexives must be c-commanded by their antecedents. To see this point, consider the examples in (139)–(142) and their abbreviated syntactic trees (the label "D" is for determiners, which will be discussed in section 12).

(139)   a.   *John's$_i$ teacher hit himself$_i$.

   b.

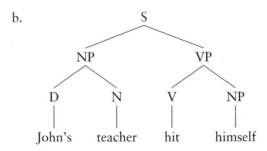

(140) a. *Mary gave himself$_i$ the book that Bill$_i$ bought.

b.

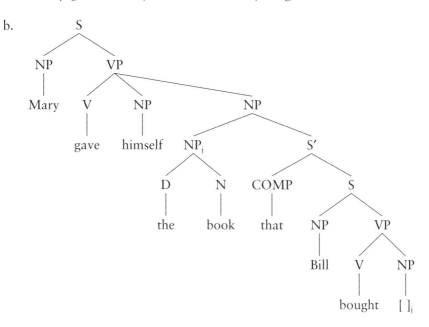

(141) a. *John$_i$-no sensei-ga   zibun$_i$-no kuruma-ni notta.
John-Gen teacher-Nom self-Gen car-onto   got into
"John's teacher got into self's car."

b.

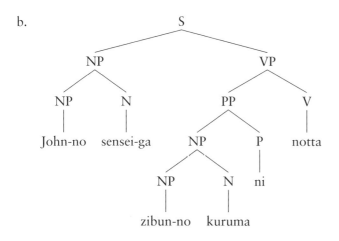

(142) a. *Mary-ga John$_i$-ga   katta   hon-o   zibun$_i$-no heya-de
Mary-Nom John-Nom bought book-Acc self-Gen room-in
yonda.
read
"Mary read the book that John bought in self's room."

(Aikawa 1993: 26)

b.

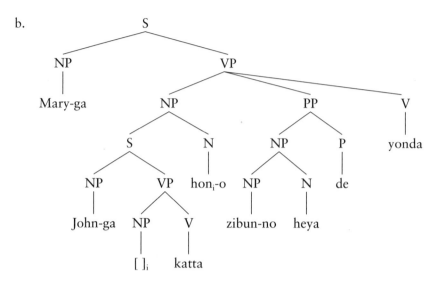

In (139) the intended antecedent *John* does not c-command the reflexive pronoun *himself*. The first branching node dominating *John*, i.e. NP, does not dominate the direct object *himself*. Similarly, in (140), the antecedent *Bill* is under the embedded S, and *Bill*, as the subject of this S, does not c-command *himself* in the matrix clause. The same situation is obtained in the Japanese sentences in (141) and (142). (141) is parallel to (139) in that the intended antecedent *John* is within the subject NP, and the first branching node dominating it, i.e. the NP, does not dominate *zibun*. In (142) the intended antecedent *John* is too "low" to c-command *zibun*. That is, the first branching node that dominates *John* is the embedded S, and this S does not dominate *zibun*. In all the examples the reflexive words are not c-commanded by their intended antecedents, leading to the ungrammaticality. Hence, the structural requirement that reflexives must be c-commanded by their antecedents holds in both English and Japanese.

The characteristics of the Japanese reflexive word *zibun* are summarized in (143).

(143) a. No agreement in person, gender, and number is required between *zibun* and its antecedent.
    b. The antecedent of *zibun* must be animate.
    c. *Zibun* can appear in the possessive position.
    d. The antecedent of *zibun* is subject.
    e. The clausemate condition need not be met, allowing for the long-distance reflexive.
    f. *Zibun* can be modified.
    g. *Zibun* allows for a discourse oriented antecedent.
    h. *Zibun* can refer to the speaker without an overtly expressed antecedent in a sentence (in some dialects only).
    i. *Zibun* must be c-commanded by its antecedent.

The various issues we have discussed above fundamentally deal with how the reflexive pronoun *zibun* is interpreted. One might wonder if those issues should be taken up in the area of semantics rather than syntax. It should be pointed out, however, that in capturing the properties inherent to *zibun*, we have crucially made reference to syntactic notions such as subject, clausemate, and c-command. That is, the way *zibun* establishes its referential relationship with a particular NP is significantly conditioned by syntactic factors. This is why reflexive pronouns in general have been one of the most explored topics in syntax.

5.2 Zibun-Zisin

Thus far, we have concentrated on the distribution of *zibun* as well as the various constraints associated with it. Although *zibun* can be regarded as the primary reflexive word in Japanese, it does not exhaust the set of reflexive words in the language. Another reflexive word, *zibun-zisin*, has recently drawn more attention since its behavior is interesting in comparison with that of *zibun*. *Zibun-zisin* is a compound word that also means "self". However, *zibun-zisin* behaves rather differently from *zibun*, as has been discussed by M. Nakamura (1987), Katada (1991), and Aikawa (1993, 1994), for instance.

First of all, we have observed above that *zibun* shows the characteristics of a long-distance reflexive. Relevant examples were examined in (121)–(122), which are repeated as (144a) and (145a), respectively. *Zibun-zisin*, by contrast, behaves more like English in that its antecedent is found within the same clause (cf. M. Nakamura 1987; Katada 1991; Aikawa 1993, 1994). That is, the clausemate condition seems to be satisfied where *zibun-zisin* appears. This is illustrated in (144b) and (145b).

(144) a. Taroo$_i$-ga   Hanako-ni [Ziroo$_j$-ga   zibun$_{i/j}$-o hihan-sita]-to   itta.
Taro-Nom Hanako-to Ziro-Nom self-Acc criticized-COMP said
"Taro said to Hanako that Ziro criticized self."

b. Taroo$_i$-ga   Hanako-ni [Ziroo$_j$-ga   zibun-zisin$_{*i/j}$-o hihan-sita]-to
Taro-Nom Hanako-to Ziro-Nom self-Acc   criticized-COMP
itta.

said
"Taro said to Hanako that Ziro criticized self."

(145) a. Taroo$_i$-ga [Ziroo$_j$-ga   zibun$_{i/j}$-no kuruma-de Tookyoo-e
Taro-Nom Ziro-Nom self-Gen   car-by   Tokyo-to
itta]-to   omotteiru.
went-COMP think
"Taro thinks that Ziro went to Tokyo in self's car."

b. Taroo$_i$-ga [Ziroo$_j$-ga   zibun-zisin$_{*i/j}$-no kuruma-de Tookyoo-e
Taro-Nom Ziro-Nom self-Gen   car-by   Tokyo-to
itta]-to   omotteiru.
went-COMP think
"Taro thinks that Ziro went to Tokyo in self's car."

As the co-indexing indicates, in the case of *zibun* the antecedent can be either the embedded subject *Ziroo* or the matrix subject *Taroo*, but *zibun-zisin* does not have such freedom and identifies the embedded subject *Ziroo* as its antecedent.

The clausemate condition, however, turns out to be too strong for *zibun-zisin*. As is discussed in Aikawa (1994), when *zibun-zisin* appears as the subject of an embedded clause, the antecedent is found in the matrix clause. This situation is illustrated by the example in (146), slightly modified from Aikawa (1994: 2).

(146)   John$_i$-wa [zibun-zisin$_i$-ga Mary-o   korosita]-to   omotte-iru.
        John-Top self-Nom   Mary-Acc killed-COMP think
        "John thinks that self killed Mary."

In this example the antecedent of *zibun-zisin* is the matrix subject. Hence, the clausemate condition is observed so far as *zibun-zisin* is not the embedded subject.

Note that *zibun-zisin* shares with *zibun* the property that its antecedent is subject. Thus, in the (b) sentences above, the antecedent of *zibun-zisin* is restricted to the embedded subject.

The second difference between *zibun* and *zibun-zisin* is that *zibun-zisin* cannot refer to the speaker, unlike *zibun* (cf. Aikawa 1993). We have seen in (137) that *zibun* can refer to the speaker without any overt antecedent expressed in the sentence although this usage of *zibun* is limited to certain dialects of Japanese. *Zibun-zisin*, on the other hand, cannot be used to refer to the speaker even in those dialects that allow such a use of *zibun*. So, the sentence in (147) is ungrammatical in all dialects of Japanese.

(147)   *Zibun-zisin-ga ikimasu.
        self-Nom   go
        "I will go."

Therefore, between *zibun* and *zibun-zisin*, the latter is more similar to English reflexive pronouns than the former on the basis of the observations made above.

Finally, in the previous subsection, we have observed that *zibun* can be modified by adjectives, numeral quantifiers, and sentence modifiers, but Aikawa (1993) points out that this property is not associated with *zibun-zisin*. Examples to illustrate this point are in (148)–(150), which should be contrasted with the examples with *zibun* in (133)–(135), repeated below.

(148)   *Taroo$_i$-ga kagami-no naka-ni **atarasii** zibun-zisin$_i$-o mituketa.
        Taro-Nom mirror-Gen inside-in new   self-Acc   found
        "Taro found a new self in the mirror."

(149)   *Hanako$_i$-ga kagami-no naka-ni **gonin-no** zibun-zisin$_i$-o mita.
        Hanako-Nom mirror-Gen inside-in five-Gen self-Acc   saw
        "Hanako saw five of self in the mirror."

(150)   *Ziroo$_i$-ga **omoidoorini   huruma-e-nakatta**   zibun-zisin$_i$-ni
        Ziro-Nom as one wishes behave-potential-didn't self-at
        gakkarisita.
        disappointed
        "Ziro was disappointed at the self that could not behave as he wished."

(133) Taroo_i-ga kagami-no naka-ni **atarasii** zibun_i-o mituketa.
Taro-Nom mirror-Gen inside-in new self-Acc found
"Taro found a new self in the mirror."

(134) Hanako_i-ga kagami-no naka-ni **gonin-no** zibun_i-o mita.
Hanako-Nom mirror-Gen inside-in five-Gen self-Acc saw
"Hanako saw five of self in the mirror."

(135) Ziroo_i-ga **omoidoorini huruma-e-nakatta** zibun_i-ni
Ziro-Nom as one wishes behave-potential-didn't self-at
gakkari-sita.
disappointed
"Ziro was disappointed at the self that could not behave as he wished."

As these examples show, *zibun-zisin* does not take any kind of modifier. In this respect, too, *zibun-zisin* has a greater similarity to English reflexive pronouns than *zibun* does.

6   The Notion of Subject

We have previously discussed the fact that in English the subject is always placed to the left of a verb, and phrase structure rules can generate the subject NP in a particular position in a syntactic tree. For this reason, we can readily define the subject as the NP that is immediately dominated by S.

What about Japanese, a language that allows for some freedom of word order, namely, scrambling? We have assumed earlier that the basic word order in Japanese is subject–object–verb, and that the scrambled sentences are derived by the application of a movement rule. Under this assumption, the subject is always defined as the NP that is immediately dominated by S, just as in English. Thus, we can always find a subject in a tree, i.e. the NP node immediately dominated by S. However, a question we shall raise now is how we identify a subject prior to a tree representation.

In this section, we will take another look at the notion of subject, setting the movement analysis of scrambling aside, because subject has not always been a notion that is straightforwardly defined (cf. Kuno 1973; Martin 1975; Harada 1976a; Shibatani 1977, 1978). Let us look at our situation slightly differently, and ask ourselves the following question: if we were to show which word, or sequence of words, is the subject in Japanese to someone who does not know much about linguistics, how should we go about it?

A possible answer to this question is to invoke Case particles; we have assumed that Case particles serve to identify NPs as subject, direct object, and indirect object. Relevant to our discussion is the Nominative Case particle *ga*. Can this particle determine subjecthood in Japanese? Let us examine the sentences in (151)–(153).

(151)   Taroo-ga   kooen-made aruita.
        Taro-Nom park-to   walked
        "Taro walked to the park."

(152)   Ziroo-ga   ringo-o   tabeta.
        Ziro-Nom apple-Acc ate
        "Ziro ate an apple."

(153)   Makoto-ga   huransugo-o yoku sitteiru.
        Makoto-Nom French-Acc   well   know
        "Makoto knows French well."

As far as these sentences are concerned, the Nominative Case particle *ga* seems
to isolate the accompanying NP as the subject of the sentence. However, the
examples in (154)–(155) cast some doubts on the assumption that the Nominative
Case particle determines which NP should be the subject of the sentence.

(154)   Taroo-ga   eigo-ga   yoku wakaru.
        Taro-Nom English-Nom well   understand
        "Taro understands English well."

(155)   Ziroo-ni(-wa)   imooto-no kimoti-ga   zenzen wakaranai.
        Ziro-Dat(-Top) sister-Gen feelings-Nom at all   not understand
        "Ziro does not understand his sister's feelings at all."

The sentence in (154) contains two NPs that are marked with the Nominative
Case particle *ga*. If we maintain that *ga* should identify the subject of the sentence,
we would be forced to say that this sentence has two subjects. Of course, we
intuitively know that this is not the conclusion we wish to reach. Furthermore,
it would be problematic to represent two NPs under the node immediately
dominated by S since there is only one node for it. The example in (155), on
the other hand, has only one NP marked with the Nominative particle, and yet
native speakers know that *Ziroo* should be the subject, rather than *imooto-no
kimoti* "his sister's feelings", which is marked with *ga*. So, again, if we maintain
the current assumption, we not only pick an NP as a subject that intuitively does
not seem to be a subject, but we also cannot isolate an NP that intuitively seems
like a subject.

   Since invoking the Nominative Case particle does not help us to establish a
way to isolate the subject, let us next examine whether the order of words can
serve our purpose. That is, can the word order determine subjecthood in Japanese,
just as in English? Can the first NP appearing in a sentence be identified as the
subject? Compare the sentences in (156a–b).

(156)   a. Hanako-ga   keeki-o   tukutta.
            Hanako-Nom cake-Acc made
            "Hanako made a cake."
        b. Keeki-o   Hanako-ga   tukutta.
            cake-Acc Hanako-Nom made
            "Hanako made a cake."

Both (156a) and (156b) convey the same meaning, and *Hanako* in both sentences has the same relationship to the verb *tukutta* "made". So, we do not want to treat the two instances of *Hanako* differently by identifying the leftmost NP of a sentence as the subject. Therefore, word order is not a reliable source for determining subjecthood, either.

Then how can we tell which NP is the subject? We have mentioned several times that native speakers "intuitively" know which NP is the subject. How, then, can we explain such an intuition in more linguistic terms? Although it has always been an issue how to define the subject internal to Japanese as well as cross-linguistically, there are at least two diagnostic tests to identify subjecthood in Japanese.

6.1 *Reflexivization*

One diagnostic for subjecthood in Japanese is found in Reflexivization (cf. Shibatani 1977, 1978). In the previous section we have observed the various characteristics of *zibun*. Recall that one of them is that the antecedent of *zibun* is the subject. So, whenever we find *zibun*, its antecedent is identified as a subject. First, consider the examples in (157)–(158).

(157) Taroo$_i$-ga Hanako$_j$-o zibun$_{i/*j}$-no heya-de korosita.
       Taro-Nom Hanako-Acc self-Gen   room-in killed
       "Taro killed Hanako in self's room."

(158) Taroo$_i$-no otooto$_j$-ga   Hanako$_k$-to zibun$_{*i/j/*k}$-no heya-de
       Taro-Gen brother-Nom Hanako-with self-Gen   room-in
       benkyoo-sita.
       studied
       "Taro's brother studied with Hanako in self's room."

The antecedent of *zibun* in (157) is *Taroo*, and hence this NP is the subject. *Hanako*, on the other hand, cannot be the antecedent of *zibun*, and thus it should not be identified as subject. Among the three NPs in (158) *zibun* picks out *Taroo no otooto* "Taro's brother", but crucially not *Taroo* or *Hanako*, as the only possible antecedent, therefore identifying Taro's brother as the subject.

Second, recall that *zibun* allows for the long-distance reflexive and that when *zibun* in an embedded clause finds its antecedent in a matrix clause, the subject orientation is observed. This is illustrated in (159).

(159) Taroo$_i$-ga Hanako-ni [Ziroo$_j$-ga zibun$_{i/j}$-o hihan-sita]-to   itta.
       Taro-Nom Hanako-to Ziro-Nom self-Acc criticized-COMP said
       "Taro said to Hanako that Ziro criticized self."

Zibun in this sentence can have two antecedents, *Taroo* and *Ziroo*, both of which are identified as subjects: *Taroo* is the subject of the matrix clause while *Ziroo* is the subject of the embedded clause. This means that the number of possible antecedents amounts to the number of the subjects existing in a sentence.

Third, this diagnostic test for subjecthood correctly picks out the subject in problematic sentences like those in (154) and (155). This is shown in (160) and (161).

(160)   Taroo$_i$-ga Hanako$_j$-ga   zibun$_{i/*j}$-no guruupu-de itiban sukida.
        Taro-Nom Hanako-Nom self-Gen   group-in   best   like
        "Taro likes Hanako the best in self's group."

(161)   Taroo$_i$-ni zibun$_i$-no kimoti-ga   wakaranai.
        Taro-Dat self-Gen   feeling-Nom not know
        "Taro does not know self's feeling."

There are two NPs that are marked with the Nominative Case particle in (160), i.e. *Taroo* and *Hanako*. The fact that *zibun* can take only *Taroo* as its antecedent leads to the conclusion that *Taroo* is the subject of the sentence while *Hanako* is not. In (161) *zibun* picks out *Taroo* as its antecedent, identifying *Taroo* as the subject of the sentence. Notice that *Taroo* is marked with the Dative Case particle *ni* while *kimoti* "feeling" is marked with the Nominative Case particle, but in this case what *zibun* selects as its antecedent is the subject regardless of the type of Case particle with which the NP is associated.

Hence, Reflexivization not only identifies the subject correctly, but also picks out all the subjects of the sentence, both matrix and embedded.[15]

6.2   *Subject Honorification*

Another diagnostic test for determining the subject is **Subject Honorification**, as is extensively discussed in Harada (1976a) and Shibatani (1977, 1978). Subject Honorification is expressed by the verbal complex of the form o-Verb-*ni naru*. That is, when a verb root ends in a vowel, o- and -*ni* are prefixed and suffixed, respectively, to the root; and when the verb root ends in a consonant, -*i*- is inserted between the root and the suffix -*ni*. Additionally the verb *naru*, which literally means "become", follows the verb complex. For instance, the Subject Honorification sentence based on the verb *yame* "quit" (a vowel-ending root) is constructed with the sequence o-yame-*ni naru*. Similarly, the complex o-kak-*i*-*ni naru* is formed from the consonant-ending root *kak* "write".

The Subject Honorification construction, characterized by the verbal complex o-Verb-*ni naru*, honors the subject, and hence serves as a good diagnostic test for subjecthood in Japanese. The examples in (162)–(165) demonstrate the role that Subject Honorification plays in identifying the subject.

(162)   Yamada-sensei-ga   gakusei-no hon-o   o-yomi-ni natteiru.
        Prof. Yamada-Nom student-Gen book-Acc is reading(hon.)
        "Prof. Yamada is reading the student's book."

(163)   *Huryoo syoonen-ga Yamada-sensei-o   o-naguri-ni natta.
        delinquent-Nom   Prof. Yamada-Acc hit(hon.)
        "A juvenile delinquent hit Prof. Yamada."

(164) Yamada-sensei-ni gakusei-no kimoti-ga   o-wakari-ni   naranai
      Prof. Yamada-Dat student-Gen feeling-Nom understand(hon.) not
      "Prof. Yamada does not understand the student's feelings."

(165) Yamada-sensei-ni syakkin-ga takusan o-ari-ni naru.
      Prof. Yamada-Dat debt-Nom lot   have(hon.)
      "Prof. Yamada has a lot of debt."

The honorific verb *o-yomi-ni natteiru* "is reading" in (162) refers to the reading
activity of *Yamada-sensei* "Prof. Yamada", and this NP is identified as the subject. In (163), on the other hand, the honorific verb picks up *huryoo syoonen*
"juvenile delinquent" as its subject, but *Yamada-sensei* is the individual that
the honorific verb should refer to, rather than *huryoo syoonen*. Because of this
discrepancy, the sentence is extremely awkward. In (164) and (165) the honorific
verbs pick out the NPs that are marked with the Dative Case particle *ni* as
subject. This suggests that the NPs that are marked with the Nominative Case
particle *ga* are not subject. Therefore Subject Honorification, *o-V-ni naru*, serves
as another diagnostic test for subjecthood in Japanese.

7 Passives

English exhibits active sentences and their passive versions, as illustrated in
(166)–(167).

(166) a. The thieves stole the painting.
       b. The painting was stolen by the thieves.

(167) a. The teacher scolded John.
       b. John was scolded by the teacher.

In forming passive sentences in English, there are several steps that need to be
taken, assuming that passive sentences are derived from their active counterparts.
First, the direct object is promoted to, or moved to, the subject position. Second,
the original subject is demoted, becoming the object of the preposition *by*.
Third, the verb form is changed to the past participle with a form of *be* placed
before it. These changes can be captured by the Passivization transformation, as
is stated in (168), where *-en* indicates the past participle.

(168) Passivization: NP V NP
                        1   2   3   → 3 be 2-en by 1

Japanese demonstrates the passive construction, but what is interesting and
different from English is that there are three types of passive sentences: they are
direct passives, indirect passives or **adversative passives**, and *ni yotte*-**passives**.
We will discuss the characteristics of these three types.

7.1 Direct Passives

Examples of direct passives in Japanese are demonstrated in (169)–(170), where the (a) sentences are active sentences and the (b) sentences are their direct passive counterparts.

(169) a. Doroboo-ga e-o   nusunda.
           thief-Nom   painting-Acc stole
           "The thief stole the painting."
       b. E-ga   doroboo-ni nusum-are-ta.
           painting-Nom thief-by   steal-pass.-past
           "The painting was stolen by the thief."

(170) a. Sensei-ga   Taroo-o   sikatta.
           teacher-Nom Taro-Acc scolded
           "The teacher scolded Taro."
       b. Taroo-ga   sensei-ni   sikar-are-ta.
           Taro-Nom teacher-by scold-pass.-past
           "Taro was scolded by the teacher."

As we have seen is the case with English, there are several changes that are involved in forming passive sentences on the basis of active ones. First, the direct object is promoted to become the subject. Notice that the direct object NPs in the (a) sentences are marked with the Accusative Case particle *o*, but once they are promoted to the subject, the NPs are followed by the Nominative Case particle *ga*. Second, the original subject of the active sentence appears with *ni*. Finally, the passive morpheme *(r)are* is suffixed to the verbal root. Thus, basically a situation parallel to English is observed here.

The status of *ni* in direct passives is an interesting question especially because *ni* could be considered either a Dative Case particle or a postposition. Miyagawa (1989a) examines the behavior of numeral quantifiers in direct passive sentences, and claims that *ni* should be analyzed as a postposition. Recall that the mutual c-command condition needs to be satisfied between a numeral quantifier and its antecedent in order to establish a proper modification relation. Keeping this condition in mind, consider the direct passive sentence in (171).

(171) *Kuruma-ga doroboo-ni sannin nusum-are-ta.
        car-Nom   thief-by   three   steal-pass.-past
        "The car was stolen by three thieves."

The NQ *sannin* "three (people)" is intended to modify *doroboo* "thief". Let us compare the syntactic structure of this sentence under the assumption that *ni* is the Dative Case particle, as in (172a), and under the assumption that *ni* is a postposition, as in (172b).

(172) a.

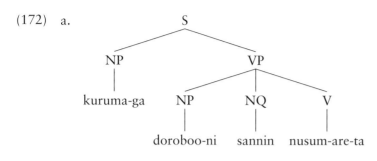

  b.

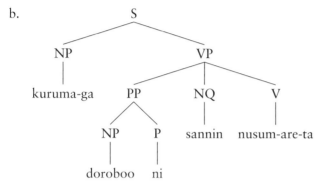

Case particles in general have been treated in a syntactic tree as part of the NP that is accompanied by them, and thus in (172a) the Dative Case is not overtly indicated although it should be understood to be under the NP. Notice that the NP and the NQ c-command each other in this structure, satisfying the mutual c-command condition, and hence the sentence should be acceptable, contrary to fact. In (172b), in contrast, *ni* is analyzed as a postposition which forms a constituent, PP, together with the NP *doroboo* "thief". In this structure, the NP and the NQ are not in mutual c-command relation. The violation of the mutual c-command condition is consistent with the ungrammatical status of the direct passive sentence in (171). Hence, on the basis of the behavior of numeral quantifiers, we will assume with Miyagawa that *ni* in direct passives is a postposition and not the Dative Case particle.

Although a traditional transformational approach that would rearrange the constituents, similar to the one stated for English in (168), might be assumed in the analysis of direct passives in Japanese, Miyagawa (1989a, 1989b) claims that passive constructions in general are treated as an instance of a movement rule that would leave a trace behind (cf. Ueda 1986b). Below, we will introduce his movement analysis of direct passives in Japanese and the motivation for it.

The movement approach advanced by Miyagawa assumes that the subject position is not filled with any word at d-structure, and that the direct object is moved to the subject position, leaving a trace behind. The d- and s-structure representations of the passive sentence of (170b), for example, are depicted in (173).

(173) a. d-structure

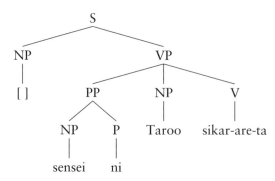

b. s-structure

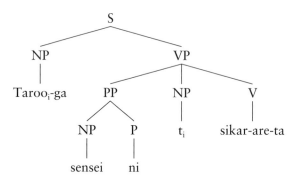

The direct object in the d-structure is moved to the subject position, leaving a trace behind, as the s-structure depicts.

Miyagawa argues that a piece of evidence for this movement analysis of the direct passive construction comes from numeral quantifiers. Keeping in mind that the mutual c-command condition must be satisfied between a NP and its numeral quantifier, consider the sentences in (174)–(175).

(174) a. E-ga   [$_{VP}$ doroboo-ni sanmai nusum-are-ta].
            painting-Nom   thief-by   three   steal-pass.-past
            "Three paintings were stolen by a thief."

       b.

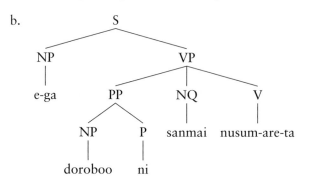

(175)   a.   Kuruma-ga [$_{VP}$ sono otoko-ni sandai kowas-are-ta].
              car-Nom   that man-by   three   break-pass.-past
              "Three cars were broken by that man."

b.

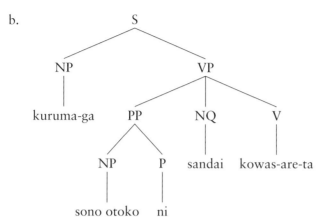

The subjects *e* "painting" and *kuruma* "car" are expected to have a mutual c-command relationship with their respective NQs, i.e. *sanmai* and *sandai*. Notice that the subjects are external to the VP while the NQs are inside the VP, and hence a mutual c-command relation cannot be established between these NPs and their NQs, as the NQs cannot c-command the subjects. For example, in (174), the first branching node that dominates the NQ is the VP, and the VP does not dominate its antecedent, *e* "painting". The sentences, then, are expected to be ungrammatical, contrary to fact. Recall, however, that the subjects in the sentences above are posited originally to be in the direct object position that is internal to VP, and upon movement, they leave traces behind. Then these traces left behind by the movement of the original direct objects and their NQs can c-command each other, satisfying the mutual c-command condition. This can be shown schematically as in (176) and (177).

(176)   (= (174))

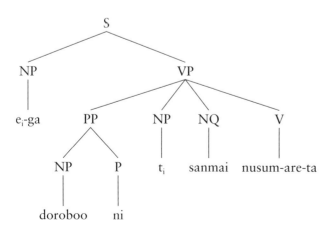

(177) (= (175))

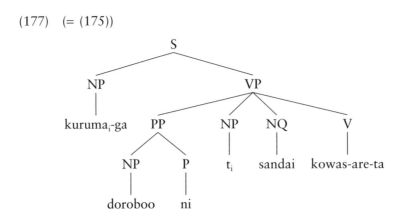

The co-indexed trace is the result of the movement of the surface subject. Notice that the trace and its NQ are in a mutual c-command relation: the first branching node that dominates the trace is the VP, and the VP also counts as the first branching node that dominates the NQ. Since the trace and the NQ are in a sisterhood relation, they are in a mutual c-command relation as well. Hence, the presence of the trace left by the movement of the direct object in the direct passive construction salvages a potential violation of the mutual c-command condition. That is, without invoking the trace of the original direct object, the unexpected grammaticality of (174) and (175) is difficult to account for. Thus, the movement analysis for direct passives is supported by the interpretation of numeral quantifiers, as was the case with scrambling.

7.2 Indirect Passives (Adversative Passives)

As we have observed above, passive sentences invariably involve transitive verbs. This is because we have assumed that the s-structure subject of a direct passive sentence is moved from the d-structure direct object position, and verbs that have direct objects are, by definition, transitive verbs.

In Japanese, there is yet another type of passive sentence, called indirect passives or adversative passives, that can be formed on the basis of either transitive or intransitive verbs. Consider the examples in (178)–(182).

(178) a. Tonari-no   gakusei-ga   piano-o   asa-made   hiita.
            neighboring-Gen student-Nom piano-Acc morning-until played
            "The neighboring student played the piano until morning."
       b. Hanako-ga   tonari-no   gakusei-ni piano-o
            Hanako-Nom neighboring-Gen student-by piano-Acc
            asa-made   hik-are-ta.
            morning-until play-pass.-past
            "Hanako was adversely affected by the neighboring student's playing the piano until morning."

(179) a. Kodomo-ga sinda.
           child-Nom died
           "A child died."
       b. Taroo-ga   kodomo-ni sin-are-ta.
           Taro-Nom child-by   die-pass.-past
           "Taro is adversely affected by his child's death."

(180) a. Ame-ga   hutta.
           rain-Nom fell
           "It rained."
       b. Ziroo-ga   ame-ni hur-are-ta.
           Ziro-Nom rain-by fall-pass.-past
           "Ziro was rained on."

(181) *John was died by a child.

(182) *Bill was rained by it.

The verb in (178) is transitive, and hence the formation of the passive is expected.
However, notice the interpretation of this sentence. As the English translation
suggests, the meaning of this type of passive is not something that is expected
in the direct passive construction. The verbs in (179) and (180) are intransitive.
Active sentences with intransitive verbs are not expected to have passive counterparts. The (b) sentences of (179) and (180) are perfectly grammatical passive
sentences, however. As (181) and (182) show, a passive sentence based on an
intransitive verb is not available in English.

There is something definitely special about indirect passives. Let us examine
the characteristics of this type of passive. First, compare the subject NP of the
(a) sentences and its realization in the (b) sentences in (178)–(180) above. The
subject NP of a base verb is demoted and occurs with *ni*.[16] In the examples above,
tonari-no gakusei "the neighboring student", *kodomo* "child", and *ame* "rain"
correspond to such an NP. As H. Hoshi (1994) notes, the *ni*-phrase in indirect
passives is obligatory (cf. Kubo 1989; Terada 1990). Compare the examples in
(183)–(185) with the (b) sentences of (178)–(180).

(183) *Hanako-ga   piano-o   asa-made   hik-are-ta.
        Hanako-Nom piano-Acc morning-until play-pass.-past

(184) *Taroo-ga sin-are-ta.
        Taro-Nom die-pass.-past

(185) *Ziroo-ga hur-are-ta.
        Ziro-Nom fall-pass.-past

As the contrast suggests, indirect passives require the presence of *ni*-phrases. On
the other hand, the *ni*-phrase in direct passives is optional.

Second, when we compare the number of NPs between the (a) sentences and (b) sentences in (178)–(180), we notice that the latter contain a new NP, i.e. a new subject. That is, a new subject is added in the indirect passive counterpart. For example, in (178b), *Hanako* is an extra NP, added to the other two NPs, i.e. *tonari-no gakusei* "the neighboring student" and *piano* "piano". Similarly, in (179b), *Taroo* is added to the NP *kodomo* "child".

Third, the resulting meaning is generally adversative: the new subject is adversely affected by the event denoted by the rest of the sentence (cf. Wierzbicka 1979; Oehrle and Nishio 1981). In (179b) Taro is the person who is adversely affected by his child's death, and in (180b) the rain adversely affected Ziro in that he did not carry an umbrella and got drenched, for instance. Notice that English does exhibit sentences similar to (180b) with the interpretation of adversity associated with them. The sentence in (186) is an example.

(186)   John was rained on.

English sentences of this sort, however, differ from Japanese indirect passives in that the adversity interpretation of (186) is not precisely what the passive construction induces, but rather the adversity meaning can be attributed to the preposition *on*. In this respect, Japanese indirect passives depart from English since adversity is inherent to the passive construction itself. Because of this specific meaning pertinent to this type of passive, indirect passives are often called adversative passives.

Nonetheless, it should be pointed out that the adversative passive may not always have adversative meaning. To demonstrate this point, consider the example in (187).

(187)   Taroo-wa sensei-ni   musuko-o home-rare-ta.
        Taro-Top teacher-by son-Acc   praise-pass.-past
        "Taro had his son praised by his teacher."

The adversative interpretation is not detected in this indirect passive sentence. Instead, the effect on Taro of the teacher's praising his son is positive and beneficial. Thus, the cover term "adversative" passives can sometimes include sentences that imply positive effects on the subject.

As Howard and Niekawa-Howard (1976) discuss in great detail, there are two approaches to the syntactic derivations of direct and indirect passives, mainly debated in the 1970s. They are termed the **uniform account** and the **non-uniform account** (cf. K. Hasegawa 1964; Kuroda 1965a, 1979; N. McCawley 1972; Kuno 1973; Howard and Niekawa-Howard 1976). According to the uniform account, both direct and indirect passives are derived in the same manner from the d-structure, as schematically illustrated in the (b) sentences of (188)–(189).

(188)   Direct Passives
        a.   Taroo-ga   hahaoya-ni sikar-are-ta.
             Taro-Nom mother-by   scold-pass.-past
             "Taro was scolded by his mother."
        b.   Taroo-ga [hahaoya-ga Taroo-o sikaru] rare-ta.

(189)   Indirect Passives
a.   Taroo-ga   sensei-ni   kodomo-o sikar-are-ta.
Taro-Nom teacher-by child-Acc   scold-pass.-past
"Taro was adversely affected by the teacher's scolding his child."
b.   Taroo-ga [sensei-ga kodomo-o sikaru] rare-ta.

Both d-structures contain embedded clauses. The analysis for direct passives in
(188b) assumes that *Taroo* within the embedded clause is deleted under identity
with the matrix subject.
   The non-uniform account assumes the same derivation as the uniform account
for indirect passives, but claims that direct passives are basically derived from
their active counterpart by applying a transformational rule that exchanges subject and object. Thus, the d-structure of the direct passive sentence of (188a) under
the non-uniform account is (190).

(190)   Hahaoya-ga Taroo-o   sikat-ta.
mother-Nom Taro-Acc scold-past
"His mother scolded Taro."

Despite the controversy over these two approaches to passives, most researchers
seem to adopt the uniform account.[17]

7.3   Ni Yotte-*Passives*

Besides the two types of passives that we have discussed above, there is a third
type that exhibits an interesting cluster of properties, called *ni yotte*-passives. *Ni
yotte*-passives basically appear to be the same as direct passives except that the
phrase *ni yotte* is used instead of the postposition *ni*. Consider the contrast in
(191a–b).

(191)   a.   Taroo-ga   dooryoo-ni   hihans-are-ta.
Taro-Nom colleague-by criticize-pass.-past
"Taro was criticized by his colleague."
b.   Taroo-ga   dooryoo-ni yotte hihans-are-ta.
Taro-Nom colleague-by   criticize-pass.-past
"Taro was criticized by his colleague."

Let us call passives of the type in (a) *ni-passives* and those of the type in (b)
ni yotte-passives. The substitution of *ni yotte* for *ni* does not invoke a striking
difference in meaning between the two. On the basis of this observation, one
might conclude that *ni* and *ni yotte* equally serve to mark an NP as the agent
of a given passive sentence and that they are interchangeably used.
   As Inoue (1976a) and Kuroda (1979) observe, however, there are instances
of *ni*-passives where *ni* cannot be substituted for by *ni yotte*, and there are also
passive sentences in which only *ni yotte* is allowed. To illustrate such cases, consider (192)–(195).

(192) a. Taroo-wa kinoo   ame-ni hur-are-ta.
          Taro-Top yesterday rain-by fall-pass.-past
          "Taro was rained on yesterday."
       b. *Taroo-wa kinoo   ame-ni yotte hur-are-ta.
          Taro-Top   yesterday rain-by   fall-pass.-past
          "Taro was rained on yesterday."

(193) a. Hanako-ga   sensei-ni   waraw-are-ta.
          Hanako-Nom teacher-by laugh-pass.-past
          "Hanako was adversely affected by her teacher's laughing at her."
       b. *Hanako-ga   sensei-ni yotte waraw-are-ta.
          Hanako-Nom teacher-by   laugh-pass.-past
          "Hanako was adversely affected by her teacher's laughing at her."

(194) a. Siroi booru-ga   Oo-ni yotte takadakato utiage-rare-ta.
          white ball-Nom Oo-by   high   hit up-pass.-past
          "A white ball was hit high in the air by Oo."
       b. *Siroi booru-ga Oo-ni takadakato utiage-rare-ta.
          white ball-Nom Oo-by high   hit up-pass.-past
          "A white ball was hit high in the air by Oo."
                                                 (Kuroda 1979: 309)

(195) a. Kaikai-ga   gityoo-ni yotte sengens-are-ta.
          opening-Nom chairperson-by announce-pass.-past
          "The opening of the meeting was announced by the chairperson."
                                                 (Inoue 1976a: 83)
       b. *Kaikai-ga   gityoo-ni   sengens-are-ta.
          opening-Nom chairperson-by announce-pass.-past
          "The opening of the meeting was announced by the chairperson."

The passives sentences in (192)–(193) are indirect (or adversative) passives. As Kuroda (1979) points out, *ni yotte* cannot be used in indirect passives. The passive sentences in (194)–(195) present the opposite situation. That is, in these examples the use of *ni yotte* is required and the substitution for *ni yotte* by *ni* results in ungrammatical passives.

Inoue (1976a) characterizes the fundamental meaning of *ni* as being the agentive influence on the subject of a passive sentence. In a *ni*-passive sentence, thus, it is required that the NP marked with *ni* serves as the agent who has direct influence on the subject of the passive sentence. When such direct influence between the agent and the subject of the passive sentence cannot be established, or when the subject of the passive sentence is conceived of as being unable to experience the agentive influence, the agent cannot be marked with *ni*. Inoue relates this account to the tendency of passive sentences with inanimate subjects to be often incompatible with *ni*-marked agents. The passives in (194)–(195) provide a good illustration of this situation. In (194) the subject is a ball, which is an inanimate object, and hence it cannot feel the direct influence of the agent. This is why the *ni*-passive sentence of (194b) is ungrammatical while its *ni yotte*-passive counterpart of (194a) is acceptable. Similarly in (195) the subject of the passive sentence is *kaikai* "the opening of the meeting", which is an abstract concept rather than a concrete object. As such, the subject of the sentence cannot be taken as experiencing the direct influence of the chairperson's announcement. Therefore, the *ni*-passive is not allowed, and the choice of the *ni yotte*-passive must be taken.

Inoue's characterization of *ni*-passives, i.e. "the influence of the agent", is further elaborated on by Kuroda (1979). Kuroda provides a detailed discussion of the semantic differences between *ni*-passives and *ni yotte*-passives. On the basis of Inoue's generalization as well as his own observations, he claims that the fundamental semantic difference between the two types of passives should be attributed to the concept of "affectivity". Note that Kuroda uses the term "affectivity" as related to the verb *affect* (cf. Kuroda 1985; Kuno 1986). That is, *ni*-passives are more appropriate in describing a situation where the subject of the sentence is consciously aware of being affected by the agent. In contrast, *ni yotte*-passives pertain to the description of an objective situation. Although the clear description of affectivity is not an easy task, as Kuroda notes, the examples in (196)–(197), taken from Kuroda (1979: 319) with minor changes in the gloss, should suffice to illustrate the difference.

(196)   John-wa moo sukosi de ki-o   usinau tokoro-o   Bill-ni
        John-Top almost   mind-Acc lose   moment-Acc Bill-by
        tasuke-rare-ta.
        rescue-pass.-past
        "John was rescued by Bill when he was about to lose consciousness."

(197)   John-wa moo sukosi de ki-o usinau tokoro-o Bill-ni yotte tasuke-rare-ta.

Kuroda explains that (196) should be assumed to have been written from John's point of view, and that it reflects John's relief, which results from Bill's timely rescue. That is, in this situation it is natural for John to feel deeply affected by Bill's rescue, in the absence of which John would have fallen unconscious.

The sentence in (197) differs from (196) minimally in that *Bill* in (197) is now marked with *ni yotte*. According to Kuroda, the *ni yotte*-passive of (197) is more appropriate when the incident is reported by someone other than John because it is stated from a more objective point of view. Thus, the choice of *ni* or *ni yotte* reflects the degree of affectivity of the agent on the subject of the passive sentence.

The illustration of affectivity inherent to *ni*-passives can further be elaborated by (198)–(199), which correspond to (196)–(197) above except that the subjects of the sentences are in the first person. These are taken from Kuroda (1979: 320), with a slightly modified gloss.

(198)   Watasi-wa (moo sukosi de ki-o   usinau tokoro-o)   Bill-ni
        I-Top   almost   mind-Acc lose   moment-Acc Bill-by
        tasuke-rare-ta.
        rescue-pass.-past
        "I was rescued by Bill when I was about to lose consciousness."

(199)   Watasi-wa (moo sukosi de ki-o usinau tokoro-o) Bill-ni yotte tasuke-
        rare-ta.

Kuroda notes that the *ni*-passive version of (198) is germane to the situation in which the speaker describes the incident as a "direct experience" (1979: 320). In this sentence, thus, the speaker depicts her or his direct involvement in the incident and the affectivity received from Bill, the agent. The *ni yotte*-passive counterpart in (199), on the other hand, describes the situation from a more neutral point of view. A possible scenario in this case would be that the speaker remembers the incident and reports it as a past experience, which she or he can describe in a more neutral perspective. So, even if the speaker reports his or her own experience, she or he is doing so as an objective depiction of the incident.

The concept of affectivity distinguishes between *ni*-passives and *ni yotte*-passives, but Kuroda points out a few more differences between the two types of passives, motivating separate treatments for them. One of the differences has to do with the temporal properties associated with the past tense morpheme *ta*. Kuroda recognizes that the morpheme *ta* can be interpreted either as "simple past" or as "perfect". By simple past he means that *ta* "can denote an event that took place at some past time", whereas *ta* in the perfect interpretation "describes a state of affairs that existed or exists as a result of an event that took place previously" (p. 328). Given two interpretations pertinent to the past tense morpheme *ta*, Kuroda claims that *ni*-passives can be used only when *ta* has the perfect interpretation, while *ni yotte*-passives do not have such a restriction. Instead, *ta* in *ni yotte*-passives can be construed with either the simple past or the perfect interpretation. To illustrate the interaction of the two types of passives with *ta*, Kuroda provides the sentences in (200)–(201) (1979: 327).

(200)   Ano mati-wa   Nippongun-ni   hakais-are-ta.
        that town-Top Japanese army-by destroy-pass.-past
        "That town was destroyed by the Japanese army."

(201)   Ano mati-wa Nippongun-ni yotte hakais-are-ta.

Although the difference is very subtle, Kuroda argues that the *ni*-passive sentence in (200) can only be interpreted as describing a state of affairs that resulted from the destruction that the Japanese army carried out. Thus it cannot be used to describe the Japanese army's destruction of the town as a historic event that happened some time in the past. The *ni yotte*-passive in (201), on the other hand, conveys either interpretation: it may describe the situation as a historical event, or it can denote the state of affairs as a result of the destruction by the Japanese army. Hence, in the presence of the past tense morpheme *ta*, *ni*-passives exhibit only the perfect interpretation while *ni yotte*-passives are ambiguous between the simple past reading and the perfect reading.

Another semantic difference that separates *ni*-passives and *ni yotte*-passives is found in the construction that contains the sequence of a verbal gerund and the verb *iru* "be". Let us call this the *-te iru* construction.[18] The *-te iru* construction is associated with two interpretations: progressive and perfect. For instance, consider the examples in (202)–(203).

(202) Taroo-ga   susi-o   tabete-iru.
      Taro-Nom sushi-Acc eat
      "Taro is eating sushi."

(203) Neko-ga sinde-iru.
      cat-Nom die
      "A cat is dead."

The sentence in (202) bears the progressive interpretation, describing that Taro's eating activity is in progress. The example in (203), on the other hand, describes a state of affairs: that is, a cat is in the state of being dead.

   Kuroda notices that the distribution of the two interpretations inherent to the *-te iru* construction displayed by the two types of passives in question is not the same. Consider first the active sentence in (204), taken from Kuroda (1979: 329).

(204) FBI-ga   Hanako-no   koto-o   tyoosasite-iru.
      FBI-Nom Hanako-Gen thing-Acc investigate
      "The FBI is investigating (things about) Hanako." or
      "The FBI has conducted an investigation of Hanako."

This active sentence in the *-te iru* construction exhibits ambiguous interpretations between the progressive and the perfect readings, as the two possible translations indicate. It can be construed as describing an ongoing activity, i.e. progressive. Or one might use the sentence after finding some evidence (e.g., a written report) to suggest that the FBI's investigation of Hanako has been conducted. Under such a situation (204) should be taken as perfect.

   Now, consider the *ni*-passive and *ni yotte*-passive version of the active sentence of (204) in (205)–(206) (Kuroda 1979: 329).

(205) Hanako-ga   FBI-ni tyoosas-are-te iru.
      Hanako-Nom FBI-by investigate-pass.
      "Hanako has been investigated by the FBI."

(206) Hanako-ga   FBI-ni yotte tyoosas-are-te iru.
      Hanako-Nom FBI-by   investigate-pass.
      "Hanako is being investigated by FBI." or
      "Hanako has been investigated by the FBI."

According to Kuroda, the *ni*-passive sentence in (205) can only have the perfect reading whereas the *ni yotte*-passive sentence in (206) can have either the progressive or perfect interpretation, as the translation suggests. Therefore, another semantic difference between the two types of passives, although apparently rather subtle, may be found in the *-te iru* construction.

Recall that we have briefly discussed the uniform and non-uniform accounts of direct and indirect passive sentences in section 7.2. On the basis of the differences between *ni*-passives and *ni yotte*-passives, however, Kuroda (1979) argues that a line should be drawn between *ni*-passives, subsuming direct and indirect passives, and *ni yotte*-passives. According to Kuroda, direct and indirect passives are given identical treatments, assuming the uniform account, while *ni yotte*-passives are derived from their active counterparts by the application of a transformational rule that permutates the subject and the object. (207)–(209) are the examples of direct, indirect, and *ni yotte*-passive sentences with their corresponding underlying structures.

(207)   Direct Passive
       a.   Taroo-ga   hahaoya-ni sikar-are-ta.
             Taro-Nom mother-by   scold-pass.-past
             "Taro was scolded by his mother."
       b.   Taroo-ga [hahaoya-ga Taroo-o sikaru] rare-ta.

(208)   Indirect Passive
       a.   Taroo-ga   sensei-ni   kodomo-o sikar-are-ta.
             Taro-Nom teacher-by child-Acc   scold-pass.-past
             "Taro was adversely affected by the teacher's scolding his child."
       b.   Taroo-ga [sensei-ga kodomo-o sikaru] rare-ta.

(209)   *Ni Yotte*-Passive
       a.   Kaikai-ga   gityoo-ni yotte sengens-are-ta.
             opening-Nom chairperson-by announce-pass.-past
             "The opening of the meeting was announced by the chairperson."
       b.   Gityoo-ga kaikai-o sengen-sita.

As we have discussed earlier, the occurrence of *Taroo* in the embedded clause of (207b) is deleted under identity with the matrix subject. Under the uniform account that is assumed by Kuroda, both direct and indirect passives sentences in (207)–(208) are derived in a similar fashion: they both contain embedded clauses. The *ni yotte*-passive sentence of (209), on the other hand, is derived from the active sentence, to which a transformation (similar to (168) for English) applies to yield the passive sentence of (209a). Kuroda notes that the different syntactic analyses for *ni*-passives and *ni yotte*-passives, outlined above, reflect their fundamental difference in semantic contributions. That is, the meaning of *ni yotte*-passives is the same as their active counterparts in their essence. The similarity in meaning, then, is explained by deriving a *ni yotte*-passive from an active sentence, thereby keeping the basic meaning of the active sentence intact. In contrast, Kuroda considers the meaning of the passive morpheme *rare* in *ni*-passives, whether direct or indirect, as vitally contributing to the meaning of *ni*-passive sentences as a whole. The presence of *rare* as a part of the under-lying structure of *ni*-passives is intended to capture such a generalization. Hence, Kuroda's separate treatments for direct and indirect passives on the one hand

and for *ni yotte*-passives on the other is largely motivated by various semantic differences between *ni*-passives and *ni yotte*-passives.

8 Causatives

8.1 O-*Causatives and* Ni-*Causatives*

The causative construction is another topic that has been well explored in Japanese (cf. Kuroda 1965b; Kuno 1973; Shibatani 1973a, 1973b, 1976, 1990; C. Kitagawa 1974; Tonoike 1978; Miyagawa 1980, 1984, 1986; Y. Kitagawa 1986). Causatives share a property with passives in that the causative morpheme *(s)ase* is suffixed to a verbal root to form a causative verb, just as was the case with *(r)are* for passives. Examples of causative sentences are illustrated in (210).

(210) a. Hanako-ga   aruita.
             Hanako-Nom walked
             "Hanako walked."
      b. Taroo-ga Hanako-o   aruk-ase-ta.
             Taro-Nom Hanako-Acc walk-caus.-past
             "Taro made Hanako walk."
      c. Taroo-ga Hanako-ni aruk-ase-ta.
             Taro-Nom Hanako-Dat walk-caus.-past
             "Taro had Hanako walk."

(210b) and (210c) are both causative versions of (210a). The causative morpheme *(s)ase* is suffixed to the verb root *aruk* "walk" to form the causative complex verb. As (210b) and (210c) show, there are two variants of causatives. Since the original subject is marked with the Accusative Case particle *o* in (210b) while accompanied by the Dative Case particle *ni* in (210c), these variants are referred to as *o-causative* and *ni-causative*, respectively. In both cases, a new subject that corresponds to the causer is added to the sentence in (210a), and the original subject is marked either with *o* or with *ni*. The NPs that are now marked either with *o* or with *ni* are referred to as the causees. The resulting causative sentences mean that the subject causes the causee to do the action denoted by the verb.

Although the rest of the sentence is exactly identical between the o-causative and the *ni*-causative exemplified by the above sentences, the meaning associated with each variant is slightly different (cf. Kuroda 1965b; Harada 1973; Kuno 1973; Shibatani 1973a, 1973b, 1976, 1990; C. Kitagawa 1974). While a detailed discussion of this issue is found in Shibatani (1976), a rough summary of the semantic difference is given by Shibatani (1990: 309): "[the o-causative] implies that the intention of the causee is ignored by the causer, while in the [*ni*-causative], the causer typically appeals to the causee's intention to carry out the caused event". Thus, generally speaking, causation in the o-causative has a more coerced interpretation than that in the *ni*-causative. For example, consider the contrast in (211a–b).[19]

(211) a. Taroo-ga   Hanako-o   muriyari aruk-ase-ta.
           Taro-Nom Hanako-Acc forcedly walk-caus.-past
           "Taro forcedly made Hanako walk."
       b. ??Taroo-ga Hanako-ni   muriyari aruk-ase-ta.
           Taro-Nom Hanako-Dat forcedly walk-caus.-past
           "Taro forcedly had Hanako walk."

The adverb *muriyari* "forcedly" modifies the *o*-causative naturally because the *o*-causative implies the coercive causation of the causer. On the other hand, the same adverb is incompatible with the *ni*-causative of (211b) because the *ni*-causative lacks the interpretation of coercive causation, and hence the presence of the adverb makes this causative sentence quite awkward.

To see a similar point, observe the examples in (212)–(213), modified from Shibatani (1990: 309–310).

(212) a. Hana-ga   migotoni   saita.
           flower-Nom beautifully bloomed
           "The flowers bloomed beautifully."
       b. Taroo-ga   hana-o   migotoni   sak-ase-ta.
           Taro-Nom flower-Acc beautifully bloom-caus.-past
           "Taro made the flowers bloom beautifully."
       c. *Taroo-ga hana-ni   migotoni   sak-ase-ta.
           Taro-Nom flower-Dat beautifully bloom-caus.-past
           "Taro had the flowers bloom beautifully."

(213) a. Hanako-ga   kizetu-sita.
           Hanako-Nom fainted
           "Hanako fainted."
       b. Taroo-ga   Hanako-o   kizetu-sase-ta.
           Taro-Nom Hanako-Acc faint-caus.-past
           "Taro made Hanako faint."
       c. *Taroo-ga Hanako-ni   kizetu-sase-ta.
           Taro-Nom Hanako-Dat faint-caus.-past
           "Taro had Hanako faint."

The unacceptability of the (c) sentences can be attributed to the fact that in the *ni*-causative, the causee acts as having the volition to undergo the action denoted by the verb. In (212c), for example, flowers do not have the volition or willingness to bloom, and hence the *ni*-causative is extremely awkward. The *o*-causative variant is perfectly acceptable, on the other hand, because the intention of the causee is absent to begin with. Similarly, the action denoted by the verb *kizetu-suru* "faint" in (213) is not something over which human beings have control. The *ni*-causative treats the NP marked with *ni* as the volitional entity, and yet the action itself is not controllable. As a result, the *ni*-causative variant is not available. If, however, *Taroo* is a movie director and *Hanako* is an actress, and he tells her to act as if she has fainted, this sentence is acceptable since the act of fainting is willingly carried out by her. The *o*-causative version of (213b) has no problem as long as this sentence is construed such that Taro did something that caused Hanako to faint, either directly or indirectly.

8.2 The Double-O Constraint

The contrast in inherent meaning between the *o*-causative and *ni*-causative that we have observed, however, can be made only with intransitive verbs. Transitive verbs can form a *ni*-causative, but *o*-causatives with transitive verbs always result in ungrammatical sentences. This situation is seen in (214).

(214) a. Taroo-ga   hon-o   yonda.
           Taro-Nom book-Acc read
           "Taro read a book."
       b. Hahaoya-ga Taroo-ni hon-o   yom-ase-ta.
           mother-Nom Taro-Dat book-Acc read-caus.-past
           "His mother made/had Taro read a book."
       c. *Hahaoya-ga Taroo-o   hon-o   yom-ase-ta.
           mother-Nom   Taro-Acc book-Acc read-caus.-past
           "His mother made/had Taro read a book."

As (214a) suggests, the verb *yomu* "read" is a transitive verb. (214b) is the *ni*-causative sentence while (214c) is the *o*-causative variant, and only the *ni*-causative is acceptable. Notice that regardless of the interpretation, i.e. whether the coercive causation is implied or the causee is construed as a volitional entity, the *o*-causative variant is not possible. Furthermore, as the English translation of (214b) suggests, when the verb is transitive, the *ni*-causative is ambiguous between the interpretation that allows the causee to be regarded as a volitional entity, which is characteristic of the *ni*-causative, and the coercive causation, which is normally the meaning associated with the *o*-causative.

As it turns out, the unavailability of the *o*-causative has nothing to do with the causative formation itself. But, rather, the *o*-causative with a transitive verb is ungrammatical due to the constraint called the **Double-*o* Constraint** by Harada (1973); see also Kuroda (1978) and Poser (1981). In brief, the Double-*o* Constraint prevents a clause from having two NPs that are marked with the Accusative Case particle *o*. So, in the causative sentence of (214c) above, by marking the NP that corresponds to the causee with *o* in forming the *o*-causative, the sentence ends up with two NPs both marked with *o*, because the base verb *yomu* "read" is a transitive and hence takes a direct object that is accompanied by the Accusative Case particle, as (214a) shows. This means that whenever a verb subcategorizes for an NP that is marked with the Accusative Case particle, an *o*-causative with the verb results in an ungrammatical sentence.

The Double-*o* Constraint is not a constraint specific to the formation of causative sentences, however (cf. Shibatani 1990). Rather, it is a more general constraint that finds its application elsewhere. For instance, sentences with verbal nouns provide an example. As was mentioned in chapter 4, verbal nouns can appear with the verb *suru* "do". When they are accompanied by *suru*, the verb *suru* can be directly compounded with the verbal noun to form a complex verb, or it can be separated from the verbal noun. In the latter case, the verbal nouns appear with the Accusative Case particle *o*. These two cases are illustrated in (215).

(215) a. Sensei-ga   kenkyuu-suru.
           teacher-Nom research-do
           "The teacher does research."
       b. Sensei-ga   kenkyuu-o   suru.
           teacher-Nom research-Acc do
           "The teacher does research."

The complex verb in (215a), *kenkyuu-suru*, can be considered transitive, and hence it is often accompanied by a direct object NP, as in (216).

(216) Sensei-ga   gengogaku-o   kenkyuu-suru.
       teacher-Nom linguistics-Acc research-do
       "The teacher does research on linguistics."

The NP *gengogaku* "linguistics" appears with the Accusative Case particle *o* as the direct object of the complex verb *kenkyuu-suru* "research". What about the situation in (215b)? If we wish to maintain the direct object in (216), what will happen? The resulting sentence, (217), is ungrammatical.[20]

(217) *Sensei-ga   gengogaku-o   kenkyuu-o   suru.
        teacher-Nom linguistics-Acc research-Acc do
        "The teacher does research on linguistics."

The ungrammaticality of this sentence can be accounted for by the Double-*o* Constraint: since there are two NPs that are marked with the Accusative Case particle within a clause, this sentence is not acceptable.

All the cases that have been shown thus far to demonstrate violations of the Double-*o* Constraint involve the Accusative Case particle *o*. However, it seems that the *o* which is stated in the constraint is not necessarily limited to the multiple occurrence of the Accusative Case *o*. Consider the sentences in (218)–(220).

(218) Taroo-ga   kooen-o   aruita.
       Taro-Nom park-Acc walked
       "Taro walked throughout the park."

(219) Hanako-ga   hasi-o   watatta.
       Hanako-Nom bridge-Acc crossed
       "Hanako crossed the bridge."

(220) Ziroo-ga   gakkoo-no mae-o   tootta.
       Ziro-Nom school-Gen front-Acc passed
       "Ziro passed by in front of the school."

These verbs appear with NPs that are marked with *o*, and it is predicted that the *o*-causative sentences of (218)–(220) should be ruled out by the Double-*o*

Constraint. This prediction is indeed borne out. Consider their *o*-causative counterparts in (221)–(223).

(221) *Sensei-ga Taroo-o kooen-o aruk-ase-ta.
      teacher-Nom Taro-Acc park-Acc walk-caus.-past
      "The teacher made Taro walk through the park."

(222) *Sensei-ga Hanako-o hasi-o watar-ase-ta.
      teacher-Nom Hanako-Acc bridge-Acc cross-caus.-past
      "The teacher made Hanako cross the bridge."

(223) *Sensei-ga Ziroo-o gakkoo-no mae-o toor-ase-ta.
      teacher-Nom Ziro-Acc school-Gen front-Acc pass-caus.-past
      "The teacher made Ziro pass by in front of the school."

Since there are two NPs marked with *o* in each sentence, none of these causative sentences is acceptable. The *ni*-causative counterparts of (218)–(220), on the other hand, are permitted, as is illustrated in (224)–(226).

(224) Sensei-ga Taroo-ni kooen-o aruk-ase-ta.
      teacher-Nom Taro-Dat park-Acc walk-caus.-past
      "The teacher made/let Taro walk throughout the park."

(225) Sensei-ga Hanako-ni hasi-o watar-ase-ta.
      teacher-Nom Hanako-Dat bridge-Acc cross-caus.-past
      "The teacher made/let Hanako cross the bridge."

(226) Sensei-ga Ziroo-ni gakkoo-no mae-o toor-ase-ta.
      teacher-Nom Ziro-Dat school-Gen front-Acc pass-caus.-past
      "The teacher made/let Ziro pass by in front of the school."

Not only are these *ni*-causative sentences grammatical, but their interpretation is also ambiguous between the *ni*-causative reading and the *o*-causative reading, as is shown by the English translation.

So far as we can see, then, the causative sentences of (221)–(226) are no different from those we have observed before. As a consequence, the Double-*o* Constraint appears to rule out the causatives in (221)–(223) and in (214c) in the same fashion. As Kuroda (1978) notes, however, the NPs that are marked with *o* in (218)–(220) demonstrate behavior different from sentences with the Accusative marked NPs (where the NP is subcategorized for by the transitive verb) like those in (227)–(228): the (b) sentences are *o*-causative versions of the (a) sentences.

(227) a. Taroo-ga hon-o yonda.
         Taro-Nom book-Acc read
         "Taro read a book."
      b. *Sensei-ga Taroo-o hon-o yom-ase-ta.
         teacher-Nom Taro-Acc book-Acc read-caus.-past
         "The teacher made Taro read a book."

(228) a. Ziroo-ga susi-o   tukutta.
           Ziro-Nom sushi-Acc made
           "Ziro made sushi."
       b. *Hahaoya-ga Ziroo-o susi-o   tukur-ase-ta.
           mother-Nom Ziro-Acc sushi-Acc make-caus.-past
           "His mother made Ziro make sushi."

The NPs that are marked with the Accusative Case particle, i.e. *hon* "book" and *susi* "sushi" in the (a) sentences above, are the NPs for which the verbs subcategorize.

   Although the ungrammatical sentences in (221)–(223) and the (b) sentences in (227)–(228) appear to show no difference, Kuroda observes that a difference emerges in so-called "pseudo-cleft" sentences. Consider (229)–(233).

(229) Sensei-ga   Taroo-o   aruk-ase-ta-no-wa   kooen(-o)-da.
       teacher-Nom Taro-Acc walk-caus.-past-fact-Top park(-Acc)-is
       "It is the park that the teacher made Taro walk in."

(230) Sensei-ga   Hanako-o   watar-ase-ta-no-wa   hasi(-o)-da.
       teacher-Nom Hanako-Acc cross-caus.-past-fact-Top bridge(-Acc)-is
       "It is the bridge that the teacher made Hanako cross."

(231) Sensei-ga   Ziroo-o   toor-ase-ta-no-wa   gakkoo-no
       teacher-Nom Ziro-Acc pass-caus.-past-fact-Top school-Gen
       mae(-o)-da.
       front(-Acc)-is
       "It is in front of the school that the teacher made Ziro pass."

(232) *Sensei-ga   Taroo-o   yom-ase-ta-no-wa   hon(-o)-da.
       teacher-Nom Taro-Acc read-caus.-past-fact-Top book(-Acc)-is
       "It is a book that the teacher made Taro read."

(233) *Hahaoya-ga Ziroo-o tukur-ase-ta-no-wa   susi(-o)-da.
       mother-Nom Ziro-Acc make-caus.-past-fact-Top sushi(-Acc)-is
       "It is sushi that his mother made Ziro make."

In these pseudo-cleft sentences, the NP that immediately precedes *da* "is" is the focus of the sentence. Setting aside the issue of how to derive pseudo-cleft sentences, notice the contrast in judgments between (229)–(231), on the one hand, and (232)–(233), on the other. The NPs that appear in the focus position, i.e. the position immediately preceding *da* "is", correspond to the NPs that are marked with *o* in the original (non-causative) sentences. This contrast indicates that although the Double-*o* Constraint rules out both sentence types as equally ungrammatical, as we have observed in (227b), (228b), and (221)–(223) above, the pseudo-cleft versions of the ungrammatical *o*-causative sentences reveal that the original *o*-marked NPs in (218)–(220) and those in the (a) sentences of (227)–(228) are somehow different in nature.

The verbs in (218)–(220) all denote traversing action, and it is typical of this group of verbs to be accompanied by NPs that are marked with *o* (cf. Martin 1975; Inoue 1978; Dubinsky 1985; Miyagawa 1989a). When an *o*-marked NP appears with a verb of traversing action, the NP-*o* normally indicates the path through which the traversing action takes place. Because of this semantic content, some researchers have analyzed the *o* occurring with a traversing verb as a postposition that has the same phonetic form as the Accusative Case particle (cf. Jorden with Noda 1987).

The "object" of a verb of traversing behaves differently from the direct object of a transitive verb with respect to the range of data involving the pseudo-cleft sentences that we have observed above. On the basis of this contrastive behavior, Kuroda (1978) claims that the two instances of *o*-markings are indeed different, and that the *o*-marked NPs that appear as "objects" of traversing verbs serve as adverbials rather than NPs for which the verbs subcategorize.[21]

It should be pointed out that the Double-*o* Constraint applies only within a single clause. So, even if a sentence contains more than one NP that is marked with *o*, the sentence would be acceptable if the NPs belonged to different clauses. This is shown in (234).

(234) [_S Taroo-ga [_S Hanako-o   nagutta] otoko-o semeta].
      Taro-Nom   Hanako-Acc hit   man-Acc blamed
      "Taro blamed the man who hit Hanako."

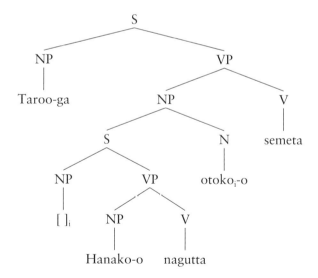

The sentence in (234) consists of a matrix clause and a sentence modifier (or relative clause) that modifies *otoko* "man". Notice that there are two NPs that are suffixed by the Accusative Case particle, *Hanako* and *otoko* "man". However, *Hanako* is within the sentence modifier, which itself forms a clause, while *otoko* "man" is in the matrix clause, and hence the Double-*o* Constraint is not effective in this sentence. That is, the two NPs marked with the Accusative Case particle are not within the same clause. Therefore, the sentence is grammatical even though there are two NPs marked with the Accusative Case particle in the sentence as a whole.

8.3 The Structure of Causatives

We have so far observed the two types of causative sentences in Japanese, but a question arises as to what kind of syntactic structure should be assigned to them. Although *o*-causatives and *ni*-causatives exhibit slightly different interpretations, we will assume an identical syntactic structure for both types of causatives. Given what we have discussed thus far, a possible structure for the causative sentence in (235) might look like (236).

(235) Taroo-ga Hanako-o/ni   benkyoo-sase-ta.
       Taro-Nom Hanako-Acc/Dat study-caus.-past
       "Taro made Hanako study."

(236)

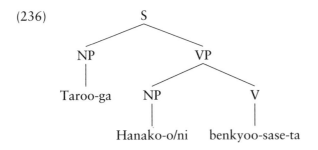

However, it has been argued that the structure of causative sentences is much more intricate than simply positing the structure depicted in (236). As Shibatani (1973b, 1976) discusses in detail, there is some evidence for the claim that a causative sentence involves an embedded clause. Consider the example in (237) with the reflexive pronoun *zibun*.

(237) Taroo$_i$-ga Hanako$_j$-o/ni   zibun$_{i/j}$-no heya-de benkyoo-sase-ta.
       Taro-Nom Hanako-Acc/Dat self-Gen   room-in study-caus.-past
       "Taro made/had Hanako study in self's room."

It should be remembered that reflexivization has been considered a diagnostic test for subjecthood in Japanese. As the co-indexing of the sentence in (237) indicates, *zibun* is ambiguous: its antecedent can be either *Taroo* or *Hanako*. Since reflexivization serves as a diagnostic test for subjecthood, both *Taroo* and *Hanako* are identified as subjects. Moreover, the fact that there are two subjects in this sentence means that there are two clauses involved in the sentence. That is, it is most natural to assume that *Taroo* is the subject of the matrix sentence while *Hanako* is the subject of the embedded sentence. On the basis of these assumptions, it has been claimed that the syntactic structure of (237) should be (238) (cf. Kuno 1973; Shibatani 1973b).

(238)

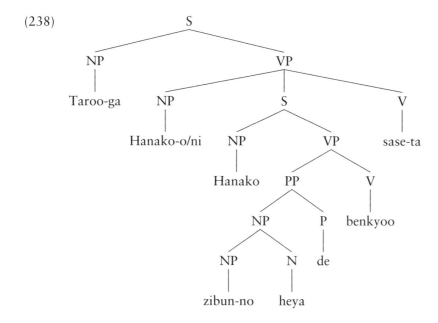

In this syntactic representation, *Taroo* and the lower *Hanako* are in NP positions immediately dominated by different Ss, consistent with the subject status diagnosed by reflexivization. The embedded subject eventually gets deleted under identity with the matrix NP. We assume that a later process applies to combine the two verbs so that the causative complex is derived to yield *benkyoo-sase-ta*.

Shibatani (1976) further claims that the "bi-clausal" (i.e. consisting of two clauses) analysis of causative sentences as is depicted in (238) is supported by the interpretation of adverbial modifications. In the examples in (239)–(240), taken from Shibatani (1976: 245), the adverbs, *damatte* "silently" and *kyuuni* "suddenly", are interpreted ambiguously.

(239) Taroo-wa Hanako-o   heya-ni   **damatte** hair-ase-ta.
       Taro-Top Hanako-Acc room-into silently   enter-caus.-past
       "Taro made Hanako come into the room silently."

(240) Taroo-wa Hanako-o   **kyuuni**   tomar-ase-ta.
       Taro-Top Hanako-Acc suddenly stop-caus.-past
       "Taro made Hanako stop suddenly."

Shibatani explains that *damatte* in (239), for example, can modify either Taro's causing event or Hanako's entering event. That is, Taro silently made Hanako enter the room or Taro made Hanako enter the room without her speaking. This ambiguity can be attributed to the bi-clausal status of causative sentences: the adverb can modify either the embedded verb *hair* "enter" or the matrix causative verb *-ase-*.

While causative sentences exhibit bi-clausal properties as was illustrated above, Miyagawa (1986) discusses that they also show properties characteristic of a single clause ("mono-clausal") structure (also Shibatani 1990). Recall that we have noted in section 8.2 that the Double-*o* Constraint is effective within a single clause; see (234), for example. If the causative structure is bi-clausal and each clause contains an NP-*o*, the sentence should be grammatical. We have already seen in (227b) that this prediction is not borne out. The example is repeated as (241) with its structure assumed under the bi-clausal analysis.

(241) a. *Sensei-ga   Taroo-o hon-o   yom-ase-ta.
           teacher-Nom Taro-Acc book-Acc read-caus.-past
           "The teacher made Taro read a book."

b.

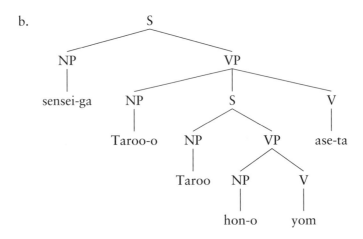

We notice that the two NPs that are marked with *o* belong to different clauses. Nevertheless, the sentence is not acceptable. If the sentence above takes a mono-clausal structure, i.e. consisting of a single clause, the ungrammaticality is straightforwardly explained by the Double-*o* Constraint. The mono-clausal representation is given as (242).[22]

(242)

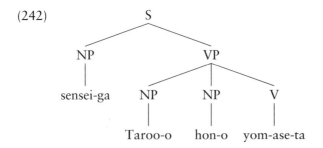

Putting these observations together, causative sentences have characteristics pertinent both to mono-clausal structures and to bi-clausal structures. From this, Miyagawa (1986) draws the conclusion that the causatives are in fact associated with both structures (cf. Y. Kitagawa 1986).

8.4 *Causative Passives*

It is interesting that causative and passive constructions can be combined to form causative passive sentences. That is, the causative morpheme *-(s)ase* and the passive morpheme *-(r)are* can both be suffixed to a verbal root at the same time. When a causative sentence is passivized, the causative morpheme is to the left of the passive morpheme, as in (243b); whereas when a causative sentence is formed on the basis of a passive sentence, the relative order between the causative and passive morphemes is reversed, as in (244b) (cf. Harada 1973; Saito 1982; Miyagawa 1989a; H. Hoshi 1994).

(243) a. Taroo-ga   Hanako-o   waraw-ase-ta. (causative)
           Taro-Nom Hanako-Acc laugh-caus.-past
           "Taro made Hanako laugh."
       b. Hanako-ga   Taroo-ni waraw-ase-rare-ta. (causative passive)
           Hanako-Nom Taro-by laugh-caus.-pass.-past
           "Hanako is made to laugh by Taro."

(244) a. Hanako-ga   Taroo-ni sikar-are-ta. (passive)
           Hanako-Nom Taro-by scold-pass.-past
           "Hanako was scolded by Taro."
       b. Ziroo-ga   Hanako-o/ni   Taroo-ni
           Ziro-Nom Hanako-Acc/Dat Taro-by
           sikar-are-sase-ta. (causative passive)
           scold-pass.-caus.-past
           "Ziro made Hanako be scolded by Taro."

There is a restriction on the formation of causative passive sentences of the type observed in (243), however, as is observed by Harada (1973) and is discussed by Miyagawa (1989a). When a passive is formed on the basis of a causative sentence and the verbal root to which the causative morpheme is suffixed is a transitive verb, as in (245a), the direct object of the transitive verb cannot be the subject of the causative passive sentence. This is shown in (245).

(245) a. Ziroo-ga   Mitiko-ni   kodomo-o home-sase-ta. (causative)
           Ziro-Nom Michiko-Dat child-Acc praise-caus.-past
           "Ziro had Michiko praise the child."
       b. *Kodomo-ga Ziroo-ni (yotte) Mitiko-ni   home-sase-rare-ta.
           child-Nom   Ziro-by   Michiko-Dat praise-caus.-pass.-past
           (causative passive)
       c. Mitiko-ga   Ziroo-ni (yotte) kodomo-o home-sase-rare-ta.
           Michiko-Nom Ziro-by   child-Acc   praise-caus.-pass.-past
           (causative passive)
           "Michiko was made to praise the child by Ziro."

The verb *home* "praise" is a transitive verb whose direct object is *kodomo* "child". The causative passive sentence of (245b) is intended to be a causative passive version, in which the direct object of the verb *home* is passivized and becomes the subject of the sentence. As is indicated, this causative passive sentence is not acceptable. The causee of the causative sentence in (245a), i.e. Michiko, on the other hand, can be passivized, as is illustrated in (245c).

8.5 Adversative Causatives

The adversative passive normally has a specific meaning: the subject is adversely affected by the event that is expressed by the rest of the sentence. Adversity constructions are not limited to passives, however. As Oehrle and Nishio (1981) demonstrate, adversity can also be expressed in causative sentences (cf. Shibatani 1976).

Let us observe the examples of adversity causatives in (246)–(247).

(246) Taroo-ga   musume-o   sin-ase-ta.
       Taro-Nom daughter-Acc die-caus.-past
       "Taro had his daughter die on him."

(247) Hanako-ga   reizooko-no   yasai-o   kusar-ase-ta.
       Hanako-Nom refrigerator-Gen vegetable-Acc spoil-caus.-past
       "Hanako had the vegetables in the refrigerator spoil on her."

The complex verbs in the sentences above have the causative morpheme *(s)ase*. The sentence in (246) is in fact ambiguous between the normal causative interpretation and the adversative causative reading. That is, the sentence can be construed as Taro causing his daughter's death or Taro being adversely affected by his daughter's death even if he did not cause the daughter's death. The adversative interpretation is observed in (247) as well. Hanako is adversely affected by the spoiled vegetable: as a result she does not have anything to eat, for example. Thus adversity is exhibited not only in passive sentences but also in the causative construction in Japanese.

8.6 Lexical Causatives

All the instances of the causative construction that we have examined thus far contain the causative morpheme *-(s)ase* that is suffixed to a verb root, and in this sense the causative sentences are productively formed. There is another type of causative that might be called **lexical causative** in Japanese (cf. Shibatani 1973a, 1973b, 1976, 1990; Miyagawa 1980, 1984, 1989a). As we have observed in chapter 4, lexical causatives are transitive verbs which often morphologically contrast with their intransitive counterpart. Unlike causative sentences with *-(s)ase*, lexical causatives are not productively formed; instead, lexical causatives are transitive verbs which bear the causative meaning inherent to them. Consider the causative (transitive) verbs and their morphologically related intransitive counterparts in (248). All the verbs are given in their citation forms, i.e. the non-past tense forms.

(248)   *causative (transitive)*   *intransitive*
      tome-ru   "stop"   tomar-u   "stop"
      age-ru   "raise"   agar-u   "rise"
      sage-ru   "lower"   sagar-u   "lower"
      okos-u   "wake up"   oki-ru   "wake up"
      nekas-u   "put to sleep"   ne-ru   "sleep"

As the paradigm in (248) shows, lexical causatives and intransitives are morphologically related. What is of interest is that the intransitive verbs in (248) have both lexical causative counterparts, as in (248), and productive causatives with *-(s)ase*. This is illustrated in (249)–(250).

(249)   a.   Taroo-ga   Hanako-o   tome-ta. (lexical causative)
            Taro-Nom Hanako-Acc stopped
            "Taro stopped Hanako."
     b.   Taroo-ga   Hanako-o   tamar-ase-ta. (productive causative)
            Taro-Nom Hanako-Acc stop-caus.-past
            "Taro made Hanako stop."

(250)   a.   Ziroo-ga   kodomo-o nekasi-ta. (lexical causative)
            Ziro-Nom child-Acc   put to sleep
            "Ziro put his child to sleep."
     b.   Ziroo-ga   kodomo-o ne-sase-ta. (productive causative)
            Ziro-Nom child-Acc   sleep-caus.-past
            "Ziro made his child sleep."

The (a) sentences are with lexical causatives while the (b) causatives are formed by suffixing the causative morpheme *-(s)ase* to the root of the intransitive verbs. Thus, if intransitive verbs have lexical causative counterparts as in (248), they are associated with two types of causative, lexical causative and productive causative.

   As Miyagawa (1984, 1989a) and Shibatani (1973a, 1973b, 1976, 1990) discuss in detail, while lexical causatives are similar to productive causatives with *-(s)ase* in that they both bear the causative meaning, they are semantically and syntactically different. First, Shibatani (1990: 317) explains their subtle meaning difference as follows: "[t]he lexical causative, e.g. *tome-ru* 'stop', typically expresses manipulative causation in which the causer brings about the caused event by physically manipulating the causee, whereas the [productive] causative, e.g. *[tomar-ase-ru]* 'make X stop', typically expresses directive causation in which the causer gives a direction to the causee to bring about the caused event". So, in the productive causative, if the causee is inanimate, the sentence sounds awkward. This is shown in the examples in (251)–(253), taken from Miyagawa (1989a: 121).

(251)   Hanako-ga   butai-ni agat-ta.
        Hanako-Nom stage-to rise-past
        "Hanako rose onto the stage."

(252) Taroo-ga Hanako/isu-o   butai-ni age-ta.
       Taro-Nom Hanako/chair-Acc stage-to raise-past
       "Taro raised Hanako/the chair onto the stage."

(253) Taroo-ga Hanako/*isu-o   butai-ni agar-ase-ta.
       Taro-Nom Hanako/chair-Acc stage-to raise-caus.-past
       "Taro caused Hanako/the chair to rise onto the stage."

(252) and (253) respectively exemplify the lexical causative and the productive
causative. In (253) the chair, being inanimate, cannot bring about an event, and
the sentence is not acceptable. When the causee is animate like Hanako, in
contrast, the productive causative has no problem. Notice that the animate vs.
inanimate difference does not influence the lexical causative of (252) because it
is the causer, rather than the causee, that brings about the event.

   Second, the lexical causative diverges from the productive causative syntactically
as well (cf. Shibatani 1973a, 1973b, 1976). Recall that we have observed above
that the reflexivization facts show that productive causative sentences consist
of two clauses, i.e. are bi-clausal. Shibatani (1976) points out, however, that the
reflexivization test demonstrates that lexical causatives consist of a single clause,
i.e. are mono-clausal. Consider the contrast in (254).

(254) a. Taroo$_i$-ga Hanako$_j$-o   zibun$_{i/*j}$-no heya-no   mae-de tome-ta.
           Taro-Nom Hanako-Acc self-Gen   room-Gen front-at stopped
           (lexical causative)
           "Taro stopped Hanako in front of self's room."
       b. Taroo$_i$-ga Hanako$_j$-o   zibun$_{i/j}$-no heya-no   mae-de
           Taro-Nom Hanako-Acc self-Gen   room-Gen front-at
           tomar-ase-ta. (productive causative)
           stop-caus.-past
           "Taro made Hanako stop in front of self's room."

Notice that while the productive causative sentence with *-(s)ase* in (254b) shows
the ambiguous interpretation of *zibun*, the reflexive pronoun is unambiguously
construed in the lexical causative sentence of (254a). It suggests lexical causative
sentences consist of only one clause.

   The conclusion that lexical causatives constitute mono-clausal structures while
productive causatives with *-(s)ase* comprise bi-clausal structures (as well as mono-
clausal structures) is also supported by the interpretation of adverbial phrases,
as Shibatani demonstrates. Examine the pair in (255a–b), taken from Shibatani
(1990: 314).

(255) a. Taroo-wa Hanako-o   **te-o   takaku age-te**   tome-ta.
           Taro-Top Hanako-Acc hand-Acc high   raise-ing stopped
           "Taro stopped Hanako with a hand raised high."
       b. Taroo-wa Hanako-o   **te-o   takaku age-te**   tomar-ase-ta.
           Taro-Top Hanako-Acc hand-Acc high   raise-ing stop-caus.-past
           "Taro made Hanako stop with a hand raised high."

The verb *tome* "stop" in (255a) is a lexical causative verb. The adverbial phrase in this sentence, *te-o takaku age-te* "with a hand raised high", unambiguously refers to the manner of Taro's action. That is, the person who raised a hand high is Taro. In contrast, the manner adverbial in (255b) is ambiguous: the person who raised a hand high can be either Taro or Hanako. The contrastive interpretation of the adverbial phrase can be explained by stating that the lexical causative sentence of (255a) consists of a single clause whereas the productive causative sentence with -(s)ase in (255b) consists of two clauses in which the adverbial phrase can modify either Taro's action or Hanako's action. Hence, lexical causatives exhibit several syntactic as well as semantic differences from productive causative sentences with -(s)ase.

9 Relative Clauses (Sentence Modifiers)

We have seen various ways of modifying nouns in Japanese. A modifier can be an adjective, an adjectival noun, a noun, or a sentence. Examples are shown in (256)–(259).

(256) Taroo-ga omosiroi hon-o kaita.
Taro-Nom interesting book-Acc wrote
"Taro wrote an interesting book."

(257) Ziroo-ga kirei-na hana-o Satiko-ni okutta.
Ziro-Nom pretty flower-Acc Sachiko-Dat sent
"Ziro sent pretty flowers to Sachiko."

(258) Hanako-ga tomodati-no uti-o katta.
Hanako-Nom friend-Gen house-Acc bought
"Hanako bought her friend's house."

(259) Satoo-sensei-ga [gakusei-ga kaita] ronbun-o yondeiru.
Prof. Sato-Nom student-Nom wrote article-Acc is reading
"Prof. Sato is reading the article that the student wrote."

The direct objects of these sentences are respectively modified by the adjective *omosiroi* "interesting", the adjectival noun *kirei* "pretty", the noun *tomodati* "friend", and the sentence *gakusei-ga kaita* "the student wrote". In (259), since the modifier is a sentence, it is called a **sentence modifier** or **relative clause**. The noun modified by a relative clause is referred to as a **head** noun. The noun *ronbun* "article" is the head noun of the relative clause in (259), for instance. In this section we will discuss various types of relative clauses (cf. J. McCawley 1976; C. Kitagawa 1982).

As we have observed earlier, the Japanese relative clauses of the type seen in (259) are slightly different from English relative clauses in that between the relative clause and its head noun there is no word connecting them in Japanese.

In English such a word is often found, and it is termed a **relative pronoun**. Compare the relative clauses in English and in Japanese in (260) and (261).

(260) a. John ate the cake (**which**) Mary baked yesterday.
       b. Bill met the student **who** hit Jane.

(261) Taroo-ga   [hahaoya-ga tukutta] susi-o   tabeta.
       Taro-Nom mother-Nom made   sushi-Acc ate
       "Taro ate the sushi that his mother made."

Notice that relative pronouns such as *which* and *who* may be required in relative clauses in English while no words equivalent to such relative pronouns exist in Japanese.

9.1 The Ga/No Conversion

In addition to the absence of relative pronouns, Japanese relative clauses depart from English with respect to the phenomenon that has been termed the *Ga/No* **Conversion** by Harada (1971) (cf. Bedell 1972; Harada 1971, 1976b; Shibatani 1976, 1977; Saito 1983; Miyagawa 1993). When a relative clause contains an NP that is marked with the Nominative Case particle *ga*, the Case can be replaced by the Genitive Case *no* without apparent difference in meaning. Observe the sentences in (262)–(264), which illustrate the *Ga/No* Conversion phenomenon.

(262) a. Taroo-ga   [Hanako-**ga**   kaita]   e-o   hometa.
           Taro-Nom Hanako-Nom painted painting-Acc praised
           "Taro praised the painting that Hanako drew."
       b. Taroo-ga [Hanako-**no** kaita] e-o hometa.

(263) a. [Kinoo   Ziroo-**ga** yondeita]   hon-ga   nakunatta.
           yesterday Ziro-Nom was reading book-Nom missing
           "The book that Ziro was reading yesterday is missing."
       b. [Kinoo Ziroo-**no** yondeita] hon-ga nakunatta.

(264) a. Taroo-ga   zitensya-o [Hanako-**ga**   tukiatteiru] otoko-ni kasita.
           Taro-Nom bicycle-Acc Hanako-Nom dating   man-to   lent
           "Taro lent his bicycle to the man with whom Hanako has been dating."
       b. Taroo-ga zitensya-o [Hanako-**no** tukiatteiru] otoko-ni kasita.

The Nominative NPs that undergo the *Ga/No* Conversion are not limited to subject NPs that are marked with *ga*. Recall that stative verbs often mark their direct objects with the Nominative Case particle *ga*. The *Ga/No* conversion applies to these Nominative Case particles that accompany the direct objects of stative verbs as long as they appear within relative clauses. Consider the examples of this sort in (265)–(266).

(265) a. Sono gakusei-ga suugaku-**ga** dekiru.
that student-Nom math-Nom be competent
"That student is good in math."

b. Taroo-ga [suugaku-**ga** dekiru] gakusei-to atta.
Taroo-Nom math-Nom be competent student-with met
"Taro met a student who is good in math."

c. Taroo-ga [suugaku-**no** dekiru] gakusei-to atta.

(266) a. Sono hito-ga eigo-**ga** wakaru.
that person-Nom English-Nom understand
"That person understands English."

b. [Eigo-**ga** wakaru] hito-ni kiite kudasai.
English-Nom understand person-to ask please
"Please ask the person who understands English."

c. [Eigo-**no** wakaru] hito-ni kiite kudasai.

Verbs like *dekiru* "be competent" and *wakaru* "understand" mark their direct objects with the Nominative Case particle, as the (a) sentences show. When a clause containing these verbs is a relative clause, as in the (b) sentences, the Nominative marked direct object can instead be marked with the Genitive Case particle *no*, as the (c) sentences indicate. There is no obvious difference in meaning between the (b) sentences and the (c) sentences.

Harada (1971) notes, however, that the *Ga/No* Conversion most notably observed within relative clauses is not allowed with any embedded clause. Consider the examples in (267)–(268).

(267) a. Taroo-ga [Hanako-ga sono gakusei-to atta]-to itta.
Taro-Nom Hanako-Nom that student-with met-COMP said
"Taro said that Hanako met the student."

b. *Taroo-ga [Hanako-**no** sono gakusei-to atta]-to itta.

(268) a. Ziroo-ga [Mitiko-ni sore-ga dekinai]-to omotteiru.
Ziro-Nom Michiko-Dat that-Nom cannot do-COMP think
"Ziro thinks that Michiko cannot do that."

b. *Ziroo-ga [Mitiko-ni sore-**no** dekinai]-to omotteiru.

The bracketed portions in these examples are not relative clauses. This can be evidenced by the fact that what follows these clauses is the complementizer *to* "that" instead of a head noun. Since the *ga*-marked NP is not within the relative clauses, the *Ga/No* Conversion does not apply to these cases.

9.2 Relative Clauses without Gaps

Recall our discussion of the syntactic structure of relative clauses. Relative clauses have been represented with a "gap" internal to them, and the gap corresponds to the head noun, as is illustrated in (269).

(269) a. Hanako-ga   [Taroo-ga kaita] hon-o   yonda.
           Hanako-Nom Taro-Nom wrote book-Acc read
           "Hanako read the book Taro wrote."

    b.

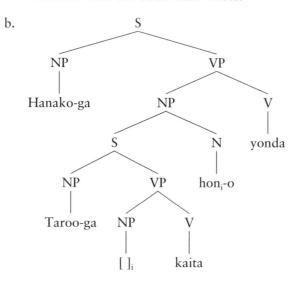

The gap within the relative clause is co-indexed with the head noun of the relative clause. Most relative clauses, not only in Japanese but also cross-linguistically, include such gaps that correspond to the head nouns.

  Japanese, however, exhibits another type of relative clause, in which a "gap" is not observed. Examples of this type of relative clause are in (270)–(273) (cf. Mikami 1960; Teramura 1971; Kuno 1973; J. McCawley 1976; C. Kitagawa 1982).

(270) [musuko-ga iede-sita]   Taroo
       son-Nom   ran away from home Taro
       "Taro whose son ran away from home"

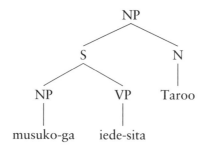

(271) [syatu-no botan-ga   torete-iru] kodomo
       shirt-Gen button-Nom missing   child
       "the child whose shirt has a missing button"

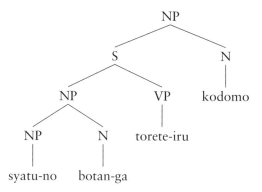

(272) [meizin-ga   ryoori-sita] azi
      expert-Nom cooked   flavor
      "flavor [that results when] an expert cooked"

(C. Kitagawa 1982: 201)

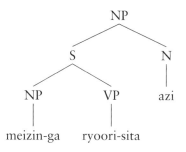

(273) [hito-ga   tooru] monooto
      person-Nom pass   sound
      "the sound of people going by"

(C. Kitagawa 1982: 202)

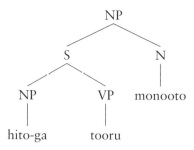

The bracketed portions are relative clauses, and the nouns that follow them are their head nouns. Notice that the relative clauses in these examples form complete Ss, rather than fragments, in that the NPs for which the verbs subcategorize as well as the subjects are all present within the relative clause. Furthermore, the head noun, which normally finds its relation to the relative clause via an index as in (269), does not have any NP with which it is co-indexed. This class of relative clauses constitutes a very special kind. As C. Kitagawa (1982) argues, the relationship between the relative clauses and their heads is not syntactic in the sense that the head nouns do not find their co-indexed NP gaps internal to the relative clause, but rather, the modification relation is normally established on semantic and pragmatic bases. For example, in (270), *musuko* "son" and *Taroo* can easily be related by kinship. Similarly, in (271), the relationship between the relative clause and its head noun can be interpreted in such a way that the shirt belongs to the child and the relative clause describes the child in terms of his shirt by referring to its missing button. The relative clauses in (272) and (273) are related to their head nouns by the attributive properties of the heads described by the relative clause: the flavor that typically results from an expert's cooking in (272), and the sound characteristic of people's passing by in (273). Hence there is always a semantic and/or pragmatic connection between the relative clauses and their heads in sentences with this type of relative clause (cf. Yoshiko Matsumoto 1988, 1990).

9.3 *Internally Headed Relative Clauses*

Japanese exhibits another interesting type of relative clause that is not observed in English. This type has been called an **internally headed relative clause**, and is exemplified by the sentences in (274)–(275) (cf. Kuroda 1992; Murasugi 1993, 1994).

(274)   Taroo-wa [ringo-ga   sara-no   ue-ni atta]-no-o totte, poketto-ni
        Taro-Top apple-Nom plate-Gen top-at be-one-Acc took pocket-to
        ireta.
        put in
        "Taro picked up an apple which was on a plate and put it in a pocket."
                                                              (Kuroda 1992: 147)

(275)   Sono omawari-wa [gakuseitati-ga CIA-no   supai-o
        that cop-Top   students-Nom CIA-Gen spy-Acc
        kumihuseta]-no-o   utikorosita.
        hold down-one-Acc shot and killed
        "The cop shot and killed the students who held down the CIA spy." or
        "The cop shot and killed the CIA spy who the students held down."
                                                              (Kuroda 1992: 153)

With an internally headed relative clause, there is no overtly expressed NP as its head. Rather, the head can be viewed as being contained within the relative clause. For example, in (274), *ringo* "apple" can be considered the head of the relative clause. Notice, as was the case with relative clauses without gaps, the relative clause of this type is complete in that all the NPs that are subcategorized for by the verb, along with the subject, are present within the relative clause. For example, in (275), the subject *gakuseitati* "students" as well as the subcategorized object NP, *CIA-no supai* "CIA spy", are overtly expressed within the relative clause. That is, there is no gap within the relative clause. What is also special about internally headed relative clauses is that where we normally find the head of a relative clause, we observe *no* "one", instead. We can regard this noun *no* as "replacing" the head that is internal to the relative clause.

As is extensively discussed in Kuroda (1992), what is of further interest is the ambiguous interpretation of (275). Notice that, as the English translation indicates, the head of the relative clause in this sentence can either be *gakuseitati* "students" or *CIA-no supai* "CIA spy". That is, the internally headed relative clause in (275) can be paraphrased into the relative clauses with head nouns in (276a–b).

(276) a. Sono omawari-wa [CIA-no supai-o kumihuseta] gakuseitati-o
          that cop-Top   CIA-Gen spy-Acc hold down   students-Acc
          utikorosita.
          shot and killed
          "The cop shot and killed the students who held down the CIA spy."
    b. Sono omawari-wa [gakuseitati-ga kumihuseta] CIA-no   supai-o
          that cop-Top   students-Nom hold down   CIA-Gen spy-Acc
          utikorosita.
          shot and killed
          "The cop shot and killed the CIA spy who the students held down."

In (276a) *gakuseitati* "students" is the the head while in (276b) *CIA-no supai* "CIA spy" is the head. The internally headed relative clause in (275), thus, is ambiguous between the two interpretations given in (276). Since internally headed relative clauses do not have a specific position internal to the relative clause that the head noun is supposed to occupy, either NP can be construed as its head so far as no semantic or pragmatic oddity arises, and consequently, two interpretations are possible.

10   Unaccusativity

We have earlier discussed the mutual c-command condition that holds between numeral quantifiers (NQs) and the NPs that they modify, as well as its relation to scrambling and passive sentences. In (277), the mutual c-command condition is satisfied between the NPs and their NQs, while the sentences in (278) fail to fulfill the condition, leading to ungrammaticality.

(277) a. Gakusei-ga   sannin [$_{VP}$ sake-o   nonde-iru].
          student-Nom three   Sake-Acc drinking
          "Three students are drinking Sake."
    b. Taroo-ga [$_{VP}$ sake-o   sanbon motte-kita].
          Taro-Nom   Sake-Acc three   brought
          "Taro brought three bottles of Sake."

(278) a. *Gakusei-ga [$_{VP}$ sake-o   sannin nonde-iru].
           student-Nom   Sake-Acc three drinking
           "Three students are drinking Sake."
       b. *Gakusei-ga [$_{VP}$ hon-o   sannin katta].
           student-Nom   book-Acc three bought
           "Three students bought books."

The mutual c-command condition has also been invoked to provide evidence
for the movement analysis of scrambling. For example, the mutual c-command
relation does not hold between the NP and its NQ in (279), but the condition
is satisfied between the trace of the scrambled NP and the NQ, providing
support for the movement of the scrambled NP.

(279) [$_S$ Sake$_i$-o [$_S$ gakusei-ga   [$_{VP}$ t$_i$ sanbon nonde-iru]]].
           Sake-Acc   student-Nom   three drinking
       "The students are drinking three bottles of Sake."

Similarly, the s-structure subject of the direct passive construction has also been
shown as being derived from the d-structure object position, by applying a
movement transformation. The grammaticality of the sentence in (280), then,
is accounted for by showing that the mutual c-command condition is satisfied
between the trace of the subject NP and its NQ.

(280) Kuruma$_i$-ga [$_{VP}$ doroboo-ni t$_i$ sandai nusum-are-ta].
       car-Nom   thief-by   three steal-pass.-past
       "Three cars were stolen by a thief."

Keeping in mind that the mutual c-command condition is often employed to
show the presence of a trace, consider the examples in (281)–(282), taken from
Miyagawa (1989b: 662), accompanied by their syntactic tree structures.

(281) a. Doa-ga   [$_{VP}$ kono kagi-de   hutatu aita].
           door-Nom   this key-with two   opened
           "Two doors opened with this key."

       b.

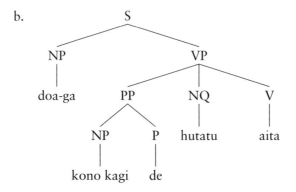

(282) a. Kyaku-ga [_{VP} ryokan-ni sannin tuita].
         guest-Nom   inn-at   three arrived
         "Three guests arrived at the inn."

b.

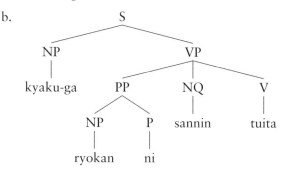

As the syntactic trees illustrate, the subject NP c-commands the NQ but the NQ does not c-command the NP, failing to satisfy the mutual c-command condition. In spite of this situation, the sentences are grammatical. Miyagawa (1989b) argues, however, that this unexpected grammaticality can be explained if we assume that the subject NP is moved from the direct object position, leaving a trace behind, and that the trace and the NQ satisfy the mutual c-command condition. According to this analysis, the s-structure representations of (281a) and (282a) can be considered as (283) and (284), respectively.

(283) Doa_i-ga [_{VP} kono kagi-de t_i hutatu aita].

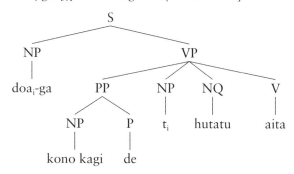

(284) Kyaku_i-ga [_{VP} ryokan-ni t_i sannin tuita].

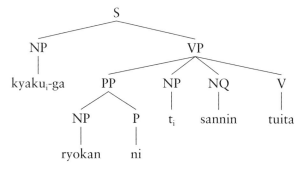

On this view, the subjects of these sentences originate from the d-structure direct object position, and are moved to the subject position. The verbs like *aku* "open" and *tuku* "arrive" whose surface subject can be analyzed as the d-structure object are called **unaccusative verbs** (cf. Perlmutter 1978; Burzio 1981, 1986; Dubinsky 1985; Miyagawa 1989a, 1989b; Terada 1990; Tsujimura 1990a, 1990b, 1990c, 1991, 1994; Levin and Rappaport Hovav 1995).

As the examples in (281)–(282) indicate, unaccusative verbs can be considered intransive verbs in that they are accompanied only by a subject. In this sense, unaccusative verbs are no different from other intransitive verbs such as *warau* "laugh" and *hasiru* "run", as exemplified in (285)–(286).

(285)   Gakusei-ga   sensei-to   waratta.
        student-Nom teacher-with laughed.
        "The students laughed with the teachers."

(286)   Gakusei-ga   awatete inu-to   hasitta.
        student-Nom hurriedly dog-with ran
        "The students hurriedly ran with a dog."

However, it has been claimed that intransitive verbs are not homogeneous, but that they should be divided into two distinct classes, namely, unaccusative verbs and **unergative verbs** (cf. Perlmutter 1978). Unaccusative verbs are verbs like those in (281)–(282) whose subjects are d-structure objects, which are moved to the subject position. The subjects of unergative verbs, on the other hand, are the subject, at both d-structure and s-structure, without involving any movement at all. This difference can be observed in the contrast between (287)–(288) and (281)–(282).

(287)   a.   *Gakusei-ga [$_{VP}$ geragerato sannin waratta].
             student-Nom   three   laughed
             "Three students laughed."

        b.

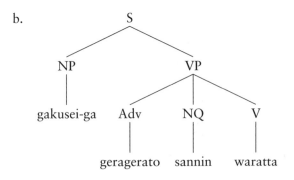

(288)   a.   *Gakusei-ga [$_{VP}$ awatete inu-to   sannin hasitta].
             student-Nom   hurriedly dog-with three   ran
             "Three students hurriedly ran with a dog."

b.

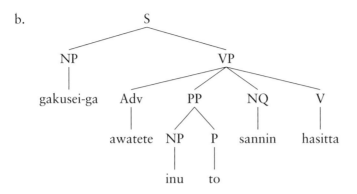

Notice that the ungrammaticality in (287)–(288) suggests that the mutual c-command condition is not satisfied in these sentences, and that the subject NPs in these sentences are always in the NP position immediately dominated by the S, so that the NQ does not c-command them. Hence, the contrast between (281)–(282) and (287)–(288) clearly shows that the two classes of verbs are different in that the subject of the former is the d-structure object and is later moved to the subject position, while the subject of the latter is the d- and s-structure subject throughout the derivation, as is depicted by the trees of (281b) and (282b) vs. (287b) and (288b).

Another piece of evidence for the underlying object status of the subject NP of an unaccusative verb comes from a construction called **resultatives**, as is discussed in Tsujimura (1990a, 1990b); (cf. Levin and Rappaport Hovav 1995). Resultative phrases describe a state as a result of some process denoted by a verb. In the examples in (289)–(291), the underlined phrases are resultatives.

(289) Taroo-ga to-o   <u>akaku</u> nutta.
       Taro-Nom door-Acc red   painted
       "Taro painted the door red."

(290) Hanako-ga   kami-o <u>mizikaku</u> kitta.
       Hanako-Nom hair-Acc short   cut
       "Hanako cut her hair short."

(291) Ziroo-ga   kuruma-o <u>kirei-ni</u> aratta.
       Ziro-Nom car-Acc   clean-to washed
       "Ziro washed his car clean."

The resultative phrases such as *akaku* "red", *mizikaku* "short", and *kirei-ni* "clean" in the above sentences all describe the state resulting from the process expressed by the verb. In (289), for instance, Taro painted the door and as a result the door became red. Similarly, in (291), Ziro washed the car, and as a result of that process, the car became clean. What is important to our discussion is that resultative phrases always describe a resulting state of the object. Thus, the resultatives in (289)–(291), *akaku* "red", *mizikaku* "short", and *kirei-ni* "clean", all refer to the resulting states of the direct objects of the sentences.

Let us call this regularity "direct object condition" (cf. Levin and Rappaport Hovav 1995). The direct object condition predicts that if the verb does not sub-categorize for an object, a resultative phrase is not compatible. This prediction is indeed borne out, as (292) shows.

(292)   *Taroo-ga kutakuta-ni hasitta/aruita/odotta.
        Taro-Nom dead tired   ran/walked/danced
        "Taro ran/walked/danced tired."

The verbs in (292) are intransitive verbs, and hence do not subcategorize for direct objects. The resultative phrase *kutakuta-ni* "dead tired" cannot appear in the absence of a direct object whose state the resultative phrase would describe.
    Assuming the direct object condition, examine the sentences in (293)–(294).

(293)   Hune-ga   suityuu   hukaku sizunda.
        ship-Nom in water deep   sank
        "The ship sank deep in the water."

(294)   Huusen-ga   sora takaku agatta.
        balloon-Nom sky high   went up
        "The balloon went up high in the sky."

Since the verbs in these examples occur only with subject NPs, and there are no direct objects, the resultative phrases *suityuu hukaku* "deep in the water" and *sora takaku* "high in the sky" should make the sentences ungrammatical. Contrary to this prediction, the examples are well-formed. Notice that the resultative phrases in (293) and (294) describe the state of the subject NPs, *hune* "ship" and *huusen* "balloon", as results of the processes of sinking and going up, respectively. That is, the ship ended up being deep in the water as a result of sinking in (293), for instance. Assuming that the direct object condition applies to sentences like (293)–(294), Tsujimura (1990a, 1990b) accounts for their grammaticality by analyzing the verbs in these examples as unaccusatives and, thus, the subject NPs originally come from the d-structure object position via movement. This analysis is described by the s-structure representations in (295)–(296).

(295)   Hune-ga$_i$ [$_{VP}$ t$_i$ suityuu hukaku sizunda].

(296)   Huusen-ga$_i$ [$_{VP}$ t$_i$ sora takaku agatta].

Under this analysis, the surface subjects are underlyingly the direct objects, and the resultative phrases describe their states resulting from the processes denoted by the verbs. Therefore, the resultative construction provides another piece of evidence for the unaccusative status of the verbs in (293)–(294).
    As mentioned above, unaccusative verbs are similar to unergative verbs in that both classes of verbs appear with only one NP. On the other hand, we can also say that unaccusative verbs resemble transitive verbs in that they both sub-categorize for the direct object NP. This latter similarity between transitive verbs

and unaccusative verbs can often be detected by the morphological resemblance between the two. Consider the transitive–unaccusative pairs in (297)–(299) (cf. Shibatani 1990; Jacobsen 1992).

(297) a. Taroo-ga   mado-o   simeta.
           Taro-Nom window-Acc closed
           "Taro closed the window."
       b. Mado-ga   simatta.
           window-Nom closed
           "The window closed."

(298) a. Hanako-ga   doa-o   aketa.
           Hanako-Nom door-Acc opened
           "Hanako opened the door."
       b. Doa-ga   aita.
           door-Nom opened
           "The door opened."

(299) a. Ziroo-ga   kabin-o   kowasita.
           Ziro-Nom vase-Acc broke
           "Ziro broke the vase."
       b. Kabin-ga   kowareta.
           vase-Nom broke
           "The vase broke."

In each pair the (a) sentence contains a transitive verb while the (b) sentence includes its unaccusative counterpart. Notice the morphological resemblance between the transitive verbs and their unaccusative correspondents. Furthermore, the object of the transitive verb in the (a) sentence is the subject of the unaccusative verb in the (b) sentence, indicating the original function of the surface subject of the unaccusative verb as the direct object. That is, a number of unaccusative verbs in Japanese can find transitive counterparts that are morphologically related to them. Therefore, along with the numeral quantifiers and the resultative construction, unaccusativity status can also be detected by the morphological component of the verbs.

11   The Light Verb Construction

One interesting type of word in Japanese is the verbal noun. When a verbal noun is compounded with the verb *suru* "do", the complex is considered a verb. The verb *suru* "do" appears with any verbal noun, carrying all the verbal inflections with it, and yet the meaning of the verb *suru* is not so vital to the meaning of the complex of verbal noun and *suru*; rather, the meaning of the entire complex primarily comes from the meaning of the verbal noun. For this reason, *suru* is termed a **light verb**, and the sentences that contain verbal nouns and light verbs are often referred to as **light verb constructions** (cf. Kageyama 1976–1977; Grimshaw and Mester 1988; Miyagawa 1989b; Terada 1990; Tsujimura 1990a, 1990b; Uchida and Nakayama 1993; Dubinsky 1994; among others).

There are two ways of expressing the sequence of a verbal noun and light verb. In one pattern, a verbal noun and light verb are morphologically merged and treated as a single complex verb. In the other, *suru* is considered the verb of a sentence and the verbal noun is separate from the light verb. In this latter situation, the verbal noun serves as a noun and is accompanied by the Accusative Case particle *o*. These two patterns are illustrated in (300).

(300)   a.   Taroo-ga   yooroppa-e ryokoo-sita.
             Taro-Nom Europe-to   traveling-did
             "Taro traveled to Europe."
        b.   Taroo-ga   yooroppa-e ryokoo-o   sita.
             Taro-Nom Europe-to   traveling-Acc did
             "Taro traveled to Europe."

As is discussed in detail by Grimshaw and Mester (1988), the light verb construction exhibits an interesting pattern of distributing NPs that are associated with a verbal noun in regard to the Case particles and postpositions that accompany them. The NPs in the light verb construction can be marked with Nominative and Accusative Case particles, among others, as well as postpositions, but they can also be marked with a Genitive Case particle resembling a prenominal modifier. These patterns are exemplified in (301)–(303).

(301)   Taroo-ga   yooroppa-e tomodati-to ryokoo-o   sita.
        Taro-Nom Europe-to   friend-with traveling-Acc did
        "Taro traveled to Europe with friends."

(302)   Taroo-ga   yooroppa-e-no tomodati-to-no ryokoo-o   sita.
        Taro-Nom Europe-to-Gen friend-with-Gen traveling-Acc did
        "Taro traveled to Europe with friends."

(303)   Taroo-ga   yooroppa-e tomodati-to-no ryokoo-o   sita.
        Taro-Nom Europe-to   friend-with-Gen traveling-Acc did
        "Taro traveled to Europe with friends."

In (301) the Case particles and the postpositions appear just as in (300) without the Genitive particle. In (302) and (303), in contrast, some of the NPs and PPs are accompanied by the Genitive Case particle *no*, which resembles the prenominal modifier pattern, as in *Taroo-no hon* "Taro's book".

Recall that we have discussed the Double-*o* Constraint in connection with the causative construction. As was mentioned, the constraint is relevant to the light verb construction. When a verbal noun appears in the pattern illustrated in (300b) and the verbal noun subcategorizes for a direct object, the Double-*o* Constraint comes into play and prevents the direct object NP from appearing with the Accusative Case particle *o*. Instead, the NP must be accompanied by the Genitive Case particle *no*, or the verbal noun must be realized in the form of a complex predicate of the pattern in (300a). This is illustrated in (304).

(304) a. *Taroo-ga suugaku-o benkyoo-o   suru.
            Taro-Nom math-Acc studying-Acc do
            "Taro studies math."
       b. Taroo-ga   suugaku-no benkyoo-o   suru.
            Taro-Nom math-Gen   studying-Acc do
            "Taro studies math."
       c. Taroo-ga   suugaku-o benkyoo-suru.
            Taro-Nom math-Acc studying-do
            "Taro studies math."

In (304a) there are two NPs that are marked with the Accusative Case particle *o*. This is exactly the situation that the Double-*o* Constraint prevents from occurring. Hence, the sentence is ungrammatical. In (304b), instead, the direct object NP is marked with the Genitive Case particle *no*, and consequently, only the verbal noun appears with the Accusative Case particle. The sentence, thus, is acceptable. (304c) exhibits another way of avoiding a violation of the Double-*o* Constraint: that is, by forming a complex predicate with *suru*, the verbal noun is no longer marked with the Accusative Case particle, and hence the direct object *suugaku* "math" is the sole NP that appears with the Accusative Case particle. Thus, the distribution of the NPs that are associated with the light verb *suru* is conditioned by the Double-*o* Constraint.

At this point, let us go back to the two patterns that we have observed earlier in (300). As it turns out, not all verbal nouns allow for these two patterns. Miyagawa (1989b) and Tsujimura (1990a, 1990b) independently demonstrate that verbal nouns of the unaccusative class disallow the pattern of (300b), where the verbal noun is marked with the Accusative Case. For instance, compare the examples in (305a–b), discussed by Miyagawa (1989b: 664).

(305) a. Tokkyuu-ga   [$_{VP}$ Ueno-eki-ni   go-dai tootyaku-sita].
            limited express-Nom   Ueno-station-at five-cl. arrival-did
            "Five limited express trains arrived at Ueno Station."
       b. *Tokkyuu-ga [$_{VP}$ Ueno-eki-ni go-dai tootyaku-o sita].

The NQ *go-dai* is intended to modify the subject *tokkyuu* "limited express". Notice that the mutual c-command condition appears to be violated, but nonetheless the sentence in (a) is grammatical. On the basis of this observation, Miyagawa concludes that the verbal noun is unaccusative and *tokkyuu* is underlyingly the object. Miyagawa further argues that when the verbal noun is unaccusative, it cannot be marked with the Accusative Case, as the (b) sentence illustrates. Unaccusative verbal nouns that exhibit the same phenomenon include *meityuu* "strike", *tanzyoo* "birth", *zyoosyoo* "ascend", and *kakudai* "enlarge", among many more.

Uchida and Nakayama (1993), on the other hand, claim that the unaccusative account for the ungrammaticality of (305b) is not quite accurate. They argue that some transitive verbal nouns such as *taiho* "arrest", *hakai* "destruction", and *tyuusi* "cancellation" resist the Accusative marking on them. They discuss the examples in (306)–(307) to illustrate their claim (p. 632).

(306) a. Keikan-ga   suri-o   taiho-sita.
           policeman-Nom pickpocket-Acc arrest-did
           "The policeman arrested the pickpocket."
       b. *Keikan-ga suri-no taiho-o sita.

(307) a. Guntai-ga hasi-o   hakai-sita.
           army-Nom bridge-Acc destruction-did
           "The army destroyed the bridge."
       b. *Guntai-ga hasi-no hakai-o sita.

They argue, instead, that the Accusative marking on verbal nouns is only possible when the verbal nouns denote events that last for a certain period of time.[23] The events denoted by *tootyaku* "arrival", *taiho* "arrest", and *hakai* "destruction" in (305)–(307) do not imply the duration of time, and the Accusative marking on them results in ungrammaticality. Consequently, the Case distribution observed in the light verb construction finds its explanation in connection with the semantic properties of verbal nouns.

12   Further Issues on Phrase Structure

This section will briefly deal with more recent developments of phrase structure rules (section 12.1) and their application to Japanese (section 12.2) to supplement our earlier discussion. This section is intended only for the reader who may be interested in pursuing more advanced issues in syntax.

12.1   X'-Theory

We have earlier examined phrase structure rules in order to generate phrases and sentences in Japanese. We can basically assume a similar set of phrase structure rules for English. Consider the examples of NPs, VPs, and PPs in English in (308)–(310).

(308) a. [NP an apple]
       b. [NP the picture]
       c. [NP this chair]

(309) a. [VP laugh]
       b. [VP eat pizza]
       c. [VP bought a table]

(310) a. [_PP_ to the park]
     b. [_PP_ with a friend]
     c. [_PP_ after dinner]

The NPs in (308) consist of the head noun and words like *an*, *the*, and *this*. Such words are called **determiners** and are abbreviated as Ds. So, the phrase structure tree of (308) looks like (311).

(311)

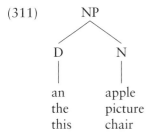

an   apple
the   picture
this   chair

The VPs in (309), as in Japanese, consist of the head V and its subcategorized NP, if any. The phrase structure tree of the VPs is depicted in (312).

(312)

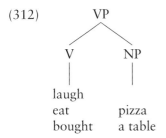

laugh
eat   pizza
bought a table

Notice that a difference between Japanese and English is that the head appears under the left branching node in English while it is under the right branching node in Japanese. Similarly, the internal structure of PPs is illustrated in (313).

(313)

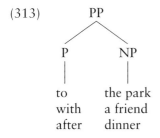

to   the park
with   a friend
after dinner

Hence, except for the presence of determiners under NPs and the position of the head, a similar set of phrase structures can be assumed in English.

Consider the NP in English in (314) and its simplified hierarchical representation.

(314)   the picture of John at school

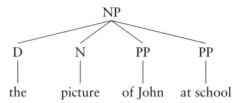

Following the phrase structure rules assumed for English, the representation of (314) appears to be reasonable.

Next, consider the sentences in (315).

(315)   a.   The [picture of John] at school is nicer than the picture of John at home.
        b.   The [picture of John] at school is nicer than the one at home.
        c.   *The [picture] of John is nicer than the one of Mary at school.

As (315b) shows, in English, the word *one* can substitute for a repeated sequence of words. So, in (315b) *one* substitutes for *picture of John*. That is, *one* refers to the N and the leftmost PP in (314). Assuming that *one* substitutes for a constituent, (315b) raises a question concerning the hierarchical representation of (314). Since the N head and the leftmost PP do not form a constituent, *one* should not be able to isolate the N and PP. In order for *one* to be able to refer to the N and the PP as a constituent, the structure would need to be modified along the lines depicted in (316), with unidentified nodes X and Y.

(316)

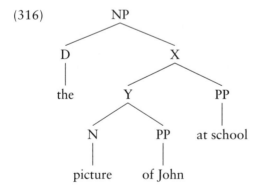

In the structure illustrated in (316), the node Y comprises the head N and PP, treating them as a constituent. The node Y, thus, can be substituted for by *one*, as is in (315b). What is the status of Y (as well as that of X)? The *one* substitution data in (315) call for the necessity of an intermediate level that can appear between an NP and its head N. Such an intermediate level is called N′ ("N-bar"). The tree in (316) can be redrawn as in (317).

(317)

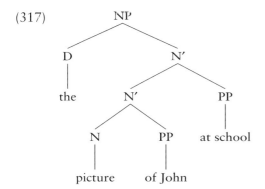

As (317) shows, the N′ level can be repeated. Notice that the contrast between the grammatical substitution in (315b) and the ungrammatical substitution in (315c) suggests that *one* makes reference only to an N′ constituent: in (315c) *one* is intended as a substitute for the N head, and the sentence is ungrammatical.

An intermediate level, like N′, is also motivated for verbs, with the V′ ("V-bar") level being invoked. Given the phrase structure rules discussed earlier, we can represent the VP of the sentence (318) as in (319).

(318)   John will buy fish at that store tomorrow.

(319)

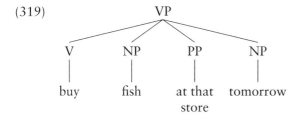

As was the case with nouns, there is a similar substition phenomenon observed within VPs. Let us call it *do-so* substitution; it is exemplified in (320), based on the sentence in (319).

(320)   a.   John will buy fish at that store tomorrow, and Mary will do so next week.
        b.   John will buy fish at that store tomorrow, and Mary will do so at the market next week.

In (320a) *do so* substitutes for *buy fish at the store*. The substituted portion corresponds to the V, first NP, and PP in (319). In (320b) the V and first NP, i.e. *buy fish*, are substituted for by *do so*. Again, the problem is that these substituted portions do not correspond to constituents. By invoking the intermediate level of V′, however, this problem is solved. Consider the modified phrase structure representation of (319) that includes V′ nodes, as is illustrated in (321).

(321)

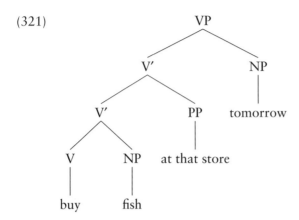

Notice, in this representation, that the V and NP *fish* form a constituent, V′, and at the same time, the V, NP *fish*, and PP are a constituent, V′. The *do-so* substitution can now refer to these V′ constituents, generating well-formed sentences like (320a) and (320b). As was the case with N′, V′ can be repeated.

The phrase structure rules that generate the hierarchical structures observed above can be schematically given as in (322)–(323), where "YP" is left unspecified for another phrasal category such as PP and NP, and "*" allows for repetition of the N′ and V′ categories.

(322)   a.   NP → ... N′ ...
        b.   N′* → ... N′ ... YP ...
        c.   N′ → ... N ...

(323)   a.   VP → ... V′ ...
        b.   V′* → ... V′ ... YP ...
        c.   V′ → ... V ...

The pattern of building a lexical category into the intermediate level and, further, into a phrasal category is identical between nouns and verbs. We can generalize this patterning by using a neutral category X, as is illustrated in (324).

(324)   a.   XP → ... X′ ...
        b.   X′* → ... X′ ... YP ...
        c.   X′ → ... X ...
        d.

The investigation regarding the hierarchical ordering of constituents, which leads to the generalization of (324), has been a primary concern of the theory called **X′-Theory** (cf. Jackendoff 1977). In the generalized structure in (324), X stands for N or V, and it is assumed to extend further to P. That is, the X′-schema of (324) is considered to hold cross-categorially.

Let us focus on the hierarchical structure depicted in (324d). In this structure, there are two nodes indicated by "...", which are not identified: one is the node that is sister to the head X, and together they form an intermediate level X′; the other is the node that is sister to the X′ building a phrasal level XP. In X′-Theory there are names for these positions. The former is called **complement** and the latter is termed **specifier**. We can now state the phrase structures in (325) using these terms.

(325) a. XP → specifier X′
       b. X′ → X complement

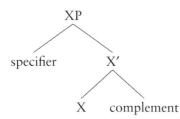

c.

Specifiers and complements have different properties. A complement usually constitutes a phrasal category, and it has a very tight relation to the head. To illustrate this property, consider the structure of the VP depicted in (321), repeated below.

(321)

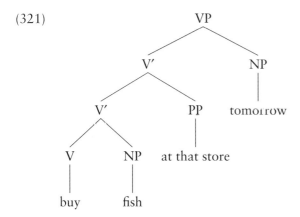

In this structure the NP *fish* is an instance of a complement. The verb *buy* is a transitive verb, and it subcategorizes for a direct object, which is exemplified by the NP *fish* in this case. Since the NP is required by the verb as its subcategorized element, the VP would be ungrammatical without it, as is demonstrated by the ill-formed phrase **buy at that store tomorrow*. Thus, the intuitive sense of "tight" relation between the verb and the direct object resides in the fact that the verb subcategorizes for the NP. For this reason, a complement consistently occupies a position that is sister to a head to reflect this tight relationship.

A similar observation is made with NPs. Consider the structure of the NP in (317), repeated below.

(317)

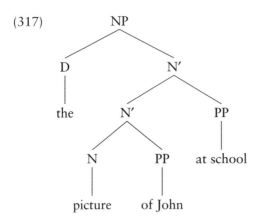

The PP that is the sister to the head N, i.e. *of John*, is an instance of a complement. Notice that the NP in (317) contains another PP, *at school*, but the relations of these two PPs to the head N are rather different. A picture would not be regarded as such without an individual or an object that is taken a picture of. In this sense *John* plays a role, as an "object" of the N head, similar to the direct object of a verb. The PP *at school*, on the other hand, does not contribute to the inherent property of a picture. Rather, the PP simply adds an optional piece of information concerning the location of the picture. Therefore, in comparison with the PP *of John*, the PP *at school* does not bear an essential relation to the head. PPs like *at school* are called **adjuncts**. The contrast between the tight relation of a complement to a head and the looser relation of an adjunct to a head is observed in the word order between a complement and an adjunct, as is illustrated in (326).

(326)   *the picture [at school] [of John]

Since the complement *of John* bears a closer relation to the head than the adjunct *at school*, the former should maintain a closer position to the head, namely, sister to the head.

As was briefly mentioned above, a specifier is sister to an intermediate level X′ forming a phrasal category XP. In our earlier examples, determiners such as *a*, *the*, and *this* serve as specifiers. Unlike complements, specifiers are not necessarily phrasal categories.

Given the X′-schema depicted in (325), we should ask ourselves a question concerning the status of S. That is, we have observed that the phrase structure rule relevant to generate a sentence in Japanese is (327).

(327)   S → NP VP

Although this rule seems to generate English sentences sufficiently, it is not consistent with the X'-schema of (325). How can we modify (327) in such a way that the X'-schema of (325) can also generate a sentence? Recall that phrases are built around heads. What, then, is an S built around? Naïvely put, a head is the most important element of the phrase. The meaning of an NP, for example, comes from the meaning of the head N. So, information concerning a phrase is judged largely on the basis of its head. What plays a similar role in a sentence? To find that out, compare (328a, b).

(328) a. John will go to Hawaii next year.
        b. John went to Hawaii last year.

These sentences are almost identical. The difference resides in the time that the event takes place. In (328a) the event will take place in the future, i.e. next year, while in (328b) the event has already happened, i.e. last year. That is, the sentence in (328a) is true only if the event will take place in the future; and it is false if it has already taken place. Similarly, the sentence in (328b) is true as long as the event has already taken place, but it is not true if it has not happened yet. So, whether the sentence is true or false can be judged by the information concerning the time of the event that is expressed by the future tense in (328a) and the past tense in (328b). What this suggests, then, is that tense plays a crucial role in judging whether sentences are true or false. For this reason, it is reasonable to identify a tense specification as the head of a sentence. That is, although we have earlier assumed that a verb and tense constitute an inseparable unit under a V, we can now separate the two, and treat tense as an independent category, **Infl**(ection). I(nfl) takes a VP as its complement to form the inter-mediate level I' ("I-bar"), which in turn takes an NP as its specifier to form a phrasal category that corresponds to a whole sentence, namely, IP. This is illus-trated in (329)–(330).

(329) a. IP → NP I'
        b. I' → I VP

(330)

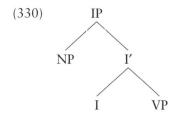

In the phrase structure depicted above, the specifier NP is the subject of the sentence. Given the X'-schema, we can illustrate the phrase structure representa-tion of the sentence (331) as in (332).

(331) John will eat pizza at home.

(332)

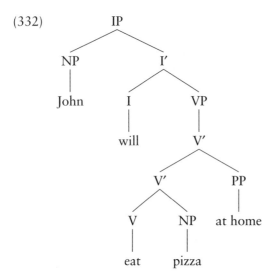

12.2 Application to Japanese

It has been accepted by many researchers that the X'-schema described in (325) basically applies to Japanese. The only difference between Japanese and English is the position of a head. Compare the Japanese sentence structure in (333) with (332).

(333) a. Taroo-ga   uti-de   susi-o   tabe-ta.
           Taro-Nom home-at sushi-Acc eat-past
           "Taro ate sushi at home."

   b.

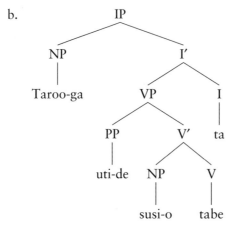

Notice that heads like I and V are on the right branching nodes in (333b) whereas in English they are on left branching nodes. Nevertheless, the rest of the structure is adequately generated by the general X'-schema of (325). Note also that while we had earlier analyzed the past tense morpheme *-ta* as part of the

V, under the X'-schema that we are currently assuming, it is regarded as the head I. By identifying a tense morpheme as constituting an independent head, i.e. I, we can now consider the structure of an S in Japanese as following the general pattern of (325) as well.

It is worth pointing out that, on the one hand, Japanese sentence structure appears to fit in with the general phrase structure pattern of (325), as we have just discussed; but, on the other, as is most notably discussed by Fukui (1986), some of the phenomena in English that have motivated the X'-schema of (325) are simply not observed in Japanese. To begin with, it should be remembered that one of the motivations for invoking the intermediate level of X' has to do with the substitution of the word *one*. The relevant examples are repeated below as (334).

(334)   a.   The [picture of John] at school is nicer than the picture of John at home.
        b.   The [picture of John] at school is nicer than the one at home.

What *one* substitutes for, i.e. *picture of John*, needs to be given the status of constituent, and for this reason, the intermediate level of N' is called for. Recall the X'-schema of (325c), which is repeated below.

(325c)

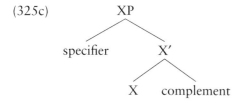

Once the X' constituent is posited, this level can be repeated, allowing for additional modifiers such as APs as adjuncts. Since *one* is considered an N', *one* can take a modifier introduced by a repeated N'. So, we have NPs like (335), which have the structure of (336).

(335)   a.   a yellow one
        b.   an old one
        c.   the delicious one

(336)

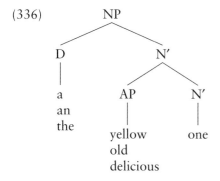

In (336), the AP constitutes adjuncts introduced by the repeated N'. In addition to the N'-level pronominal form *one*, English also employs NP-level pronominal forms that include *it*, *he*, and *himself*. These pronominal forms constitute NPs, and therefore cannot allow prenominal modifiers to precede them. That is, given an NP structure like (336), for example, a prenominal modifier must occur under the NP, modifying either the N' or the N head. This is why the phrases in (337) are ungrammatical.

(337)   a.   *big it
        b.   *short he
        c.   *yesterday's himself

                                                    (Fukui 1986: 231)

Since *it*, *he*, and *himself* by themselves constitute a phrasal level, NP, there is no way they can take further modification. The distinction between the two types of pronominal forms, *one*, on the one hand, and words like *it*, *he*, and *himself*, on the other, provides evidence that English exhibits both N'- and NP-level pronominals, motivating an intermediate level X' in addition to a phrasal level XP and a head X.

   If Japanese observed the same type of distinction, namely, between an N'-level pronominal form and an NP-level pronominal form, it would motivate the three levels, i.e. N, N', and NP. However, Fukui points out that Japanese pronominal forms equivalent to English *it*, *he*, and *himself*, for instance, should all be considered N' levels and that there is no NP-level pronominal form in Japanese. Compare (337) with Fukui's examples in (338)–(340).

(338)   *sore* "it"
        Tookyoo-no biru-no   okuzyoo-kara mita   Haree-suisei-wa
        Tokyo-Gen building-Gen top-from   (I) saw Halley's Comet-Top
        smog-no   tame   bonyarito nigotte-ita   ga, <u>Okinawa-no   Naha-de</u>
        smog-Gen due to faintly   blurred-was but Okinawa-Gen Naha-in
        <u>mita</u>   *sore*-wa yozora-ni   kukkirito kagayaite-ita.
        (I) saw it-Top   night sky-in vividly   shining-was
        "Halley's Comet that (I) saw from the top of a building in Tokyo was
        blurred by the smog, but it that (I) saw in Naha City in Okinawa was
        vividly shining in the night sky."

                                                    (Fukui 1986: 232)

(339)   *kare* "he"
        Kinoo   Taroo-ni   atta ka-i?
        yesterday Taro-with met Q
        "Did you see Taro yesterday?"
        un, demo <u>kinoo-no</u>   *kare*-wa sukosi   yoosu-ga   hendat-ta.
        yes but   yesterday-Gen he-Top   somewhat state-Nom be strange-past
        "Yes, but yesterday's he was somewhat strange."

                                                    (Fukui 1986: 233)

(340) *zibun* "self"

Kukyoo-ni tatasare-ta   Saburoo-wa nanno kuroo-mo
hardship-in forced to face-past Saburo-Top not any sufferings-even
siranakat-ta <u>mukasi-no</u> <u>zibun</u>-ni modoritai-to
not know-past old days-Gen self-to wanted to go back-that
omotta.
thought
"Saburo, who was stranded in hardships, wanted to go back to old day's
himself who did not know any sufferings."

(Fukui 1986: 233)

The fact that these pronominal forms can be modified means that they cannot
be NP-level pronominals; rather, they demonstrate a behavior pattern similar
to the English N'-level pronominal form *one*. Hence, in Japanese, (338)–(340)
provide evidence for the N' level, but there is no motivation suggesting that
the phrasal level of NP is needed in addition to N' and N. A conclusion drawn
from this is that a maximal level built around an N head should be considered
an N', rather than an NP, and that the phrasal level of NP need not be invoked
in Japanese.

 Fukui demonstrates that another problem arises concerning the status of
determiners in Japanese. Recall that in English, determiners occupy the specifier
position. The specifier is a unique position in that, together with its sister N', it
forms a phrasal category, namely, NP. Having a unique specifier position explains
the fact that determiners cannot be repeated in English, as is illustrated in (341).

(341) a. *a the pen
   b. *the your cat
   c. *the the ship
   d. *Mary's this magazine

 In Japanese, Fukui argues, there are no determiners. Consider the sentences
in (342), focusing on the direct objects.

(342) a. Taroo-ga kuruma-o katta.
     Taro-Nom car-Acc bought
     "Taro bought a/the car."
   b. Hanako-ga keeki-o tabeta.
     Hanako-Nom cake-Acc ate
     "Hanako ate a/the cake."
   c. Masao-ga isu-o tukutta.
     Masao-Nom chair-Acc made
     "Masao made a/the chair."

The direct objects of these sentences are not accompanied by determiners, and
yet the sentences are grammatical. In contrast, English equivalents would not be
acceptable without determiners. Hence, Japanese does not exhibit determiners
in NPs.

On the other hand, demonstrative words such as *kono* "this", *sono* "that", and *ano* "that over there" can accompany nouns, and might be regarded as determiners. However, when they occur with nouns, they can further be preceded by prenominal modifiers. Consider the examples in (343).

(343) a. kono e
           this painting
           "this painting"
      b. Taroo-no kono e
           Taro-Gen this painting
           "Taro's this painting (i.e. this painting of Taro's)"

(344) a. ano hanasi
           that story
           "that story"
      b. Hanako-no ano hanasi
           Hanako-Gen that story
           "Hanako's that story"
      c. kinoo-no Hanako-no ano hanasi
           yesterday-Gen Hanako-Gen that story
           "yesterday's Hanako's that story"

Let us suppose that demonstratives such as *kono* "this" and *ano* "that" in the above examples can be analyzed as determiners. The demonstratives should then be treated as specifiers, and form NPs with their sisters. Under this assumption, the phrases in the (a) examples above, for instance, are NPs. However, if *kono e* "this painting" in (343a) and *ano hanasi* "that story" in (344a) were NPs, they should not be able to take further modifications preceding them, because an NP is the maximal level. Contrary to this prediction, such modification is possible, as the (b) and (c) examples in (343)–(344) indicate. This observation suggests that demonstrative words in Japanese do not serve as specifiers. A specifier, together with its sister node, builds a phrasal category, but without a specifier, a phrasal category need not be posited. As we have seen above, since there is no determiner in Japanese and hence no specifier, an N can build into an N' level, without invoking a further phrasal category NP.

While the general phrase structure pattern depicted in (325) can be posited in Japanese, it should be kept in mind that some of the phenomena in English that have motivated it are not necessarily detected in Japanese.

Notes

1 The Dative Case particle *ni* has the phonological form identical with the postposition *ni* "to". Instances where the Dative Case particle *ni* surfaces are observed primarily with verbs of giving, such as *ageru* "give" and *yaru* "give", as well as verbs like *au* "meet". An argument for the treatment of *ni* associated with these verbs as the Dative

Case particle rather than the postposition comes from the behavior of numeral quantifiers, as is extensively discussed in Miyagawa (1989a).

2 For the discussion of head concerning (22a) and (22b), see section 12 below.

3 One may wonder if yes–no questions in English can be formed by a transformational rule parallel to (44), which would move an auxiliary word and leave a trace behind, rather than the rule of (39). Such an approach has indeed been proposed. See Haegeman (1991), for example, for a detailed discussion of the analysis.

4 Saito's analysis of scrambling as an instance of movement is not unprecedented. For example, Harada (1977) argues that scrambled sentences should be derived by a transformational rule.

5 As for (83b, c), presumably it is not totally impossible to consider them instances of Right Dislocation, especially if a pause is given after the verb as well as after each constituent following it.

6 For an analysis of this type of rightward movement, see Saito (1985).

7 It should be pointed out that many native speakers, to various degrees, can accept sentences like (98b) and (99b). The constraints on scrambling observed in (98)–(99) are discussed in terms of the "Crossing-Over Constraint" by Kuno (1980) and Tonoike (1980a).

8 The label "cl." is the abbreviation of classifier.

9 Kuroda (1965a), Huang (1984), and N. Hasegawa (1986) all take the position that the null anaphora in the embedded object position cannot be interpreted as referential with the matrix subject. Contrary to this claim, a number of native speakers find such an interpretation perfectly acceptable.

10 Aikawa (1993) makes an interesting observation concerning the interpretation of the plural antecedent (cf. Ishii 1989; J. Abe 1991). Consider the example in (i), taken from Aikawa (1993: 30) with minor modifications.

(i) [John$_i$ to Mary$_j$]-ga zibun$_{\{i,j\}/*\{i+j\}}$-no uti-o tateta.
John and Mary-Nom self-Gen house-Acc built
a. John built his house and Mary built her house (i.e. two houses are built.)
b. *John and Mary built their house (i.e. one house is built.)

In this sentence, the antecedent of *zibun* is *John to Mary* "John and Mary". Notice that *zibun* cannot be interpreted to refer to two individuals as a group. Rather, the sentence must be construed such that *zibun* refers to *John* and *Mary* separately. That is, John built his own house and Mary built her own house. Hence, as Aikawa notes, it may be possible to assume that *zibun* must agree with a singular antecedent. For discussion regarding a different assumption, see Aikawa (1993) and the references cited there.

11 While overwhelming support for the subject orientation of *zibun* is found in a great many of the investigations on this topic, it has also been noted that the antecedent of *zibun* can be a constituent other than subject. Some of the counter-examples, like the one in (i), are discussed in Iida and Sells (1988: 23), for example.

(i) Takasi-wa Taroo$_i$-kara [Yosiko-ga zibun$_i$-o nikundeiru koto]-o kiita.
Takashi-Top Taro-from Yoshiko-Nom self-Acc was-hating fact-Acc heard
"Takashi heard from Taro that Yoshiko hated him."

12 A syntactic account for this phenomenon within the Government and Binding framework is explored in Aikawa (1993).

13 Semantics deals primarily with the meaning of linguistic expressions, as will be discussed in chapter 6. Pragmatics deals with how the role of context and the shared beliefs that the participants in a discourse have about the world affect the interpretation of a phrase or sentence.

14 English exhibits expressions like *John and myself will go*, where the reflexive pronoun, referring to the speaker, is used as a part of the subject. The distribution of a reflexive of this type, however, is rather restricted in that it occurs only in a conjoined NP. So, the single occurrence of a reflexive as referring to the speaker is still unacceptable, as the example in (138) suggests. This phenomenon in English may be related to sentences like *John and me will go*, where the occurrence of the pronoun *me* is possible in colloquial English as part of the subject only when it is conjoined, as is evidenced by the ungrammaticality of *Me will go*.

15 As was noted in note 11, however, although Reflexivization serves as a reliable diagnostic test for subjecthood in Japanese, there are some counter-examples in which *zibun* picks out a non-subject constituent. Additional examples include (i)–(ii), as discussed in Sells (1987: 453–454).

(i) [Yosiko-ga   zibun$_i$-o nikundeiru koto]-ga Mitiko$_i$-o   zetuboo-e
   Yoshiko-Nom self-Acc hate   fact-Nom Michiko-Acc desperation-to
   oiyatta.
   drove
   "The fact that Yoshiko hates self drove Michiko to desperation."

(ii) Taroo-wa Takasi$_i$-kara [Yosiko-ga   zibun$_i$-o nikundeiru koto]-o kiita.
    Taro-Top Takashi-from Yoshiko-Nom self-Acc hate   fact-Acc heard
    "Taro heard from Takashi that Yoshiko hates self."

In (i)–(ii) above the antecedents of *zibun* are not the subject: rather, they are the direct object in (i) and the object of the postposition in (ii). For the analyses of these counter-examples, see Sells (1987) and Aikawa (1993).

16 As is discussed by Miyagawa (1989a), the status of *ni* in indirect passives should be given a treatment separate from the postposition *ni* in direct passives. Compare the indirect passive sentence (i) with (171).

(i) Hahaoya-ga kodomo-ni   hutari sin-are-ta.
   mother-Nom children-Dat two   die-pass.-past
   "Two children died on their mother."

(Miyagawa 1989a: 169)

If the occurrence of *ni* in this sentence were analyzed as a postposition, as in the case of *ni* in (171), the mutual c-command condition would be violated and, as a result, the sentence should be unacceptable. The fact that the sentence is not ungrammatical suggests that *ni* in (i) above is better analyzed as Dative Case particle.

17 A thorough summary of the uniform and non-uniform accounts is found in Howard and Niekawa-Howard (1976). They discuss the various arguments that have motivated each account.

18 This construction will be discussed further in chapter 6.

19 The label "??" indicates that a sentence is not totally ungrammatical but induces some awkwardness.

20 Sells (1989) notes that the violation of the Double-*o* Constraint observed with verbal nouns accompanied by *suru* as in (217) is not as bad as in causative sentences like

(214c). In some instances, especially when the direct object of a verbal noun is scrambled to sentence-initial position, the grammaticality improves. Such an improvement, however, cannot be observed with causative sentences.

21 It might be added that the Double-*o* Constraint seems to be lenient with traversal object cases. In particular, the acceptability appears to increase when two *o*-marked NPs are not immediately adjacent to each other. For example, when *mayonaka-ni* "midnight-at" intervenes between the two *o*-marked NPs in (221), the sentence improves.

22 There is another piece of evidence for the mono-clausal status of the causatives. The *sika-nai* sequence, inducing the meaning of "only", serves as a diagnostic test for a single clause (cf. Muraki 1978; McGloin 1986). The grammaticality of the causative sentence in (i) suggests that *sika* and *nai* are within the same clause, indicating that the causative sentence consists of a single clause.

(i) Sensei-ga   Taroo-ni hon-sika   yom-ase-nakat-ta.
     teacher-Nom Taro-Dat book-SIKA read-caus.-neg.-past
     "The teacher made Taro read only books."

23 Uchida and Nakayama identify this group of verbal nouns with "activity" and "accomplishment", which are the terms that characterize the aspectual properties of verbs. We will discuss verbal classification on the basis of aspectual properties in chapter 6.

Suggested Readings

General theoretical issues in syntax: Chomsky (1957, 1965, 1981, 1986a, 1986b), Jackendoff (1977), Newmeyer (1980), Cook (1988), Radford (1988), Haegeman (1991), Napoli (1993), Webelhuth (1995), Culicover (1997), Ouhalla (1999), among many others. Newmeyer (1990) provides a summary of the historical development of syntactic theories. Those who are interested in Chomsky's theory but do not have much background in syntax might appreciate Cook (1988) for a start. Radford (1988) and Haegeman (1991) are also good textbooks for beginning students who are interested in pursuing syntactic issues. Webelhuth (1995, ed.), Culicover (1997), and Ouhalla (1999) introduce the Minimalist program. Jackendoff (1977) provides a good introduction to X′-syntax.

General issues in Japanese syntax: Kuroda (1965a), Kuno (1973, 1983), Inoue (1976a, 1978), Shibatani (1990), Tsujimura (1999, ed.). Both Kuroda (1965a) and Kuno (1973) contain crucial initial observations concerning the various phenomena in Japanese syntax. Tsujimura (1999, ed.) contains overview articles of several syntactic phenomena including scrambling, reflexives, passives, and causatives.

Phrase structure, configurationality, and scrambling: Hinds (1973), Harada (1977), Whitman (1979, 1986), Farmer (1980, 1984), Hale (1980, 1981, 1983), Saito and Hoji (1983), Lasnik and Saito (1984, 1992), Hoji (1985), Saito (1985, 1992), Fukui (1986), Miyagawa (1997), Saito and Fukui (1998), Ueyama (1998), Nemoto (1999), Takano (1999), Yatsushiro (2003). Farmer (1980, 1984) and Hale (1980, 1981, 1983) argue for the non-configurational analysis of Japanese, while

Saito and Hoji (1983), Hoji (1985), and Saito (1985) are proponents of the con-figurational approach to Japanese. Fukui (1986) and Whitman (1986) suggest alternaltive analyses. Saito (1992), Miyagawa (1997), Saito and Fukui (1998), Ueyama (1998), Nemoto (1999), Takano (1999), and Yatsushiro (2003) discuss more recent (and technical) issues of scrambling.

Numeral quantifiers: Harada (1976c), Kamio (1977), Shibatani (1977, 1978), Inoue (1978), Kuno (1978), Haig (1980), C. Kitagawa (1980), Kuroda (1980, 1983), Miyagawa (1989a), Katagiri (1991), Fukushima (1993).

Null anaphora/zero pronouns: Kuroda (1965a), Ohso (1976), Huang (1984), Kameyama (1985), N. Hasegawa (1986). N. Hasegawa (1986) and Huang (1984) discuss the distribution and interpretation of null anaphora within the Govern-ment and Binding framework while Kameyama provides an analysis under the Lexical Functional Grammar approach.

Reflexives: Inoue (1976b), N. McCawley (1976), C. Kitagawa (1981), M. Nakamura (1987), Sells (1987), Iida and Sells (1988), Katada (1990, 1991), Aikawa (1993, 1994, 1999), Iida (1996). N. McCawley (1976) presents a tradi-tional transformational approach to *zibun*, while Inoue (1976b) proposes an interpretive approach. Katada (1990, 1991) and Aikawa (1993, 1994) discuss the range of phenomena that *zibun* and *zibun-zisin* demonstrate in terms of the binding theory within the Government and Binding theory. Sells (1987) and Iida and Sells (1988) take discourse factors for *zibun* into consideration and formalize them. Iida (1996) analyzes how *zibun* is interpreted in various contexts and gives formal representations within Head-Driven Phrase Structure Grammar.

Subject: Mikami (1960), Kuno (1973), Shibatani (1977, 1978), Y. Kitagawa (1986), Tateishi (1991). These works deal with the notion of the subject as well as syntactic issues related to the subject in Japanese. The last two assume the Government and Binding theory. See Harada (1976a) for a detailed discussion of Subject Honorification as well as "Object" Honorification.

Passives: Kuroda (1965a, 1979), N. McCawley (1972), Makino (1972), Kuno (1973), Howard and Niekawa-Howard (1976), Inoue (1976a), Oehrle and Nishio (1981), Y. Kitagawa (1986), Ueda (1986b), Miyagawa (1989a, 1989b), Washio (1989/1990), H. Hoshi (1994, 1999). Howard and Niekawa-Howard (1976) provide a detailed discussion of the uniform and non-uniform accounts of passives. Oehrle and Nishio (1981) (as well as Wierzbicka 1979) contains a discussion on adversity. H. Hoshi (1999) gives an overview of syntactic issues surrounding passives. Y. Kitagawa (1986), Miyagawa (1989a, 1989b), and H. Hoshi (1994, 1999) all assume the Government and Binding framework.

Causatives: Kuroda (1965a, 1965b), Harada (1973), Kuno (1973), Shibatani (1973a, 1973b, 1976), C. Kitagawa (1974, 1980), Tonoike (1978), Farmer (1980), Miyagawa (1980, 1984, 1986, 1989a, 1999), Oehrle and Nishio (1981), Y. Kitagawa (1986), H. Hoshi (1994), Harley (1995). An overview of the topic is found in Miyagawa (1999). Kuroda (1965b), Kuno (1973), Harada (1973), Shibatani (1973a, 1973b, 1976), and C. Kitagawa (1974) all discuss the semantic differences between *o*-causative and *ni*-causative, and Tonoike (1978) provides a summary of these works. Farmer (1980), Miyagawa (1980, 1984, 1986, 1989a), Y. Kitagawa (1986), and H. Hoshi (1994) deal with issues concerning the status of causative verbs as well as the structural representation of the causative construction. Oehrle and Nishio (1981) discuss adversative causatives. (For the Double-*o* Constraint, see Harada 1973; Kuroda 1978; Poser 1981.)

Relative clauses and the *Ga/No* Conversion: Mikami (1960), Harada (1971, 1976b), Teramura (1971), Bedell (1972), J. McCawley (1976), C. Kitagawa (1982, 2005), Saito (1983), Yoshiko Matsumoto (1988, 1990, 1997), Kameshima (1989), Kuroda (1992), Miyagawa (1993), Murasugi (1993, 1994), K. Hoshi (1995), Ohara (1996, 2002), Shimoyama (1999), Matsuda (2002). Issues on relative clauses including the discussion of different types of relative clauses are found in Mikami (1960), Teramura (1971), J. McCawley (1976), C. Kitagawa (1982), and Kuroda (1992). Kameshima (1989) assumes the Government and Binding theory. Kuroda (1992), in particular, provides an extensive discussion of internally headed relative clauses. A more recent analysis of internally headed relative clauses is found in Murasugi (1993, 1994). K. Hoshi (1995), Ohara (1996, 2002), Matsuda (2002), and C. Kitagawa (2005) discuss various aspects of internally headed relative clauses from different theoretical frameworks. The *Ga/No* Conversion is discussed in Harada (1971, 1976b), Bedell (1972), Saito (1983), and Miyagawa (1993), the last two of which deal with the issue within the Government and Binding theory. Yoshiko Matsumoto (1988, 1990, 1997) investigates various pragmatic factors relevant to relative clauses in general.

Unaccusativity: Perlmutter (1978), Burzio (1981, 1986), Dubinsky (1985), Grimshaw (1987), Miyagawa (1989a, 1989b), Terada (1990), Tsujimura (1990a, 1990b, 1990c, 1991), Van Valin (1990), Levin and Rappaport Hovav (1995). Discussions of the general theoretical issues concerning unaccusativity are found in Perlmutter (1978), Burzio (1981, 1986), Grimshaw (1987), and Levin and Rappaport Hovav (1995). Issues on unaccusativity related to Japanese are discussed in the rest of the above references.

The light verb construction: Kageyama (1976–1977, 1991), Saiki (1987), Miyagawa (1987a, 1989a, 1989b), Grimshaw and Mester (1988), Sells (1989), Terada (1990), Tsujimura (1990a, 1990b), Uchida (1991), Yo Matsumoto (1992, 1996), H. Hoshi and Saito (1993), Sato (1993), Uchida and Nakayama (1993), Dubinsky (1994), H. Hoshi (1994), Miyamoto (1999).

One issue not taken up in this chapter is the syntactic behavior of wh-words. Readers who are interested in this issue should see Nishigauchi (1990, 1999) and Watanabe (1995).

EXERCISES

1   The items under list A are the linguistic terms that have been introduced in this chapter. The items in list B are examples of those terms. Match the terms in list A with appropriate examples in list B that represent them.

List A

a. dominate
b. scrambling
c. mutual c-command condition
d. null anaphora
e. adversative passive
f unaccusative verbs
g. internally headed relative clauses
h. Double-*o* Constraint

List B

a. Taroo-ga   tukutta.
   Taroo-Nom made
   "Taro made (it)."
b. *Hanako-ga   kodomo-o ninzin-o   tabe-sase-ta.
   Hanako-Nom child-Acc carrots-Acc eat-caus.-past
   "Hanako made her child eat carrots."
c. Ziroo-ga   musuko-ni sin-are-ta.
   Ziro-Nom son-by   die-pass.-past
   "Ziro was adversely affected by his son's death."
d. Hanako-ga   sensei-ni   sikar-are-ta.
   Hanako-Nom teacher-by scold-pass.-past
   "Hanako was scolded by her teacher."
e. Taroo-ga   hahaoya-ga   tukutta sebiro-o kiteiru.
   Taro-Nom mother-Nom made   suit-Acc be wearing
   "Taro is wearing the suit that his mother made."
f. Kodomo-o Hanako-ga   aruk-ase-ta.
   child-Acc   Hanako-Nom walk-caus.-past
   "Hanako made her child walk."
g. Hanako-wa [Ziroo-ga reitoo-no   keeki-o   tokasita]-no-o
   Hanako-Top Ziro-Nom frozen-Gen cake-Acc defrosted-one-Acc
   tabeta.
   ate
   "Hanako ate the frozen cake that Ziro defrosted."
h. Roopu-ga nihon-ni kireta.
   rope-Nom two-to   cut
   "The rope has been cut into two."
(For i–k, see the tree structure on the right.)
i. relation of A to F
j. relation of B to G
k. relation between B and C

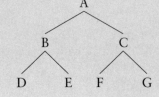

2 In the following phrase structure tree, give all the node labels that C c-commands.

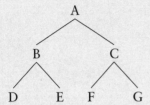

3 (This is an exercise intended for students who are familiar with Japanese.) List an appropriate sentence in Japanese that would fit each of the following structures.

a.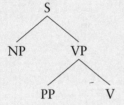

b.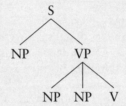

c.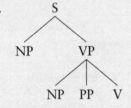

d.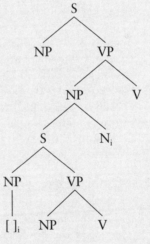

e.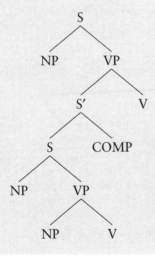

4 Draw tree diagrams for the following sentences.

   a. Etuko-ga   waratta.
       Etsuko-Nom laughed
       "Etsuko laughed."
   b. Ziroo-ga   kooen-de aruita.
       Ziro-Nom park-at   walked
       "Ziro walked at the park."
   c. Satoko-ga   Taroo-to odotta.
       Satoko-Nom Taro-with danced
       "Satoko danced with Taro."
   d. Itiroo-ga   sukiyaki-o   tukutta.
       Ichiro-Nom Sukiyaki-Acc made
       "Ichiro made Sukiyaki."
   e. Hanako-ga   takai   kuruma-o katta.
       Hanako-Nom expensive car-Acc   bought
       "Hanako bought an expensive car."
   f. Taroo-ga   honya-de   yasui hon-o   katta.
       Taro-Nom bookstore-at cheap book-Acc bought
       "Taro bought a cheap book at the bookstore."
   g. Ziroo-ga Tomoko-ni okasi-o   ageta.
       Ziro-Nom Tomoko-Dat sweets-Acc gave
       "Ziro gave Tomoko sweets."
   h. Hanako-ga   Ziroo-ni hurui zassi-o   okutta.
       Hanako-Nom Ziro-Dat old   magazine-Acc sent
       "Hanako sent Ziro an old magazine."
   i. Yosiko-ga   Taroo-ga   sensei-ni   Ginza-de atta-to   itta.
       Yoshiko-Nom Taro-Nom teacher-with Ginza-in met-COMP said
       "Yoshiko said that Taro met with his teacher in Ginza."
   j. Taroo-ga   Hanako-ga   omosiroi hon-o   katta-to
       Taro-Nom Hanako-Nom interesting book-Acc bought-COMP
       omotteiru.
       think
       "Taro thinks that Hanako bought an interesting book."
   k. Ziroo-ga Hanako-ga   katta hon-o   yonda.
       Ziro-Nom Hanako-Nom bought book-Acc read
       "Ziro read the book Hanako bought."
   l. Tomoko-ga   hometa hito-ga   gakkoo-e kita.
       Tomoko-Nom praised person-Nom school-to came
       "The person Tomoko praised came to school."
   m. Hanako-ga   Taroo-ga   honya-de   katta   zassi-o
       Hanako-Nom Taro-Nom bookstore-in bought magazine-Acc
       otooto-ni   ageta.
       brother-Dat gave
       "Hanako gave her brother the magazine that Taro bought at the
       bookstore."

5 State the explanation for the ungrammaticality of the following sentences.

    a. *Taroo-ga tabeta kinoo   oisii   ringo-o.
        Taro-Nom ate   yesterday delicious apple-Acc
        (intended meaning) "Taro ate a delicious apple yesterday."

    b. *Hanako$_i$-ga tukutta keeki-ga   zibun$_i$-no hahaoya-o
        Hanako-Nom made   cake-Nom self-Gen mother-Acc
        yorokobaseta.
        pleased
        "The cake Hanako made pleased self's mother."

    c. *Kodomo-no neko-ga awatete   sannin hasitta.
        child-Gen   cat-Nom hurriedly three   ran
        (intended meaning) "Three children's cat hurriedly ran."

    d. *Ziroo-ga musuko-o ringo-o   kaw-ase-ta.
        Ziro-Nom son-Acc   apple-Acc buy-caus.-past
        "Ziro made his son buy apples."

    e. *Suugaku-ga Taroo-ga   amari dekinai.
        math-Nom   Taro-Nom very   not competent
        (intended meaning) "Taro is not so good in math."

6 The syntactic construction called "pseudo-cleft" was introduced in relation to our discussion of causative sentences in section 8.2 of this chapter. The examples in (b)–(g) are the pseudo-cleft sentences of (a). Give an appropriate description of how to form pseudo-cleft sentences in Japanese.

    a. Taroo-ga   sono sakanaya-de maguro-o katta.
        Taro-Nom that fish store-at tuna-Acc bought
        "Taro bought tuna at that fish store."

    b. Taroo-ga   sono sakanaya-de katta-no-wa   maguro-da.
        Taro-Nom that fish store-at bought-one-Top tuna-is
        "What Taro bought at that fish store is tuna."

    c. Taroo-ga   maguro-o katta-no-wa   sono sakanaya-de-da.
        Taro-Nom tuna-Acc bought-one-Top that fish store-at-is
        "The place that Taro bought tuna is at that fish store."

    d. Sono sakanaya-de maguro-o katta-no-wa   Taroo-da.
        that fish store-at tuna-Acc bought-one-Top Taro-is
        "The person who bought tuna at that fish store is Taro."

    e. Taroo-ga   sono sakanaya-de sita-no-wa maguro-o kau-koto-da.
        Taro-Nom that fish store-at did-one-Top tuna-Acc buy-fact-is
        "What Taro did at that fish store is buy tuna."

    f. *Taroo-ga maguro-o sita-no-wa   sono sakanaya-de kau-koto-da.
        Taro-Nom tuna-Acc did-one-Top that fish store-at buy-fact-is
        "*What Taro did tuna is buy at that fish store."

    g. *Taroo-ga sono sakanaya-de maguro-o sita-no-wa   kau-koto-da.
        Taro-Nom that fish store-at tuna-Acc did-one-Top buy-fact-is
        "*What Taro did tuna at that fish store is buy."

7 In the following pairs, neither of the (b) sentences is ambiguous in the
   way that the (a) sentences are.

   (1) a. Taroo-ga   Hanako-ga   zibun-o hihansita-to   itta.
            Taro-Nom Hanako-Nom self-Acc criticize-COMP said
            "Taro said that Hanako criticized herself/him."
        b. Taroo-ga   zibun-ga Hanako-o   hihansita-to   itta.
            Taro-Nom self-Nom Hanako-Acc criticize-COMP said
            "Taro said that he criticized Hanako."

   (2) a. Taroo-ga   Hanako-ga   zibun-o sensei-ni
            Taro-Nom Hanako-Nom self-Acc teacher-to
            syookaisita-to   itta.
            introduced-COMP said
            "Taro said that Hanako introduced herself/him to the teacher."
        b. Taroo-ga   zibun-ga Hanako-o   sensei-ni
            Taro-Nom self-Nom Hanako-Acc teacher-to
            syookaisita-to   itta.
            introduced-COMP said
            "Taro said that he introduced Hanako to the teacher."

   A. Draw a syntactic tree diagram for (1b).
   B. What is the syntactic difference between the two sets of sentences
       that accounts for the fact that the (b) sentences have only one inter-
       pretation whereas the (a) sentences have two?

8 Consider the following sentences.

   (1) a. Taroo-ga   zibun-o hihansita.
            Taro-Nom self-Acc criticized
            "Taro criticized himself."
        b. Zibun-o Taroo-ga hihansita.
   (2) a. Taroo-ga   zibun-o sensei-ni   syookaisita.
            Taro-Nom self-Acc teacher-to introduced
            "Taro introduced himself to the teacher."
        b. Zibun-o Taroo-ga sensei-ni syookaisita.
   (3) a. Mieko-ga   zibun-o keibetusiteiru.
            Mieko-Nom self-Acc despise
            "Mieko despises herself."
        b. Zibun-o Mieko-ga keibetusiteiru.

   A. In the (b) sentences, one of the conditions on reflexivization in
       Japanese is apparently violated (although the sentence is unex-
       pectedly grammatical). Which condition is supposed to be observed?
       State the condition.

B. Discuss why the (b) sentences are grammatical in spite of the apparent violation of the condition mentioned in (i) above.

9 We have examined two types of causatives that are structurally contrastive. Consider the following example.

   a. Hanako$_i$-ga   kodomo$_j$-o zibun$_{i/j}$-no heya-de nak-ase-ta.
       Hanako-Nom child-Acc self-Gen   room-in cry-caus.-past

A. Discuss which type of causative (a) is, explaining why.

We have also examined various types of passives in Japanese. On the basis of (1), we can form the following causative passive sentence (ignoring the PP).

   b. Yamada-san-ga   Hanako-ni kodomo-o nak-ase-rare-ta.
       Mr Yamada-Nom Hanako-by child-Acc cry-caus.-pass.-past

B. Which type of passive is (b)? Explain why, and state the meaning of (b).

6 Semantics

In the previous three chapters we have discussed how sounds pattern, how words are formed, and how words are put together to build into grammatical sentences. However, if understanding of phonology, morphology, and syntax were all that constitutes the knowledge of a native speaker of a language, say English, the sentence in (1) would be perfectly acceptable.

(1) Colorless green ideas sleep furiously.   (Chomsky 1957: 15)

What is wrong with (1) is that the sentence is not meaningful: it disregards the meaning of each word and the meaning of combinations of words. Thus, it is critical to consider what meaning properties a word has and what meaning arises when words are combined in a particular way. The area of linguistics that is concerned with the meaning of words, phrases, and sentences is **semantics**.

Consider the Japanese cartoon that describes the following situation. In a crowded elevator of a department store, a man with a long umbrella stands behind a woman. The umbrella accidentally pokes the woman's buttocks. She thinks that the man behind her is a pervert, trying to touch her buttocks. In response to her accusatory look, he says, *gokai-desu yo* "it's *gokai*". Upon hearing the man's statement, another woman gets off the elevator. When the elevator door closes, this woman realizes that she is on the wrong floor, and utters, *gokai-zya-nai zyanai* "it's not *gokai*". A native speaker of Japanese finds this cartoon funny because she or he knows that the word *gokai* can mean either "misunderstanding" or "the fifth floor". So, in the cartoon, the man uses the word with the meaning of "misunderstanding" but the second woman interprets it as "the fifth floor".

Think about another cartoon, in English this time. At a "Pizza To Go" restaurant, a customer complains to the manager by saying, "I'd like to return this 'pizza to go with everything'." The manager responds, "What's wrong with it?" The customer goes on to say, "It doesn't go with my living room drapes." Those who find this cartoon funny or who at least understand the intention of the cartoon know that the meaning of the phrase "pizza to go with everything" can be either "pizza with everything on it that you take out" or "pizza that in appearance matches everything around it such as the living room drapes". These two instances of "word play" are not possible unless we take into consideration the meaning of each word and the meanings of certain combinations of words.

In considering meaning, it is important to distinguish between **linguistic meaning** and **speaker's meaning** (or **utterance meaning**). To illustrate the difference, consider (2).

(2)   This room is cold.

The linguistic meaning refers to what the sentence in (2) means, i.e. the room temperature is very low. This meaning is based on the meaning of each word in the sentence and the meaning as a result of putting the four words together. The same sentence can also be uttered with the hope that a listener will close the windows. In this situation, the speaker uses the sentence in order to achieve a communicative goal, i.e. a request. This is an example of speaker's meaning. Understanding speaker's meaning calls for information about the context in which an utterance is used for the purpose of communication. Because of its independent importance, the study of speaker's meaning is often dealt with in a separate area of linguistics, i.e. **pragmatics**. In this chapter we will primarily focus on linguistic meaning, introducing some relevant semantic notions and discussing their manifestations, but will briefly touch on some issues of pragmatics pertinent to Japanese in the final section.

1   Word Meaning and Sentence Meaning

As we have seen in the two cartoon examples above, word meaning and composition of word meaning may give rise to intriguing semantic phenomena. This section illustrates the semantic nature of various types of words and discusses some basic semantic notions useful for characterizing the meanings of words, phrases, and sentences.

1.1   Word/Phrase Meaning and Types of Relationships

There are different ways of characterizing word meanings, but observing relationships in meaning between two or more words can serve the purpose. When two or more words are pronounced identically but bear different meanings, they are referred to as **homonyms**. The Japanese cartoon described above illustrates an example of homonyms. The form *gokai* can be viewed as two different words each having its meaning (and each written with a different set of Chinese characters) but with identical pronunciation: one meaning is "misunderstanding" and the other is "the fifth floor". Confusion between the two meanings is the source of the comic nature of the cartoon. Such confusion can be attributed to another semantic notion, that of **ambiguity**. Ambiguity arises when a word, phrase, or sentence exhibits more than one meaning, and its source can be either lexical or syntactic. In the case of the Japanese cartoon, the source of the ambiguity is the form *gokai*, and hence it illustrates an instance of lexical ambiguity. Another example of lexical ambiguity in relation to homonyms is observed in the request, *Itte-kudasai*. A request is made by using the gerund form of a verb followed by *kudasai* "please". So, *tabete kudasai* means "please eat (it)". It turns out that the verb *iku* "go" and the verb *iu* "say" have the identical gerund form *itte*. So, if someone says *Itte-kudasai*, especially without a specific context, we would not know whether the person means "Please go" or "Please say (it)." This ambiguity results from the fact that the gerund *itte* can mean either "go" or "say". Thus, homonyms display lexical ambiguity. Additional examples of homonyms include: *kai* "shell" vs. *kai* "organization", *tika* "basement" vs. *tika* "land price", *titi* "father" and *titi* "milk/breast", and *sumu* "live" vs. *sumu* "finish". Each of these pairs has exactly the same pronunciation including the accentuation pattern, but the meaning is quite different. Note that each pair contains words of the same category, but homonyms are not subject to such a categorial restriction. For instance, *matu* "wait (verb)" vs. *matu* "pine tree (noun)" and *tikai* "near (adjective)" vs. *tikai* "oath (noun)" are equally explicatory examples of homonyms. So, the only characteristic that is shared by homonyms is the pronunciation.

If words exhibit different phonological realizations but have the same or nearly the same meaning, the words are said to be **synonyms**. For example, *kirei* "pretty" and *utukusii* "beautiful" have a very similar meaning. The verbs *hanasu* "speak" and *syaberu* "speak" also bear nearly analogous meaning although there are some occasions in which only one can be appropriate. As is the case with homonyms, synonyms do not have to share part of speech categories, as the first example mentioned above illustrates: *kirei* "pretty" is an adjectival noun while *utukusii* "beautiful" is an adjective. Hence, identical, or near identical, meaning is the minimal requirement for synonyms. Other examples of synonyms include: *kowai* "fearful" vs. *osorosii* "scary", *hasiru* "run" vs. *kakeru* "run", and *tabemono* "food" vs. *syokuryoo* "food".

The converse situation of synonyms is **antonyms**, which refer to words that have opposite meanings. Included in this group are *ookii* "big" vs. *tiisai* "small", *nagai* "long" vs. *mizikai* "short", *ue* "up" vs. *sita* "down", and *takai* "high" vs. *hikui* "low". Antonyms can be morphologically formed as well. For example, the word *antei* is an adjectival noun that means "stable", and by adding the prefix *hu-* to it, the adjectival noun meaning "unstable" is derived, as in *hu-antei*. The antonym pair, *kansei* "complete" and *mi-kansei* "incomplete", is another example that is morphologically derived. Antonyms also include opposites that can be defined by their relation to each other. For instance, pairs like *sensei* "teacher" vs. *seito* "student" and *kau* "buy" vs. *uru* "sell" are opposites not in terms of the meaning of each word but in terms of the relationship between the two individuals or events. For example, if Taro is Ziro's teacher, then Ziro is Taro's student. This type of relational opposite is subsumed under antonyms.

When a word has more than one meaning, often related to one another, it is considered **polysemous**. Examples of polysemy are abundant. The noun *kagi* has at least two meanings: (i) a key, and (ii) a clue to solve a problem. Another common noun, *te*, has a number of meaning entries in a dictionary. The following are just a few: (i) a hand, (ii) a worker, (iii) a handle, (iv) a way/means, and (v) skill. The verb *miru* appropriately illustrates the polysemous nature as well. Its meanings include: (i) look, (ii) examine, (iii) judge, (iv) look after, and (v) examine a patient. In some of these meaning entries, the relatedness is easily detected.

Notice that the English cartoon described earlier may be analyzed to present an instance of polysemy. The two meanings that lead to the comical nature of the cartoon match the following two definition entries in *Webster's New World College Dictionary* (fourth edition): one is "to be or act in harmony; fit in" and the other, appearing in *to go*, "to be taken out". This suggests, then, that just like homonyms, polysemy can be a source of lexical ambiguity. It is interesting to observe, furthermore, that the polysemous case of *go* in the English cartoon phrase, a *pizza to go with everything*, further elicits an instance of syntactic ambiguity as well. Under the first meaning, "to be in harmony", *to go with everything* forms a constituent that modifies *a pizza*; whereas under the second meaning, *a pizza to go* and *with everything* form separate constituents, and the PP *with everything* modifies the NP *a pizza (to go)*. Thus, a *pizza to go with everything* illustrates an interesting interaction between the multiple meanings of a word and their corresponding phrasal structures.

Focusing a bit more on syntactic ambiguity, let us recall an instance of syntactic ambiguity in Japanese that was discussed in chapter 5. The example introduced there is in (3).

(3) akai hon-no   hyoosi
     red   book-Gen cover

This example is syntactically ambiguous because of the two syntactic structures that can be posited for this phrase, as in (4).

(4) a.   b.

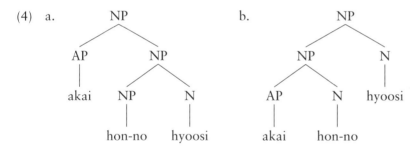

The AP *akai* "red" can modify the NP *hon-no hyoosi* "book cover" as a whole or the noun *hon* "book", depending on which interpretation is intended. When we assume the structure of (4a), the meaning of the phrase is such that the cover is red and the book itself is not necessarily red; in contrast, the structure of (4b) is associated with the interpretation of the book itself being red. Unlike the English cartoon phrase we have discussed above, the phrase in (3) does not involve lexical ambiguity: each word bears a unique meaning, and the meaning of the individual word is identical under both interpretations of (4a) and (4b). Thus, the phrase in (3) is an instance of ambiguity solely induced by its ambiguous structures.

The phrase in (5) serves as another example of syntactic ambiguity.

(5) Taroo-to Hanako-no   hahaoya
     Taro-and Hanako-Gen mother

This coordinated phrase can be represented in two different ways: *Taroo* is combined with *Hanako-no hahaoya* "Hanako's mother"; or *Taroo* and *Hanako* are conjoined and the mother belongs to both of them, "the mother of both Taro and Hanako". That is, in the former structure, the meaning is "Taro and the mother of Hanako" and the phrase refers to two individuals, while in the latter, only one person is referred to, namely, the mother, who has two children, Taro and Hanako. Again, the ambiguity in (5) cannot be traced back to homonyms or the polysemy of individual words in the phrase, but rather it is an ambiguity that is triggered by more than one syntactic way of representing the phrase, i.e. a case of syntactic ambiguity.[1]

1.2 Sentence Meaning

Chapter 4 introduced **thematic** (or semantic) **roles**. These roles specify relationships between semantic participants in events and in states that sentences describe, and thus play a crucial role in capturing sentence meaning. We have seen that agent, theme, source, goal, and experiencer comprise a major set of thematic roles. Each verb is identified with an argument structure that lists thematic roles as its required arguments, as is illustrated in (6) for the verbs *taberu* "eat" and *ageru* "give".

(6)   a.   taberu: (agent, theme)
      b.   ageru: (agent, theme, goal)

Because of the information concerning thematic roles like (6a), for instance, we are able to understand that a sentence with the verb *taberu* refers to an event in which an "agent" individual acts on a "theme" entity that undergoes a change of state or transfer. Recall that we have discussed subcategorization in chapter 5. Subcategorization lists the number and category of the constituents (besides subject), but does not say anything about the semantic relationship between them. While a subcategorization is a basis for building a sentence structure, thematic roles serve as partial input to the meaning of the sentence. Thus, thematic roles and subcategorization go hand in hand, providing semantic and syntactic information about the constituents in a sentence.

The knowledge that speakers have of their language enables them to judge sentences of their language as being true or false. The judgment of a sentence that a speaker makes based on its **truth value**, i.e. true or false, is another semantic notion relevant to sentence meaning. For example, a speaker of Japanese knows that the statement in (7) is linguistically true whereas (8) is linguistically false.

(7)   Taroo-no musuko-wa otoko-da.
      Taro-Gen son-Top   male-be
      "Taro's son is a male."

(8)   Taroo-no musko-wa onna-da.
      Taro-Gen son-Top   female-be
      "Taro's son is a female."

In (7), given the meanings of *musuko* "son" and *otoko* "male", among other things, the sentence must be true. That is, regardless of any specific context, the speaker knows that the word *musuko* means a male child, the word *otoko* means a male person, and therefore what is said in the sentence is consistent with how these words are defined. The speaker knows that the sentence in (8), on the other hand, is false not because of the specific context in which the sentence is uttered, but because the linguistic definition of the word *musuko* and that of the word *onna* are incompatible with each other: that is, a male child cannot be a female individual.

Some sentences are necessarily true, like (7), and others are necessarily false, like (8), regardless of non-linguistic considerations. There are, however, yet other sentences whose truth values depend on particular circumstances which may vary according to the world we live in. Consider the sentence in (9).

(9)   Taroo-wa Hanako-no   sensei-da.
      Taro-Top Hanako-Gen teacher-be
      "Taro is Hanako's teacher."

Unlike the cases in (7)–(8) above, the truth value of (9) is determined only upon consideration of the circumstances. For example, if there is a situation in which there is a teacher–student relation between Taro and Hanako, and in that relation Taro is the teacher while Hanako is the student, the sentence is true. If, in contrast, there is a situation in which there is a teacher–student relation between Taro and Hanako, but in that relation Taro is the student while Hanako is the teacher, then the sentence is false. So, the truth value of this sentence is dependent upon these circumstances. These circumstances, on the basis of which the truth value is determined, are called **truth conditions**.

Another illustration of truth conditions is provided by (10).

(10)   Ziroo-wa tyomusukii-ga   gengo-gakusya-da-to   omotte-iru.
       Ziro-Top Chomsky-Nom linguistic-scholar-be-COMP think-be
       "Ziro thinks that Chomsky is a linguist."

This sentence is true if there is an individual called Ziro who actually thinks that Chomsky is a linguist. Under the condition that there is no such individual (i.e. Ziro), in contrast, the sentence is false. Thus, the speaker's ability to judge whether a sentence is linguistically true or false, or to determine the circumstances under which a statement is true or false, comes from the speaker's knowledge of sentence meaning.

We have discussed types of relationships in word meaning in the previous section. Similarly, there are types of semantic relations between sentences based on truth in such a way that the truth value of one sentence may sometimes lead to the truth value of another. One such truth relation is **entailment**. X is said to entail Y when the relation between the two is such that if X is true, then Y is also true. To see how an entailment relation holds, let us examine the two sentences in (11)–(12).

(11)   Taroo-ga   Ziroo-o   korosita.
        Taro-Nom Ziro-Acc killed
        "Taro killed Ziro."

(12)   Ziroo-ga   sinda.
        Ziro-Nom died
        "Ziro died."

If (11) is true, then (12) must also be true: if Taro killed Ziro, it is necessarily true that Ziro died. Thus, (11) entails (12).

Another important semantic relation is **presupposition**. An assumption is often made in order for a statement to be appropriate. Such an assumption is called presupposition. Consider the relationship between the two sentences in (13)–(14).

(13)   Hanako-no   otto-wa   amerikazin-da.
        Hanako-Gen husband-Top American-be
        "Hanako's husband is American."

(14)   Hanako-ni   otto-ga   iru.
        Hanako-Dat husband-Nom be
        "Hanako has a husband."

(13) is said to presuppose (14): if the statement is made that Hanako's husband is American, it is assumed or implied that Hanako has a husband.

We can observe an interesting implication of truth relations to word meaning. When we consider "translation equivalents" of verbs cross-linguistically, as is most typically done in English–Japanese dictionaries and the like, many critical semantic differences between languages compared are often not recorded, understandably leading us to believe that they are "equivalents". Take an example of the English verb *drown* and its Japanese "equivalent" *oboreru*. A semantic difference between the two verbs can be illuminated by examining entailment relations, as in (15)–(16).

(15)   a.   John drowned in a river.
        b.   John died.

(16)   a.   Taroo-ga   kawa-de oboreta.
              Taro-Nom river-in   "drowned"
              "Taro 'drowned' in the river."
        b.   Taroo-ga   sinda.
              Taro-Nom died
              "Taro died."

In English, if John drowned, it automatically follows that he died. Thus, (15a) entails (15b). The same relation, on the other hand, does not always hold in Japanese. The truth of (16a) does not guarantee the truth of (16b): Taro could be dead or alive in (16a). So, (16a) does not entail (16b). In order for the entailment to hold in parallel with (15), the verb *oboreru* in (16a) needs to form a compound verb with verb *sinu* "die", deriving *obore-zinu* "drown (to death)". Thus, English and Japanese verbs with nearly identical meaning do not necessarily encode the same entailment relations.

A similar contrast in the availability of entailment relations between English and Japanese is frequently found in morphologically related transitive and intransitive pairs as discussed in chapter 4, such as *moyasu-moeru* "burn", *tokasu-tokeru* "melt", and *wakasu-waku* "boil". Compare the Japanese sentence pair in (17) with its English counterpart in (18).

(17) a. Taroo-wa otiba-o   moyasita. (transitive)
          Taro-Top fallen leaves-Acc burned
          "Taro burned the fallen leaves."
      b. Otiba-ga   moeta. (intransitive)
          fallen leaves-Nom burned
          "The fallen leaves burned."

(18) a. John burned the leaves.
      b. The leaves burned.

As is the case with (16), an entailment relation does not hold in (17): the truth of (17a) does not automatically guarantee the truth of (17b). (18a), in contrast, entails (18b), as expected. In fact, the lack of entailment relations in Japanese in pairs like (16) and (17) makes seemingly contradictory sentences like (19)–(20) fully acceptable (although there are speakers who entirely reject this pattern) (Ikegami 1985; Kageyama 1996; Tsujimura 2003). Needless to say, their English counterparts do not make sense at all. (19)–(20) are adopted from Ikegami (1985).

(19) Wakasita-kedo, wakanakatta
      boiled-but   didn't boil
      "I boiled it, but it didn't boil."

(20) Reito-syokuhin-o tokasita-kedo, tokenakatta.
      frozen-food-Acc melted-but   didn't melt
      "I melted the frozen food, but it didn't melt."

Japanese is not an isolated language in making available this pattern between sentences that is apparently paradoxical: languages that exhibit a similar phenomenon include Chinese, Hindi, Russian, Tamil, and Thai, although the range of phenomena and exact details may vary from language to language (Tai 1984; Singh 1991; Pederson 1995; Tsujimura 2003; Koenig and Muansuwan 2005).

1.3   Metaphors and Idioms

We have thus far examined word meaning, principally considering what words mean. If what words literally mean is all that the speaker has to be concerned with, the sentences in (21) should strike us odd or anomalous.

(21) a. Yosiko-wa syokuba-no <u>hana</u>-da.
          Yosiko-Top work place-Gen flower-be
          "Yoshiko is a flower in the office."

      b. Yamada-san-wa <u>sokonasi</u>-da.
          Yamada-Top bottomless-be
          "Yamada is bottomless."

      c. Sono otoko-ga ziken-no <u>kagi</u>-da.
          that man-Nom case-Gen key-be
          "That man is a key to the case."

      d. Kyoo-wa <u>asi</u>-ga nai-kara kaisya-ni ikenai.
          today-Top leg-Nom not have-because company-to can't go
          "I don't have legs today, so I can't go to the company."

Oddity would arise if we attempted to understand the meaning of the under-lined words literally. A native speaker of Japanese, however, finds no anomaly here because she or he knows that the underlined words are not meant to be taken literally. When we try to describe individuals and entities, we often refer to other individuals and entities that have similar characteristics. The under-lined words in (21) are interpreted non-literally for that purpose. This type of **non-literal** use of words leads to **metaphors**. In (21a) *hana* literally means "flower", and since Yoshiko is human while flowers are plants, the literal inter-pretation of the word generates a senseless statement. The word, instead, serves as a metaphor to describe the beauty of Yoshiko at her workplace. *Sokonasi* in (21b) is a noun that is literally used to describe something does not have a bottom, such as swamp. As a metaphor, it can refer to an unlimited degree. In this particular case, the metaphor is used to describe Yamada's capacity to drink alcoholic beverages, i.e. that he drinks a lot. In (21c) the primary meaning of *kagi* "key" refers to an essential instrument for opening locked objects such as doors, but this essential nature is metaphorically extended to describe a person: the man is regarded as a critical clue to solve a case. The literal interpretation of the first clause in (21d) does not make sense because a person cannot be handicapped without legs just today. Instead, *asi* in this sentence is metaphoric-ally used to refer to a transportation means like a car. Metaphors are ubiquitous in Japanese as well as other languages. Many English examples are so commonly used that we often may not realize they are metaphors. Those examples include: *time is money*, his son is *a monster*, time *flies*, native *tongue*, his answer is *fishy*, and many more.

It is often difficult to distinguish between metaphors and polysemy. Recall that we have earlier considered the word *kagi* as illustrating polysemy, having at least the following two meanings: (i) a key, and (ii) a clue to solve a problem. We have treated the second as one of multiple meanings that the word has. The same word appears in (21c), and we have treated it as an instance of a meta-phor, i.e. a non-literal interpretation of the word. Neither approach should be deemed incorrect, because the distinction is often extremely difficult to make between the two situations. That is, many of the multiple meanings associated with a single word, i.e. an instance of polysemy, may be considered metaphoric-ally extended meanings.

Another instance of the non-literal meaning of a word is observed with **idioms**. Examples of idioms in English and Japanese are given in (22)–(23).

(22) a. pull someone's leg "make fun of or fool by playing on a person's credulity"
b. kick the bucket "die"
c. look up to "respect"
d. spill the beans "divulge secret information"
e. give someone a break "stop treating harshly, critically"

(23) a. te-o kiru "cut one's connection with"
hand-Acc cut
b. asi-o hakobu "walk to, visit"
legs-Acc move
c. te-ni noru "be fooled by someone's trick"
hand-by get on
d. otya-o nigosu "evade a situation"
tea-Acc make muddy
e. keti-o tukeru "speak ill of"
stinginess-Acc attach

An idiom is a phrase whose meaning cannot be understood by putting together the literal meaning of each word. Instead, idiomatic meaning renders itself as a semantic property specific to a particular combination of words. The non-literal nature of idioms, however, does not mean that idioms like those in (22)–(23) do not have the literal meanings based on the literal meaning of each word. The English phrase in (22a), for example, can be interpreted literally or idiomatically. Literally it simply means to undergo a physical action of pulling by applying the movement to someone's leg. Idiomatically, by contrast, it means making fun of someone. Notice that this idiomatic interpretation cannot be deduced by putting together the literal meanings of the words that the phrase consists of. Similarly, (23a) can literally mean injuring a hand by cutting it, putting together the literal meaning of *te* "hand" and that of *kiru* "cut". As an idiom, however, it means breaking a relationship.

1.4 Deixis

When we hear someone say "dog" or "eat", we know that a specific kind of animal or a specific kind of action is referred to. What about expressions like *yesterday* and *two days ago*? The exact date that is referred to as *yesterday* or *two days ago* all depends on when the time of the speech is. If the speech occurs on Monday, *yesterday* would refer to a particular Sunday that immediately precedes the Monday, for example. Personal pronouns such as *I* and *you* present similar situations. These pronouns refer to particular individuals under a particular context, and depending on that context, the individuals picked out could be *Mary*, *Steve*, *Taro*, *Hanako*, etc. The semantic concept underlying such a shift in reference depending on various contexts is called **deixis**.

Deixis is described by Fillmore (1975: 38) as aspects of language that are called for "when the sentences in which they occur are understood as being anchored in some social context, that context defined in such a way as to identify the time during which the communication act is performed". The examples of *I* and *you* are instances of personal deixis, and expressions like *yesterday* and *two days ago* are examples of temporal deixis. There are two areas of Japanese in which the notion of deixis is particularly important: (i) demonstrative words, and (ii) verbs of giving and receiving.

Japanese exhibits a set of demonstrative words that are regarded as examples of spatial deixis, and they are used in reference to the speaker. The basic criteria are (i) near the speaker, (ii) slightly removed from both the speaker and the listener, or slightly removed from the speaker, but close to the listener, and (iii) far from both the speaker and the listener. These three spatial notions are systematically represented by words whose initial morae are *ko-*, *so-*, and *a-*, respectively. Normally added to this three-way division are interrogative words, whose initial mora is *do-*. Because of such a regular semantic–phonological correlation, these demonstrative words are called *ko-so-a-do* words. For each series, there are several members, as is illustrated in (24). The basic spatial deictic notions that distinguish among *ko*, *so*, and *a* apply to each category. (25)–(30) provide example sentences in which these deictic terms are used.

(24)

		ko-	*so-*	*a-*	*do-*
a.	*independent noun*	kore "this one"	sore	are	dore "which one"
b.	*pronominal modifier*	kono "this (N)"	sono	ano	dono "which (N)"
c.	*location*	koko "here"	soko	asoko	doko "where"
d.	*direction*	kotira "this direction"	sotira	atira	dotira "which direction"
e.	*kind (pronominal)*	konna "this kind of (N)"	sonna	anna	donna "what kind of (N)"
f.	*manner (adverbial)*	koo "in this manner"	soo	aa	doo "how"

(25)   <u>Kore</u>-o   itutu kudasai.
       this-Acc five   please give me
       "Please give me five of these."

(26)   <u>Sono</u> ringo-wa   ikura-desu-ka.
       that   apple-Top how much-be-Q
       "How much is that apple?"

(27)   <u>Asoko</u>-ni   ookina tatemono-ga   aru.
       over there-at big   building-Nom there is
       "There is a big building over there."

(28) Kotira-ni   kite-kudasai.
      this direction-to come-please
      "Please come here (= to this direction)."

(29) Sonna   mono-wa iranai.
      that kind thing-Top not need
      "I don't need that kind of thing."

(30) Koo   kaite-kudasai.
      in this way write-please
      "Please write it this way."

These *ko-so-a-do* words are extended to something more abstract than physical distance. A typical example of such an abstract application of spatial deixis includes the use of demonstrative words, particularly the *so-* and *a*-series, to refer to an individual or an object mentioned in discourse. Consider the examples in (31)–(32).

(31) A: Sakki   depaato-de   atta otoko-no hito,   dare?
          a while ago department store-at met male-Gen person who
          "Who is the man who you met at the department store a while ago?"
      B: Aa, ano hito-wa   daigaku-no toki-no   tomodati.
          Oh that person-Top college-Gen time-Gen friend
          "Oh, that person is a friend from my college days."

(32) A: Asita   atarasii gakusei-ga   kimasu-yo.
          tomorrow new   student-Nom will come
          "A new student will come tomorrow."
      B: Sono gakusei-mo nihongo-o   osieru-n-desu-ka.
          that   student-also Japanese-Acc teach-is it the case?
          "Is that student also going to teach Japanese?"

Unlike the sentences in (25)–(30), the actual location of the speaker and the physical distance between the speaker and the individuals referred to in (31)–(32) are not relevant, but rather, the presence or absence of the knowledge shared by the speaker and the listener plays a more essential role in accounting for the demonstratives. Although the characterization of the *so*-series and *a*-series in this discoursal function and the distinction between the two are often hard to determine, Kuno (1973: 290) gives the explanation in (33).

(33) a. The *a*-series is used for referring to something (at a distance either in time or space) that the speaker knows both he and the hearer know personally or have shared experience in.
      b. The *so*-series is used for referring to something that is not known personally to either the speaker or the hearer or has not been a shared experience between them.

In (31), assuming that A was present when B met with a friend from her college days, both the speaker (B) and the listener (A) share the experience of encountering B's friend. This background makes it appropriate to use *ano*, according to (33a). In (32), on the other hand, the speaker (B) has no personal knowledge of a new student, so the use of *sono* is consistent with (33b). It also follows from (33) that the converse use of *ano* and *sono* in (31)–(32) makes the sentences very odd.

Another illustration of deixis can be found in verbs of giving and receiving, as is described in detail in Kuno (1973), Kuno and Kaburaki (1977), Jorden with Noda (1988), and Shibatani (1990), among others. In Japanese there are several verbs that correspond to the English verbs *give* and *receive*, and the distinction among them invokes diverse factors that include the following: (i) whether a given transfer is to be described as a giving or receiving event, (ii) where the speaker stands in the giving/receiving event, and (iii) what the social status or the relationship is of the participants of the giving/receiving event. Verbs of giving and receiving describe transfer of possession events, but the selection of "give" or "receive" depends on from whose perspective a transfer event is perceived. Moreover, consideration of the social status of event participants serves as a factor indispensable to the unique selection of the verb. Such a social consideration, in particular, may be viewed as an instance of social deixis (Finegan 1994). We will discuss giving and receiving verbs in Japanese not simply because a verb inventory of this sort displays a pattern rather different from and richer than the English counterparts, but also because the use of giving and receiving verbs in Japanese illustrates an intricate mixture of various deictic elements.

There are at least five Japanese verbs that correspond to the English verb *give* and two Japanese verbs that correspond to the English verb *receive*. Those giving verbs include *sasiageru*, *ageru*, *yaru*, *kudasaru*, and *kureru*; and the receiving verbs are exemplified by *itadaku* and *morau*. The event described by these verbs is that of the transfer of some material that always involves a giver and a receiver, along with the material itself, as the participants of the transfer. It is logically possible, then, to view a given transfer either as a giving event or as a receiving event. For ease of description, let us assume that the speaker is one of the participants in a given transfer.

There are two situations in which the speaker can view the transfer as a giving event. In one situation the speaker is the giver, and the event can be expressed in English as "I give something to someone." Under this situation *sasiageru*, *ageru*, and *yaru* are used. In the other situation the speaker is the receiver, and the corresponding English sentence would be "Someone gives me something." In this second situation, *kudasaru* and *kureru* are chosen.

As for the situation in which the speaker views the transfer as receiving, there is only one instantiation: that is, the speaker is almost always the receiver, and it can be described in English as "I receive something from someone." In this situation, *itadaku* and *morau* are used. It is extremely rare in Japanese to say a sentence corresponding to the English sentence, "Someone receives something from me."

We have thus far discussed giving and receiving situations, centering on the speaker as a participant of the transfer. As it turns out, however, there is another set of participants that should be grouped together with the speaker, with respect to the use of giving and receiving verbs. The participants relevant to our discussion may be characterized as what Jorden with Noda (1988) call the speaker's "in-group". The term **in-group** is a rather deictic word itself, and the group of individuals to be referred to as the speaker's "in-group" varies depending on the social status of the individuals in relation to that of the speaker. For example, let us assume a company in which the speaker holds her or his employment. Internal to the company, the speaker forms her or his own in-group, and hence, she or he would treat the president of the company as an out-group person. On the other hand, in the presence of members of another company, the president of the company to which the speaker belongs would be considered to be in the speaker's in-group, while a member of another company would be considered an out-group member.

Given the notion of in-group, then, we can restate the three situations given earlier, replacing the speaker with "the speaker and her or his in-group". A new set of descriptions is summarized in (34)–(36).

(34) Situation Viewed as Giving
When the speaker or the speaker's in-group is the giver (the situation corresponding to "I, or my in-group, give something to someone"), use: *sasiageru, ageru, yaru.*

(35) Situation Viewed as Giving
When the speaker or the speaker's in-group is the receiver (the situation corresponding to "Someone gives me, or my in-group, something"), use: *kudasaru, kureru.*

(36) Situation Viewed as Receiving
When the speaker or the speaker's in-group is the receiver (the situation corresponding to "I, or my in-group, receive something from someone"), use: *itadaku, morau.*

Given the descriptions of the giving and receiving verbs above, how are they distinguished in each category? The next thing we need to take into consideration is the social status of the other participants in relation to that of the speaker. Let us examine each case of (34)–(36).

I **The speaker or the speaker's in-group = the giver "I, or my in-group, give someone something"**

In this case the speaker or her or his in-group is the giver. If the receiver's status is higher than the speaker's, with respect to age and/or social status, *sasiageru* is used. If the receiver's status is equal to the giver's, either *ageru* or *yaru* is used, with a preference for *ageru* over *yaru*. When the receiver is lower in status than the speaker, again, either *ageru* or *yaru* is used, although it seems that women tend to use *ageru* more often than *yaru* in this situation. Examples of these three situations are given in (37)–(42). The symbols ">", "=", and "<" represent higher, equal, and lower status, respectively.

A   the receiver > the speaker: *sasiageru*

(37)   (Watasi-ga)   sensei-ni   hon-o   sasiageta.
       (I-Nom)   teacher-Dat book-Acc gave
       "I gave a book to my teacher."

(38)   Imooto-ga   sensei-ni   hana-o   sasiageta.
       younger sister-Nom teacher-Dat flower-Acc gave
       "My younger sister gave flowers to the teacher."

B   the receiver = the speaker: *ageru, yaru*

(39)   (Watasi-ga) tomodati-ni eiga-no   ken-o   ageta.
       (I-Nom)   friend-Dat   movie-Gen ticket-Acc gave
       "I gave my friend a movie ticket."

(40)   Haha-ga   tomodati-no Yamada-kun-ni susi-o   ageta.
       mother-Nom friend-Gen   Yamada-Dat   sushi-Acc gave
       "My mother gave sushi to my friend Yamada."

C   the receiver < the speaker: *yaru, ageru*

(41)   (Watasi-ga) imooto-ni   hurui tokei-o   yatta/ageta.
       (I-Nom)   younger sister-Dat old   watch-Acc gave
       "I gave my younger sister an old watch."

(42)   Otooto-ga   hana-ni   mizu-o   yatta.
       younger brother-Nom flower-Dat water-Acc gave
       "My younger brother watered the flowers." (Lit.: "My younger brother
       gave water to the flowers.")

When the verb *sasiageru* is used, the giver is the speaker, as in (37), or someone in the speaker's in-group, e.g., *imooto* "younger sister" in (38), while the
receiver in these examples is the teacher, who is considered to have a higher social
status than the giver. (39)–(40) represent the equal relation between the giver,
i.e. the speaker or her or his in-group, and the receiver: in (39) the receiver is the
speaker's friend; and in (40) the giver is in the speaker's in-group, i.e. her or his
mother, and the receiver is the speaker's friend. In (40), although the speaker's
mother may not maintain an equal status with the speaker's friend, because of
the age difference, for instance, the speaker's mother is a member of the speaker's
in-group, and crucially, the relation between the speaker's mother and the speaker's
friend is viewed like that between the speaker and the speaker's friend.[2] Hence,
it is essential to keep in mind that where the participants of a given exchange
stand, in terms of their social status, is determined from the speaker's point of
view. The examples in (41)–(42) illustrate the relation in which the receiver's
status is lower than that of the speaker or the speaker's in-group, i.e. the giver.
The status lower than the speaker's can include inanimate objects like flowers,

as in (42). As was pointed out above, female speakers tend to use *ageru* in this situation, thereby making no difference between categories B and C.

II The speaker or the speaker's in-group = the receiver "someone gives me, or my in-group, something"

Under this category, the exchange is still regarded as giving, but in this case the speaker or the speaker's in-group is the receiver. The verbs that are suitable for this situation are *kudasaru* and *kureru*. When the giver is socially higher than the speaker or the speaker's in-group, *kudasaru* is used; otherwise, *kureru* is selected. That is, when the giver's status is equal to or lower than that of the speaker or the speaker's in-group, *kureru* is appropriate. Examples of these two situations are given in (43)–(47).

A   the giver > the speaker: *kudasaru*

(43)   Sensei-ga   watasi-ni tizu-o   kudasatta.
        teacher-Nom I-Dat   map-Acc gave
        "My teacher gave me a map."

(44)   Sensei-ga   musuko-ni hon-o   kudasatta.
        teacher-Nom son-Dat   book-Acc gave
        "The teacher gave my son a book."

B   the giver = or < the speaker: *kureru*

(45)   Tomodati-ga watasi-ni zisyo-o   kureta.
        friend-Nom I-Dat   dictionary-Acc gave
        "My friend gave me a dictionary."

(46)   Tanaka-san-ga   imooto-ni   okasi-o   kureta.
        Mr Tanaka-Nom younger sister-Dat sweets-Acc gave
        "(My friend) Mr Tanaka gave my younger sister sweets."

(47)   Imooto-ga   watasi-ni hana-o   kureta.
        younger sister-Nom I-Dat   flower-Acc gave
        "My younger sister gave me flowers."

In (43)–(44) the giver is a teacher, who is regarded as socially higher than her or his students and their parents. In (43) the giver is the teacher and the receiver is the speaker, and hence *kudasaru* is used. (44) presents an interesting case in that the speaker herself or himself does not directly participate in the exchange: the giver in this case is the teacher while the receiver is the speaker's son, i.e. the speaker's in-group. It can readily be seen that the teacher's status is higher than that not only of the speaker's son but also of the speaker herself or himself. It should be remembered that it is the speaker's status in relation to the other participant of the exchange that is crucial to the distinction of giving and receiving verbs. So, even if the speaker is older than the teacher, for instance, the teacher's status is socially considered higher than the speaker's, the giver still has a higher status than the speaker, and hence *kudasaru* is used. The category under IIB represents situations in which the giver is equal to or lower than the speaker or the speaker's in-group in social status. (45) is straightforward: the speaker's friend, the giver, has a status equal to that of the speaker, the receiver. Accordingly, *kureru* is used. (46) is another instance in which the speaker does not directly participate in the exchange. The receiver is in the speaker's in-group, her or his younger sister, and the giver is the speaker's friend. Although the friend may not have a status equal to that of the speaker's younger sister, i.e. the receiver, the friend maintains an equal status to that of the speaker and hence *kureru* is used.

(47) is also an interesting example. Thus far, we have considered the speaker's family members as her or his in-group. In the case of (47), however, the speaker's younger sister is treated as belonging to the speaker's out-group since the speaker herself or himself is the receiver, forming her or his own in-group. Thus, the speaker's younger sister is lower in status than the speaker because of the age difference, and as a result, *kureru* is used. The contrast between (46), in which the speaker's younger sister is viewed as the speaker's in-group, and (47), where the speaker's younger sister is treated as the speaker's out-group, also provides an excellent example illustrating that the notion of deixis is in effect: that is, the treatment of the speaker's younger sister varies depending on particular contexts.

III The speaker or the speaker's in-group = the receiver "I, or my in-group, receive something from someone"

A major difference of this category from the previous two is that a given exchange is viewed as receiving in this case, rather than giving. This category involves only one situation in which the speaker or her or his in-group is the receiver. When the speaker or the speaker's in-group is the giver, the situation is viewed only as giving, i.e. the situation that has been described under the category I above. That is, it is extremely rare, or impossible, to describe a receiving event as the Japanese equivalent of "Someone receives something from me or my in-group."

When the giver is higher in status than the speaker or her or his in-group under this category, *itadaku* is used. Otherwise, *morau* is the verb that describes the receiving event. These two situations are illustrated by the examples in (48)–(52).

A   the giver > the speaker: *itadaku*

(48)   Watasi-wa sensei-ni/kara   eigo-no   sinbun-o   itadaita.
       I-Top   teacher-Dat/from English-Gen newspaper-Acc received
       "I received an English newspaper from my teacher."

(49)   Imooto-ga   sensei-ni/kara   nihon-no tizu-o   itadaita.
       younger sister-Nom teacher-Dat/from Japan-Gen map-Acc received
       "My younger sister received a map of Japan from the teacher."

B   the giver = or < the speaker: *morau*

(50)   Watasi-wa tomodati-ni/kara zassi-o   moratta.
       I-Top   friend-Dat/from   magazine-Acc received
       "I received a magazine from my friend."

(51)   Ane-ga   tomodati-no Tanaka-san-ni/kara   mezurasii
       older sister-Nom friend-Gen   Mr Tanaka-Dat/from rare
       kitte-o   moratta.
       stamp-Acc received
       "My older sister received a rare stamp from my friend Tanaka."

(52)   Watasi-wa imooto-ni/kara   hana-o   moratta.
       I-Top   younger sister-Dat/from flower-Acc received
       "I received flowers from my younger sister."

As these examples show, the giver is marked either with *ni* or with *kara* in these situations that are viewed as receiving. A teacher, i.e. the giver, in (48) is of a higher status than the speaker, who is the receiver, and the receiving event is described with the verb *itadaku*. The receiving situation expressed in (49) does not physically involve the speaker as a participant of the exchange. However, the speaker is related to the receiver by the in-group relation of the receiver to the speaker. Since the teacher is higher than the speaker or her or his sister in social status, *itadaku* is again appropriate.

In (50) the giver is the speaker's friend, who maintains an equal relation to that of the speaker, and thus *morau* is sufficient. The receiver in (51) is the speaker's in-group, rather than the speaker herself or himself. Although the speaker's older sister might be considered higher in status than the speaker's friend, Tanaka, because of the sister's greater age, what is crucial here is the relation between the speaker herself or himself and the friend Tanaka. Since the speaker and Tanaka maintain a compatible relation, *morau* is used.

(52) presents a situation parallel to (47), above, in that the speaker's younger sister is considered the speaker's out-group in this example. Since the younger sister is "lower" than the speaker with respect to age, *morau* is appropriate.

We have observed that the use of giving and receiving verbs presents an instance of deixis, in that the choice of a particular verb requires a specific contextualization that calls for the speaker's viewpoint of a given exchange, in/out-group difference, and relative social status among the participants including the speaker, among others. A summary of this categorization, among the giving and receiving verbs, is given in (53).

(53)   Exchange Viewed as Giving

       I   The speaker or the speaker's in-group = the giver
            "I, or my in-group, **give** someone something"
            A   the receiver > the speaker: *sasiageru*
            B   the receiver = the speaker: *ageru, yaru*
            C   the receiver < the speaker: *yaru, ageru*

II The speaker or the speaker's in-group = the receiver
    "someone **gives** me, or my in-group, something"
    A the giver > the speaker: *kudasaru*
    B the giver = or < the speaker: *kureru*

Exchange Viewed as Receiving

III The speaker or the speaker's in-group = the receiver
     "I, or my in-group, **receive** something from someone"
     A the giver > the speaker: *itadaku*
     B the giver = or < the speaker: *morau*

We have above observed that the verbs of giving and receiving in Japanese display an interesting case of deixis, and that their variety, as well as the several factors that contribute to the determination of their specific use, instantiate a system rather distinct from the verbs of giving and receiving in English. What is, furthermore, intriguing with these verbs is that the same set can serve as auxiliary verbs. When they are used as auxiliary verbs, they suffix to the gerund form of a verb. The meaning associated with such a construction is parallel to the meaning of giving and receiving that they denote as full-fledged verbs. The event denoted by a gerundive verb, to which a giving or receiving verb is suffixed, is perceived as a favor or benefit, and the favor or benefit of the event denoted by the gerundive verb is considered the target of an exchange or transfer.[3] Moreover, the deictic aspects of the verbs summarized in (53) apply to this case as well.

The examples illustrating the auxiliary use of the giving and receiving verbs are provided below, according to the categories adopted in (53). Let us begin with the giving situation in which the giver is the speaker or the speaker's in-group.

I **The speaker or the speaker's in-group = the giver**
   "I, or my in-group, give someone something"

A the receiver > the speaker: *sasiageru*

(54) Watasi-ga sensei-ni zyuusyo-o   kaite-sasiageta.
      I-Nom teacher-Dat address-Acc write-gave
      "I wrote the address for my teacher."

(55) Haha-ga   sensei-ni   keeki-o   tukutte-sasiageta.
      mother-Nom teacher-Dat cake-Acc make-gave
      "My mother made a cake for my teacher."

B the receiver = the speaker: *ageru, yaru*

(56) (Watasi-ga) tomodati-ni zisyo-o   misete-ageta.
      (I-Nom)   friend-Dat dictionary-Acc show-gave
      "I showed my friend a dictionary."

(57) Titi-ga   Yamada-kun-no kuruma-o naosite-ageta.
    father-Nom Yamada-Gen   car-Acc   fix-gave
    "My father fixed (my friend) Yamada's car (for him)."

C   the receiver < the speaker: *yaru, ageru*

(58) Musume-ni   hon-o   yonde-yatta/ageta.
    daughter-Dat book-Acc read-gave
    "I read a book for my daughter."

(59) Otooto-ga   tori-no   mizu-o   kaete-yatta.
    younger brother-Nom bird-Gen water-Acc change-gave
    "My younger brother changed the water for the bird."

Notice that the giving and receiving verbs are used as auxiliary verbs suffixed to the gerundive form of a verb. The event denoted by each verb is considered a beneficial act by the "giver" for the "receiver". In (54), for instance, the speaker's writing the address for the teacher is viewed as a transfer of a favor from the speaker to the teacher. In this case, the teacher is higher than the speaker in social status and therefore *sasiageru* is suffixed to the gerund of the verb *kaku* "write".[4] Similarly, in (55), the cake-making event is regarded as a transfer of a favor directed from the speaker's in-group, i.e. the speaker's mother, to the teacher. In this case, the teacher occupies a socially higher status than the speaker's mother (who is considered to be in the speaker's in-group), and thus *sasiageru* is suffixed to the verb that denotes the actual event. The remaining examples also parallel the range of data that we have seen illustrating giving and receiving verbs as full-fledged verbs.

The two other situations parallel to II and III of (53), when the giving and receiving verbs are used as auxiliary verbs, are exemplified in (60)–(69).

II **The speaker or the speaker's in-group = the receiver**
    "someone gives me, or my in-group, something"

A   the giver > the speaker: *kudasaru*

(60) Sensei-ga   watasi-ni tizu-o   kaite-kudasatta.
    teacher-Nom I-Dat   map-Acc write-gave
    "My teacher drew a map for me."

(61) Sensei-ga   musuko-ni hon-o   misete-kudasatta.
    teacher-Nom son-Dat   book-Acc show-gave
    "The teacher showed my son the book."

B   the giver = or < the speaker: *kureru*

(62) Tomodati-ga (watasi-ni) zitensya-o   kasite-kureta.
    friend-Nom (I-Dat)   bicycle-Acc lend-gave
    "My friend lent me his bicycle."

(63)   Tanaka-san-ga imooto-ni   okasi-o   tukutte-kureta.
       Tanaka-Nom younger sister-Dat sweets-Acc make-gave
       "(My friend) Mr Tanaka made sweets for my younger sister."

(64)   Imooto-ga   watasi-ni hana-o   katte-kureta.
       younger sister-Nom I-Dat   flower-Acc buy-gave
       "My younger sister bought me flowers."

III   The speaker or the speaker's in-group = the receiver
       "I, or my in-group, receive something from someone"

A   the giver > the speaker: *itadaku*

(65)   Watasi-wa sensei-ni/kara   tegami-o okutte-itadaita.
       I-Top   teacher-Dat/from letter-Acc send-received
       "I had my teacher send a letter to me (on my behalf)."

(66)   Musuko-ga sensei-ni   sakubun-o   naosite-itadaita.
       son-Nom   teacher-Dat composition-Acc correct-received
       "My son had his teacher correct his composition (for him)."

B   the giver = or < the speaker: *morau*

(67)   Watasi-wa tomodati-ni/kara zyuusyo-o   osiete-moratta.
       I-Top   friend-Dat/from   address-Acc teach-received
       "I had my friend let me know the address."

(68)   Ane-ga   Tanaka-san-ni   conpyuutaa-o naosite-moratta.
       older sister-Nom Mr Tanaka-Dat computer-Acc fix-received
       "My older sister had (my friend) Mr Tanaka fix her computer (for her)."

(69)   Watasi-wa imooto-ni   kaimono-ni itte-moratta.
       I-Top   younger sister-Dat shopping-to go-received
       "I had my younger sister go shopping (for me)."

In summary, the use of giving and receiving verbs as auxiliaries suffixed to gerundive forms exactly parallels the use of those verbs as full-fledged verbs.

1.5   Mimetics

The discussion in this chapter thus far assumes that the words we use are associated with a definable set of meanings, as we see with word definitions in a dictionary. Mimetics present a challenging situation to such a view. Mimetic words are symbolic, whether what are symbolized are sounds, manner, or psychological states, and thus rephrasing them often amounts to giving a common situation or context in which a given mimetic word can be used, frequently accompanied by mimicking sounds or gestures (Diffloth 1972). The challenge also stems from the fact that some mimetics are not restricted to particular word categories, such as nouns and verbs, and therefore the "meaning" of a mimetic word varies depending on what category it is used in a sentence.

Consider the mimetic word *don*, which appears with *-to* to function as an adverb. The meaning descriptions of *don* found in an extensive mimetic dictionary (Kakehi et al. 1996: 269–271) are given in (70)–(71) along with examples.

(70) A dull, resonant exploding sound; a dull, resonant sound made when relatively hard objects collide with force.
    a. <u>Don-to</u> naru tabini, hanabi-wa oozora-ni tairin-no hana-o sakaseru.
        "With each <u>boom</u>, fireworks burst in the night sky like huge flowers blooming."
    b. Sumoo-no keiko-de, otooto-desi-ga ani-desi-no mune-o megakete <u>don-to</u> butukatta.
        "During the sumo wrestling practice, the junior trainee <u>ran crashing</u> into his senior's chest."

(71) The manner of doing something to a great degree.
    Benrida-kara-to itte kurezittokaado-o atikoti-de tukatteiru-to, ato-de <u>don-to</u> tuke-ga mawattekite taihenna koto-ni naru.
    "If you run around using your credit card everywhere simply because it's convenient, then you're going to be in real trouble later on when the bills show up <u>with a vengeance</u>."

The description in (70) symbolizes the sound that is associated with the mimetic word. As the example sentence in (70b) shows, however, the sound symbolism can be extended in such a way that the sound does not necessarily accompany the depicted situation: whether the sound is present or not, the mimetic in this example has the effect of presenting a symbolic image of a forceful collision. The "definition" in (70) is more concrete than that in (71), but they are both within the range of *don*'s symbolic image as perceived by the speakers.

Another example can be seen with *hirahira*. This mimetic word can be used as an adverb, a verb, and a noun, and its "meaning" varies accordingly. Its descriptions and their corresponding examples are given in (72)–(74), adapted from Kakehi et al. (1996: 522–524).

(72) hirahira-to (Adv.): The manner in which small, light, thin and usually dry objects, typically leaves, flutter or fall fluttering; the manner in which a flame wavers.
    a. Sakura-no hana-ga kaze-ni <u>hirahira-to</u> tiru sama-wa, nantomo ienu huzei-ga aru.
        "There is something aesthetically very pleasing about the way cherry blossoms <u>flutter down</u> in the breeze."
    b. . . . Kayako-wa, tiisai te-o <u>hirahira-to</u> hurimasita.
        ". . . Kayako <u>fluttered</u> her little hand."

(73) hirahira-suru (V): to flutter
      . . . kakkoku-no kokki-ga kaze-ni <u>hirahira-site</u>, . . .
      ". . . the national flags of all the participating countries . . . <u>were flapping
      gently</u> in the wind . . ."

(74) hirahira (N): lace frill
      . . . suso-to sode-ni <u>hirahira</u>-no tuita kawaii huku-o katte-yatta.
      ". . . I bought her a pretty dress with <u>frills</u> on the sleeves and hem."

While the "meaning" of each instance of *hirahira* varies, the wide gamut is still
within the range that the symbolic image of the mimetic word allows according to the speaker's perception. In other words, unlike conventional words with
specific categories, symbolic images are the foundation of mimetics, from which
their semantic characterizations in precise instances are drawn.[5]
   A further difference between mimetics and non-mimetics with respect to
their meaning properties is that the former may interact with morphology more
closely than the latter. Reduplicated mimetics may have a semantic repercussion
especially when a reduplicated mimetic and its base are both available.[6] In many
situations like that, a reduplicated mimetic word often describes a repeated action
or a continuous state of what is depicted by its base. The contrast is shown in
(75)–(76) (taken from Hamano 1998: 105).

(75) a. Toogarasi-ga   sita-ni   <u>pirit</u>-to kita.
          hot pepper-Nom tongue-to   came
          "The hot pepper (momentarily) burned my tongue."
      b. Hiyake   sita tokoro-ga   <u>piripiri</u> suru.
          sun burn did place-Nom   do
          "I have a (continuous) burning pain in the sun-burned places."

(76) a. Namida-ga <u>porot</u>-to koboreta.
          tear-Nom   rolled down
          "A teardrop rolled down [the cheek]."
      b. Namida-ga <u>poroporo</u> koboreta.
          tear-Nom   rolled down
          "Tears rolled down [the cheek]."

As these pairs illustrate, the morphological process of reduplication displays an
interesting contribution to the interpretation of mimetics.
   In a similar vein, it has been shown that the nature of consonants and vowels
that comprise a mimetic word contributes to the determination of the semantic
scope to which a common symbolic image applies. This line of investigation
has been extensively followed by Hamano (1986, 1998). Hamano (1998: 172–
173), for instance, examines individual consonants and their respective ranges
of symbolism in C_1VC_2V-based mimetic adverbs as in (77)–(78). (C = consonant;
V = vowel.) For example, the mimetic adverb *patapata* contains the C_1VC_2V
base *pata*, where C_1 and C_2 correspond to /p/ and /t/, respectively.

(77) C_1

p	taut surface	light; small; fine
b	taut surface	heavy; large; coarse
t	lack of surface tension; subduedness	light; small; fine
d	lack of surface tension; subduedness	heavy; large; coarse
k	hard surface	light; small; fine
g	hard surface	heavy; large; coarse
s	non-viscous body; quietness	light; small; fine
z	non-viscous body; quietness	heavy; large; coarse
h	weakness; softness; unreliability; indeterminateness	
m	murkiness	
n	viscosity; stickiness; sliminess; sluggishness	
y	leisurely motion; swinging motion; unreliable motion	
w	human noise; emotional upheaval	

(78) C_2

p, b	explosion; breaking; decisiveness
t	hitting of a surface; coming into close contact; complete agreement
k	opening; breaking up; swelling; expanding; puffing out; emission from inside; surfacing; in–out movement
s	soft contact; friction
h	breath
m	?
n	bending; elasticity; unreliability; lack of force; weakness
y	sound from many sources; haziness; childishness
w	softness; faintness; haziness
r	rolling; fluid movement

According to Hamano, C_1 represents the tactile nature of the object, and C_2 the type of movement. Examples that illustrate the correlation between the consonant selection and its symbolism are given in (79) (Hamano 1998: 170).

(79)　a.　<u>kusukusu</u> warau.
　　　　　　　　 laugh
　　　　　"to giggle softly"
　　　b.　<u>sukusuku</u> sodatu
　　　　　　　　　 grow
　　　　　"to grow healthy　without a problem"

The /k-s-/ combination corresponds to "friction on a hard surface", while the /s-k-/ sequence means "involvement of a smooth surface in an outward movement", leading to "smooth growth". These semantic characteristics, thus, separate mimetics from more conventional word classes.

2 Tense and Aspect

When we describe a situation like John's running, numerous sentences can serve the purpose, including those in (80).

(80) a. John will run tomorrow.
     b. John ran yesterday.
     c. John is running.
     d. John has run.

The basic situation of John's running is expressed in all the sentences in (80), but they are different with respect to temporal interpretations. (80a–c) are contrastive in regard to the time in which the event is located: it is placed in the future in (80a), in the past in (80b), and in the present or at the time of utterance in (80c). The division is based on how the event is related to the time of speech, and this concept is called **tense**. Tense is generally partitioned into three: present (at the time of speech), future (after the time of speech), and past (before the time of speech). (80c–d) are also contrastive but in a different way: in these two sentences, the event of John's running is viewed internally in terms of continuity and termination. This mode of viewing a situation is **aspect**. Comrie (1976) defines these concepts as follows: tense "locates the time of a situation relative to the situation of the utterance" (p. 2), while aspects "are different ways of viewing the internal temporal constituency of a situation" (p. 3). Since temporal information is crucial to sentence meaning, both tense and aspect are considerable ingredients in linguistic meaning (cf. Reichenbach 1947; Comrie 1976).

Discussions of tense and aspect in Japanese have traditionally centered on morphemes such as *-(r)u* and *-ta* for tense, and *-te iru* for aspect, as grammatical markers. This section follows the tradition and examines their semantic roles, but will also include illustrations of how aspectual properties are encoded internally to verbs (lexical aspect) and how they are represented in the form of compounds (aspectual verbs). Throughout the section, our discussions will be restricted to simple sentences.

2.1 Tense

In chapter 4 we have referred to the verbal suffixes *-(r)u* and *-ta*, as well as their equivalents for adjectives and nouns, as non-past and past tense markers, respectively, but the temporal information that these two morphemes convey is actually more complicated than those labels may suggest (Soga 1983; Ogihara 1999). Their analyses thus have been controversial between the view that they are tense markers and the one that they are aspect markers (Ogihara 1999). In fact, because of the temporal properties they exhibit and their controversial analysis, they have received different names, including present vs. past, non-past vs. past, and imperfective vs. perfective. In the remainder of this chapter and throughout the book, the terms "non-past" and "past" will continue to be used for convenience to refer to *-(r)u* and *-ta* and their equivalents for adjectives and nouns; and the terms "present", "past", and "future" will refer to times in relation to the time of utterance, as is characterized above.

Let us first examine *-(r)u* (for verbs), *-i* (for adjectives), and *-da* (for nouns). These non-past markers refer to states or events in the present or the future. Examples of these situations are given in (81)–(84).

(81) Present State
      a. Tanaka-san-wa suugaku-ga yoku deki-ru.
          Tanaka-Top   math-Nom well is competent
          "Mr Tanaka is strong in math."
      b. Kono uti-wa   totemo huru-i.
          this house-Top very   old
          "This house is very old."
      c. Hanako-wa daigakusei-da.
          Hanako-Top college student-is
          "Hanako is a college student."

(82) Future State
      Musuko-ga   daigaku-ni iku-node, rainen   kane-ga   i-ru.
      my son-Nom college-to go-because next year money-Nom need
      "Because my son will start college, I will need money next year."

(83) Present Event
      Watasi-wa sore-ga   ii-to   omo-u.
      I-Top   that-Nom good-COMP think
      "I think that it's good."

(84) Future Event
      Asita   tomodati-to eiga-ni   ik-u.
      tomorrow friend-with movie-to go
      "I will go to a movie with a friend tomorrow."

These examples illustrate the fact that the non-past markers in Japanese are sometimes called such because they serve as locating states and events in the present or future time, i.e. times other than the past.

There are at least two more situations for which the non-past marker *-(r)u* may be used: to describe habitual events and to give instructions and directions, such as in cook books. Examples of these situations are given in (85) and (86), respectively.

(85) Watasi-wa maiasa   go-mairu hasir-u.
      I-Top   every morning 5-mile   run
      "I run 5 miles every morning."

(86) a. Zairyoo-o   mazeawase-ru.
          ingredients-Acc mix
          "Mix the ingredients."
      b. Remonziru-o   kuwae-ru.
          lemon juice-Acc add
          "Add lemon juice."

As the adverb *maiasa* "every morning" indicates in (85), the sentence refers to a routine of running 5 miles, an event repeated every morning. Those in (86) are typical sentences used as cooking instructions; they contrast with their English counterparts, in which imperative sentences are customarily used.

   The intriguing range of situations to which the past tense markers *-ta* (for verbs), *-katta* (for adjectives), and *-datta* (for nouns) refer are wide enough to lead to controversy over the determination of the nature of these markers. To start with, relatively straightforward situations they describe are states, events, and habits in the past. An example of each is given in (87)–(89).

(87) Past State
      a. Musuko-wa tyuugaku-no   toki suugaku-ga deki-ta.
          my son-Top middle school-Gen when math-Nom was competent
          "My son was strong in math when he was in middle school."
      b. Kono mati-wa   mukasi   totemo ooki-katta.
          this   town-Top in old days very   was big
          "This town was very big in the old days."
      c. Hanako-wa Mitiko-to   kodomo-no toki   tomodati-datta.
          Hanako-Top Mitiko-with child-Gen   when were friends
          "Hanako was friends with Mitiko in child days."

(88) Past Event
      Hanako-wa kyonen igirisu-e   it-ta.
      Hanako-Top last year England-to went
      "Hanako went to England last year."

(89) Past Habit
      Gakusei-no toki   yoku sanzi-made   benkyoo-si-ta.
      student-Gen when often 3 o'clock-until studied
      "When I was a student, I often studied until 3:00 a.m."

   While the function of *-ta* for referring to events in the past as in (88) seems straightforward, its interpretation is in fact the center of a controversy. Nakau (1976), for one, considers the sentence in (90) ambiguous between the past tense reading and the present perfect interpretation that resembles the English *have V-ed*.

(90) Boku-wa ano hon-o   yon-da.
      I-Top   that book-Acc read
      a. "I read that book (yesterday)."
      b. "I have (already) read that book."

                                          (adapted from Nakau 1976: 427)

Under the past tense interpretation, i.e. (90a), the event of book-reading took place at some time prior to the speech time, and adverbs indicating the past time such as *kinoo* "yesterday" or *sensyuu* "last week" may be added to the sentence to highlight this interpretation. (90) is also compatible with the interpretation in (90b), focusing on the present state resulting from having read the book. This reading is reinforced by adverbs like *moo* "already", the same type of adverbs that co-occur with the English present perfect *have V-ed*. It should be pointed out that the latter interpretation of *-ta* analyzes the morpheme as an aspectual, rather than tense, marker. Evidence for the dual status of *-ta* has been shown by the way that question–response patterns differ in the two situations. Compare (91) and (92), adapted from Nakau (1976: 427–428).

(91) a. Kimi-wa **kinoo**   ano hon-o   **yon-da**-ka.
          you-Top yesterday that book-Acc read-Q
          "Did you read that book yesterday?"
      b. Un, (boku-wa **kinoo**   ano hon-o)   **yon-da**.
          yes I-Top   yesterday that book-Acc read
          "Yes, I did (I read that book yesterday)."
      c. Iya, (boku-wa **kinoo**   ano hon-o)   **yomana-katta**.
          no I-Top   yesterday that book-Acc didn't read
          "No, I didn't (read that book yesterday)."

(92) a. Kimi-wa **moo** (**sudeni**) ano hon-o   **yon-da**-ka.
          you-Top already   that book-Acc read-Q
          "Have you already read that book?"
      b. Un, (boku-wa **moo** (**sudeni**) ano hon-o)   **yon-da**.
          yes I-Top   already   that book-Acc read
          "Yes, I have (already read that book)."
      c. Iya, (boku-wa **mada** ano hon-o)   **yonde-ina-i**.
          no I-Top   yet   that book-Acc haven't read
          "No, I have not (read that book) yet."

In (91a) the adverb *kinoo* "yesterday" is included to highlight the past event reading. (92a), on the other hand, is intended to bear the present perfect interpretation, facilitated by the adverb *moo* "already/yet", and refers to the present state resulting from a past event. The contrast to be emphasized according to the proponents of the dual status of *-ta* is (91c) and (92c). In (91c) the verb appears with the past tense marker *-ta*, agreeing with *kinoo* "yesterday", whereas *-i* in *yonde-ina-i* in (92c) is in the non-past tense, supporting the claim that the described state applies to the present. Some, however, say in refutation that if *-ta* should be analyzed as the present perfect marker, the *-(kat)ta* in (91c) should also be so analyzed, allowing for the adverbial substitution of *mada* "(not) yet" for *kinoo* "yesterday" (Ogihara 1996, 1999). The sentence would look like (93).

(93) *Boku-wa **mada** ano hon-o   **yomana-katta**.
        I-Top   yet   that book-acc didn't read
       "(intended) I haven't read that book yet."

Contrary to the prediction, the adverb and the verbal morphology are not compatible with each other. This latter camp maintains that -*ta* is a past tense marker with a modified notion of tense to extend to instances like those in (92a–b) (Ogihara 1999).

Returning to additional functions that -*ta* exhibits, there are at least three other situations of interest. First, -*ta* can refer to a situation in the immediate future where an expected completion or realization of an event or state is readily foreseeable. This corresponds to what Soga (1983) calls "future completed state", and may be viewed as analogous to the English progressive, as in "A bus is coming." Examples in (94), taken from Soga (1983: 65–66), illustrate the function of -*ta*.

(94) a. Aa, dekita,   dekita.
          oh got done got done
          "Oh, (it's) coming, (it's) coming." (Lit. "(It's) got done, (it's) got done."
          May be used when one is making something and its completion is near.)
      b. Yoku natta,   yoku natta.
          well became
          "(It's) getting better, (it's) getting better." (Lit. "(It) got well, (it) got
          well." May be used by a doctor, for example, to a patient who is
          getting better.)
      c. Kita! Kita!
          Came
          "(He) is coming, (he) is coming!/There he comes!" (Lit. "(He) came,
          (he) came.")

Consider (94c), for example. This can be used to refer to an approaching bus at a bus station or stop, although once the bus comes to halt, (94c) is no longer appropriate (McClure 2000). Recall that the present tense marker -*ru* refers to a future event, so the situation in which a bus is approaching a bus stop can also be described with -*ru*. Thus, (95) and (94c) can both refer to the same situation.

(95) Basu-ga   kuru-yo.
      bus-Nom come
      "A bus is coming/will come (soon)."

Second, facts that are relevant to the present or future moment can be stated with -*ta* as a sign of the speaker's attempt to recall them. The examples in (96) illustrate this situation.

(96) a. Kyoo-wa   kayoobi-datta-ne.
          today-Top Tuesday-was-isn't it
          "Today is Tuesday, isn't it?"
      b. Asita   eigo-no   tesuto-ga at-ta?
          tomorrow English-Gen test-Nom there was
          "Will there be an English test tomorrow?"

The past tense for the purpose of recall is also observed in English, as is frequently used in utterances like "I'm sorry, but what <u>was</u> your name again?" and "The test <u>was</u> tomorrow, right?"

Finally, the past tense marker *-ta* can appear in commands, as in (97).

(97) a. Kutta kutta.
          eat   eat
          "Eat up!"
      b. Doita   doita.
          Get out of the way get out of the way
          "Get out of the way!"
      c. Kaetta kaetta.
          leave leave
          "Leave!"

This type of command is considered fairly strong and abrupt, and as all the examples in (97) illustrate, the verbal form is regularly repeated twice.

2.2 Aspect

As we have seen in the definition by Comrie earlier, aspect is considered to be the various ways of viewing a situation with respect to internal constituency, so questions like whether an event is ongoing or completed become an issue. Such aspectual information can be encoded by varied modes in Japanese: (i) by grammatical morphemes, (ii) internally to individual verbs, and (iii) by compounds.

2.2.1 Grammatical Aspect

The most notable and well-investigated grammatical marker of aspect is *-te iru*: the first part of this complex, *-te*, corresponds to the gerundive form of a verb (Kindaichi 1976b; Teramura 1982; Soga 1983; Jacobsen 1992; McClure 1994; Ogihara 1999; Shirai 2000; among many others). The primary meanings of *-te iru* are the progressive and resultative (state), but to them the habitual interpretation is sometimes added. Examples of each situation are given in (98)–(100).

(98) Progressive
      a. Kodomo-ga waratte-iru.
          child-Nom   laugh
          "A child is laughing."
      b. Satosi-ga   susi-o   tabete-iru.
          Satosi-Nom sushi-Acc eat
          "Satoshi is eating sushi."

(99) Resultative
      a. Sakana-ga sinde-iru.
          fish-Nom   die
          "The fish is dead."
      b. Kuruma-ga tomatte-iru.
          car-Nom   stop
          "The car is parked."

(100)   Habitual
      a.   Watasi-wa maiasa   go-mairu hasitte-iru.
           I-Top   every morning 5-mile   run
           "I run 5 miles every morning."
      b.   Ano gakusei-wa yoku nihongo-no   teepu-o kiite-iru.
           that student-Top often Japanese-Gen tape-Acc listen
           "That student often listens to Japanese tapes."

In all the examples above, the verbs occur in the gerundive form, *waratte*, *tabete*, *sinde*, *tomatte*, *hasitte*, and *kiite*, immediately followed by the verb *iru* "be".

In (98) the verbs in the *-te iru* form induce the progressive meaning: the examples are construed such that the activities of laughing and eating sushi are in progress at the present, speech time. Under this reading, the V-*te iru* complex corresponds to the English progressive *be V-ing*.

In (99), by contrast, *-te iru* refers to a state resulting from an event that has occurred at some point, and for that reason, this type of interpretation is sometimes termed "perfect" in the sense of Comrie (1976) (cf. Jacobsen 1992), although we will continue using "resultative", following the literature. (99a), for instance, assumes that the fish died at some unspecified point in the past, and refers to the situation that describes the state of the fish being dead. Similarly, (99b) describes the state of the parked car as a result of its having stopped. Crucially, these sentences make no reference to the process of the fish dying or the process of the car being parked. That is, they are not the equivalents of English sentences "The fish is dying" and "The car is being parked." This is why the resultative interpretation of *-te iru* is often considered comparable to the English present perfect *have V-ed* in that it refers to a state resulting from an event and the state remains to hold true now. As we will discuss in section 2.2.2 below, not all verbs in the *-te iru* form are associated with both the progressive and resultative meanings, and the determination as to which verbs can bear which interpretation is largely related to the aspectual property that individual verbs have (lexical aspect).

The *-te iru* in (100) means that the event described by the verb is repeated everyday as a present habit. Recall that the non-past tense marker *-(r)u* also refers to habitual events, as was illustrated by (85), repeated below.

(85)   Watasi-wa maiasa   go-mairu hasi-ru.
      I-Top   every morning 5-mile   run
      "I run 5 miles every morning."

These sentences are identical except for the verbal morphology, and both describe practically the same habit of running 5 miles every morning. Although the semantic difference between the two is very subtle, Teramura (1982: 129) explains that the routine described with *-te iru* is of a more temporary nature, implying that it started at some time in the past but it is possible that it stops at some time in the future. This is why habitual events in the *-te iru* form often sound more natural with adverbial phrases like *kono goro* and *saikin* "recently".

According to Teramura, the non-past tense marker -*(r)u*, on the other hand, suggests that the habit described refers to a situation in which the same pattern of action is repeated without giving the impression that it started some time in the past or that it may stop in the future. Thus, habitual situations described with -*(r)u* may be regarded as more permanent.

The grammatical marker of aspect, -*te iru*, interacts with the tense markers, -*(r)u* and -*ta*. We have in fact already observed its interaction with the non-past marker in the range of examples in (98)–(100). That is, the progressive, resultative, and habitual situations in those examples are temporally placed at the time of speech. Their past counterparts are given in (101)–(103).

(101) Progressive
    a. (Kinoo)   kodomo-ga waratte-ita.
        (yesterday) child-Nom laugh
        "A child was laughing (yesterday)."
    b. (Kinoo)   Satosi-ga   susi-o   tabete-ita.
        (yesterday) Satosi-Nom sushi-Acc eat
        "Satoshi was eating sushi (yesterday)."

(102) Resultative
    a. (Kinoo)   sakana-ga sinde-ita.
        (yesterday) fish-Nom die
        "The fish was dead (yesterday)."
    b. (Kinoo)   kuruma-ga tomatte-ita.
        (yesterday) car-Nom   stop
        "The car was parked (yesterday)."

(103) Habitual
    a. (Ano koro) watasi-wa maiasa   go-mairu hasitte-ita.
        (that time) I-Top   every morning 5-mile   run
        "(Back then) I used to run 5 miles every morning."
    b. (Mukasi)   ano gakusei-wa yoku nihongo-no   teepu-o
        (in the past) that student-Top often Japanese-Gen tape-Acc
        kiite-ita.
        listen
        "(In the past) that student often used to listen to Japanese tapes."

The temporal location of the situations described in (101)–(102) becomes clear once temporal phrases like *kinoo* "yesterday" are added to them. (101) describes a child's laughing or Satoshi's consumption of sushi as in progress at some time yesterday. Similarly, in (102), the state of the dead fish or the state of the parked car, resulting from the event of the fish having died and of the car having been parked respectively, existed at some time yesterday. The examples in (103) describe past habitual events, the time adverbials that imply a long span of time such as *ano koro* "those days, back then" and *mukasi* "in the past" making the situation more explicit: running and listening to tapes were habitual activities that continued at least for some time in the past.

Another grammatical aspect marker is *-te aru* (Martin 1975; Teramura 1982; Miyagawa 1989a; Yo Matsumoto 1990). The *-te aru* form semantically resembles the resultative interpretation of *-te iru* in that they both refer to a state resulting from an action. Some examples with *-te aru* are shown in (104)–(106).

(104)   Denki-ga   tukete-aru.
        lights-Nom turn on
        "The lights have been turned on." (Lit: "The lights are in the state of having been turned on.")

(105)   Bangohan-ga tukutte-aru.
        dinner-Nom make
        "Dinner has been made." (Lit: "Dinner is in the state of having been made.")

(106)   Syatu-ga   aratte-aru.
        shirt-Nom   wash
        "The shirt has been washed." (Lit: "The shirt is in the state of having been washed.")

As is the case with the resultative *-te iru*, *-te aru* assumes the existence of an action from which a state resulted. An important difference between the resultative *-te iru* and *-te aru* is that the latter further assumes the existence of a volitional agent that was engaged in the action. The difference between (104) and (107), thus, is such an assumed agent.

(107)   Denki-ga   tuite-iru.
        light-Nom   turn on
        "The lights are on."

Both (104) and (107) describe the state in which the lights are on, but while (104) additionally suggests that there is an individual who actually turned the lights on, (107) has no mention of the presence or absence of such an individual.

Besides the semantic role as a grammatical aspect marker, *-te aru* exhibits properties that reflect an important interface between syntax and semantics. One of the restrictions on the formation of *-te aru* is that the verb must be transitive and its argument structure consists of agent and theme. Once this condition on the type of the verb is met, the subject of the *-te aru* sentence always corresponds with the theme (Miyagawa 1988, 1989a), while the agent does not have a syntactic realization. That is, the *-te aru* sentences are constructed based on transitive verbs, but end up in the intransitive structure. For this reason, sentences with *-te aru* are often called "intransitivizing resultative construction" (Martin 1975; Miyagawa 1989a; Jacobsen 1992).[7] Examples in (108)–(110) illustrate the relation between the transitive argument structure and the intransitive syntactic structure triggered by the *-te aru* morphology, corresponding to (104)–(106).

(108) a. tukeru "turn on": (agent, theme)
 b. Hanako-ga   denki-o tuketa.
   Hanako-Nom light-Acc turned on
   "Hanako turned on the lights."
 c. Denki-ga   tukete-aru.
   lights-Nom turn on
   "The lights have been turned on."

(109) a. tukuru "make": (agent, theme)
 b. Otto-ga   bangohan-o tukutta.
   husband-Nom dinner-Acc made
   "My husband made dinner."
 c. Bangohan-ga tukutte-aru.
   dinner-Nom make
   "Dinner has been made."

(110) a. arau "wash": (agent, theme)
 b. Yosio-ga   syatu-o aratta.
   Yosio-Nom shirt-Acc washed
   "Yoshio washed the shirt."
 c. Syatu-ga   aratte-aru.
   shirt-Nom wash
   "The shirt has been washed."

All the verbs in (108)–(110) are transitive with agent and theme as their arguments. Their agent arguments are marked with the Nominative Case for subjects and the theme arguments are marked with the Accusative Case for direct objects, as the (b) sentences demonstrate. The same set of verbs takes the *-te aru* morphology in the (c) sentences, where the theme arguments, which serve as the direct objects in the (b) sentences, are the sole arguments that have their syntactic realization, i.e. subjects with the Nominative Case.

Recall that in chapter 4 we discussed transitive and intransitive verb pairs like *taosu* (Vt)–*taoreru* (Vi) "fell/fall" and *naosu* (Vt)–*naoru* (Vi) "repair/be repaired". It is interesting to note that transitive and intransitive verb pairs reflect a minimum contrast concerning *-te iru* and *-te aru* constructions. Since the *-te aru* construction requires that a base verb be transitive, this condition excludes the intransitive verbs of morphologically related verb pairs from entering into the construction. The *-te iru* construction, however, does not impose a constraint on transitivity, and the intransitive counterparts can still take the *-te iru* morphology. As a result, the *-te aru* construction with transitive verbs and the *-te iru* construction with intransitive counterparts have virtually the same meaning: both refer to states resulting from action. The only difference is the presence or absence of an implied agent who undertook the actions. This situation holds throughout the morphologically related transitive and intransitive verb pairs. The parallel situation between the two constructions and corresponding verb selection is illustrated in (111)–(112) for the *taosu–taoreru* pair and (113)–(114) for the *tukeru–tuku* pair.

(111) taosu "fell": (agent, theme)
     a. Yosio-ga   ki-o   taosita.
        Yosio-Nom tree-Acc felled
        "Yoshio felled a tree."
     b. Ki-ga   taosite-aru.
        tree-Nom fell
        "A tree has been felled (by someone)."

(112) taoreru "fall": (theme)
     a. Ki-ga   taoreta.
        tree-Nom fell
        "A tree fell."
     b. Ki-ga   taorete-iru.
        tree-Nom fall
        "A tree is down."

(113) tukeru "turn on": (agent, theme)
     a. Hanako-ga   denki-o tuketa.
        Hanako-Nom light-Acc turned on
        "Hanako turned on the lights."
     b. Denki-ga   tukete-aru.
        light-Nom turn on
        "The lights have been turned on (by someone)."

(114) tuku "turned on": (theme)
     a. Denki-ga   tuita.
        light-Nom turned on
        "The lights are turned on."
     b. Denki-ga   tuite-iru.
        light-Nom turn on
        "The lights are on."

The verbs in (111) and (112) share the identical root *tao-*, to which additional morphemes are suffixed to form a transitive verb and its intransitive counterpart, respectively. Both of the (b) sentences refer to a state resulting from the action described in the corresponding (a) sentences. While (111b) and (112b) depict the state of a tree being on the ground, for instance, they differ in that the former assumes an agent who brought about the state of the tree whereas the latter does not. The verbs in (113) and (114) are also morphologically related, sharing the root *tuk-*. The transitive verb takes the *-te aru* construction while its intransitive counterpart appears in the *-te iru* construction, and the resulting sentences have very similar meanings except that only the former assumes the presence of the agent leading to the described state. These examples manifest a systematic pattern in the way syntax and semantics interact via morphological operations. We will return to the relationship between the *-te iru* interpretations and morphologically related transitive and intransitive verb pairs in section 2.2.2.

Finally, the last grammatical aspect we will examine is *-te simau* (Teramura 1982), which emphasizes the completion of an action. Consider the examples in (115)–(117).

(115) Piza-o   zenbu hitoride   tabete-simatta.
       pizza-Acc all   by myself eat
       "I ate all the pizza by myself."

(116) Hon-o   issatu yonde-simatta.
       book-Acc one   read
       "I read the whole book."

(117) Kono sigoto-o   gozi-madeni site-simatte-kudasai.
       this   work-Acc 5 o'clock-by do-please
       "Please complete this work by 5 o'clock."

Completing a task generally presupposes that it takes some time to complete it. Furthermore, in order to complete a task, it ought to have a natural ending point. So, the nature of semantic compatibility that the *-te simau* construction requires restricts the range of verbs that can appear with *-te simau*. For example, verbs that describe actions that take place instantaneously, like *sinu* "die" and *tuku* "arrive", and verbs that refer to actions that do not have natural ending points, such as *hasiru* "run" and *warau* "laugh", are not compatible with *-te simau* in the completion sense.[8]

2.2.2 Lexical Aspect

We have thus far observed that aspect is marked grammatically in a variety of morphological forms, as is exemplified by *-te iru*, *-te aru*, and *-te simau*. Aspectual properties are also encoded internally to verbs (or VPs), and researchers have used this lexical aspect to classify verbs. For English, Vendler (1967) and Dowty (1979) argue that verbs display different ranges of sensitivity to the various linguistic environments in which they appear, and that they should be categorized into four distinct classes according to their aspectual properties. The four classes are States, Activities, Accomplishments, and Achievements, and their examples are illustrated in (118).

(118)

States	*Activities*	*Accomplishments*	*Achievements*
know	run	paint a picture	recognize
believe	walk	make a chair	spot
have	swim	deliver a sermon	find
desire	push a cart	draw a circle	lose
love	drive a car	push a cart	reach
		recover from illness	die

(Dowty 1979: 54)

States refer to static situations. For example, the sentence *Mary knows French* describes the static situation that refers to Mary's knowledge of French. It does not involve any dynamic movement or change. Activities, on the other hand, involve dynamic movements. They further imply continuous movements that do not bear natural endpoints. For instance, the sentence *John swam* expresses that the swimming event homogeneously continued, and that the event of swimming does not have a natural endpoint. Like Activities, Accomplishments refer to dynamic events that last a certain amount of time, but unlike Activities, they imply that the events reach natural endpoints. It requires a certain amount of time to paint a picture, for instance, and yet, when the painting event reaches an endpoint, we can say that we painted a picture. Similar to this situation is Achievement. Both Accomplishments and Achievements have natural endpoints, and yet the difference between them is that Accomplishments imply that the event before reaching the endpoint requires a certain amount of time while Achievements refer to instantaneous events. For example, the event of reaching a summit takes place instantaneously. Of course, one would repeat the climbing activity to get to the top, but such an activity is not part of what *reach a summit* denotes. The climbing activity is what we know one would have to do in the process of reaching a summit, based on our knowledge of the world. Thus, the linguistic expression *reach a summit* refers to an instantaneous event.

Besides these inherent aspectual differences that the four classes of verbs and VPs display, as Dowty (1979) shows, they exhibit diverse distributions in various linguistic environments. We will make reference to a few of these environments. First, all the classes except States appear in the progressive form. This is demonstrated in (119).

(119) a. *John is loving Mary. (State)
       b. John is running. (Activity)
       c. John is painting a picture. (Accomplishment)
       d. John is reaching the summit. (Achievement)

Second, adverbials that imply the duration of time, such as *for an hour*, can co-occur with Activities but not with Accomplishments; whereas adverbials referring to a point in time, like *in an hour*, can appear with Accomplishments but not with Activities. Consider the contrasts in (120)–(121).

(120) a. John swam for an hour. (Activity)
       b. *John swam in an hour.

(121) a. Mary made a chair in a week. (Accomplishment)
       b. *Mary made a chair for a week.

Third, accomplishments can follow the verb *finish* while achievements cannot, as (122) shows.

(122) a. Bill finished making a chair. (Accomplishment)
       b. *Bill finished finding his wallet. (Achievement)

Hence, the verbal classification based on aspectual properties, as is depicted in (118), is well motivated by the range of data given in (119)–(122).

A similar verbal classification to the one for English introduced above was proposed for Japanese by Kindaichi (1976b). Kindaichi categorizes Japanese verbs into four classes: they are Stative, Continuative, Instantaneous, and Type 4 (the English terms for these are from Jacobsen 1992). Examples of each class are given in (123).

(123) a. *Stative*   aru "be", dekiru "can do", hanaseru "can speak",
                          mieru "be visible", yoo-suru "require"
      b. *Continuative*   yomu "read", kaku "write", warau "laugh", utau
                          "sing", aruku "walk", miru "look", nomu "drink",
                          osu "push", hataraku "work"
      c. *Instantaneous* sinu "die", kieru "turn off", sawaru "touch",
                          kimaru "decide", sameru "wake", hazimaru "begin",
                          tootyaku-suru "arrive"
      d. *Type 4*   sobieru "tower", sugureru "be outstanding", zub-
                          anukeru "be outstanding", arihureru "be common"

Stative, Continuative, and Instantaneous in (123) are equivalent to States, Activities, and Achievements in (118), respectively. Type 4 verbs do not find their equivalents in (118), but the motivation for this class will be clarified shortly.

It is clear that, like the Vendler/Dowty-style classification illustrated in (118), Kindaichi's classification is also based on the aspectual properties of verbs. Unlike the classification of (118), however, which is motivated by a number of diagnostic tests, the distinction among the four classes for Japanese verbs that Kindaichi proposes relies solely on the interpretation that arises in the *-te iru* construction, i.e. the progressive and resultative interpretations, as we have discussed in section 2.2.1.

First, Stative verbs do not appear in the *-te iru* construction. This is illustrated by the ungrammatical (a) sentences in (124)–(126).

(124) a. *Koko-kara umi-ga   miete-iru.
         here-from ocean-Nom see
         "We can see the ocean from here."
      b. Koko-kara umi-ga   mieru.
         here-from ocean-Nom see
         "We can see the ocean from here."

(125) a. *Taroo-wa suugaku-ga yoku dekite-iru.
         Taro-Top   math-Nom well competent
         "Taro is very good in math."
      b. Taroo-wa suugaku-ga yoku dekiru.
         Taro-Top math-Nom well competent
         "Taro is very good in math."

(126) a.   *Hanako-wa huransugo-ga hanasete-iru.
             Hanako-Top French-Nom can speak
             "Hanako can speak French."
       b.   Hanako-wa huransugo-ga hanaseru.
             Hanako-Top French-Nom can speak
             "Hanako can speak French."

As the contrast in these pairs shows, Stative verbs cannot be used in the *-te iru* construction with either the progressive or the resultative interpretation. Instead, they must appear in the citation form (i.e. in the present tense) or the past tense equivalent of it, as is shown by the (b) sentences. As we will see immediately below, other classes of verbs can appear in this construction and receive appropriate interpretations. In this respect, Stative verbs depart from the rest of the verb classes.

Second, Continuative verbs such as *yomu* "read" and *kaku* "write" can appear in the *-te iru* construction, and receive the progressive interpretation. For instance, consider the examples in (127)–(129).

(127) Taroo-wa ima zassi-o   yonde-iru.
       Taro-Top now magazine-Acc read
       "Taro is reading a magazine now."

(128) Mary-wa kinoo   Ziroo-to kooen-o   aruite-ita.
       Mary-Top yesterday Ziro-with park-throughout walk (past)
       "Mary was walking with Ziro at the park yesterday."

(129) Kodomo-ga mizu-o   nonde-iru.
       child-Nom water-Acc drink
       "A child is drinking water."

All the verbs in (127)–(129) belong to the Continuative class. As the translation shows, when they appear in the *-te iru* construction, the interpretation associated with them is the progressive one. In (127), for example, the reading activity is in progress at the speech time. Similarly, in (128), where the *-te iru* construction has the past tense suffix, the walking activity was in progress at some time yesterday. Thus, it is a characteristic of this class of verbs that they bear the progressive reading in the *-te iru* construction.

Third, verbs belonging to the Instantaneous class, of which *sinu* "die" and *hazimaru* "begin", for instance, are members, can also be in a sentence construction with *-te iru*. However, the interpretation obtained in this construction is resultative rather than progressive. For example, the sentences in (130)–(132) all describe the resulting state rather than the situations in which given events are in progress.

(130) Kaeru-ga sinde-iru.
       frog-Nom die
       "A frog is dead."

(131) Zyugyoo-ga moo   hazimatte-iru.
       class-Nom   already begin
       "The class has already begun."

(132) Kekkonsiki-no hidori-wa moo   kimatte-iru no?
       wedding-Gen date-Top already decide   Q
       "Has the date for the wedding already been set?"

Notice that none of these examples describes the instantaneous event itself that the verb denotes: rather, they all refer to the states of affairs that result from the instantaneous events. (130), for instance, describes the state of a frog being dead instead of referring to the very moment of the frog's death. Likewise, (131) depicts the state of the class that has already been in session rather than the moment of the starting of the class.

Type 4 verbs are unique in that they MUST appear in the *-te iru* construction, namely, almost the opposite situation of the Stative class. Consider (133)–(134).

(133) a. Tanakasan-no   musukosan-wa totemo sugurete-iru-sooda.
           Mr Tanaka-Gen son-Top   very   outstanding-I hear
           "I hear that Mr Tanaka's son is outstanding."
       b. *Tanaksan-no   musukosan-wa totemo sugureru.
           Mr Tanaka-Gen son-Top   very   outstanding
           "Mr Tanaka's son is outstanding."

(134) a. Kono syu-no   seihin-wa   arihurete-iru.
           this   type-Gen merchandise-Top common
           "This type of merchandise is common."
       b. *Kono syu-no   seihin-wa   arihureru.
           this   type-Gen merchandise-Top common
           "This type of merchandise is common."

The (b) sentences indicate that if these verbs do not appear in the *-te iru* construction, the sentences with the verbs are ungrammatical. The (a) sentences, in contrast, suggest that the Type 4 class of verbs is much more natural in the *-te iru* construction. In summary, the inherent aspectual properties of individual verbs together with their (mostly semantic) behavior in the *-te iru* construction has led Kindaichi to the four-way classification of Japanese verbs.

Kindaichi's work has drawn a great deal of further investigation on this issue (cf. Fujii 1976; Yoshikawa 1976; Okuda 1978a, 1978b; Soga 1983; Jacobsen 1992; Shirai 2000). Jacobsen (1992), for one, provides a detailed survey of the relation between the interpretation of the *-te iru* construction and the aspectual properties of verbs. He first attempts to capture the function of *-te iru* as "presenting a state of affairs as existing in a homogeneous, unchanging fashion over a given interval of time" (p. 200), regardless of whether it invokes a progressive reading or a perfect interpretation.

Under this conception of the role that *-te iru* plays, then, what is referred to in the *-te iru* construction is uniformly captured. Recall, for instance, that verbs like *aruku* "walk" present an ongoing, continuous activity, and because of such an aspectual property, they are termed Activities or Continuative. When they appear in the *-te iru* construction, the *-te iru* complex refers to a segment of this homogeneous event and presents it as a state of the ongoing event. Since the event itself is of a dynamic nature, the construction receives the progressive interpretation, as is shown in (135).

(135)   Taroo-ga   kooen-o   aruite-iru.
        Taro-Nom park-throughout walk
        "Taro is walking in the park."

Verbs like *sinu* "die", which belong to the Achievement or Instantaneous class, based on their aspectual properties, present a different situation. It should be remembered that these verbs describe momentary events. This means that the aspectual properties pertinent to these verbs do not include any interval of time that can be captured as a homogeneous state. This is why the progressive interpretation is normally not obtained with these verbs. However, the states as a result of those momentary changes can be referred to as homogeneous states. For instance, the state of a frog being dead in (130) will last without a natural endpoint. Thus, even Achievements (or Instantaneous) can induce a homogeneous state as long as the *-te iru* complex refers to the state of an affair that follows the instantaneous event. Since such a resulting state can only be static in nature without involving a dynamic movement or change, the resultative reading is obtained, as the translation of (130) suggests.

It should be noted that Kindaichi's classification does not include the class that would correspond to the Accomplishments of the Vendler/Dowty system. For instance, the phrase *eat an apple* implies a natural endpoint while the phrase *eat apples* does not. That is, *eat an apple* is an Accomplishment while *eat apples* is an Activity. Notice that although the verb *eat* itself does not seem to have an explicit aspectual specification, the type of direct object that the verb takes can change the aspectual properties of the verb phrase as a whole. As Dowty (1979) argues, it is the aspectual properties in the VP as a whole that we need to capture, rather than the aspectual properties of individual verbs. This is why Kindaichi lacks the verb class that corresponds to Accomplishments: his focus has been on the aspectual properties that each verb, and verb alone, inherently has, and the criteria he uses are exclusively the *-te iru* morphology and its interpretation.

Under Dowty's interpretation of verbal aspect, Japanese VPs like *hon-o kaku* "write a book" belong to the Accomplishment class. Notice that the situation referred to by this phrase can be considered as consisting of two composite events. Writing a 300-page book, for instance, does not happen in one second, and so it requires a homogeneous activity. At the same time, the homogeneous activity does not last forever: rather, when the writer reaches page 300, the natural endpoint of the activity is reached. Thus, the *-te iru* complex has two options in terms of its reference. On the one hand, it can refer to the ongoing writing activity before the endpoint arrives, and with such a reference, it induces the progressive reading. On the other hand, it can refer to the static state after the natural endpoint is reached as a (static) homogeneous state. In such a case, the resultative interpretation is obtained. Consider the examples in (136)–(137).

(136) Tanaka-sensei-wa kongakki   hon-o   kaite-iru.
       Tanaka-Prof.-Top this semester book-Acc write
       "Prof. Tanaka has been writing a book this semester."

(137) Tanaka-sensei-wa moo   hon-o   gosatu-mo   kaite-iru.
       Tanaka-Prof.-Top already book-Acc five-as many as write
       "Prof. Tanaka has already written as many as five books."

The VP *hon-o kaku* "write (a) book" with *-te iru* can be ambiguous between the progressive reading and the perfect interpretation, as has been discussed above. The expression *kongakki* "this semester" in (136), furthermore, puts forward the interpretation that refers to an ongoing event. The word *moo* "already" in (137), on the other hand, implies that some event has already happened, and hence it invokes the resultative reading. The choice of the progressive or resultative interpretations associated with the *-te iru* construction and its interaction with the aspectual properties that verbs and VPs have, hence, are accounted for given the conception of *-te iru* advanced by Jacobsen (1992).

   One of the interesting consequences of the investigation of the relation between the *-te iru* interpretations and the aspectual properties of verbs and VPs can be found in the consideration of transitive and intransitive verb pairs that are morphologically related, as has been discussed by Okuda (1978a, 1978b) and Jacobsen (1981, 1992), among others. Some morphologically related transitive and intransitive verb pairs and contrastive examples of them are illustrated in (138)–(141).

(138) | *transitive* | *intransitive* | *gloss* |
| --- | --- | --- |
| akeru | aku | "open" |
| simeru | simaru | "close" |
| ageru | agaru | "raise/rise" |
| sageru | sagaru | "lower" |
| kowasu | kowareru | "break" |
| taosu | taoreru | "fell/fall" |
| okosu | okiru | "wake" |
| tokasu | tokeru | "melt" |

(139) a. Taroo-ga   mado-o   aketa. (transitive)
         Taro-Nom window-Acc open
         "Taro opened the window."
     b. Mado-ga   aita. (intransitive)
         window-Nom opened
         "The window opened."

(140) a. Kodomo-ga isu-o   taosita. (transitive)
         child-Nom   chair-Acc let fall
         "The child let the chair fall."
     b. Isu-ga   taoreta. (intransitive)
         chair-Nom fell
         "The chair fell."

(141) a. Ziroo-ga kabin-o kowasita. (transitive)
           Ziro-Nom vase-Acc broke
           "Ziro broke a vase."
       b. Kabin-ga kowareta. (intransitive)
           vase-Nom broke
           "A vase broke."

We have earlier noted the connection between the *-te iru* construction with intransitive verbs of morphologically related transitive and intransitive pairs and the *-te aru* construction with their transitive counterparts, as is illustrated in (111)–(114). As our discussion there may in part suggest, the *-te iru* construction with these verb pairs demonstrates an overwhelming tendency for the transitive verbs in (138) to induce the progressive reading and for their intransitive counterparts to bear the resultative interpretation. The examples of the *-te iru* construction in (142)–(144) correspond to the pairs in (139)–(141), respectively.

(142) a. Taroo-ga mado-o   akete-iru. (transitive-progressive)
           Taro-Nom window-Acc open
           "Taro is opening the window."
       b. Mado-ga   aite-iru. (intransitive-resultative)
           window-Nom open
           "The window is open."

(143) a. Kodomo-ga isu-o   taosite-iru. (transitive-progressive)
           child-Nom chair-Acc let fall
           "The child is letting the chair(s) fall."
       b. Isu-ga   taorete-iru. (intransitive-resultative)
           chair-Nom fall
           "The chair has fallen (and it is on the ground)."

(144) a. Ziroo-ga kabin-o kowasite-iru. (transitive-progressive)
           Ziro-Nom vase-Acc break
           "Ziro is breaking a vase(s)."
       b. Kabin-ga kowarete-iru. (intransitive-resultative)
           vase-Nom break
           "A vase is broken."

All the (a) sentences, which consist of transitive verbs, have the progressive interpretation, while the (b) examples, where intransitive counterparts are used, are construed as resultative. This generalization holds for all the words featured in the paradigm listed in (138).

Notice that for the intransitive counterparts in (138), the subjects of these verbs bear the thematic role of theme, that is, an entity that undergoes change of state or location. As Jacobsen (1992) points out, the change of state inherent in the intransitive counterparts of the paradigm plays a crucial role in explaining the resultative interpretation of the *-te iru* construction. It should be remembered that under Jacobsen's account, having a change of state as part of an aspectual characterization of a verb suggests that the resulting state can be regarded as a homogeneous state to which the -*te iru* complex can refer. As a static state, the resulting state associated with the intransitive counterparts of (138) can readily relate to the resultative interpretation.

As for the transitive verbs in the paradigm, the subject is agent and the object is theme. Having a theme, then, may suggest that the -*te iru* complex can refer to a static state after the change of state that the verb denotes. Jacobsen, however, notes that the change of state inherent in the transitive counterparts is rather weakened in its focus. On the basis of a strong correlation between the progressive interpretation and the agentive subject, Jacobsen further claims that the agentivity pertinent to the subject of the transitive counterparts of (138) crucially contributes to the progressive reading of the -*te iru* construction. Therefore, rather than relying on the simple correlation between transitive–intransitive verbs and the progressive–resultative interpretation of -*te iru*, notions such as agentivity and change of state, coupled with the fundamental aspectual properties of verbs, contribute to accounting for the range of data in (142)–(144).

As Jacobsen further demonstrates, some transitive verbs indeed exhibit the resultative interpretation while some intransitive verbs display the progressive reading in the -*te iru* construction. This situation is not expected if we base our analysis solely on the transitive vs. intransitive opposition, but finds a natural explanation on the basis of aspectual properties. Consider the examples in (145)–(148), taken from Jacobsen (1992: 184–189) with minor changes in translation.

(145) Kare-wa tokkuni   tegami-o okutte-iru sooda.
       he-Top   long since letter-Acc send   I hear
       "He says that he has long since sent the letter."

(146) Dareka-ga   kuruma-o hooti-site-iru.
       someone-Nom car-Acc   leave (unattended)
       "Someone has left their car unattended."

(147) Kodomotati-wa yabu-no   naka-ni/de kakurete-iru.
       children-Top   bushes-Gen inside-in/at hide
       "The children are hiding in the bushes." or
       "The children have hidden in the bushes."

(148) Akatyan-wa nikai-ni/de   nete-iru.
       baby-Top   second floor-in/at sleep
       "The baby is sleeping on the second floor." or
       "The baby has fallen asleep on the second floor."

(145) and (146) are transitive verbs while (147) and (148) are intransitive verbs. The subjects of the first two sentences are agents, and are regarded as being intentional entities that bring about the action denoted by the verb. As such, they should invoke the progressive reading. Instead, the more natural interpretation of these sentences is the resultative one. Jacobsen explains that in these cases the completion of the activity, presumably leading to the notion of change of state,

is implied sufficiently to invoke the perfect interpretation. The sentences in (147) and (148) are indeed ambiguous between the two readings. Such ambiguity arises depending on the manner in which the subject is conceived of. If it is considered an agentive entity that has the intention of bringing about the action, the progressive interpretation is forced. If, on the other hand, it is regarded as an entity that undergoes a change of state, the *-te iru* complex refers to the static state as a homogeneous state, giving rise to the resultative reading. In sum, the aspectual properties of verbs and VPs together with the notion of agentivity play a significant role in accounting for the distribution of the semantic interpretations underlying the *-te iru* construction.

Let us return to the verbal classification described in (123), this time focusing on the Stative class. Stative verbs and more generally Stative predicates are important in Japanese as they exhibit an interesting set of semantic and syntactic properties. Stative predicates include Stative verbs like those in (123a), *aru* "be", *dekiru* "can do", *hanaseru* "can speak", *mieru* "be visible", *yoo-suru* "require", and *wakaru* "understand", as well as adjectives like *hosii* "want" and *umai* "be good at" and adjectival nouns such as *zyoozu* "be good at". We have discussed earlier that the hallmark of Stative verbs is that they do not appear in the *-te iru* construction. Examples demonstrating this property are repeated as (149)–(151).

(149)   *Koko-kara umi-ga   miete-iru.
        here-from   ocean-Nom see
        "We can see the ocean from here."

(150)   *Taroo-wa suugaku-ga yoku dekite-iru.
        Taro-Top   math-Nom well competent
        "Taro is very good in math."

(151)   *Hanako-wa huransugo-ga hanasete-iru.
        Hanako-Top French-Nom can speak
        "Hanako can speak French."

Despite this characterization, there are some instances in which Stative verbs can take the *-te iru* morphology. Compare the pairs in (152)–(153).

(152)   a. Taroo-wa suugaku-ga yoku dekiru/*dekite-iru.
            Taro-Top math-Nom well competent
            "Taro is very good in math."
        b. Taroo-wa kyoo-no   siken-wa dekite-iru.
            Taro-Top today-Gen exam-Top competent
            "Taro did well in today's exam."

(153)   a. Taroo-wa eigo-ga   yoku wakaru/*wakatte-iru.
            Taro-Top English-Nom well understand
            "Taro understands English well."
        b. Taroo-wa kono riron-ga   yoku wakatte-iru.
            Taro-Top this theory-Nom well understand
            "Taro has a good understanding of this theory."

Both (a) sentences and (b) sentences contain Stative verbs, and yet only the latter are grammatical with *-te iru*. (152a) and (153a) describe Taro's competence in math and English as an inherent property of Taro's, and this is consistent with the profile of Stative verbs: that is, they refer to static situations. The verbs in the (b) sentences, on the other hand, have more dynamic meanings: in (152b) the verb *dekiru* means "complete, perform well", and in (153b) the verb *wakaru* implies coming to comprehension. These verbs under the interpretations available in the (b) sentences, thus, can be classified as Achievements. In fact, it makes more sense for *dekiru* and *wakaru* to be able to appear with *-te iru* if they are Achievement verbs; as such, they induce the resultative reading with *-te iru*. That is, (152b) refers to a high-scored exam as a result of Taro's good performance on it; and (153b) describes Taro's high comprehension level as a result of his reaching such a level. The contrast in (152)–(153) suggests that some verbs may show aspectual ambiguity. The Japanese verbs *dekiru* and *wakaru*, for example, can be classified either as Stative or as Achievements, and the contrastive behavior we have observed is a consequence of such aspectual ambiguity. A similar phenomenon is commonly detected in English, as (154) shows.

(154)   Q: How do you like this linguistics class?
       A: Oh, I'm loving it.

The verb *love* is a Stative verb, and as such it is normally odd to use it in the progressive form, as in "*I am loving my parents", or "*I am loving mountains." But, the fact that the response in (154) is perfectly acceptable in this situation indicates that the verb can also be classified as Activity (McClure 1994).[9]

Stative predicates, which are grouped together on the basis of their aspectual property above, have been investigated as a coherent class of verbs beyond the aspectual motivation. In chapter 5 we mentioned that there is a group of verbs whose subject and object are both marked with the Nominative Case particle *-ga*. These verbs in fact correspond to Stative predicates. The subject of a Stative predicate, alternatively, can be marked with the Dative Case particle *ni*, while the object can be marked with the Nominative Case particle, in some cases. A question we address here is whether they can also be given a narrow semantic characterization other than the aspect-based one that Kindaichi originally observed. That is, do Stative predicates constitute a semantically coherent class? Let us see the range of predicates that can take two Nominative marked NPs in order to examine their semantic properties. The predicates listed in (155)–(157) are Stative predicates that take two NPs both marked with the Nominative Case particle, taken from Kuno (1973: 90–91). Some examples of these Stative predicates are in (158)–(160).

(155)   *verbs*

V-reru/rareru	"be able to"
aru/nai	"have/not to have"
dekiru	"be able to do"
iru	"need"
kikoeru	"hear"
mieru	"see"
wakaru	"understand"

(156) *adjectives*   V-tai   "be anxious to"
                          arigatai   "be grateful for"
                          hazukasii   "be bashful of, be ashamed of"
                          hosii   "want"
                          itosii   "think tenderly of"
                          kawaii   "hold dear"
                          osorosii   "be afraid of, be fearful of"
                          umai   "be good at"
                          urayamasii   "be envious of"

(157) *adjectival nouns* heta   "be bad at"
                          kanoo   "be able to"
                          suki   "be fond of"
                          tokui   "be good at"
                          kirai   "dislike"
                          zyoozu   "be good at"
                          zannen   "regret"

(158) a. Dare-ga   suugaku-ga   dekiru   no?
           who-Nom   math-Nom   be able to Q
           "Who is good in math?"
       b. Dare-ga   huransugo-ga hanas-e-ru   no?
           who-Nom   French-Nom   speak-can   Q
           "Who can speak French?"

(159) a. Taroo-ga   eigo-ga   wakaru   no?
           Taro-Nom   English-Nom understand   Q
           "Does Taro understand English?"
       b. Anata-ga kono oto-ga   kikoenai-no-wa   toozendesu.
           you-Nom   this sound-Nom not hear-fact-Top natural
           "It is natural that you should not hear this sound."
                                                              (Kuno 1973: 89)
       c. Anata-ga kokuban-no   zi-ga   mienai-no-wa
           you-Nom   blackboard-Gen letters-Nom   not see-fact-Top
           toozendesu.
           natural
           "It is natural that you should not see what is written on the
           blackboard."

(160) a. Anata-ga okane-ga   aru koto-wa minna-ga   sitte-imasu.
           you-Nom   money-Nom   have fact-Top everyone-Nom   know
           "Everyone knows that you have money."
                                                              (Kuno 1973: 89)
       b. Anata-ga okane-ga   nai   koto-wa minna-ga
           you-Nom   money-Nom   not have   fact-Top everyone-Nom
           sitte-imasu.
           know
           "Everyone knows that you don't have money."

c. Watasi-wa okane-ga   iru.
    I-Top   money-Nom need
    "I need money."

As is discussed in detail in Kuno (1973), when we concentrate on the verbs illustrated in (158)–(160), we can reach the following generalizations. The verbs *dekiru* "be able to" and *hanas-e-ru* "can speak" in (158) indicate "competence". The verbs *wakaru* "understand", *kikoeru* "can hear", and *mieru* "hear" in (159) suggest "non-intentional perception". Finally, the verbs in (160), *aru* "have", *nai* "not have", and *iru* "need", imply "possession" or "need". These semantic properties are also shared by many of the adjectives in (156) and the adjectival nouns in (157) as well. In addition, some of the adjectives and adjectival nouns suggest psychological states, as is shown by *hosii* "want", *osorosii* "be afraid of, be fearful of", *suki* "be fond of", and *kirai* "dislike". Thus, the Stative predicates are not arbitrary in their semantic properties, and it is not impossible to give an adequate characterization on the basis of their meanings denoted by the predicates. Interestingly, furthermore, the same set of semantically coherent predicates exhibits an equally consistent syntactic property reflected in the array of Case particles on their arguments.

Another matter that should be pointed out concerning Stative predicates is that among these verbs that allow subject and object to appear with the Nominative Case particle *ga*, some of them can also show the substitution of the Dative Case particle *ni* for *ga* for the subject NP. This is the phenomenon that Kuno (1973) calls "*Ga/Ni* Conversion". Consider the examples in (161)–(162).

(161) a. Dare-ga   sonna   koto-ga   dekiru   no?
           who-Nom that sort of thing-Nom be able to do Q
           "Who can do such a thing?"
       b. Dare-ni sonna   koto-ga   dekiru   no?
           who-Dat that sort of thing-Nom be able to do Q
           "Who can do such a thing?"

(162) a. Dare-ga   susi-ga   tukur-e-ru no?
           who-Nom sushi-Nom can make Q
           "Who can make sushi?"
       b. Dare-ni susi-ga   tukur-e-ru no?
           who-Dat sushi-Nom can make Q
           "Who can make sushi?"

Notice that the subject marked with the Nominative particle in the (a) sentences can appear with the Dative Case particle instead, as the (b) sentences show. Thus, with these predicates both the NP-*ga* NP-*ga* and the NP-*ni* NP-*ga* patterns are possible.

It should be mentioned, at this point, that one of the Stative predicates, namely, the potential expression consisting of V-*e-ru* "be able to V", can optionally mark its object with the Accusative Case particle, as is illustrated in the (a) sentences of (163) and (164).[10] However, if the object of this verb appears with

the Accusative particle, the Nominative particle on the subject cannot be substituted for by the Dative Case particle *ni*. This is shown in the (b) sentences of
(163) and (164).

(163) a. Dare-ga   kono uta-o   uta-e-ru no?
           who-Nom this   song-Acc sing-can Q
           "Who can sing this song?"
       b. *Dare-ni kono uta-o   uta-e-ru no?
           who-Dat this   song-Acc sing-can Q
           "Who can sing this song?"

                                                              (Kuno 1973: 88)

(164) a. Dare-ga   eigo-no   hon-o   yom-e-ru no?
           who-Nom English-Gen book-Acc read-can Q
           "Who can read English books?"
       b. *Dare-ni eigo-no   hon-o   yom-e-ru no?
           who-Dat English-Gen book-Acc read-can Q
           "Who can read English books?"

Hence, the substitution of *ni* for *ga* for the subject marking observed with
some of the Stative verbs is possible only when the object is also marked
with *ga*.
    Note, however, that not all the Stative predicates can allow the NP-*ni* NP-*ga*
pattern. This fact is illustrated in (165)–(167).

(165) a. Dare-ga   huransugo-ga zyoozu-desu ka?
           who-Nom French-Nom good at-be   Q
           "Who is good at French?"
       b. *Dare-ni huransugo-ga zyoozu-desu ka?
           who-Dat French-Nom   good at-be   Q
           "Who is good at French?"

(166) a. Dare-ga   okane-ga   iru   no desu ka?
           who-Nom money-Nom need that is   Q
           "Who is it that needs money?"
       b. *Dare-ni okane-ga   iru   no desu ka?
           who-Dat money-Nom need that is   Q
           "Who is it that needs money?"
                                  (Kuno 1973: 89 – judgments are his)

(167) a. Taroo-ga Hanako-ga   suki-da.
           Taro-Nom Hanako-Nom like
           "Taro likes Hanako."
       b. *Taroo-ni Hanako-ga   suki-da.
           Taro-Dat Hanako-Nom like
           "Taro likes Hanako."

Thus, not all the Stative predicates that allow for the NP-*ga* NP-*ga* pattern demonstrate the NP-*ni* NP-*ga* pattern, but the opposite situation seems to hold. That is, if a Stative predicate exhibits the NP-*ni* NP-*ga* pattern, then it can allow for the NP-*ga* NP-*ga* pattern as well.

2.2.3 Aspectual Verbs

As we have discussed in chapter 4 as an instance of syntactic V–V compounds, compounding provides yet another way of marking aspect. In that chapter we have introduced verbs with aspectual meaning such as *hazimeru* "begin", *dasu* "begin", *owaru* "finish", *oeru* "finish", *agaru* "finish", *tuzukeru* "continue", and *kakeru* "be about to" as the second member of V–V compounds, to indicate whether the action denoted by the first verb of a compound has started, continues, or is completed. On the basis of their semantic contribution, we will call the second member of these compounds **aspectual verbs**. These aspectual verbs are suffixed to the stem form of a verb, deriving aspectual compounds like *tabe-hazimeru* "begin to eat", *nomi-owaru* "finish drinking", and *yomi-tuzukeru* "continue to read".

The aspectual information that these aspectual verbs have ranges from inception and continuation to completion. The aspectual verbs that denote inception include *hazimeru*, *dasu*, and *kakeru*; those that imply continuation of an event are *tuzukeru* and *tuzuku*; and those that indicate completion or termination are *ageru*, *agaru*, *kiru*, and *yamu*. Some of these aspectual verbs have a function as an independent verb besides serving as the second member of a V–V compound. Others are used only as a part of a compound when they bear aspectual meanings. In other words, these verbs are not aspectual as independent (main) verbs. The former includes *hazimeru*, *tuzukeru*, *tuzuku*, *oeru*, *owaru*, and *yamu*; and the latter *ageru*, *dasu*, *kakeru*, and *kiru*. Examples of the former are illustrated in (168)–(169), and those of the latter in (170)–(172).

(168) a. Sensei-ga   zyugyoo-o hazimeta/tuzuketa/oeta.
            teacher-Nom class-Acc   started/continued/finished
            "The teacher started/continued/finished class."
       b. Gakusei-ga   hon-o   yomi-hazimeta/tuzuketa/oeta.
            student-Nom book-Acc read-started/continued/finished
            "The student started/continued/finished reading the book."

(169) a. Ame-ga   yanda.
            rain-Nom stopped
            "The rain stopped."
       b. Kodomo-ga naki-yanda.
            child-Nom   cry-stopped
            "The child stopped crying."

(170) Kyooko-wa ronbun-o kaki-ageta.
        Kyoko-Top   paper-Acc write-finished
        "Kyoko finished writing a paper."

(171)   Yuki-ga   huri-dasita.
        snow-Nom fall-started
        "Snow started to fall (= It started to snow)."

(172)   Ziroo-wa huruhon-o   issyuukan-de uri-kitta.
        Ziro-Top used books-Acc in a week   sell-finished
        "Ziro sold out the used books in a week."

Recall that in chapter 4 we discussed the two senses that certain aspectual verbs bear, i.e. the non-intentional beginning reading and the intentional initiation reading (Shibatani 1973c; Kuno 1983; Yo Matsumoto 1996). These two meanings most notably emerge when the aspectual verbs in V–V compounds are *hazimeru* "begin", *tuzukeru* "continue", and *owaru* "finish". The representative examples for each sense are repeated in (173)–(174).

(173)   The Non-Intentional Beginning Reading
        a. Hanako-wa   hutori-hazimeta.
            Hanako-Top become fat-began
            "Hanako began to become fat."   (Shibatani 1973c: 88)
        b. Ame-ga   huri-hazimeta.
            rain-Nom fall-began
            "It began to rain."   (Matsumoto 1996: 171)

(174)   The Intentional Initiation Reading
        a. Taroo-ga   susi-o   tabe-hazimeta.
            Taro-Nom sushi-Acc eat-began
            "Taro began to eat sushi."
        b. Hanako-ga   tegami-o kaki-hazimeta.
            Hanako-Nom letter-Acc write-began
            "Hanako began to write a letter."

In the case of the non-intentional beginning reading, although the aspectual verb *hazimeru* "begin" is compounded with the verbs *hutori* "become fat" and *huri* "fall", the aspectual range is not simply restricted to what these verbs imply; rather, the semantic range of "beginning" is the entire sentence, *Hanako-wa hutoru* "Hanako becomes fat" and *Ame-ga huru* "It rains." Thus, in these sentences what started are Hanako's weight gain and rainfall, and the subjects are not responsible for their inceptions. Under the intentional initiation reading in (174), on the other hand, the aspectual verb is compounded with the verbs *tabe* "eat" and *kaki* "write", and the aspectual range is also effective on the same verbs. That is, what started in these sentences are eating and writing, and at the same time the subjects, Taro and Hanako, are considered to have intentionally initiated the events of eating and writing.

As we noted before, while the different senses the aspectual verbs induce may largely be influenced by the semantic and aspectual nature of V1, the determination of a specific interpretation is not all that straightforward, as Yo Matsumoto (1996) points out in the examples in (175)–(176) (adapted from Yo Matsumoto 1996: 172–173).

(175)   John-wa sono koro-kara   ii   ronbun-o kaki-hazimeta.
      John-Top that period-since good paper-Acc write-began
      "John's writing of good papers began around that time."

(176)   John-wa kinoo   ronbun-o kaki-hazimeta.
      John-Top yesterday paper-Acc write-began
      "John (intentionally) began to write the paper yesterday."

While the compound is identical in both examples, (175) refers to the beginning of a non-intentional event while (176) describes John's intentional initiation of an event. The event of writing a paper is in itself an intentional action, which suggests that the semantic nature of V1 does not always lead us to a unique interpretation.

   We have above listed several examples of aspectual verbs according to specific aspectual information such as inception, continuation, and completion/termination, but not all the members of the same class mean exactly the same (Teramura 1982). For example, *hazimeru* and *dasu* both imply the inception of the event denoted by their V1 members, but there are contrastive pairs in which only one is appropriate. Compare the examples in (117)–(118), adapted from Teramura (1982: 175).

(177)   Akatyan-ga watto   naki-dasita/*hazimeta.
      baby-Nom burst out cry-begin
      "The baby burst out crying."

(178)   Onaka-ga   suitekita-kara   otoosan-wa madada-keredo
      stomach-Nom is getting empty-because father-Top   not yet-but
      tabe-*dasoo/hazimeyoo.
      eat-lets begin
      "Although our father won't eat yet, since we are getting hungry, let's begin to eat."

Teramura explains that *hazimeru* and *dasu* have similar aspectual meanings, but *hazimeru* does not seem to be suitable for events that are impulsive and uncontrollable by humans. Examples of such situations include crying and laughing, and this is why (177) sounds odd with *hazimeru*. Teramura goes on to comment on *dasu* and states that *dasu* adds a stronger sense of suddenness than *hazimeru* (p. 176), which may be the reason why (178) is peculiar with *dasu*, because a suggestion to start eating requires some degree of planning. In a similar vein, the two aspectual verbs of completion or termination, *owaru* and *yamu*, exhibit a subtle difference. According to Teramura, *owaru* is generally used for volitional actions while *yamu* is more suitable for natural phenomena. This difference may be captured by the contrast in (179)–(180).

(179)   Yosio-ga   sinbun-o   yomi-owatta/*yanda.
      Yoshio-Nom newspaper-Acc read-finish
      "Yoshio finished reading the newspaper."

(180) Kaze-ga   huki-*owatta/yanda.
       wind-Nom blow-finish
       "The wind stopped blowing."

(181) summarizes aspectual verbs, as a part of V–V compounds, and their aspectual meanings.

(181) *inception*   V-hazimeru, V-dasu, V-kakeru
       continuation   V-tuzukeru, V-tuzuku
       completion/termination V-ageru, V-agaru, V-kiru, V-yamu

Since V1 bears its inherently specified lexical aspectual properties and the V2 aspectual verbs, by definition, also provide aspectual information, it is important to take into consideration the question of whether the two sets of aspectual properties are compatible between V1 and V2 in order to derive aspectually acceptable V–V compounds. Such a consideration is particularly crucial to verbs of the Achievement or Instantaneous class like *sinu* "die", *kieru* "turn/go off", and *kimaru* "decide". These verbs describe events that take place instantaneously and do not have a time span. For these events, then, there is no way to refer to beginning and termination points and a continuing phase. This is why aspectual verbs are normally incompatible with these verbs, as is shown in (182)–(184).

(182) *Inu-no Poti-ga   sini-hazimeta/tuzuketa/owatta.
       dog-Gen Poti-Nom die-began/continued/finished
       "My dog, Pochi, began/continued/finished dying."

(183) *Roosoku-ga kie-hazimeta/tuzuketa/owatta.
       candle-Nom   go off-began/continued/finished
       "The candle began/continued/finished going out."

(184) *Kaigi-no   hi-ga   kimari-hazimeta/tuzuketa/owatta.
       meeting-Gen date-Nom decide-began/continued/finished
       "The date of the meeting began/continued/finished being decided on."

The only type of situation under which some combinations of Achievement V1 and aspectual V2 are acceptable is when a repeated event is described, as in (185).

(185) Sono mura-de-wa AIDS-de   ooku-no   hito-ga
       that villege-in-Top AIDS-due to many-Gen people-Nom
       sini-hazimeta/tuzuketa.
       die-began/continued
       "In that village, many people began/continued to die of AIDS."

In (185) the event of a single individual's dying happens instantaneously, but succession of more than one deaths indeed yields a duration of time, and in such repeated events, it is possible to perceive the beginning and the continuation. Even in this situation, however, the ending point is not foreseeable and hence the selection of *owaru* "finish" as V2 is not acceptable, *sini-owatta*.

Another aspectual verb class with which aspectual compatibility is critical is the Activity class (or some verbs in the Continuative class). Events described by Activity verbs like *aruku* "walk", *warau* "laugh", *kangaeru* "think", and *omou* "think" do not have ending points as an intrinsic property, unlike events that depict building a house or writing a book. Thus, these Activity verbs are incompatible with *owaru*, which indicates the completion or termination of an event: for example, **aruki-owaru*, **warai-owaru*, **kangae-owaru*, and **omoi-owaru* are all extremely odd. An apparent exception to this generalization is *naki-yamu* (cry-stop) "stop crying" and *huki-yamu* (blow-stop) "(wind) stop blowing" (cf. **naki-owaru*, **huki-owaru*): although *yamu* is an aspectual verb to indicate the termination of an event, unlike *owaru*, it can be suffixed to Activity verbs like *naku* "cry" and *huku* "blow". While Teramura's explanation that *yamu* is more suitable for natural phenomena (or presumably an event beyond human control) than *owaru* is may contribute to its relatively relaxed situation concerning the aspectual compatibility at issue, a parallel situation is observed in English, between *stop* and *finish*: there is a contrast in *The child stopped/*finished crying* and *The wind stopped/*finished blowing*. Thus, whatever operative principle exists in distinguishing between the two aspectual verbs in terms of aspectual compatibility, it seems to hold in both languages.

A final issue to be taken up concerning aspectual verbs is the morphological and syntactic repercussions of some aspectual verbs that employ morphologically related transitive and intransitive verb pairs (Shibatani 1973c, 1990; Kuno 1983, 1987; Yo Matsumoto 1996). The verb pairs under consideration are V-*tuzukeru* (Vt) vs. V-*tuzuku* (Vi) "continue to V", V-*oeru* (Vt) vs. V-*owaru* (Vi) "finish V-ing", and V-*ageru* (Vt) vs. V-*agaru* (Vi) "complete V-ing". Of these three pairs, the first two may be used as independent verbs with aspectual meanings while the verbs in the last pair do not bear aspectual meanings when they stand as independent verbs. As we have discussed in chapter 4, the argument realization in syntax of morphologically related transitive and intransitive verb pairs is such that the object of a transitive verb is realized as the subject of its intransitive counterpart. Independent verbs with aspectual meanings, *tuzukeru/tuzuku* "continue" and *oeru/owaru* "finish", follow the same argument distribution pattern, as is illustrated in (186)–(187).

(186) a. Mitiko-ga   piano-no   rensyuu-o   tuzuketa. (Vt: tuzukeru)
      Michiko-Nom piano-Gen practice-Acc continued
      "Michiko continued her piano practice."
    b. Piano-no   rensyuu-ga   tuzuita. (Vi: tuzuku)
      piano-Gen practice-Nom continued
      "The piano practice continued."

(187) a. Mitiko-ga   piano-no   rensyuu-o   oeta. (Vt: oeru)
      Michiko-Nom piano-Gen practice-Acc finished
      "Michiko finished her piano practice."
    b. Piano-no   rensyuu-ga   owatta. (Vi: owaru)
      piano-Gen practice-Nom finished
      "The piano practice is finished."

The transitivity dichotomy of these verb pairs, however, does not transfer to aspectual V–V compounds, and furthermore the transitivity relations of V1 and V2 differ between *tuzukeru/tuzuku* and *oeru/owaru*. Examine the range of transitivity relations each pair exhibits.

(188) V1 = Intransitive Verb (Agentive)
    a. Hanako-ga   aruita.
        Hanako-Nom walked
        "Hanako walked."
    b. Hanako-ga   aruki-tuzuketa.
        Hanako-Nom walk-continued (Vt)
        "Hanako continued to walk."
    c. *Hanako-ga   aruki-tuzuita.
        Hanako-Nom walk-continued (Vi)

(189) V1 = Transitive Verb
    a. Mayumi-ga   susi-o   tabeta.
        Mayumi-Nom sushi-Acc ate
        "Mayumi ate sushi."
    b. Mayumi-ga   susi-o   tabe-tuzuketa.
        Mayumi-Nom sushi-Acc eat-continued (Vt)
        "Mayumi continued to eat sushi."
    c. *Mayumi-ga   susi-o   tabe-tuzuita.
        Mayumi-Nom sushi-Acc eat-continued (Vi)
    d. *Susi-ga   tabe-tuzuketa/tuzuita.
        sushi-Nom eat-continued (Vt/Vi)

(190) V1 = Intransitive Verb (Natural Phenomena)
    a. Ame-ga   hutta.
        rain-Nom fell
        "It rained."
    b. Ame-ga   huri-tuzuketa.
        rain-Nom fall-continued (Vt)
        "It continued to rain."
    c. Ame-ga   huri-tuzuita.
        rain-Nom fall-continued (Vi)
        "It continued to rain."

(191) V1 = Intransitive Verb (Non-Intentional Subject)
    a. Kane-ga   natta.
        bell-Nom rang
        "The bell rang."
    b. Kane-ga   nari-tuzuketa.
        bell-Nom ring-continued (Vt)
        "The bell continued to ring."
    c. *Kane-ga nari-tuzuita.
        bell-Nom ring-continued (Vi)

(192) V1 = Intransitive Verb (Agentive)
   a. Masao-ga   Yooko-to hanasita.
      Masao-Nom Yoko-with spoke
      "Masao spoke with Yoko."
   b. Masao-ga   Yooko-to hanasi-oeta.
      Masao-Nom Yoko-with speak-finished (Vt)
      "Masao finished talking to Yoko."
   c. Masao-ga   Yooko-to hanasi-owatta.
      Masao-Nom Yoko-with speak-finished (Vi)
      "Masao finished talking to Yoko."

(193) V1 = Transitive Verb
   a. Masaru-ga   hon-o   yonda.
      Masaru-Nom book-Acc read
      "Masaru read a book."
   b. Masaru-ga   hon-o   yomi-oeta.
      Masaru-Nom book-Acc read-finished (Vt)
      "Masaru finished reading a book."
   c. Masaru-ga   hon-o   yomi-owatta.
      Masaru-Nom book-Acc read-finished (Vi)
      "Masaru finished reading a book."
   d. *Hon-ga   yomi-oeta/owatta.
      book-Nom read-finished (Vt/Vi)

(194) V1 = Intransitive Verb (Non-Intentional)
   a. Kane-ga natta.
      bell-Nom rang
      "The bell rang."
   b. *Kane-ga nari-oeta.
      bell-Nom ring-finished (Vt)
      "The bell finished ringing."
   c. Kane-ga nari-owatta.
      bell-Nom ring-finished (Vi)
      "The bell finished ringing."

As we have discussed earlier, the lexical aspectual properties of V1 influence the range of aspectual verbs it compounds with, but aside from that, there is a lack of consistency between the *tuzukeru/tuzuku* pair and the *oeru/owaru* pair with regard to the transitivity relation between V1 and V2. More importantly, there does not seem to be any coherent pattern in transitivity between V1 and V2. For example, in the case of V-*tuzukeru/tuzuku*, regardless of the transitivity of V1, the transitive *tuzukeru* can be suffixed, while its intransitive counterpart is only allowed for sentences that describe natural phenomena. The aspectual verb pair *oeru/owaru*, on the other hand, both transitive and intransitive verbs are almost equally suffixed to V1, again regardless of the transitivity of V1. The only exception is (194b), where the non-intentional intransitive verb, *naru* "ring", cannot appear with the transitive verb *oeru* "finish". In light of (186)–(187), it is interesting to note that the argument realization pattern in syntax observed with transitive and intransitive verb pairs, i.e. the object of a transitive verb is the subject of its intransitive counterpart, is not a consequence of the aspectual compounds under consideration: neither (189d) nor (193d) is acceptable.

This last point is significantly different in aspectual compounds with the *ageru/agaru* pair. The aspectual meaning of completion emerges only when these verbs serve as the V2 member of a compound (hence aspectual compound), and the argument realization parallels that of (186)–(187). The range of transitivity relations with this pair of aspectual verbs is given in (195)–(198).

(195) V1 = Transitive Verb
    a. Satosi-ga   ronbun-o kaita.
        Satoshi-Nom paper-Acc wrote
        "Satoshi wrote a paper."
    b. Satosi-ga   ronbun-o kaki-ageta/*agatta.
        Satoshi-Nom paper-Acc write-finished (Vt/*Vi)
        "Satosi finished writing a paper."
    c. Ronbun-ga kaki-*ageta/agatta.
        paper-Nom write-finished (*Vt/Vi)
        "The paper has been completed."

(196) V1 = Transitive
    a. Masao-ga   hoorensoo-o yudeta.
        Masao-Nom spinach-Acc boiled
        "Masao boiled spinach."
    b. Masao-ga   hoorensoo-o yude-ageta/*agatta.
        Masao-Nom spinach-Acc boil-finished (Vt/*Vi)
        "Masao finished boiling spinach."
    c. Hoorensoo-ga yude-*ageta/agatta.
        spinach-Nom boil-finished (*Vt/Vi)
        "Spinach has been finished boiling."

(197) V1 = Intransitive (Natural Phenomena)
    a. Sora-ga   hareta.
        sky-Nom cleared
        "The sky cleared."
    b. Sora-ga   hare-*ageta/agatta.
        sky-Nom clear-finished (*Vt/Vi)
        "The sky is cleared up."   (adapted from Himeno 1999: 42)

(198) V1 = Intransitive (Natural Phenomena)
    a. Mizu-ga   sunda.
        water-Nom cleared
        "The water cleared."
    b. Mizu-ga   sumi-*ageta/agatta
        water-Nom clear-finished (*Vt/Vi)
        "The water is cleared up."   (adapted from Himeno 1999: 42)

As (195)–(196) show, the transitive syntactic pattern of the V1 is only compatible with the transitive aspectual verb, *ageru*, as the (b) sentences indicate.
The situation under which the intransitive aspectual verb, *agaru*, is suffixed to
the transitive V1 is when the original direct object of the V1 is realized as the
subject with the Nominative Case particle, as in the (c) sentences; and in this
case, the transitive aspectual verb, *ageru*, is not acceptable. Thus, the transitivity
of the aspectual verbs and the syntactic realization of the arguments of V1 are
systematic. (197)–(198) are the instances where V1 is an intransitive verb that
describes natural phenomena. In these examples, only the intransitive aspectual
verb, *agaru*, is allowed, keeping the transitivity of V1 and that of V2 parallel.

3 Verb Semantics

Of a number of topics dealt with in the area of semantics, the study of verb
meaning has increasingly gained attention (Levin 1993). Investigation of what a
verb means is important because the number and type of arguments and adjuncts
and the manner in which they are distributed in a sentence greatly depend on
the meaning of the verb. Moreover, grouping verbs on the basis of their meanings
often provides insight into which syntactic phenomena are possible and which
are impossible with a set of verbs of similar meaning. This area of investigation
is also interesting cross-linguistically because translation equivalents of a verb in
two or more languages may or may not show identical syntactic behavior of the
verb's arguments and adjuncts. In this section we examine some issues relevant
to the syntax–semantics interface.

3.1 *Linking Regularity and Unaccusativity*

When we consider the thematic roles such as agent and theme that we have discussed in chapter 4, and how they surface in a syntactic configuration, we notice
a striking regularity (Fillmore 1968; Carter 1988). For example, when a verb is
associated with agent and theme roles, it is always the case in English that the
agent is realized as subject and the theme as object in syntax; similarly in Japanese,
the agent surfaces as NP with the Nominative Case particle and the theme as NP
with the Accusative Case. Conversely, when the English and Japanese sentences
with mystery verbs in (199)–(200) are presented, the speaker of each language
would not identify an apple as agent and John and Hanako as theme.

(199)   John xxxxx-ed an apple.

(200)   Hanako-ga   ringo-o   xxxxx-ta.
        Hanako-Nom apple-Acc xxxxx-Past

That is, even though the speaker does not understand the meaning of the verb,
she or he can at least ascertain that John and Hanako instigated an action that

involves an apple and the apple most likely underwent some change. Such regularity in linking between thematic roles and syntactic positions, then, is a part of the speaker's knowledge of the language.

Focusing on the association between agent and subject, it is expected that the subject of an intransitive verb is invariably understood as bearing the agent role. This, however, is not the case. Recall our discussion of morphologically related transitive and intransitive verb pairs in chapter 4, as exemplified by the examples in (201)–(202).

(201) a. Susumu-ga   kabin-o kowasita. (kowasu: transitive)
           Susumu-Nom vase-Acc broke
           "Susumu broke the vase."
       b. Kabin-ga   kowareta. (kowareru: intransitive)
           vase-Nom broke
           "The vase broke."

(202) a. Kokku-ga bataa-o   tokasita. (tokasu: transitive)
           cook-Nom butter-Acc melted
           "The cook melted the butter."
       b. Bataa-ga   toketa. (tokeru: intransitive)
           butter-Nom melted
           "The butter melted."

In the (a) sentences, the subjects are agent and the objects are theme. The subjects of the (b) sentences, the vase and the butter, undergo a change of state, and thus are theme. The themehood of the subjects in the (b) sentences is also confirmed by considering the thematic role of the same NPs in their corresponding (a) sentences: that is, in the transitive (a) sentences, the NPs are also theme. Intransitive sentences like those in (201b)–(202b) indicate that the subject of an intransitive sentence is sometimes theme, as is the case with (201b)–(202b), but sometimes agent, as the examples in (203) show.

(203) a. Satosi-ga   kawa-de oyoida.
           Satoshi-Nom river-in swam
           "Satoshi swam in the river."
       b. Yooko-ga   geragerato waratta.
           Yoko-Nom   laughed
           "Yoko laughed."

This situation leads us to wonder if the regularity in linking between thematic roles and syntactic positions is not systematic after all when it is applied to intransitive sentences.

It should be remembered that in chapter 5 we discussed the fact that there are two kinds of intransitive verbs, namely, unaccusative verbs and unergative verbs: the s-structure subject of an unaccusative verb is underlyingly the direct object while that of an unergative verb is the subject at both d-structure and s-structure. If it is shown that theme-subject sentences like those in the (b) sentences

of (201)–(202) are unaccusative whereas agent-subject sentences such as those
in (203) are unergative, the linking regularity between thematic roles and syntactic positions is still maintained. The numeral quantifier test can be applied to
determine the types of intransitive verbs. Relevant data are given in (204)–(207).

(204)   Kabin-ga   [$_{VP}$ konagonani mittu kowareta]
        vase-Nom   into pieces three broke
        "Three vases broke into pieces."

(205)   Bataa-ga   [$_{VP}$ zikabi-de   san-pondo   toketa]
        butter-Nom   open fire-with three-pound melted
        "Three pounds of butter melted over an open fire."

(206)   *Kodomo-ga [$_{VP}$ kawa-de sannin oyoida]
        child-Nom   river-in three swam
        "Three children swam in the river."

(207)   *Gakusei-ga [$_{VP}$ geragerato sannnin waratta]
        student-Nom   three   laughed
        "Three students laughed."

In (204)–(205) the subjects of the sentences and the numeral quantifiers are not
in a mutual c-command relation, and yet the sentences are not ungrammatical.
As we have discussed in chapter 5, this can be attributed to the fact that the
surface subjects, *kabin* "vase" and *bataa* "butter", are originally the direct objects
at d-structure and are moved to the subject position, leaving traces. It is with these
traces that the numeral quantifiers can maintain a mutual c-command relation.
The mutual c-command condition is satisfied in these sentences, and hence they
are grammatical. The d-structure object status of the surface subject is thus syntactically justified. The ungrammatical status of (206)–(207), by contrast, suggests
that there are no traces with which the mumeral quantifiers can hold a mutual
c-command relation. That is, in these sentences, the subjects are always the subjects, both at d-structure and s-structure. The numeral quantifier test shows that
the verbs in (204)–(205) are unaccusative while those in (206)–(207) are uncrg-
tive. The theme role associated with unaccusative verbs is indeed realized as
the object at d-structure, and such an association is entirely consistent with the
general linking regularity that we have observed above: that is, the agent is mapped
onto the subject and the theme onto the object. It implies, furthermore, that the
association pattern of the theme role with the syntactic object, observed with
unaccusative verbs, is in fact semantically motivated as well, given the regularity
in correspondence between thematic roles and syntactic positions.

3.2   Semantic Classes of Verbs and their Syntactic Patterns

Verbs can be grouped together on the basis of similarities in meaning. Such
semantically coherent classes of verbs often exhibit uniform syntactic behavior.

An example to illustrate the correlation between verb semantics and syntax comes from the phenomenon called locative alternation (or the hypallage phenomenon) (Kageyama 1980; Fukui et al. 1985), observed in both Japanese and English. Consider (208)–(211).

(208) a. Satoko-ga   akai penki-o   kabe-ni nutta.
           Satoko-Nom red   paint-Acc wall-on smeared
           "Satoko smeared red paint on the wall."
       b. Satoko-ga   kabe-o   akai penki-de   nutta.
           Satoko-Nom wall-Acc red   paint-with smeared
           "Satoko smeared the wall with red paint."

(209) a. Mari-ga   hana-o   heya-ni kazatta.
           Mari-Nom flowers-Acc room-in decorated
           "Mari put flowers (to decorate) in her room."
       b. Mari-ga   heya-o   hana-de   kazatta.
           Mari-Nom room-Acc flowers-with decorated
           "Mari decorated her room with flowers."

(210) a. John smeared butter on the toast.
       b. John smeared the toast with butter.

(211) a. The server cleared dirty dishes from the table.
       b. The server cleared the table of dirty dishes.

Focusing on the Japanese instances of the locative alternation as illustrated in (208)–(209), we notice that the (a) sentences have the materials to be applied marked with the Accusative Case particle while the location to which the materials are applied appear as postpositional phrases. In the (b) sentences, it is the location that is marked with the Accusative Case particle while the material NPs form postpositional phrases. Other verbs that exhibit locative alternation of the sort in (208)–(209) include *sasu* "stick", *tumeru* "fill", *tumaru* "fill", *tirakasu* "litter", *mitasu* "fill", *haru* "paste", *ahureru* "overflow", and *tatekomu* "get crowded" (cf. Kageyama 1980). These verbs form a semantically consistent group in that the general meanings of these verbs can be captured by "putting something/somebody (or being put) at some location". Thus, they share not only a fundamental meaning but also the syntactic phenomenon of locative alternation as a property associated with this semantic class of verbs.

Locative alternation furthermore provides an interesting characteristic to be captured in terms of a semantics–syntax correspondence. It has been observed for English as well as for Japanese that the interpretations of the two variants in locative alternation sentences are not identical (Anderson 1971, 1977; Schwartz-Norman 1976; Kageyama 1980; Fukui et al. 1985). When the location NP surfaces as the direct object, as in the (b) sentences of (208)–(211), the entire surface of the area is affected. This is called the "holistic" interpretation. When the material NP is the direct object, as in the (a) sentences, it does not imply that the entire area is affected. This is the "partitive" interpretation. In (208b), for example, it is understood that the entire wall is painted red; in (208a), however, some parts of the wall may be left unpainted. Thus, this illustrates that a particular mapping of a semantic participant of an event onto a syntactic position influences a specific interpretation the sentence should receive.

In light of cross-linguistic variation, locative alternation demonstrates an intriguing contrast between Japanese and English. In English the locative alternation also applies to a class of verbs whose meaning is generalized to "removing something from somewhere", such as *clear*, *clean*, *drain*, and *empty* (Levin 1993). An example was given in (211). Japanese equivalents of these verbs, however, do not show the alternant of the (b) pattern where the location NP is the direct object. So, the only patterns available for removal verbs such as *katazukeru* "clear", *akeru* "empty", *nomi-hosu* "drain", *toku* "undo", and *sebiru* "tease (a person for money)" are the one in which the material NP is the direct object and the location surfaces as a postpositional phrase, and the one in which the location NP is the direct object with no inclusion of the material NP (Kageyama 1980). This is shown in (212)–(213).

(212) a. Kodomo-ga sara-o teeburu-kara katazuketa.
child-Nom dish-Acc table-from cleared
"The child cleared the dishes from the table."
b. Kodomo-ga teeburu-o (*sara-de) katazuketa.
child-Nom table-Acc (dish-with) cleared
"The child cleared the table (*of dishes)."

(213) a. Hirosi-ga nakami-o yooki-kara aketa.
Hiroshi-Nom content-Acc container-from emptied
"Hiroshi emptied the contents from the container."
b. Hirosi-ga yooki-o (*nakami-de) aketa.
Hiroshi-Nom container-Acc (*content-with) emptied
"Hiroshi emptied the container (*of the contents)."

The range of comparison shown above indicates that translation equivalents of verbs across languages sometimes exhibit an interesting parallelism, as is the case with the locative alternation available to verbs of putting things as well as the holistic vs. partitive interpretations associated with the alternation; on the other hand, such parallelism can often break down, as is evidenced by the lack of one alternant in Japanese verbs of removal.

3.3 Lexicalization

We have just seen that verbs of seemingly parallel meanings in two languages do not necessarily exhibit the same range of syntactic distribution of arguments and adjuncts, as is observed with locative alternation above. When we investigate what constitutes the meaning of a verb in one language and compare it with its translation equivalent in another language, we realize that the two verbs often turn out to have quite different semantic properties. That is, what constitutes a verb's meaning can vary across languages in interesting ways.

A good example is drawn from motion verbs in Japanese and English. In English specific manners describing certain motion events can serve as a meaning component of a verb, and individual verbs can contrast in those specific manners. For instance, a simple walking event may be differentiated by using a variety of verbs depending on the exact manner of walking. So, *waddle, trudge, trot, lumber, plod, stroll, stagger,* and *toddle,* among others, all refer to a walking motion but differ in specific manners associated with the walking motion. Japanese, by contrast, does not have a large inventory of individual verbs to describe various modes of walking as in English, but instead expresses specific manners of walking by mimetics that modify the generic verb of walking, *aruku.* The translation equivalents for specific manners of walking are contrasted in (214).

(214)　*tyoko-tyoko*　aruku　"waddle"
　　　　teku-teku　　aruku　"trudge"
　　　　toko-toko-to　aruku　"trot"
　　　　dosi-dosi　　aruku　"lumber"
　　　　tobo-tobo-to　aruku　"plod"
　　　　bura-bura　　aruku　"stroll"
　　　　yota-yota　　aruku　"stagger"
　　　　yoti-yoti　　aruku　"toddle"

(214) suggests that the two languages use different devices to represent specific manners of an action: in English they are encoded internally to individual verbs as their semantic properties, i.e. **lexicalized**, while Japanese differentiates the detailed manners by mimetics that are expressed externally to a verb of a more general meaning.

A similar observation is made with verbs that describe emission of sounds in English, such as *clatter, rumble,* and *rustle* (Levin and Rappaport Hovav 1995). These English verbs can be used to describe motion accompanied by sounds. So, individual verbs like *clatter, whistle, rumble,* and *rustle* contrast in the sounds to illustrate distinct manners. As is the case with (214) above, Japanese does not employ individualized verbs to differentiate the sound-based manner distinction, but rather it takes advantage of its rich mimetic inventory. The contrast in (215)–(216) demonstrates this difference between the two languages.

(215)　a.　The truck rumbled out of the tunnel.
　　　　b.　Torakku-ga gata-gata(-to) tonneru-kara dete-kita.
　　　　　　truck-Nom　　　　　　　　　tunnel-from　exit-came

(216)　a.　The bullet whisled toward the palace.
　　　　b.　Dangan-ga pyuu(-tto) kyuuden-no hoo-e　　　tonde-itta.
　　　　　　bullet-Nom　　　　　　palace-Gen　direction-to fly-went

In English, the verb lexicalizes the manner of motion distinguished by particular sounds accompanying the motion event. Japanese, by contrast, does not lexicalize sound-based manners with motion, and hence the sounds that characterize various manners of motion are described externally to verbs by separate mimetic words. Thus, languages may differ in **lexicalization** patterns, i.e. patterns in which semantic bits of information are encoded internally to a verb serving as its meaning, and also in ways in which semantic bits that are not lexicalized may be expressed externally to a verb.

Another illustration of what is lexicalized and what is not is seen again with motion verbs (Talmy 1985). In English, motion verbs that lexicalize manner of motion, such as *walk*, *run*, *fly*, and *swim*, can appear with phrases that express the direction of the motion. So, the sentences in (217) raise no problem.

(217) a. John walked to the park.
      b. The bird flew to the big tree over there.
      c. Mary swam to the other side of the river.

The translation equivalents of (217) in Japanese (as well as in Spanish and French), however, are low in acceptability (Yoneyama 1986; Tsujimura 1990c, 1991, 1994). Consider the Japanese equivalents in (218).

(218) a. ??Satoko-ga kooen-ni aruita.
          Satoko-Nom park-to   walked
          "Satoko walked to the park."
      b. ??Tori-ga mukoo-no   ki-ni   tonda.
          bird-Nom over there-Gen tree-to flew
          "A bird flew to the tree over there."
      c. ??Midori-ga kawa-no mukoogawa-ni   oyoida.
          Midori-Nom river-Gen the other side-to swam
          "Midori swam to the other side of the river."

English verbs like *walk*, *run*, *fly*, and *swim* lexicalize manner of motion and direction of motion at the same time. In (217a), for example, *walk* expresses that the manner of motion is walking and that the walking event is directed toward an unspecified goal. Accordingly, the specification of the goal, *to the park*, is compatible with the verb. In Japanese, manner of motion verbs like *aruku* "walk", *tobu* "fly", and *oyogu* "swim", among others, lexicalize manner of motion alone and cannot further imply that the motion is directed toward an unspecified goal. This is why these manner of motion verbs cannot co-occur with directional phrases in (218). In order to express both manner of motion and direction of motion within the same clause in Japanese, a periphrastic expression consisting of the gerundive form of a manner verb and a direction verb is utilized. (219) corresponds to (217a), and expresses both manner and direction of motion.

(219) Satoko-ga   kooen-ni aruite   itta.
      Satoko-Nom park-to   walking went
      "Satoko walked to the park." (Lit. "Satoko went to the park by walking.")

Lexicalization patterns thus often illuminate cross-linguistic differences as to what syntactic expressions are possible with what range of verbs.

4 Pragmatics

The remainder of the chapter will be spent discussing speaker's meaning as well as the nature of the information that speech participants share and the relevance of context. These topics are investigated in the area of **pragmatics**.

4.1 Speaker's Meaning

In carrying out a conversation, speech participants intend the conversation to be successful. To this end, interlocutors attempt to show cooperation and mutual understanding, and cultural background often serves as a vital element in the attempt. As is well known, Grice (1975: 45) elaborates on the general principle of this mutual effort between interlocutors, referred to as **the cooperative principle**: "Make your conversational contribution such as is required, at the stage at which it occurs, by the accepted purpose or direction of the talk exchange in which you are engaged." The cooperative principle consists of four categories, namely, quantity, quality, relation, and manner, and each category is explained in terms of maxims, as is shown in (220)–(223) (taken from Grice 1975: 45–46).

(220) Quantity
     a. Make your contribution as informative as is required (for the current purposes of the exchange).
     b. Do not make your contribution more informative than is required.

(221) Quality – "Try to make your contribution one that is true."
     a. Do not say what you believe to be false.
     b. Do not say that for which you lack adequate evidence.

(222) Relation – "Be relevant."

(223) Manner – "Be perspicuous."
     a. Avoid obscurity of expression.
     b. Avoid ambiguity.
     c. Be brief (avoid unnecessary prolixity).
     d. Be orderly.

These are the contents of the cooperative principle that each speech participant expects the other to share for the purpose of effective communication.

When the speaker uses an utterance to communicate more than what the sentence directly means, e.g., request, threat, and apology, the utterance is considered **indirect**, and indirect speech may result from a violation of a maxim in the cooperative principle. Consider the examples in (224)–(226).

(224) Anata-wa nani-o   yattemo   ozyoozu-desu-ne.
      you-Top what-Acc even if you did very good
      "You are good at anything you put your hands on."

(225) Ninzin-o   tabenai-to ookiku-narenai-yo.
carrots-Acc not eat-if big-can't become
"If you don't eat carrots, you won't be able to grow."

(226) A: Kihukin   onegaisimasu.
donation please make
"Please make a donation."
B: Sengetu   sinsya-o   kattyattanda-yo-ne.
last month new car-Acc bought
"I bought a new car last month."

These examples show that any utterance can be used indirectly given the right context. (224), for example, can be interpreted as sarcasm, where the speaker does not believe that the addressee is a highly competent person or does not have sufficient evidence for it. So, the statement violates the maxim of quality. (225), taken directly, is obviously a false statement, and is another violation of the maxim of quality. This utterance is used indirectly as a mild threat from a parent to her or his child who refuses to eat carrots. Under the context in (226) where B tries to express his unwillingness to make a donation, the statement by B is a violation of the maxim of relation: a purchase of a new car made last month apparently has no relation to the request to make a donation, but in this context, the utterance is used indirectly to achieve the speaker's goal of declining the request made by A. In order for an instance of indirect speech to be successful, the hearer must realize that a maxim of the cooperative principle is being violated so she or he can figure out the speaker's intended meaning.

A number of expressions in indirect speech acts in Japanese have been standardized and have come to be commonly used as a part of rituals. The two examples in (227)–(228) illustrate ritualistic expressions typical of the Japanese culture.

(227) Tumaranai mono-desu-ga doozo.
insignificant thing-is-but   please take
(Lit. "Please take this insignificant thing.")

(228) Kitanai tokoro-desu-ga o-agari-kudasai.
dirty   place-is-but   please come in
(Lit. "Please come into this dirty place.")

In (227)–(228) the speaker's intention is to be modest and polite toward the addressee. (227) is an expression uttered when giving a gift: taken literally, it is extremely odd to offer something the giver sincerely thinks insignificant. The speaker does not believe that the gift is insignificant at all, but it is a way of humbling herself or himself. In a similar vein, one would not invite a guest to come into the house when the house is in a very messy condition. (228) is another indirect speech act where the speaker does not truly think the house is messy, but uses the sentence as a humbling expression. Both ritualistic expressions are viewed as a part of a sociocultural norm, which reflects the relevance of indexing a social hierarchy.

4.2   The Nature of Information

Even though a sentence may have nothing grammatically wrong with it from the phonological, morphological, syntactic, and semantic perspectives, it could still be considered unacceptable by native speakers. Such a problem often arises when the utterance is not consistent with the nature of information that is constrained by context. Put differently, linguistic forms, or a specific choice of one linguistic form over another, may be influenced by contextual consideration. The best-known instance of this sort in Japanese is found in the distinction between the particles -*wa* and -*ga* (Kuno 1973; Hinds et al. 1987; Matsuda 1997; McClure 2000; Fiengo and McClure 2002).

4.2.1   Wa *vs.* Ga

Numerous examples in previous chapters contain subjects marked with -*wa* or -*ga*, and furthermore other grammatical functions like direct objects can also be marked with -*wa*. Central to the understanding of the *wa/ga* contrast are the notions of **new information** and **given information** (or shared information). The basic distinction between the two particles is made on the basis of the nature of the knowledge of a subject matter that speech participants have, namely, whether the knowledge is new or given: roughly, *ga* for new information and *wa* for given information. Consider the context in (229).

(229)   Mukasi   aru   tokoro-ni   <u>oziisan-ga</u>   sundeimasita.
        Long ago some place-at   old man-Nom   was living
        Sono <u>oziisan-wa/#ga</u> maiasa   gozi-ni   okite   sigoto-o
        the   old man   every morning 5 a.m.-at got up work-Acc
        hazimemasita.
        began
        "A long time ago, there was an old man living some place. The old man
        got up at 5:00 a.m. every morning and started working."

The NP, *oziisan* "old man", is marked with *ga* in the first sentence but with *wa* in the second. The particle *ga* is appropriate to mark the NP when it is first mentioned so that it introduces new information. Once the initial presentation of the NP is made, *oziisan* is now considered given information shared between speech participants, so the NP at the second mention is marked with *wa*. That is, the NP *oziisan* is now viewed as topic. The use of *ga* in the second sentence thus results in a pragmatic oddity, as the diacritic "#" indicates, although either choice of the particle would not have an effect on the sentence meaning.

A parallel phenomenon is observed in English (Kuno 1973). One method of distinguishing between new and given information in English is the use of definite and indefinite articles, *the* vs. *a*. New information is introduced or presented by the indefinite article, as in *an apple*, but once such presentation is given, the same apple is referred to as *the apple*, serving as given information or the topic. English phrases like *as for* and *speaking of* occur with the topic of a sentence, and as such, it becomes pragmatically odd if they appear with indefinite NPs. For example, it is odd to say, "#speaking of an apple, it was very sour", while replacing *an* with *the* would make the sentence pragmatically natural, "speaking of the apple, it was very sour".

Information need not be newly introduced every time in an overt form with the particle *ga* as a sort of prerequisite to serving as given information, i.e. topic. Information that the speaker assumes the listener shares helps establish a topic without overt prior mention of it, as is exemplified by the sentences in (230)–(231).

(230)   Kono ringo-wa   totemo suppai.
        this   apple-Top very   sour
        "This apple is very sour."

(231)   Tanaka-sensei-wa kyoo yasumi-desu.
        Tanaka-Prof.-Top today absent-is
        "Professor Tanaka is absent today."

The demonstrative *kono* of the NP *kono ringo* "this apple" in (230) helps establish the apple as the topic since its presentation is deictically achieved. *Tanaka-sensei* in (231) is an individual whose relationship to the speech participants has already been established and hence it is pragmatically natural to treat her or him as the topic. In both cases, the speaker at least expects that reference to the apple and Professor Tanaka constitute knowledge shared by her or him and the listener.

It should be pointed out that the notion of new vs. given information is independent of grammatical functions such as subject and object. The separation of the two can be illustrated by the fact that a *wa*-marked topic and a *ga*-marked subject can co-occur within a single sentence. Consider the examples in (232)–(233), adapted from Kuno (1973: 62–64).

(232)   Sakana-wa tai-ga   oisii.
        fish-Top   red snapper-Nom delicious
        "Speaking of fish, red snapper is the most delicious."

(233)   Kono kurasu-wa dansei-ga   yoku dekiru.
        this   class-Top   male-Nom well able
        "Speaking of this class, the boys do well (at studies)."

In both sentences, the *wa*-marked NP serves as the topic of the sentence, but is not the argument of the predicates, *oisii* "be delicious" and *dekiru* "be able". The *ga*-marked NP, instead, is an argument of the predicate, and plays a role as the subject of the sentence.

Kuno (1973), in his detailed investigation of *wa* and *ga*, further states that the topic can be a generic NP, i.e. an NP that refers to a general class whose members share a common attribute. For example, *nihonzin* "Japanese people", *inu* "dogs", and *sensinkoku* "advanced countries" may be considered generic NPs. Examples of a generic NP as the topic are given in (234)–(235).

(234) Nihonzin-wa gohan-o yoku taberu.
Japanese-Top rice-Acc a lot eat
"Japanese people eat a lot of rice."

(235) Sensinkoku-wa   tozyookoku-o   tasukeru-bekida.
advanced countries-Top developing countries-Acc help-should
"Advanced countries should help developing countries."

The topic marker *wa*, on the other hand, does not occur with interrogative words (Kuno 1973). When an interrogative word is the subject of a sentence, the particle is *ga*, instead. This is shown in (236)–(237).

(236) Dare-*wa/ga   kinoo   paatii-ni kimasita-ka.
who-Top/Nom yesterday party-to came-Q
"Who came to the party yesterday?"

(237) Dore-*wa/ga   oisii?
which-Top/Nom delicious
"Which one is delicious?"

In addition to the role as a topic marker, the particle *wa* has a contrastive function. In each of the following examples, the two NPs marked with *wa* are contrasted: in (238) they are both subjects while in (239) they are both objects.

(238) Satoko-wa paatii-ni kita-kedo, Masao-wa konakatta.
Satoko-Top party-to came-but Masao-Top didn't come
"Satoko came to the party, but Masao didn't."

(239) Sakana-wa taberu-kedo, niku-wa   tabemasen.
fish-Top   eat-but   meat-Top don't eat
"I eat fish, but not meat."

Recall that the topic marker *wa* cannot appear with interrogative words, as is shown in (236)–(237) above. When *wa* serves as a contrastive marker, however, the combination is possible (Miyagawa 1987b). (240) is taken from Miyagawa (1987b: 186).

(240) Dare-wa kite dare-wa konakatta-no?
who-Top came who-Top didn't come
"Who came and who didn't?"

In this sentence, two groups of individuals are contrasted, those who came and those who didn't. Under this kind of contrastive situation, an interrogative word with *wa* is allowed. Put differently, interrogative words marked with *wa* always receive the contrastive interpretation.

4.2.2 *Interaction with Syntax and Morphology*

Pragmatic notions such as new vs. given information as instantiated by *wa* and *ga* exhibit interactions with morphology and syntax in an interesting way. An example of such an interaction is observed with Quantifier Floating (Downing 1993). We have introduced in chapter 5 the facts that numeral quantifiers can be placed prenominally as prenominal modifiers marked with the Genitive Case *-no*, or can be "floated" postnominally. Examples illustrating the two positional possibilities of numeral quantifiers are repeated in (241)–(242).

(241) a. <u>Sannin</u>-no kodomo-ga uti-e   kita.
            three-Gen child-Nom house-to came
            "Three children came to my house."
      b. Kodomo-ga <u>sannin</u> uti-e   kita.
            child-Nom   three   house-to came
            "Three children came to my house."

(242) a. Taroo-ga   <u>sanmai</u>-no kami-o   katta.
            Taro-Nom three-Gen paper-Acc bought
            "Taro bought three sheets of paper."
      b. Taroo-ga   kami-o   <u>sanmai</u> katta.
            Taro-Nom paper-Acc three   bought
            "Taro bought three sheets of paper."

The numeral quantifiers modify the subject in (241) and the object in (242). In both pairs the numeral quantifiers are prenominal modifiers in the (a) sentences while they are in the "floated" position in the (b) sentences. While there is very little, if any, difference between the prenominal pattern and Quantifier Floating in terms of sentence meaning, Downing (1993) observes a pragmatic constraint that seems to explain the frequency of the two patterns in the texts that she surveyed. According to her, the floating structure, corresponding to the (b) sentences in (241)–(242), is more frequently adopted (87.5 percent) when the information about the number is new in the discourse. The prenominal pattern, in contrast, is less constrained in that it can appear regardless of whether the number information is new or repeated. The contrast shown in (243) (taken from Downing 1993: 75) suggests the difference. (CLASS = classifier; COLL = collective marker; Loc = location)

(243) a. Kenzyuu-o kosi-ni   sageta heisi-ga   NI-MEI,
            pistol-Acc waist-Loc hung   soldier-Nom 2-CLASS
            doa-o   akete   ikioiyoku tobi-orita.
            door-Acc opening vigorously jumping-descended
            "TWO soldiers with pistols at their hips opened the door and ener-
            getically jumped down."
      b. Kogara-no   HUTA-RI-no heisi-tati-no   yoko-de
            small stature-Gen 2-CLASS-Gen soldier-COLL-Gen side-Loc
            kare-ra-no   sei-ga   amarini   takai.
            he-Coll-Gen height-Nom excessively tall
            "They were excessively tall next to the TWO small soldiers."

Downing explains that in (243a) the subject NP *heisi* "soldier" is introduced in the discourse along with its quantity as new information, while its later mention appears in the prenominal pattern, as in (243b).

Another pragmatic distinction between the two numeral quantifier structures that Downing draws is that the NP modified by a numeral quantifier in the prenominal pattern is generally specific and its individuality is emphasized. Thus, when a modified noun is specific, it tends to take the prenominal pattern; otherwise, it is likely to appear with a floating quantifier. The contrast is shown in (244)–(245), taken from Downing (1993: 78).

(244)   a.   SAN-NIN-no tomodati-o matte-imasu.
             3-CLASS-Gen friend-Acc is waiting
             "(I) am waiting for THREE friends."
        b.   ?Tomodati-o SAN-NIN matte-imasu.

(245)   a.   ?SAN-NIN-no hisyo-o   sagasite-imasu.
             3-CLASS-Gen secretary-Acc looking for
             "(I) am looking for THREE secretaries (e.g., to hire)."
        b.   Hisyo-o SAN-NIN sagasite-imasu.

The modified noun in (244) refers to a specific group of friends for whom the speaker is waiting, and in such a context, the prenominal pattern is preferable to the floating structure. (245) presents an opposite situation: it is not intended that a specific set of secretaries is sought, and hence the floating pattern is more natural in this context.

A similar explanation can be given for the contrast in (246)–(247).

(246)   a.   ?IP-PON-no   tabako-o   sutte-mimasyoo.
             1-CLASS-Gen cigarette-Acc smoke-let's try
             "Let's have a cigarette."
        b.   Tabako-o IP-PON sutte-mimasyoo.

                                             (Downing 1993: 79)

(247)   a.   ?Ippai-no koohii-o   nomanai?
             1 cup-Gen coffee-Acc won't you drink
             "Won't you have some coffee?"
        b.   Koohii-o ippai nomanai?

In these examples, the quantity is immaterial, and it is irrelevant whether the speaker ends up smoking more than one cigarette or drinking more than a cup of coffee. That is, individuation of the NP is not intended in these situations, and hence the prenominal pattern is quite unnatural.

Another illustration of interaction that pragmatic notions may exhibit is observed with the choice of predicate morphology, as is reported in Maynard (1991). The predicate morphology of *-da* and *-desu/masu* has been understood to be contrastive on the basis of style. The *-da* ending is generally assumed to be informal, abrupt, and more suitable for written language; and, the opposite criteria have been applied to the *-desu/masu* ending. Consider the pairs in (248)–(249).

(248)　a.　Yamada-san-wa gakusei-<u>desu</u>.
　　　　　Yamada-Top　　student-be
　　　　　"Mr Yamada is a student."
　　　b.　Yamada-san-wa gakusei-<u>da</u>.

(249)　a.　Asita　　　gakkoo-ni iki<u>masu</u>.
　　　　　tomorrow school-to　go
　　　　　"I will go to school tomorrow."
　　　b.　Asita gakkoo-ni <u>iku</u>.

The (a) sentences end with the *-desu/masu* morphology while the (b) sentences end with the *-da* morphology and its verbal equivalent. The sentence meanings of the pair, regardless of the predicate morphology, are the same, and the difference has been considered one of style.

　Maynard (1991), after surveying both spoken and written texts from different genres, observes that a mixing of the two "styles" of speech is frequently found in a single conversation. Maynard cites the following lines (p. 552) spoken by a single individual in contemporary Japanese fiction, and gives the narrative setting of (251) as background of the utterances in (250).

(250)　a.　Hitori　　　dete-<u>kita</u>. (abrupt)
　　　　　one person appeared
　　　　　"A person is coming out."
　　　b.　Ano ko　<u>desu</u>-yo. (formal)
　　　　　that child be
　　　　　"That is the very girl."

(251)　Two police officers – Officer Tadokoro and Oono – are on duty secretly observing female high school students – suspected of prostitution – coming out of a local bar. Of particular interest to these men hiding behind the billboard across the bar is Kimie, the daughter of the couple who interact with the protagonists of the mystery novel. Tadokoro notices a girl coming out of the bar; he pokes at his partner and utters [(250)]. (Maynard 1991: 560)

In (250), the informal/abrupt "style" of the *-da* ending and the formal "style" of the *-desu* ending are used by the same speaker, and the utterance of (b) immediately follows (a). Maynard relates a switch from one predicate ending to another as in (250) to the speaker's awareness of or sensitivity toward her or his audience. The higher the speaker's awareness of the addressee, the more likely that the *-desu/masu* ending is used. Conversely, when the speaker expresses her or his internal thoughts or emotional reactions, whereby the degree of awareness of the addressee is lower, the *-da* ending is more likely to be used. In the situation described in (251), the use of the abrupt form, *dete-kita* "appeared", reflects his surprise, excitement, or internal thoughts to himself. That is, (250a) can be regarded as an utterance addressed toward himself, and thus his level of awareness of his partner, Oono, is low. In (250b), by contrast, the use of the more formal -*desu*/*masu* ending indicates that the spearker is more conscious of the addressee, making his utterance addressed directly to Oono.

Maynard further gives a scenario different from (251), i.e. (252), in which the opposite choice of the predicate morphology is more appropriate, as is illustrated in (253).

(252) Tadokoro describes to Oono that a girl is coming out of the bar; he calmly describes the situation in the style that he uses most often, i.e., [(253a)]. Then all of a sudden he realizes that the girl he has just described is the one that he and Oono were looking for. At this point Tadokoro exclaims [(253b)]. (Maynard 1991: 561)

(253) a. Hitori   dete-kimasita. (formal)
           one person appeared
       b. Ano ko da. (abrupt)
           that girl be

In the situation in (252), the use of the -*desu*/*masu* ending in (253a) is viewed as the reflection of the speaker's higher awareness of the addressee; while the use of the -*da* ending in (253b) mirrors the speaker's internal emotion, i.e. surprise. Thus the choice of the two kinds of predicate morphology may be influenced by pragmatic considerations such as the degree to which the speaker is aware of the addressee.

4.3   Relevance of Contextual Information

Even if a sentence does not violate phonological, syntactic, or semantic constraints or rules, it can be contextually odd or awkward. Furthermore, semantically ambiguous sentences may receive a specific interpretation depending on the context. In this section we will show cases in which contextual information plays a relevant role in certain syntactic constructions.

The first example comes from the relative clause construction without gap discussed in chapter 5 (C. Kitagawa 1982; Yoshiko Matsumoto 1990, 1997). Examples are repeated in (254).

(254) a. [musuko-ga iede-sita]   Taroo
           son-Nom   ran away from home Taro
           "Taro whose son ran away from home"
       b. [meizin-ga   ryoori-sita] azi
           expert-Nom cooked   flavor
           "flavor [that results when] an expert cooked"

It should be remembered that since there are no NP gaps internal to the relative clauses with which the head nouns can be co-indexed, the nature of modification between the head noun and the relative clause largely relies on semantic and pragmatic factors. Interestingly, contextual information of the sort that is involved in the interpretation of relative clauses without gaps like those in (254) may override a seemingly straightforward interpretation of relative clauses with gaps. Consider the example in (255) along with the two possible interpretations in (256), taken from Yoshiko Matsumoto (1990: 122).

(255) [Kookoo nyuusi-ni   zettai   ukaru] katei-kyoosi-o
       high scool entrance exam-Dat absolutely pass   tutor-Acc
       sagasiteimasu.
       be searching for

(256) a. (I) am searching for a tutor (with whose assistance) (one) can be sure
           to pass the high school entrance exam.
       b. (I) am searching for a tutor (who) can be sure to pass the high school
           entrance exam.

The relative clause in (255) has a gap in the subject position with which the head noun can be co-indexed, and on the basis of this structural property, it is expected to have interpretation (256b). As Matsumoto explains, the preferred interpretation of (255), however, is that in (256a), and such a preference results from a pragmatic consideration, which requires knowledge of Japaense society. That is, *katei-kyoosi* "tutor" is commonly hired by a family for a child in preparation for an entrance exam, and a competent tutor is one of the important keys leading to a success in passing an entrance exam. Given such a social understanding as the background context in which (255) is uttered, it is more natural to interpret the relative clause as in (256a).

To illustrate a similar pragmatic effect, Yoshiko Matsumoto (1990: 123) provides the pair in (257)–(258).

(257) [Donarudo toranpu-ga katta] mise-wa doko?
       Donald Trump-Nom   bought store-Top where
       "Where is the store (which) Donald Trump bought?"

(258) [Tomo-tyan-ga katta] mise-wa doko?
       Tomo-Nom   bought store-Top where
       "Where is the store (in which) little Tomo bought (it)?"

The syntactic structures of the two relative clauses seem identical, with an apparent gap corresponding to the direct object of the verb, *katta* "bought". Their (preferred) interpretations, however, are quite different: in (257) the relative clause is interpreted with a gap that corresponds to the direct object of the verb, while in (258) it is construed as a relative clause without a gap. The difference in interpretation, despite the parallel structure, can be ascribed to our knowledge of the world. We know that Donald Trump is a millionaire and can easily buy commercial stores; with little Tomo, on the other hand, it is more natural to understand that the store is the place at which she made a purchase. The examples that we have considered above suggest that contextual information can sometimes give preferences as to whether and/or where a gap is located in a relative clause, leading to a preferred interpretation of the sentence.

Another example of the relevance of pragmatic factors to the interpretation of a sentence is observed with the *-te aru* construction ("intransitivizing resultative construction") discussed earlier in this chapter. Recall that the *-te aru* construction is formed based on a transitive sentence, and the theme of a transitive verb surfaces as the subject. Some of the examples discussed earlier are repeated as (259)–(260).

(259) Denki-ga   tukete-aru.
       lights-Nom turn on
       "The lights have been turned on." (Lit: "The lights are in the state of having been turned on.")

(260) Bangohan-ga tukutte-aru.
       dinner-Nom   make
       "Dinner has been made." (Lit: "Dinner is in the state of having been made.")

While it has been argued that the subject of the *-te aru* construction must correspond to the theme argument of a transitive verb (Miyagawa 1988, 1989a), Yo Matsumoto (1990) demonstrates that the theme condition does not always account for the well-formedness of the construction. Relevant to his argument are examples like those in (261)–(262), taken from Yo Matsumoto (1990: 275–276).

(261) #Doa-ga   tataite-aru.
        door-Nom beat
       "The door is in the state of having been knocked upon."

(262) #Ishi-ga   nigitte-aru.
        stone-Nom grasp
       "The stone is in the state of having been grasped (e.g., its shape is changed)."

Native speakers find these sentences unacceptable although there is nothing wrong with respect to their structures. Matsumoto claims that a pragmatic condition is necessary in order to explain the unacceptable status of sentences like (261)–(262), and proposes the Describability Condition, as stated in (263).

(263) It must be evident that the state being described in the *-te aru* construction has resulted from a previous action of an agent. (Yo Matsumoto 1990: 275)

According to the Describability Condition, (261) is odd because when we knock on a door, there is usually no detectable mark left on it. Similarly, the state of a stone normally does not change by being grasped. If, on the other hand, the sentences are modified so that they describe a state where one could recognize some evidence of the agent's action leading to a state, then they are acceptable, as illustrated by (264)–(265).

(264) Doa-ga   itamu-hodo   tataite-aru.
       door-Nom be damaged- degree beat
       "The door is in the state of having been beaten to the degree of being damaged."

(265) (?)Nendo-ga nigitte-aru.
       clay-Nom   grasp
       "The clay is in the state of having been grasped (i.e. its shape is changed)."

The additional expression, *itamu-hodo* "to the degree of being damaged", in (264) provides further information that directly connects the agent's action and the detectable result. The change in subject from *ishi* "stone" to *nendo* "clay" in (265) makes it easier to interpret that an effect of grasping is much more readily recognizable. Thus, pragmatic constraints often play a role in offering explanations for an oddity or a preferred interpretation of some sentences.

Notes

1 The phrase in (5) has a third meaning: Taro's mother and Hanako's mother, namely, two female individuals. The nature of coordination under this interpretation is slightly different. Discussions of this type of coordination are found under the term "Right Node Raising". See Radford (1988), for discussion.

2 This shift in viewpoint is technically called empathy, as Kuno and Kaburaki (1977) explain in detail.

3 The giving verb *yaru* as an auxiliary verb can also be used to express the speaker's strong will. Under such an interpretation, *yaru* does not give rise to any sense of transfer in favor or benefit. One such example is given in (i), taken from Takami and Kato (2003: 97).

   (i) Rainen-koso-wa   kitto toodai-ni   gookaku-site-yaru-zo.
        next year-definitely-Top surely Univ. of Tokyo-in pass exam-give
        "I will surely do everything to get myself accepted by the University of Tokyo definitely next year."

4 The same situation can be expressed without a giving verb. The verbal complex *o-V(stem)-suru* is generally considered a humble expression to describe the situation that V-*sasiageru* is intended to express. So, for example, the following sentence can replace (54): *Watasi-ga sensei-ni zyuusyo-o o-kaki-sita.*

5 While the "meaning" associated with each mimetic word is often conventionalized and is thus found in a dictionary entry, the mimetic word can also invoke an

innovative use to the extent that it is still within its symbolic or imagery scope. The degree of acceptance of such an innovative use, however, may vary depending on individuals.

6 There are some mimetics that take the morphological forms of reduplication and yet do not have their corresponding non-reduplicated bases. Examples of this situation include (i).

(i) a. gatugatu (a manner of devouring)   vs.   *gatu(tto)
     b. uturautura (a manner of dozing)   vs.   *utura(tto)
     c. ityaitya (a manner of flirting)   vs.   *itya(tto)
     d. sekaseka (a manner of hurrying)   vs.   *seka(tto)

7 Because of these semantic and syntactic properties, the resemblance between the intransitivizing resultative construction and passives has been pointed out.

8 These verbs, on the other hand, may appear in the *-te simau* construction under the interpretation of regret of some sort, "end up doing something". The latter meaning is expressed in (i)–(ii).

(i)   Kawaigatteita inu-ga   sinde-simatta.
      dear   dog-Nom die
      "My dear dog ended up dying."
(ii) Okasii hanasi-ni tui   waratte-simatta.
      funny story-at involuntarily laugh
      "I ended up laughing at the funny story involuntarily."

9 It should be understood, however, that not just any Stative verb in Japanese exhibits aspectual ambiguity of the sort that we have observed in (152)–(153). For example, Stative verbs such as *iru* "be", *aru* "be", and *iru* "need" resist *-te iru*. Stative verbs are normally incompatible with imperatives, and *aru* "be" and *iru* "need" cannot form imperative sentences, while *iru* "be" can, as in *koko-ni ite-kudasai* (here-at be-please) "please be/stay here". Thus, within an apparently uniform aspectual class there is some degree of variation that could lead to aspectual ambiguity.

10 This type of Accusative Case marking on the object is also observed with the desiderative construction comprising V-*tai* "want to".

Suggested Readings

General issues in semantics: Ullmann (1962), Jackendoff (1972), Chierchia and McConnel-Ginet (1990), Kearns (2000), Saeed (2003).

General semantic issues in Japanese: Kuroda (1965a), Kuno (1973), Inoue (1976a).

Word meaning: Ullmann (1962), Dowty (1979), Lakoff and Johnson (1980), Levin (1985, 1993), Chierchia and McConnel-Ginet (1990). Ullmann (1962), in particular, provides a detailed discussion of lexical ambiguity. Lakoff and Johnson (1980) examine a number of metaphors and discuss concepts underlying them. Levin (1993) contains an impressive collection of various classes of English verbs with comments on their semantic and syntactic properties.

Verbs of giving and receiving: Kuno (1973), Kuno and Kaburaki (1977), Jorden with Noda (1988). Kuno (1973) and Jorden with Noda (1988) provide descriptions of giving and receiving verbs. Kuno and Kaburaki (1977) deal with issues related to verbs of giving and receiving using the notion of empathy. (Note: For the notion of deixis, see Fillmore 1975.)

Mimetics: Diffloth (1972), Hamano (1986, 1998), Kita (1997, 2001), Tamori and Schourup (1999), Tsujimura (2001, to appear), Tsujimura and Deguchi (to appear). Diffloth (1972) discusses the semantic characteristics of mimetic words in general. Hamano (1986, 1998) and Tamori and Schourup (1999) give an extensive survey of mimetics in Japanese. Kita (1997, 2001) and Tsujimura (2001) exchange different semantic views of Japanese mimetics. Tsujimura (to appear) and Tsujimura and Deguchi (to appear) re-examine the relevance of mimetics in linguistic theories.

Tense: Reichenbach (1947), Nakau (1976), Soga (1983), Teramura (1984), Comrie (1985), Hornstein (1990), Binnick (1991), Ogihara (1996). Reichenbach (1947), Comrie (1985), Hornstein (1990), Binnick (1991), and Ogihara (1996) give theoretical views of tense in general. Nakau (1976), Soga (1983), Teramura (1984), and Ogihara (1996) give descriptive and theoretical analyses of Japanese tense.

Aspect: Vendler (1967), Comrie (1976), Fujii (1976), Kindaichi (1976b), Yoshikawa (1976), Okuda (1978a, 1978b), Dowty (1979), Soga (1983), Teramura (1984), Binnick (1991), Smith (1991), Jacobsen (1992), McClure (1994, 1997), Tenny (1994), Levin and Rappaport Hovav (1995), Ogihara (1998), Shirai (2000), Kusumoto (2003). Detailed discussions concerning the notion of aspect are found in Comrie (1976), Binnick (1991), and Smith (1991). Kindaichi (1976b) presents an analysis of verbal classification in Japanese. McClure (1994) investigates the aspectual properties of Japanese verbs from the perspective of formal semantics. Rich literature on the *-te iru* construction in recent years particularly from various theoretical perspectives is found in McClure (1994, 1997), Ogihara (1998), Shirai (2000), and Kusumoto (2003).

Verb semantics: Talmy (1985, 2000a, 2000b), Levin (1993), Goldberg (1995), Levin and Rappaport Hovav (1995), Kageyama (1996), Yo Matsumoto (1996), Croft (1998), Rappaport Hovav and Levin (1998), Tsujimura (1999). The introduction of Levin (1993) lays out motivations for research in verb semantics. Levin and Rappaport Hovav (1995), Goldberg (1995), Croft (1998), and Rappaport Hovav and Levin (1998) argue for various theoretical approaches to issues in verb semantics, focusing on English. Discussion of Japanese on this topic is found in Kageyama (1996), Yo Matsumoto (1996), and Tsujimura (1999). Talmy (1985) gives an introduction to lexicalization, surveying a number of languages in the world, and Talmy (2000a, 2000b) develops an extensive analysis of it in Cognitive Grammar.

General issues in pragmatics: Searle (1969), Levinson (1983), Chierchia and McConnell-Ginet (1990), Horn and Ward (2004). A number of issues surrounding pragmatic matters in Japanese have often been dealt with in the realm of discourse analysis. Works along these lines include Maynard (1987, 1993a, 1993b, 1997, 1999), Iwasaki (1993), Okamoto (1995), and Kamio (1997).

EXERCISES

1   Give English and Japanese examples of the following.

    a.   homonyms
    b.   synonyms
    c.   antonyms
    d.   lexical ambiguity

2   Explain why the following sentences (with the intended meanings) are ungrammatical.

    a.   *Kodomo-ga warat-te aru.
        child-Nom   laugh
    b.   *Tori-ga   sin-de iru.
        bird-Nom die
        "The bird is dying."
    c.   *Tokei-ga kowasi-te iru. (kowasu: Vt)
        "A watch is broken."

3   List all the deictic expressions in the following sentences.

    a.   Konna   mazui   mono-wa tabe-rare-nai.
        this kind of tasteless thing-Top eat-Potential-Negative
        "I can't eat such a tasteless food."
    b.   Kyonen   tomodati-ni eigo-o   osie-te ageta.
        last year friend-Dat   English-Acc teach   gave
        "Last year I taught my friend English."
    c.   Taroo-ni asita   asoko-made itte-morai-tai.
        Taro-Dat tomorrow there-to   go-receive-want
        "I want Taro to go there tomorrow."

4   The following sentences are ambiguous. On the basis of the discussion in chapters 5 and 6, describe the ambiguity in detail.

    a.   Hanako-ga   kinoo   katta   okasi-o   otto-to   tabeta.
        Hanako-Nom yesterday bought sweets-Acc husband-with ate
    b.   Haha-ni   te-o   kir-are-ta.
        mother-by hand-Acc cut-Passive-Past

5   In the following sets of sentences one or more words are used metaphorically. Provide a general statement describing the principle that underlines these sets of metaphors. The example below is taken from Finegan (1994: 191).

Example:
a. I let my manuscript <u>simmer</u> for six months.
b. She <u>concocted</u> a report that readers will appreciate.
c. There is no easy <u>recipe</u> for writing effective business letters.

General statement: The writing process is viewed as cooking.

A. a. Kare-no kenryoku-ga agatta.
 he-Gen power-Nom rose
 "His power rose."
 b. Kare-no kenryoku-wa kudari-zaka-ni aru.
 he-Gen power-Top down-hill-at exist
 "His power is on the decline."
 c. Kare-wa kenryoku-no za-kara koroge-otita.
 he-Top power-Gen seat-from roll-fell
 "He fell from power."

B. a. Kangae-o ikani hoosoo-suru-ka-ga taisetu-da.
 idea-Acc how package-Q-Nom important-is
 "It's important how you package your idea."
 b. Sonna kangae-wa urenai.
 that sort of idea-Top won't sell
 "Such an idea won't sell."
 c. Sore-wa kati-no nai kangae-da.
 that-Top value-Gen there isn't idea-is
 "That is a worthless idea."

C. a. Watasi-wa mitita seikatu-o site-kita.
 I-Top filled life-Acc have done
 "I have had a full life."
 b. Kare-ni totte zinsei-wa karappo-da.
 he-for life-Top empty-is
 "Life is empty for him."
 c. Kanozyo-no seikatu-wa iroirona katudoo-de tumatteiru.
 she-Gen life-Top various activity-with fill
 "Her life is crammed with activities."

6 Answer the following questions concerning the *-te aru* construction.

A. Sentences (a–b) below are ungrammatical for reasons other than pragmatic oddity. Explain why.
 a. *Ki-ga taore-te aru.
 tree-Nom fall
 b. *Kodomo-ga nikun-de aru.
 child-Nom hate
 (cf. Titioya-ga kodomo-o nikunda.
 "father-Nom child-Acc hated")

B. In sentences (c–d) the identical verb *miru* is used to form the *-te aru* construction. As you can see from the accompanying sentences, the argument structure of the verb is also identical in both sentences. Consulting a dictionary, if necessary, explain the difference in grammaticality.

    c. *Umi-ga mi-te aru.
       sea-Nom
       (cf. Taro-ga umi-o miru "Taro-Nom sea-Acc <verb>")
    d. Ronbun-ga mi-te aru.
       thesis (or academic paper)-Nom
       (cf. Taro-ga ronbun-o miru "Taro-Nom thesis-Acc <verb>")

7 Japanese is famous for having what are called multiple-subject sentences. Consider (a–b).

    a. Tanaka-sensei-ga   musuko-san-ga nakunatta.
       Prof. Tanaka-Nom son-Nom   died
       "It is Professor Tanaka whose son died."
    b. Yahari natu-ga   biiru-ga   umai.
       after all summer-Nom beer-Nom tasty
       "After all, it's during the summer that beer tastes good."

In (a–b), there are two NPs that are both marked with the particle that typically goes with the subject. It has been claimed that the second NP in each of these sentences is the true subject, whereas the first NP-*ga* is to be distinguished as a MAJOR Subject. The first NP-*ga* typically receives a stress peak and is followed by a pause.

A. Looking at (a–b), what difference can you see regarding thematic roles between subjects and major subjects?

B. Compare (c–d) below with (b).

    c. *Yahari wain-ga   biiru-ga   umai.
       after all wine-Nom beer-Nom tasty
       "After all, wine, beer is tasty."
    d. *Yahari Taro-ga   biiru-ga   umai.
       after all Taro-Nom beer-Nom tasty
       "After all, Taro, beer is tasty."

(c–d) are semantically anomalous. A native speaker of Japanese would be unsure of what you might possibly mean by saying them. How do (c–d) contrast with (b) semantically? Look particularly at the lexical choice of major subject in the overall sentence.

8 Recall the sentences with the reflexive word *zibun* and the discussion of them. Now, consider the following examples (modified from Kuno 1973: 309–310).

    a. i.   Taroo$_i$-ga Hanako-ga   zibun$_i$-o korosooto sita toki,
                Taro-Nom Hanako-Nom self-Acc try to kill did when
                Yooko-to   neteita.
                Yoko-with was sleeping
                "Taro was sleeping with Yoko when Hanako tried to kill him."

        ii.   *Taroo$_i$-ga Hanako-ga   zibun$_i$-o korosita toki, Yooko-to
                Taro-Nom Hanako-Nom self-Acc killed   when Yoko-with
                neteita.
                was sleeping
                "Taro was sleeping with Yoko when Hanako killed him."

    b. i.   Taroo$_i$-ga zibun$_i$-o korosootosita sono otoko-to maeni
                Taro-Nom self-Acc tried to kill   that man-with before
                atta koto-ga atta.
                met had
                "Before Taro had met the man who tried to kill him."

        ii.   *Taroo$_i$-ga zibun$_i$-o korosita sono otoko-to maeni atta
                Taro-Nom self-Acc killed   that man-with before met
                koto-ga atta.
                had
                "Before Taro had met with the man who killed him."

    c. i.   Taroo$_i$-ga kazoku ya   sinsekitati-ni, zibun$_i$-ga sinu maeni,
                Taro-Nom family and relatives-to   self-Nom die before
                denwa-o   kaketa.
                phone-Acc called
                "Taro called up his family and relatives before he died."

        ii.   *Taroo$_i$-ga zibun$_i$-ga sinda toki, issen mo   motte inakatta.
                Taro-Nom self-Nom died when penny even have not
                "Taro, when he died, didn't have a penny."

Does the ungrammaticality of the (ii) sentences have to do with a violation of any of the conditions we discussed? If so, which one? If not, what do you think might be the problem with these sentences?

7 Language Variation

People who speak the same language do not all speak alike. They may speak differently from one another depending on where they are from, their social status, and what sex they are. Social and cultural factors like gender and style, among others, as well as geographical region make up a set of variables that account for how linguistic forms are realized under a specific speech situation in a given speech community. Japanese serves as a particularly interesting language to investigate from the perspective of sociolinguistics because besides a wide range of regional dialectal variation, it exhibits rich and complex linguistic systems of speech style, honorification, and gender differences and indexing. In this chapter we shall briefly examine language variation in Japanese from the perspectives of dialects, styles and levels of speech, and gender differences.

1 Dialectal Variation

Unlike the United States, Japan is a very small island country, and yet people from different regions of the country speak differently. This type of variation in the language reflects different dialects. Differences among regional dialects can be found in phonetic, accentual, lexical, morphophonological, or morphosyntactic properties (or any combination of them). A major split in Japanese can be found between eastern and western dialects. The former includes Tokyo while the latter covers Osaka and the Kansai areas. This section will discuss some of the aspects of dialectal variation in Japanese.

One of the major factors pertinent to dialectal variation is sound-related differences among dialects of various regions. An example comes from the nature of the high back vowel /u/, between the eastern and the western parts of Japan. We have discussed in chapter 2 the fact that the high back vowel in Japanese is unrounded. Shibatani (1990) observes, however, that the unrounded high back vowel is more frequently observed in the eastern part of Japan, and speakers of the western dialects tend to pronounce the high back vowel more rounded.

Another instance of regional variation in terms of the pronunciation of certain phonemes is reported in Shibatani (1990) concerning the number and nature of vowels that different dialects employ. In chapter 2 we have stated that Japanese has five vowels: /i, e, a, o, u/. Although this five-vowel system seems to be wide-spread, there exist dialects that exhibit fewer than five vowels, as well as dialects that have more than five vowels. According to Shibatani, Ryukyuan dialects exemplify these cases. The Yonaguni dialect, for instance, has three vowels, /i, a, u/, while the Hateruma dialect shows seven vowels, /i, ï, u, e, ë, o, a/, where /ï/ and /ë/ indicate that these sounds are centralized versions of /i/ and /e/, respectively.

An interesting difference between eastern and western dialects is that while eastern dialects have one-mora words such as *ki* "tree" and *me* "eye", these tend to be lengthened in the western dialects and are pronounced as [ki:] and [me:], respectively. A lengthening phenomenon is also observed in the Nakizin dialect of Okinawan Japanese, as is discussed in Haraguchi (1991; see also Nakasone 1983). In Nakizin verbs and adjectives, the second and fourth syllables are lengthened. This is depicted in (1) (slightly modified from Haraguchi 1991: 39).

(1) a. hakuu-na   "don't write"
     b. pʰataarakuu-na   "don't work"
     c. haraamakuu-na   "don't wind"

In (1a) the second syllable is lengthened while in (1b) and (1c) the second and fourth syllables become long. The corresponding phrase for (b) in the Tokyo dialect, for example, is *hataraku-na*, in which the second and fourth syllables are short.

The dialects spoken in the Tohoku region, the northern part of Honshu, demonstrate several interesting characteristics, as is discussed in detail in Shibatani (1990). Shibatani reports that in the Tohoku dialects it is common to see the centralization of high vowels /i/ and /u/: that is, the front vowel /i/ is pronounced more back and the back vowel /u/ is pronounced more front. Specifically, in these dialects the distinction between /i/ and /u/ has been lost. For instance, in Tokyo, the words *sisi* "lion" and *susi* "Sushi" are clearly distinguished: they are pronounced [šiši] and [suši], respectively. On the other hand, in Akita, the northern part of the Tohoku region, both words are pronounced as [šïšï], while in Sendai, the southern part of the Tohoku region, both words are phonetically realized as [süsü]. The same observation is made with the words *tizi* "governor" and *tizu* "map", which are pronounced as [čiǰi] and [čizu] in Tokyo. Both words are pronounced as [čïǰï] in Akita and as [tˢüzü] in Sendai. Similarly, the distinction between *kuti* "mouth" pronounced as [kuči] and *kutu* "shoe" pronounced as [kutˢu] in Tokyo is completely lost in these Tohoku dialects: they are both pronounced as [kïčï] in Akita, while they are realized as [kütˢü] in Sendai. So, in these Tohoku dialects, the distinction between the high vowels is neutralized: they are realized as [ï] in Akita and [ü] in Sendai.

According to Shibatani, in southern Tohoku, voiceless stops become voiced, thereby resulting in the loss of the distinction between the voiced and voiceless stops. For example, *ito* "string" and *ido* "well" are both realized as [ido]; *mato* "target" and *mado* "window" are pronounced as [mado]; and *taka* "hawk" and *taga* "hoop" are pronounced as [taga]. This phenomenon should be contrasted

Prefectures	Cities	Islands	
1 Aomori	37 Sendai	48 Hachijōjima	53 Tokunoshima
2 Akita	38 Mito	49 Oki	54 Miyako
3 Miyagi	39 Yokohama	50 Ibukijima	55 Ishigaki
4 Yamagata	40 Kanazawa	51 Kikaijima	56 Hateruma
5 Ibaraki	41 Nagoya	52 Amami-ōshima	57 Yonaguni
6 Chiba	42 Takajōchō		
7 Tōkyō	43 Miyakonojō		
8 Nīgata	44 Nago		
9 Toyama	45 Naha (Shuri)		
10 Ishikawa	46 Suzu		
11 Shizuoka	47 Hirara		
12 Gifu			
13 Aichi			
14 Mie			
15 Shiga			
16 Kyōto			
17 Nara			
18 Ōsaka			
19 Okayama			
20 Hiroshima			
21 Yamaguchi			
22 Kagawa			
23 Tokushima			
24 Kōchi			
25 Fukuoka			
26 Ōita			
27 Nagasaki			
28 Kumamoto			
29 Miyazaki			
30 Kagoshima			
31 Okinawa			
(32) Hōki			
(33) Izumo			
(34) Chikugo			
(35) Hizen			
(36) Higo			

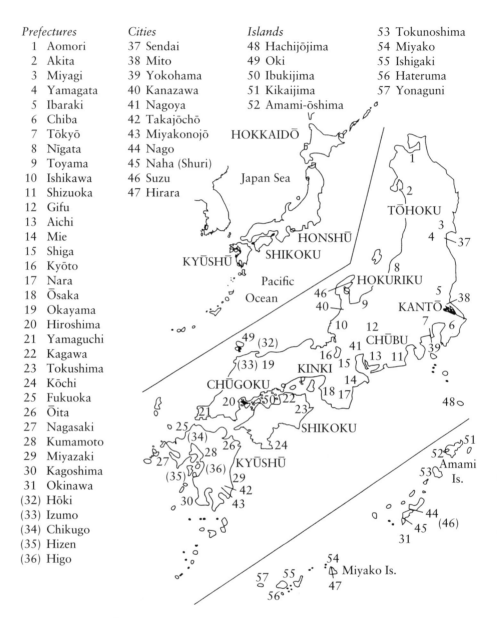

Map 7.1 Map of Japan

with a similar voicing phenomenon observed in northern Tohoku. There the voicing of voiceless stops is also observed, but the stops that are voiced in other dialects have prenasalization in northern Tohoku. So, *ito* "string" is pronounced as [ido] while *ido* "well" is realized as [iⁿdo]. Similarly, *mato* "target" and *mado* "window" surface are realized as [mado] and [maⁿdo], respectively. As for the velar stop /g/, it is replaced by the velar nasal [ŋ]. For example, *taka* "hawk" and *taga* "hoop" are realized as [taga] and [taŋa], respectively. Thus, in both southern and northern Tohoku, the voicing of voiceless stops is observed, but in southern Tohoku the difference between the voiced and voiceless stops is neutralized, while in northern Tohoku the distinction is still made by way of the nasalization of the voiced stops.

The type of variation in Japanese that is most extensively discussed in the literature is the diversity among the dialects in accentuation and pitch patterns. Here we will briefly indicate a few of these differences in comparing Tokyo with other dialects (see Shibatani 1990 and Haraguchi 1977 for a fuller discussion). First, the forms in (2) contrast the pitch patterns of various words in the Tokyo dialect with that of the Osaka dialect.

(2)

				Tokyo	*Osaka*
a.	miyako	"capital"		LHH	HHH
b.	kokoro	"heart"		LHL	HLL
c.	inoti	"life"		HLL	HLL
d.	atama	"head"		LHH	HHL
e.	sora	"sky"		HL	LH
f.	take	"bamboo"		LH	HH
g.	yama	"mountain"		LH	HL
h.	suzume	"sparrow"		LHH	LLH
i.	kabuto	"helmet"		HLL	LHL
j.	tukemono	"pickles"		LHHH	LLLH
k.	niwatori	"chicken"		LHHH	HHHH
l.	bentoo	"box lunch"		LHHL	HHLL
m.	uguisu	"Japanese nightingale"		LHLL	HLLL
n.	nokogiri	"saw"		LHHL	LHHL
o.	kaminari	"thunder"		LHHH	LHHL

Second, the differences in the pitch pattern can also be observed between the Tokyo dialect and the Takamatsu dialect of Shikoku as well as between the Tokyo dialect and the Kagoshima dialect of Kyushu. What is particularly interesting is that the Takamatsu dialect shows falling pitch (on a single mora) as well as high and low pitch. Observe (3)–(4), where "F" stands for falling pitch (cf. Haraguchi 1977).

(3)

			Tokyo	*Takamatsu*
a.	kasa	"umbrella"	HL	LL
b.	isi	"stone"	LH	HL
c.	uta	"song"	LH	LF
d.	usagi	"rabbit"	LHH	LLL
e.	azuki	"red beans"	LHH	LHL
f.	kabuto	"helmet"	HLL	LLF
g.	niwatori	"chicken"	LHHH	LLLL
h.	murasaki	"purple"	LHLL	LLHL
i.	mayoigo	"missing child"	LHHL	LLLF
j.	garasudo	"glass door"	LHHL	LHHF

(4)   *Tokyo*   *Kagoshima*
   a. hana   "nose"   LH   HL
   b. hana   "flower"   LH   LH
   c. sakura   "cherry"   LHH   LHL
   d. usagi   "rabbit"   LHH   LLH
   e. meirei   "order"   LHHH HHLL
   f. kyuusyuu "Kyushu"   HLLL HHLL
   g. kookoo   "filial piety" HLLL LLHH
   h. kantan   "simple"   LHHH LLHH

			Tokyo	*Kagoshima*
a.	hana	"nose"	LH	HL
b.	hana	"flower"	LH	LH
c.	sakura	"cherry"	LHH	LHL
d.	usagi	"rabbit"	LHH	LLH
e.	meirei	"order"	LHHH	HHLL
f.	kyuusyuu	"Kyushu"	HLLL	HHLL
g.	kookoo	"filial piety"	HLLL	LLHH
h.	kantan	"simple"	LHHH	LLHH

As a final observation, we note that the different pitch patterns in the dialects may be reflected by their different realizations on minimal pairs. The difference in (5) between the Tokyo and Kyoto dialects illustrates the point.

(5)   *Tokyo*   *Kyoto*

			Tokyo	*Kyoto*
a.	hasi	"chopsticks"	HL	LH
b.	hasi	"bridge"	LH	HL
c.	hasi	"edge"	LH	HH

The Tokyo dialect has a two-way distinction while the Kyoto dialect has a three-way distinction. That is, in isolation, the Kyoto dialect can make a specific distinction among these three words by way of the pitch pattern, whereas in the Tokyo dialect, two of the words are realized as bearing the identical phonetic and pitch realization. More generally, the HH tone pattern on a two-syllable CVCV word is not found in the Tokyo dialect.

Somewhat related to the accentuation pattern is the intonational pattern among dialects. It is usually the case that in Tokyo, assertions tend to have falling intonation toward the end of the sentence, while the ending of a question bears rising intonation. So, for instance, in Tokyo (6a–b) are different only in their intonation pattern toward the end of the sentences.

(6) a. Satoo-san-wa asita   kimasu. (falling intonation)
        Mr Sato-Top tomorrow come
        "Mr Sato will come tomorrow."
    b. Satoo-san-wa asita   kimasu(ka)? (rising intonation)
        Mr Sato-Top tomorrow come (Q)
        "Will Mr Sato come tomorrow?"

In Japanese, question sentences often end with the question particle *ka*, but it need not be present as long as the sentence has rising intonation, as (6b) indicates. Without the question particle, then, the assertion of (6a) and the question of (6b) are identical. The only way to differentiate these two is by the intonation: the assertion sentence ends with falling intonation while the question sentence bears rising intonation.

The use of the intonation pattern to differentiate assertions from questions is not observed in all dialects. For example, Fujiwara (1964) reports that the Kansai dialects, which include Osaka and Kyoto, have level intonation for both assertions and questions. That is, regardless of the sentence type, there is no intonation contour. Observe (7)–(9), taken from Fujiwara (1964: 220).

(7) Mookarimakka? "Are you having good business?"

(8) Ikkooni sirimasen. "I don't know a thing."

(9) Nagete mitarooka? "Shall I throw (it)?"

The sentences in (7) and (9) are questions while (8) is an assertion. According to Fujiwara, in spite of this difference in the type of sentence, all these sentences bear the same intonation pattern: that is, regardless of whether these sentences are assertions or questions, they maintain level intonation toward the end, rather than display rising or falling intonation. Hence, not all dialects of Japanese use intonation contours to differentiate questions from assertions.

Let us now examine variation among lexical items and expressions that are frequently used in everyday conversation. The opposition between eastern and western regions has been observed above with respect to sound and accent-related variation. Opposition between these regions is also clearly detected in individual lexical items. For example, Tojo (1955: 55) lists various lexical differences between the Tokyo dialect and the Osaka/Kyoto dialect, some of which are illustrated in (10).

(10)

Tokyo	*Osaka/Kyoto*	*gloss*
kaeru	inu	"return, go home"
sawaru/iziru	irau	"touch"
korobu	kokeru	"stumble"
niru	taku	"cook, simmer"
osorosii	kyootoi	"scary"
isogasii	seturosii	"busy"
ugoku	inoku	"move"
ikenai	akan	"no good"
kimyoona	kettaina	"strange"

It is interesting to observe that some of the contrasting words seem to share certain phonological aspects while others do not.

Another instance of dialectal variation is observed in certain common expressions such as "thank you", "good morning", and "good evening". Yoshimoto (1991) observes that *arigatoo* "thank you" in Tokyo is expressed as *kinodokuna* or *dandan* in Toyama prefecture, the area north of Tokyo, facing the Sea of Japan. What is interesting here is that *kinodokuna* in the Tokyo dialect means "pitiful". In Mie prefecture, the western part of the Kii peninsula, *sumimasen*, which can mean "I'm sorry" or "excuse me" in the Tokyo dialect, is used to express "thank you". It is also well known that *ookini* or *ookeni* is used in the Kansai area to express gratitude.

Similar types of variation are reported by Yoshimoto (1991), who surveys dialectal diversity for the expressions "good morning" and "good evening". (11)–(12) list some of his examples (pp. 24–28).

(11) *expression for "good morning"*
Tokyo   ohayoo
Akita   ohayansi
Iwate   ohayagansi
Fukushima   hayainasi
Kyoto   ohayoosan
Nagasaki   ohinnarimasita
Kagoshima   sameyansitaka

(12) *expression for "good evening"*
Tokyo   konbanwa
Kagoshima   konbanna
Iwate   oban/obandegansu
Fukushima   eebandasina
Tochigi   obankadarenasarimasita
Shimane   banzimasite
Tottori   bannarimasina

Thus, quite a wide variety of expressions is detected for simple greetings that are used in everyday conversation.

Finally, as an illustration of morphosyntactic variation among dialects of Japanese, let us examine verbal conjugation patterns. According to the report by Kokuritsu Kokugo Kenkyujo (National Language Research Center: 1959), the verbal conjugation forms in (13) for *kaku* "write" are listed.

(13)

place	*present*	*negative*	*provisional*	*past*
Yamagata	kagu	kagane	kageba	kagita/da
Ishikawa	kaku	kakan	kakya	kaita
Aichi	kaku	kakanai	kakya	kakita
Nara	kaku	kakahen	kakeba	kaita
		kakan		
Ehime	kaku	kakan	kakeba	kaita
Tokyo	kaku	kakanai	kakeba	kaita

As (13) shows, there are wide varieties of conjugation types attested across dialects.

2   Styles and Levels of Speech

Every language seems to have at least some kind of strategy for marking, in one way or another, a speaker's admiration or respect for, or politeness to, a hearer: it could be manifested, for instance, as intonation, specific choice of words, or a particular selection of syntactic constructions. In order to communicate with members of various speech communities in diverse settings, it is often necessary and sometimes more effective for particular purposes to make use of varying degrees of politeness and different styles. Taking an example from English, when a student asks a professor to write a letter of recommendation, the student is more likely to say something similar to "Would you be able to write a recommendation letter for me?" than to say "Hey, write me a recommendation letter, will you?" It is clear that the former strikes one as more polite and appropriate for this request situation than the latter.

Japanese is known to be rich in linguistic encoding of styles and levels of speech, which has been referred to as **honorification**. Honorification is reflected most distinctively in predicates, and is primarily divided into two types, **referent honorifics** and **addressee honorifics** (Shibatani 1990; Okamoto 1997; Iwasaki 2002). Referent honorifics serve to mark respect for an individual referred to, and can further be branched into **respectful forms** and **humble forms**. Respect forms are used for an individual or the individual's activities in order to honor him or her. This individual is a person who holds a rank socially higher than the speaker (or the speaker's in-group), and thus is to be respected. The basic role that humble forms play is to humble the speaker or the speaker's in-group, whereby respect is paid to the referent. Thus, the effect of respectful forms and humble forms is roughly the same in that they ultimately exalt the individual referred to. Referent honorifics are manifested in several verbal forms, by irregular verbs in some cases and by more regular verbal morphology in others, as we will see from examples below. Addressee honorifics are also referred to as "polite forms", and are mainly used when a conversational situation calls for some formality. This type of honorific is marked in the inflectional ending. The inflectional paradigms for verbs, adjectives, and adjectival nouns that are introduced in chapters 3 and 4, repeated in (14)–(16) below, are citation forms, but they are considered to be a casual style and an informal level of speech when they are used sentence-finally. Their corresponding addressee honorific forms, which typically end in *-masu* for verbs and *-desu* for other word categories, are given in (17)–(19).

(14) verb
    a. *non-past*   tabe-ru   "eat"
    b. *non-past neg.* tabe-nai
    c. *past*   tabe-ta
    d. *past neg.*   tabe-na-kat-ta
    e. *tentative*   tabe-ru-daroo

(15) adjective
    a. *non-past*   ooki-i   "big"
    b. *non-past neg.* ooki-ku na-i
    c. *past*   ooki-kat-ta
    d. *past neg.*   ooki-ku na-kat-ta
    e. *tentative*   ooki-i daroo

(16)   *nouns*   *adjectival nouns*

		nouns "book"	adjectival nouns "pretty"
a.	*non-past*	hon-da	kirei-da
b.	*non-past neg.*	hon-zya na-i	kirei-zya na-i
c.	*past*	hon-dat-ta	kirei-dat-ta
d.	*past neg.*	hon-zya na-kat-ta	kirei-zya na-kat-ta
e.	*tentative*	hon-daroo	kirei-daroo

(17)   *verb (addressee honorific)*
    a.   *non-past*   tabe-masu   "eat"
    b.   *non-past neg.*   tabe-masen
    c.   *past*   tabe-masita
    d.   *past neg.*   tabe-masen desita
    e.   *tentative*   tabe-ru desyoo

(18)   *adjectives (addressee honorific)*
    a.   *non-past*   ookii-desu   "big"
    b.   *non-past neg.*   ooki-ku arimasen
    c.   *past*   ooki-katta desu
    d.   *past neg.*   ooki-ku arimasen desita
    e.   *tentative*   ookii-desyoo

(19)   *noun/adjectival noun (addressee honorific)*
    a.   *non-past*   hon/kirei-desu   "book/pretty"
    b.   *non-past neg.*   hon/kire-zya arimasen
    c.   *past*   hon/kire-desita
    d.   *past neg.*   hon/kire-zya arimasen-desita
    e.   *tentative*   hon/kire-desyoo

Let us give an illustration of how respectful forms, humble forms, and addressee honorific forms are used in a modern-day conversation. The verbal forms for *iku* (citation form) "go" corresponding to these three classes are *irassyaru* (respectful), *mairu* (humble), and *ikimasu* (addressee honorific), respectively. Consider the hypothetical dialogue in (20) between the student Tanaka and his teacher, focusing on the distribution of these verbal forms.

(20)   Tanaka: Sensei, asita-no   kaigi-ni   <u>irassyaimasu</u> ka?
                      teacher tomorrow-Gen conference-to go (hon.)   Q
                      "Are you going to the conference tomorrow?"
       Prof.:   Ee, <u>ikimasu</u>. Tanakakun-wa?
                      yes go (pol.) Tanaka-Top
                      "Yes, I will. How about you, Mr Tanaka?"
     Tanaka: Hai, watasi-mo <u>mairimasu</u>.
                      yes I-also   go (hum.)
                      "Yes, I will go, too."

The student, Tanaka, uses the respectful form, *irassyaimasu*, to refer to the professor's activity. This is to show his respect toward the professor. The professor, on the other hand, does not use the respectful form or the humble form in reference to his own action of attending the meeting; instead, he uses the addressee honorific form, *ikimasu*. The use of this form by the professor in this example can be viewed as his attempt to keep a formal relationship between the two parties in order to maintain social distance. The student's response contains the humble form, *mairimasu*. The student refers to his own activity of going, and in the presence of his professor as the addressee, the humble form is used as an indication of respect for the teacher: that is, by humbling himself the speaker achieves the effect of exalting the professor. Note that referent honorifics are used in combination with addressee honorifics, as is shown in the forms like *irrasyaimasu* and *mairimasu* in this example.

Not all the verbs in Japanese exhibit the morphologically distinguished forms of respectful, humble, and addressee honorific in the manner shown by the set of verbs *irassyaimasu*, *mairimasu*, and *ikimasu*. The majority of verbs, instead, make use of a morphologically more productive way of forming honorific forms. For the respectful form, for instance, *o* is prefixed to a verbal root and at the same time *ni naru* is added to the right of it. When a verbal root is prefixed by *o*, and is followed by *suru*, on the other hand, a humble form is derived. And, as the inflectional paradigm in (17) exhibits, a verbal root suffixed by *masu* corresponds to an addressee honorific form. So, for example, the respectful, humble, and addressee honorific forms of the verb *kik(u)* "ask, listen to" are *o-kiki-ni naru/narimasu*, *o-kiki-suru/simasu*, and *kiki-masu*, respectively.[1] The use of these forms is demonstrated by the hypothetical dialogue in (21) between Tanaka and his teacher, parallel to that of (20).

(21) Tanaka: Sensei, hisyo-ni   sono hon-no   namae-o
               teacher secretary-of that book-Gen name-Acc
               o-kiki-ni narimasu ka.
               hon.-ask   Q
               "Are you going to ask the secretary the name of that book?"
      Prof.:   Iie, kiki-masen.
               No, ask-pol.neg
               "No, I'm not going to."
      Tanaka: Zyaa, watasi-ga o-kiki-simasu.
               then I-Nom   hon.-ask
               "Then, I will ask (her for you)."

The student Tanaka asks his teacher a question concerning the professor's possible activity of asking the secretary the name of the book by using the respectful form, *o-kiki-ni narimasu*, which is formed by the morphologically productive way of deriving this type of referent honorifics. The use of a respectful verb thus indicates the student's respect for his teacher. The teacher, on the other hand, does not have to use the respectful form or the humble form for his own activity when he is speaking with his student, who is considered to be at a lower social rank. In fact, if the professor used either a respectful or humble form, in the current situation, the sentence would be extremely awkward. This is why the professor uses the addressee honorific form. Notice that the use of the addressee honorific form also suggests that the style of the conversation is formal, and is used to maintain some social distance between the two participants. Finally, the student's response contains the humble expression *o-kiki-simasu* to refer to his own activity of asking. By humbling his activity, the student expresses respect for the teacher.

It is indisputable that honorification, manifested in several linguistic forms in Japanese, is an example of language variation, in which people speak differently depending on their social status. This socially and culturally rooted linguistic phenomenon, nevertheless, should be examined with great caution. The generalizations of honorific forms that we have assumed in the discussion above are prevalently thought of as mirroring the actual language use commonly observed in Japanese speech communities. That is, it has been believed and stated time and again that any formal setting that involves interlocutors of different social ranks necessarily calls for appropriate linguistic forms of honorification. It is crucial to realize, however, that what we have described thus far may sometimes represent an ideological, normative language use (i.e., the speech pattern that we are supposed to use), and real situations may involve a far wider range of social and cultural variables beyond what has been customarily understood.

An important case in illustration, for example, comes from Okamoto's (1997) sociolinguistic study and other related works (Okamoto and Shibamoto Smith 2004). In this investigation, Okamoto compares two similar business settings, and notes the difference in the use of honorification: one setting involves a salesperson and a customer at a department store, as in (22); and in the other, a dialogue takes place between a fish vendor in a market and a customer, as in (23). Both are taken from Okamoto (1997: 106), with slight modifications.

(22)   (at a women's clothes section of the department store in Kyoto; a saleswoman, talking to a customer)
    S: Irassyaimase. Doozo goran kudasaimase.
        "Welcome. Please take a look at them."

(23)   (at a fish shop in the market in Osaka; a male vendor, talking to customers, trying to catch their attention)
    S: Tyuu-toro ya, tyuu-toro. Ii no haitte ru yo. Mite itte yo, mite itte.
        "(It's/We have) tyuu-toro, tyuu-toro (a kind of fish – fatty tuna). Good ones are in. Take a look at them, take a look at them."

In theory, both situations involve a setting for an exchange between a salesperson and a customer, and as is normally considered appropriate, may call for the use of honorification on the part of the salespersons. The salesperson at a department store in (22) follows such a norm, but the fish vendor does not. In (23), the inflectional ending -*desu* for *tyuu-toro* is missing; the addressee honorific form of *haitte-imasu* is replaced by the casual speech form of *haitte ru (yo)*; and the verbal gerund form of *(mite) itte* represents a very informal request. The use of honorific forms in (22) and the lack thereof in (23) by salespersons indeed reflect truly authentic language use. If the fish vendor were to use the same kind of language as the saleswoman in (22), it would be extremely inappropriate and would be considered even comical or absurd. In the rather friendly atmosphere that street markets in downtown areas try to create, the lack of rigid formality is not only suitable but desirable. Thus, the decision by a speaker to use a particular form of honorification is not so easily reduced to an ideological norm, but is controlled by the interaction of numerous factors, of which linguistic, social, and cultural ones are just a few.

3   Gender Differences

Many languages exhibit different speech patterns between men and women (Tannen 1990). That is, the way men speak and the way women speak are different, and we will refer to such differences as gender differences, and regard them as another instance of language variation. Even in languages that do not have apparent systematic gender differences, there are always certain characteristics that can distinguish the speech patterns of male and female speakers. English, for example, does not seem to have a systematic way of marking gender differences. However, women arguably have a tendency to use more detailed color terms such as *magenta, aquamarine,* and *cobalt blue* that males use less frequently.

   Japanese is one of the languages that explicitly exhibits various gender differences in speech. The clearest instances of such gender differences in Japanese that are often referred to include the use of personal pronouns and sentence-final particles. First, Japanese demonstrates quite a rich pronominal system particularly with regard to the speaker, i.e. the first person, and the hearer, i.e. the second person. The selection of these personal pronouns depends on the gender of the first and second persons that participate in the conversation as well as on the formality of the situation in which the conversation takes place. The list in (24), taken from Ide (1990: 73), illustrates varieties of ways to refer to "I" and "you".

(24)

		men's speech	*women's speech*
first person			
formal		watakusi	watakusi
		watasi	atakusi*
plain		boku	watasi
			atasi*
deprecatory		ore	Ø
second person			
formal		anata	anata
plain		kimi	anata
		anta*	anta*
deprecatory		omae	
		kisama	Ø

(*marks variants of a social dialect.) All the first person pronouns mean "I" and all the second person pronouns mean "you". Notice that among the first person pronouns, *watakusi* and *watasi* can be used both by male and female speakers whereas *boku* and *ore* are rarely used by females in a normal speech situation.[2] Similarly, for the second person pronouns, the typical female use of *anata* is often adopted in male speech, but *kisama* is not normally used by females. To illustrate briefly their uses in sentences, consider the male and female speech in (25)–(26), in which first person pronouns are exemplified.

(25) Male Speech
   a. **Watakusi/Watasi**-ga itasimasu.
      I-Nom   do
      "I will do (it)."
   b. **Boku**-ga simasu/suru-yo.
      I-Nom   do
      "I will do (it)."
   c. **Ore**-ga suru-yo.
      I-Nom do
      "I will do (it)."
   d. ??**Ore**-ga simasu.
      I-Nom   do
      "I will do (it)."

(26) Female Speech
   a. **Watakusi**-ga simasu.
      I-Nom   do
      "I will do (it)."
   b. **Watasi**-ga simasu/suru-wa.
      I-Nom   do
      "I will do (it)."

Careful attention should be paid to the relationship between the first person pronouns and the verbal endings that indicate formality. (25) demonstrates the range of first person pronouns uttered by male speakers. Male speakers use either *watakusi* or *watasi* to refer to themselves in a formal situation, although *watakusi* is more formal than *watasi*. So, when a company employee speaks to the company president, for example, it is most likely that the employee refers to herself or himself as either *watakusi* or *watasi*. This is observed by (25a). The verbal ending *itasimasu* "will do" is a respectful verbal form with the inflectional ending typical of addressee honorifics, -*masu*, and indicates that the situation in which the conversation takes place is formal. The plain form, *boku*, in (25b) can be used in a formal situation, especially with the choice of *simasu*, an addressee honorific form, although less formal than the situation in (25a); or in a casual setting such as in a conversation between two male colleagues or friends. The verbal ending *suru-yo* is a sign of informality, and hence it is compatible with *boku*. *Ore*, on the other hand, is used in a very casual situation, as in the conversation between very close friends. Furthermore, Ide classifies this pronoun as deprecatory. Notice that the verbal ending that is compatible with this pronoun is *suru-yo*, which is also very casual, as is illustrated in (25c). When *ore* is used with the addressee honorific form of *simasu*, as in (25d), there arises a conflict in style between the very casual pronoun and the formal verbal ending, and hence the sentence is awkward.

   In contrast with the wide range of first person pronouns used by male speakers, first person pronouns that refer to female speakers are more restricted. When the situation is formal, *watakusi* or *watasi* is used, but the latter can also be used in a casual speech situation. This is confirmed by the examples in (26). As (26a) demonstrates, *watakusi* is normally used in very formal circumstances, while as (26b) shows, *watasi* can be used with either the formal verbal ending *simasu* or the casual verbal ending *suru-wa*. Hence personal pronouns, especially those for the first and second persons, demonstrate a clear difference between male and female speech patterns.

Second, there are a number of sentence-final particles, some of which emphasize assertion and some of which signal that the sentence is a question. However, not all the sentence-final particles are used identically by male and female speakers: some of them exhibit predominant use by males while others are used mainly by females. Consider the examples in (27)–(29).

(27) a. Kaeru **zo**.
         go home
         "I will go home."
      b. Iku **ze**.
         go
         "I will go."
      c. Dekiru **sa**.
         be competent
         "You can do it."

(28) a. Satoo-san-wa kuru **kasira**.
         Mr Sato-Top come Q
         "I wonder if Mr Sato will come."
      b. Basu-ga kita **wa**. (rising intonation)
         bus-Nom came
         "The bus has come."
      c. Asita   yasumu **no**. (falling intonation)
         tomorrow be absent
         "I will be absent tomorrow."

(29) a. Iku **yo**.
         go
         "I will go."
      b. Kuru **ne**. (rising intonation)
         come
         "You are coming, aren't you?"

The sentence-final particles in (27) are primarily used by men, although the use of *sa* in (27c) is increasingly being extended to female speech in informal situations. The particles in (28), in contrast, are used mainly by female speakers. That is, in a normal speech situation, we do not consider the sentences in (28) (particularly (a) and (b)) typical of men's speech; and, similarly, we do not normally expect a woman to speak those sentences in (27), especially (27a–b). However, the use of the sentence-final particles in (27) by female speakers has been observed in very informal conversations, including recent advertisements. The particles in (29), in contrast, can be used almost equally by both men and women. Therefore, the range of sentence-final particles illustrated in the sentences in (27)–(29) demonstrates that the addition of a particle generally reflects gender difference in Japanese.[3]

In addition to personal pronouns and sentence-final particles, women's speech is distinct from men's in various other respects. Ide (1990) claims that women do not use words and expressions that suggest "profanity" or "obscenity", although what she refers to as "profane and obscene" words might better be termed slang. For example, men can employ slang words like *kuu* "eat" and *dekee/dekai* "big" whereas women would, instead, say *taberu* and *ookii*, which are more neutral vocabulary terms meaning "eat" and "big", respectively. As we will discuss further below, however, this generalization may not accurately describe the actual state of the speech situation, as an increasing number of researchers have been reporting the use of the above-mentioned slang words and the like as well as expressions that have traditionally been classified as male speech by female speakers.

Ide further adds the use of "beautification honorifics" and hypercorrected use of honorifics as characteristics of female speech. As was discussed in the previous section, Japanese has a rich honorification system. In particular, expressions in respectful forms are directed toward individuals that possess higher social status while those in humble forms, by humbling the speaker herself or himself, have the effect of exalting the hearer. The prefix *o/go-* is normally used as an honorific expression similar to respectful forms, as the examples in (30)–(31) indicate.

(30)   sensei-no   **go**-zitaku
       teacher-Gen hon.-house
       "teacher's house"

(31)   sensei-no   **o**-kuruma
       teacher-Gen hon.-car
       "teacher's car"

The prefix *go-* is attached to Sino-Japanese words while *o-* is prefixed to native words (Harada 1976a).[4] The prefix *o/go-* in these examples expresses the speaker's respect toward the teacher. When we refer to the house and the car that belong to some individual for whom the use of honorific expressions is not necessary, the bare forms *zitaku* and *kuruma* are used without the prefix. Besides this type of honorific use, the prefix *o/go-* is often used by women to "beautify" the entity under discussion even when the entity does not belong to someone to whom the speaker expresses respect. As Harada (1976a) explains, such a use of the prefix plays a role in making the speech "soft and feminine" (p. 542). For example, when men normally say *kane* "money", *susi* "sushi", and *soba* "soba noodle", women tend to refer to the same set of objects as *o-kane*, *o-susi*, and *o-soba*. Compare the male and female speech in (32)–(33).

(32) a. *male*   Motto kane-ga   hosii-yo.
                   more money-Nom want
                   "I want more money."
      b. *female* Motto o-kane-ga   hosii-wa.
                   more hon.-money-Nom   want
                   "I want more money."

(33) a. *male*   Kyoo-wa susi-ga   tabe-tai.
                   today-Top sushi-Nom eat-want
                   "I want to eat sushi today."
      b. *female* Kyoo-wa o-susi-ga   tabe-tai-wa.
                   today-Top hon.-sushi-Nom eat-want
                   "I want to eat sushi today."

The casual verbal endings suggest that these sentences are uttered in informal situations, and we can assume that the use of honorific forms is not called for.

Ide mentions that women's speech can be characterized by the hypercorrected use of honorifics as well. The example she uses is (34) (Ide 1990: 74).

(34) Haha-ga   o-kaeri-**ni narimasita**.
      mother-Nom hon.-return.-hon.
      "My mother returned."

The *o . . . ni naru* construction derives respectful forms, and is used to refer to the action of an individual that possesses higher status than the speaker. For this reason, this expression is not normally used to refer to the speaker herself or himself or the speaker's in-group, such as her or his own family members. Thus, the fact that this referent honorific expression is used to refer to the speaker's mother in (34) is somewhat unexpected since a humble expression would instead be anticipated. According to Ide, however, this sort of "hypercorrected" use of honorifics is typical of female speech since women's speech tends to be more formal than men's speech, and the use of honorific expressions in sentences like (34) would contribute to the expression of formality.

Intriguing gender differences in Japanese can also be found with respect to syntax. The statistical study of gender differences that Shibamoto (1985) conducted reveals interesting results. First, men and women show different degrees of word order scrambling depending on which constituents of a sentence are scrambled. Shibamoto's investigation indicates that men exhibit the scrambling of sentential and temporal adverbials, placing them before the subject, more frequently than women do, while women display other scrambling types such as the scrambling of direct object and indirect object, placing them before the subject. As a result, women demonstrate more overall application of scrambling than men.

Second, the phenomenon of Right Dislocation, which we have briefly discussed in chapter 5 in connection with scrambling, is more distinctly observed in female speech than in male speech. Right Dislocation is the phenomenon in which a word(s) or a phrase(s) can appear to the right of the verb. The (b) sentences in (35)–(36) are examples of Right Dislocation.

(35) a. Kono okasi tabeta?
          this   sweet ate
          "Did you eat this sweet?"
      b. Tabeta, kono okasi?
          ate   this   sweet
          "Did you eat this sweet?"

(36) a. Taroo-wa gakkoo-e itta-yo.
          Taro-Top school-to went
          "Taro went to school."
      b. Taroo-wa itta-yo, gakkoo-e.
          Taro-Top went   school-to
          "Taro went to school."

In the (b) sentences, a constituent can follow the verb with a pause between them. Shibamoto's study reveals that Right Dislocation is more common in female speech than in male speech. She further observes that men do apply Right Dislocation, but when they do, the dislocated constituent has its pronominal form, or at least the element that refers to the dislocated constituent, in the original position of the sentence. Some of her examples are shown in (37)–(39) (Shibamoto 1985: 142).

(37) **Sore-wa** hurui kamo siremasen yo, **wareware-no kankaku-wa.**
      that-Top old   maybe we-Gen   feelings-Top
      "They may be old[-fashioned], our feelings."

(38) **Watasi** tuitui   yuttyaundesu ne, **watasi-no baai-wa.**
      I   unguardedly end up saying I-Gen   case-Top
      "In unguarded moments, I say everything, in my case."

(39) **Kodomo-to asondari suru-no-wa** tanosii ne, **are.**
      child-with play   do-that-Top fun   that
      "Playing with the children and so on is fun, isn't it, that."

These are sentences spoken by male speakers. As the examples illustrate, there are elements within the sentences that refer to the same thing as the dislocated constituents: *sore-wa* in (37), *watasi* in (38), and *kodomo-to asondari suru-no-wa* in (39). This phenomenon occurs more frequently in male speech than in female speech, and Shibamoto explains that men apply Right Dislocation as a means of emphasis or restatement.

Finally, Shibamoto finds that Case particles are more often dropped by women than by men. Specifically, she reports that in women's speech, particles are more frequently dropped than in male speech when the accompanying nouns are the subject and direct object. According to her, moreover, females drop the subject particle more often when the subject is scrambled. Notice that this is somewhat unexpected, given our discussion of the function that particles are supposed to display with scrambling. That is, we have discussed how native speakers of Japanese know which NP serves as subject and which NP as object when they are scrambled, perhaps because Case particles such as Nominative and Accusative serve to signal the syntactic functions that the scrambled NPs have. Given this assumption, we would expect scrambling to be less frequently observed when particles are dropped, because particles which would indicate the syntactic roles of the NPs, such as subject and object, are no longer associated with the NPs.

The result that Shibamoto reports suggests that the functional explanation of Case particles assumed above may not be so appropriate.

Another experimental study, by Haig (1990), is worth mentioning in relation to gender differences in Japanese. He investigated the gender differences observed with high-school and junior high-school students in Nagoya in Aichi prefecture (the area west of Tokyo). In the Nagoya dialect, the use of the negative suffix *n*, as in *ikan* "I won't go", the standard equivalent of which is *ikanai*, and the gerund plus *oru* where the standard Japanese would have the gerund plus *iru* to mean "be V-ing", are frequently observed. Haig finds that these dialectal expressions, i.e. the use of *n* and the gerund plus *oru*, are more distinctly observed among male students than among female students. Female students use the standard versions more often, namely, *ikanai* and the gerund plus *iru*. On the basis of this result, Haig concludes that the female speech in this region is on its way toward standardization. Furthermore, these dialectal expressions are more commonly used by male students in high school than by male students in junior high school. Haig relates this age difference to masculinity, and concludes that the non-standard forms are expressions of masculinity. Hence, in this study, women tend to standardize their speech by using more standard expressions, while men incline to maintain the dialectal expressions which are considered a sign of masculinity.

In the previous section we have noted that prescriptive and ideological descriptions of honorification should not be interpreted as accurately illustrating the actual use of linguistic forms of honorification. The same criticism has been raised in the research area of gender differences, and a need to widen the scope of investigations in this area has been adovocated, with intriguing results. Many of the observations and generalizations on gender indexing discussed earlier, which had been widely accepted for quite some time and are still prevalent in some aspects, have recently been re-evaluated from diverse perspectives. A central concern underlying the recent criticism has to do with wide diversity among a specific gender group, and therefore the traditional gender-specific generalizations such as women's more frequent use of a higher level of politeness than men simply does not capture an accurate picture.

One of the variables relevant to adequate characterizations of gender differences that has drawn a great deal of attention is the age factor. Okamoto (1997), for instance, examined the conversations of five pairs of college students, ranging from 18 to 20 years old, and five pairs of middle-aged women of 43–57 years of age, and concludes that older women tend to use what are considered "feminine" forms, realized in sentence-final forms, more often than younger female speakers. The study shows that of the gender-indexed forms used by older speakers, 36 percent were feminine forms, 12 percent masculine forms, and 51 percent neutral forms. In the younger speakers' speech, in contrast, 12 percent were feminine forms, 19 percent masculine forms, and 69 percent neutral forms. Expressions that are classified as "strongly feminine", such as the sentence-final particle sequence *wa yo*, as is illustrated in (40), for example, were present in the older women's speech more than three times as frequently as in the younger speakers' speech.

(40)   Ha ni kita no. Moo doo siyoo mo nai <u>wa yo</u>, watasi . . .
       "It (the symptoms of strain) came to my teeth. I'm hopeless."
                                         (adapted from Okamoto 1997: 103)

This should be contrasted with the more common use of what were labeled
"strongly masculine" forms like the underlined expressions in (41)–(42) by the
younger female speakers (adapted from Okamoto 1997: 104–105). Not surpris-
ingly, the use of "strongly masculine" forms was virtually non-existent in the
middle-aged women's speech.

(41)   (students, talking about the location of an office)
       A: Ii na. Watasi Maruno-uti de hatarakitakatta naa.
            "That's nice. I wanted to work in Maruno-uchi."
       B: Iya datte tooi <u>zo</u>.
            "But it's far away."

(42)   (students, talking about a ski trip)
       A: Gondora.
            "It's a gondola."
       B: Gondoro ka.
            "I see, it's *gondoro* (gondola)."
       A: Gondoro <u>ja nee</u>, gondora. [laughter]
            "It's not *gondoro*, it's *gondora*."

(43)   (a student, responding to the interlocutor's teasing remark)
       Katte ni <u>itte ro</u> tte.
       "Say whatever you want to say."

The sentence-final particles *zo* in (41) and *ro* in (43) have been conventionally
analyzed as exclusive markers of the male gender of the speaker; and the sentence-
final expression *ja nee* in (42) could even have been considered vulgar. This
study thus makes it explicit that the actual situation of so-called "gender differences" reflected in the language is not a simple matter of the gender indexing
of the speaker.

   On a similar premise, there have been studies that investigate the relevance of
dialectal variation to gender differences. Contrary to the familiar assumption
that so-called "women's speech" is a wide-spread speech pattern that applies to
Japanese women in general, it has been pointed out that gender-specific linguistic
characteristics are in fact much more commonly observed in urban areas of Japan,
and more specifically Yamanote regions of the Tokyo dialect (C. Kitagawa 1977;
Sunaoshi 1995, 2004; Miyake 1995; Okamoto 1997). To highlight the significant regional differences in the research area of "women's speech" in general,
Sunaoshi (2004) examined the speech of women in the rural agricultural area
of Ibaraki (north of Tokyo). The women in this study predominantly spoke in
Ibaraki dialect, and neither honorification, which according to Sunaoshi is nearly
absent in the dialect, nor what has been perceived as "women's language" was
detected.

Interestingly, some of the expressions in Ibaraki dialect that these farm women used may be felt as "masculine" and even "vulgar", perhaps, from the standpoint of the so-called standard dialect, as is illustrated by the sentences in (44)–(45).

(44) [Ibaraki dialect] <u>Ore</u> ge sa kita ra . . .
      [standard dialect] watasi no uti ni kita ra . . .
                          "If you come over to my place . . ."
                                              (adapted from Sunaoshi 2004: 193)

(45) toochan nantsuoo-to kantsuoo-to <u>kama-nee</u> yaa to omotte
      "I thought I wouldn't care no matter what my husband says [about my going on the trip]."
                                              (adapted from Sunaoshi 2004: 196)

The first person pronoun in (44), *ore*, appears in (24) as a "deprecatory" pronoun indexing the male speaker in standard Japanese. This pronoun is obviously gender neutral in Ibaraki dialect, and thus does not register gender differences. The underlined predicate in (45), *kama-nee* "I wouldn't care", corresponds to *kamawa-nai* in the standard Japanese. The negative inflection of *-nee* in the standard dialect is considered typical of male speech and particularly a "coarse" expression, but again in Ibaraki dialect, the coarseness is absent.

Sunaoshi explains that the farm women's almost exclusive use of the dialect, which is devoid of the normative features of female speech, reflects their strategy to create rapport and solidarity. In fact, a similar sense of closeness and intimacy, crucially as opposed to an expression of masculinity, apparently contributes to the choice that younger women (especially teenagers) make in using first person pronouns such as *ore* and *boku* and sentence-final particles like *zo* which have been labeled as men's speech (see note 3). The same explanation can be given for the use of "strongly masculine" forms by younger speakers illustrated earlier in (41)–(43). Interestingly, some of these women feel female-specific particles and other similar expressions create distance, or even sarcasm, between the speaker and the listener (Okamoto 1997). Thus it is evident that gender differences in language are far more complex than merely indexing the gender of the speaker.

Finally, a recent work by H. Abe (2004) on lesbian bar talk provides a further motivation to distinguish between linguistic ideology and actual language use with respect to gender differences. Abe interviewed female speakers in lesbian bars in Tokyo, and reports that the use of first person pronouns varies depending on the speaker's sense of identity. There are basically three groups: transsexual/transgendered, lesbian, and *onabe* (literally, "pan"). H. Abe (2004) describes the three groups as follows: the first group refers to female-to-male transsexual/transgendered people; lesbian is "a woman who feels comfortable with her female body (in other words, with her biologically female sex) and who chooses a woman as a partner. Unlike straight women, however, her identity as a woman is constructed through a relationship with another woman" (p. 209); and *onabe* is described as a woman who "loves women and chooses a woman as a partner, but an *onabe*'s social and emotional identity is male" (p. 209). Abe finds that transsexual/transgendered people use *boku* as a first person pronoun, lesbians use *watasi*, and *onabe* use *zibun* "self", although she cautions at the same time that these speakers vary their use of first person pronouns depending on the context and that this illustration is by no means their unique choice of the first person pronoun. Note that as we have discussed above, *boku* is commonly considered a pronoun for male speakers, and *zibun* is generally a reflexive pronoun, but is also used as a first person pronoun in Kansai (western) dialects. Therefore the non-uniform selection of first person pronouns by these women, as well as what could be viewed as the "deviant" use of the male-oriented pronoun by transsexual/transgendered speakers, adds another reason why an accurate description of how male and female speakers actually use (or do not use) gender indexing in the language must go beyond ideological and normative language use by referencing a broad range of factors.

Notes

1   Since *kik-* "ask, listen to" is a consonant-ending root, *-i-* is inserted between the root and *ni naru/suru*.
2   Note that Ide's list in (24) implies that *atakusi* and *atasi* are never used by male speakers. However, their use by males is not as rare as the use of *boku* and *ore* by female speakers. The "unexpected" use of male speech by female speakers will be discussed later.
3   There is an apparently increasing tendency for female speakers, particularly those of the younger generation, to use more readily words and particles that have been described as characteristic of male speech. We will have more discussions on this point later.
4   Examples such as *o-tya* "tea" and *o-denwa* "telephone", however, are counter to this generalization: both *tya* and *denwa* are of Sino-Japanese origin.

Suggested Readings

Dialectal variation: Tojo (1955), Fujiwara (1964), Haraguchi (1977, 1991), Shibatani (1990), Yoshimoto (1991). Both Haraguchi (1977) and Shibatani (1990) provide detailed descriptions of accentuation patterns observed in a wide range of regional dialects. Haraguchi (1977, 1991) discusses theoretical issues concerning dialectal variation of accent within the autosegmental and metrical theories.

   Styles and level of speech: Harada (1976a), Jorden with Noda (1987), Yoshiko Matsumoto (1997), Okamoto (1997), Ide and Yoshida (1999).

   Gender differences in general: Tannen (1990, 1993), Coats (1998). Tannen (1990) discusses in a non-technical fashion a number of general characteristics of women's and men's speech that are observed in American English and those that are reflective of different gender roles in American society. Some of these characteristics may be relevant for Japanese as well.

Gender differences in Japanese: Shibamoto (1985), Ide and McGloin (1990), Ide and Yoshida (1999), Okamoto and Shibamoto Smith (2004). Shibamoto (1985) presents results from her statistical study of characteristics of female speech in Japanese. Ide and McGloin (1990) is an edited volume containing ten articles dealing with women's language in Japanese. Okamoto and Shibamoto Smith (2004) compiles intriguing articles on the topic from a more recent research point of view.

EXERCISES

1 Find a speaker who comes from an area different from yours, and interview her or him. Observe any difference between your speech and her or his speech.

2 Why do many people believe that they speak WITHOUT an accent? What would it mean to speak without an accent? And what is your opinion about such a view? Explain the basis for your opinion.

3 Find examples in English that come closest to honorifics (referent and addressee honorifics).

4 Japanese speakers of the younger generation increasingly find the use of honorification difficult. What do you think are the positive and negative aspects of the honorification system? What do you think about relaxing or even eliminating the use of honorification?

5 Describe ways in which the speech of women and men differs in greetings, threats, swearing, and promises in either English or Japanese. What do you think accounts for these differences? Do you think the differences are increasing or decreasing? Explain the basis for your answers.

6 What do you think about the gender differences linguistically encoded in Japanese, such as the different sets of sentence-final particles and pronouns for males and females? Could they be eliminated or neutralized somehow? What do you think would happen in that case? Do you think English should have such a dichotomy? Argue for a particular position.

8 Language Acquisition

How do children learn their native tongue? This is one of the fundamental questions with which linguists are concerned in their pursuit of the nature of the knowledge that we have of our first language. As a quick answer, we may think that children's language acquisition takes place through their experience in the environment in which they exist: children may imitate what their parents say to them; or they may observe the world around them when their parents say something and try to connect the words and the surrounding situations. This way of understanding how children learn their language is illustrated by the following statement by the philosopher John Locke (1690: 233):

> If we will observe how children learn languages, we shall find that to make them understand what the names of simple ideas or substances stand for, people ordinarily show them the thing, whereof they would have them have the idea; and then repeat to them the name that stands for it, as white, milk, sugar, cat, dog. But as for mixed modes, especially the most material of them moral words, the sounds are usually learned first, and then to know what complex ideas they stand for, they are either beholden to the explication of others, or (which happens for the most part) are left to their own observation and industry.

If this hypothesis about how children learn language were correct, blind and deaf children would have a very difficult time in acquiring language, if it were at all possible. Barbara Landau and Lila Gleitman's work on blind children has been instrumental in refuting this approach. Landau and Gleitman (1985) emphasize dissociation between the manner in which language is learned and experience in the environment, and demonstrate how blind children learn English as their native tongue. Landau and Gleitman's findings are not only important to show that the observation-based language acquisition hypothesis is not on the right track, they are also intriguing in their own right. In one of their experiments, a blind 3-year-old child, Kelli, and four sighted blindfolded children who were about the same age were asked to respond to commands like "Look up", "Look down", and "Look in front of you." If visual observations of what is happening around the children provided the basis for language acquisition, it would be predicted that Kelli would not be able to respond to these commands because she would not understand the meaning of "Look". The result was that Kelli responded to the command "Look up" by raising both hands without tilting her head; on the other hand, sighted blindfolded children uniformly looked up, tilting their heads but without raising their hands. The responses to the other commands were similar: Kelli used her hand movement without moving her head while sighted children all used head movement. It suggests that Kelli is capable of learning what appear to be sight-oriented words without experiencing what it is like to see things, although the word "Look" does not mean the same to her as to sighted children. "Look" means "contact with the hands" to Kelli and blind children (Landau and Gleitman 1985: 56).

The hypothesis of language acquisition by observation or imitation is further countered by the creative or novel nature of words, phrases, and sentences children utter, as well as the systematic nature of the errors that they make, as was briefly mentioned in the introduction to this book. It is important to remind ourselves that caregivers do not give children formal instructions in novel words and sentences, or expose them to error-bound expressions. The creativity and regularity with which children approach language indicate that language acquisition involves children's subconscious effort to analyze the language into rules and generalizations, whether they turn out to be correct or error-ridden.

In this chapter we will provide evidence for the rule-governed mode or regularity observed in the process of language acquisition, drawing on data from Japanese children's speech. In observing acquisition data, both naturally occurring and obtained in experimental settings, we will notice that children's generalizations make reference to linguistic units and concepts that are discussed in previous chapters.

1 Regularity in Language Acquisition

1.1 *Phonological Unit – Mora*

When children speak, their pronunciations of words are often "incomplete" or "modified" because certain sounds are still underdeveloped, and certain sequences of sounds have not been accurately acquired. The modified pronunciations are reflections of their attempt to pronounce such sounds and sound sequences. Research reveals that the way in which children modify speech is systematic and is consistent with restrictions on what constitute phonological units in the language. One such unit relevant to child language that has received a good deal of attention cross-linguistically is the foot. Recall that we have discussed a number of instances in chapter 3 where constraints are imposed on the length of a word as an output of word formation in Japanese, and of particular importance was the notion of the bimoraic foot. Investigations of Japanese child phonology demonstrate that this same unit (the bimoraic foot) underlies the way children modify their pronunciation (Ota 1999, 2003).

One of the ways that children modify their pronunciations is by truncation. Examples of truncated words are shown in (1) (taken from Ota 1999: 199 – transcription modified; originally from Ingram 1996, Okubo 1981). The leftmost phonemic transcription reflects adult pronunciations, and the phonetic transcription is the child's (named "T"); and the numbers in square brackets correspond to the child's age (i.e. year; month. day).

(1) a. /nai/   [na:]   "not"   [1;0.12]
     b. /ta:čaN/   [ta:]   (T's nickname)   [1;0,12]
     c. /koara/   [ko:]   "koala"   [1;0;14]
     d. /basɯ/   [ba:]   "bus"   [1;1.16]
     e. /ita/   [ta:]   "there it is"   [1;1.16]
     f. /koinobori/   [bo:] [ba:] "carp steamer"   [1;2.0]
     g. /ari/   [a:]   "ant"   [1;3.22]

T's words in (1) are truncated in a uniform manner with the remaining vowel being lengthened to form a two-mora output. That is, T's utterance is consistent with the bimoraic constraint we have observed in adult language that an output should be minimally bimoraic. The phenomenon is not restricted to a single child. According to Ota (1999), who surveyed several other children, the bimoraic minimality requirement is detected throughout his data. He reports that the subjects in his data, namely, Hiromi, Takeru, and Kenta, all produce truncated outputs within the bimoraic minimality requirement, as is illustrated in (2). It is not that there are no monomoraic truncated words (i.e. no vowel lengthening) in these children's speech, and there are indeed such instances, as in (3). However, their number is not more than 10 percent of that of bimoraic truncated outputs and so is low.

(2) a. /kani/   [ka:]   "crab"   Hiromi [1;3.4]
     b. /bo:rɯ/   [bo:]   "ball"   Hiromi [1;3.25]
     c. /bo:rɯ/   [bo:]   "circle"   Takeru [1;4.24]
     d. /ǰɯ:sɯ/   [zɯ:]   "juice"   Takeru [1;6.21]
     e. /motto/   [mo:]   "more"   Takeru [1;9.5]
     f. /marɯ/   [ma:]   "circle"   Kenta [2;1.21]
     g. /banana/   [ba:]   "banana"   Kenta [2;3.22]
     h. /Φo:kɯriΦɯto/   [bɯ:]   "forklift"   Kenta [2;3.22]
                                      (Ota 1999: 201 – transcription modified)

(3) a. /ba:ni:/   [ba]   "Barney"   Takeru [1;6.21]
     b. /pasɯ/   [pa]   "pass"   Takeru [1;9.19]
     c. /motto/   [mo]   "more"   Takeru [1;10.16]
     d. /hači/   [gi]   "bee"   Kenta [2;1.25]
     e. /inɯ/   [nɯ]   "dog"   Kenta [2;3.22]
     f. /kiša/   [da]   "train"   Kenta [2;4.6]

                                                              (Ibid.)

The bimoraic minimality requirement is observed in another way. There are one-mora words in Japanese, and when children try to pronounce these monomoraic words, they lengthen the vowels, deriving the outputs in (4).

(4) a. /me/ [me:] "eye"   Hiromi [1;9.11]
     b. /te/ [te:] "hand"   Hiromi [1;9.11]
     c. /ki/ [ki:] "tree"   Hiromi [1;9.28]
     d. /e/   [he:] "picture" Hiromi [1;9.28]
     e. /me/ [me:] "eye"   Takeru [1;8.13]
     f. /te/ [te:] "hand"   Takeru [1;11.2]
     g. /ji/ [di:] "letter"   Kenta [2;2.27]

        (Ota 1999: 210 – transcription modified)

These data suggest that while children truncate words for ease in pronunciation, they do so in a rule-governed or systematic fashion: the output reflects a minimal word requirement that the truncation consists of two morae. It is further important to realize that it is the same bimoraic minimality requirement that underlies various morphophonological phenomena that we have seen in chapter 3. This may also suggest that the notion of "mora" already plays a crucial role in children's production of these truncated forms as a primary unit for constructing outputs like those in (1), (2), and (4), in particular. Thus, the speaker of the language has access to fundamental principles of language from early on.

Regularity in child phonology continues to be observed as children's speech production becomes more than bimoraic in length. Recall that the mora in Japanese is not simply a vowel but also includes a moraic nasal and a geminate consonant. So, these segments are equally critical in the recognition of a phonological unit and the internal structure of that unit. The young Japanese speakers that Ota (1998) investigates demonstrate in their speech production that they preserve the prosodic structure of a word in a very similar way to the one we saw in the Japanese speech error data in chapter 3. It should be remembered, for instance, that the characteristics of speech errors in Japanese we discussed in the earlier chapter, which are repeated in (5), are all possible because a vowel, the first part of a long consonant (or a geminate), and a moraic nasal each constitutes a single mora.

(5) a. Long vowels can split into two components.
     b. Long consonants can split into two parts.
     c. Vowels can be replaced by consonants, and vice versa.

When children modify their pronunciation, they appear to be sensitive to what counts as a mora in Japanese, and their outputs result in the same number of morae as the corresponding adult words. This is shown in (6). (The symbol ~ indicates some variation.)

(6) a. ta:.ta   ta:.ta ~ tat.to   "shoes"   S [1;8]
     b. Φɯ:.sen   geŋ.ken ~ Φɯ:.čen   "balloon"   A [2;0]
     c. to:.kʸo: tat.ča: "Tokyo"   A [2;3]
     d. çi.ko:.ki   çi.kuk.ki ~ çi.go:.ki   "plane"   N [1;8]
     e. am.pam.man   am.pam.man   (cartoon   N [1;11]
                       ~ a:.pa:.man   character)

        (Ota 1998: 337 – transcription modified)

In (6b), the long vowel in the first syllable is realized as a moraic nasal; in (6c), the long vowel in the second syllable is pronounced as a geminate consonant; and in (6e), the moraic nasal in the first and second syllables may sometimes be pronounced as a long vowel. This is consistent with the observation in (5c). Thus, the parallel treatment of a vowel, the first member of a geminate, and a moraic nasal indicates that the mora is a phonological unit to which children are sensitive.

The data in (6) have an interesting implication for the structure of syllables. We have discussed the fact that a syllable can consist of an onset (an initial consonant), a nucleus (a vowel), and a coda (a final consonant), of which the first and the last can be optional. When a coda is present or a nucleus consists of a long vowel (or a diphthong), the syllable is said to be **heavy**; otherwise, the syllable is **light**. From looking at syllables by their weight, it is significant that the heavy syllables in (6) are recognized and produced by children as such. That is, a long vowel, a geminate, and a moraic nasal are all heavy-syllable-forming elements, and in this sense, the syllable weight is kept intact in the children's production.

With respect to the mora, the data in (7) are of further interest.

(7) a. tˢɯ.me.tai   tˢɯː.tai ~ met.tai   "cold"   S [1;6]
     b. a.ge.han   geː.an   (type of food)   S [1;10]
     c. pa.to.kaː   pak.kaː   "police car"   A [2;1]
     d. ba.na.na   ban.ǰa   "banana"   A [2;3]
     e. o.me.me   oːme   "eye"   N [2;0]
     f. ha.bu.ra.ši haː.ba.ši   "toothbrush"   N [2;0)]

(ibid.)

The target words in (7) do not contain heavy syllables, at least in relevant respects. The children in these cases skip a mora of a target word, but instead compensate for the skipped mora by either lengthening a vowel (e.g., (a, b, e, f)), forming a geminate (e.g., (a, c)), or adding a moraic nasal (e.g., (d)). That is, these compensated segments are full-fledged morae, and the resulting words have the same number of morae as the target word. In their attempt to pronounce target words like adult speakers, thus, children in their modified manner preserve a prosodic structure which very much resembles the adult's counterpart, and the underlying notion of what constitutes a basic phonological unit appears to prevail even in child phonology.

1.2 Lexicalization Pattern and Mimetics

One of many puzzling facts about children's language acquisition is that child language is remarkably rich in mimetics, although there is some individual variation. Mimetics are ubiquitous in Japanese, and as we have discussed in earlier chapters, their linguistic characteristics are often considered unique. It may come as no surprise that adult learners of Japanese have a very difficult time in understanding the meaning of mimetic words and in learning how to use them properly. It is peculiar, then, that many Japanese children exhibit rapid and accurate acquisition of this word class (Oda 2000; Tsujimura, to appear). While it still calls for a great deal of research before fully understanding how speakers capture the meaning of mimetics given their iconic and symbolic nature, there are some interesting acquisition data particularly with respect to their implications for lexicalization patterns that we have discussed in chapter 6.

Japanese does not lexicalize various manners of motion in motion verbs, unlike English. Manner, instead, is often expressed by adverbs, and mimetic words particularly are extensively used to specify manner of motion. Examples of different manners of walking are repeated in (8).

(8)   *tyoko-tyoko*   aruku   "waddle"
      teku-teku   aruku   "trudge"
      toko-toko-to   aruku   "trot"
      dosi-dosi   aruku   "lumber"
      tobo-tobo-to   aruku   "plod"
      bura-bura   aruku   "stroll"
      yota-yota   aruku   "stagger"
      yoti-yoti   aruku   "toddle"

Exclusion of the manner component in the lexicalization pattern is in fact not restricted to motion verbs in Japanese, and the same pattern is observed with verbs describing pain and verbs of looking. They are illustrated in (9) and (10): in these examples mimetics serve as specifying manners of pain and looking, respectively.

(9)   *zuki-zuki*   itamu   "throb"
      chiku-chiku   itamu   "prick"
      hiri-hiri   itamu   "smart"
      piri-piri   itamu   "tingle"
      siku-siku   itamu   "griping"
      gan-gan   itamu   "splitting"

(10) *jiro-jiro*   miru   "stare"
      jitto   miru   "gaze"
      chira-chira   miru   "glance"
      maji-maji   miru   "look hard"
      kyoro-kyoro   miru   "look around"

Children are very quick to pick up mimetic words from very early on, but they do not start from the beginning to use mimetics as manner expressions external to individual verbs like (8)–(10). In the case of a monolingual child, Sumihare, whose speech was recorded by his father (Noji 1973–1977), a few steps were taken before frequent use of the pattern in (8)–(10) (Tsujimura, to appear). First, mimetics emerge at the one-word stage. Many instances are sound-symbolic, and Sumihare utters them as an accompaniment of his or his caregiver's actions. Examples at this stage are in (11).

(11)   poi: as he throws a ball [1;1]
        pan: when his father uses a flyswatter [1;4]
        toon: when he gets down from a big stone [1;4]
        bata bata: as he opens his father's fan and shakes it [1;5]
        pachin pachin: as he repeatedly pulls a string of a light to turn it on/off
                [1;6]

Sumihare then starts using mimetic words with the verb *suru*, whose semantic
content does not make much contribution to the meaning of a resulting complex verb. Some samples are given in (12), where *shita* is the past tense form
of *suru*.

(12)   a.   poi-shita [1;8]
             "I threw it away" (after throwing away chopsticks)
        b.   paan-shita [1;9]
             "I broke it" (He hit a bottle against concrete and broke it.)
        c.   chan-shita [1;9]
             "I sat down"
        d.   ringo pan-shi-tai [1;10]
             apple (mimetic)-*suru*-want
             "I want to have the apple split (into two)."
        e.   toon-shita [1;10]
             "I hit (my head)" (after hitting his head against a corner of a box)
        f.   shii-shita [1;10]
             "I peed"

The complex verb form comprising a mimetic word and *suru* is extremely common
in adult speech. This stage of complex verbs precedes the phase at which lexical
verbs, i.e. verbs of the native word class, are learned. Interestingly, from the
end of his first year to the beginning of his second year, Sumihare's vocabulary
starts containing a number of lexical verbs of the native class, and at the same
time, he starts using mimetic words directly suffixed by the past tense morpheme
-*ta*. (13) and (14), respectively, show the initial group of lexical verbs and the
inventory of mimetics suffixed by the past tense morpheme.

(13)   *atta* "there was/I found" [1;10], *kita* "came" [1;11], *ochita* "fell" [1;11], *itta*
        "went" [1;12], *kau* (present) "buy" [2;1], *iu* "say" (present) [2;1], *denai*
        "won't come out" (present, negative) [2;1], *deta* "came out" [2;1], *waitenai*
        "hasn't boiled" (present) [2;1], *achobu* (for *asobu*) "play" [2;1], *noru*
        "ride" (present) [2;1], *hutta* "rained" [2;1], *yanda* "stopped raining" [2;1],
        kieta (for *kireta*) "was cut" [2;2], *tootta* "passed" [2;2]

(14)   a.   tonton-ta(a) [1;11]
             "I hit it" (after hitting a tile)
        b.   taachan tabi pai-ta(a) [1;12]
             Mommy sock
             "Mommy, I threw my sock away"

c. okaze byuut-ta [1;12]
   wind
   "The wind blew hard (in a *byuu*-way)" (describing the cold wind during his outing with his father)

d. pachin-ta-yo [2;1]
   "(it) bursted" (describing the firewood bursting)

e. pachin pachin-ta(a)-naa [2;1]
   "I turned it on and off" (as he has repeatedly turned the light on and off)

f. pyuut-ta-yo [2;1]
   "(it) blew in a *pyuu*-way" (asked by his father to describe the rainy wind outside)

g. ton-ta-yo [2;3]
   "I tripped over" (upon falling)

h. jan jaat-ta [2;3] (upon hearing a metallic noise made in a neighbor's house resulting from having dropped something)

While the forms in (14) are not acceptable in adult speech, it is readily detectable that the morphological analysis the child gives to the mimetic words in (14) is regular and parallel to the morphological process involved in the verbs in (13). In building up his verb vocabulary as in (13), Sumihare recognizes that -*ta* is a morpheme suffixed to a verb to mark an event denoted by it as past. The mimetic words in (14) all refer to events, and as he identifies their function as similar to that of verbs like those in (13), thereby analyzing the word category of the mimetics as parallel to verbs, he adds the past tense morpheme to the mimetic words.

Special attention should be paid to what is lexicalized in the mimetic forms in (14). In each instance an event is described, but crucially the manner that depicts the event, which is for the most part a sound associated with it, is a part of the meaning of the mimetic. That is, in verbal use of the mimetic words in (14), manner is lexicalized as one of the semantic components that are built into the meaning of each mimetic verb. In (14a), for example, *tonton-ta* "I hit it" refers to a hitting motion with a specific instrument like a hammer that characterizes the manner of hitting that perhaps induces a typical noise. Similarly in (14b), *pai-ta* "I threw it" describes a motion of throwing something away, typically a small, light material being thrown into the air. Thus the specific manners in which these motions are brought about are described quite explicitly by the whole mimetic words, which have been morphologically (and semantically) analyzed as verbs. Recall that lexicalization of manner is not a typical pattern that native Japanese verbs exhibit, as we have observed in (8)–(10). But at the time when the child is just learning native verbs and is building up its inventory, an event appears to be holistically captured and hence so lexicalized, including semantic components that are not normally incorporated in the adult's verb lexicon. Thus, as Sumihare increases the number of native verbs and at the same time gets exposed to examples in which manner is expressed externally to a verb rather than being lexicalized, he seems to learn the more conventional lexicalization pattern, as the set of examples in (15) demonstrates.

(15) a. Ame <u>zaazaa</u> hutteru [1;12]
          rain   is raining
          "It's raining in a *zaazaa* manner."
      b. Denki tsuita. <u>Patto</u> tsuita [2;3]
          light   got on   got on
          "The light got (turned) on. It got on in a *paQ* way."
      c. <u>Buubuu jaajaa</u> deru-yo [2;3]
                          come out
          "(The water) comes out in a *buubuu jaajaa* way."
      d. Kore-ne, <u>kachaan</u>-te koboreta [2;4]
          this   fell
          "These (sweets) fell in a *kachaan* way."
      e. Omote-de <u>sutoon</u>-te korondan-yo [2;4]
          outside-at   tripped over
          "I tripped over in a *sutoon* way outside."
      f. Hukuya-no booru-wa-ne, <u>putsun</u>-to kirete nakunattan-to [2;4]
          Fukuya-Gen ball-Top   cut   lost
          "The Fukuya department's advertising balloon got its string cut off
          and got lost"
      g. Imani <u>zaat</u>-to huru-yo [2;5]
          soon   will rain
          "It will rain in a *zaa* way soon."
      h. Konnani <u>moo moo</u> moeteta [2;5]
          this way   was burning
          "It was burning in a *moo moo* way."
      i. Bunbu-ga konnani <u>bachan bachan</u> yureru-yo [2;6]
          boat-Nom this way   shake
          "The boat is shaking in a *bachan bachan* way"
      j. Michin   <u>kuru kuru</u> ugoku-desho [2;7]
          sewing machine   move
          "The sewing machine moves in a *kuru kuru* way, doesn't it?"
      k. <u>guru guru</u> maashitoru [2;8]
                      is stirring
          "I'm stirring (the egg)"
      l. Koko-kara <u>pyuut</u>-to deta [2;8]
          here-from   came out
          "(The medicine) came out from here in a *pyuuQ* way."

As should be clear from Sumihare's age for each speech, these speech samples
emerge after native verbs like those in (13) have frequently been uttered and also
after expressions as in (14) have been observed. Strikingly in (15), not only are
mimetic words no longer analyzed morphologically as parallel to Japanese native
verbs, but also they are used predominantly as adverbs modifying native verbs.
This is, of course, the adult pattern, and is fully acceptable. Once such an adult-
like pattern is acquired, the child never uses forms like those in (14).

    The several sets of data presented here illustrate that the child initially captures
the Japanese lexicalization pattern as of a rather holistic nature, but that as he

increases his inventory of native verbs, he learns the conventional lexicalization pattern in which manner is not an incorporated semantic component in Japanese verbs. The nature of the transition in Sumihare's use of mimetics that we have just observed above, particularly the emergence of forms like those in (14) that are unacceptable by adults, is not all that rare; in fact it is typical especially when the size of the child's vocabulary is still small and limited. Clark (1993, 2003), for instance, points out English-speaking children's coinage of new words like *to car* for *to drive*, *to piano* for *to play the piano*, and *to bell* for *to ring*, and explains that children coin new words when they do not yet have a term to fit the meaning they want to express so that they can temporarily fill the gap. In so doing, they use lexical items and morphemes that are already familiar to them. Once they have learned a more conventional word to replace the coined word, however, they stop using the coined word (Clark 2003: 283). Sumihare's morphological and semantic analysis of the mimetic words as parallel to native verbs, as in (14), may thus be viewed as a coinage stage at which he is yet to learn the conventional lexicalization pattern of Japanese verbs. Since he does not have a sufficient number of native verbs to describe a particular event, and does not know the conventional way of lexicalization (i.e. how or whether to lexicalize manner), he coins a new word comprising a mimetic root and the past tense morpheme. Thus, Sumihare's coinage that results in unacceptable forms by the adult's standard, and his transition toward acquisition of the conventional way of expressing the manner component, follow a natural path of language acquisition in general.

1.3 Tense/Aspect Marking

As we have discussed in chapter 6, tense and aspect are important semantic notions that exhibit intriguing interactions with morphology. Researchers who investigate child language acquisition in various languages have looked into the relationship between tense morphology and lexical aspect. Terms in lexical aspect relevant to our current discussion include the four-way classification of State, Activity, Accomplishment, and Achievement. In examining English-speaking children, it was found that children demonstrate a strong tendency to use the past tense morpheme with Accomplishment and Achievement verbs such as *find*, *fall*, and *break*, while the present progressive form with *-ing* appears with Activity verbs like *play*, *ride*, and *write* (Brown 1973; L. Bloom et al. 1980; Tomasello 1992; Shirai and Andersen 1995; Clark 1996; among others). Similar tendencies have been reported in other languages, such as Italian (Antinucci and Miller 1976), French (Bronckart and Sinclair 1973), and Turkish (Aksu-Koç 1988).

A parallel situation is obtained in Japanese with respect to the past tense morpheme *-ta*. Li and Shirai (2000: 133), in their reanalysis of Rispoli (1981), report that when a child used the past tense marker *-ta*, it almost always occurred with Accomplishment and Achievement verbs at an earlier developmental stage, 1;6 to 1;8, but that the use of the past tense morpheme was broadened to include Activity and Stative verbs at the age period of 1;10 to 2;0. There does not seem to be individual variation among the children examined: basically the same results have been obtained in the examinations of three Japanese-speaking children. Shirai (1998) reports the strong correlation between the past tense marker and Achievement verbs. For example, one of the children whose longitudinal data Shirai examined is understood to start using the past tense morpheme productively at 2 years old, and after that the morpheme is more frequently used with Achievement verbs than other verb classes. Shirai's statistical analysis of this child indicates that the combination of *-ta* and Achievement verbs ranges between 57.1 percent and 78.8 percent. Examples of Achievement verbs used by the child include *tomaru* "stop", *mitsukeru* "find", and *hairu* "go in". In contrast, the past tense morpheme with Activity verbs appears at the 5 percent to 21.4 percent range, and with Stative verbs at the 8.9 percent to 25 percent range. This pattern is very similar with the other two children in Shirai's investigation.

The grammatical aspect represented by the morphological complex *-te iru* induces two interpretations, progressive and resultative, as we have discussed in chapter 6. So, *-te iru* cannot be equated exclusively with the English progressive *-ing*. The situation closest to the correlation between *-ing* and Activity verbs in English would be *-te iru* with Activity verbs in the progressive interpretation. Shirai's examination of three children exhibits a great deal of individual variation, and very little correlation, if any at all, between the grammatical aspect marker and the verb class. That is, there is no conclusive association of *-te iru* with Activity verbs in the progressive interpretation, no strong connection between *-te iru* and Achievement verbs in the resultative reading, and no relative order of emergence between the progressive and resultative uses of *-te iru*. (cf. Horiguchi 1981; Rispoli and Bloom 1985; Shirai 1993).

To the extent that the cross-linguistic and Japanese-specific data point to a similar tendency concerning the relationship between tense markers and aspectual classes reflected in verbs, it is an often observed pattern that children connect past tense markers with Accomplishment and Achievement verbs. That is, children's morphological selection may well be sensitive to semantic distinctions based on the aspectual nature of events denoted by verbs.

2   Generalizations in Children's Errors

Children in acquiring their native tongue make a number of mistakes, but as has been frequently pointed out, those mistakes are not random but result from children's attempt to make linguistic generalizations. An often-cited example is the irregular past tense formation of English verbs such as *go–went*, *eat–ate*, *bring–brought*, and *come–came*. Children's errors like *goed* for *went* and *bringed* for *brought*, for instance, reflect the generalization that the past tense form of an English verb is generated by adding *-ed* to the verb root. When the child has not yet quite figured out the precedence of irregular verbs over regular ones, she or he applies the generalization based on regular verbs to all English verbs. That is, errors like *goed* and *bringed* are instances of overgeneralization of the regular past tense formation in English. By examining the range and the nature of errors that children make, we can ascertain a great deal about the process and mechanism of first language acquisition. In this section we will look at several cases of the errors that Japanese-speaking children make. In particular, we shall observe areas like inflectional morphology, Case particle and word order, and prenominal modification, to illustrate errors that primarily reflect language-specific properties.

2.1   *Inflectional Morphology*

Inflectional morphology is an area in which many types of children's errors have been reported (Okubo 1967; Hatano 1968; Iwabuchi and Muraishi 1968; Sanches 1968; Fujiwara 1977; Yamamoto 1981; Clancy 1985). Most notable are errors involving negative suffixes and their occurrence with the present/past tense markers. The inflectional morphology may be complex to young children particularly because the inflectional paradigms are different depending on the morphological category of words: nouns and adjectival nouns pattern identically, but adjectives have their own patterns that are different from nouns and adjectival nouns, and so do verbs. The inflectional patterns of verbs, adjectives, and nouns and adjectival nouns are given in (16)–(18).

(16)   *verbs*
    a.   *non-past*   tabe-ru   "eat"
    b.   *non-past neg.* tabe-nai
    c.   *past*   tabe-ta
    d.   *past neg.*   tabe-na-kat-ta
    e.   *tentative*   tabe-ru-daroo

(17)   *adjectives*
    a.   *non-past*   ooki-i   "big"
    b.   *non-past neg.* ooki-ku na-i
    c.   *past*   ooki-kat-ta
    d.   *past neg.*   ooki-ku na-kat-ta
    e.   *tentative*   ooki-i daroo

(18)

		nouns "book"	*adjectival nouns* "pretty"
a.	*non-past*	hon-da	kirei-da
b.	*non-past neg.*	hon-zya na-i	kirei-zya na-i
c.	*past*	hon-dat-ta	kirei-dat-ta
d.	*past neg.*	hon-zya na-kat-ta	kirei-zya na-kat-ta
e.	*tentative*	hon-daroo	kirei-daroo

Clancy (1985) gives detailed descriptions of inflectional errors that children frequently make. In spite of the three-way inflectional paradigms in adult Japanese illustrated in (16)–(18), children make a generalization that the negative suffix *-nai* is a unique morpheme that can be added to a root of any word category. So, the N-*nai* form like **hikooki-nai* "airplane-NEG" for *hikooki-zya-nai* "it's not an airplane" to replace the noun negation pattern of (18b) is very common, particularly among 2-year-olds. The same negative suffix is also used for verbs, adjectives, and adjectival nouns. Examples of this sort, taken from Clancy (1985) including those cited in her work, are given in (19).

(19) *verbs*
    a. *tabe-ru-nai   for   tabe-nai "(I) won't eat"
        eat-pres.-NEG
        *kaer-u-nai   for   kaer-a-nai "(I) won't go home"
        return-pres.-NEG
    b. *ar-u-nai   for   na-i "there isn't"
        be-pres.-NEG
    c. *deki-ta-nai   for   deki-na-kat-ta "(I) couldn't do it"
        complete-past-NEG
        *at-ta-nai   for   na-kat-ta "there wasn't"
        be-past-NEG

(20) *adjectives*
    a. *atu-i-nai   for   atu-ku nai "it's not hot"
        hot-pres.-NEG
    b. *oisi-kat-ta-nai   for   oisi-ku na-kat-ta "it wasn't delicious"
        delicious-past.NEG

(21) *adjectival nouns*
    *suki-nai   for   suki-zya nai "(I) don't like it"
    like-NEG

Verbal and adjectival roots cannot stand by themselves, but it is interesting to note that children put the present and past tense morphemes before the negative suffix. In (19a), (19b), and (20a), the present tense markers of verbs and adjectives appear internal to *-nai*; and in (19c) and (20b), the respective past tense markers are again placed before the negative suffix. Furthermore, the verb *aru* "be" in (19b) has its suppletive negative form of *nai* as an irregular pattern, but the child's error, *arunai*, is consistent with the negative formation with other verbs and word categories. While there is no question about the erroneous status of these forms, they are systematic, based on a single generalization about the negative morpheme and its order relative to other inflectional morphemes.

    Clancy further elaborates on the extent to which the negative suffix (of the adult paradigms) is difficult for children to acquire. The tense markers *-ru/-ta* are acquired before 2½ years of age while children do not start using the negative past sequence until later. Children around 3 years old are cited whose errors include *oisi-katta-nai* for *oisi-ku-na-katta* "it wasn't delicious" and *yo-katta-ku-nai* for *yo-ku-na-katta* "it wasn't good". Clancy points out that these errors consistently keep the relative order of "the past tense before negative" even though the order is the reverse in the correct forms. She reasons that this persistent placement of the negative morpheme is a sign of children's preference for giving salience to the negative information, and the word-final position is the right place for that purpose.

In connection with inflectional errors, categorial crossover between adjectives and adjectival nouns is a well-known finding. As the paradigms in (17) and (18) show, adjectives and adjectival nouns belong to distinct inflectional patterns. Children, however, put the two word classes together, and apply the adjectival paradigm to both vocabulary types. Resulting errors include, for example, *kiree-kunai* for *kiree-zya nai* "it's not pretty" and *kiree-katta* for *kiree-datta* "it was pretty", where *kiree* "pretty" is an adjectival noun. Other adjectival nouns such as *ippai* "full", *kirai* "dislike", and *suki* "like" are claimed to induce the same type of inflectional error (Okubo 1967; Hatano 1968; Fujiwara 1977; Clancy 1985). A possible explanation for this categorial crossover, according to Clancy, is that although adjectives and adjectival nouns may be distinct in terms of inflectional patterns, they are semantically very alike: both word classes bear descriptive meanings. Children thus group them together on the basis of their meanings and apply a unique inflectional paradigm to both (Slobin 1973; Clancy 1985).

2.2   Case Particles

It has been observed that Case particles such as *wa*, *ga*, *o*, *ni*, and *no*, as well as postpositions including *de* (instrumental), *ni* (locative), *kare* (source), and *e* (goal), appear in children's speech between 1;8 and 2;6 (Clancy 1985). It should be noted, however, that there are instances of optional Case drop, as is frequently observed in adult Japanese, and the lack of children's use of Case particles does not necessarily reflect absence of acquisition. Several researchers report that children often replace *o* with *ga* in the "N-*ga* N-*o* V" sentence structure. Clancy (1985: 389), for instance, gives an example of a child of 2;1 years who once said (22) with the correct use of particle but then made a mistake by using *ga* for *o*, as in (23).

(22)   mama-ga   mizu ire-ta-no-ne
       mama-Nom water put in-past
       "Mama put in water"

(23)   *omizu-ga ire-ta-noni
       water-Nom put in-past-although
       "although she put in water"

The verb in these examples is the transitive verb *ireru* "put (something) in". In (22) the child marks the subject with *ga* while she does not mark the object with the Accusative Case *o*. Both the use of *ga* and the instance of Case drop in (22) are consistent with the adult Japanese. The same child in (23), however, does not express the subject NP, *mama*, and ends up marking the object *omizu* "water" with *ga*. Morikawa (1997) examined the longitudinal data in Noji (1973–1977), and lists a similar kind of particle error, those in (24), according to the child's age. Morikawa states that the child, Sumihare, does not make many errors of this sort, but that when he does make errors, they are observed with transitive verbs while no particle errors are detected in sentences where intransitive verbs and adjectives are predicates. The correct forms for Sumihare's errors are given in square brackets.

(24) a. *1;11–2;1*
           To-*wa[o]   *aite[akete].
           Door-Top[Acc] please open
           "(Please) open the door."
           Raazi-*ga[o]   akatyan miteru-yo
           radio-Nom[Acc] baby   look at
           "The baby is looking at the radio."
      b. *2;2–2;4*
           Akatyan-*ga[o] turete iku
           baby-Nom[Acc] take   go
           "(We will) take the baby along."
           Taitai-*ga[o]   totta
           fish-*Nom[Acc] caught
           "(I) caught a fish."
           Katyan haimoo-*ga[o] tensuru no-wa?
           Mom   fly-Nom[Acc] swat   thing-Top
           "Mom, (where is) the thing to swat flies?"
      c. *2;5–2;7*
           Atama-*ga[o]   utu-kara.
           head-*Nom[Acc] hit-because
           "Because (I will) hit (my) head."
      d. *2;8–2;10*
           Ototyan-ga o-*ga[o]   kitta
           Dad-Nom   thong-Nom[Acc] cut
           "Dad cut the thong."

Clancy explains the children's overextension of the particle *ga* as a marker for the first nominal argument of a sentence. This "positional hypothesis" does not account for all the children's particle errors ((24d), for example), but it may explain the errors in (25)–(26), reported in Fujiwara (1977) (taken from Clancy 1985: 390–391).

(25) *jiichan-ga   kita   kitaa
       grandfather-Nom came came

(26) *jiichan-ga   maatta (= moratta)
       grandfather-Nom received

The child consistently used *ga* to replace the directional postposition *ni* when the verb was *kuru* "come", *iku* "go", and *kaeru* "return". In (25), the child was carried over to her grandfather and hence intended to say that she has come to her grandfather. So, the correct form should be *jiichan-no tokoro-<u>ni</u>* "to (the place of) grandfather", with the postposition *ni* to mark the goal of the motion. Similarly in (26) the child's intended speech was that she received something from her grandfather, and *jiichan* should be marked with the Dative Case, *ni*, or the postposition of source, *kara* "from". Thus this child seems consistent in her use of *ga* with the first NP of the sentence, whether it replaces a Case particle or a postposition.

2.3   Prenominal Modification

Prenominal modification of various sorts is another commonly noted error type observed in children's acquisition. The child in Clancy's (1985) sample started using N-*no*-N correctly at 2;2–2;4, as in (27), but around the same time errors like (28) also emerged even though he had produced correct forms of the A–N modification pattern, e.g., *akai buubuu* "red car", prior to the error stage of (28).

(27)   a.   Yotchan-no   o-chinchin
            Yotchan-Gen penis
            "Yotchan's penis"
       b.   Oosaka-no ojiichan
            Osaka-Gen grandpa
            "grandpa who lives in Osaka"   (Clancy 1985: 458)

(28)   a.   *aoi-**no**   buubuu   for aoi buubuu
            blue-Gen car
            "a blue car"
       b.   *chiichai-**no** buubuu   for chiichai buubuu
            tiny-Gen   car
            "a tiny car"

The prenominal modifiers in (28) are both adjectives, so the addition of the Genitive Case is not appropriate. However, the child uses the prenominal modification pattern of X-*no*-N uniformly, perhaps following the N-*no*-N pattern of (27).

   The overgeneration of the prenominal modification exemplified in (28) is in fact quite extensive, not just limited to instances where the modifiers are adjectives. The same X-*no*-N schema is applied regardless of the category or structure of X. Clancy (1985) and Murasugi (1991) provide a number of examples to illustrate this phenomenon: the modifying X element can be an adjective, an adjectival noun, or a relative clause with or without a gap, as shown below. The examples in (29)–(32), taken from Murasugi (1991: 221–225) with some modification, are the errors that a child at 2;11–4;2 made. The correct forms are give in parentheses.

(29) X = *adjective*
  a. *suppai-**no** zyuusu (cf. suppai zyuusu)
     sour-Gen   juice
     "sour juice"
  b. *ookii-**no** tako (cf. ookii tako)
     big-Gen   octopus
     "a big octopus"

(30) X = *adjectival nouns*
  a. *kirei-**no**   hana (cf. kirei-na hana)
     pretty-Gen flower
     "a pretty flower"
  b. *gennki-**no**   onnanoko (cf. genki-na onnanoko)
     cheerful-Gen girl
     "a cheerful girl"
  c. *kirai-**no**   papa (cf. kirai-na papa)
     dislike-Gen daddy
     "Daddy, who (I) dislike"

(31) X = *relative clauses with gaps*
  a. *hasitteru-**no**   baabaa (cf. hasitteru baabaa)
     is running-Gen Babar
     "the Babar, who is running"
  b. *odotteru-**no**   sinderera (cf. odotteru sinderera)
     is dancing-Gen Cinderella
     "Cinderella, who is dancing"
  c. *Emityan-no kaita-**no**   sinderera (cf. Emityan-no kaita sinderera)
     Emi-Gen   drew-Gen Cinderella
     "the Cinderella that Emi drew"
  d. *Mama tukutta-**no** syuukuriimu (cf. Mama tukutta syukuriimu)
     Mother made-Gen cream puffs
     "the cream puffs that Mother made"

(32) X = *relative clauses without gaps*
  a. *asoko-**no** doa-no   simatta-**no** oto
     there-Gen door-Gen shut-Gen   sound
     "the sound that the door over there shut"
                                  (cf. asoko-no doa-no simatta oto)
  b. *shuukuriimu tukutten-**no**   nioi-yo
     cream puffs   is making-Gen smell
     "(that's) the smell of (her) making cream puffs"
                                  (cf. shuukuriimu tukutten nioi-yo)

These examples illustrate the fact that a variety of prenominal modification relations existing in adult Japanese, as is summarized in (33), are all generalized into one pattern, i.e. (34).

(33) a. *adjectives*   aka-i hon (red-book)
      b. *adjectival nouns* kirei-na hon (pretty-book)
      c. *nouns*   Mama-no hon (Mom-book)
      d. *relative clauses*   Mama-ga katta hon ([Mom bought]-book)

(34) X-*no*-N

Interestingly, Murasugi (1991) demonstrates that the child also made errors of the opposite type, i.e. an instance of undergeneration. The range of modifiers placed immediately before a noun is not restricted to those in (33): PPs can also modify nouns, and in such a situation, the Genitive Case *no* intervenes between a modifying PP and a modified noun, i.e. PP-*no*-N, as in *tomodati-kara-no tegami* (friend-from-Gen letter) "a letter from a friend". The child in Murasugi's longitudinal study omitted *no* when a noun is modified by a PP, resulting in errors like those in (35).

(35) a. *Santasan-kara purezento   (cf. Santasan-kara-no purezento)
          Santa-from   present
          "a present from Santa"
      b. *Emityan-e purezento   (cf. Emi-tyan-e-no purezento)
          Emi-to   present
          "a present to Emi"
      c. *Toronto-kara kippu   (cf. Toronto-kara-no kippu)
          Toronto-from   ticket
          "a ticket from Toronto"

According to Murasugi, the child, in addition to errors like those in (35), sometimes dropped postpositions while she kept *no*, generating *Santasan-no purezento* for (35a), for example. Thus, prenominal modification involving *no* exhibits instances of both overgeneration and undergeneration, although the former seem to constitute a much more common error type in language acquisition data.

We have thus far been assuming that the instances of *no* that appear in the errors that children make in prenominal modification such as in (28)–(32) are the Genitive Case (Clancy 1985). Murasugi (1991), however, casts doubt on this assumption, drawing on data from the Toyama dialect. The prenominal modification with a noun modifier in the Toyama dialect patterns with Tokyo Japanese, as in *John-no hon* (John-Gen book) "John's book". In the Tokyo dialect, *no* also appears as a form of pronoun often replacing understood nouns, corresponding the English *one* as in *a big one*; and it also shows up as a sentential subject of a cleft sentence, which according to Hoji's (1990) proposal is analyzed as a complementizer. Examples of these two situations are given in (36)–(37).

(36) siroi-**no**
      white-pro
      "a white one"

(37) [Yamada-ga   atta] **no**-wa   Russell-da.
     Yamada-Nom met Comp-Top Russell-is
     "It was Russell that Yamada met"   (Murasugi 1991: 93)

In Toyama, in contrast, the pro-form of *no* in (36) and the complementizer *no* in (37) are realized as *ga*, instead. So, the Toyama dialect versions of (36)–(37) are (38)–(39), respectively.

(38)   siroi-**ga**

(39)   [Yamada-ga atta] **ga**-wa Russell-da.

Thus, the Toyama dialect makes a distinction between the Genitive Case on the one hand and the pro-form and the complementizer on the other: the former is realized as *no*, as is the case with the Tokyo dialect, while the latter is *ga*, unlike the case with the Tokyo. The contrast between the two dialects is summarized in (40).

(40)   *Tokyo*   *Toyama*
       prenominal modification   no   no
       pro-form   no   ga
       complementizer   no   ga

Errors parallel to (28)–(32) by a child using the Toyama dialect show a similar phenomenon to that in the errors made by the child using the Tokyo dialect, but crucially it is *ga* rather than *no* that intervenes between a modifier and a modified noun. This is shown in (41)–(42), spoken by a child at 2;11 (taken from Murasugi 1991: 179).

(41)   *akai-**ga** boosi
       red-GA   cap
       "a red cap"

(42)   *anpanman   tuitoru-**ga**   koppu
       "anpanman"   attaching-GA cup
       "a cup which has on it pictures of 'anpanman'"

On the basis of these acquisition data that highlight the dialectal variation, Murasugi questions the assumption that the instances of *no* in children's errors like those in (28)–(32) are the Genitive Case.

3   Theoretical Approaches to Verb Acquisition

It is clear by now that the question of how children learn their first language is a very important issue to investigate in linguistic research. In this pursuit, researchers propose various language acquisition hypotheses which are tested against longitudinal and experimental data in different areas of investigation ranging from phonetics, phonology, syntax, and semantics to pragmatics. This section will introduce two theoretical approaches to the pursuit, taking an example from research on lexical acquisition, in particular, verb acquisition. In looking at both approaches and the difficulties arising from their applications to languages like Japanese, we will see how important it is to take language-specific characteristics into consideration and how relevant typological variation is to forming acquisition hypotheses.

An underlying key question for hypotheses that are concerned with verb acquisition revolves around the question of what sort of information children make reference to in forming generalizations toward the correct use of verbs. This inquiry has been rigorously made in what have been called bootstrapping hypotheses, most notable of which are the **syntactic bootstrapping** and **semantic bootstrapping hypotheses** (Pinker 1987). These hypotheses have been contrasted because they depart from each other in what they regard as basic information children use in verb learning: the syntactic structure in which a verb appears is crucial for the syntactic bootstrapping hypothesis, and the semantic representation of a verb is relevant to the semantic bootstrapping hypothesis.

The basic principle of the syntactic bootstrapping hypothesis is that the child uses the syntactic structure as the initial cue leading to verb meaning (Landau and Gleitman 1985). Building on the earlier claim, Gleitman (1993: 175) more recently elaborates on syntactic bootstrapping:

> The idea here is that children deduce the verb meanings in a procedure that is sensitive to their syntactic privileges of occurrence. They *must* do so, because either (a) there is *not enough* information in the whole world to learn the meaning of even simple verbs, or (b) there is *too much* information in the world to learn the meanings of these verbs. [italics original]

This is a lexical acquisition hypothesis that was originally constructed as a challenge to the "observational learning hypothesis", which is reflected in the quotation from John Locke given at the beginning of this chapter. The observational learning hypothesis claims that children's verb learning takes place by observing real-world events with which a verb co-occurs. That is, the child learns the meaning and the use of a verb when she or he sees the event that is supposedly described by the verb or the event that occurs at the time the verb is uttered. The child associates the verb with the event, and this is how the child accomplishes verb learning.

Gleitman (1993) gives a number of arguments against such an observation-based acquisition hypothesis. For example, as was briefly mentioned earlier, Landau and Gleitman (1985) report a study that compares blind and sighted children in their patterns of verb learning. If the observational learning hypothesis were correct, blind children would experience more difficulties in learning vision-related verbs, such as *look* and *see*, than do sighted children. Contrary to this prediction, however, Landau and Gleitman found no difference in the extent of knowledge these two sets of children acquired of vision-related verbs. The only difference is that blind children understood *look* and *see* as describing haptic perceptions whereas sighted children interpreted them as representing visual perceptions. Gleitman also argues that a single event can be described by a set of verbs like *buy/sell*, *chase/flee*, and *give/receive*, and hence a mere observation of a real-world event will not be sufficient for the child to acquire knowledge of a verb. Furthermore, the observational learning hypothesis assumes that there exists an event to be observed for the purpose of verb learning, but there is overwhelming evidence that not all occurrences of verbs are accompanied by their corresponding events. Mental verbs like *think* and *know* as well as verbs describing psychological states like *worry* and *love* are such examples. Instead, Gleitman claims that syntax, more precisely information regarding subcategorization frames, plays an important role in helping the child deduce verb meaning. This line of reasoning has been the underlying force motivating the syntactic bootstrapping hypothesis.

There are a number of experimental studies on children's verb learning that have been conducted to support the syntactic bootstrapping hypothesis. Niagles (1990), for example, uses the preferential-looking paradigm, which assumes that if the child understands a sentence correctly, she or he will pay more attention to a visual cue that is consistent with what the sentence means. Niagles reports that children focus on causal events when they are presented with transitive sentences while they pay more attention to non-causal events when they hear intransitive sentences. Twenty-four children, whose average age was 25 months, were divided into two groups. In the training session, one group of children heard nonsense verbs such as *gorp*, *blick*, *krad*, and *dax* in the transitive frame: "Look! The duck is gorping the bunny!" The other group heard the same set of nonsense verbs in the intransitive frame: "Look! The duck and the bunny are gorping!" Both groups of children were shown two videos, one depicting a causative action and the other a non-causative action, with the prompt "Where is gorping now? Find gorping!" The results strongly indicate that children's visual fixation is on the causative action when they hear transitive sentences and on the non-causative action when they hear intransitive sentences. Thus, the transitivity of sentences that children hear, which is reflected in the syntactic subcategorization frames, and the event type, causative vs. non-causative, are congruent to each other. On the basis of this experimental investigation, Niagles concludes that the children in the study used syntactic frames to deduce the meaning of the verbs, and that especially with the use of nonsense verbs, it provides a piece of evidence for the syntactic bootstrapping hypothesis.

Fisher et al. (1994) illustrate another testing ground for syntactic bootstrapping in their experimental study on children's acquisition of verb meaning. There are many real-world situations that can be described by a pair of verbs. They include *eat/feed*, *push/fall*, *flee/chase*, and *give/receive*, among many more. For example, a transfer of possession can be described either as *John gave candy to Mary* or as *Mary received candy from John*. Fisher et al. hypothesize that children would interpret nonsense verbs like *biff* more like "give" if the verb appeared in a syntactic environment like (43); and they would interpret the verb more like "receive" if it were used in sentences like (44). Fisher et al. claim that these biases are in part guided by the syntactic information supplied by the PPs that are headed by *to* and *from*.

(43) The rabbit is biffing the ball to the elephant.

(44) The elephant is biffing the ball from the rabbit.

(Fisher et al. 1994: 339)

Similarly, under this hypothesis, it is predicted that the child would more likely interpret the nonsense verb *zike* as "push" upon hearing transitive sentences like (45), while intransitive sentences like (46) would lead her or him to interpret the verb as "fall". This is because causation is encoded in transitivity: transitive sentences imply causative events while intransitive sentences imply non-causative events.

(45) The rabbit is ziking the duck.

(46) The duck is ziking.   (Fisher et al. 1994: 340)

Thus, in this approach, syntactic information serves as a primary medium for mapping between words and concepts.

   In the experimental study Fisher et al. (1994) report, 54 3-year-old and 4-year-old children were tested in two groups for the validity of this hypothesis on the basis of nonsense verbs like *zike*, *blick*, *pilk*, *dack*, *moke*, and *nade*. The children were shown several scenes such as one where a rabbit feeds an elephant with a spoon. These scenes were presented with an accompanying sentence of the intransitive frame, *The rabbit is V-ing*, for the first group, with a sentence of the transitive frame, *The elephant is V-ing the rabbit*, for the second group, and with a sentence without any clue of transitivity, *Look, V-ing*, for both groups. Children were then asked to explain what the verb meant at the prompt "What does V-ing mean?" According to Fisher et al., the results demonstrate a strong correlation between the syntactic frame of the sentence presented and the meaning of the nonsense verb that children deduce. For example, children who heard *The elephant is pilking the rabbit* interpreted the verb *pilk* to mean *feed* while those who heard *The rabbit is pilking* guessed the verb means *eat*. Thus, Fisher et al. conclude that syntactic information triggers meaning in children's acquisition of nonsense verbs.

   While syntactic bootstrapping has often characterized as "sentence-to-world" mapping, semantic bootstrapping has contrastively been portrayed as "word-to-world" mapping (Gleitman 1993). In a series of works (Pinker 1984, 1987, 1989, among others), Pinker has developed the semantic bootstrapping hypothesis. This hypothesis claims that the child deduces the meaning of a verb by observing real-world events, and then applies a set of linking rules that map the semantic properties of the verb onto syntax. An informal illustration of linking rules, for instance, is that an argument that corresponds to the causer of an event, i.e. the agent, is linked to the subject position.

   The mapping of semantic properties of lexical items onto syntactic properties as a step in semantic bootstrapping can further be illustrated by various examples. On the basis of work by Slobin (1973), Bowerman (1973), and Brain (1971), Pinker (1984) observes that children tend to use Case markers such as Accusative

Case and Ergative Case "to refer only to semantically restricted set of entities" (p. 57) like the agents and patients of physical actions; and that they use sound-symbolic words as verbs when they refer to actions with agents as subjects, as in *Mummy oops* and *Doggie wuf-wuf*. Clancy (1985), moreover, demonstrates that Japanese children exhibit a similar tendency to use grammatical markers based on the semantic properties of lexical items. As we have mentioned in section 2.1 above, adjectives such as *ookii* "big" and *takai* "expensive" on the one hand, and adjectival nouns like *kirei* "pretty" and *benri* "convenient" on the other, follow distinctive inflectional paradigms in adult Japanese; but the Japanese children reported in Clancy (1985) and Hatano (1968) apply the inflectional pattern of adjectives both to adjectives and to adjectival nouns, treating them non-distinctively. This of course results in inflectional errors. This type of error by the child points to a bias in favor of semantic grounds in determining grammatical markers such as inflectional forms.

Semantic-based mapping onto syntax, the central thesis of the semantic bootstrapping hypothesis, has been shown to extend to children's acquisition of verb meaning. Bowerman's (1982) data on children's errors suggest that children deduce the syntax of a verb from its meaning. For instance, some English verbs exhibit alternation as in (47)–(48).

(47)   a.   John broke the vase.
       b.   The vase broke.

(48)   a.   The sun melted the ice cream.
       b.   The ice cream melted.

The (a) sentences are causative counterparts of the (b) sentences. On the basis of the observation that causation is represented as the transitive pattern of the (a) sentences, children make mistakes like *You can drink me the milk*, and *Remember me what I came in for*, where they intend to mean *Feed me with the milk* and *Remind me what I came in for*, respectively. In these error sentences, children are clearly using *drink* and *remember* under the causative interpretation as in (47a) and (48a), and thus assign novel meanings to these verbs that are not available in adult English. With these novel causative meanings associated with *drink* and *remember* in mind, they link the agent (or the causer) of the event to the subject and the patient/theme to the object. So, these errors are understood to have resulted from overextension of semantic-based mapping onto syntax to verbs that turn out not to allow for the causative alternation in adult grammar.

Experimental work has also supported the semantic bootstrapping hypothesis. Assuming that verb meaning is systematically represented and contains the information of the verb's agentive, causal, and temporal properties, Gropen et al. (1991), for example, examined whether the child uses semantic notions such as "cause to change" or "affectedness" in order to predict the syntactic properties of the verb. In English it has been observed that "figure–object" verbs like *pour* have the canonical linking pattern, while "ground–object" verbs like *fill* are known to have the non-canonical linking pattern. This difference is reflected in the sets of examples in (49)–(50).

(49) a.   pour water into the glass   (water = figure → object)
      b.   *pour the glass with water

(50) a.   *fill water into the glass
      b.   fill the glass with water   (the glass = ground → object)

Gropen et al. state that the linking patterns of (49a) and (50b) are subsumed under the linking rule in (51) (1991: 159), where "change" refers to either change of state or change of location.

(51)   Link the argument that is specified as "caused to change" in the main event of a verb's semantic representation to the grammatical object.

This linking rule picks out an "affected" entity, and Gropen et al. consider affectedness is a crucial semantic notion to determine the syntactic array of a verb's arguments. That is, once an affected entity is identified, the choice of (49a) or (50b) should follow straightforwardly: in the case of "figure–object" verbs like *pour* in (49a), *water* is the affected entity since it undergoes change of location; with "ground–object" verbs like *fill* in (50b), in contrast, *the glass* is viewed as the affected entity because the state of the glass undergoes a change.

On this premise, Gropen et al. ran experiments with adults and children using nonsense verbs, and report the following conclusions. Subjects tend to select the goal of motion as the direct object when the goal undergoes change of state regardless of the nature of the change (e.g., shape, color, and fullness). Furthermore, when change of state and manner (e.g., zig-zagging and bounding) both describe an event where the former is the end result and the latter is a means, the entity that is affected in the end result is realized as the direct object. Hence, this experimental work attests to the validity of the linking rule of (51), which in turn supports semantic-based mapping onto syntax.

We have thus far reviewed two hypotheses of verb acquisition, syntactic bootstrapping and semantic bootstrapping, and have observed the conceptual position and observational and experimental justification for each approach. Ideally such theoretical hypotheses should achieve the goal of accounting for verb learning in any given language. This is because one of the goals of linguistic research is to investigate the nature of innateness in the human cognitive system. That is, the bootstrapping hypotheses, in theory, should have cross-linguistic bearing. Gleitman (1993: 202) points out this very question: "The first proviso to the semantic usefulness of syntactic analysis for learning purposes is that the semantic/syntactic relations have to be materially the same across languages. Otherwise, depending on the exposure language, different children would have to perform completely different syntactic analyses to derive aspects of the meaning. And that, surely, begs the question at issue."

Evaluation of these bootstrapping hypotheses along with other theoretical approaches to verb acquisition and to language acquisition in general calls for a great deal of careful examination of cross-linguistic and language-internal properties. It is not our goal to give a specific endorsement for a particular bootstrapping hypothesis discussed above, but some of the assumptions of syntactic bootstrapping, at least, seem to be problematic once languages like Japanese are taken into consideration. First, syntactic bootstrapping assumes that subcategorization frames can be figured out from the number of overtly expressed NPs that appear in a sentence in English, as is exemplified by the transitive vs. intransitive dichotomy, but this situation does not always obtain in Japanese because of null anaphora, as is illustrated in (52).

(52) a. Taroo-ga   keeki-o   tabeta.
            Taro-Nom cake-Acc ate
            "Taro ate a cake."
      b. Taroo-ga   tabeta.
            Taro-Nom ate
            "Taro ate (it)."
      c. Keeki-o   tabeta.
            Cake-Acc ate
            "(She or he) ate a cake."
      d. Tabeta.
            Ate
            "(She or he) ate (it)."

(52a) is a sentence in which all the subcategorized NPs are overtly expressed. (52b–d) are equally full-fledged, grammatical Japanese sentences, and frequently occur in natural conversation: the missing NPs are contextually interpreted. So, if the child hears any of the (52b–d) sentences, it should not give sufficient syntactic information for the meaning of the verb to be deduced under the syntactic bootstrapping hypothesis.

The optional status of subcategorized NPs is not the only obstacle. English sentences not only contain all the NPs that are subcategorized for by a verb but also put a restriction on the order in which the NPs are aligned, i.e. in the order of the subject NP, the verb, and the object NP. Japanese, in contrast, exhibits scrambling effects, by which the subcategorized NPs do not necessarily have to appear in the basic order Subject–Object–Verb. Thus, (53) does not bear any difference in meaning from (52a), for example.

(53) Keeki-o   Taroo-ga   tabeta.
      Cake-Acc Taro-Nom ate
      "Taro ate a cake."

In scrambled sentences like (53), the Case particles that accompany the NPs can indicate the grammatical functions of the NPs. On the other hand, Case particles can also be optional, as in (54).

(54) Taroo-ga   keeki tabeta.
      Taro-Nom cake ate
      "Taro ate a cake."

Again, if the syntactic bootstrapping hypothesis were to account for the child's verb learning in Japanese just the way it applies to English, the presence of the scrambling phenomenon and Case particle drop as well as the combination of the two would prevent the child from receiving sufficient syntactic information for her or him to figure out the meaning of the verb. In this scenario, then, we might picture a tremendous delay in Japanese children's language acquisition compared to English-speaking children, but studies show that this is far from true (Clancy 1985).

Second, underlying the relevance of subcategorization frames is an explicit categorial identification of nouns, but as was already mentioned above, Japanese presents an interesting instance that illustrates categorial ambiguity. Recall Clancy's (1985) and Hatano's (1968) reports of the Japanese children's approach to adjectival nouns. This class of words are categorially nouns, following the same inflectional patterns as nouns, but bear a semantic property on a par with adjectives. Hatano's study suggests that it is by semantic coherence and regularity that children seem to interpret the meaning of lexical items.

Third, the syntactic bootstrapping hypothesis assumes that the acquisition of nouns precedes that of verbs, since the identification of nouns and the number of nouns lead to the information about subcategorization frames that is relevant to the deduction of a verb's meaning. The bias toward nouns in acquisition order, in fact, has been defended by some researchers such as Gentner (1982) and Markman (1989). While such an assumption may be sustained for English, it does not apply to all languages. For example, Choi and Gopnik (1995) report that nouns and verbs are equally accessible to Korean children's vocabulary learning from an early stage of acquisition.

Finally, the potentially problematic implications of the syntactic bootstrapping hypothesis for languages like Japanese as pointed out above are experimentally confirmed (Rispoli 1995). Rispoli (1989) examined sentences containing 300 Action verbs spoken by six Japanese caregivers to their 2-year-old children, and showed that only 13 percent of transitive verbs appeared with their complete array of subcategorized arguments in their utterance. He further calculated that a child would have to hear a transitive verb eight times before the verb occurred with a full range of subcategorized arguments in a sentence. Along similar lines, Rispoli (1991) surveyed 226 caregivers' transitive sentences, which are expected to appear in the syntactic form [NP-*ga* NP-*o* V] in its full expansion. The patterns of a verb alone, [V], and of a verb with a single NP without a Case particle, [NP V], constituted the overwhelming majority (78 percent) of all the sentence types he examined. The entire picture of this survey is given in (55) (Rispoli 1991: 342).

(55)	sentence type	frequency	percentage of total
a.	V	73	32
b.	NP V	103	46
c.	NP-o V	15	7
d.	NP-ga V	8	4
e.	NP-ga V (passive)	2	1
f.	NP NP V	18	8
g.	NP-ga NP	3	1
h.	NP NP-o V	2	1
i.	NP-ga NP-o V	2	1

What is of interest is that despite such impoverished input stimuli, children do not make mistakes in the number of NPs that are required by Action verbs (Rispoli 1995). Assuming that children are exposed to their caregivers' inputs as the source from which a particular subcategorization frame is figured out, the statistical situation Rispoli provides seems to be quite "costly" and inefficient for children's verb acquisition, and yet it requires an explanation as to why children are able to select the right number of arguments for an Action verb.

Recall that Case particles in Japanese can be a crucial piece of information concerning the role that an NP plays in a sentence: Nominative normally corresponds to the subject and Accusative to the object. In order for syntactic bootstrapping to be relevant, the syntactic information as to which grammatical function a given NP (if overt at all) is assigned by the verb should be available in a sentence. We have observed ample instances in which such information is not always given. On the basis of studies by Hakuta (1982) and Hayashibe (1975), furthermore, Rispoli (1995) reports that the proper use of Case particles is still not adequately acquired by older children, as late as 5 years old. This developmental observation suggests that crucial pieces of syntactic information that allegedly aid the child in deducing verb meaning may not be fully acquired until much later than one would expect under acquisition approaches like the syntactic bootstrapping hypothesis.

While Rispoli (1987) is critical of the syntactic bootstrapping approach to verb acquisition in Japanese, he points out that the relatively late acquisition of Case particles by Japanese children raises some problems with the semantic bootstrapping hypothesis as well. In his longitudinal study of two Japanese children, Rispoli finds that (i) out of 20 sentences that denote planned actions they produced, 19 were transitive sentences where there was no Case particle on the theme arguments; and (ii) they generally produced more intransitive than transitive sentences, but when the theme argument was inanimate, the number of transitive sentences exceeded that of intransitive sentences. Thus, Rispoli concludes from this study that the distinction between transitive and intransitive sentences is made on the basis of semantic notions like planned action and animacy of theme rather than the syntactic information of Case particles. It should be remembered that under the semantic bootstrapping hypothesis, while it is semantic information like thematic roles by which children are essentially guided, linking rules are still called for in order to map semantic information to syntactic configuration. In the study with the two Japanese children above, however, such linking rules would involve Case particles to map semantic roles to grammatical functions, but the children are not using Case particles to mediate linking by the time they figure out the transitivity dichotomy. Thus, the late acquisition of Case particles also presents some obstacle to the semantic bootstrapping hypothesis. Rispoli instead argues that the combination of semantics and context is at play to account for the acquisition situation in Japanese.

While each hypothesis is built upon a strong conceptual foundation, we have seen that languages like Japanese particularly raise challenging questions concerning the cross-linguistic implications of the syntactic bootstrapping hypothesis. Arguments surveyed in this section seem to point to a semantics-based approach to verb acquisition as preferable, although a strict version of the semantic bootstrapping hypothesis would face some difficulties. It goes without saying that a wide range of typological and language-specific studies regarding acquisition theories is needed, and an increasing number of scholars have been engaged in the pursuit (Bowerman 1996; Slobin 2001).

4   Pragmatic Acquisition

We have thus far been concerned with how children acquire the internal structure of a language, but an investigation of children's pragmatic acquisition and development constitutes another interesting research area. Especially in Japanese, there are a number of linguistic forms that are important with respect to social context, such as honorification, politeness, and gender variation, and thus an inquiry in this area particularly enriches our understanding of the acquisition of pragmatic knowledge.

Let us begin our discussion with politeness in children's speech. As we have discussed in chapter 7, politeness in adult Japanese is marked most notably by inflectional ending, and this has been referred to as addressee honorifics. The inflectional paradigms for nouns, adjectives, adjectival nouns, and verbs that are introduced in chapters 3 and 4 are citation forms (see also (16)–(18) in this chapter), but they are considered an informal and casual level of speech when they are used sentence-finally. Their corresponding formal and polite forms (i.e. addressee honorific forms) are displayed in (56)–(58).

(56)   *nouns/adjectival nouns*: hon "book", kirei "pretty"
    a. *non-past*   hon/kirei-desu
    b. *non-past neg.* hon/kire-zya arimasen
    c. *past*   hon/kire-desita
    d. *past neg.*   hon/kire-zya arimasen-desita
    e. *tentative*   hon/kire-desyoo

(57)   *adjectives*: ooki- "big"
    a. *non-past*   ookii-desu
    b. *non-past neg.* ooki-ku arimasen
    c. *past*   ooki-katta desu
    d. *past neg.*   ooki-ku arimasen desita
    e. *tentative*   ookii-desyoo

(58)   *verbs*: tabe- "eat"
    a. *non-past*   tabe-masu
    b. *non-past neg.* tabe-masen
    c. *past*   tabe-masita
    d. *past neg.*   tabe-masen desita
    e. *tentative*   tabe-ru desyoo

These addressee honorific forms, which are often characterized as *desu/masu* forms, appear in children's spontaneous speech early on, as early as 2 years of age, and by 3 years of age, children's use of polite forms is quite solid (Clancy 1985; K. Nakamura 2002). Children's speech environment is largely restricted to the household situation where dialogues take place with their caregivers, and it does not normally form a typical context for addressee honorifics. Researchers thus point out that children's use of addressee honorifics is characteristically observed in role-play (such as doctor–patient, restaurant server–customer, hostess–guest), telephone conversations, and disciplinary situations. In a monologue in (59), a 2-year-old girl plays an (adult) hostess role and an (adult) visitor role at the same time, and the level of politeness is what we expect in adult Japanese.

(59) *(Both A (visitor) and B (hostess) are uttered by the same child.)*
    A: Gomen kudasai.
        hello
        "Hello."
    B: Irassyaimase.
        welcome
        "Come in."
    A: Minasan   o-genki-desu-ka.
        everybody healthy-Q
        "Are you all well?"
    B: Hai. O-genki-desu.
        yes   healthy
        "Yes. We're fine."
    A: Kore rika-tte   yuu namae-desu.
        this Rika-Quotative say name
        "This one's name is Rika."
    B: Maa, ookiku nari-masita-ne.
        my   big   become
        "My, how big she's gotten."
                        (Clancy 1985: 445–446 (modified); original source
                                     Iwabuchi and Muraishi 1968)

This monologue contains some formal ritual exchanges like *gomen kudasai* "hello" and *irassyaimase* "come in", and even referent honorific expressions like *minasan* "everybody" and *ogenkidesuka* "are you all well?"

    K. Nakamura (2002: 26–27) gives the following examples to illustrate that children at age 2;6 and 2;4 can readily use a polite level of speech when speaking to a stranger. (60) is a situation where a stranger speaks to the child at a park, and (61) presents a phone conversation.

(60) Adult: O-namae wa nan <u>desu</u> ka?
            "What is (your) name?"
      Child: Horikawa Yuuki <u>desu</u>.
            "(My name) is Yuuki Horikawa."

Adult:	Nan-sai <u>desu</u> ka?
	"How old are (you)?"
Child:	Ni-sai <u>desu</u>.
	"(I) am two."
Adult:	Yoochien itteru no?
	"Are (you) going to kindergarten?"
Child:	Iie, <u>chigaimasu</u>.
	"No, (I)'m not."

(61)
Caller:	Moshimoshi.
	"Hello."
Child:	Sano <u>desu</u>.
	"(This) is the Sano (residence)."
Caller:	Okaasan <u>irasshaimasu</u> ka?
	"Is (your) mother there?"
Child:	Hai, <u>imasu</u>.
	"Yes, (she)'s here."
Caller:	<u>Kawatte-kuremasu</u> ka?
	"Could (you) change (with her)?"
Child:	Hai, chotto <u>matte-kudasai</u>.
	"Yes, please wait a little."

Both children use the *desu/masu* forms correctly and adequately for these formal situations. In disciplinary situations adults are viewed as people of authority, and hence a formal speech level can be more appropriate. K. Nakamura (2002: 28), for example, reports that a child at 2;6 apologizes for spilling milk and says, *Moo shimasen* "I won't do it again", where *shimasen* is a polite negative verbal form.

Referent honorifics (respectful forms and humble forms), in comparison to addressee honorifics, have been understood to show late acquisition. Clancy (1985) explains that one of the reasons for the late acquisition of respectful and humble forms is that they present linguistic complexity in their variety of forms, ranging from several morphologically productive formations to idiosyncratic forms that must be individually memorized, each one of them associated with intricate semantic and pragmatic properties. This linguistic complexity is made more difficult because respectful and humble expressions need to be used appropriately with full understanding of the social hierarchy. Children are certainly not exposed early on to situations that lead them to full social understanding. K. Nakamura (2002) discusses a few referent honorific expressions that children as young as 3 years old use, but they tend to be ritualistic and sometimes frozen expressions specifically used by companies when they deal with their customers. Her examples of children's utterances (K. Nakamura 2002: 30–31) include those in (62), with modification.

(62) a. Ojama-<u>itashimasu</u> [humble]
          "I'm sorry to intrude."
      b. <u>Itadakimasu</u> [humble]
          "I will eat." (ritual before eating)

c. Kono denwa bangoo wa tsukawarete-<u>orimasen</u>.   [humble]
    "This telephone number is not being used." (recording)
d. Nani ni <u>nasaimasu</u> ka?   [respectful]
    "What would you like to have?" (restaurant server's frozen expression)
e. Doozo <u>meshiagare</u>.   [respectful]
    "Please eat." (frozen expression to urge a guest to eat)

As for gender distinctions, K. Nakamura (2002) reports that children at around 3 years old start using gender-indexing expressions, like pronouns and sentence-final particles, as they attend kindergarten, where children of both sexes interact with each other. Nakamura notes that boys in particular begin to use the first person pronouns *boku* and *ore*, the (somewhat vulgar) second person pronouns *omae* and *temee*, and the sentence-final particles *zo* and *ze*. Girls appear to show a slightly different tendency from boys in that they do not use gender-indexing expressions as much as boys do and keep gender-neutral language. Girls, however, are able to use female speech forms as well as male speech forms in role-play situations, as the examples in (63)–(64) attest (taken from K. Nakamura 2002: 35).

(63) *Girl (2;6) pretending to be a woman looking for someone*:
      Koko ni inai <u>wa</u>.   "She is not here."

(64) *Girl (2;3) pretending to be a boy taking turns*:
      Ja <u>boku</u> wa tsugi.   "I'll (be) next."

The sentence-final particle *wa* in (63) is typical of female speech, while *boku* is a first person pronoun for a male speaker; but both are spoken by a girl in role-play. Thus, while there are differences between boys and girls as well as among individuals, Japanese children seem to be aware of gender differences reflected in the language from early on.

Suggested Readings

General issues in language acquisition: Slobin (1985), P. Bloom (1993), Pinker (1994, 1999), Bowerman and Levinson (2001), Tomasello and Bates (2001), Clark (2003).

Japanese language acquisition: Clancy (1985), Murasugi (1991), Yamashita (1995), Nakayama (1996), Morikawa (1997), Ota (1999, 2003), Otsu (1999), Li and Shirai (2000), Aoyama (2001), Nakayama et al. (to appear). Clancy (1985) is rich in data that describe Japanese children's acquisition patterns in various linguistic aspects. Nakayama et al. (to appear) brings together overview articles of a number of topics related to language acquisition, both first and second language. The other references given above are mostly on specific topics.

EXERCISES

1 The following data illustrate a type of mispronunciation by some Japanese children. (The data are taken from Davis and Ueda 2003.)

A.		*target forms*	*children's pronunciation*	*gloss*
	(a)	rappa	dappa	"trumpet"
		roosoku	doosoku	"candle"
		remoŋ	demoŋ	"lemon"
		risu	disu	"squirrel"
	(b)	daruma	daruma	"tumbler"
		doobutˢueŋ	doobutˢueŋ	"zoo"
		denša	denša	"tram car"
	(c)	parašu:to	parašu:to	"parachute"
		guro:bu	guro:bu	"glove"
		terebi	terebi	"television"
		sora	sora	"sky"
	(d)	ǰido:ša	ǰiro:ša	"automobile"
		namida	namira	"tear"
		budo:	buro:	"grape"

Describe the children's mispronunciation illustrated in (a–d) above. What is the relationship between the sounds [d] and [r] in these children's speech?

B. There is another type of mispronunciation found in some children. Consider the following set of data.

		target forms	*children's pronunciation*	*gloss*
	(e)	rap:a	dap:a	"trumpet"
		roosoku	doosoku	"candle"
		remoŋ	dcmoŋ	"lemon"
		risu	disu	"squirrel"
	(f)	daruma	daduma	"tumbler"
		doobutˢueŋ	doobutˢueŋ	"zoo"
		denša	denša	"tram car"
	(g)	parašu:to	padašu:to	"parachute"
		guro:bu	gudo:bu	"glove"
		terebi	tedebi	"television"
		sora	soda	"sky"
	(h)	ǰido:ša	ǰido:ša	"automobile"
		namida	namida	"tear"
		budo:	budo:	"grape"

Describe the mispronunciation pattern illustrated in (e–h). How do these children's speech differ from that in (A) above?

2   In the literature on language acquisition, the term "baby-talk" refers to the way adults speak to babies. The following are common baby-talk expressions in Japanese.

target	baby-talk	gloss
me	omeme	"eye"
te	otete	"hand"
kuči	okuči	"mouth"
mimi	omimi	"ear"
hana	ohana	"nose"
sakana	ototo	"fish"
tamago	tamatama	"egg"
kutˢu	kuk:u	"shoes"
aši	anyo	"leg, foot"
onaka	pompo	"stomach"
gohan	mam:ma	"meal, food"

A. What patterns are common to these forms?
B. Baby-talk expressions in English are exemplified by such forms as *tummy, doggy, choo-choo, bow-wow,* and *poo-poo.* How are their patterns similar to those of the baby-talk in Japanese? How are they different?

Bibliography

Abe, H. (2004) Lesbian bar talk in Shinjuku, Tokyo. In: Okamoto, S. and Shibamoto Smith, J. (eds), 205–221.

Abe, J. (1991) *Zibun* as distributor and its interaction with pronominal *kare*. Manuscript. University of Connecticut.

Aikawa, T. (1993) Reflexivity in Japanese and LF-analysis of *zibun*-binding. PhD dissertation, Ohio State University.

Aikawa, T. (1994) Logophoric use of the Japanese reflexive *zibun-zisin* "self-self". *MIT Working Papers in Linguistics* 24, 1–22.

Aikawa, T. (1999) Reflexives. In: Tsujimura, N. (ed.), 154–190.

Akmajian, A., Demers, R. A., and Harnish, R. M. (1984) *Linguistics: An Introduction to Language and Communication*, second edition. Cambridge, MA: MIT Press.

Aksu-Koç, A. (1988) *The Acquisition of Aspect and Modality: The Case of Past Reference in Turkish*. Cambridge: Cambridge University Press.

Anderson, S. (1971) On the role of deep structure in semantic interpretation. *Foundations of Language* 7, 387–396.

Anderson, S. (1977) Comments on the paper by Wasow. In: Culicover, P., Wasow, T., and Akmajian, A. (eds), 361–377.

Antinucci, F. and Miller, R. (1976) How children talk about what happened. *Journal of Child Language* 3, 169–189.

Aoyama, K. (2001) *A Psycholinguistic Perspective on Finnish and Japanese Prosody*. Dordrecht: Springer.

Aronoff, M. (1976) *Word Formation in Generative Grammar*. Cambridge, MA: MIT Press.

Aronoff, M. and Fudeman, K. (2005) *What is Morphology?* Oxford: Blackwell.

Bach, E. and Harms, R. T. (eds) (1968) *Universals in Linguistic Theory*. New York: Holt, Rinehart, and Winston.

Bauer, L. (1983) *English Word-Formation*. Cambridge: Cambridge University Press.

Beckman, M. E. (1982) Segmental duration and the "mora" in *Japanese*. *Phonetica* 39, 113–135.

Beckman, M. E. (1986) *Stress and Non-Stress Accent*. Dordrecht: Foris.

Bedell, G. (1972) On *no*. *UCLA Papers in Syntax* 3, 1–20.

Bedell, G., Kobayashi, E., and Muraki, M. (eds) (1979) *Explorations in Linguistics: Papers in Honor of Kazuko Inoue*. Tokyo: Kenkyusha.

Binnick, R. (1991) *Time and the Verb*. Oxford: Oxford University Press.

Bloch, B. (1950) Studies in colloquial Japanese IV: phonemics. *Language* 26, 86–125.

Bloom, L., Lifter, K., and Hafitz, J. (1980) Semantics of verbs and the development of verb inflection in child language. *Language* 56, 386–412.

Bloom, P. (ed.) (1993) *Language Acquisition*. Cambridge, MA: MIT Press.

Bloom, P., Peterson, M. A., Nadel, L., and Garrett, M. F. (eds) (1996) *Rethinking Linguistic Relativity*. Cambridge: Cambridge University Press.

Bowerman, M. (1973) *Early Syntactic Development: A Cross-Linguistic Study with Special Reference to Finnish*. Cambridge: Cambridge University Press.

Bowerman, M. (1982) Evaluating competing linguistic models with language acquisition data: implications of developmental errors with causative verbs. *Quaderni di Semantica* 3, 5–66.

Bowerman, M. (1996) Learning how to structure space for language: a crosslinguistic perspective. In: Bloom, P., Peterson, M. A., Nadel, L., and Garrett, M. F. (eds), 145–176.

Bowerman, M. and Levinson, S. C. (eds) (2001) *Language Acquisition and Conceptual Development*. Cambridge: Cambridge University Press.

Brain, M. D. S. (1971) On two types of models of the internalization of grammars. In: Slobin, D. (ed.), 153–186

Bronckart, J.-P. and Sinclair, H. (1973) Time, tense and aspect. *Cognition* 2, 107–130.

Brown, R. (1973) *A First Language*. Cambridge, MA: Harvard University Press.

Burzio, L. (1981) Intransitive verbs and Italian auxiliaries. PhD dissertation, MIT.

Burzio, L. (1986) *Italian Syntax: A Government-Binding Approach*. Dordrecht: Reidel.

Butt, M. and Geuder, W. (eds) (1998) *The Projection of Arguments: Lexical and Compositional Factors*. Stanford: CSLI.

Carter, R. (1988) Some linking regularities. In: Levin, B. and Tenny, C. (eds), 1–92.

Chierchia, G. and McConnell-Ginet, S. (1990) *Meaning and Grammar*. Cambridge, MA: MIT Press.

Choi, S. and Gopnik, A. (1995) Early acquisition of verbs in Korean: a cross-linguistic study. *Journal of Child Language* 22, 497–529.

Chomsky, N. (1957) *Syntactic Structure*. The Hague: Mouton.

Chomsky, N. (1965) *Aspects of the Theory of Syntax*. Cambridge, MA: MIT Press.

Chomsky, N. (1980) *Rules and Representations*. New York: Cambridge University Press.

Chomsky, N. (1981) *Lectures on Government and Binding*. Dordrecht: Foris.

Chomsky, N. (1986a) *Barriers*. Cambridge, MA: MIT Press.

Chomsky, N. (1986b) *Knowledge of Language: Its Nature, Origin, and Use*. New York: Praeger.

Clark, E. (1993) *The Lexicon in Acquisition*. Cambridge: Cambridge University Press.

Clark, E. (1996) Early verbs, event types and inflections. In: Johnson, C. E. and Gilbert, J. H. V. (eds), 61–73.

Clark, E. (2003) *First Language Acquisition*. Cambridge: Cambridge University Press.

Clancy, P. M. (1985) *The Acquisition of Japanese*. Hillsdale, NJ: Lawrence Erlbaum.

Coates, J. (ed.) (1998) *Language and Gender: A Reader*. Oxford: Blackwell.

Cole, P. and Morgan, J. L. (eds) (1975) *Syntax and Semantics 3: Speech Acts*. New York: Academic Press.

Comrie, B. (1976) *Aspect*. Cambridge: Cambridge University Press.

Comrie, B. (1985) *Tense*. Cambridge: Cambridge University Press.

Comrie, B. and Polinsky, M. (eds) (1993) *Causatives and Transitivity*. Amsterdam: John Benjamins.

Cook, V. J. (1988) *Chomsky's Universal Grammar: An Introduction*. Oxford: Blackwell.

Croft, W. (1998) Event structure in argument linking. In: Butt, M. and Geuder, W. (eds), 21–63.

Culicover, P. (1997) *Principles and Parameters: An Introduction to Syntactic Theory*. Oxford: Oxford University Press.

Culicover, P., Wasow, T., and Akmajian, A. (eds) (1977) *Formal Syntax*. New York: Academic Press.

Davis, S. (1988) *Topics in Syllable Geometry*. New York: Garland.

Davis, S. and Tsujimura, N. (1991) An autosegmental account of Japanese verbal conjugation. *Journal of Japanese Linguistics* 13, 117–144.

Davis, S. and Ueda, I. (2003) Mora augmentation processes in Japanese. *Journal of Japanese Linguistics* 18, 1–23.

Di Sciullo, A.-M. and Williams, E. (1987) *On the Definition of Word*. Cambridge, MA: MIT Press.

Diffloth, G. (1972) Notes on expressive meaning. *CLS* 8, 440–447.

Downing, P. (1993) Pragmatic and semantic constraints on numeral quantifier position in Japanese. *Journal of Linguistics* 29, 65–93.

Dowty, D. R. (1979) *Word Meaning and Montague Grammar*. Dordrecht: Reidel.

Dubinsky, S. (1985) Japanese union constructions: a unified analysis of "-sase" and "-rare". PhD dissertation, Cornell University.

Dubinsky, S. (1994) Syntactic underspecification: a minimalist approach to light verbs. *MIT Working Papers in Linguistics* 24, 61–81.

Farmer, A. K. (1980) On the interaction of morphology and syntax. PhD dissertation, MIT.

Farmer, A. K. (1984) *Modularity in Syntax: A Study of Japanese and Syntax*. Cambridge, MA: MIT Press.

Farmer, A. K. and Kitagawa, C. (eds) (1981) *Coyote Papers 2*. University of Arizona.

Farmer, A. K. and Otsu, Y. (eds) (1980) Theoretical Issues in Japanese Linguistics. *MIT Working Papers in Linguistics* 2.

Ferguson, C. and Slobin, D. (eds) (1973) *Studies of Child Language Development*. New York: Holt, Rinehart and Winston.

Fery, C. and van de Vijver, R. (eds) (2003) *The Syllable in Optimality Theory*. Cambridge: Cambridge University Press.

Fiengo, R. and McClure, W. (2002) On how to use *-wa*. *Journal of East Asian Linguistics* 11, 5–41.

Fillmore, C. (1968) The case for case. In: Bach, E. and Harms, R. T. (eds), 1–88.

Fillmore, C. (1975) *Santa Cruz Lecture on Deixis 1971*. Bloomington, IN: IULC.

Finegan, E. (1994) *Language: Its Structure and Use*, second edition. Fort Worth, TX: Harcourt Brace.

Fisher, C., Hall, D. G., Rakowitz, S., and Gleitman, L. (1994) When it is better to receive than to give: syntactic and conceptual constraints on vocabulary growth. *Lingua* 92, 333–375.

Fried, M. and Boas, H. C. (eds) (to appear) *Construction Grammar: Back to the Roots*. Amsterdam: John Benjamins.

Fromkin, V. (1971) The non-anomalous nature of anomalous utterances. *Language* 47, 27–52.

Fromkin, V. (1973) *Speech Errors as Linguistic Evidence*. The Hague: Mouton.

Fromkin, V. and Rodman, R. (1993) *An Introduction to Language*, fifth edition. Fort Worth, TX: Harcourt Brace Jovanovich.

Fujii, T. (1976) "Dooshi + te iru" no imi [The meaning of "verb + *te-iru*"]. In: Kindaichi, H. (ed.), 97–116.

Fujiwara, Y. (1964) *Hogen Kenkyuho*. Tokyo: Tokyodo Shuppan.

Fujiwara, Y. (1977) *Yooji no Gengo Hyoogen Nooryoku no Hattatsu* [Children's Development of Linguistic Ability]. Hiroshima: Bunka Hyoron.

Fukui, N. (1986) A theory of category projection and its applications. PhD dissertation, MIT.

Fukui, N., Miyagawa, S., and Tenny, C. (1985) *Verb Classes in English and Japanese: A Case Study in the Interaction of Syntax, Morphology and Semantics*. Lexicon Project Working Papers 3, MIT.

Fukushima, K. (1993) Model theoretic semantics for Japanese floating quantifiers and their scope properties. *Journal of East Asian Linguistics* 2, 213–228.

Fukushima, K. (2005) Lexical V–V compounds in Japanese: lexicon vs. syntax. *Language* 81, 568–612.

Gentner, D. (1982) Why nouns are learned before verbs: linguistic relativity vs. natural partitioning. In: Kuczaj II, S. A. (ed.), 301–334

Georgopoulos, C. and Ishihara, R. (eds) (1990) *Interdisciplinary Approaches to Language: Essays in Honor of S.-Y. Kuroda.* Dordrecht: Kluwer.

Gleitman, L. (1993) The structural sources of verb meanings. In: Bloom, P. (ed.), 174–221.

Goldberg, A. (1995) *Constructions: A Construction Grammar Approach to Argument Structure.* Chicago: University of Chicago Press.

Goldsmith, J. (ed.) (1995) *The Handbook of Phonological Theory.* Oxford: Blackwell.

Grice, H. P. (1975) Logic and conversation. In Cole, P. and Morgan, J. L. (eds), 41–58.

Grimshaw, J. (1987) Unaccusatives – an overview. *NELS* 17, 244–258.

Grimshaw, J. and Mester, R. A. (1988) Light verbs and theta-marking. *Linguistic Inquiry* 19, 181–205.

Gropen, J., Pinker, S., Hollander, M., and Goldberg, R. (1991) Affectedness and direct objects: the role of lexical semantics in the acquisition of verb argument structure. In: Levin, B. and Pinker, S. (eds), 153–195.

Gruber, J. (1965) Studies in lexical relations. PhD dissertation, MIT.

Haegeman, L. (1991) *Introduction to Government and Binding Theory.* Oxford: Blackwell.

Hagiwara, H., Ito, T., Sugioka, Y., Kawamura, M., and Shiota, J. (1999) Neurolinguistic evidence for rule-based nominal suffixation. *Language* 75, 739–763.

Haig, J. (1980) Some observations on quantifier float in Japanese. *Linguistics* 18, 1065–1083.

Haig, J. (1990) A phonological difference in male–female speech among teenagers in Nagoya. In: Ide, S. and McGloin, N. H. (eds), 5–22.

Hakuta, K. (1982) Interaction between particles and word order in the comprehension and production of simple sentences in Japanese children. *Developmental Psychology* 18, 62–76.

Hale, K. (1980) Remarks on Japanese phrase structure: comments on the papers on Japanese syntax. In: Farmer, A. K. and Otsu, Y. (eds), 185–203.

Hale, K. (1981) *On the Position of Warlpiri in a Typology of the Base.* Bloomington, IN: IULC.

Hale, K. (1983) Warlpiri and the grammar of non-configurational languages. *Natural Language and Linguistic Theory* 1, 5–47.

Halle, M. and Vergnaud, J.-R. (1987) *An Essay on Stress.* Cambridge, MA: MIT Press.

Hamano, S. (1986) The sound-symbolic system of Japanese. PhD dissertation, University of Florida.

Hamano, S. (1998) *The Sound-Symbolic System of Japanese.* Tokyo: Kurosio/CSLI.

Harada, S. (1971) *Ga–no* conversion and idiolectal variations in Japanese. *Gengo Kenkyuu* 60, 25–38.

Harada, S. (1973) Counter equi NP deletion. *Annual Bulletin* 7, Research Institute of Logopedics and Phoniatrics, University of Tokyo, 113–147.

Harada, S. (1976a) Honorifics. In: Shibatani, M. (ed.), 499–561.

Harada, S. (1976b) *Ga–no* conversion revisited. *Gengo Kenkyuu* 70, 23–38.

Harada, S. (1976c) Quantifier float as a relational rule. *Metropolitan Linguistics* 1, 44–49.

Harada, S. (1977) Nihongo ni henkei wa hitsuyoo da [Transformations are needed in Japanese]. *Gengo* 6, 88–103.

Haraguchi, S. (1977) *The Tone Pattern of Japanese: An Autosegmental Theory of Tonology.* Tokyo: Kaitakusha.

Haraguchi, S. (1991) *A Theory of Stress and Accent.* Dordrecht: Foris.

Harley, H. (1995) Subjects, events and licensing. PhD dissertation, MIT.

Hasegawa, K. (1964) Nihongo bunpo shiron [Essays on Japanese Grammar]. *Gengo Bunka* 1, 3–46.

Hasegawa, N. (1979) Casual speech vs. fast speech. *CLS*, 126–137.

Hasegawa, N. (1986) On the so-called "zero pronouns" in Japanese. *Linguistic Review* 4, 289–342.

Hasegawa, N. (ed.) (1993) *Japanese Syntax in Comparative Grammar.* Tokyo: Kurosio.

Hasegawa, N. and Kitagawa, Y. (eds) (1986) *University of Massachusetts Occasional Papers in Linguistics: Oriental Linguistics.* University of Massachusetts.

Haspelmath, M. (1993) More on the typology of inchoative/causative verb alternations. In: Comrie, B. and Polinsky, M. (eds), 87–120.

Haspelmath, M. (2002) *Understanding Morphology.* London: Arnold.

Hatano, K. (1968) Kotoba no hattatsu shinri [Developmental psychology of language]. In: Iwabuchi, E. (ed.).

Hayashibe, H. (1975) Word order and particles: a developmental study in Japanese. *Descriptive and Applied Linguistics* 8, 1–18.

Higurashi, Y. (1983) *The Accent of Extended Word Structure in Tokyo Standard Japanese.* Tokyo: Educa.

Himeno, M. (1999) *Fukugoodoosi no Koozoo to Imiyoohoo* [The Structure and Meaning of Compound Verbs]. Tokyo: Hituzi Shobo.

Hinds, J. (1973) On the status of VP node in Japanese. *Language Research* 9, 44–57.

Hinds, J. and Howard, I. (eds) (1978) *Problems in Japanese Syntax and Semantics.* Tokyo: Kaitakusha.

Hinds, J., Maynard, S., and Iwasaki, S. (eds) (1987) *Perspectives on Topicalization: The Case of Japanese Wa.* Amsterdam: John Benjamins.

Hoji, H. (1985) Logical form constraints and configurational structures in Japanese. PhD dissertation, University of Washington.

Hoji, H. (1990) Sloppy identity in Japanese. Manuscript. University of Southern California.

Holt, J. (1943) *Etudes d'aspect. Acta Jutlandica* 15.2.

Hori, M. and Peng, F. C. C. (eds) (1981) *Gengo Syuutoku no Syosoo* [Aspects of Language Acquisition]. Hiroshima: Bunka Hyoron.

Horiguchi, S. (1981) Nensyoozi no asupekuto [Aspect in young infants]. In: Hori, M. and Peng, F. C. C. (eds).

Horn, L. and Ward, G. (eds) (2004) *The Handbook of Pragmatics.* Oxford: Blackwell.

Hornstein, N. (1990) *As Time Goes By.* Cambridge, MA: MIT Press.

Hoshi, H. (1994) Passive, causative, and light verbs: a study of theta role assignment. PhD dissertation, University of Connecticut.

Hoshi, H. (1999) Passives. In: Tsujimura, N. (ed.), 191–235.

Hoshi, H. and Saito, M. (1993) The Japanese light verb construction: a case of LF theta marking. In: Saito, M. (ed.), 45–62.

Hoshi, K. (1995) Structural and interpretive aspects of head-internal and head-external relative clause. PhD dissertation, University of Rochester.

Howard, I. and Niekawa-Howard, A. (1976) Passivization. In: Shibatani, M. (ed.), 201–238.

Huang, J. (1984) On the distribution and reference of empty pronouns. *Linguistic Inquiry* 15, 531–574.

Hyman, L. M. (1975) *Phonology: Theory and Analysis.* New York: Hold, Rinehart, and Winston.

Hyman, L. M. (1977) On the nature of linguistic stress. In: Hyman, L. M. (ed.), 37–83.

Hyman, L. M. (ed.) (1977) *Studies in Stress and Accent*. Southern California Occasional Papers in Linguistics 4. USC.

Ide, S. (1990) How and why do women speak more politely in Japanese? In: Ide, S. and McGloin, N. H. (eds), 63–79.

Ide, S. and McGloin, N. H. (eds) (1990) *Aspects of Japanese Women's Language*. Tokyo: Kurosio.

Ide, S. and Yoshida, M. (1999) Sociolinguistics: honorifics and gender differences. In: Tsujimura, N. (ed.), 444–480.

Iida, M. (1987) Case assignment by nominals in Japanese. In: Iida, M., Wechsler, S., and Zec, D. (eds), 93–138.

Iida, M. (1996) *Context and Binding in Japanese*. Stanford: CSLI.

Iida, M. (1999) Meishikagenshoo no goironnteki koosatsu [Lexical consideration of nominalization]. Manuscript. Inxight Software.

Iida, M. (2002) Meishikagenshoo no goironnteki koosatsu [Lexical consideration of nominalization]. In: Ito, T. (ed.), 9–32.

Iida, M. and Sells, P. (1988) Discourse factors in the binding *zibun*. In: Poser, W. (ed.), 23–46.

Iida, M., Wechsler, S., and Zec, D. (eds) (1987) *Working Papers in Grammatical Theory and Discourse Structure*. Stanford: CSLI.

Ikegami, Y. (1985) "Activity" – "accomplishment" – "achievement" – a language that can't say "I burned it, but it didn't burn" and one that can. In: Makkai, A. and Melby, A. K. (eds), 265–304.

Imai, T. and Saito, M. (eds) (1986) *Issues in Japanese Linguistics*. Dordrecht: Foris.

Ingram, D. (1996) The acquisition of prosodic structure in Japanese: a case study. Manuscript. University of British Columbia, Vancouver, BC.

Inoue, K. (1976a) *Henkei-bunpoo to Nihongo* [Transformational Grammar and Japanese]. Tokyo: Taishukan.

Inoue, K. (1976b) Reflexivization: an interpretive approach. In: Shibatani, M. (ed.), 117–200.

Inoue, K. (1978) *Nihongo no Bunpoo Kisoku* [Grammatical Rules in Japanese]. Tokyo: Taishukan.

Ishii, Y. (1989) Reciprocal predicates in Japanese. *ESCOL*, 150–161.

Ito, J. (1990) Prosodic minimality in Japanese. *CLS* 26, 213–239.

Ito, J. and Mester, R. A. (1986) The phonology of voicing in Japanese: theoretical consequences for morphological accessibility. *Linguistic Inquiry* 17, 49–73.

Ito, J. and Mester, R. A. (1993) *Japanese Phonology: Constraint Domains and Structure Preservation*. UCSC Linguistics Research Center.

Ito, J. and Mester, R. A. (1995) Japanese phonology. In: Goldsmith, J. (ed.), 817–838.

Ito, J. and Mester, R. A. (1999) The phonological lexicon. In: Tsujimura, N. (ed.), 62–100.

Ito, J. and Mester, R. A. (2003) *Japanese Morphophonemics: Markedness and Word Structure*. Cambridge, MA: MIT Press.

Ito, J., Kitagawa, Y., and Mester, R. A. (1996) Prosodic type preservation in Japanese: evidence from *zuuja-go*. *Journal of East Asian Linguistics* 5, 217–294.

Ito, T. (ed.) (2002) *Bunpoo Riron: Rekishikon to Toogo* [Grammar and Theory: Lexicon and Syntax]. Tokyo: University of Tokyo Press.

Iwabuchi, E. (ed.) (1968) *Kotoba no Tanjoo: Ubugoe kara Gosai made* [From Birth to 5 Years Old]. Tokyo: Nihon Hoosoo Shuppan Kyookai.

Iwabuchi, E. and Muraishi, S. (1968) Kotoba no syuutoku [Language acquisition]. In: Iwabuchi, E. (ed.).

Iwasaki, S. (1993) *Subjectivity in Grammar and Discourse*. Amsterdam: John Benjamins.

Iwasaki, S. (2002) *Japanese*. Amsterdam: John Benjamins.

Jackendoff, R. (1972) *Semantic Interpretation in Generative Grammar*. Cambridge, MA: MIT Press.

Jackendoff, R. (1977) *X' Syntax: A Study of Phrase Structure*. Cambridge, MA: MIT Press.

Jacobsen, W. M. (1981) Transitivity in the Japanese verbal system. PhD dissertation, University of Chicago.

Jacobsen, W. M. (1992) *The Transitive Structure of Events in Japanese*. Tokyo: Kurosio.

Jaeggli, O. (1980) Remarks on *to* contraction. *Linguistic Inquiry* 11, 239–246.

Johnson, C. E. and Gilbert, J. H. V. (eds) (1996) *Children's Language. Vol. 9*. Nahwah, NJ: Lawrence Erlbaum.

Jorden, E. with Noda, M. (1987) *Japanese: The Spoken Language* Part 1. New Haven, CT: Yale University Press.

Jorden, E. with Noda, M. (1988) *Japanese: The Spoken Language* Part 2. New Haven, CT: Yale University Press.

Kageyama, T. (1976–1977) Incorporation and Sino-Japanese verbs. *Papers in Japanese Linguistics* 5, 117–155.

Kageyama, T. (1980) The role of thematic relations in the spray paint hypallage. *Papers in Japanese Linguistics* 7, 35–64.

Kageyama, T. (1982) Word formation in Japanese. *Lingua* 57, 215–258.

Kageyama, T. (1989) The place of morphology in the grammar. *Yearbook of Morphology* 2, 73–94.

Kageyama, T. (1991) Light verb constructions and the syntax–morphology interface. In: Nakajima, H. (ed.), 169–205.

Kageyama, T. (1993) *Bunpoo to Gokeisei* [Grammar and Word Formation]. Tokyo: Hitsuji Shobo.

Kageyama, T. (1996) *Dooshi Imiron* [Verb Meaning]. Tokyo: Kurosio.

Kageyama, T. (1999) Word formation. In: Tsujimura, N. (ed.), 297–325.

Kageyama, T. (2001a) Polymorphism and boundedness in event/entity nominalizations. *Journal of Japanese Linguistics* 17, 29–57.

Kageyama, T. (2001b) *Dooshi no imi to koobun* [Verb Meaning and Structure]. Tokyo: Taishukan.

Kageyama, T. (2002) Doosashumeisi ni okeru goi to toogo no kyookai [The boundary between lexicon and syntax with respect to agentive noun]. *Kokugogaku* 53, 44–55.

Kakehi, K., Tamori, I., and Schourup, L. (1996) *Dictionary of Iconic Expressions in Japanese*. The Hague: Mouton.

Kameshima, N. (1989) The syntax of restrictive and nonrestrictive clauses in Japanese. PhD dissertation, University of Wisconsin.

Kameyama, M. (1985) Zero anaphora: the case of Japanese. PhD dissertation, Stanford University.

Kamio, A. (1977) Suuryoosi no sintakkusu [The syntax of numeral quantifiers]. *Gengo* 8, 83–91.

Kamio, A. (1997) *Territory of Information*. Amsterdam: John Benjamins.

Katada, F. (1990) The representation of anaphoric relations in logical form. PhD dissertation, USC.

Katada, F. (1991) The LF representation of anaphora. *Linguistic Inquiry* 22, 287–313.

Katagiri, M. (1991) Review article. *Studies in Language* 15, 399–414.

Katayama, M. (1998) Optimality theory and Japanese loanword phonology. PhD dissertation, UCSC.

Kearns, K. (2000) *Semantics*. New York: St. Martin's Press.

Kindaichi, H. (1976a) Rendaku no kai [On explaining Rendaku]. *Sophia Linguistica* 2, 1–22.

Kindaichi, H. (1976b) Kokugo dooshi no ichibunrui [A classification of Japanese verbs]. In: Kindaichi, H. (ed.), 5–26.

Kindaichi, H. (ed.) (1976) *Nihongo Dooshi no Asupekuto* [Aspect in Japanese Verbs]. Tokyo: Mugi Shobo.

Kita, S. (1997) Two-dimensional semantic analysis of Japanese mimetics. *Linguistics* 35, 379–415.

Kita, S. (2001) Semantic schism and interpretive integration in Japanese sentences with a mimetic: a reply to Tsujimura. *Linguistics* 39, 419–436.

Kitagawa, C. (1974) Case marking and causativization. *Papers in Japanese Linguistics* 3, 43–56.

Kitagawa, C. (1977) A source of femininity in Japanese: In defense of Robin Lakoff's "Language and woman's place". *Papers in Linguistics* 10, 275–298.

Kitagawa, C. (1980) Review article. *Language* 56, 435–440.

Kitagawa, C. (1981) Anaphora in Japanese: *kare* and *zibun*. In: Farmer, A. K. and Kitagawa, C. (eds), 61–75.

Kitagawa, C. (1982) Topic constructions in Japanese. *Lingua* 57, 175–214.

Kitagawa, C. (2005) Typological variations of head-internal relatives in Japanese. *Lingua* 115, 1243–1276.

Kitagawa, Y. (1986) Subjects in Japanese and English. PhD dissertation, University of Massachusetts.

Koenig, J. and Muansuwan, N. (2005) The syntax of aspect in Thai. *Natural Language and Linguistic Theory* 23, 335–380.

Kokuritsu Kokugo Kenkyujo (1959) *Nihon Hoogen no Kijututeki Kenkyuu* [Descriptive Work on Dialects of Japanese].

Koster, J. (1982) Counter-opacity in Korean and Japanese. Manuscript. Tilburg University.

Kubo, M. (1989) Japanese passives. Manuscript. MIT.

Kubozono, H. (1985) Speech errors and syllable structure. *Linguistics and Philology* 6, 220–243.

Kubozono, H. (1989) The mora and syllable structure in Japanese: evidence from speech errors. *Language and Speech* 32, 249–278.

Kubozono, H. (1993) *The Organization of Japanese Prosody*. Tokyo: Kurosio.

Kubozono, H. (1993/1994) The syllable in Japanese. Manuscript. Osaka University of Foreign Studies.

Kubozono, H. (1995) *Go-keisei to Onin-koozoo* [Word Formation and Phonological Structure]. Tokyo: Kurosio.

Kubozono, H. (1999) Mora and syllable. In: Tsujimura, N. (ed.), 31–61.

Kubozono, H. (2002) *Shingo wa Kooshite Tsukurareru* [How New Words Are Formed]. Tokyo: Iwanami.

Kubozono, H. (2003) The syllable as a unit of prosodic organization in Japanese. In: Fery, C. and van de Vijver, R. (eds), 99–122.

Kubozono, H. and Mester, R. A. (1995) Foot and accent: new evidence from Japanese compound accentuation. Paper presented at LSA meeting, New Orleans.

Kuczaj II, S. A. (ed.) (1982) *Language Development. Vol. 2: Language, Thought, and Culture*. Hillsdale, NJ: Lawrence Erlbaum.

Kunihiro, T. (ed.) (1980) *Nichi-ei Hikaku Koza II: Bunpo* [Lectures on Japanese-English Comparison: Grammar]. Tokyo: Taishukan.

Kuno, S. (1973) *The Structure of the Japanese Langauge*. Cambridge, MA: MIT Press.

Kuno, S. (1978) Theoretical perspectives on Japanese linguistics. In: Hinds, J. and Howard, I. (eds), 213–285.

Kuno, S. (1980) A note on Tonoike's intra-subjectivization hypothesis. In: Farmer, A. K. and Otsu, Y. (eds), 149–156.

Kuno, S. (1983) *Shin-Nihon Bunpoo Kenkyuu* [New Studies in Japanese Grammar]. Tokyo: Taishukan.

Kuno, S. (1986) Ukemi-bun no imi [The meaning of passives]. *Nihongogaku* 5, 70–87.

Kuno, S. (1987) *Functional Syntax: Anaphora, Discourse and Empathy*. Chicago: University of Chicago Press.

Kuno, S. and Kaburaki, E. (1977) Empathy and syntax. *Linguistic Inquiry* 8, 627–672.

Kurisu, K. (2005) Gradient prosody in Japanese. *Journal of East Asian Linguistics* 14, 175–226.

Kuroda, S.-Y. (1965a) Generative grammatical studies in the Japanese language. PhD dissertation, MIT.

Kuroda, S.-Y. (1965b) Causative forms in Japanese. *Foundations of Japanese* 1, 31–50.

Kuroda, S.-Y. (1978) Case-marking, canonical sentence patterns and counter equi in Japanese. In: Hinds, J. and Howard, I. (eds), 30–51.

Kuroda, S.-Y. (1979) On Japanese passives. In Bedell, G., Kobayashi, E., and Muraki, M. (eds), 305–347.

Kuroda, S.-Y. (1980) Bun no kozo [Sentence structure]. In: Kunihiro, T. (ed.), 23–62.

Kuroda, S.-Y. (1983) What can Japanese say about government and binding? *WCCFL* 2, 153–164.

Kuroda, S.-Y. (1985) Ukemi ni tuite no Kuno setsu o kaisyaku suru [Reconsideration of Kuno's account of passives]. *Nihongogaku* 4, 69–76.

Kuroda, S.-Y. (1992) *Japanese Syntax and Semantics: Collected Papers*. Dordrecht: Kluwer.

Kuroda, S.-Y. (2002) Rendaku. *Japanese/Korean Linguistics* 10, 337–350.

Kusumoto, K. (2003) The semantics of *-te iru* in Japanese. *Japanese/Korean Linguistics* 11, 367–380.

Ladefoged, P. (1982) *A Course in Phonetics, Second Edition*. New York: Harcourt Brace Jovanovich.

Lakoff, G. and Johnson, M. (1980) *Metaphors We Live By*. Chicago: University of Chicago Press.

Landau, B. and Gleitman, L. (1985) *Language and Experience: Evidence from the Blind Child*. Cambridge, MA: Harvard University Press.

Lasnik, H. and Saito, M. (1984) On the nature of proper government. *Linguistic Inquiry* 15, 235–290.

Lasnik, H. and Saito, M. (1992) *Move Alpha: Conditions on its Application and Output*. Cambridge, MA: MIT Press.

Levin, B. (1985) Lexical semantics in review: an introduction. In: Levin, B. (ed.), 1–62.

Levin, B. (ed.) (1985) *Lexical Semantics in Review*. Lexicon Project Working Papers 1, MIT.

Levin, B. (1993) *English Verb Classes and Alternations: A Preliminary Investigation*. Chicago: University of Chicago Press.

Levin, B. and Pinker, S. (eds) (1991) *Lexical and Conceptual Semantics*. Cambridge, MA: Blackwell.

Levin, B. and Rappaport Hovav, M. (1995) *Unaccusativity: At the Syntax–Semantics Interface*. Cambridge, MA: MIT Press.

Levin, B. and Tenny, C. (eds) (1988) *On Linking: Papers by Richard Carter*. Lexicon Project Working Papers 25, MIT.

Levinson, S. C. (1983) *Pragmatics*. Cambridge: Cambridge University Press.

Li, P. and Shirai, Y. (2000) *The Acquisition of Lexical and Grammatical Aspect*. Berlin: Mouton de Gruyter.

Locke, J. (1690) *An Essay Concerning Humane Understanding*, London: Eliz. Holt.

Lovins, J. B. (1975) *Loanwords and the Phonological Structure of Japanese*. Bloomington, IN: IULC.

McCawley, J. D. (1968) *The Phonological Component of a Grammar of Japanese*. The Hague: Mouton.

McCawley, J. D. (1976) Relativization. In: Shibatani, M. (ed.), 295–306.

McCawley, J. D. (1977) Accent in Japanese. In: Hyman, L. M. (ed.), 261–302.

McCawley, J. D. (1993) A Japanese and Ainu linguistic feast (review article). *Journal of Linguistics* 29, 469–484.

McCawley, N. A. (1972) On the treatment of Japanese passives. *CLS* 8, 256–270.

McCawley, N. (1976) Reflexivization: a transformational approach. In: Shibatani, M. (ed.), 51–116.

McClure, W. (1994) Syntactic projections of the semantics of aspect. PhD dissertation, Cornell University.

McClure, W. (1997) Morphosyntactic realization of aspectual structure. *Japanese/Korean Linguistics* 7, 445–461.

McClure, W. (2000) *Using Japanese: A Guide to Contemporary Usage*. Cambridge: Cambridge University Press.

McGloin, N. H. (1986) *Negation in Japanese*. Alberta: Boreal Scholarly.

MacWhinny, B. (ed.) (1987) *Mechanisms of Language Acquisition*. Hillsdale, NJ: Lawrence Erlbaum.

Makino, S. (1972) Adverbial scope and the passive construction in Japanese. *Papers in Linguistics* 5, 73–98.

Makino, S. (1976) Nominal compounds. In: Shibatani, M. (ed.), 483–498.

Makkai, A. and Melby, A. K. (eds) (1985) *Linguistics and Philosophy: Essays in Honor of Rulon S. Wells*. Amsterdam: John Benjamins.

Markman, E. (1989) *Categorization and Naming in Children: Problems of Induction*. Cambridge, MA: MIT Press.

Masuoka, T. and Takubo, Y. (1992) *Kiso Nihon Bunpoo* [Basic Japanese Grammar]. Tokyo: Kurosio.

Martin, S. (1952) Morphophonemics of standard colloquial Japanese. Supplement to *Language*: Language Dissertation No. 47.

Martin, S. (1975) *Reference Grammar of Japanese*. New Haven, CT: Yale University Press.

Martin, S. (1987) *A Reference Grammar of Japanese*. Rutland: Charles E. Tuttle.

Matsuda, Y. (1997) Representation of focus and presupposition in Japanese. PhD dissertation, USC.

Matsuda, Y. (2002) Event sensitivity of head-internal relatives in Japanese. *Japanese/Korean Linguistics* 10, 629–643.

Matsumoto, Y(o). (1990) Constraints on the "intransitivizing" resultative -*te aru* construction in Japanese. *Japanese/Korean Linguistics*, 269–283.

Matsumoto, Y(o). (1992) On the wordhood of complex predicates in Japanese. PhD dissertation, Stanford University.

Matsumoto, Y(o). (1996) *Complex Predicates in Japanese: A Syntactic and Semantic Study of the Notion "Word"*. Stanford: CSLI.

Matsumoto, Y(oshiko). (1988) Grammar and semantics of adnominal clauses in Japanese. PhD dissertation, University of California.

Matsumoto, Y(oshiko). (1990) The role of pragmatics in Japanese relative clause constructions. *Lingua* 82, 111–129.

Matsumoto, Y(oshiko). (1997) *Noun-Modifying Constructions in Japanese*. Amsterdam: John Benjamins.

Matthews, P. H. (1976) *Morphology: An Introduction to the Theory of Word Structure*. Cambridge: Cambridge University Press.

Maynard, S. (1987) Thematization as a staging device in the Japanese narrative. In: Hinds, J., Maynard, S., and Iwasaki, S. (eds), 57–82.

Maynard, S. (1991) Pragmatics of discourse modality: a case of *da* and *desu/masu* forms in Japanese. *Journal of Pragmatics* 15, 551–582.

Maynard, S. (1993a) *Kaiwa Bunseki* [Discourse Analysis]. Tokyo: Kurosio.

Maynard, S. (1993b) *Discourse Modality: Subjectivity, Emotion and Voice in the Japanese Language*. Amsterdam: John Benjamins.

Maynard, S. (1997) *Japanese Communication: Language and Thought in Context*. Honolulu: University of Hawaii Press.

Maynard, S. (1999) Discourse analysis and pragmatics. In: Tsujimura, N. (ed.), 423–443.

Mester, R. A. and Ito, J. (1989) Feature predictability and underspecification: palatal prosody in Japanese mimetics. *Language* 65, 258–93.

Mikami, A. (1960) *Zoo wa Hana ga Nagai* [Elephants Have Long Noses]. Tokyo: Kurosio.

Miller, R. (1971) *Japanese and the Other Altaic Languages*. Chicago: University of Chicago Press.

Miyagawa, S. (1980) Complex verbs and the lexicon. PhD dissertation, University of Arizona.

Miyagawa, S. (1984) Blocking and Japanese causatives. *Lingua* 64, 177–207.

Miyagawa, S. (1986) Restructuring in Japanese. In: Imai, T. and Saito, M. (eds), 273–300.

Miyagawa, S. (1987a) Lexical categories in Japanese. *Lingua* 73, 29–51.

Miyagawa, S. (1987b) *Wa* and the WH phrase. In Hinds, J., Maynard, S., and Iwasaki, S. (eds), 185–217.

Miyagawa, S. (1988) Predication and numeral quantifier. In: Poser, W. (ed.), 157–192.

Miyagawa, S. (1989a) *Structure and Case Marking in Japanese*. San Diego: Academic Press.

Miyagawa, S. (1989b) Light verbs and the ergative hypothesis. *Linguistic Inquiry* 20, 659–668.

Miyagawa, S. (1993) Case-checking and minimal link condition. *MIT Working Papers in Linguistics* 19, 213–254.

Miyagawa, S. (1997) Against optional scrambling. *Linguistic Inquiry* 28, 1–25.

Miyagawa, S. (1999) Causatives. In: Tsujimura, N. (ed.), 237–268.

Miyake, Y. (1995) A dialect in the face of the standard: a Japanese case study. *BLS* 21, 217–225.

Miyamoto, T. (1999) *The Light Verb Construction in Japanse: The Role of the Verbal Noun*. Amsterdam: John Benjamins.

Morikawa, H. (1997) *Acquisition of Case Marking and Argument Structures in Japanese*. Tokyo: Kurosio.

Muraki, M. (1978) The *sika nai* construction and predicate restructuring. In: Hinds, J. and Howard, I. (eds), 155–177.

Murasugi, K. (1991) Noun phrases in Japanese and English: a study in syntax, learnability and acquisition. PhD dissertation, University of Connecticut.

Murasugi, K. (1993) Two notes on head-internal relative clauses. *Treatises and Studies by the Faculty of Kinjo Gakuin University*, 233–242.

Murasugi, K. (1994) Head-internal relative clauses as adjunct pure complex NPs. *Synchronic and Diachronic Approaches to Language*, 425–437.

Nakajima, H. (ed.) (1991) *Current English Linguistics in Japan*. Berlin: Mouton de Gruyer.

Nakajima, H. and Otsu, Y. (eds) (1993) *Argument Structure: Its Syntax and Acquisition*. Tokyo: Kaitakusha.

Nakamura, K. (2002) Pragmatic development in Japanese monolingual children. *Studies in Language Sciences* 2, 23–41.

Nakamura, M. (1987) Parameterized extension of binding theory. *MIT Working Papers in Linguistics* 9, 193–223.

Nakasone, S. (compile) (1983) *Okinawa Nakizin Hoogen Jiten* [A Dictionary of the Nakijin Dialect in Okinawa]. Tokyo: Kadokawa Shoten.

Nakau, M. (1976) Tense, aspect, and modality. In: Shibatani, M. (ed.), 421–482.

Nakayama, M. (1996) *Acquisition of Japanese Empty Categories*. Tokyo: Kurosio.

Nakayama, M., Mazuka, R., Shirai, Y., and Li, P. (eds) (to appear) *Handbook of East Asian Psycholinguistics: Japanese*. Cambridge: Cambridge University Press.

Napoli, D. J. (1993) *Syntax: Theory and Problems*. Oxford: Oxford University Press.

Napoli, D. J. (1996) *Linguistics*. Oxford: Oxford University Press.

Napoli, D. J. (2003) *Language Matters: A Guide to Everyday Questions about Language*. Oxford: Oxford University Press.

Nemoto, N. (1999) Scrambling. In Tsujimura, N. (ed.), 121–153.

Newmeyer, F. (1980) *Linguistic Theory in America*. New York: Academic Press.

Niagles, L. (1990) Children use syntax to learn verb meaning. *Journal of Child Language* 17, 357–374.

Nishigauchi, T. (1990) *Quantification in the Theory of Grammar*. Dordrecht: Kluwer.

Nishigauchi, T. (1999) Quantification and *wh*-constructions. In: Tsujimura, N. (ed.), 269–296.

Nishiyama, K. (1998) The morphosyntax and morphophonology of Japanese predicates. PhD dissertation, Cornell University.

Noji, J. (1973–1977) *Yoojiki no Gengoseikatsu no Jittai* [The Language Development of a Child]. Hiroshima: Bunka Hyoron Shuppan.

Oda, H. (2000) An embodied semantic mechanism for mimetic words in Japanese. PhD dissertation, Bloomington, Indiana University.

Oehrle, R. and Nishio, H. (1981) Adversity. In: Farmer, A. K. and Kitagawa, C. (eds), 163–185.

Ogihara, T. (1996) *Tense, Attitude, and Scope*. Dordrecht: Kluwer.

Ogihara, T. (1998) The ambiguity of the -*te iru* form in Japanese. *Journal of East Asian Linguistics* 7, 87–120.

Ogihara, T. (1999) Tense and aspect. In: Tsujimura, N. (ed.), 327–348.

Ohara, K. H. (1996) A constructional approach to Japanese internally headed relativization. PhD dissertation, University of California.

Ohara, K. H. (2002) From relativization to clause-linkage: a constructional account of Japanese internally headed relativization. *Japanese/Korean Linguistics* 10, 279–292.

Ohkado, M. (1991) On the status of adjectival nouns of Japanese. *Lingua* 83, 67–82.

Ohso, M. (1976) A study of zero pronominalization in Japanese. PhD dissertation, Ohio State University.

Okamoto, S. (1995) Pragmaticization of meaning in some sentence-final particles in Japanese. In: Shibatani, M. and Thompson, S. (eds), 219–246.

Okamoto, S. (1997) Social context, linguistic ideology, and indexical expressions in Japanese. *Journal of Pragmatics* 28, 795–817.

Okamoto, S. and Shibamoto Smith, J. (eds) (2004) *Japanese Language, Gender, and Ideology*. Oxford: Oxford University Press.

Okubo, A. (1967) *Yooji Gengo no Hattatsu* [Development of Child Language]. Tokyo: Tookyoodoo.

Okubo, A. (1981) *Yooji no Kotoba Siryoo* [Records of Child Language]. Tokyo: Syuuei Syuppan.

Okuda, Y. (1978a) Asupekuto no kenkyuu o megutte I [On the study of aspect I]. *Kokugo Kyoiku* 53, 33–44.

Okuda, Y. (1978b) Asupekuto no kenkyuu o megutte II [On the study of aspect II]. *Kokugo Kyoiku* 4, 14–27.

Okutsu, K. (1995) Jidooka, tadooka oyobi ryookyokuka tennkei [Intransitivization, transitivization, and bi-directional derivation]. In: Suga, K. and Hayatsu, E. (eds), 57–81.

Ota, M. (1998) Minimality constraints and the prosodic structure of child Japanese. *Japanese/Korean Linguistics* 8, 331–344.

Ota, M. (1999) Phonological theory and the acquisition of prosodic structure: evidence from child Japanese. PhD dissertation, Georgetown University.

Ota, M. (2003) *The Development of Prosodic Structure in Early Words*. John Benjamins.

Otsu, Y. (1980) Some aspects of Rendaku in Japanese and related problems. In: Farmer, A. K. and Otsu, Y. (eds), 207–228.

Otsu, Y. (1999) First language acquisition. In: Tsujimura, N. (ed.), 378–397.

Ouhalla, J. (1999) *Introducing Transformational Grammar*, second edition. London: Arnold.

Parker, F. and Riley, K. (1994) *Linguistics for Non-Linguists*. Boston, MA: Allyn and Bacon.

Pederson, E. (1995) Event realization in Tamil. Paper presented at the International Cognitive Linguistics Association Meeting, Albuquerque, New Mexico.

Perlmutter, D. (1978) Impersonal passives and the unaccusative hypothesis. *BLS* 4, 157–189.

Pierrehumbert, J. and Beckman, M. E. (1988) *Japanese Tone Structure*. Cambridge, MA: MIT Press.

Pinker, S. (1984) *Language Learnability and Language Development*. Cambridge, MA: Harvard University Press.

Pinker, S. (1987) The bootstrapping problem in language acquisition. In: MacWhinny, B. (ed.), 399–441.

Pinker, S. (1989) *Learnability and Cognition: The Acquisition of Argument Structure*. Cambridge, MA: MIT Press.

Pinker, S. (1994) *The Language Instinct: How the Mind Creates Language*. New York: William Morrow.

Pinker, S. (1999) *Words and Rules*. New York: Basic Books.

Port, R. F., Dalby, J., and O'Dell, M. (1987) Evidence for mora timing in Japanese. *Journal of Acoustic Society of America* 81, 1574–1585.

Poser, W. (1981) The "double-*o* constraint": evidence for a direct object relation in Japanese. Manuscript. MIT.

Poser, W. (1984) The phonetics and phonology of tone and intonation in Japanese. PhD dissertation, MIT.

Poser, W. (ed.) (1988) *Papers From the Second International Workshop on Japanese Syntax*. Stanford: CSLI.

Poser, W. (1990) Evidence for foot structure in Japanese. *Language* 66, 78–105.

Postal, P. and Pullum, K. P. (1982) The contraction debate. *Linguistic Inquiry* 13, 122–138.

Radford, A. (1988) *Transformational Grammar*. Cambridge: Cambridge University Press.

Rappaport Hovav, M. and Levin, B. (1998) Bulding verb meanings. In: Butt, M. and Geuder, W. (eds), 97–134.

Reichenbach, H. (1947) *Elements of Symbolic Logic*. New York: Macmillan.

Rispoli, M. (1981) The emergence of verb and adjective tense–aspect inflection in Japanese. MA thesis, University of Pennsylvania.

Rispoli, M. (1987) The acquisition of transitive and intransitive action verb categories in Japanese. *First Language* 7, 183–200.

490 *Bibliography*

Rispoli, M. (1989) Encounters with Japanese verbs: caregiver sentences and the categorization of transitive and intransitive action verbs. *First Language* 9, 57–80.

Rispoli, M. (1991) The acquisition of verb subcategorization in a functionalist framework. *First Language* 11, 41–63.

Rispoli, M. (1995) Missing argument and the acquisition of predicate meaning. In: Tomasello, M. and Merriman, W. E. (eds), 331–352.

Rispoli, M. and Bloom, L. (1985) Incomplete and continuing: theoretical issues in the acquisition of tense and aspect. *Journal of Child Language* 12, 471–474.

Rosch, E. (1978) Principles of categorization. In: Rosch, E. and Lloyd, B. (eds), 27–48.

Rosch, E. and Barbara Lloyd, B. (eds) (1978) *Cognition and Categorization*. Hillsdale, NJ: Lawrence Erlbaum.

Saeed, J. I. (2003) *Semantics (Second Edition)*. Oxford: Blackwell.

Saiki, M. (1987) Grammatical functions in the syntax of Japanese nominals. PhD dissertation, Stanford University.

Saito, M. (1982) Case marking in Japanese: a preliminary study. Manuscript. MIT.

Saito, M. (1983) Case and government in Japanese. WCCFL 2, 247–259.

Saito, M. (1985) Some asymmetries in Japanese and their theoretical implications. PhD dissertation, MIT.

Saito, M. (1992) Long distance scrambling in Japanese. *Journal of East Asian Linguistics* 1, 69–118.

Saito, M. (ed.) (1993) *Japanese Grammar (II)*. Second Annual Report for the Research Project "Development of a Formal Grammar of Japanese". University of Connecticut.

Saito, M. and Fukui, N. (1998) Order in phrase structure and movement. *Linguistic Inquiry* 29, 439–474.

Saito, M. and Hoji, H. (1983) Weak crossover and move alpha in Japanese. *Natural Language and Linguistic Theory* 1, 245–259.

Sanches, M. (1968) Features in the acquisition of Japanese grammar. PhD dissertation, Stanford University.

Sato, Y. (1993) Complex predicate formation with verbal nouns in Japanese and Korean: argument transfer at LF. PhD dissertation, University of Hawaii.

Schwartz-Norman, L. (1976) The grammar of "content" and "container". *Journal of Linguistics* 12, 179–187.

Searle, J. (1969) *Speech Acts: An Essay in the Philosophy of Language*. Cambridge: Cambridge University Press.

Sells, P. (1987) Aspect of logophoricity. *Linguistic Inquiry* 18, 445–481.

Sells, P. (1989) More on light verbs and theta-marking. Manuscript. Stanford University.

Shibamoto, J. (1985) *Japanese Women's Language*. New York: Academic Press.

Shibatani, M. (1973a) A linguistic study of causative constructions. PhD dissertation, University of California.

Shibatani, M. (1973b) Semantics of Japanese causativization. *Foundation of Language* 9, 327–373.

Shibatani, M. (1973c) Where morphology and syntax clash: a case in Japanese aspectual verbs. *Gengo Kenkyu* 64, 65–96.

Shibatani, M. (1976) Causativization. In: Shibatani, M. (ed.), 239–294.

Shibatani, M. (ed.) (1976) *Syntax and Semantics* vol. 5: *Japanese Generative Grammar*. New York: Academic Press.

Shibatani, M. (1977) Grammatical relations and surface cases. *Language* 53, 789–809.

Shibatani, M. (1978) Mikami Akira and the notion of "subject" in Japanese grammar. In: Hinds, J. and Howard, I. (eds), 52–67.

Shibatani, M. (1990) *The Languages of Japan*. Cambridge: Cambridge University Press.

Shibatani, M. and Kageyama, T. (1988) Word formation in modular theory of grammar: post-syntactic compounds in Japanese. *Language* 64, 451–484.

Shibatani, M. and Thompson, S. (eds) (1995) *Essays in Semantics and Pragmatics.* Amsterdam: John Benjamins.

Shimoyama, J. (1999) Internally headed relative clauses in Japanese and e-type anaphora. *Journal of East Asian Linguistics* 8, 147–182.

Shinohara, S. (2000) Default accentuation and foot structure in Japanese: evidence from Japanese adaptations of French words. *Journal of East Asian Linguistics* 9, 55–96.

Shirai, Y. (1993) Inherent aspect and the acquisition of tense/aspect morphology in Japanese, In: Nakajima, H. and Otsu, Y. (eds), 185–211.

Shirai, Y. (1998) Tense–aspect morphology in Japanese. *First Language* 18, 281–309.

Shirai, Y. (2000) The semantics of the Japanese imperfective *-te iru*: an integrative approach. *Journal of Pragmatics* 32, 327–361.

Shirai, Y. and Andersen, R. W. (1995) The acquisition of tense–aspect morphology: a prototype account. *Language* 71, 743–762.

Shopen, T. (ed.) (1985) *Language Typology and Syntactic Description 3: Grammatical Categories and the Lexicon.* Cambridge: Cambridge University Press.

Singh, M. (1991) The perfective paradox: or how to eat your cake and have it too. *BLS* 17, 469–478.

Slobin, D. (ed.) (1971) *The Ontogenesis of Grammar: A Theoretical Symposium.* New York: Academic Press.

Slobin, D. (1973) Cognitive prerequisites for the development of grammar. In: Ferguson, C. and Slobin, D. (eds), 175–208.

Slobin, D. (ed.) (1985) *The Crosslinguistic Study of Language Acquisition. Vol. 1: The Data.* Hillsdale, NJ: Lawrence Erlbaum.

Slobin, D. (2001) Form–function relations: how do children find out what they are? In: Bowerman, M. and Levinson, S. C. (eds), 406–449.

Smith, C. (1991) *The Parameter of Aspect.* Dordrecht: Kluwer.

Soga, M. (1983) *Tense and Aspect in Modern Colloquial Japanese.* Vancouver: University of British Columbia Press.

Spencer, A. (1991) *Morphological Theory.* Oxford: Blackwell.

Spencer, A. and Zwicky, A. (eds) (1998) *The Handbook of Morphology.* Oxford: Blackwell.

Suga, K. (1995) Jita chigai [Transitivity difference]. In Suga, K. and Hayatsu, E. (eds), 122–136.

Suga, K. and Hayatsu, E. (eds) (1995) *Dooshi no Jita* [Verb Transitivity]. Tokyo: Hitsuji Syobo.

Sugioka, Y. (1986) *Interaction of Derivational Morphology and Syntax in Japanese and English.* New York: Garland.

Sunaoshi, Y. (1995) Japanese women's construction of an authoritative position in their communities of practice. MA thesis, University of Texas, Austin.

Sunaoshi, Y. (2004) Farm women's professional discourse in Ibaraki. In: Okamoto, S. and Shibamoto Smith, J. (eds), 187–204.

Suzuki, H. (1995) Minimal words in Japanese. *CLS* 31, 448–463.

Tabusa, T. (1982) *Kotoba no Tochiri* [Speech Errors]. Yonago: Imai Shoten.

Tagashira, Y. and Hoff, J. (1986) *Handbook of Japanese Compound Verbs.* Tokyo: Hokuseido Press.

Tai, J. (1984) Verbs and times in Chinese: Vendler's four categories. *CLS* 20, 289–296.

Takami, K. and Kato, K. (2003) "-te yaru" hyoogen-no imi-no tayoosei to kihontekiimi [Diverse meanings and the basic meaning of the *-te yaru* expression]. *Gengo* 32, 96–101.

Takano, Y. (1999) Object shift and scrambling. *Natural Language and Linguistic Theory* 16, 817–889.

Talmy, L. (1985) Lexicalization patterns: semantic structure in lexical forms. In: Shopen, T. (ed.), 57–149.

Talmy, L. (2000a) *Toward a Cognitive Semantics. Volume I: Concept Structuring Systems*. Cambridge, MA: MIT Press.

Talmy, L. (2000b) *Toward a Cognitive Semantics. Volume II: Typology and Process in Concept Structuring*. Cambridge, MA: MIT Press.

Tamori, I. and Schourup, L. (1999) *Onomatope* [Onomatopoeia]. Tokyo: Kurosio.

Tannen, D. (1990) *You Just Don't Understand: Women and Men in Conversation*. New York: William Morrow.

Tannen, D. (ed.) (1993) *Gender and Conversational Interaction*. Oxford: Oxford University Press.

Tateishi, K. (1989) Theoretical implications of Japanese musicians' language. *WCCFL* 8, 384–98.

Tateishi, K. (1991) The syntax of "subject". PhD dissertation, University of Massachusetts.

Tenny, C. (1986) Tone and cyclicity in Tokyo Japanese. Manuscript. MIT.

Tenny, C. (1994) *Aspectual Roles and the Syntax–Semantics Interface*. Dordrecht: Kluwer.

Terada, M. (1990) Incorporation and argument structure in Japanese. PhD dissertation, University of Massachusetts.

Teramura, H. (1971) The syntax of noun modification in Japanese. *Journal-Newsletter of the Association of Teachers of Japanese* 6, 64–74.

Teramura, H. (1982) *Nihongo no Shintakkusu to Imi* [The Syntax and Semantics of Japanese]. Vol. 1. Tokyo: Kurosio.

Teramura, H. (1984) *Nihongo no Shintakkusu to Imi* [The Syntax and Semantics of Japanese]. Vol. 2. Tokyo: Kurosio.

Tojo, M. (1955) *Nihon Hogengaku* [Japanese Dialectology]. Tokyo: Yoshikawa Hiroshi Bunkan.

Tomasello, M. (1992) *First Verbs: A Case Study of Early Grammatical Development*. Cambridge: Cambridge University Press.

Tomasello, M. and Bates, E. (eds) (2001) *Language Development: The Essential Readings*. Oxford: Blackwell.

Tomasello, M. and Merriman, W. E. (eds) *Beyond Names for Things: Young Children's Acquisition of Verbs*. Hillsdale, NJ: Lawrence Erlbaum.

Tonoike, S. (1978) On the causative construction in Japanese. In: Hinds, J. and Howard, I. (eds), 3–29.

Tonoike, S. (1980a) Intra-subjectivization. In: Farmer, A. and Otsu, Y. (eds), 137–147.

Tonoike, S. (1980b) More on intra-subjectivization. In: Farmer, A. and Otsu, Y. (eds), 157–170.

Tsujimura, N. (1989) Some accentuation properties in Japanese and lexical phonology. *Linguistic Inquiry* 20, 334–338.

Tsujimura, N. (1990a) Ergativity of nouns and case assignment. *Linguistic Inquiry* 21, 277–287.

Tsujimura, N. (1990b) Unaccusative hypothesis and noun classification. *Linguistics* 28, 929–957.

Tsujimura, N. (1990c) Unaccusative mismatches in Japanese. *ESCOL* 6, 264–276.

Tsujimura, N. (1991) On the semantic properties of unaccusativity. *Journal of Japanese Linguistics* 13, 91–116.

Tsujimura, N. (1992) Licensing nominal clauses: the case of deverbal nominals in Japanese. *Natural Language and Linguistic Theory* 10, 477–522.

Tsujimura, N. (1994) Unaccusative mismatches and resultatives in Japanese. *MIT Working Papers in Linguistics* 24, 335–354.

Tsujimura, N. (1999) Lexical semantics. In: Tsujimura, N. (ed.), 349–377.

Tsujimura, N. (ed.) (1999) *The Handbook of Japanese Linguistics*. Oxford: Blackwell.

Tsujimura, N. (2001) Revisiting the two-dimensional approach to mimetics: a reply to Kita (1997). *Linguistics* 39, 409–418.

Tsujimura, N. (2003) Event cancellation and telicity. *Japanese/Korean Linguistics* 12, 388–399.

Tsujimura, N. (to appear) A constructional approach to mimetic verb. In: Fried, M. and Boas, H. C. (eds).

Tsujimura, N. and Davis, S. (1987) The accent of long nominal compounding in Tokyo Japanese. *Studies in Language* 11, 199–206.

Tsujimura, N. and Davis, S. (1989) The morphophonemics of Japanese verbal conjugation: an autosegmental account. *ESCOL*, 488–499.

Tsujimura, N. and Deguchi, M. (to appear). Semantic integration of mimetics in Japanese. *CLS* 39.

Uchida, Y. (1991) Verbal noun constructions in Japanese. MA thesis, Ohio State University.

Uchida, Y. and Nakayama, M. (1993) Japanese verbal noun constructions. *Linguistics* 31, 623–666.

Ueda, M. (1986a) Notes on a Japanese (reflexive) pronoun *zibun*. Manuscript. University of Massachusetts.

Ueda, M. (1986b) On quantifier float in Japanese. In: Hasegawa, N. and Kitagawa, Y. (eds), 263–309.

Uehara, S. (1998) *Syntactic Categories in Japanese: A Cognitive and Typological Introduction.* Tokyo: Kurosio.

Ueyama, A. (1998) Two types of dependency. PhD dissertation, USC.

Ullmann, S. (1962) *Semantics: An Introduction to the Science of Meaning.* New York: Barnes and Noble.

Van Valin, R. D. (1990) Semantic parameter of split intransitivity. *Language* 66, 221–260.

Vance, T. J. (1980) Comments on "some aspects of Rendaku in Japanese and related problems". In: Farmer, A. K. and Otsu, Y. (eds), 229–235.

Vance, T. J. (1982) On the origin of voicing alternation in Japanese consonants. *Journal of the American Oriental Society* 102, 333–341.

Vance, T. J. (1986) Review article. *Papers in Japanese Linguistics* 11, 222–231.

Vance, T. J. (1987) *An Introduction to Japanese Phonology.* New York: SUNY Press.

Vendler, Z. (1967) *Linguistics in Philosophy.* Ithaca, NY: Cornell University Press.

Washio, R. (1989/1990) The Japanese passive. *Linguistic Review* 6, 227–263.

Watanabe, A. (1995) Aspects of questions in Japanese and their theoretical implications. PhD dissertation, USC.

Webelhuth, G. (ed.) (1995) *Government and Binding Theory and the Minimalist Program.* Oxford: Blackwell.

Whitman, J. (1979) Scrambled, over easy, or sunny side up? *CLS* 15, 342–352.

Whitman, J. (1986) Configurationality parameter. In: Imai, T. and Saito, M. (eds), 351–374.

Wierzbicka, A. (1979) Are grammatical categories vague or polysemous? The Japanese "adversative" passive in a typological context. *Papers in Linguistics* 12, 111–162.

Wilbur, R. (1993) The phonology of reduplication. PhD dissertation, University of Illinois.

Williams, E. (1981) On the notions "lexically related" and "head of a word". *Linguistic Inquiry* 12, 245–274.

Williams, N. K. (1990) *Japanese Intonation: Meaning and Intonational Phrase.* PhD dissertation, Georgetown University.

Yamamoto, M. (1981) The semantic development of negation in English and Japanese in a simultaneously bilingual child. MA thesis, University of Hawai'i.

Yamamoto, M. (1984) Fukugoo-dooshi no kaku-shihai [Case government of compound verbs]. *Todai Ronshuu* 21, 32–49.

Yamashita, Y. (1995) The emergence of syntactic categories: evidence from the acquisition of Japanese. PhD dissertation, University of Hawai'i.

Yatsushiro, K. (2003) VP internal scrambling. *Journal of East Asian Linguistics* 12, 141–170.

Yoneyama, M. (1986) Motion verbs in conceptual semantics. *Bulletin of the Faculty of Humanities* 22, 1–15.

Yoshikawa, T. (1976) Gendai nihongo dooshi no asupekuto no kenkyuu [Research on the aspect of verbs in modern Japanese]. In: Kindaichi, H. (ed.), 155–328.

Yoshimoto, K. (1991) *Hogen Zogo* [Dialectal Diversity]. Toyama: Hurusato no bunka o hagukumu kai.

Yumoto, Y. (2005) *Hukugoodooshi, Haseidooshi no Imi to Toogo* [Syntax and Semantics of Compound Verbs and Derived Verbs]. Tokyo: Hitsuji.

Index